International Max Planck Research School (IMPRS)
for Maritime Affairs
at the University of Hamburg

Hamburg Studies on Maritime Affairs
Volume 9

Edited by

Nicolai Lagoni

The Liability of Classification Societies

Springer

Dr. Nicolai Lagoni
International Max Planck Research School
for Maritime Affairs
Max-Planck-Institut für ausländisches
und internationales Privatrecht
Mittelweg 187
20148 Hamburg
n.lagoni@gmail.com

Inaugural-Dissertation zur Erlangung des Grades eines Doktors
der Rechtswissenschaft der Fakultät für Rechtswissenschaft
der Universität Hamburg
Erstgutachter: Professor Dr. Dr. h.c. Jürgen Basedow, LL.M. (Harvard)
Zweitgutachter: Professor Dr. Dr. h.c. Rüdiger Wolfrum
Tag der mündlichen Prüfung: 31. Januar 2007

Library of Congress Control Number: 2007928574

ISBN 978-3-540-72915-0 Springer Berlin Heidelberg New York

Springer is a part of Springer Science+Business Media

springer.com

Production: LE-TEX Jelonek, Schmidt & Vöckler GbR, Leipzig
Cover-design: WMX Design GmbH, Heidelberg

SPIN 12072255 64/3180YL - 5 4 3 2 1 0 Printed on acid-free paper

To my parents

Preface

The topic of this study originated in a discussion with my doctoral advisor Professor Dr. Dr. h.c. Jürgen Basedow, Director of the Max Planck Institute for Comparative and International Private Law in Hamburg. I am most grateful for his inspiring advice and constant intellectual support which he gave me throughout the two years of my research and writing. I would further like to thank Professor Dr. Dr. h.c. Rüdiger Wolfrum, Director of the Max Planck Institute for Comparative Public Law in Heidelberg for the timely submission of the second opinion on my dissertation.

The interdisciplinary discussions in the International Max Planck Research School Maritime Affairs were very helpful and have furthered this study. I feel obliged to the Directors of the Research School. Furthermore the Research School supported my research with a generous scholarship and provided me with a grant for the publication of this book. From February until May 2005, I have been researching at Columbia Law School, New York City. This was supported by the German Academic Exchange Service (DAAD). I owe particular thanks to the Research School and to the DAAD for this financial support.

In the course of researching and preparing this study, many friends and experts have provided me with information, advice or assistance, I am indebted to all of them. But only a few can be mentioned here: Prof. Dr. Peter Ehlers (Präsident des Bundesamtes für Seeschifffahrt und Hydrographie); Regierungsdirektoren Peter Escherich und Gert-Jürgen Scholz (Bundesministerium für Verkehr, Bau- und Wohnungswesen); William France Jr. (Healy & Baillie); Gesa Heinacher-Lindemann (Germanischer Lloyd); Brian Starer (Holland & Knight). Warmest thanks go to Prof. Dr. Yesim Atamer (Istanbul Bilgi University), Prof. Juan Luis Pulido (Universidad de Cadiz) and Dr. Wolfgang Wurmnest, (Max-Planck Institute for Comparative and International Private Law) for many controversial and encouraging discussions as well as to all friends and colleagues at the Max Planck Institute and at the International Max Planck Research School Maritime Affairs.

Last but not least I would like to thank my family. Their continuous support and encouragement have helped to make this book a reality.

This Study takes into account literature and documents available until November 2006.

Hamburg, March 2007 Nicolai Lagoni

Outline Table of Contents

Table of Contents

Abbreviations

ABS	American Bureau of Shipping
A.C.	Appeal Cases
AcP	*Archiv für die civilistische Praxis*
ACP	United States Coast Guard Alternate Compliance Program
aff'd	affirmed
AJIL	*American Journal of International Law*
ALR	*American Law Reports*
All E.R.	All England Law Reports
All E.R. Annual Review	All England Law Reports Annual Review
A.M.C.	American Maritime Cases
Am.J.Comp.L.	*American Journal of Comparative Law*
App.Cas.	Appeal Cases
Asp.	*Aspinall, Reports of Cases Relating to Maritime Law, London 1896.*
ATS	Australian Treaty Service
Aus.	Australia
BauR	*Zeitschrift für Baurecht*
Bevans	Treaties and Other International Agreements of the United States of America 1776-1949
BGB	Bürgerliches Gesetzbuch (German Civil Code)
BGHZ	Entscheidungen des Bundesgerichtshofes in Zivilsachen (Decisions of the Bundesgerichtshof in civil cases)
BGH	Bundesgerichtshof
BIMCO	The Baltic and International Maritime Council
BIMCO Bull.	*BIMCO Bulletin*
BV	Bureau Veritas
C.A.	Court of Appeal
Cal.W.Int'l L.J.	*California Western International Law Journal*
Cambridge L.J.	*Cambridge Law Journal*
C.B.	Court of Common Bench
CCS	China Classification Society
Central Crim.Ct.	Central Criminal Court
CERCLA	Comprehensive Environmental Response, Compensation and Liability Act
cert. denied	*certiorari denied*
CFR	United States Code of Federal Regulations
Ch.	Chancery Division
chap.	chapter
Civ.Div.	Civil Division
CLC	International Convention on Civil Liability for Oil Pollution Damage

C.L.J.	*Canada Law Journal*
ClassNK	Nippon Kaiji Kyokai
CMI	Comité Maritime International
Cmnd.	Command Paper [United Kingdom Parliament]
CMR	Convention on the Contract for the International Carriage of Goods by Road
cmt.	comment
Coastal Mgmt.	*Coastal Management*
COGSA	Carrriage of Goods by Sea Act
col.	Column
COLREG 1960	International Regulations for Preventing Collisions at Sea
Com.Ct.	Commercial Court
Comm.	Commercial
Comm.Law.	*Commercial Lawyer*
Con.L.R.	*Construction Law Reports*
Const.L.J.	*Construction Law Journal*
COTIF	Convention concerning International Carriage by Rail
CSC 1972	International Convention for Safe Containers, 1972
CTS	Canada Treaty Series
CWA	Clean Water Act
Dist.	District
DMF	*Le droit maritime français*
DNV	Det Norske Veritas
Doc.	Document
Duke Envtl. L. & Pol'y F.	*Duke Environmental Law and Policy Forum*
E.C.	Treaty establishing the European Community
E.G.	Estates Gazette
E.G.L.R.	Estates Gazette Law Reports
EMSA	European Maritime Safety Agency
Eng.Rep.	English Reports
Envtl. Pol'y & L.	*Environmental Policy and Law*
EPIL	Encyclopaedia of Public International Law
ETS	European Treaty Series
EWHC	High Court
Ex.	Exchequer Reports (1847–1856)
Exch.	Court of Exchequer
F.2d	Federal Reporter, Second Series
F.3d	Federal Reporter, Third Series
FAA	Federal Aviation Agency
FONASBA	The Federation of National Associations of Ship Brokers and Agents
found.	founder
F.Rep.	Federal Reporter
F.Supp.	Federal Supplement
FTCA	Federal Tort Claims Act
GBS	Goal based standards
GG	Grundgesetz
GL	Germanischer Lloyd
Geo.Wash.L.Rev.	*George Washington Law Review*
H.C.(Aus.)	High Court (Australia)
HGB	*Handelsgesetzbuch* (German Commercial Code)

H.L.	House of Lords
HNS	Hazardous and Noxious Substances
HNS Convention	International Convention on Liability and Compensation for Damage in Connection with the Carriage of Hazardous and Noxious Substances by Sea
Hofstra L.R.	*Hofstra Law Review*
HSSC	Harmonized system of ship survey and certification
IACS	International Association of Classification Societies
IAEA	International Atomic Energy Agency
I.B.L.	*International Business Lawyer*
ICAO	International Civil Aviation Organization
I.C.C.L.R.	*International Company and Commercial Law Review*
I.C.J.	International Court of Justice
I.C.J. Reports	International Court of Justice Reports
I.C.R.	Incorporated Council of Law Reporting for England and Wales, The Law Reports
I.J.S.L.	*International Journal of Shipping Law*
ILM	International Legal Materials, American Society of International Law
IMCO	Intergovernmental Consultative Organization
IMF	International Monetary Fund
IMO	International Maritime Organization
INMARSAT	Convention on the International Maritime Satellite Organization
Int.Enc.Comp.L.	International Encyclopedia of Comparative Law
Int.I.L.R.	*International Insurance Law Review*
Int.J.Mar. & Coast.L.	*International Journal of Marine and Coastal Law*
Int.M.L.	*International Maritime Law*
Inter.L.For.du droit intern.	*International Law FORUM du droit international*
Int. Oil Spill Conf.	*International Oil Spill Conference* [Journal]
IOPCF Doc.	Documents of the International Oil Pollution Compensation Funds
IOPC Funds	International Oil Pollution Compensation Funds
ISM Code	International Safety Management Code
ISPS Code	International Ship and Port Facility Security Code
I.T.L.O.S.	International Tribunal for the Law of the Sea
J.Air L.&Com.	*Journal of Air Law and Commerce*
J. Econ. Persp.	*Journal of Economic Perspectives*
J.I.M.L.	*Journal of International Maritime Law*
J.Mar.L.&Com.	*Journal of Maritime Law and Commerce*
JW	*Juristische Wochenschau*
JZ	*Juristenzeitung*
K.B.	Kings Bench Division
K.C.L.J.	*Kings College Law Journal*
K.B.	*Law Reports, King's Bench*
KRS	Korean Register of Shipping
Law & Pol'y	*Law & Policy*
Law & Pol'y in Int'l Bus.	*Law & Policy in International Business*
LDC	Convention on the prevention of marine pollution by dumping of wastes and other matter
LL	*Lloyd's List*

LL 1966	Load Lines 1996
Ll.L.Rep.	Lloyd's List Law Reports
L.M.C.L.Q.	*Lloyd's Maritime and Commercial Law Quaterly*
Lloyd's Rep.	Lloyd's Law Reports
LLMC	Convention on Limitation of Liability for Maritime Claims
LNTS	League of Nations Treaty Service
LR	Lloyd's Register
L.R. Exch.	Law Reports Court of Exchequer
Mar. Law.	*The Maritime Lawyer*
Mar.Pol.Bull.	*Marine Pollution Bulletin*
Marit. Pol. Mgmt.	*Maritime Pollution Management*
Mar. Pol'y	*Marine Policy*
MARPOL	International Convention for the Prevention of Pollution from Ships
MDR	*Monatsschrift für deutsches Recht*
MEPC	Documents of the Marine Environment Protection Committee
M.L.A.A.N.Z.J.	*The Maritime Law Association of Australia & New Zealand Journal*
M.L.R.	*Modern Law Review*
MSC	Documents of the IMO Maritime Safety Committee
MV	Motor Vessel
Neb. L. Rev.	*Nebraska Law Review*
NJW	*Neue Juristische Wochenschau*
NJW-RR	*Neue Juristische Wochenschau Rechtsprechungs Report*
NJWE-VHR	*NJW Entscheidungsdienst Versicherungs- und Haftungsrecht*
No.	Number
Nor.J.I.L.	*Nordic Journal of International Law*
Notre Dame L.Rev.	*Notre Dame Law Review*
Nott.L.J.	*Nottingham Law Journal*
NVwZ	*Neue Zeitschrift für Verwaltungsrecht*
N.Z.B.L.Q.	*New Zealand Business Law Quaterly*
N.Z.C.A.	*Court of Appeal of New Zealand Reports*
NZG	*Neue Zeitschrift für Gesellschaftsrecht*
N.Z.L.R.	*New Zealand Law Review*
NZTS	New Zealand Treaty Series, New Zealand Government
NZV	*Neue Zeitschrift für Verkehrsrecht*
Ocean Dev. & Int'l L.	*Ocean Development & International Law*
OECD	Organisation for Economic Co-operation and Development
OILPOL	International Convention for the Prevention of Pollution of the Sea by Oil, 1954
OJ	Official Journal of the European Union
OPA	Oil Pollution Act
OPPR	IMO Documents from the Conference on International Co-operation on Oil Pollution Preparedness and Response
OPRC 1990	International Convention on Oil Pollution Preparedness, Response and Co-operation
O.R.	Official Referee
p.	page
P.	*Law Reports Probate, Divorce and Admiralty*

PAL 1974	Athens Convention Relating to the Carriage of Passengers and Their Luggage by Sea, 1974
P.C.	Privy Council
P.C.I.J.	Permanent Court of International Justice
P&I	Protection and Indemnity
P&I Int.	*P& I International*
P.N.L.R.	Professional Negligence and Liability Reports
Q.B.	Law Reports, Queen's Bench
Q.B.D.	Queens Bench Division
Q.S.C.	Supreme Court of Queensland, Australia
RECIEL	*Review of European Community and International Environmental Law*
Rep.	Reports
Res.	Resolution
RGZ	Entscheidungen des Reichsgerichts in Zivilsachen
RINA	Registro Italiano Navale
RMC	The Ratification of Maritime Conventions. Edited by the Institute of Maritime Law, University of Southampton. London: 1990.
RS	Russian Maritime Register of Shipping
Santa Clara L.Rev.	*Santa Clara Law Review*
SchSV	Schiffssicherheitsverordnung
S.Ct.	United States Supreme Court
SDR	Standard Drawing Right of the International Monetary Fund
Sect.	Section
Seton Hall Legis.J.	*Seton Hall Legislative Journal*
SIAA	Suits in Admiralty Act
SOLAS	Convention for the Safety of Life at Sea
Spill Science & Tech.Bull.	*Spill Science and Technologie Bulletin*
Stan.L.Rev.	*Stanford Law Review*
STCW 1978	International Convention on standards of training, certification and watchkeeping for seafarers, 1978
STP	Special Trade Passenger Ships Agreement
suppl.	supplement
TIAS	Treaties and other International Act Series, United States Government
TranspR	*Transportrecht*
Tul.L.Rev.	*Tulane Law Review*
Tul.Mar.L.J.	*Tulane Maritime Law Journal*
U.Chi.L.Rev.	*The University of Chicago Law Review*
UCTA	Unfair Contract Terms Act 1977
UKTS	United Kingdom Treaty Series
UNCLOS	United Nations Convention on the Law of the Sea
UNIDROIT	International Institute for the Unification of Private Law
UNTS	United Nations Treaty Series
U.Pa.J.Int'l Econ.L.	*University of Pennsylvania Journal of International Economic Law*
U. Pa. L. Rev.	*University of Pennsylvania Law Review*
U.S.	United States Supreme Court
USCG	United States Coast Guard
USLW	BNA United States Law Week

UST	United States Treaty Series 1778-1945, merged into TIAS.
US Treaty Doc.	United States Congress, Senate, Treaty Document
VersR	*Zeitschrift für Versicherungsrecht*
vol.	volume
WL	Westlaw
W.L.R.	*Weekly Law Reports*
W.M.	*Wertpapier-Mitteilungen*
Yale L.J.	*Yale Law Journal*
ZEuP	*Zeitschrift für europäisches Privatrecht*
ZHR	*Zeitschrift für das gesamte Handelsrecht und Wirtschaftsrecht*
ZIP	*Zeitschrift für Wirtschaftsrecht*
ZPO	*Zivilprozessordnung* (German Code of Civil Procedure)

Introduction

Classification societies have assumed the control of all kinds of maritime technology for both private entities and governments. In many instances they possess even more detailed knowledge about a vessel than its shipowner or flag State. Representations that are made by classification societies are not only relied upon by the maritime industry. These societies also participate in the development of the safety standards they enforce and apply. However, despite the fact that their control is of superior importance to the shipowner, to third parties, and to the flag State, classification societies often argue that their role is subordinate to their contracting parties and that they do not assume liability for their acts. They argue that the activity of the classification society does not in itself cause a risk to third parties. These societies could only state that a vessel is safe which proves not to be, but the risk is usually caused by the vessel rather than by the incorrect representation. Whether or not such representation provides an actionable claim for persons such as the shipowner, the insurance company of the vessel, crew members, passengers, or even coastal States which suffer from the consequences of an incident will be the subject of this thesis. If there is such liability, the question arises of how it may be integrated in the sophisticated system of limitations of liability in shipping.

In order to be able to analyse the liability of these societies under English, United States and German law, it is not only necessary to define their scope of activities, to scrutinise their duties and to develop their relevance to the system of maritime safety. The first part of this thesis also provides a brief history of classification and gives an overview of modern challenges to classification societies, which are required to understand the implications of their liability. Besides, in order to facilitate a comprehensive legal analysis, the legal framework in which a classification society acts is thereafter portrayed in relation to both its public and private functions.

Until today, there have been only a few decisions in which a court held a classification society liable for its action in a civil procedure.[1] In the approximately 175

---

1 A very recent case in which the classification society has been held liable under *United States* law is *Otto Candies, L.L.C. v. Nippon Kaiji Kyokai Corp.*, 2002 WL 1798767 (E.D.La. 2002), 346 F.3d 530, 2003 A.M.C. 2409 (5th.Cir.(La.)2003), 2004 WL 179442, 72 USLW 3668, 72 USLW 3672 (U.S.2004). In *Psarianos v. Standard Marine Ltd. et al.* injured seamen and the relatives of the dead were awarded damages totalling USD 22 million., 728 F. Supp. 438 (E.D.Tex.1989); the award against ABS has not

years of classification societies, one can assume that there have been human errors by surveyors which have caused damage.[2] There are two explanations why there is

---

been published. In the *United Kingdom*, only the Ramsgate trial lead to a condemnation of a classification society, however by a criminal court, *see Health and Safety Executive v. Port Ramsgate Ltd. (and Lloyd's Register)* (Unreported, 1997) (Central Crim.Ct.), discussed by Barber, 'Ramsgate Walkway Collapse: Legal Ramifications', 17 *Const.L.J.* 25 (2001). For an analysis of the liability of classification societies under *German* law *see* Basedow/Wurmnest, *Die Dritthaftung von Klassifikationsgesellschaften* (2004) as well as Basedow/Wurmnest, *Third-Party Liability of Classification Societies* (2005). The other cases under English, German and United States law will be discussed *infra* in Part 2.

[2] In *France* the Cour d'Appel de Versailles held the classification society liable in the cases "*Elodie II*", 21 March 1996, [1996] *DMF* 721 (with case-comment by Delebecque, 'Observations–La responsabilité extra-contractuelle des sociétés de classification: quel régime juridique?', [2005] *DMF* 318) and *"Wellborn"*, 9 December 2004, [2005] *DMF* 313. *See also* Cour de Cassation (Chambre de requêtes) 15 May 1923, *Revue de droit maritime comparé*, vol. 3 (1923), p. 384; Chambre Arbitrale Maritime de Paris, Sentence n° 115 du 5 April 1974, [1974] *DMF* 635; Tribunal de commerce de Marseille 6 January 1978, [1978] DMF 510. In other cases such as Cour de Cassation (1ère Chambre civile) 11 May 1999, [2000] *DMF* 39 (with case comment Bonassies, [2000] *DMF* 41), Cour d'Appel de Tunis 23 February 1955, [1956] *DMF* 87 and Cour d'Appel de Paris 9 June 1999, [2000] *DMF* 326 – "*Mamer*" (with case comment Coste, [2000] *DMF* 332) their liability has been rejected. Moreover, there have been some criminal actions against classification societies in *France*, *e.g.* against a manager of BV after the sinking of the "*Cap-de-la-Hague*", Cour d'Appel de Douai 6 July 1978, [1981] *DMF* 153, Cour de Cassation (Chambre criminelle) 30 May 1980, [1981] *DMF* 146, with comments by Langavant/Boisson, 'L'affaire du naufrage de la drague « Cap-de-la-Hague » et le problème de la responsabilité des sociétés de classification', [1981] *DMF* 131. *Compare* also Tribunal de Grande Instance d'Avrances 12 January 1982, Cour d'Appel de Caen 12 January 1983, Cour de Cassation (Chambre criminelle) 8 October 1985 – "*Compass Rose III*" (unpublished); Cour de Cassation (Chambre criminelle) 7 July 1998, [1999] *DMF* 106 – "*Snekkar Arctic*" (case comment Morin, [1999] *DMF* 118, notably at 120); Cour de Cassaction (Chambre criminelle) 29 March 2001, [2002] *DMF* 14; Tribunal correctionnel de Saint-Nazaire 18 March 2003, [2003] *DMF* 1068 (with case comment Proutière-Maulion, 'Observations', [2003] *DMF* 1088). The liability under *French* law is analysed by Coffi, *Les sociétés de classification à l'épreuve de la sécurité maritime* (2001), Mémoire de la Faculté de Droit et de Sciences Politiques d'Aix-Marseille, accessible at <http://www.cdmt.droit.u-3mrs.fr/memoires/2001/m01coch.doc>, last accessed 19 March 2007; Ferrer, *La Responsabilité des Sociétés de Classification* (2004); Govare, 'Le Bureau Véritas', in: Associazione Italiana di Diritto Marittimo, *Studi in Onore di Francesco Berlingieri* (1933), at 250; Saunière, *Le Buréau Véritas* (1932) ; *compare also* Boisson, 'Classification Society Liability: Maritime Law Principles Must be Requestion (sic !)?', [1994] *CMI Yearbook* 235, Boisson, 'Responsabilité des sociétés de classification: Faut-il remettre en cause les principes du droit maritime?', [1995] *DMF* 109.

only a limited body of case-law regarding classification societies. First of all, classification societies have settled disputes in order to avoid negative precedents. Secondly, considerations of public policy have favoured classification societies for a long time. Most of the reported cases refer to issues such as the possibility for a shipowner to limit his liability and the argument that if classification societies were to be held liable, they would in effect become a super-insurer of all seaborne traffic. Moreover, it is stated that classification societies act for the public benefit and should therefore not be liable.

In order to analyse whether classification societies are liable for their actions, and if so to what extent, this thesis focuses in its second part on German, English and United States law. The liability of these entities towards their contracting parties and towards third parties will be dealt with, both in the performance of private and public functions. The case-law will be analysed and commented upon. Situations which have not yet been tried shall also be taken into consideration. Furthermore, the implications of a liability of such societies shall be reviewed.

Under *Greek law* there has been the case of the Court of the First Instance of Athens 8909/1985, Hellenic Justice Review (*Elleniki Dikaiosini*) 26, 1409, 1415, which is analysed by Antapassis, 'Classification Societies' Liability: A Comparison with Emphasis to Greek Law', in: Huybrechts, *Marine Insurance at the Turn of the Milennium*, Vol. 2 (2000), 57, at 68.

In *Italy* there has been the criminal case of the "Tito Campanella", Tribunale di Savona 29 October 1990, [1991] *Il Diritto Marittimo* 423. *Italian* law is covered by Lopez de Gonzalo, 'La Responsabilità delle Società di Classifica', [1997] *Diritto del Commercio Internazionale* 651, at 656 *et seq.*; Comenale Pinto, 'La Responsabiltà delle Società di Classificazione di Navi', [2003] *Il Diritto Marittimo* 3.

A detailed analysis of their liability under *Spanish* law is undertaken by Pulido Begines, *La responsabilidad frente a terceros de las sociedades de clasificación de buques* (2006), as well as Gómez Prieto, 'Las sociedades de clasificación de buques', 11 *Anuario de Derecho Marítimo* 257 (1994).

For the legal situation in the *Nordic* countries, *see* Krüger, 'Fault Liability for Classification Societies Towards Third Parties?', in: Gorton, *Festskrift till Kurt Grönfors* (1991), at 271.

Under *Australian* law, there is a case for the negligent classification of the new built 14.3 meter catamaran *"Sundancer"*, *Natcraft Pty & Henlock Party Ltd. v. Det Norske Veritas & Peter Colley,* [2001] Q.S.C. 348 (file No. SC No. 7976/2000), *accessible at* <http://www.courts.qld.gov.au>, last accessed 19 March 2007. *"Sundancer"* is also the name of the vessel in a different *United States* case, *Sundance Cruises Corp. v. American Bureau of Shipping,* 799 F.Supp. 363 (S.D.N.Y.1992), *aff'd,* 7 F.3d 1077 (2d Cir.1993). The sale of the vessel *"Nivanga"* gave rise to the *New Zealand* case *The Attorney-General v. Wright & ORS,* [2003] NZCA 48, *accessible* at <http://www.austlii.edu.au>, last accessed 19 March 2007. For case comments *see* Beever, 'All at Sea in the Law of Negligent Misrepresentation', 9 *N.Z.B.L.Q.* 101 (2003); Myburgh, 'Review: Shipping Law', (2003) *N.Z.L.R.* 287, at 299–302; Underdown, 'Surveys and Negligence', 18 *M.L.A.A.N.Z.J.* 24 (2004).

One of the main problems of the liability of classification societies is its interrelation with the limited liability of the shipowner. The shipowner can limit his liability, whereas classification societies would be liable to an unlimited extent, despite of not being primarily responsible for the vessel. In an attempt to re-establish a coherent system of liability, the third part of this paper will consider a limitation of the liability of classification societies by way of a European or international regulation. The scope of existing international conventions which limit the liability of parts of the maritime industry will be scrutinised, and the question of whether these laws can be applied or extended to classification societies will be analysed. And finally, the paper will consider whether there is not only a need for a new regulation but also sufficient justification for it, and what the essential principles of such a regulation should be.

Part 1 [Factual Situation and Legal Foundations]

A. The Classification of Vessels

I. The Concept of '*Classification*'

The term 'classification' might imply that ships were arranged in different classes.[3] This was indeed the practice of classification societies in former times, but has long been abolished. The classes of those days depended on the condition of the hull and the equipment. Usually, the hull was classified according to its construction and condition and its class was indicated by the capital letters A, E, I, O or U, according to its construction and condition, as first defined by Lloyd's Register of Shipping.[4] The equipment of the vessel was either good (G), middling (M) or bad (B). This was later replaced by numbers from 1 to 3. 'A1' therefore represented the highest available class of a ship. Some classification societies used numbers or letters instead in order to indicate which percentage of their safety rules was satisfied by the vessel. Often there was also a number for the duration of the class. German Lloyd (GL), for example, awarded to ships which were in conformity with all its rules at the beginning of a class period the class sign '*100 A 5*'. The '*100*' indicated that all requirements were complied with, and the '5' implied that the ship would stay in that class for a period of five years. If GL revised its rules and the ship consequently no longer complied with all of them, the '*100*' would be changed to a lower figure (e.g. '*90*') which represented the percentage of the rules complied with after the revision. It was, however, not indicated which of the requirements were met.

Nowadays, the class symbols still reflect this tradition. Mostly, class symbols still contain an '*A1*' or a '*100*', which is also illustrated by most of the members of the International Association of Classification Societies (IACS), who use their own class symbols to denote that a ship built under their special survey is in com-

---

3 Under '*classification*' the Oxford English Dictionary (*The Oxford English Dictionary*, vol. II C, (1933, Reprinted: 1978)) understands: '1. The action of classifying or arranging in classes, according to common characteristics or affinities; assignment to the proper class. 2. The result of classifying; a systematic distribution, allocation, or arrangement, in a class or classes; esp. of things which form the subject-matter of a science or a methodic inquiry.'

4 Lay, *Marine Insurance* (1925), at 161, 177.

pliance with their rules and thus qualifies for unrestricted sea-going services.[5] But these symbols no longer indicate which percentage of the rules is satisfied. A vessel which is classified must correspond to the minimum standard which is laid down in the rules. It is no longer accepted that a vessel fails to meet this standard. When surveying a vessel, the classification society solely establishes whether the vessel is 'in' or 'out' of class.

The classification of a vessel is always carried out in a similar way. It is a process which consists of several different activities. For example, the American Bureau of Shipping (ABS) describes it in the following way:[6]

> 'The classification process consists of
> a) the development of Rules, Guides, standards and other criteria for the design and construction of marine vessels and structures, for materials, equipment and machinery,
> b) the review of design and survey during and after construction to verify compliance with such Rules, Guides, standards or other criteria,
> c) the assignment and registration of class when such compliance has been verified, and
> d) the issuance of a renewable classification certificate with annual endorsements valid for five years. [...]
>
> For classification, vessels are to comply with both the hull and the machinery requirements of the Rules.'

In accordance with that, the classification society analyses the design, construction, integrity and condition of a vessel of any nationality. It examines and approves drawings, inspects the materials used, surveys[7] the construction in the shipyard and attends the ship's test runs.[8] If the vessel is built in accordance with the society's rules and regulations, the classification society issues the classifica-

---

[5] ABS: ≅ A1; Bureau Veritas (BV): I; China Classification Society (CCS): H CSA 5/5; Det Norske Veritas (DNV): ≅ 1A1; GL: ≅ 100 A5; Korean Register of Shipping (KRS): ≅ KRS1; Lloyd's Register (LR): ≅ 100A1; Nippon Kaiji Kyokai (ClassNK): NS Θ; Registro Italiano Navale (RINA): 100-A-1.1 or C; Russian Maritime Register of Shipping (RS): KM H.

[6] Part 1, Chapter 1, Section 1/1 of the Rules of ABS. *Compare* IACS, *Classification Societies – What, Why and How?* (2005) (accessible at <http://www.iacs.org.uk/_pdf/Class_WhatWhy&How.PDF>, last accessed 19 March 2007). CMI Code of Conduct for Classification Societies, [1995] *CMI Yearbook* 100-106; also reprinted in Annex A & B to Wiswall, 'Classification societies: issues considered by the Joint Working Group', 2 *I.J.S.L.* 171 (1997), at 183, 185; Wiswall, 'Report and Panel Discussion concerning the Joint Working Group on a Study of Issues Re Classification Societies', [1995] *Il Diritto Marittimo* 66, at 274, 277.

[7] '*Survey*', as defined by the IACS Recommendation 82 of July 2003 'Surveyor's Glossary, Hull Terms and Hull Service Terms' (<http://www.iacs.org.uk/guidesandrecs.htm>, last accessed 19 March 2007), is a collective term for examination, testing and evaluation of results and decision-making.

[8] Boisson, 'The Liability of Classification Societies in the Marine Industry Context', in: Lux, *Classification Societies*, (1993), at 3.

tion certificate and publishes the name of the vessel in its Register of Ships. The inspection by the society, however, does not guarantee its seaworthiness; this would require a very thorough and time–consuming inspection.[9] The classification of the vessel aims at improving its seaworthiness, but cannot guarantee it. The surveys aim to balance safety with economically reasonable requirements.

The vessel continues to be '*in class*' as long as it is maintained in a condition which corresponds to the rules. The classification society examines the ship at all scheduled surveys. If the vessel is deficient, it cancels or suspends the class. The Registers of Ships of the members of IACS are publicly accessible. So is the information about vessels of which the class has been cancelled or suspended and on which grounds.[10] Smaller, national classification societies, however, do not usually provide such information.

A vessel usually does not only have a class. Additionally, a '*classification notation'* or specific symbol may be granted to a special type of vessel or equipment. Such *classification notation* may indicate, for example, that the vessel is specifically equipped for the carriage of oil or chemicals in bulk, suitable for ferry service or that it disposes of a specific installation such as a refrigeration system. Just as there are multiple purposes for vessels and seaborne traffic, there are multiple rules for the construction of ships. Moreover, whilst most of the ships are intended for unrestricted ocean service, some trade only in certain geographically limited regions, such as vessels which only operate on internal waterways. Accordingly, particular classification notations and specific rules have been developed for the different types of ships. It is evident that an oil tanker requires substantially different rules from a passenger vessel or a reefer. However, the rules do not cover all aspects of the design and construction or equipment on board a vessel. Every vessel is included in the society's record book with an appropriate classification notation.[11] Vessels of special design, such as vessels designed for ferry service, for dredging or for fishing, will be distinguished in the record book by a notation of the trade for which they have been approved by the classification society. A classification notation may be withdrawn by the classification society if its requirements are no longer fulfilled. The ship however may continue to be *in class* despite losing this classification notation. For example, a vessel equipped with automatic steering appliances can be granted the classification notation '*AUT'*. If these appliances no longer satisfy the requirements of the rules regarding automatic steering appliances, the classification notation *'AUT'* will be withdrawn. In spite of

9 *See* Miller, 'Liability of Classification Societies', 22 *Tul.Mar.L.J.* 75 (1997), at 83.

10 On the homepages of the classification society in question, through a list published by the IACS (<www.iacs.org.uk>, last accessed 19 March 2007) of the ships of which the classification has been withdrawn, and via *Equasis* (<www.equasis.org>, last accessed 19 March 2007).

11 The American Bureau of Shipping, for example, distinguishes between Oil Carrier, Ore Carrier, Bulk Carrier, Ore or Oil Carrier, Oil or Bulk/Ore (OBO) Carrier, Passenger Vessel, Vehicle Carrier, Container Carrier, Towing Vessel, Refrigerated Cargo Vessel, as stated in their Rules, Part 1, Chapter 1, Section 3 §3.

this, the vessel may continue to sail if the crew keeps the watch in the way it has to be kept for ships without such automatic steering equipment.

The process of classification is governed by private law and finds its basis in a private contract with either the shipowner or the shipyard. Classification societies have, however, extended their business to services for public entities. They secure the application of international and national regulations on maritime safety and security, as well as the prevention of marine pollution. Such statutory surveys are effected on the basis of a contract with a flag State and they are governed by public law.[12] Hence, a classification society offers usually both the Classification of a vessel and Statutory Services – two distinct services which are to be distinguished in the following pages. The one is a private, the other a public function. When the term *'classification'* is used, only the private function is meant.

II. The Historical Development of Classification Societies

The classification of vessels has a long history, which can be traced back to a London Coffee House in the 17th century. In 1652, the first Coffee House (not the one of *Edward Lloyd*) was opened in the City of London, and many others soon followed.[13] Coffee was one of the few public diversions that were accepted in those puritan times.[14] As English Coffee Houses were meeting places for all kinds of businessmen, they became important localities for trading and commerce. Various sections of commerce were organised and centralised in them, such as the services of merchants, shippers, marine underwriters, charterers and bankers. Some Coffee Houses became famous spots for a certain commerce and evolved into centres of great commercial activity. Their guests also distributed news, discussed political events and personalities, and exchanged gossip. The place to be for people whose business had to do with shipping was *Lloyd's Coffee House*, which opened in 1688.[15] It was first situated in Tower Street and moved in 1691 to the corner of Lombard Street and Abchurch Lane, across the road from the Royal Exchange and in the centre of the merchant's district of London.[16] Its owner *Edward Lloyd* compiled information on all matters which might be of value and interest to his clien-

---

12 '*Statutory Survey*', as defined by the IACS Recommendation 82 of July 2003 'Surveyor's Glossary, Hull Terms and Hull Service Terms' (<http://www.iacs.org.uk/guidesandrecs.htm>, last accessed 19 March 2007) are collective terms of surveys required to meet requirements by international convention such as Load Line (LL), International Convention for the Safety of Life at Sea (SOLAS 74) and MARPOL 73/78.

13 Lay, *Marine Insurance* (1925), 20; Brown, *300 years of Lloyds* (1988), 17.

14 Brown, *300 years of Lloyds* (1988), 16.

15 It is first mentioned in an advertisement in the *London Gazette* dated February 18, 1688, with which Mr *Edward Bransby* of Derby sought information about watches which had been stolen from him. Notice could be given to him or at *Edward Lloyd's* Coffee House in Tower street.

16 Brown, *300 years of Lloyds* (1988), 18.

tele,[17] and from 1696 he had this information printed on a news-sheet. This circular included the arrivals and departures of vessels, general shipping intelligence, and happenings at home and abroad that were likely to affect the business of his guests.[18] In total, *Edward Lloyd* published 76 numbers of *'Lloyd's News'*.[19] It was discontinued after *Lloyd* was ordered by the House of Lords to rectify a statement criticising proceedings in Parliament that he had made in his newspaper.[20] But Lloyd preferred to stop printing *'Lloyd's News'* rather than obey the orders. Nonetheless, he continued to provide his customers with intelligence in a hand-written form and included this information in the *'Ships' Lists'*, which he kept in his Coffee House. The *Ships' Lists* cited the names of the ships and the kind of transports they had been used for and gave brief descriptions of ships that were likely to require insurance.[21]

After his death in 1712, *Lloyd's* successors continued to hand out such news-sheets, up until the printed newspaper *'Lloyd's List'* was first circulated in 1726.[22] *'Lloyd's List'* is a Shipping and Mercantile daily paper, which is still published today. Its first issues in 1726 included the ships' lists that had been drawn up in Lloyd's Coffee House. The information was intended for the general use of shipowners, merchants, masters of vessels and underwriters.

In 1760, a society of underwriters established the first register called *'Register of Shipping'* in London. It laid down previous and present names of the vessels, names of the owners and the masters, the ports between which the vessel traded, the tonnage, number of crew, and number of guns carried, the port and year of construction, as well as a classification stating the condition of hull and equipment.[23] For the first time, such a classification required a survey of the ship, but there existed no classification society at the time. The first book was printed in 1764 and dated 1764-65-66. Initially, the information in this *'Green Book'* was also obtained from the Ships' Lists that were kept in Lloyd's Coffee House.[24] The *'Register of Shipping'* was for the exclusive use of the enrolled underwriters; persons who forwarded its information were heavily fined. The only revenue of the

---

17 In the beginning they were read out loud by a waiter called 'the kidney' from a pulpit, which was a special feature of *Edward Lloyd's* Coffee House, see Brown, *300 years of Lloyds* (1988), 18; Martin, *The History of Lloyd's* (1876), 105. *Compare* also Boisson, 'Classification societies and safety at sea–Back to basics to prepare for the future', 18 *Mar. Pol'y* 363 (1994), at 364.

18 Lay, *Marine Insurance* (1925), 24; Ferrer, *La Responsabilité des Sociétés de Classification* (2004), 19.

19 The Bodleian Library, Oxford, keeps copies of Nos. 8 to 76 of *'Lloyd's News'*, the earliest is dated 19 September 1696.

20 Lay, *Marine Insurance* (1925), 25.

21 Saunière, *Le Bureau Véritas* (1932), 34.

22 Martin, *The History of Lloyd's* (1876), 107.

23 Lay, *Marine Insurance* (1925), 161.

24 For this reason, some authors trace the establishment of Lloyd's Register of British and Foreign Shipping back to 1726 when Lloyd's List was founded, *see* Martin, *The History of Lloyd's* (1876), 327.

Register were the subscriptions of the underwriters, who received copies of the book on an annual basis.

In 1797, the criteria of this *'Green Book'* were changed. The classification of the vessel was solely based on its place of construction and its age. Shipbuilders in the southern ports of the United Kingdom were considered more satisfactory than those in the northern ports. A vessel built on the Thames was therefore awarded a class for a period of thirteen years, whereas one built in a northern port was only allowed to hold it for eight years.[25] This discrimination led to unrest among northern shipbuilders and shipowners and ultimately to the founding of a competitor to the *'Green Book'*, the *'The New Register Book of Shipping'*. This list, which is also known as the *'Red Book'*, was issued by a society of shipowners from 1799 onwards.[26] The market however could not sustain two independent registers. It took 35 years of fierce competition before the two registers merged in *Lloyd's Register of British and Foreign Shipping* in 1834, which is nowadays called *Lloyd's Register of Shipping* (LR). Its Register Book was intended not only for insurers, but for the use of the entire shipping community. The first volume recorded all vessels of 50 tons and upwards that were registered in the United Kingdom, whether these vessels had been classed or not.[27] In eleven columns, information was provided concerning the name and description of the vessel, the name of the master, the tonnage, the port and the year of construction, the name of the owner, the port of registry, a classification, if assigned, and the port at which the classification survey was carried out, as well as abbreviated descriptions of the materials of which the vessels were constructed and the repairs executed.[28] At the time of the reprint of the Register Book in 1838, all vessels that had not been surveyed by the exclusive surveyors of the classification society were omitted. Only the committee of the society had the power to grant a class, not the individual surveyor. The society developed its own rules that were based on recommendations by the Committee of Inquiry that had been appointed in 1826. *Lloyd's Register of British and Foreign Shipping* already functioned in the same way as LR does today.

However, as it had already been established in Antwerp in 1828, the first classification society in a modern sense was *Bureau Veritas* (BV).[29] It controlled its registered vessels according to certain rules and was based in Paris as from 1832.[30] *'Lloyd's News'* and *Lloyd's Register of British and Foreign Shipping,* together

---

[25] Lay, *Marine Insurance* (1925), 165.

[26] Boisson, 'Classification societies and safety at sea–Back to basics to prepare for the future', 18 *Mar. Pol'y* 363 (1994), at 365; Lay, *Marine Insurance* (1925), 164; Martin, *The History of Lloyd's* (1876), 332; Saunière, *Bureau Véritas* (1932), 35.

[27] Lay, *Marine Insurance* (1925), 175.

[28] Lay, *Marine Insurance* (1925), 175 *et seq.*

[29] The history of BV is covered by Govare, 'Le Bureau Véritas', in: Associazione Italiana di Diritto Marittimo, *Studi in Onore di Francesco Berlingieri* (1933), at 250; Saunière, *Bureau Véritas* (1932), 36–85. *See also* Boisson, 'Classification societies and safety at sea–Back to basics to prepare for the future', 18 *Mar. Pol'y* 363 (1994), at 365.

[30] Saunière, *Bureau Véritas* (1932), 34.

with BV, were the nucleus of the system of classification of vessels that was copied in many countries. At a time of fierce competition between national merchant fleets, it was considered prestigious to possess a national classification society. Subsequently, many of the international classification societies were set up in the course of the nineteenth century.[31]

III. The Relevance of Classification Societies for the Maritime Industry

1. The Necessity of a Classification of Vessels

There is no general legal obligation that ships must have a class. There were indeed times when the ships of the *British India Steamship Company* or of *Furness Whitney* were not classed because these shipowners were self-insurers.[32] This illustrates the principal reason why shipowners apply for a classification of their vessels. The first and foremost reason is insurance. Hull insurance companies require that a ship is classed by one of the members of IACS, as the standard insurance clause illustrates.[33] Furthermore, only classed vessels can be registered with a P&I club.[34] However, apart from insurance, a carrier will also face problems to contract for cargo if the ship is unclassified or out of class. Even though cargo insurance policies do not generally require the cargo owner to use a classified vessel, cargo underwriters have the right to revoke coverage at reasonable notice if a shipment is carried on a vessel whose classification has been revoked.[35] Moreover, representations made by the classification society can be important for both the seller and the purchaser of a vessel.[36] Also, chartering practice requires the ser-

---

31 ABS was founded in 1862, BV in 1828, China Classification Society (CCS) in 1956, Germanischer Lloyd (GL) in 1867, Det Norske Veritas (DNV) in 1864, Korean Register of Shipping (KRS) in 1960, Nippon Kaiji Kyokai (ClassNK) in 1899, Registro Italiano Navale (Rina) in 1861, and Russian Maritime Register of Shipping (RS) in 1913. For the history of the GL *see* Germanischer Lloyd, *Germanischer Lloyd-Internationales Register, 1867-1992* (1992); Lehmann/Lau, *Geprüfte Sicherheit–Der Germanische Lloyd im Wandel der Zeiten* (1997).

32 There are still some ships registered in the least reliable flags of convenience which are unclassed and uninsured, *compare* Goss, 'Maritime Insurance and Economic Welfare', 30 *Marit. Pol. Mgmt.* 357 (2003), at 361.

33 Regarding the Institute Classification Clause *see infra* Part 1 A III 2. There may, however, be certain regions of the world where this requirement is not enforceable.

34 *See for instance Rule 5 section K of the Rules of The United Kingdom Mutual Steam Assurance Association (Bermuda) Ltd.,* reprinted in Benedict, *On Admiralty* (2002), vol. 7A § 1.01 at 1-29 to 1-30; *Rule 8 of The Rules of The London Steam-Ship Owners' Mutual Insurance Association Ltd.,* reprinted in Benedict, *On Admiralty* (2002), vol. 7A § 1.02 at 1-140 to 1-41.

35 Templeman/Lambeth, *On Marine Insurance* (1986), at 46, Brown/Novitt, *Marine Insurance–Cargo Practices* (1985), 53-57.

36 *See infra* Part 1 A III 3.

vices of a classification society as an independent entity that ensures the safety of a vessel which is to be chartered.[37] Since chartering is a highly volatile market, a prospective charterer may need a vessel at a moment's notice. When a charter is cancelled, a vessel may instantly need to be chartered out. There is usually no time to survey the vessel. Instead, the shipowner informs the chartering broker that the vessel is in class and is in possession of a certain classification notation. This indicates that the vessel corresponded at the time of the last survey to the rules of the society and therefore to a certain standard of safety. It is a standard condition of the charter party that the shipowner keeps the vessel in class.[38]

Surveys by an independent organization have the major advantage that underwriters, chartering brokers, or cargo owners need not survey the vessel themselves. A multiplicity of surveys would be technically redundant, costly and a waste of time. In addition, a classification society gains better insights into the condition of a vessel than any other party. It has considerable experience in marine engineering because of its research and development department, and as a result of the analysis of many accidents over the years. By analysing sister vessels, it can also identify more effectively the problems that vessels of a certain construction face.

However, there are also some reasons for a classification that are based on the enforcement of safety by the government. A shipowner may also want to have his ship classified because of the simplicity of receiving a Cargo Ship Safety Construction Certificate pursuant to SOLAS Rule I/12 for a classified vessel. The sole precondition for this certificate is that the vessel is classified by a classification society that is recognised by the flag State. Depending on the domestic regulations, this certificate may be issued directly either by the classification society or by the flag State, which solely checks that the vessel has a valid class. If the ship is not classified, a thorough survey and control of the blueprints of the vessel by the flag State is required. However, if the Cargo Ship Safety Construction Certificate is issued only because the vessel has a valid class, its private classification, which is governed by private law, influences a certificate that is governed by public law. Apart from this aspect of flag State control, port State control (PSC) is also of importance. A vessel which does not have a class or which is registered with a dubious classification society may face considerable disadvantages during PSC. Such a vessel will be considered as a possible hazard, and it will be more often and more closely inspected. Therefore, such vessels have to be used in coastal traffic in regions where PSC is ineffective or they must be put out of service.

In principle, the powers of a classification society are limited. Neither can it order the repair of a vessel nor can it require that certain safety equipment be implemented or that the condition of a vessel be improved in a certain way. Nevertheless, the aforementioned example proves that the society's powers are in fact quite effective. It can require improvements to the safety of the vessel at the threat of otherwise suspending or withdrawing the class. As it is in the shipowner's in-

---

[37] *See also* Part 1 A III 4.

[38] *See infra* Part 1 A III 4.

terests to have a classed vessel, he is likely to follow the recommendations or conditions of the society. However, the classification society only surveys the vessel pursuant to a certain survey cycle, unless the shipowner requests a particular survey. Most classification societies have therefore adopted a rule that they may survey the vessel for reasons of quality control at all times without the request of the shipowner, but this possibility is of hardly any relevance in practice.

2. *Marine Insurance and Classification Societies*

To analyse the relevance of classification societies for insurance matters in further detail, one should keep in mind that marine insurance is carried out in two different ways.[39] The first way is the insurance by one or several insurers by way of an insurance contract. If there are several insurers, the risk is spread between individuals or companies called underwriters. As an example, *Lloyd's of London* is such a society of underwriters consisting of more than 17,000 individual and 95 corporate members.[40] The second way is by mutual insurance through Protection and Indemnity Clubs (P&I Clubs). The members of these clubs are shipowners, who form an association to protect one another against large financial loss. If a loss occurs to one of their members, all others have to contribute according to a ratio that is fixed beforehand. P&I Clubs cover liabilities which are otherwise not insurable, such as the costs of defending claims made by a cargo owner.[41]

It goes without saying that underwriters and P&I Clubs[42] should seek to insure safe vessels. There are different ways to ascertain that a ship is safe and that the risk assumed is to a certain degree a limited one which can be rated and calculated. In former times, hull clubs[43] used to survey all ships which applied for membership.[44] The *Jersey Mutual*, for example, even bought a chain-testing machine with the intention of checking that its insured vessels had reliable cables.[45] The purpose of hull surveys, however, was to establish different ratings for underwriting purposes and not necessarily to prevent loss.[46] Strategies to prevent damage only started when the P&I Clubs started to offer indemnity cover in respect of liabilities for cargo damage. Thereafter they started to analyse the correla-

---

39 For an introduction to Marine Insurance *see* Schoenbaum, *Admiralty and Maritime Law* (2004), § 19, at 244–364.

40 Sullivan, *Marine Encyclopaedic Dictionary*, at the term "*Lloyd's*". In the 19th century, *Lloyd's* and the *Institute of London Underwriters* developed standardised clauses for the use in marine insurance. These claused have been maintained and are known as the *Institute Clauses*.

41 See Sullivan, *Marine Encyclopaedic Dictionary*, at "*Protection and Indemnity Club*".

42 Throughout this thesis the term *insurance company* includes both underwriters and P&I Clubs.

43 Hull clubs are the predecessors of modern P&I clubs; a brief historical introduction to this subject can be found in Hazelwood, *P&I Clubs, Law and Practice* (2000), 1.

44 Hazelwood, *P&I Clubs* (2000), 39.

45 Hazelwood, *P&I Clubs* (2000), 39.

46 Hazelwood, *P&I Clubs* (2000), 39.

tion between the condition and cargo-worthiness of the ship and the number of cargo claims. Modern P&I Clubs, as well as underwriters, require that the vessel remains in class throughout the period of coverage, and that every incident which might affect class is brought to the attention of its classification society. The vessel has to comply with all the rules, recommendations and requirements of the society. In the case of non-compliance, the vessel will no longer be insured and the insurance company is exempt from liability.

Marine underwriters generally demand that the vessel be submitted to a condition survey at the time of entry. In addition to that, the insurance contract obliges the shipowner to have the vessel inspected by an IACS member society or a National Flag Society; the vessel must be *'in class'* and maintained in such a condition.[47] Typically, the insurance contract compels the owners to follow all the recommendations of the vessel's society which relate to the vessel's seaworthiness; otherwise the underwriters are discharged from liability.[48] The insurance coverage may even terminate if the vessel's class is suspended.[49]

---

[47] See e.g. the Institute Clauses, which are published by the Institute of London Underwriters in collaboration with Lloyd's in *Reference Book of Marine Insurance* Clauses (2004):

INSTITUTE CLASSIFICATION CLAUSE 01/01/2001 (CL354-2001)

'1. This insurance and the marine transit rates as agreed in the policy or open cover apply only to cargoes and/or interests carried by mechanically self-propelled vessels of steel construction classed with a Classification Society which is:

1.1 a Member or Associate Member of the International Association of Classification Societies (IACS *), or

1.2 a National Flag Society as defined in Clause 4 below, but only where the vessel is engaged exclusively in the coastal trading of that nation (including trading on an inter-island route within an archipelago of which that nation forms part). [...]

4. A National Flag Society is a Classification Society which is domiciled in the same country as the owner of the vessel in question, which must also operate under the flag of that country.

* For a current list of IACS Members and Associate Members please refer to the IACS website at <www.iacs.org.uk>.'

For an analysis of this clause, *see* Gooding, *Institute Classification Clause Revision* (2000), accessible at <www.iumi.com/conferences/2000_london/docs/Nick Gooding.doc>, last accessed 19 March 2007.

[48] INSTITUTE TIME CLAUSES HULLS 01/11/95, Clause 4–Classification states:

'4.1 It is the duty of the Assured, Owners and Managers at the inception of and throughout the period of this insurance to ensure that

4.1.1 the Vessel is classed with a Classification Society agreed by the Underwriters and that her class within that Society is maintained,

4.1.2 any recommendations, requirements or restrictions imposed by the Vessel's Classification Society which relate to the Vessel's seaworthiness or to her maintenance in a seaworthy condition are complied with by the dates required by that Society.

4.2 In the event of any breach of the duties set out in Clause 4.1 above, unless the Underwriters agree to the contrary in writing, they will be discharged from liability under this insurance as from the date of the breach provided that the Vessel is

P&I Clubs do not put as much emphasis on the classification certificate and ordinary classification surveys. The classification society primarily examines whether the vessel may safely put to sea throughout the time a usual policy of marine insurance is in effect. Since P&I Clubs do not insure the hull of the vessel, but liabilities towards cargo owners, passengers, the crew and other third parties such as coastal States, they often demand a special survey before a vessel may be registered with the club in order to minimise these risks.[50]

Both marine underwriters and P&I Clubs receive information about the date of all class surveys, the expiry date of the classification certificate and overdue surveys, as well as the text of overdue conditions of class and recommendations.[51] If the insurance contract incorporates such an obligation, it may also learn about both the contents of classification certificates and reports and the text of new con-

---

at sea at such date the Underwriters' discharge from liability is deferred until arrival at her next port.

4.3 Any incident, condition or damage in respect of which the Vessel's Classification Society might make recommendations as to repairs or other action to be taken by the Assured, Owners or Managers must be promptly reported to the Classification Society.

4.4 Should the Underwriters wish to approach the Classification Society directly for information and/or documents, the Assured will provide the necessary authorisation.' Explanations of this clause can be found in Howard/Davenport, 'English Maritime Law Update 1994/95', 27 *J.Mar.L.&Com.* 427 (1996), at 441–448; Hudson, *The Institute Clauses* (1999), at 95–97; Thomas, *The Modern Law of Marine Insurance* (1996), 62.

49 Excerpt from INSTITUTE TIME CLAUSES HULLS 01/11/95, Clause 5–Termination: 'Unless the Underwriters agree to the contrary in writing, this insurance shall terminate automatically at the time of

5.1 change of the Classification Society of the Vessel, or change, suspension, discontinuance, withdrawal or expiry of her Class therein, or any of the Classification Society's periodic surveys becoming overdue unless an extension of time for such survey be agreed by the Classification Society, provided that if the Vessel is at sea such automatic termination shall be deferred until arrival at her next port. However where such change, suspension, discontinuance or withdrawal of her Class or where a periodic survey becoming overdue has resulted from loss or damage covered by Clause 6 of this insurance or which would be covered by an insurance of the Vessel subject to current Institute War and Strikes Clauses Hulls–Time such automatic termination shall only operate should the Vessel sail from her next port without the prior approval of the Classification Society or in the case of a periodic survey becoming overdue without the Classification Society having agreed an extension of time for such survey.'

An analysis of this clause is provided by Hudson, *The Institute Clauses* (1999), at 97–99.

50 Hazelwood, *P&I Clubs* (2000), 40.

51 *See* IACS Procedural Requirement No. 3 'Transparency of Classification and Statutory Information' (accessible at <http://www.iacs.org.uk/preqs/main.htm>, last accessed 19 March 2007).

ditions of class and recommendations.[52] The insurers will be informed about the due dates of statutory surveys and the expiry date of statutory certificates. On top of that, they may consult the registered and overdue statutory recommendations.[53] The fact that both marine insurers and P&I Clubs only insure vessels that are in class illustrates that they rely on the information about the ships which is contained in class records[54] and have identified classification societies as an important component of the marine safety system.[55]

3. *The Norwegian Saleform and a Confirmation of Class*

The purchaser of a ship will always want to ascertain that she is in good condition. This may be achieved by inspecting the ship or by investigating the vessel's classification record. The Norwegian Saleform,[56] which is one of the forms most

---

52 *See* IACS Procedural Requirement No. 3 'Transparency of Classification and Statutory Information' (accessible at <http://www.iacs.org.uk/preqs/main.htm>, last accessed 19 March 2007).

53 *See* IACS Procedural Requirement No. 3 'Transparency of Classification and Statutory Information' (accessible at <http://www.iacs.org.uk/preqs/main.htm>, last accessed 19 March 2007).

54 A typical example of the information provided and the information policy of a classification society is included in 1-1-1-3.5 of the Rules of ABS:
'The Bureau will release certain information to the vessel's hull underwriters and P&I clubs for underwriting purposes. Such information includes text of overdue conditions of classification, survey due dates, and certificate expiration dates. The Owners will be advised of any request and/or release of information.
In case of overdue conditions of classification, the Owners will be given the opportunity to verify the accuracy of the information prior to release.'

55 However, they could do more according to the OECD, *see* OECD, Maritime Transport Committee, *Report on the Removal of Insurance from Sub-standard Shipping* (2004). *See also* Bennett, 'Governing environmental risk: regulation, insurance and moral economy', 23 *Progress in Human Geography* 189 (1999), at 204; Bennett, 'Mutual Risk: P&I Insurance Clubs and Maritime Safety and Environmental Performance', 25 *Mar. Pol'y* 13 (2001), at 17; Furger, 'Accountability and Systems of Self-Governance: The Case of the Maritime Industry', 19 *Law & Pol'y* 445 (1997), at 458–461, 464–465; Richardson, 'Mandating Environmental Liability Insurance', 12 *Duke Entl. L. & Pol'y F.* 293 (2002), at 325.

56 Norwegian Shipbrokers' Association's Memorandum of Agreement for sale and purchase of ships. Adopted by the Baltic and International Maritime Council (BIMCO) in 1956. Codename SALEFORM 1993, revised in 1966, 1983 and 1986/87. A copy of it is attached as Appendix VIII to Gorton/Hillenius//Ihre/Sandevärn, *Shipbroking and Chartering Practice* (2004), Hodges/Hill, *Principles of Maritime Law* (2001), Appendix 4. See also Breitzke, *Norwegian Saleform* (1970); Hodges/Hill, *Principles of Maritime Law* (2001), 31-66; Strong/Herring, *Sale of Ships, The Norwegian Saleform* (2004). For an interpretation of Clause 9 see *Rank Enterprises Ltd. and Others v. Gerard,* Times Law Reports, Feb. 28, 2000; as regards Clause 11 of the Norwegian Saleform (1983

commonly used for the sale of ships,[57] requires that the vessel's classification society mediates between the buyers and the sellers in a certain way. The vessel's classification records remain in the possession of the sellers, but the buyers may inspect them. Moreover, the classification society will either survey the vessel's underwater parts in a dry dock or have it inspected by a diver at the buyers' request. Those inspections are carried out in accordance with the classification society's rules. The buyers may be present at the dry dock as long as they do not interfere with the work or the decision of the classification society. On the occasion of such inspections, the classification society might require repairs, which have to be carried out at the seller's expense. Just before delivery, a confirmation of class is to be provided by the classification society. It contains information about the ship's classification rating, any class recommendations or memoranda for the owners. Overdue surveys may be included, as well as outstanding debts to the society.[58] When delivered, the vessel shall be delivered with her class maintained without conditions or recommendations.[59]

Revision), *see Niobe Maritime Corporation v. Tradax Ocean Transportation S.A.* [1995] 1 *Lloyd's Rep.* 579.

57 Other forms are Nipponsale '93 and Barecon '89, which is a bareboat charter form published by BIMCO that contains an optional instalment sale agreement in its Part IV. Nipponsale includes a classification clause similar to the one of the Norwegian Saleform '93.

58 Goldrein/Turner, *Ship Sale and Purchase* (2003), 110, 192, 194.

59 'Clause 11. Condition on Delivery
The Vessel with everything belonging to her shall be at the Sellers' risk and expense until she is delivered to the Buyers, but subject to the terms and conditions of this Agreement she shall be delivered and taken over as she was at the time of inspection, fair wear and tear excepted.
However, the Vessel shall be delivered with her class maintained without condition/recommendation*, free of average damage affecting the Vessel's class, and with her classification certificates and national certificates, as well as all other certificates the Vessel had at the time of the inspection, valid and unextended without condition/recommendation* by Class or the relevant authorities at the time of delivery.
"Inspection" in this Clause 11, shall mean the Buyers' inspection according to Clause 4 a) or 4 b), if applicable, or the Buyer's inspection prior to the signing of this Agreement. If the Vessel is taken over without inspection, the date of this Agreement shall be the relevant date.
* Notes, if any, in the surveyor's report which are accepted by the Classification Society without condition/recommendation are not to be taken into account.'
For an interpretation of Clause 11 of the Norwegian Saleform (1983 Revision) under English law, see *Niobe Maritime Corporation v. Tradax Ocean Transportation S.A.* [1995] 1 *Lloyd's Rep.* 579.

As stated in Clause 4,[60] the purchase contract may be concluded in a way that the buyers are allowed to inspect the ship themselves. In such a case, the statements and certificates of the classification society are naturally of importance to them, but they have the opportunity to verify them. Whenever only Clause 4 b) is applicable, the buyer may not inspect the vessel by himself. He is therefore forced to rely upon the representations of the classification society unless it is stipulated that the vessel is surveyed in a dry dock and the buyer has the right to be present at the time of the survey. The buyer of the ship is therefore in possession of all ship-related information which is included in the Classification Records and will usually rely on this information.

Pursuant to Clause 8 c), the seller has to deliver a confirmation of class within 72 hours prior to delivery of the ship. The aim of a confirmation of class is a very distinct one. It informs whether or not any class-related deficiencies are included in the files of the classification society, or whether the class or class notation of the vessel is subject to any conditions. The vessel is not entirely surveyed once again on the issuance of the confirmation of class, because of the costs and the time that an additional survey would require. Due to this fact, a confirmation of class does not claim to reflect exactly the condition of the vessel; it only reflects the status as ascertained in the course of the last surveys. This status has been laid down in the files, which are the basis of the confirmation of class. As a result, the condition of the vessel may have changed since the last time a survey was executed. Nonetheless, unless the shipowner has informed the classification society of any subsequent deficiency, it will provide a clean confirmation of class. If this situation has changed since the last surveys, one cannot hold the classification society liable for such a change for the worse. Whenever there are existing conditions related to the class, the shipowner will request the society to conduct surveys to check whether these conditions have to be upheld or can be withdrawn. Only in this respect will surveys be executed.

4. Charter Parties and Classification Societies

The charterer does not receive any specific ship-related information from the classification society. He knows whether or not the vessel is in class. In addition to that, he may consult the information contained in the classification society's Register of Ships. The charterer of the ship will either transport cargo which belongs to himself or to someone else, or sub-charter the boat. Therefore, if an incident oc-

---

[60] 'Clause 4. Inspections

a)* The Buyers have inspected and accepted the Vessel's classification records. The Buyers have also inspected the vessel at/in [...] on [....] and have accepted the Vessel following this inspection and the sale is outright and definite, subject only to the terms and conditions of this Agreement.

b)* The Buyers shall have the right to inspect the Vessel's classification records and declare whether the same are accepted or not within [...]

* *4a) and 4b) are alternatives; delete whichever is not applicable. In the absence of deletions, alternative 4a) to apply.'*

curs, he may be affected if it is his own property or be held liable by the owner of the cargo. In cases in which he sub-charters the vessel, he may be subject to recourse, unless he exempts himself from these obligations.[61] Charter parties usually contain a clause that a chartered vessel has to be classified by a classification society.[62] The charterer may only rely on the fact that the ship is classified and on the information given in the Register of Ships.

5. *The Rules of a Classification Society*

As the process of classification is governed by the individual rules of the society, it is of relevance what these rules imply. They are not designed from the point of view of a perfectly safe ship – which in fact would be impossible to design and too expensive to build. One can never be entirely safe. On the contrary, there are always incidents which have never happened before and which are entirely new and

---

61 An exemption clause is common in charter-parties, *see* Gorton/Hillenius/Ihre/ Sandevärn, *Shipbroking and Chartering Practice* (2004), at 212–214.

62 In order to illustrate this fact, several standard form clauses are included as follows. According to the Americanized Welsh Coal Charter, issued by the Association of Ship Brokers and Agents (U.S.A.) Inc., the vessel has to be classed at the time the contract is concluded (Williams, *Chartering Documents* (1999), 184). Similarly, the Baltic and International Maritime Conference Uniform Time-Charter (BALTIME FORM) requires the vessel to be classed (see Wilford/Coghlin/Kimball, *Time Charters* (2003), 21). In the same way, the Deep Sea Time Charter issued by the Baltic and International Maritime Conference, called LINERTIME, demands the vessel to be classed (included in Gorton/Hillenius//Ihre/Sandevärn, *Shipbroking and Chartering Practice* (2004), Appendix II). New York Produce Exchange Form Time Charter 1993 (Code Name: 'NYPE 93') (A copy of the NYPE 93 is included in Gorton/Hillenius//Ihre/Sandevärn, *ibid.*, Appendix IV, and Wilford/Coghlin/Kimball, *ibid.,* 7) issued by the Association of Ship Brokers and Agents (U.S.A.), Inc., and recommended by The Baltic and International Maritime Council (BIMCO), as well as The Federation of National Associations of Shipbrokers and Agents (FONASBA). The North American Grain Charterparty 1973 (NORGRAIN 89), issued by the Association of Ship Brokers and Agents (U.S.A.) Inc. requires information about the vessel's classification and its current status (see Williams, *ibid.*, 174). SHELLTIME 4 (issued December 1984, a copy of which is included in Gorton/Hillenius//Ihre/Sandevärn, *ibid.*, Appendix V, as well as Wilford/Coghlin/ Kimball, *ibid.,* 27), which is used by Shell International Shipping Limited also requires that the vessel be classed. The form which is used by the same company as a Voyage Carter Party (SHELLVOY 5), issued July 1987 (text printed in Gorton/Hillenius/ Ihre/Sandevärn, *ibid.*, Appendix VI) demands that '*Part I (A) Owners guarantee that at the date hereof the vessel:- (i) is classed [...]*'. Similar statements are in the Tanker Time Charter Party (STB TIME Form) (see Wilford/Coghlin/Kimball, *ibid.,* 37). By contrast, there is no clause with regard to classification societies in the form recommended by the Baltic and International Maritime Council for trades for which no specially approved form is in force, which is called Uniform General Charter (as revised 1922, 1976, and 1994) (GENCON) (included in Gorton/Hillenius/Ihre/Sandevärn, *ibid.,* Appendix I).

unexpected. The rules are generally developed in retrospect, but they are being constantly improved by knowledge gained through marine engineering. In the same way, the rules for new units or products are developed from the experience gained from existing products. They have evolved in the course of time and have always been updated whenever accidents have happened. It is not the ship in total, but all of its parts which have been identified as potentially hazardous or vital to its safety that are covered. The rules of the classification societies contain a large number of requirements as to the way the hull, the superstructures and the equipment (including *e.g.* anchoring, towing and mooring equipment) have to be constructed and maintained. There are regulations on what materials are to be employed for which usage, how the welding has to be carried out and tested, in which way fire safety measures are to be implemented, how the vessel systems and machinery (including propulsion, boilers, deck and other machinery, electrical systems) are to be constructed, and how optional items and systems (such as cargo refrigeration installations) are to be developed and maintained. This list is not exhaustive. For all specific class notations there are detailed regulations on how the installation is to be constructed and in which condition it is to be maintained. It is, however, not possible to use the rules as a blueprint for building a ship. They only imply that the ship fulfils all measures known to avoid common deficiencies at the time of its inspection.

As all major classification societies develop their own rules, the rules allow some competition between the societies.[63] Classification societies may develop their rules on their own unless they have to implement unified requirements that have been decided upon at IACS.[64] A shipowner who intends to build a new vessel will therefore make inquiries about the societies' rules and their consequences in practice. For instance, a difference of a few millimetres in the scantlings may considerably change the price of a large vessel.[65] This example illustrates that the rules have to balance the public interest concerning the safety of a ship and the interest of the shipyards and shipowners to build not only safe but also affordable ships at competitive prices. Despite considerations of economic necessities, it must be ensured that the rules are state-of-the-art and that these safety requirements are effectively met against any pressure from the industry. In a given case, it may, however, be very difficult to ascertain what precisely the state of the art requires.

It can be concluded from these reflections concerning the rules that the classification of a vessel is very different from the quality control of a product. A classification society does not guarantee or confirm that a vessel is built in a perfect way

---

[63] The process of rule-making by the classification societies is analysed by Furger, 'Accountability and Systems of Self-Governance: The Case of the Maritime Industry', 19 *Law & Pol'y* 445 (1997), at 456–457. *Compare also* Smith, 'The role of classification societies in the regulatory regime', 95 *BIMCO Bull.* 18 (2000).

[64] *See also* Part 1 A V.

[65] O'Gray, 'Why don't classification societies admit liability?', [1998] *BIMCO Review* 109, at 110; *LL*, May 20, 2005, at 10, 'Teamwork paying dividends in safety drive'.

or even suitable for the trade it is intended for. It only states that the standard of its own rules is fulfilled by the ship. A certification of parts of the equipment of the vessel only states that they are safe in general, and not that every such product in fact is safe. However, this is already quite substantial.

6. *Marine Surveyors*

One needs to distinguish between classification societies and marine surveyors. Marine surveyors are the people that actually carry out a survey. There are marine surveyors for all kinds of maritime activities. They usually act at the request of a shipowner, charterer, potential purchaser of a vessel or of the owners of cargo or a classification society itself. Marine surveyors may conduct damage surveys, surveys of the condition of a vessel, check how a vessel is loaded and the cargo is stowed, check the quality of the cargo and survey it on- and off-charter.[66] Most classification societies call upon a number of exclusive and non-exclusive marine surveyors who are based in almost every major port and shipyard in the world. Since many sea-going vessels are operated world-wide and rarely, if ever, return to their port of registry, it is indispensable that classification societies offer world-wide services. A shipowner seeking advice for the repair of his vessel will need the service without delay to ascertain that the vessel can complete its journey as soon as possible. Moreover, surveyors must be available at any dry dock in order to survey the structure of the hull of a vessel in dry dock. Only major classification societies have such a network of surveyors.

If a marine surveyor acts on behalf of a classification society, his liability is closely linked to the question of the liability of classification societies. However, since marine surveyors exercise a large variety of different activities, which may or may not be in any relation to the obligation of the shipowner to provide a seaworthy vessel, and because of the limited financial capability of a single marine surveyor, their liability will not be included in this thesis.[67]

7. *Other Activities*

The scope of activities of classification societies has expanded significantly in the course of time. No longer do they only class vessels, but they also give technical advice for structures that are based on land. The societies control international standards that are laid down in quality management systems such as ISO 9001, certify systems, types or projects of offshore installations and provide various other forms of technical assistance to the industry. For these services they act like every other technical adviser and are accordingly subject to the same obligations

---

[66] *See i.e. Coastal (Bermuda) Ltd. v. E.W. Saybolt & Co.*, 826 F.2d 424 (5th Cir.1987).

[67] For a closer analysis of their liability, *see* Beck, 'Liability of Marine Surveyors for Loss of Surveyed Vessel', *Notre Dame L.Rev.* 246 (1989); Goldsmith, 'River Pilot, Marine Surveyor, and Third-Party Inspector Liability', 26 *Tul. Mar. L.J.* 463 (2002); Gordon, 'The Liability of Marine Surveyors and Ship Classification Societies', 19 *J. Mar. L. & Com.* 301 (1988), Stuart/Caffrey, 'Liability of Marine Surveyors, Adjusters, and Claims Handlers', 22 *Tul. Mar. L.J.* 1 (1997).

and the same regime of liability. Hence, they are in the same way liable for their actions as every other technical adviser. Only in the case of the survey and classification of ships may specific principles of maritime law influence their liability. For this reason, their activities as a developer and surveyor of the 'class' and as a chartered surveyor who analyses the condition of a vessel will be dealt with in the following sections. Moreover, the situation of statutory surveys will also be considered.

IV. The Relevance of Classification Societies for the International Community

Public authorities have assigned an increasing number of functions to classification societies. These societies conduct surveys for the flag State administration and issue statutory certificates. In some cases they have effectively taken over the place of flag State control or at least exercise a more effective control than the administration. As regards surveys of ships world-wide, classification societies perform statutory surveys for almost every flag State administration.[68] They are an integral part of the system of maritime safety. According to public international law, a flag State cannot exercise its power on foreign territory and therefore has to call upon a classification society if it wants to survey a vessel in a foreign port. Classification societies facilitate the smooth international operation of ships and make it possible that ships do not have to return to their ports of registry at least once a year. One can either see this development as an advantage, because it saves resources and promotes efficiency, or one can disapprove of it due to the fact that ships no longer have a link to their port of registry.[69] The lack of flag State control means that there can be sub-standard shipping. Vessels that do not fulfil the safety requirements may be considerably cheaper to operate and therefore provide shipowners with competitive advantages. Sub-standard operators can save an enormous amount of money, which allows them to offer dumping prices and thus have economic advantages in a highly competitive market.

---

[68] For a complete list of all 59 classification societies that carry out statutory surveys on behalf of flag States *see* FSI/Circ.10 of 4 June 2001. A list of authorisations given by administrations to IACS classification societies and the precise scope of authorisation is included in Annex 2 to FSI 12/7/3 of 12 December 2003. This document is accessible online at <http://www.iacs.org.uk/submissions.htm>, last accessed 19 March 2007.

[69] 'Genuine link' in the sense of Article 91 (1) 2nd sentence UNCLOS means today that the ship is under survey and control with respect to the international standards, as spelled out in Article 94 UNCLOS, *see* I.T.L.O.S. *MV Saiga (No. 2) Case*, 1 July 1999, 37 para. 83. The genuine link is therefore, in fact, assured by the classification society.

Such vessels may only be controlled by classification societies or port State control.[70] In areas where there is not even effective port State control, classification societies may be the only guarantors of a minimum standard of safety. If the vessel is classed by a national classification society which does not enforce the safety standards nor has sufficient experience and knowledge, the shipowner may be able to operate a sub-standard vessel within a certain regional market. Safety, sub-standard shipping and the fairness of competition between shipowners are therefore interrelated. The example of the oil industry shows that certain classification societies still might have to improve their services. All major oil companies have their own surveyors who check whether a chartered vessel is fit for the transport of oil. Such surveys are called *'vetting inspections prior to accepting a tanker'*.[71] For the companies, the classification certificate is not sufficient to prove that the vessel is in a safe condition to transport oil.

Whether or not flag State control is carried out by the maritime administration, there are at least classification societies which are obliged to control the vessel once in a while. If the flag State does not look after its vessels and is thus in violation of Article 94 of the Law of the Sea Convention (UNCLOS), it is likely not to control the classification society either. In such a case it is highly doubtful whether statutory surveys achieve the safety they should, especially if major classification societies operating world-wide do not carry out the checks, but small national ones.

States often decide at international level to introduce new legal instruments and obligations. When it comes to their implementation, they rely, *inter alia*, on the help of classification societies. There are basically two reasons for this development. First, restraints with regard to administrative staff require the help of private bodies. The flag State either completely delegates flag State control to classification societies or solely undertakes those surveys which generate the most income. Secondly, the specific knowledge of marine engineering which classification societies possess is another reason for their participation in the process. Most administrations discuss technical matters with classification societies, and it is quite usual that these societies are represented on technical committees of the administrations for the purpose of consultations, the exchange of information and the provision of advice. As a result, classification societies are no longer only concerned with maritime safety and the protection of the marine environment. They

---

[70] The exercise of port State control may not be delegated to classification societies. However, classification societies may co-operate with port State control, *see* Boisson, 'Classification Society Cooperation with Port State Control: a Move Towards the End of Substandard Practices', 24 *I.B.L.* 352 (1996), at 353.

[71] *See* Boisson, 'Classification societies and safety at sea–Back to basics to prepare for the future', 18 *Mar. Pol'y* 363 (1994), at 373–374; Martowski, 'Vetting Clauses', 26 *Tul.Mar.L.J.* 123 (2001); Özçayir, 'The "Erika" and its Aftermath', 7 *Int.M.L.* 230 (2000), at 231.

have even assumed functions with regard to maritime security, as their functions under the ISPS Code on maritime security of 2002 illustrate.[72]

V. The International Association of Classification Societies (IACS)

Presently ten classification societies are members of IACS.[73] This is a non-governmental organisation which was formally established in 1968. It was based on the experience that a number of classification societies had gathered in different working parties on specific topics, which can be traced back to the first working groups on Load Lines in the 1930s.[74] The aim of IACS is to standardise the different rules and regulations of its members, to facilitate the exchange of knowledge and to offer training for surveyors. As each and every society defines its own Rules and Class Notations, only IACS promotes minimum standards for its member societies through Unified Interpretations, Unified Requirements, Recommendations and Procedural Requirements. Its member societies are obliged to implement Unified Requirements in their rules within a certain period of time. Unified Interpretations relate to the uniform interpretation of a large number of international conventions. In the absence of authentic or official interpretations, Unified Interpretations standardise by way of self-regulation. IACS carries out technical discussions in its permanent and ad-hoc working groups, which generally consist of representatives from each member society.[75] Time and again some members aim at further measures. For example, ABS, LR and DNV have aimed to unify their rules on tankers.[76] Nevertheless, until today the competition between these

---

72 International Ship and Port Facility Security Code (ISPS Code), December 2002 Amendment to SOLAS, adopted on 12 December 2002, Entry into force: 1 July 2004 (tacit acceptance), SOLAS/CONF.5/32, SOLAS/CONF.5/33, SOLAS/CONF.5/34, RMC II.3.47.

73 American Bureau of Shipping (ABS), Bureau Veritas (BV), China Classification Society (CCS), Det Norske Veritas (DNV), German Lloyd (GL), Korean Register of Shipping (KRS), Lloyd's Register (LR), Nippon Kaiji Kyokai (ClassNK), Registro Italiano Navale (RINA), and Russian Maritime Register of Shipping (RS). The Polish classification society Polski Rejestr Statkow (PRS) was excluded in 1999. This action was taken, because according to IACS PRS did not guarantee a sufficient degree of experience and safety. The Indian Register of Shipping (IRS) is an Associate Member. Associate Membership has, however, been phased out.

74 Sullivan, 'International Association of Classification Societies' in *The Marine Encyclopaedic Dictionary* (1999).

75 The list of Permanent Working Groups includes: Bulk Chemicals, Containers, Drilling Units, Electricity, Engines, Fire Protection, Gas Tankers, Inland Waterways, Vessels, Marine Pollution, Materials and Welding, Mooring and Anchoring, Pipes and Pressure Vessels, Strength of Ships, and Subdivision and Load Lines.

76 'Big three tanker drive steals march on rivals.' DNV, LR and ABS forge ahead with new steel measures, leaving IACS behind again, *LL*, 5 June 2002, at 1.

member societies has been so strong that most initiatives of only a small number of members were doomed to fail.[77] But in spite of these difficulties, a considerable amount of unification of rules takes place within IACS.[78]

These Unified Requirements and Unified Interpretations are also vital for the shipping industry. Whenever IACS develops a new Unified Requirement, ship architects, shipyards, manufacturers of the goods concerned and shipowners will implement the new technical specifications in their construction of ships in order to keep their designs up-to-date and fulfil their contractual obligations *vis-à-vis* the buyer or class. IACS can therefore accelerate the speed of implementation of safety measures by revising the Unified Requirements or Unified Interpretations.[79] As an example, IACS can accelerate the implementation of regulations of the IMO Sub-Committee on Flag State Implementation, which considers, *inter alia*, questions of survey and certification. Nonetheless, IACS does not generally duplicate the requirements of international conventions such as the International Convention for the Safety of Life at Sea (SOLAS) in its rules.

Another activity of IACS is the analysis of casualties involving ships. IACS collects information on the types of defects and ships in question. If a certain kind of construction shows weaknesses, the classification societies will exchange information within IACS in order to identify ships[80] with the same hazards. Since the members of IACS class more than 90% of the world's tonnage,[81] such an exchange of information can be highly effective in increasing the safety of vessels. IACS takes part in working committees on ship safety, and it is a permanent representative with consultative status at the International Maritime Organization (IMO).

---

77 ABS denied allegations that LR, DNV and itself brought an end to competition of the "Big Three" classification societies, SEATRENDS WEB, 7 June 2002, 3.

78 This may, however, change if the IMO continues its efforts to define "Goal-based standards" which define a certain standard of safety that has to be achieved by each and every classification society, *see supra* Part 1 A VI 5.

79 The pivotal safety role of the major classification societies is reaffirmed by the latest IMO recommendations on bulk carriers. In particular, the unified requirements of IACS are relevant in this regard, *see LL*, 28 March 2003, at 7. While the members of IMO were still discussing a set of proposals on new bulk-carrier safety proposals, IACS had already announced a similar initiative and had the measures implemented in the rules of its member societies (*TRADEWINDS*, 6 December 2002, at 46). Nonetheless, some of the measures were withdrawn later (*FAIRPLAY SOLUTIONS*, January 2003, at 4). *See also* Simpson, 'Die Klassifikationsgesellschaften heute', [1980] *Hansa* 1726, at 1729; Vorbach, 'The Vital Role of Non-Flag State Actors in the Pursuit of Safer Shipping', 32 *Ocean Dev. & Int'l L.* 27 (2001), at 32–33, 37.

80 *E.g.* after the sinking of the vessel ERIKA, its sister ships were identified. A certain type of deck failure has been reported on those sister ships. See IACS Press Release of 7 June 2000 (accessible at <www.iacs.org.uk/press/2000/PressSis.pdf>, last accessed 19 March 2007); see also *LL*, 11 February 2000, at 1.

81 According to IACS, 'What are classification societies?' at 2 (accessible at <www.iacs.org.uk/_pdf/Class%20monograph.pdf>, last accessed 19 March 2007).

Further to this, IACS has established a general procedure for the shipowner to change the classification society.[82] Whenever the shipowner has to carry out repairs, he may try to avoid the costs by registering his vessel with another society which has different rules or which is not as strict in enforcing its own rules. Especially small national non-IACS classification societies may accept such a vessel, which as a result continues to trade in certain local markets and still poses a risk. Although the members of IACS share a minimum standard of rules and none of them is considered sub-standard or less strict than the others, it can happen that another classification society will class the ship without any modifications. The IACS procedure for the change of classification society tries to minimise this phenomenon, which one might call '*classification society shopping*' or '*class hopping*'.[83]

VI. Current Challenges for Classification Societies

Being an old and elaborate system, classification societies nevertheless face a number of challenges. Some of them are old problems which occur in a new context. Others have developed because of increased competition between the societies or the quest for claimants with a "*deep pocket*".

1. The Dual Role of Classification Societies

Classification societies usually work at the same time for the flag State and for the shipowner. With regard to flag State control, they are obliged to check whether the ship corresponds to certain safety regulations which are laid down in international and national regulations. This control of the ship is exercised by way of statutory surveys. The scope and location of these statutory surveys depend on their relationship with the flag State. Some flag States use classification societies only for surveys in foreign ports, which the State itself cannot perform. Others authorise a society to perform the entire control of all vessels registered under its flag wherever they are. Evidently, there may be a lack of control of the classification society in such instances. As a result, the breach of both class and statutory requirements may not be uncovered.[84]

At the same time, the classification societies act on behalf of the shipowner when carrying out classification services. In the majority of cases, the shipowner

---

82 IACS Procedural Requirement 1A, 'Procedures for Changing Classification Status' (accessible at <http://www.iacs.org.uk/preqs/main.htm>, last accessed 19 March 2007).

83 Boisson, 'Classification societies and safety at sea–Back to basics to prepare for the future', 18 *Mar. Pol'y* 363 (1994), at 373; Furger, 'Accountability and Systems of Self-Governance: The Case of the Maritime Industry', 19 *Law & Pol'y* 445 (1997), at 463; Özçayir, *Port State Control* (2004), § 12.49, at 507.

84 *Compare* Commission of the European Communities, Commission Working Document on the control of recognised organisations by the Commission of 11 October 2006, COM(2006) 588 final, at 3.2.2.

asks the society to carry out the mandatory statutory surveys. Accordingly, the classification society is paid by the shipowner for these surveys. Only in some cases are they paid by the flag State. Hence, although they are operating on the basis of an official authorisation when they perform statutory surveys, classification societies are the clients of the shipowners who ordered them to carry out the surveys and who are paying for this service. This dual role of classification societies carrying out public functions on the basis of a private contract may cause a conflict of interest, especially when the shipowner has a large fleet and/or the classification society is economically dependent upon the shipowner. However, to make this very clear here, this would not mean that classification societies principally operate in the economic interest of the shipowners. In the long run, this would be the end of their public functions regarding statutory surveys.

In the light of this conflict of interest, the lack of control over classification societies which carry out the entire flag State control has been criticised.[85] Some flag States seem to be convinced that audits of the classification societies can solve this problem. Such audits are carried out on the European level by the European Maritime Safety Agency (EMSA) and in other countries, such as the United States, by private auditors.[86] But these audits are only of a general nature and do not analyse the work which has been conducted by the classification society. Members of the European Commission have also addressed this problem:

> 'He [Mr Karamitsos of the European Commission's energy and transport directorate] said that "class had a lot to do" and "the current system where flag States subordinate their responsibilities to the private sector has deficiencies. The situation where the same private company offers statutory and classification certificates, paid by the operator, is wrong".'[87]

In fact, it has been discussed for a long time whether or not statutory surveys should be carried out by classification societies.[88] The international community has refrained from changing this assignment of power to classification societies, even though it has identified this problem. Practically all flag States, whether they

---

85 *E.g.* by the International Commission on Shipping, *see* Hayashi, 'Toward the Elimination of Substandard Shipping: The Report of the International Commission on Shipping', 16 *Int.J.Mar. & Coast.L.* 501 (2003), at 508. *Compare also* Hutchison, 'Practical and Political Considerations', in: Lux, *Classification Societies* (1993), 27, at 32-35; Lentz/Felleman, 'Oil Spill Prevention: A Proactive Approach', (2003) *Int. Oil Spill Conf.* 1, at 11; Vorbach, 'The Vital Role of Non-Flag State Actors in the Pursuit of Safer Shipping', 32 *Ocean Dev. & Int'l L.* 27 (2001), at 31. This has also been criticised by the International Union of Marine Insurers from 1987 onwards, *compare* Boisson, 'Classification societies and safety at sea–Back to basics to prepare for the future', 18 *Mar. Pol'y* 363 (1994), at 372–373.

86 *See i.e.* the Memorandum of Understanding between the USCG and ABS, accessible at <http://www.uscg.mil/hq/g-m/mse/acp/abs.htm>, last accessed 19 March 2007.

87 Mr Karamitsos of the European Commission's energy and transport directorate, *LL*, 18 September 2003.

88 Anderson, *ISM* Code (1998), 38–40 .

are strict enforcers of safety regulations or offer flags of convenience, require the help of the societies. Some of these States do not simply have the manpower to control their registered vessels. Apparently there is currently only a very limited number of people world-wide who possess the required knowledge. From an economic point of view, it is also more efficient to have only a limited number of specialists with such knowledge to survey a large vessel. Moreover, shipping is an international business and there is no time to return to the port of registry once a year in order to submit the vessel to flag State control. As the statutory survey of a vessel is a public measure, the flag States would need permission to perform it in a foreign territory with its own State officials. It is therefore a much easier way to have this control of vessels in foreign ports assigned to a private survey organisation such as a classification society.

A first option to minimise this conflict of interest would be to ensure that the classification society is only paid by the flag State when it exercises statutory surveys. As an effect, the classification society would consider the flag State as its client rather than the shipowner who currently pays for these surveys. However, such a solution would not really put an end to this conflict.

As a second possibility, flag States could require that classification societies either perform classification services or statutory surveys, but not both at the same time. The aim would be to have some classification societies which only do private classification and others which are only involved in flag State control. Distinguishing between classification societies in such a way depends on the co-operation of the societies. If no classification society were willing to perform statutory surveys, such an initiative would prove ineffective. As the ten major classification societies are organised in IACS and co-ordinate their activities in this forum, it is not unlikely that such an initiative would fail.

Finally, the third way to minimise this conflict of interest is to abolish class as it exists today. There have been several initiatives to extend IMO regulations and to define standards for areas of the law that are still left open to private regulation by the classification societies.[89] Initiatives such as the IMO *goal-based standards* could be taken even one step further than only harmonising what the classification societies have to achieve by their controls.[90] One could expand the scope of international conventions such as SOLAS and establish new statutory certificates for safety aspects, which are until today only covered by the rules of the classification societies. Even though one would not stop classification societies from offering their services to shipowners, one would indirectly eliminate private classification. Nevertheless, one could not prevent classification societies from developing new services for shipowners, such as different kinds of computer-aided analysis of the vessel or the fleet, which might replace the information that is currently provided by private classification. If they offer such new services, the conflict of interest to work both for the flag State and the shipowner may re-emerge. The only way to reduce the conflict effectively between public safety and private economic interest

---

89 IMO C 89/12/1 of 21 October 2002; MSC 77/2/5 of 26 March 1993.

90 *See supra* Part 1 A VI 5.

is to ensure that the classification societies are neutral organisations working in the interest of both the flag State and the shipowner. It is therefore necessary to submit them to strict control as to whether they really exercise their services in an independent way and to provide them as a flag State with sufficient funds so that they can act freely and independently of shipowners.

2. *Selling Safety in a Competitive Environment*

The second conflict of interest addresses the contradiction of selling safety to someone else and competing for clients at the same time. The market for classification of vessels has become highly competitive and volatile. Currently, most of the societies try to raise their market share. Due to fewer periodic surveys, marine income of LR went down by 11% in the business year from 2002 to 2003, whereas it increased by 6% from 2004 to 2005 because of the classification of more than 120 million gross tons, which represents 18.3% of the world fleet in terms of gross tonnage, a record in LR's long history.[91] In 2005, the fleet classed by ABS grew by 5.7% to 120.9m gross tons. The aggregate tonnage of all vessels order grew in the same period by 13%.[92] In 2003, BV managed to increase its marine income by 4% and in 2004 the revenue generated by marine services even increased by 11%.[93] GL informed the press that it managed to double its registered fleet from 20 million gross tons in 1994 to 40.8 million gross tons in 2000, with a high market share for new orders.[94] About every second container vessel is built with a GL class. In 2005, GL had classed vessels of 55.7 million gross tonnage, which represented a growth of 16.5%.[95] Competition amongst societies in order to increase market share is expressly encouraged by IACS, as long as marketing methods involving deliberate misrepresentation are not used.[96]

---

[91] Press release 2003 LR/051/03 of 11December 2003, and 2005 LR/26/05 of 20 October 2005 (accessible at <www.lr.org>, last accessed 19 March 2007).

[92] ABS, *Annual Review 2005*, 7 (accessible at < http://www.eagle.org/news/pubs/pdfs/AR05.pdf>, last accessed 19 March 2007.

[93] BV Press release 08/05 of 6 June 2005 (accessible at <www.veristar.com>, last accessed 19 March 2007).

[94] In 2003, GL had an order level of 10 million GT, corresponding to 11.3 percent of the world order level, GL Press Release of 2 September 2003 (*see* <www.gl-group.com>, last accessed 19 March 2007).

[95] Germanischer Lloyd, *Annual Report 2005*, 9 (accessible at < http://www.gl-group.com/images/glgroup/Annual_Report_2005_E.pdf >, last accessed 19 March 2007).

[96] IACS Code of Ethics:

'3.1 General: Competition among Societies must not be prevented, restricted or distorted. Competition helps to keep the Societies flexible, alert and cost-conscious to the benefit of the entire marine community. Competition between Societies shall be on the basis of services (technical and field) rendered to the marine industry but must not lead to compromises on safety of life and property at sea or to the lowering of technical standards.

3.2 Marketing: 3.2.1 Each Member Society is free to market its technical and related activities in a manner considered necessary to achieve its objectives. However,

A classification society must find ways to stabilise or raise its market share in such a competitive environment. The society has a choice between five possible ways of competing for clients in such a market. It may aim at promoting the highest standards of all classification societies and thereby attract shipowners who are risk-averse and strong enforcers of safety measures.[97] To achieve such a standing, the society can focus on certain kinds of vessels, such as cruise ships or container vessels, concentrate its research and development (R&D) on such vessels and develop the largest degree of experience in that area. Especially shipowners who transport valuable goods or goods and passengers involving the risk of a high exposure to liability or publicity, such as cruise vessels, react positively to such an approach. If, however, ships enter its register which do not meet this high standard, the classification society needs to be firm in its approach and require immediate improvement. Otherwise it risks losing its standing and thereby its clients. Yet even the most risk-averse shipowner needs to aim at profits. The classification society therefore needs to find a reasonable balance between the benefits of safety standards and the costs which such safety incurs. If it becomes too expensive to operate a vessel in the way the classification society requires, clients tend to turn away.

As a second possibility, the classification society could cut its prices for the classification of a newly built vessel and/or for the periodical surveys and try to be cheaper than the other societies. The difficulty of such an approach is that research and development require considerable investments, as does the training of the staff. In the long run, it will be quite difficult for a classification society to keep up such an approach. In order to be at the forefront of technological development, the classification society needs to earn and invest money.

Another approach is to define rules in a way that the building of the vessel is cheaper than with other societies. Due to the costs of steel, the thickness of the scantlings is an important issue for someone who constructs or orders a vessel. Rather than being the cheapest classification society as regards their fees, a classification society which requires thinner scantlings than all the others could considerably reduce the overall costs for the construction of the vessel. This third possibility has the advantage for the classification society that it may generate a high revenue, since its fees are not as relevant as the overall costs of the vessel, and still be competitive, as it provides the shipowner with a cheaper vessel than other clas-

---

> marketing methods should not be pursued to a position which involves deliberate misrepresentation in order to obtain business to the detriment of other members.'

Nonetheless, in 2000 Intertanko warned against inter-class society rivalry, which might hamper efforts to improve ship safety, *TRADEWINDS*, 14 January 2000, 4. *Compare also* Grey, 'Classification societies under renewed scrutiny', 96 *BIMCO Bull.* 44 (2001), at 46.

[97] Lord Donaldson points out that the members of IACS compete against each other in terms of service and not in terms of being soft on shipowners, Lord Donaldson, '"Safer Ships; Cleaner Seas"–full speed ahead or dead slow?' [1998] *L.M.C.L.Q.* 170, at 173.

sification societies. The main loser of such behaviour is the safety of the vessel and competition, as such behaviour is likely to provoke a race to the bottom.

As a fourth possibility, a classification society could try to be present in a protected market. This is especially the situation of small national societies, which otherwise could hardly survive. Such a classification society is to a certain degree protected if a flag State has delegated the control of its vessels to a single society or to the oligopoly of a small number of societies. Especially if this monopolistic or oligopolistic market is opened for classification societies with high standards, the small national society is likely to attract sub-standard operators who would not be registered by other societies.

A classification society has also the fifth option to raise its market share by lowering its requirements and accepting sub-standard ships.[98] It is obvious that such an approach is in the long run particularly dangerous–even more so if taken by members of IACS, as their ships have the seal of a class of good standing and quality. IACS promotes high standards and tries to identify and ban such members, as it did in the case of the Polish classification society in May 1997.[99]

The promotion of the highest possible standard of safety will not work if the costs for the safety exceed the value of the vessel. Such is the case with substandard operators. If the main interest of the shipowner is to make money as quickly as possible without caring about the future, he will buy the cheapest ship available, invest as little as is required in order to keep it going and get freight of little value which is owned or forwarded by someone who is just as unscrupulous. Safety is expensive. The value of a sub-standard ship, however, is low. Moreover, if the operator has established a company structure that protects his assets and solely subjects his one-ship company to legal proceedings, his exposure to liability is highly limited. For such an operator, the incentives in this race to the bottom to invest in his ship are low. Only the fear of criminal proceedings might be a motivation. If the shipowner or operator comes from a country which does not strictly enforce criminal law, or if he has set up a complex system with owners and operators located in multiple jurisdictions,[100] he may not even be motivated by such a threat. As long as he finds insurance, which is compulsory for certain trades such as the transport of oil, or engages in other trades, he may not need any classifica-

[98] The financial advantages of the sub-standard operator are analysed in Organisation for Economic Co-operation and Development (OECD), *Competitive Advantages Obtained by Some Shipowners as a Result of Non-Observance of Applicable International Rules and Standards* (1996), with examples at 10–16 and 29–30 and OECD, Maritime Transport Committee, *Cost Savings Stemming from Non-Compliance with International Environmental Regulations in the Maritime Sector* (2003), with examples at 17, 43–46, 49–50, 53. The financial burdens of the users of such vessels are considered in OECD, *The Costs to Users of Substandard Shipping* (2001), at 26–29.

[99] IACS Press Release of 16 October 1997, and of 29 August 2000 (accessible at <http://www.iacs.org.uk/>, last accessed 19 March 2007).

[100] Such company structures are analysed in OECD, Maritime Transport Committee, *Ownership and Control of Ships* (2003).

tion society at all. Or he will try to find a classification society which nonetheless accepts his vessel, whether that is justified or not.

It does not even have to be a sub-standard operator. One of the main problems of the system is that it is the shipowner who pays for the classification, but who is at the same time the person in charge of the vessel which is to be controlled. This problem has already been referred to in the preceding section. There are several shipowners who try to take advantage of the competition between the classification societies. The most dubious ones are those shipowners who register the vessel with a classification society that is known for having high standards, but that does not really want to achieve these standards. The ship is maintained in such a way that it just fulfils the standards at the time of the surveys. Despite being in possession of all necessary certificates, the vessel is not a safe one. Like sub-standard operators with rusting hulks that operate merely in a national market because PSC would otherwise detect them, these shipowners act on the fringe of safety and legality.[101] Classification societies can only avoid this by generally raising the standards so that the margin left to these societies becomes narrower. Raising the standards may, however, be rather difficult. Shipowners are normally members of the committees of the classification societies and often hold parts of their shares, and so they have some influence on the standards as well.

At the end of the 1980s and at the beginning of the 1990s, class had a lot of problems with its credibility and standing. In 1992, some London insurers entrusted ship inspections to the Salvage Association.[102] They wanted to make sure that the ships they insured were in observance of the international conventions on ship security and maritime safety.[103] The survey carried out was called the Structural Condition Survey, known in the market as JH. 722.[104] Its terms were very specific and the scope of the survey was so extensive that it might require several days to complete such a survey.[105] If the owners did not comply with the recom-

---

101 OECD, Maritime Transport Committee, *Report on the Removal of Insurance from Substandard Shipping* (2004), at 23.

102 The Salvage Association was founded in London in 1856 and provides services to hull and machinery underwriters and P&I Clubs. It is not a classification society, but provides all kinds of maritime surveys to the insurance industry, especially whenever incidents occur, *see* < http://www.wreckage.org/>, last accessed 19 March 2007.

103 Boisson, 'Classification societies and safety at sea–Back to basics to prepare for the future', 18 *Mar. Pol'y* 363 (1994), at 372; Durr, *An Analysis of the Potential Liability of Classification Societies: Developing Role, Current Disorder & Future Prospects*, § 2.3.1 (accessible at <http://www.uctshiplaw.com/theses/durr.htm>, last accessed 19 March 2007); Furger, 'Accountability and Systems of Self-Governance: The Case of the Maritime Industry', 19 *Law & Pol'y* 445 (1997), at 464; Harling, 'The Liability of Classification Societies to Cargo Owners', [1993] *L.M.C.L.Q.* 1, at 7; Ulrik, 'The Underwriter's Perspective', in: Lux, *Classification Societies* (1993), 37, at 40.

104 *JH* stands for the London Market Joint Hull Committee. *See* also Boisson, 'Classification societies and safety at sea–Back to basics to prepare for the future', 18 *Mar. Pol'y* 363 (1994), at 373.

105 *LL*, 22 December 1992.

mendations of the Salvage Association, the underwriter was discharged from liability.[106] The surveyed ships were mainly old vessels and the statistics published in September 1993 showed that 80% of those ships which were all '*in class*' needed extensive repairs.[107] The original survey is no longer carried out today, but it has been replaced by a similar one.[108]

Neutrality and credibility is an essential precondition for the system of classification. At the beginning of the last century, classification societies were described as occupying *'a public and quasi-judicial position'*.[109] Many classification societies still present themselves as having a non-profit-making character.[110] This designation as not-for-profit allows them to appear neutral, since they are only interested in improving the safety of the Maritime Sector and in conducting research to achieve that aim. Whether they still are not-for-profit organisations may be disputed. Despite being relevant as concerns neutrality and credibility, a non-profit-making character does not give any implications about liability. *Lord Steyn* presented classification societies in the House of Lords as acting in the public interest and fulfilling a *'role which in its absence would have to be fulfilled by States.'*[111] However, he also stated that '*classification societies do not have a blanket immunity from all tortious liability.*'[112] The status of being a public interest organisation

---

[106] *LL*, 22 December 1992.

[107] 'By early December this year [1992], the Salvage Association had received instructions to carry out 187 structural surveys under the JH. 722 provisions, 60% of which involved bulkers, 25% tankers and 15% vessels of other types. The Salvage Association says that 80% of those ships surveyed have required significant repairs,' *LL*, 22 December 1992.

[108] This survey is carried out under the brand *ShipShape* and identifies the high points and low points of a vessel in a specific grading system, *compare* <http://www.wreckage.org/>, last accessed 19 March 2007. *Compare also* Boisson, 'Classification societies and safety at sea–Back to basics to prepare for the future', 18 *Mar. Pol'y* 363 (1994), at 373.

[109] Mr Justice Wright in *W. Angliss and Co. (Australia) Proprietary Ltd. v. Peninsular and Oriental Steam Navigation Co. Ltd.*, [1927] 28 *Ll.L.Rep.* 202, at 214. In a decision of 1995, Lord Steyn presented classification societies as acting in the public interest and fulfilling a 'role which in its absence would have to be fulfilled by states' (Lord Steyn in *Marc Rich & Co. AG v. Bishop Rock Marine Co. Ltd.* (and ClassNK) *("The Nicholas H.")* [1995] 2 *Lloyd's Rep.* 299 (H.L.), at 316.

[110] CCS claims to 'provide services for the public interest', and KRS calls itself 'non-profit ship classification society'. According to the introduction to LR on its homepage, 'Lloyd's Register Group is a non-profit distributing organisation; income derived from our fees and the sale of publications is used for research and development, training our staff and to improve services.' ClassNK 's what is known under Japanese law as a public service foundation' And ABS presents itself as 'not-for-profit' and is tax exempt in the United States as a non-governmental organisation (NGO).

[111] Lord Steyn in *Marc Rich & Co. AG v. Bishop Rock Marine Co. Ltd.* (and ClassNK) *("The Nicholas H.")* [1995] 2 *Lloyd's Rep.* 299 (H.L.), at 316 col. 1.

[112] At 315 col. 2.

does not allow a general immunity from liability in tort, but needs to be taken into consideration, for instance under English law, for the analysis of a duty of care towards third parties.[113]

3. Shipowners/Operators Have to Report Damage

The third conflict of interest is one which is practically impossible to solve: the shipowner or operator has to report any possible deficiencies of the vessel which require repair and call upon the classification society to have them surveyed.[114] As classification societies depend on this co-operation, they are not a fully independent survey organisation. They cannot survey the vessel on their own initiative, but are dependent on their contracting party. One should be aware of the societies' importance for maritime safety, but one should not overestimate their possibilities either. Despite the fact that they aim at minimising sub-standard shipping, they cannot control their registered vessels at all times. This limits their possibilities. The assistance of the shipowner is necessary, and it is very difficult to imagine a system which is not based on such co-operation. As long as there are shipowners or operators who try to save money by not putting in place safety measures, classification societies will not always get the necessary information as the ship is not constantly under their control.

It is far from ideal that those who must be controlled need to allow the control, and even have to report that they require to be controlled. Still, the schedule for survey activities of a vessel is based on the co-operation of shipowners. It assumes normal maintenance and repairs. The owners have to be interested in keeping their ships safe and seaworthy, otherwise the condition of their vessel might deteriorate within a very short time. Additionally, there can be a very strong pressure on the surveyor. Not only that he has to control the vessel in a minimum period of time. He also has to deal with the representatives of the owners or operators, resist pressure exerted by them and bring to light any hidden defects.[115] The classification society may try to increase the ship's safety, and yet it is reliant on the very people

---

113 Lord Steyn in *Marc Rich & Co. AG v. Bishop Rock Marine Co. Ltd.* (*and ClassNK*) *("The Nicholas H.")*, [1995] 2 *Lloyd's Rep.* 299 (H.L.), at 316, col. 1.

114 This conflict of interests is also referred to by France, 'Classification societies: their liability-an American lawyer's point of view in light of recent judgments', 1 *I.J.S.L.* 67 (1996), at 71.

115 The prescription by IACS that at least two surveyors conduct special surveys in order to see more and be able to resist pressure from the owner or his superintendent illustrates this threat (*see* <www.iacs.org.uk/role.htm>, last accessed 19 March 2007). *See also* Commission of the European Communities, Commission Working Document on the control of recognised organisations by the Commission, COM(2006) 588 final, at 3.2.7.

to report defects who themselves might wish to cover them up. With regard to a sub-standard operator, the system can be too lax for these reasons.[116]

4. *Sub-standard Classification Societies*

The number of classification societies increased significantly in the course of the second half of the twentieth century. Today, there are at least 65 classification societies world-wide.[117] However, according to the European Commission, a great number of them do not possess the required expertise to conduct surveys.[118] The

---

116 The competitive advantages of a sub-standard operator have been analysed by the Organisation for Economic Co-operation and Development (OECD), *Competitive Advantages Obtained by Some Shipowners as a Result of Non-Observance of Applicable International Rules and Standards* (1996), especially at 10–16, and OECD, Maritime Transport Committee, *Cost Savings Stemming from Non-Compliance with International Environmental Regulations in the Maritime Sector* (2003), with examples at 17, 43–46, 49–50, 53. The ownership structure of such vessels and ways to create anonymity are discussed in OECD, Maritime Transport Committee, *Ownership and Control of Ships* (2003).

117 The IMO Document FSI 13/10/2 of 23 December 2004 identifies the following classification societies: Alfa Register of Shipping, American Bureau of Shipping, Belize Maritime Bureau Inc., Belize Register Corporation, Biro Klasifikasi Indonesia, Bulgarski Koraben Registar, Bureau Securitas, Bureau Veritas, Ceskoslovensky Lodin Register, China Classification Society, China Corporation Register of Shipping, Compañía Nacional de Registro e Inspección de Naves, Croatian Register of Shipping, Cyprus Bureau of Shipping, Det Norske Veritas, Fidenavis SA, Germanischer Lloyd, Global Marine Bureau, Hellenic Register of Shipping, Honduras Bureau of Shipping, Honduras International Surveying and Inspection Bureau, Honduras Maritime Inspection, INCLAMAR, Indian Register of Shipping, Inspección y Clasificación Marítima, S. de R.L., International Merchant Marine Registry of Belize, International Naval Surveys Bureau, International Register of Shipping, Isthmus Bureau of Shipping, Korea Classification Society (former Joson Classification Society), Korean Register of Shipping, Lloyd's Register of Shipping, Marconi International Marine Company Ltd., Maritime Technical Systems and Services, Mongolia Ship Registry, National Cargo Bureau Inc., National Shipping Adjusters Inc, Nippon Kaiji Kyokai, NV Unitas, Panama Bureau of Shipping, Panama Maritime Surveyors Bureau Inc, Panama Maritime Documentation Services, Panama Register Corporation, Panama Shipping Certificate Inc., Panama Shipping Registrar Inc., Polski Rejestr Statkow, R.J. Del Pan, Register of Shipping (Albania), Register of Shipping (DPR Korea), Registro Cubano de Buques, Registro Italiano Navale, Registro Internacional Naval S.A., Regjistri Laknori Shqiptar, RINAVE Portuguesa, Romanian Naval Register, Russian Maritime Register of Shipping, Russian River Register, Seefartsaht Helsinki, Shipping Register of Ukraine, Sociedad Clasificadora de Colombia, Sociedad de Registro y Clasificación Mexicana SA, Société Anonyme Internationale de Télégraphie sans fil, Société Générale de Surveillance, Turkish Lloyd, Viet Nam Register of Shipping.

118 'Whereas worldwide a large number of the existing classification societies do not ensure either adequate implementation of the rules or reliability when acting on behalf of

European Commission believes that only the members of IACS have sufficient knowledge and experience to conduct statutory surveys for the Member States.[119] Similarly, the Memoranda of Understanding issue each year a report on the classification societies of detained vessels and categorises the classification societies in different risk categories.[120] Sub-standard classification societies are also more likely to be influenced by the threat of a shipowner to change to another society. Moreover, they usually do not have enough money to conduct the necessary re-

national administrations as they do not have adequate structures and experience to be relied upon and to enable them to carry out their duties in a highly professional manner; [...]
Whereas EN 45004 and EN 29001 standards combined with International Association of Classification Societies (IACS) standards constitute an adequate guarantee of performance quality of organizations.' (Council Directive 94/57/EC of 22 November 1994 On Common Rules and Standards for Ship Inspection and Survey Organizations and for the Relevant Activities of Maritime Administrations (OJ L 319, 12 December 1994, 20, amended by: Commission Directive 97/58/EC of 26 September 1997, OJ L 274, 7 October 1997, 8; Directive 2001/105/EC of the European Parliament and of the Council of 19 December 2001, OJ L 19, 22 January 2002, 9; Directive 2002/84/EC of the European Parliament and of the Council of 5 November 2002, OJ L 324, 29 November 2002, 53) Consideration No. 6 and 9).

119 But even the recognised classification societies do not always fulfil their tasks to the satisfaction of the European Commission: 'The Commission has examined a considerable number of ship files [...]. This examination has yielded a sometimes bleak picture, with instances where important errors had been made by the surveyors or certain inspections or tests had simply been omitted, while the subsequent internal controls sometimes failed to detect obvious occurences or provide appropriate follow up', *see* Commission of the European Communities, Commission Working Document on the control of recognised organisations by the Commission of 11 October 2006, COM(2006) 588 final, at 3.2.2.

120 Paris Memorandum of Understanding (MoU) on Port State Control, *The year detention rate per Classification Society (2003-2005)*, accessible at <http://www.parismou.org/upload/anrep/RO%20performance%20list%202005.pdf>. A more detailed analysis is provided in the Paris MoU, *Annual Report 2005*, at 34–37, accessible at <http://www.parismou.org/upload/anrep/Paris%20MOU%20JV%202004-LR.pdf>. Comparable statistics are published by the Tokyo MoU, *Annual Report on Port State Control in the Asia-Pacific Region 2005,* at 39–40, accessible at <http://www.tokyo-mou.org/ANN05.pdf>; the Latin American Agreement on Port State Control of Vessels [Viña del Mar Agreement], *Summary of Annual Report 2005*, at 3, accessible at <http://200.45.69.62/index_i.htm>; Indian Ocean MoU, *Annual Report 2005,* at 14, 21–22, 29, 35–36, accessible at <http://www.iomou.org/annrep05.pdf>; Black Sea MoU, *Annual Report for 2005,* at 11–12, accessible at <http://www.bsmou.org/PDF/2005ANNUALREPORT.pdf>. The report by the USCG for 2004 'Classification Society Performance' is accessible at <http://www.uscg.mil/hq/g-m/pscweb/2004_ Classification_Society. pdf>. An explanation of the Performance Statistics can be found at <http://www.uscg.mil/hq/g-m/pscweb/class.htm>. All homepages were accessed on 19 March 2007.

search and do not dispose of a sufficient number of surveyors. Whenever they assume the work of flag States and issue statutory certificates, no effective flag State control is carried out at all. This leads to an increase in the duties of port State control.

Since the second half of the 1980s, ABS, LR and DNV have considered several times setting up a "*Super IACS*" consisting of only these three largest classification societies in order to gain competitive advantages over the other IACS members. These companies regarded themselves as having the most experience.[121] Today, they have registered more than 50% of the world's fleet in tonnage terms.[122] The other seven member societies of IACS account for about 44%. However, these initiatives have always been discontinued for reasons which have not been aired.

The standing of IACS member societies makes it very difficult for smaller societies to increase their market share. For them it is almost impossible to meet the criteria fixed by the European Commission to become a recognised survey organisation[123] or the criteria to become a member of IACS.[124] A small classification society is most likely to remain small. It is its fate to survive either by state protectionism, low prices or because of a low level of enforcement of safety standards. But since vessels which are classed by small national classification societies usually trade only in the respective national markets, it is rather difficult to displace such small sub-standard classification societies.

121 *See* IACS Press Release of 19 March 2001; FAIRPLAY, 24 August 2000, at 33; 22 March 2001, at 20-21; *LL*, 15 March 2001, at 1; 1 June 2001, at IX.

122 The combined share with ClassNK is even more than 70%.

123 E.g. Annex to Council Directive 94/57/EC of 22 November 1994 (OJ L 319, 12 December 1994, 20). Minimum Criteria for Organisations referred to in Article 3: '2.The organisation must have in its class a fleet of at least 1,000 ocean-going vessels (over 100 GRT) totalling no less than one million GRT. 3.The organisation must employ a technical staff commensurate with the number of vessels classed. As a minimum, 100 exclusive surveyors are needed to meet the requirements in paragraph 2.'
Apart from the RINAVE Portuguesa, the Hellenic Register of Shipping (HRS) is the only non-IACS society which is recognised by the European Union, but as it does not make its own rules and does not have a sufficient number of ships in its register, it is prohibited from access to IACS. HRS claims that without being a member of IACS, it is very hard to achieve such numbers; *FAIRPLAY*, 13 November 2003, at 6-7.

124 In order to become a member, a classification society must have 30 years of experience with its own classification rules, a classed fleet of not less than 1,500 ocean-going vessels (over 100 GT each) with an aggregate total of not less than 8 million GT, and professional staff of 150 exclusive surveyors and 100 technical specialists trained in accordance with IACS procedures.

5. *Current International Developments: Goal-based Standards*

Some States have been critical about the aforementioned independence[125] of classification societies in regard of the development of the classification societies' rules. They claim that in the interest of safe shipping and transparency of the market, at least the level of safety should be standardised between all classification societies. These States believe that the conflicts of interests could be minimized if the international community were to assume further functions in regard of the precise definition of standards which ships must attain. Additionally, classification societies would be monitored more closely. For classification societies, this could imply a further restriction of their liberties and deprive them of one of their principal means to compete against each other.

At the IMO Council in 2002, the Bahamas and Greece initiated a discussion about the development of regulations on private classification by an IMO subcommittee and no longer by the classification societies.[126] Although this initiative was discontinued in July 2003,[127] it was the nucleus of a new move currently under discussion, which is called "*goal-based standards*" (GBS).[128] *Goal-based standards* are defined as

> '.1 broad, over-arching safety, environmental and/or security standards that ships are required to meet during their lifecycle;
> .2 the required level to be achieved by the requirements applied by class societies and other recognized organizations, Administrations and IMO;
> .3 clear, demonstrable, verifiable, long standing, implementable and achievable, irrespective or ship design and technology; and
> .4 specific enough in order not to be open to differing interpretations.'[129]

GBS will be included in SOLAS and consist of five different tiers. The principal tier contains the '*goals*', the second is called "*functional requirements*", the third "*verification of compliance criteria*", and the fourth and fifth tiers include the actual rules developed by classification societies, other recognized organisations and industry organisations.[130] Tier IV is "*Technical procedures and guidelines, classification rules and industry standards*", and Tier V is "*Codes of practice and safety and quality systems for shipbuilding, ship operation, maintenance, training, manning, etc.*" The Working Group has developed Tier I and II, which is an ongoing process. While the development of Tier I leads to the development of Tier II, the results of Tier II require reconsideration of Tier I. Tier III essentially defines the

---

[125] *See supra* Part 1 A III 5.

[126] IMO C 89/12/1 of 21 October 2002; MSC 77/2/5 of 26 March 2993; *LL*, February 28, 2003, at 1.

[127] *LL*, 24 July 2003, at 1.

[128] *LL*, 20 November 2003.

[129] IMO MSC 80/6 of 22 December 2004, Annex 1; MSC 80/WP.8 of 18 May 2005, Annex 1.

[130] *LL,* 13 December 2004, at 3, 'Back to basics push over safety rules: Maritime Safety Committee talks reveal widely divergent views on definition of goal-based standards'; *LL*, 30 March 2005, at 14, 'IMO wary of allowing class to verify common scantlings'.

verification process, which guarantees that the detailed requirements of the classification societies meet the functional requirements of Tier II.[131] It is still an open issue which authority should control this implementation through the classification societies, as it is evident that the classification societies should not define the rules of Tier IV and V and control whether they conform to Tier I and II.

The principal aim of GBS is to determine the fundamental standards according to which ships are built. IMO does not intend to take over the work of classification societies to develop detailed rules, but rather states in a general way what has to be achieved. It is the task of classification societies, ship designers, naval architects, marine engineers and ship-builders to fill these regulations with life and meet the required standards. The IMO Working Group seeks to introduce a system defining standards that would be a benchmark against which the safety of a vessel can be assessed during its design and construction, as well as during its time of operation, regardless of the type of ship. The design life of ships is not to be shorter than 25 years, so they should be designed in accordance with North Atlantic environmental conditions and relevant long-term sea state scatter diagrams.[132] GBS are not yet mandatory and will in any case not apply retroactively at the time when they become mandatory.

One of the major achievements of GBS is that they harmonise the aims to be fulfilled by all classification societies. Once these standards become mandatory, classification societies can no longer argue that their rules embody solely a general standard of safety which has with hindsight proved to be sufficient. They are under an obligation to develop their rules in conformity with the standards laid down in GBS. However, since there are no precise requirements how a standard of Tier I or II has to be implemented, the classification societies have to define the precise requirements that are imposed on a vessel in Tier IV and V. The duties of classification societies and safety standards will thereby be more precisely determined than they are today. Furthermore, the classification societies will have less room to grant exemptions from their rules or to implement less strict regulations as regards, for example, scantlings.[133]

At the same time, several classification societies are working on their own *common structural rules for double-hull oil tankers*, which aim at applying the same rules throughout all IACS member societies.[134] Such rules are also developed for dry-bulk tankers, and the IACS plans to take a similar approach to all kinds of standard vessels.[135] This activity is similar to GBS in that it aims at harmonising the rules of all member societies. It could lead in the long run to those definitions that are required by Tier IV and V. The development of *common struc-*

131 IMO MSC 81/6 of 13 July 2005, at 2.

132 MSC 80/WP.8 of 18 May 2005, Annex 3, II.1/II.2.

133 *See also supra* Part 1 A VI 2.

134 *LL*, 20 September 2005, at 3, 'Tanker and bulker rules scheduled for November: IACS structural standards set to enter force next April'.

135 *LL,* 20 May 2005, at 12, 'Common rules to take tankers into the future'.

tural rules however illustrates that classification societies understand GBS as a threat to their liberty to develop rules at their own discretion.

6. Classification Societies in Litigation

Another challenge to the system of classification is the increasing legal pressure which has arisen since the beginning of the 1990s. Before, class seemed to have been considered as almost immune from legal suits. Over the years, there were only a few reported cases in which someone sought damages against a classification society.[136] As the question of their liability came more and more into the focus of lawyers in those years, an increasing number of law suits ensued. This development has continued until today.

The main challenge of this litigation is not only the multitude of jurisdictions in question, as the societies offer their services in almost every port or shipyard of the world and their negligence may have consequences virtually everywhere in the world. Also and especially the amount of damages sought is at issue in these cases. An impressive example is the suit against ABS, which had classified the vessel '*Prestige*', a tanker with a cargo of 76,972 metric tons of heavy fuel oil which sank off the Spanish coast on 19 November 2003, resulting in a major oil spill.[137] On 16 May 2004, the Kingdom of Spain initiated an action before the U.S.

---

[136] English law: *Braginton v. Chapman and Others (Trustees of Lloyd's Register of Shipping) (The "Midas")* [1878] 7 Asp. 77 (Q.B. Div.); *Thiodon v. Tindall and Others (the Committee of Lloyd's Register) (The "Ibex")* [1891] 7 Asp. 76 (Q.B. Div.). United States law: *Great American Insurance Co. v. Bureau Veritas*, 338 F.Supp. 999 (S.D.N.Y.1972), *aff'd*, 478 F.2d 235 (2d Cir.1973); *Steamship Mutual Underwriting Association Ltd. v. Bureau Veritas*, 380 F.Supp. 482 (E.D.La. 1973); *Gulf Tampa Drydock Co. v. Germanischer Lloyd*, 634 F.2d 874 (5th Cir.1981); *Continental Insurance Co. v. Daewoo Shipbuilding & Heavy Machinery Ltd.*, 707 F.Supp. 123 (S.D.N.Y. 1988); *Somarelf v. American Bureau of Shipping*, 720 F.Supp. 441 (D.N.J.1989); *Psarianos v. Standard Marine Ltd. et al.*, 728 F.Supp. 438 (E.D.Tex. 1989), the award against ABS has not been published. German law: OLG Hamburg 26 October 1906, [1907] *Hanseatische Gerichtszeitung, Hauptblatt,* 37 (*Theodor Schiff, Heinecke & Co. und Bergeest & Siemers v. Bureau Veritas (Schoonergaliote "Industrie"));* LG Hamburg 18 January 1972, 10 O 176/70 (unpublished). French law: '*Cap-de-la-Hague*', Cour d'Appel de Douai, [1981] *DMF* 153, Cour de Cassation (Ch. crim.), [1981] *DMF* 146. Italian law: Tribunale di Savona 29 October 1990, "Tito Campanella", [1991] *Il Diritto Marittimo* 423.

[137] Also, the International Oil Pollution Compensation Funds (IOPC) have considered to file a suit against ABS before a Spanish court in order to take recourse action for claims regarding settlements for the Prestige incident, IOPC Funds, *Report on the Activities of the International Oil Pollution Compensation Funds in 2004* (accessible at <http://www.iopcfund.org/npdf/AR2004English.pdf>, last accessed 19 March 2007), 102-104. They have decided not to take recourse against the classification society in the United States, and have deferred a recourse action in Spain. With regard to the details of this incident, *see* IOPC Funds, *Report on the Activities of the International Oil Pollution Compensation Funds in 2005* (accessible at <http://en.iopcfund.org/npdf/

District Court (Southern District of New York) against ABS and its group of companies for USD 700 million in damages, which was later increased to an estimated USD 1 billion.[138] However, this sum does not include damages for injuries to health, well-being and security of the inhabitants of the affected regions, environmental damages, and loss of income or earnings with regard to tourism. At the beginning, it was reported that the Spanish government was going to file a USD 5 billion suit,[139] but it finally turned out that 'only' USD 1 billion are being claimed.[140]

The action is based upon a negligent, wilful and wanton behaviour of the classification society. Under the auspices of ABS, the *Prestige* had been repaired in China in May 2001 and was surveyed in Dubai a year later. It is argued that, in contradiction with its own rules, ABS had not internally checked the ballast water tanks adjacent to tanks with heating coils. It is further argued that ABS was informed by the master of sub-standard conditions aboard the vessel and that it therefore should not have endorsed the classification certificate or withdrawn it at a later date. According to the Kingdom of Spain, the vessel would otherwise not have been permitted to load its cargo of heavy fuel oil that was released or discharged into the waters off the coast of Spain. For this reason, ABS would have to answer for its misbehaviour. In a parallel procedure against ABS, the Basque Region, jointly with the local governments of Bizkaia, Gipuzkoa and Donosti-San

AR05_E.pdf>, last accessed 19 March 2007), 99-123. Other examples of similar litigations are the *Erika* suit against the RINA, which is pending in Italy, *compare* Harrison, 'The Accountability of Classification Societies, The Role of Classification and Market-oriented Policy Issues (The "Erika"), [2000] *J.I.M.L.* 299. And the litigation against BV subsequent to the *Estonia* casualty, *see infra* Part 3 B II.

138 Case No. 03Civ.3573(LTS)(RLE), increase made by the amended complaint of 30 July 2004. The court has published a first decision which relates to a motion of Spain seeking to dismiss the counterclaims of ABS, *see Reino de Espana v. American Bureau of Shipping,* 328 F.Supp.2d 489 (S.D.N.Y.2004). Due to the lack of subject matter jurisdiction as laid down in the Foreign Sovereign Immunities Act (FSIA), the counterclaim, which aimed at a declaratory judgment that 'as between [Spain] and ABS, [Spain] is wholly or principally liable for any damages arising out of the *Prestige* casualty and must wholly indemnify ABS and/or contribute to payment of damages assessed in any judgment against ABS anywhere in the world [...]' has been dismissed. An overview over the Prestige casualty is provided by Garcia, 'Comment: "Nunca Mais!" How Current European Environmental Liability and Compensation Regimes are Addressing the Prestige Oil Spill of 2002', 25 *U.Pa.J.Int'l Econ.L.* 1395 (2004).

139 *LL*, 15 May 2003.

140 *LL*, 1 July 2003.

Sebastian, has filed a USD 50 million lawsuit at a Court in Texas.[141] Meanwhile the cases have been transferred to the Southern District of New York.[142]

ABS rejects all claims of the Kingdom of Spain as well as the Spanish regions. It submits that the regions have no right of action to raise such claims; in any case, their claims would be barred by the concurring claims of the Kingdom of Spain. It further submits against the action of the Kingdom of Spain that there was no negligent behaviour on its side, and that the action did not furnish proof of a causality between its conduct and the pollution of the seas.

Furthermore, ABS has counter-claimed against the Kingdom of Spain, requiring the Kingdom of Spain to indemnify ABS against all liability put forward against ABS world-wide due to the average of the *Prestige*. In addition, it has initiated action in a Spanish court against the Kingdom of Spain and the Spanish regions, claiming a breach of Spanish material and procedural law by the actions in United States courts.

In this context, the Kingdom of Spain and the Spanish regions have decided to call upon the European Commission to withdraw ABS' status as a recognised classification society.[143] The reason for such a measure by the State might not only be its concern regarding the enforcement of maritime safety, but rather the intention to open a second theatre of actions in order to distract from its own faults. However, the European Commission has not reacted to the Spanish initiative.

The *Prestige* case shows the risks for classification societies of being submitted to legal action when the damages exceed the compensation paid by the P&I Clubs of the shipowner or the International Oil Pollution Compensation Funds (IOPC Funds). In addition, the societies may be subject to a claim of recourse by the insurance company and the IOPC Funds in certain situations. They are the only subjects which might be held liable without being able to limit their liability at first hand; and the amount of damages involved can be enormous. The Executive Committee of the IOPC Funds decided to make initial payments covering 15% of approved claims filed by those affected by the *Prestige* disaster. The level of payments reflected the widespread view that claims arising from the accident will vastly exceed the total USD 198 million that are available through the fund. According to some estimates, the combined cost of the damage caused by the accident in Spain, France and Portugal could exceed € 1 billion.[144] This example shows that it is almost certain that the question of the liability of classification societies will come up again in the future.

---

[141] *LL*, 14 May 2003.

[142] The cases of the constituents of the Basque Country of Spain is pending as *Communidad Autonoma Del Pais Vasco, et al. v. ABS,* 04 Civ. 671 (LTS)(RLE). Only the criminal procedure against the master is still pending in Spain (Juzgado de Primera Instancia e Instrucción nº1 de Corcubión, procedimiento: PREVIAS 960/02).

[143] *LL*, 14 May 2003.

[144] *LL*, 15 May 2003.

B. Private Operations and Public Functions in Detail

Although the application form for surveys undertaken by a classification society usually includes both statutory services and classification, because both a class as well as a number of statutory certificates are required to operate a ship,[145] one needs to distinguish clearly between private operations and public functions exercised by the classification society. Private classification rests upon a private contract between the shipowner or shipyard and the classification society, whereas the statutory survey is a public function mandated by the government. This section explains in more detail the legal structure of these two different activities and their legal foundations, as well as the obligations involved.

I. Private Operations

1. *Contracts and Contracting Parties*

When exercising the activities with regard to the class survey, the society acts pursuant to a '*classification contract*' with the shipowner (or the shipyard, as appropriate). The terms of the contract are agreed upon by the two parties in accordance with the rules of the classification society. Most classification societies base the price of a classification on a system of different factors according to the size and type of ship. A country factor is applied, which reflects the difference in costs for surveying a ship abroad. In total, the price is more influenced by the tonnage of the ship and the power of the engines than by the services rendered and the time used.

Two different phases of development of the classification contract can be identified. The first phase leads to the issuance of the classification certificate and the registration of the ship in the society's ship's register. This may be achieved in two different ways. One way is the classification of a new construction. For a new construction, the shipyard requests a classification and indicates the classification notations which shall be assigned. The society analyses whether these notations meet the requirements of the services the ship is intended to provide and sends an

[145] For a list of certificates and documents required to be carried on board ships, see IMO Circular of 3 July 2000, FAL/Circ.90, MEPC/Circ.368, MSC/Circ.946. There are the following Statutory Certificates: Load Line Certificate, Cargo Ship Safety Construction Certificate (SOLAS), Cargo Ship Safety Equipment Certificate (SOLAS), Cargo Ship Safety Radio Certificate (SOLAS), Safety Management Certificate (SOLAS), Passenger Ship Safety Certificate (SOLAS), International Oil Pollution Prevention Certificate (MARPOL 73/78), International Pollution Prevention Certificate for the Carriage of Noxious Liquid Substances in Bulk (MARPOL 73/78), International Tonnage Certificate, Grain Loading Booklet, Certificate of Fitness for the Carriage of Dangerous Chemicals in Bulk, Certificate of Fitness for the Carriage of Liquefied Gases in Bulk, Certificate of Fitness for Ship Carrying Dangerous Goods, Sewage Pollution Prevention Certificate.

offer, which also contains the price. If the shipyard accepts, the classification society will review the blueprints, survey the ship and issue an interim certificate to the shipyard. The final certificate will not be handed out until some weeks or even months after delivery, at the time when all relevant material has been handed over by the shipyard. The contract with the shipyard has already ended at that time, since all duties towards the shipyard have been executed.

Vessels which have already been built at the time of classification are classed in a different way. A shipowner requests the classification of one of his ships which has either been classed by another classification society or not at all and submits the blueprints of the ship. If the type of ship has already been classed or if the plans have been certified by a classification society that is considered of similar standing in the application of its rules, only a survey of the vessel according to the rules of the classification society is required before a class is assigned. Otherwise a review of the design is necessary, which may be very time-consuming.

After the assignment of the class and the class notations, the classification society checks during its periodical surveys whether the vessel may keep its class. It checks whether the standards laid down in its rules are still met and whether the ship adheres to new standards. Instead of the contract with the shipyard, a similar contract is concluded with the shipowner, or the contract which has been concluded for the classification of an existing vessel is continued. At the request of the shipowner, the classification society offers its services for the maintenance of class, for which certain obligations have to be fulfilled, that are described in the following section. This contract is generally intended to last throughout the whole life of the ship. In most cases, the price for the services of the classification society is fixed for a five-year period. The contract is automatically renewed for another period of five years after the price for the second period has been (tacitly) accepted by the shipowner.

Apart from the classification contract, a classification society may verify the condition of a vessel on the basis of several other contracts with private entities. All these contracts, which are governed by private law, have the one aspect in common that they are concluded for an expert opinion by the classification society. Depending on the provisions of the classification contract, repair surveys may or may not need a separate contract. Either it is stipulated that the fees include all services during the five-year period, or they only include the periodical ones. In the latter case, an extra contract needs to be concluded before such services are performed. Similarly, the issuance of a confirmation of class may be included in the contract.

The survey of the conversion of a vessel is generally not included in the package of the classification society, but in a contract of its own. Whenever the vessel is converted, it has to be checked whether the conversion fulfils the rules and whether class notations have to be withdrawn or others assigned. In the same way, the owner may ask the classification society to supervise the shipyard at the time of the building or conversion of the vessel.[146] Such a contract would also contain very specific provisions, unlike a classification contract.

Similarly, an *'on hire'* survey at the request of the charterer can give rise to such an individual contract[147] as well as at the request of someone who buys a vessel. The latter alternative is nonetheless a rare occasion, because the Norwegian Saleform,[148] under which most vessels are bought and sold, already determines in Art. 8 c) the obligation of the seller to present a certification (called '*confirmation of class'*), which states that the ship is still in class.

Other examples of individual contracts are contracts for weight measurements, necessary, for example, for a passage through the Suez Canal.[149] Also, an insurance company may want to check the condition of a ship which applies for insurance. Nevertheless, this appears to be a rather theoretical possibility, because insurance companies either seem to trust the classification certificates and the information they receive[150] or have such services conducted by undertakings such

---

146 *See* e.g. the German case BGH 3 March 1998, [1998] *NJW-RR* 1027.

147 As an example of such a survey, please refer to *Great American Insurance Co. v. Bureau Veritas*, 338 F.Supp. 999, 1010 (S.D.N.Y.1972), *aff'd*, 478 F.2d 235 (2d Cir.1973).

148 *See* Breitzke, *Die Norwegian Saleform* (1970); Hodges/Hill, *Principles of Maritime Law* (2001), 31-66; Strong/Herring, *Sale of Ships, The Norwegian Saleform* (2004). *See also supra* Part 1 A III 3.

149 There is also a contract for the certification of items. A manufacturer will contract with a classification society for the certification of items in order to show that the certified product corresponds to the rules of the society, and may be built as a new construction without any further analysis of its safety. Not each and every product is tested which leaves the chain of production, but only the construction of it once and for all. The effect of the certificate is that the general safety of the product does not have to be analysed again. However, this does not necessarily imply that the product will not be surveyed once it is put into place in a vessel. There, it may deteriorate due to fatigue or stress. Due to the fact that a product is only in rare cases designed to meet the criteria of the rules, a classification society has to discuss with the manufacturer how the standard of safety can be established and, if necessary, whether exemptions from the rules may be granted, since the product fulfils an equivalent standard of safety by other means. The manufacturer of an item only needs to have it certified once. There are no periodical examinations or the like. The plans of the product need to be reviewed and approved and, in general, the test results which have been worked out by the manufacturer are also analysed. In general, there are no or only a limited number of tests which are executed by the classification society. The manufacturer guarantees that he has tested the product and that it is safe and the classification society places its confidence in this representation.

150 According to IACS Procedural Requirement No. 3 'Transparency of Classification and Statutory Information' (accessible at <http://www.iacs.org.uk/preqs/main.htm>, last accessed 19 March 2007), the Insurance Company receives information about the date of all Class Surveys, the expiry dates of classification certificates, overdue surveys, and the text of overdue Conditions of Class/Recommendations, as well as the due dates of

as the Salvage Association.[151] To sum up, there are a number of contracts which are different from a classification contract. All have the same character in so far as they are expert opinions on the question of whether the object concerned satisfies the rules of the classification society.

2. *Obligations of the Classification Society*

The classification process begins with the review of the plans and the first surveys at the time of the construction of the ship. The shipyard contracts with a classification society in order to sell a classified vessel, a condition preceding its contract with the future owner of the ship.[152] Before the building of the vessel begins, the classification society approves the drawings and issues formal letters in view of this approval.[153] The society examines plans showing the scantlings, arrangements and details of the principal parts of the hull structure of the vessel.[154] Later on, it certifies important equipment and surveys the construction. Ships which are surveyed whilst being built will later receive a special class symbol in the ship's register, often a Maltese Cross or an A1.

Statutory Surveys and the expiry dates of Statutory Certificates. Unless prevented by the agreement with the flag State, it also receives the overdue Statutory Recommendations. When accepted by the owners or through a special clause in the insurance contract, it may also obtain the Certificates and Reports, the text of Conditions of Class and Recommendations and the registered Statutory Recommendations. The Executive Hull Summary is available during a visit on board.

151 *See supra* Part 1 A III 2.

152 E.g. Shipbuilding Contract of the Association of West European Shipbuilders (AWES Contract (July 1972)), Art. 1 lit. (c): 'The VESSEL shall be built under the survey of .... to............ Class and in accordance with normal shipbuilding practices in .... for new vessels of the type and general characteristics of the VESSEL. Classification, survey and testing charges relating to the CONTRACTOR'S obligations and items of supply under this CONTRACT shall be for the account of the CONTRACTOR [the shipyard].'
A copy of an AWES Contract is attached as Appendix I to Clarke (ed.), *Shipbuilding Contracts*, 2nd ed. (1992).

153 It should be noted that classification rules cannot be used as a design code, due to their structure and the fact that they only cover parts of the ship.

154 ABS Rule 1-1-7/1 demands the following plans to be submitted: Vessel Specifications, Bow framing; General Arrangement; Stem; Midship section; Stern framing; Scantling profile and decks; Stern frame and rudder; Bottom construction, floors, girders, etc.; Shaft struts; Framing plan; Spectacle frames and bossing details; Inner bottom plating; Docking plan; Shell expansion; Hatches and hatch-closing arrangements; Deck plans; Ventilation system on weather decks; Pillars and girders; Capacity plan; Watertight and deep-tank bulkheads; Lines and body plan; Miscellaneous non-tight bulkheads which are used as structural supports; Superstructures and deckhouses, and their closing arrangements; Shaft tunnels; Anchor handling arrangements; Machinery casings, boiler, engine and main auxiliary foundations.

The situation changes at the time the ship is delivered. The contract between the shipyard and the society expires and a new contract with the shipowner is concluded. It becomes the responsibility of the shipowner to ensure that all periodical surveys for the maintenance of class are executed at the appropriate time.[155] These surveys follow a certain schedule. Once a year, the vessel must be inspected at the annual survey. Surveyors will inspect the hull externally, the equipment and machinery of the ship and conduct further tests to ascertain that the vessel remains in a general condition which satisfies the requirements of the rules.[156] Depending upon age, size, type and condition of the vessel, the annual survey may require from several hours to a few days to complete.[157] Further periodical surveys are the intermediate survey that is carried out every two and a half years, which involves closer scrutiny of the vessel's structure. According to the type and age of the vessel, the classification society may demand dry-docking and ultrasonic measurements of the thickness of the hull to observe corrosion, search for cracks and determine their size. The special survey once in five years is executed in a dry dock and involves thorough surveys of all parts of the ship which are covered by the rules. It may take up to a few weeks to complete. Instead of a time-consuming special survey once in five years, the shipowner may opt for a Continuous Survey in which not all the check-ups are conducted simultaneously. Instead, each and every part is surveyed at times favourable to the schedule of the ship. Nonetheless, all parts covered by the classification must be checked at least once in five years.

The contracts oblige shipowners to inform the classification society of all occasions when the vessel can be inspected in a dry dock or on a slipway.[158] A minimum of two examinations of the outside of the ship's bottom and related items has to be conducted within a five-year period, one of them in combination with the special survey.[159] The shipowners also have to provide information on all repairs which might affect the classification and on damages, defects, deterioration or breakdown which could invalidate the conditions for which a class has been assigned.[160] Whenever there is damage to the vessel, a Damage Survey has to be completed before the vessel can continue its journey. In the case of an average, the vessel loses its class and must be classified once again. If the ship is not made accessible to a survey, if necessary repairs which are required by the surveyor are

---

155 *See* e.g. ABS Rule 1-1-2/3.

156 IMO Resolution A.746(18) 'Survey Guidelines Under the Harmonized System of Survey and Certification' identifies the minimum survey requirements of annual and intermediate surveys.

157 IACS, 'What are classification societies?' (2004), available at <www.iacs.org.uk/pdf/Class%20monograph.pdf>, last accessed 19 March 2007.

158 IACS Unified Requirement Z3.1.1 (Corr. Feb. 2004) 'Periodical Survey of the Outside of the Ship's Bottom and Related Items', accessible at <http://www.iacs.org.uk/ureqs/main.htm>, last accessed 19 March 2007.

159 IACS Unified Requirement Z3.1.2, accessible at <http://www.iacs.org.uk/ureqs/main.htm>, last accessed 19 March 2007.

160 ABS Rule 1-1-8/1.1; KRS Rule Pt 1, Ch 1, 701.

not carried out in time or if the vessel is used for different purposes from those it is designed and approved for, the class is either automatically suspended or the classification society may withdraw it at any time and expel the ship from its register.[161]

How can the classification society breach a duty of care? That depends on what precisely its activities and functions are. Many of the declarations of the members of IACS aim at the protection of life at sea and the marine environment.[162] But such statements are generally not intended to be legally binding. Therefore, it is not the slogans, but the services that need to be analysed. As has been described in a preceding section, a classification society classifies ships and parts of ships according to rules it has developed from a retrospective point of view.[163] The services it provides are somewhat of a compromise between the guarantee of safety and economic considerations. Shipowners and insurance companies are represented on its General Committee, as well as shipyards. As has also been explained above, the rules do not cover every piece of structure or item, but set forth a certain standard of safety, which has to be state-of-the-art.[164] Therefore a classification society does not guarantee that a vessel is absolutely safe or suitable for intended services. The aim of classification and certification is to ascertain that a certain vessel or item is state-of-the-art at the time of its inspection. A classification society is obliged to assist in securing the safety of the vessel, an obligation it carries out by regular surveys. Owing to the fact that these surveys are only carried out once a year, it is the duty of the owner to ensure that the standard of safety does not deteriorate in the meantime. Similarly, for the certification of parts, the safety of the item is checked only in a general way, by examining the blueprints and a number of samples. The safety of each and every such item produced by the manufacturer is not ensured by the classification society. Such a service would be a quality control, not a certification. An analysis of the interests and the intentions of the contractual parties confirm this result. In general, the shipowner is interested in having the safest ship for the lowest price. From his point of view, safety

---

161 *See for instance* ABS Rules Part 1 Chapter 1 Section 2 §§ 7, 11.

162 ABS: 'Promoting the safety of life, property, and the marine environment', <http://www.eagle.org>; BV: 'For the benefit of business & people', <http://www.veristar.com>; the objective of DNV is to 'Safeguard life, property and the environment', <http://www.dnv.com/maritime/about_us/index.asp>; GL: 'Operating 24/7', <http://www.gl-group.com>; LR: 'As a classification society, Lloyd's Register is an essential link in the overall safety chain of the marine industry', <http://www.lr.org/Industries/Marine/Services/Classification/>; ClassNK defines as its ultimate goal: 'To contribute to the development of maritime service for the protection of human life and property at sea', <http://www.classnk.or.jp/hp/nk_e/About_NK/AboutNKintro.htm>; RINA: 'Together for excellence', <http://www.rina.org>; RS states that its main objectives are 'providing safety of life at sea; providing safe navigation of ships; safe carriage of goods by sea and in inland waters; promoting environmental protection', <http://www.rs-head.spb.ru/English/rsh_main.html> (all homepages last accessed 19 March 2007).

163 *See supra* Part 1 A III 5.

164 *See supra* Part 1 A III 5.

has to be affordable; otherwise he will make much more money by operating an unsafe vessel.[165] For this reason, it is a compromise between safety and expense if a classification society neither checks each and every product used for the building of the vessel nor supervises the vessel at all times. A certain standard is already guaranteed if samples of products are tested before their use and surveys of the vessel in its entirety are carried out once a year.

As the classification society depends upon its credibility and reputation, it is highly interested in a small number of detentions by PSC and few averages of its classed vessels. But this does not imply that it guarantees that all its registered ships are safe at all times. Even though classification societies fulfil a very important role in the system of maritime safety, the price level of a classification or certification reflects the fact that there is no intention to guarantee the safety and operability of the vessel towards the whole shipping industry at all times. In order to achieve this result, the owner also plays a very important part.

3. The Contents of the Classification Certificate, the Confirmation of Class and the Register of Ships

A classification certificate appears to contain the same information as a confirmation of class and the ship's register. However, this is only partly correct. All three of them provide information about the current class and class notation of the vessel. The classification certificate only states that the vessel has been assigned a certain class and class notation. It does not give information about when the last survey has taken place or whether the class is subject to certain conditions or recommendations. Additionally, the year and place of construction and the name of the shipyard as well as the registered tonnage are included. A classification certificate therefore differs from what the purchaser of a vessel may expect. This certificate only relates to safety issues and does not give any information about the value of the vessel or whether the vessel can be used for a certain trade. These issues are of no concern to classification societies, which are mainly interested in safety measures, the prevention of marine pollution and to a certain degree in maritime security (as related to the ISPS Code), as well as ship management as required by the ISM Code. The class notations (such as *i.e.* '*chemical bulker*') imply certain minimum criteria, but only those which relate to safety matters. When analysing the kind of trust that a certain classification certificate may evoke, one needs to refer to the rules. The rules set the scope of what has precisely been analysed by the classification society before granting the certificate and what exactly this certificate implies. A certificate may only state what has been, or according to the rules should have been, analysed and surveyed. It does not give any further information. For this reason, there may be a difference in what a shipowner or purchaser believes the certificate should imply and what it really does.

---

165 The profits of operating a sub-standard vessel are already enormous. Thanks to PSC and the risks involved in such a business, the costs of a safe ship do not outweigh such risks yet.

A confirmation of class by contrast reflects the condition of the vessel as it is included in the files. Not all information contained in the files will be given. Only information about whether or not the vessel is currently subject to conditions or recommendations is included. Also, no extra survey will be carried out for the confirmation of class and the data will not be updated unless the shipowner requests the re-survey of a deficiency leading to a condition or recommendation. For this reason, the last survey of some parts of the vessel might have been a long time ago, in an extreme case up to five years. The main objective of a confirmation of class is not to guarantee that a vessel entirely satisfies the rules but to report the current status of the files and to ensure that the vessel is currently not subject to any conditions or recommendations.

All members of IACS and some other classification societies enter their vessels in a ship register that is openly accessible to the public. These private ship registers can usually be accessed on-line. They contain not only information about the class and class notations, but also the vessel's IMO number, the name of the owner or operator, the flag, the year and construction of the vessel, its gross tonnage, and particulars such as the freeboard, information about the engine and refrigeration installations, as well as the date when the class was issued and until when it is valid. It is not stated whether the classification certificate of a certain vessel is subject to conditions. All vessels of which the class is suspended or withdrawn are not included in the register, but shown in a list that contains the current suspensions and withdrawals which have lasted more than seven days. Sometimes even reinstatements are included and the reasons for suspensions and withdrawals. All lists of suspensions and withdrawals are collected by IACS and included in a list which is published on the homepage of IACS.[166]

II. Public Functions

The high seas are open to all States as Art. 87 (1) UNCLOS[167] provides. Every State has the right to sail ships flying its flag on the high seas.[168] If a flag State grants nationality to a ship,[169] it thereby obtains the right and obligation to exercise exclusive jurisdiction and control over it on the high seas.[170] These obligations are *inter alia* defined in Art. 94 UNCLOS. They include the duty to take measures to ensure safety at sea.[171] Accordingly, a flag State needs to adopt and enforce laws in order to prevent, reduce and control the pollution of the marine environment from vessels flying its flag.[172] The various international conventions on maritime

166 At <www.iacs.org.uk>, last accessed 19 March 2007.
167 United Nations Convention on the Law of the Sea.
168 Art. 90 UNCLOS.
169 Art. 91 (1) UNCLOS.
170 Art. 92 (1) UNCLOS.
171 Art. 94 (3) UNCLOS.
172 Art. 211 (2) UNCLOS.

safety and the prevention of pollution of the marine environment, which have been elaborated mainly by the International Maritime Organization (IMO), set up specific obligations of the flag States telling them how to satisfy these aims.[173] The flag State has to exercise surveys of all ships flying its flag with regard to these conventions. The duty to exercise statutory surveys is carried out because of international obligations and is of a public nature.

The flag State may choose how to fulfil these international obligations. It may either carry out the necessary statutory surveys itself through its own government by a sovereign act. Public international law does not allow a State to exercise its power on the territory of another State unless permission is granted. In foreign ports, therefore, such an act cannot be undertaken without the approval of the port State. The flag State may also choose to assign these functions to a private legal subject, such as a classification society. If the private body acts under private law, a classification society may, for instance, carry out statutory surveys and award or renew certificates. The territorial sovereignty of the port State is not affected by such private acts. For this reason, most flag States have either authorised classification societies to undertake certain statutory surveys on their behalf or even granted a full authorisation to issue all necessary statutory certificates, whether the vessel is in its port of registry or not. Classification societies are present in every major port world-wide or at least have a dense network of exclusive and non-exclusive surveyors. In such a case, the classification society performs quasi-

[173] *Maritime Safety*: Convention on the International Maritime Satellite Organization (INMARSAT), 1976, Convention on the International Regulations for Preventing collisions at Sea (COLREG), 1972, International Convention on Load Lines (LL), 1966, International Convention for Safe Containers (CSC), 1972, International Convention for the Safety of Life at Sea (SOLAS), 1974, International Convention on Maritime Search and Rescue (SAR), 1979, International Convention on Standards of Training, Certification and Watchkeeping for Seafarers (STCW), 1978, International Convention on Standards of Training, Certification and Watchkeeping for Fishing Vessel Personnel (STCW-F), 1995, Special Trade Passenger Ships Agreement (STP), 1971, Protocol on Space Requirements for Special Trade Passenger Ships, 1973. In preparation is a Wreck Removal Convention, which shall be considered by a Diplomatic Conference in 2004-2005.
Marine Pollution: International Convention for the Prevention of Pollution of the Sea by Oil, 1954, as amended (OILPOL), International Convention Relating to Intervention on the High Seas in Cases of Oil Pollution Casualties, 1969 (INTERVENTION), Convention on the Prevention of Marine Pollution by Dumping of Wastes and Other Matter (LDC), 1972, International Convention for the Prevention of Pollution from Ships, 1973, as modified by the Protocol of 1978 relating thereto (MARPOL 73/78), International Convention on Oil Pollution Preparedness, Response and Co-operation (OPRC), 1990, Protocol on Preparedness, Response and Co-operation to pollution Incidents by Hazardous and Noxious Substances, 2000 (HNS Protocol). Both the International Convention on the Control of Harmful Anti-fouling Systems on Ships, 2001 and the International Convention for the Control and Management of Ships' Ballast Water and Sediments are not in force yet.

governmental functions on behalf of the government and issues Statutory Certificates. Even highly regulated States which are strong enforcers of safety measures, such as the United States of America, call upon classification societies in order to exercise flag State control. The U.S. Coast Guard (USCG) has acknowledged ABS, DNV, GL, and LR to provide support and issue Statutory Certificates on behalf of the United States abroad.[174] Such an arrangement is very common, as the example of the largest classification societies shows. There is even a number of flag States which do not have the means to conduct the surveys of their registered fleet. Instead, they make use of classification societies for all statutory surveys and the issuance of the appropriate certificates. DNV, GL and LR each conduct statutory surveys for more than 120 flag States, BV for more than 110, ABS for more than 100 and ClassNK for more than 90. Compliance with safety measures and marine pollution protection is to a large degree controlled by class.

The lack of an effective flag State control by several countries has led to an increasing importance of port State control (PSC). When exercising PSC, a State inspects foreign ships in its ports, *i.e.*, under its territorial jurisdiction, in order to ensure that the ship, its equipment, its manning and the way it is operated satisfies the requirements of international rules and regulations. In many regions of the world, PSC assures the compliance of all vessels with the international conventions. There are regional arrangements for port State control based on so-called Memoranda of Understanding (MOU).[175] Port States usually keep a database to identify sub-standard vessels and to minimise the number of controls of vessels that fulfil the regulations.[176] The MOUs try to minimise lay-over time for vessels that have already been controlled and focus on vessels that have previously been identified as being dangerous and sub-standard. Under a council directive, governments exercising PSC may not call upon the services of a classification society.[177] However, at the request of a port State, a classification society will provide

[174] The foundation is each a Memorandum of Understanding (MOU) between USCG and the classification society in question. These agreements are in accordance with Title 46, United States Code of Federal Regulations, section 8.130. ABS signed on 12 January 1995 (MOU and further information available at <http://www.uscg.mil/hq/g-m/mse/acp/abs.htm>), GL on 7 September 2001 (<http://www.uscg.mil/hq/g-m/mse/acp/gl.htm>), LR on 3 October 1997 (<http://www.uscg.mil/hq/g-m/mse/acp/lr.htm>), and DNV on 12 December 1997 (<http://www.uscg.mil/hq/g-m/mse/acp/dnv.htm>) (all last accessed 19 March 2007).

[175] There is the Paris MOU for Europe and the north Atlantic, the Tokyo MOU for Asia and the Pacific, the Acuerdo de Viña del Mar for Latin America, the Caribbean MOU, the Abuja MOU for West and Central Africa, the Black Sea MOU, the Mediterranean MOU, and the Indian Ocean MOU.

[176] The Paris MOU, for instance, has a central database, which is located in Saint Malo, France (<http://www.parismou.org/>, last accessed 19 March 2007). It is not accessible by the public. However, some of the data is contained in the publicly accessible database Equasis (<http://www.equasis.org/>, last accessed 19 March 2007).

[177] *See* Council Directive 95/21/EC of 19 June 1995 (OJ L 157, 7 July 1995, 1-19) concerning the enforcement, in respect of shipping using Community ports and sailing in

certain information with regard to any of its registered vessels.[178] The problem of sub-standard shipping has been practically banned in those areas where there is effective PSC. Such vessels have moved to regional markets where there is still less control.

1. The Agreement with the Flag State on the Delegation of Power and the Statutory Survey Contract with the Shipowner or Shipyard

With regard to statutory services, there is a complex contractual situation. The flag State is obliged to issue the Statutory Certificates for each of its registered vessels. It needs to ensure that all these vessels correspond to the respective international conventions. The flag State may engage in an agreement with one or several classification societies and assign the inspection of the vessels.[179] Whenever a society carries out statutory work, it is in fact bound by two contracts. The first with the flag State (the general assignment of power to act for it) can be called "*agreement on the delegation of power*". The contract with the shipowner for the performance of statutory surveys is a contract which shall be named "*statutory survey contract*". Once again, it has to be reiterated that a Flag State is not obliged to dele-

---

the waters under the jurisdiction of the Member States, of international standards for ship safety, pollution prevention and shipboard living and working conditions (port state control) as amended by Council Directive 98/25/EC of 27 April 1998 (OJ L 133, 7 May 1998, 19-20), and Commission Directive 98/42/EC of 19 June 1998 (OJ L 184, 27 June 1998, 40-46). PSC is subject to mutual recognition in Europe. This has the effect that fewer ships are controlled in total numbers, but more sub-standard ships are identified.

178 According to IACS Procedural Requirement No. 3 'Transparency of Classification and Statutory Information' (accessible at <http://www.iacs.org.uk/preqs/main.htm>, last accessed 19 March 2007), the classification Societies are obliged to hand out information to the port State about the date of all Class Surveys, the expiry date of the classification certificate, overdue surveys, and the text of all Conditions of Class or Recommendations including overdue ones, as well as the due dates of Statutory Surveys and expiry date of Statutory Certificates. It also receives the text of registered and overdue Statutory Recommendations. Information on Class Transfer and Class Withdrawal will be provided. When accepted by the owners or the master of the ship, it may also see all classification certificates and Reports. The Executive Hull Summary is available during a visit on board.

179 A list of details of the authorisations granted to IACS Member Societies by flag Administrations to undertake statutory surveys and issue certificates on their behalf has been published by the IMO Sub-Committee on Flag State Implementation in its 11th Session on 3 January 2003 (FSI 11/7/1) (accessible at <http://www.iacs.org.uk/ submissions.htm>), last accessed 19 March 2007; there is also a list sorted by flag States including information about where the agreements are published (<http://www.imo.org/ includes/blastDataOnly.asp/data_id%3D8487/11.pdf>, last accessed 19 March 2007).

gate the power of issuance; it is only an option it may choose.[180] A shipowner, by contrast, has no such choice. He needs to be in possession of the Statutory Certificates, whether they are issued by the flag State authorities or by a classification society on behalf of the authority. If his ship does not hold the required Statutory Certificates, it will be detained by port State control in the case of an examination.

The distinction between the classification contract and the statutory survey contract is also reflected in the applicable regulations. With respect to the classification contract, the society applies solely its own rules. As regards the statutory survey contract, it employs the national maritime safety regulations of the flag State in question, which in many cases incorporate the international conventions on this question. It is the right of the flag State to interpret these regulations and it may notify its classification societies in which way it interprets the international conventions. Whenever there is no such authentic interpretation, the society follows its own regulations. Moreover, IACS issues common interpretations of these regulations for its members.

2. Obligations of the Classification Society

The Agreements on the Delegation of Power vary enormously in extent and content. In some cases it is just a one-page letter, in others it is a folder of many pages.[181] The classification society is obliged to exercise the control of the vessels effectively, as laid down in the applicable international conventions. Generally, there are duties of information and of discussion, especially with regard to interpretations as regards the conventions. The surveyors need to know how the flag State expects the surveys to be carried out. There are provisions that the examination may only be performed by exclusive surveyors who only act for this special classification society. Sometimes the agreement on the delegation of power stipulates that the activity of the classification society is supervised by the flag State or by a neutral audit group. Furthermore, it is usually agreed that the flag State accepts the approval of plans by a classification society in the same way as if it had been carried out by its own officials. The results of inspections, examinations, reviews and approvals often have to be forwarded to the flag State. The classification society also has to grant access to information concerning any deficiencies

---

[180] *E.g.* in Germany, the issuance of Statutory Certificates is not delegated to classification societies. A different, more complex construction has been chosen, which is explained in detail in the chapter concerning liability under German law.

[181] For instance, in the case of the agreement between the Danish flag administration and six classification societies, it is a 48-page agreement (accessible under <http://soefart.inforce.dk/graphics/Synkron-Library/DMA/UK_PDF/STCW/dk_class_agreement_2003.pdf>, last accessed 19 March 2007). The Agreement of the United States Coast Guard is much shorter. It can be downloaded at <http://www.uscg.mil/hq/ gm/mse/acp/uscgabs.pdf>, last accessed 19 March 2007.

that are related to delegated functions. If agreed to by the shipowner, the classification society will also give information about deficiencies that are related to private classification. If a vessel does not correspond with the details of the certificate of inspection or if it is not fit to proceed to sea, the flag State administration has to be informed as well. It is self-evident that the classification society has to keep records of all information and surveys and is obliged to observe strict secrecy.

C. Non-Delegable Duty of the Shipowner to Make the Vessel Seaworthy and Presumption of Unseaworthiness

Even though it may not appear necessary to discuss duties of the shipowner when classification societies are at issue, a reference thereto is necessary for a more precise determination of the duties of the classification society. The duty of a classification society is different from the duty of the shipowner. It is not the classification society that is responsible for the seaworthiness of the vessel, but the shipowner. Under common law, a shipowner implicitly undertakes that his ship is seaworthy.[182] He guarantees to those who are transported or ship their goods that the vessel is seaworthy.[183] This duty is a stimulus to do everything necessary to make the vessel safe, including, *inter alia*, surveys by a classification society. The duty of seaworthiness is absolute and independent of negligence.[184] Whenever the Hague-Visby Rules apply, the shipowner has a duty to exercise due diligence to make the ship seaworthy before and at the beginning of the voyage. However, even if a classification society performs such surveys, the shipowner is not relieved from his duty, as the survey does not cover all parts of the ship and some

182 Scrutton/Boyd, *On charterparties and bills of Lading* (1996), Stahl, *Die Zeitcharter nach englischem Recht* (1989), 33.

183 *Ford v. Compagnie Furness* [1922] 2. K.B. 797, at 802, 804.

184 *The Osceola,* 189 U.S. 158, 23 S.Ct. 483, 47 L.Ed. 760 (1903); *Mahnich v. Southern S.S. Co.*, 321 U.S. 96, 64 S.Ct. 455, 88 L.Ed. 561, 1944 AMC 1 (1944); *Mitchell v. Trawler Racer, Inc.*, 362 U.S. 539, 80 S.Ct. 926, 4 L.Ed.2d 941 (1960); *compare also Usner v. Luckenbach Overseas Corp.*, 400 U.S. 494, 91 S.Ct. 514, 27 L.Ed.2d 562, 1971 AMC 277 (1971); Schoenbaum, *Admiralty and Maritime Law*, 4th ed. (2004), § 6-25, at 362. The test for an unseaworthy condition is whether the vessel, equipment or appurtenances were '*reasonably fit for their intended use*' (*Jordan v. United States Lines, Inc.*, 738 F.2d 48 (1st Cir.1984)). The violation of a statute or regulation relating to safety will justify a finding of unseaworthiness *per se* (*Smith v. Trans-World Drilling Co.,* 772 F.2d 157 (5th Cir.1985)).

time may have passed since the last survey.[185] As it is a non-delegable duty, the shipowner cannot transfer it to a third person. It must always be possible to hold the shipowner liable in the case of an average.

German law obliges the carrier (*Verfrachter*) to provide a seaworthy vessel on the basis of a fault-based liability.[186] The carrier is the person who undertakes the carriage of goods by sea in his own name; this can be, but does not necessarily have to be, the shipowner.

Seaworthiness implies that the vessel must not only be fit to meet the perils of the sea. It also has to be suitable for the transport of the particular cargo. The owner warrants that the vessel is seaworthy for the particular journey and the vessel intends to undertake the particular cargo which it will carry.[187] The English House of Lords came to similar conclusions with regard to classification societies in *The Muncaster Castle*[188] and the *Marc Rich*[189] cases. Under German law, the carrier has to answer for failures of a classification society in the exercise of surveys during the lifetime of a vessel, as these surveys relate to the performance of the contract for the carriage of goods at sea.[190]

---

185 *See In re Tecomar S.A.*, 765 F.Supp. 1150, 1991 A.M.C. 2432 (S.D.N.Y.1991). Even though a certificate may not be non- conclusive evidence, it may serve as *prima facie* evidence, *Union of India v. N.V. Rederij* [1963] 2 *Lloyd's Rep.* 223; RG [1937] *JW* 1920; Liesecke, 'Die Seetüchtigkeit des Schiffs beim Frachtvertrag in der Rechtsprechung, insbesondere des Bundesgerichtshofes', in: Baumann, *Festschrift für Sieg* (1976), 345, at 355 *et seq.*

186 § 559 HGB, Rabe, *Seehandelsrecht* (2000), § 559 at no. 31.

187 'The test of seaworthiness is whether the vessel is reasonably fit to carry the cargo which she has undertaken to transport' (Mr. Justice Gray in *The Sylvia*, 171 U.S. 462). 'What has been said is not to suggest that the owner is obliged to furnish an accident-free ship. The duty is absolute, but it is a duty only to furnish a vessel and appurtenances reasonably fit for their intended use. The standard is not perfection, but reasonable fitness; not a ship that will weather every conceivable storm or withstand every imaginable peril of the sea, but a vessel reasonably suitable for its intended service.' (*Mitchell v. Trawler Racer, Inc.*, 362 U.S. 539, 80 S.Ct. 926, 4 L.Ed.2d 941 (1960)). *See also* Benedict, O*n Admiralty* (2002), vol. 2A § 84 at 8-4 with further reference.

188 *The Muncaster Castle,* [1961] A.C. 807, [1961] 2 *Lloyd's Rep.* 57.

189 *Marc Rich & Co. AG v. Bishop Rock Marine Co. Ltd.* (*and ClassNK*) *("The Nicholas H."),* [1995] 2 *Lloyd's Rep.* 299; *see* also "*The Amstelslot*" [1963] 2 *Lloyd's Rep.* 236; "*The Yamatogawa*" [1990] 2 *Lloyd's Rep.* 39.

190 *See* Rabe, *Seehandelsrecht* (2000), § 559 at no. 37; Kronke, 'Seefrachtvertragliche Gehilfenhaftung', [1988] *TranspR* 89, 93; Herber, *Seehandelsrecht* (1999), 314. This question used to be discussed controversely. The arguments against a responsibility were that although the shipowner had to answer for an independent contractor according to § 278 BGB, a classification society was somewhat special, as the shipowner was practically forced to have a vessel classed and there used to be a monopoly of GL. Nowadays this argumentation can no longer apply, as such a monopoly no longer exists. Argumentations against a responsibility of the shipowner towards the classification society are therefore to be considered as outdated. Against a responsibility argued *inter*

The fact that a vessel has a valid classification certificate gives only a first indication that the vessel is seaworthy. It does not relieve the shipowner of this duty.[191] By contrast, if a vessel is surveyed by a classification society, but not considered fit enough to be classed, it is evident that it has to be considered unseaworthy. A ship must be kept up-to-date according to the standard practices (or established usage) of safety. It is not seaworthy if it does not possess the required Statutory Certificates. This does not mean that the ship has to be equipped with every technical feature which is possible, as technical standards change all the time. It only requires those which are used on all ships of that particular kind.

It should be added that in United States courts the notion of seaworthiness is also important in all cases in which the vessel is lost without any explanation in weather which was not unusual.[192] Under such circumstances, it is presumed that the vessel was not seaworthy, as she must be able to withstand expectable action of the seas and expectable vicissitudes.[193] However, in order to recover for unseaworthiness, the plaintiff must show that the unseaworthy condition played a substantial part in bringing about or actually causing the injury and that the injury was either a direct result or a reasonably probable consequence of the unseaworthiness.[194] The presumption of unseaworthiness corresponds to the obligation to pro-

---

alia: Schaps/Abraham, *Das Seerecht in der Bundesrepublik Deutschland* (1978), vol. 1 § 559 no. 8; Ballin, *Die Verantwortlichkeit des Verfrachters für Seetüchtigkeit unter der Einbeziehung der anglo-amerikanischen Rechtsprechung* (1965), 106-108; Liesecke, 'Die Seetüchtigkeit des Schiffs beim Frachtvertrag', in: Baumann, *Festschrift für Sieg* (1976), 345, at 357; Wüstendörfer, *Neuzeitliches Seehandelsrecht* (1950), 240. In favour of it: Pappenheim, *Handbuch des Seerechts* (1918), vol. 3, 142.

191 Expressly stated for Canadian law: Gold/Chircop/Kindred, *Maritime Law* (2003), 157. *Compare* Schoenbaum, *Admiralty and Maritime Law* (2004), § 6-26, 368-372; Scrutton/Boyd, *On charterparties and bills of Lading* (1996), 94-100; Goldsmith, 'River Pilot, Marine Surveyor, and Third-Party Inspector Liability', 26 *Tul.Mar.L.J.* 463 (2002), at 505–508.

192 Mangone, *United States Admiralty Law* (1997), at 128–133; Schoenbaum, *Admiralty and Maritime Law* (2004), § 6–25 to 6–27, at 360–375. When suing a shipowner, the injured party only has to prove that its loss was caused by the unseaworthiness of the vessel, not that the vessel was unseaworthy at the time of the journey (Rabe, *Seehandelsrecht* (2000), § 559 at no. 40). The burden of proof lies with the carrier to show that neither he himself nor the people he was responsible for made a mistake.

193 *Commercial Melasses Corp. v. New York Tank Barge Corp.,* 114 F.2d 248 (2d Cir.1940), *aff'd* 314 U.S. 104, 62 S.Ct. 156, 86 L.Ed. 89 (1941); *South, Inc. v. Moran Towing and Transportation Co.*, 360 F.2d 1002, 1005 (2d Cir.1966); *Leka & Drivas, Inc. v. Goulandris*, 306 F.2d 426 (2d Cir.1962); *Federazione Italiana Dei Corsorzi Agrari v. Mandask Compania de Vapores, S.A.*, 388 F.2d 434, 436 (2d Cir.1968); Bendict, *On Admiralty* (2002), vol. 2A § 63, at 7–4 with further references.

194 *Alvarez v. J. Ray McDermott & Co., Inc.*, 674 F.2d 1037, 1042, 1984 A.M.C. 302 (5th Cir.1982); *Philipps v. Western Company of North America*, 953 F.2d 923, 1993 A.M.C. 1815 (5th Cir.1992); *McClow v. Warrior & Gulf Navigation Co.,* 842 F.2d 1250 (11th Cir.1988). Schoenbaum, *Admiralty and Maritime Law* (2004), § 6-25, at 361.

vide a seaworthy vessel. The burden of proof shall be imposed on those who are obliged to provide a seaworthy vessel. A classification society is not under such an obligation; only the shipowner is. For this reason, the presumption of unseaworthiness does not work against the classification society. If a vessel is lost without any explanation under usual weather conditions, one might, however, discuss a presumption of imperfect performance of the survey. As regards the shipowner, it is presumed that the vessel was unseaworthy. This might imply that the society did not perform the survey in the way it should have done. As regards third parties, such presumption would, however, not be appropriate to the position of the classification society. The society does not have the ship under control at all times. Moreover, it is not under a duty towards the third party to provide a seaworthy vessel, as this is a duty that only extends to the shipowner because of the contract of carriage. The classification society is not even under such presumption of faulty performance of the survey as regards the shipowner. Not only is the shipowner primarily responsible for his vessel, but the last survey might also be nearly a year ago. As the condition of a vessel may considerably change within a year's time, such presumption would not be fair. The shipowner has access to his vessel at all times and can assess the condition of the vessel at all times; but the classification society cannot. Also, the classification society does not guarantee that due to its surveys the vessel is seaworthy. It only guarantees that the ship corresponds to a certain standard as defined in its rules, resulting in a certain standard most likely to ensure a certain level of seaworthiness.

Part 2 [Legal Analysis]

A. Private Functions: The Protection of Contracting Parties

I. English Law

Parties that have contracted with classification societies could theoretically hold these societies liable for either the breach of a contractual duty, the breach of an implied contractual duty to exercise reasonable care and skill or a breach of a duty which the classification society owes to its client irrespective of the contract.[195] As there is no case-law on this question yet, the principles which English courts have developed in regard to similar cases will be applied in order to provide a guideline on how contracting parties are protected.

The classification society agrees by contract to render certain services and therefore undertakes certain duties, and the client agrees to pay a certain fee. There is generally implied a term by law that the classification society will exercise reasonable skill and care as it is a professional person.[196] The main advantage of an action in tort over an action in contract is a different limitation period of the claim. The cause of action in contract will arise when the surveyor breaches his contract, for example by giving a negligent survey report.[197] In tort, by contrast, the action will come about only when the client suffers loss; usually this occurs only after he acts in reliance on the report.[198]

Liability in contract and tort may concur.[199] One of the main problems is to identify the exact scope of the terms of engagement of the classification society. Since *Hedley Byrne*,[200] it is established law that someone who provides incorrect

---

195 Jackson & Powell, *On Professional Negligence* (1997), § 3–71. *See also Caparo Industries Plc v. Dickman,* [1990] 2 A.C. 605 (H.L.), at 619C per Lord Bridge, who describes the duty in tort which the professional man owes to his own client.

196 The common law principle that there is such an implied term in a contract with a professional person is incorporated in s. 13 of the Supply of Goods and Services Act 1982.

197 Jasckson/Powell, *On Professional Negligence* (1997), § 3–08.

198 *See for example Secretary of State for the Environment v. Essex Goodman & Suggitt* [1986] 1 W.L.R. 1432.

199 *Henderson v. Merrett Syndicates Ltd.*, [1995] A.C. 145, [1994] 2 Lloyd's Rep. 468.

200 *Hedley Byrne & Co. Ltd. v. Heller & Partners*, [1963] 2 All E.R. 575, [1964] A.C. 465 (H.L.).

advice or information can be liable not only for death or personal injury but also for economic loss if there is a special relationship between these two persons. A contractual relationship between two persons leads to such duty to prevent economic loss.[201] Whether a classification society owes a duty to prevent economic loss to third parties will be answered *infra* in Part B.

1. Liability for Breach of Contractual Duty

According to Common law, someone who enters into a contract impliedly guarantees that he has the capacity to perform stipulated obligations. In general, there is no requirement to prove a fault of the defendant, but the latter has a strict liability for the contractual obligations.[202] The main issue is to define the scope of obligations of the contract and the warranties implied. Classification societies owe a number of contractual duties to their clients. If a society breaches such duties, it is liable for the damage it causes to its contracting party regardless of the fault. The individual duties depend on the contract, which needs to be carefully construed.

The precise duties of the classification society and therefore the instances in which they are breached depend on the individual contract. It is, however, possible to enumerate and order the breaches of duty which may occur. This enumeration is therefore instructive but not exhaustive.[203]

The first category of a breach of duty consists of the direct causation of harm to others. This is the example of the surveyor who negligently drops his torch and causes damage to the ship's engine. From a legal point of view, such damage is not very interesting as liability for such an action is evident.

The second category relates to damage which has been caused by the classification or a certification in an indirect way. "Indirect" in this sense means that it is not solely the action of the classification society that causes the injury. Someone else has to act before something happens. This additional action may not even be a breach of duty in itself. To give but one example, a classification society certifies the engines of a vessel as according to its rules, but in fact they do not meet the criteria or standards implied. This certification does not cause damage in itself. Damage can only occur if the vessel is operated. Either the engines will be physically damaged or their breakdown will cause damage to other property. They may even cause the loss of life or the pollution of the marine and coastal environment if the vessel gets out of control due to the breakdown of its engines. Similarly, the owner of the vessel or of the goods which are transported may suffer a loss because of the delay of the vessel, caused by its breakdown. In brief, the certification

---

[201] *See* Lord Reid at 483 and Lord Devlin at 528–529, *ibid.*

[202] Lord Edmund-Davies in: *Raineri v. Miles* [1981] A.C. 1050: 'It is axiomatic that, in relation to claims for damages for breach of contract, it is, in general, immaterial why the defendant failed to fulfil his obligation, and certainly no defence to plead that he had done his best.'

[203] This enumeration is influenced by Jackson/Powell, *On Professional Negligence* (1997), § 3-71.

of the engines does not harm others in itself, but it can be part of the chain of causation which causes the damage.

A different kind of damage may occur if one of the engines is sold to a third party. If it is only bought because it has been certified by a (specific) classification society, the buyer might argue he suffered pure economic loss due to the certification. He would have paid less if he had known the correct condition of the article. Only in a particular case will such damage be caused by the classification society. As mentioned before, a classification and likewise a certification by a classification society should not be mistaken for a quality control.[204] Such a certificate does not imply that the checked product is, *inter alia,* of the highest quality, matches the services it is intended for or is worth its price.[205] It only implies that the surveyed product has fulfilled the rules at the time of inspection. If only samples have been inspected, these samples must have matched the obligations imposed by the rules. However, if this was not the case at the time of inspection and if this lack has solely or partly caused the pure economic loss, the classification society can be liable for the issuance of this certification.

Several services of a classification society can cause such indirect damage. The society may calculate and vet the blueprints incorrectly, which causes the vessel to be unstable, insecure, slower, less spacious in its cargo holds or more expensive in its construction. As the rules do not include each and every possible construction, the certificate will still be granted if their safety standard is nevertheless met. If such an exemption is awarded but not justified, the classification society will also cause indirect damage.

Moreover, the society may fail to perform a survey according to its rules. Just like any other kind of surveyor, a classification society is under a duty to carry out the surveys of the vessel as contracted. An instance of default is if it does not survey the vessel at all or not to the extent that has been stipulated. It needs to be ascertained from the contract what the classification society was obliged to do and whether it achieved this standard. Moreover, the society has an obligation to possess sufficient knowledge and experience. It may only engage surveyors who have sufficient knowledge and experience to perform the surveys in question.[206] In addition to that, the classification society has a duty to analyse the design plans of the vessel, attend the building process and subsequently inspect the vessel in a proper way. It has to verify compliance of a new vessel with the applicable rules by providing a technical review of design plans and other related documents and must attend the construction of the vessel in the shipyard. A failure to inspect properly constitutes an incident of default. The precise definition of a proper standard of inspection can, however, be difficult at times. To this end, one may have

[204] *See supra* in this chapter, Part 1 A I and Part 1 A III 5.

[205] An individual contract with a chartered surveyor for an expert opinion concerning the worth of the ship may be concluded. However, classification societies generally do not offer such services.

[206] Regarding a valuation survey of a building *Kenney v. Hall, Pain and Foster* [1976] 2 EGLR 29.

recourse to IACS standards, the CMI code of conduct and IMO Resolutions, which specify the standard of care that needs to be assured whenever statutory surveys are carried out.[207] Despite the fact that these IMO Resolutions only refer to the standard of care which is relevant to statutory surveys, they need to be taken into account because they sum up the relevant standard of the industry as regards the survey of vessels. In any given case, the plaintiff may argue that the standard of care is even more advanced, but will need to present sufficient evidence to prove his point. As an example of a failure to inspect the vessel properly, the surveyor of the classification society may not have surveyed all those parts that have to be surveyed according to the survey cycle and the extent of the survey (annual, intermediate or special survey). He may also have failed to enter confined spaces which should have been checked or did not uncover and open up hidden spots, even though there was specific reason for suspicion.[208] A classification society, just like any surveyor, must be 'judging what you cannot see by what you can see'.[209] An incorrect calibration of measuring equipment may also constitute such a default, as well as an incorrect measurement of the thickness or a visual inspection of the hull under water despite the fact that according to the survey cycle the vessel should have been put in a dry dock. Another example is the duty to observe all deficiencies. Despite the fact that the classification society's surveyor has inspected the defective area or item, he may not necessarily observe all deficiencies, which constitutes a breach of contract.[210] A limited survey may constitute another breach of the duty to inspect properly. The scope of an annual survey is rather limited; the classification society is, however, only obliged to carry out the survey in the way that has been contracted. At the annual survey only a sampling is tested and this involves testing those parts of the vessel or its machinery that are especially exposed to corrosion, subject to the highest incidence of stress or especially threatened by fatigue or damage.

The safety of the construction does not need to be checked each time again, as this is thoroughly analysed at the time the vessel enters the society's register. As the scope is contractually defined by the rules of the classification society, there is no duty towards the contracting party to expand the scope of these surveys further.

---

[207] IMO, *Guidelines for the authorization of organizations acting on behalf of the Administration*, Resolution A.739(18); IMO, *Specifications on the survey and certification functions of recognized organizations acting on behalf of the Administration,* Resolution A.789(19); IMO, *Guidelines under the Harmonized System of Survey and Certification,* Resolution A.948(23).

[208] See *Roberts v. J. Hampson & Co.,* [1990] 1 W.L.R. 94 (Q.B.D.) , approved by Lord Templeman in *Smith v. Eric S. Bush* [1990] 1 A.C. 831 (H.L.), at 851.

[209] There are no cases yet which relate to classification societies, but the following cases regarding building surveyors are directly comparable, as they also relate what such surveyors have to discover and what not. *Hacker v. Thomas Deal & Co.* [1991] 2 EGLR 161; *see also Bere v. Slades* [1989] 2 EGLR 160; *Whalley v. Roberts & Roberts* [1990] 1 EGLR 164.

[210] For example, *Cross v. David Martin and Mortimer* [1989] 1 EGLR 154.

However, if the society discovers deficiencies or has justified suspicions that such deficiencies are present, it may have to enlarge the scope of its survey in order to be able to provide the information on how the vessel may retain its class.

Moreover, the classification society is also under a duty to report its findings adequately. If the class is assigned, the society is under a duty to issue a certificate. If the vessel is subject to a number of defects, it has to provide advice on how the vessel can be brought to class standard. Finally, the classification society has to develop its rules in a proper manner. It is obliged to analyse common defects and include appropriate provisions in its set of rules.

Last but not least, such "indirect" damage may also occur whenever the survey has been executed correctly, but, contrary to the results of the survey, the class or class notation is granted, although the prerequisites of a classification certificate were not fully met by the vessel.[211]

The third category of breaches of duty includes certain negligent behaviour. Whenever the certificate or the class is awarded under certain conditions, these conditions may only be revoked if the factual situation has changed and the reason for their imposition no longer exists. Such conditions may be that the ship is only employed in coastal regions. Whenever the conditions are no longer applied, even though the situation as regards the vessel has not changed, the classification society can be liable for this withdrawal.

The fourth category concerns the rules. As an example of this category, an engine is classed as according to the rules and the rules are effectively fulfilled, but it turns out that the standard of safety included in the rules was not high enough. For the contractual parties, the contract needs to be interpreted in the light of the rules. According to the statutes of a classification society, it provides services in accordance with its rules. For that reason, the rules are part of the contract. The societies subject their rules to continual revisions. Whenever major breakdowns to certain types or models of ships occur, their cause will be evaluated in order to avoid similar occurrences to other vessels. The results of such an evaluation process usually lead to an update of the rules. But they might also be changed due to regulatory requirements. Whenever the rules are changed, the owner has to act in accordance with the new requirements within a certain period of time and keep his vessel in an up-to-date condition.

It may be concluded that it is a breach of contract if the rules are no longer state-of-the-art, and therefore from a general point of view a vessel or parts of it cannot be considered as safe. If the society departs from its rules, its exception must guarantee the same level of safety. A "new" defect which has never been seen before and which was until then not foreseeable imposes no liability. For a "new" imperfection which has never occurred before, but which has been foresee-

211 Similarly, several mistakes with regard to the issuance of the certificates may occur. There might be a difference between the provisional and the final Classification Certificate and between the Classification Certificate and the ship's register. These are, however, cases which are based on negligent behaviour as regards administration. In the age of computers, they should not occur.

able, one might discuss liability in a particular case. Whenever "old" shortcomings have not been correctly analysed due to the negligence of the classification society, the rules are no longer state-of-the-art. Evidently, the same applies to "old" faults which have been analysed but not yet included in the rules.

All other contracts which have been mentioned before oblige the classification society to perform one single duty, such as the supervision of the conversion or the issuance of a confirmation of class.

2. *Implied Contractual Duty to Exercise Reasonable Care and Skill*

If neither the application form for a classification contract or some kind of Special Contract with a classification society nor the rules of the society specify the express terms of the engagement, one may have recourse to implied contractual duties. There is a term implied by law that the classification society will carry out its contractual activities with reasonable care and skill.[212] Just as with any other professional person, the standard of care required of a classification society is that of the ordinary skilled man exercising the same skill as itself.[213] Such skill is defined by the courts in the following way:

> 'From these general statements it follows that a professional man should command the corpus of knowledge which forms part of the professional equipment of the ordinary member of his profession. He should not lag behind other ordinary assiduous and intelligent members of his profession in knowledge of new advances, discoveries and developments in his field. He should have such an awareness as an ordinarily competent practitioner would have of the deficiencies in his knowledge and the limitations on his skill. He should be alert to the hazards and risks in any professional task he undertakes to the extent that other ordinarily competent members of the profession would be alert. He must bring to any professional task he undertakes no less expertise, skill and care than other ordinarily competent members of his profession would bring, but need bring no more. The standard is that of the reasonable average. The law does not require of a professional man that he be a paragon combining the qualities of polymath and prophet.'[214]

The standard of care and skill must be determined by reference to members of the profession concerned. In all cases in which there are no authorities, as in the case of classification societies, the standard of care must be that care and skill which members of the profession ought to achieve.[215] For a claim against a classification society, this implies that the society must have failed to exercise the standard of care and skill which the court deems to be compulsory for an ordinary member of the profession of classification societies. As a guideline, one may refer

---

212 *See* §§ 13 and 16 of the Supply of Goods and Services Act 1982.

213 Jackson & Powell, *On Professional Negligence* (1997), § 3–49; *Daisley v. B.S. Hall & Co.* (1972) 225 EG 1553, at 1555; *Corisand Investments Ltd. v. Druce & Co.* (1978) 248 E.G. 315, at 318.

214 *Eckersley v. Binnie*, [1988] 18 Con. L.R. 1, at 79 *per* Bingham L.J.

215 *Midland Bank Trust Co. Ltd. v. Hett, Stubbs & Kemp* [1979] 1 Ch. 384; *Brown v. Gould & Swayne* [1996] P.N.L.R. 130.

to the standard of care that has been laid down in the IMO conventions on classification societies and the exercise of flag State control.[216]

3. *Tort of Negligence*

Concurring with a claim in contract, the contracting party may also have a cause of action based on the tort of negligence. This tort has three preconditions.[217] The defendant must owe a duty of care to the plaintiff, the defendant has acted or spoken in such a way as to break that duty of care, and the plaintiff has suffered damage as a consequence of the breach. This damage must be within the scope of the defendant's duty. The main problem of the tort of negligence is whether or not a duty of care exists towards the plaintiff and how the scope of such duty can be defined. As the section regarding the protection of third parties will illustrate,[218] the establishment of the duty of care can be rather difficult, and the courts continue to differ in their approach to this question. Usually, it must be considered fair, just and reasonable to impose a duty of care on the defendant.[219] This test is employed to determine whether there is a special relationship between the plaintiff and the defendant that justifies the imposition of a duty of care on the defendant. In a contractual situation, the contract already provides sufficient justification to impose such a duty. In *Smith v. Eric S. Bush* it was therefore held that surveyors 'not only entered into contractual relations with the building society but also came under a duty in tort to it to exercise reasonable care in carrying out their survey and preparing their report.'[220] Where parties have entered into a contract which defines their obligations, the law of tort, however, does not impose any wider duties.[221] For classification societies, this implies that their duties in tort correspond to the duties that are owed to the contracting parties in contract.

---

[216] IMO, *Guidelines for the authorization of organizations acting on behalf of the Administration*, Resolution A.739(18); IMO, *Specifications on the survey and certification functions of recognized organizations acting on behalf of the Administration,* Resolution A.789(19); IMO, *Guidelines under the Harmonized System of Survey and Certification,* Resolution A.948(23).

[217] Jackson & Powell, *On Professional Negligence* (1997), § 1–13.

[218] *See infra* Part 2 B I.

[219] Regarding the development of the duty of care from *Donough v. Stevenson* until today, please refer to Charlesworth & Percy, *On Negligence* (2006), §§ 2–07 to 2–191; Jackson & Powell, *On Professional Negligence* (1997), §§ 1–22 to 1–61.

[220] *Smith v. Eric S. Bush,* [1990] 1 A.C. 831, at 870 E per Lord Jauncey (with whom Lord Keith and Lord Brandon agreed).

[221] *Tai Hing Cotton Mill Ltd. v. Liu Chong Hing Bank Ltd.* [1986] A.C. 80; *Greater Nottingham Co-operative Society Ltd. v. Cementation Piling and Foundations Ltd.* [1989] Q.B. 71; *Scally v. Southern Health & Services Board* [1992] 1 A.C. 294; *Downsview Nominees Ltd. v. First City Corporation* [1993] A.C. 295.

4. Exemption and Limitation Clauses

Classification societies usually include exemption or limitation clauses in their contracts. If they are valid and enforceable, such clauses not only relate to contractual liability, but also to liability in tort towards the contracting party. Traditionally, English judges first ascertain the liability of the defendant apart from the exemption clause and then consider whether the exemption clause has any effect on that liability.[222] Such clauses must be expressed clearly and without ambiguity; otherwise they will not be effective.[223] Clauses which are so broad and general in scope that they would defeat the main purpose of the contract or absolve one party of all its rights and duties can be deemed inapplicable.[224]From a general point of view, there are three different types of exemption clauses. First of all, there are clauses which limit what would otherwise be the defendant's duty under the contract, for instance by excluding express or implied terms or limiting liability to cases of wilful neglect.[225]

The second type of clauses purports to exclude or limit liability that would otherwise attach to a breach of contract. Such a clause may be inserted, but needs to be analysed rather critically. The Unfair Contract Terms Act 1977 (UCTA) largely limits the possible extent of exemption clauses. For death or personal injury resulting from negligence, one cannot contractually exclude or limit liability at all despite sufficient indication in the contract that the parties intended to do so.[226] If other loss or damage occurs, such exclusion or restriction is only possible if the requirement of *reasonableness* is met.[227] The onus of proof is on the party that relies on the clause.[228] According to the test of reasonableness, 'the term shall have been a fair and reasonable one to be included having regard to the circumstances which were, or ought reasonably to have been, known to or in the contemplation of the parties when the contract was made'.[229] The time for determining the reasonableness of the term is the time the contract was made.[230] There is no precise definition of *reasonableness*. Schedule 2 to the Act however provides some guidelines,[231] which are frequently considered to be of general application.[232] Additional

---

222 *Rutter v. Palmer* [1922] 2 K.B. 87, at 92.

223 Chitty, *On Contracts* (2004), § 14–05 with further references.

224 *See for example Suisse Atlantique Société d'Armement Maritime S.A. v. N.V. Rotterdamsche Kolen Centrale* [1967] 1 A.C. 361 (H.L.), at 398; *Tor Line A.B. v. Alltrans Group of Canada Ltd.* [1984] 1 W.L.R. 48.

225 Chitty, *On Contracts* (2004), § 14–03.

226 § 2 (1) of the Unfair Contract Terms Act 1977.

227 § 2 (2) of the Unfair Contract Terms Act 1977.

228 § 11 (5) of the Unfair Contract Terms Act 1977.

229 § 11 (1) of the Unfair Contract Terms Act 1977.

230 Chitty, *On Contracts* (2004), § 14–84 with further references.

231 '(a) the strength of the bargaining positions of the parties relative to each other, taking into account (among other things) alternative means by which the customer's requirements could have been met;

criteria have been added by the courts. In the course of his judgment in *Smith v. Eric S. Bush*, Lord Griffiths acknowledged that the decision on whether the requirement of reasonableness has been met is a very difficult one to make and that it is impossible to draw up an exhaustive list of the factors that must be taken into account.[233] However, he identified four matters which, in his view, should always be considered, and which have been adhered to in subsequent judgments. Of prime interest is the bargaining power of the parties. If they have equal bargaining power and have concluded the relevant clause after a discussion, the clause is more likely to be reasonable than if it has been imposed by one party on the other which has no effective power to bargain.[234] Secondly, in a contract for the provision of information or advice, it is of relevance whether the advice could be obtained from an alternative source at reasonable cost and in a reasonable time.[235] Thirdly, whether such a clause is reasonable also depends on the nature of the performance that is promised by the contract. If it is difficult or dangerous and entails a high risk of failure, it will be more reasonable to exclude liability as a condition of the work.[236] However, whenever there is no such difficulty, it is less appropriate to limit or exclude the liability. Last but not least, an additional pointer towards or against the reasonableness of the term are the practical consequences of the decision, with regard to the sums of money potentially at stake, the ability of the re-

(b) whether the customer received an inducement to agree to the term, or in accepting it had an opportunity of entering into a similar contract with other persons, but without having to accept a similar term;
(c) whether the customer knew or ought reasonably to have known of the existence and extent of the term (having regard, among other things, to any custom of the trade and any previous course of dealing between the parties);
(d) where the term excludes or restricts any relevant liability if some condition is not complied with, whether it was reasonable at the time of the contract to expect that compliance with that condition would be practicable;
(e) whether the goods were manufactured, processed or adapted to the special order of the customer.'

232 *Flamar Interocean Ltd. v. Denmac Ltd,* [1990] 1 Lloyd's Rep. 434, at 438–439; *Stewart Gill Ltd. v. Horatio Myer and Co. Ltd.*, [1992] Q.B. 600, at 608; *Overseas Medical Supplies Ltd. v. Orient Transport Services Ltd.,* [1999] 2 Lloyd's Rep. 273, at 277. For further references *see* Chitty, *On Contracts* (2004), § 14–085 at no. 424.

233 *Smith v. Eric S. Bush,* [1990] 1 A.C. 831, at 858–859 *per* Lord Griffiths.

234 *See also Overseas Medical Supplies Ltd. v. Orient Transport Services Ltd.,* [1999] 2 Lloyd's Rep. 273, at 277.

235 *See also Overseas Medical Supplies Ltd. v. Orient Transport Services Ltd.,* [1999] 2 Lloyd's Rep. 273, at 277.

236 *Compare Sonicare International Ltd. v. East Anglia Freight Terminal Ltd.*, [1997] 2 Lloyd's Rep. 48, at 55 per Judge Hallgarten, Q.C.; *Overseas Medical Supplies Ltd. v. Orient Transport Services Ltd.,* [1999] 2 Lloyd's Rep. 273, at 277.

spective parties to bear the losses involved and the availability of insurance to meet such losses.[237]

As regards classification societies, the bargaining power of the contracting party cannot be answered in general, because a shipowner who owns a large fleet has substantially more bargaining power than a one-ship company. However, as there is considerable competition between classification societies, every shipowner may choose between several classification societies, and not all classification societies employ the same disclaimers. In *Smith v. Bush*, one of the problems was that one party was inexperienced with the kind of contract in question and not accustomed to disclaimers. In the view of the court, that party needed protection. Parties such as shipowners, by contrast, are accustomed to disclaimers and do not necessarily require such protection. If the parties are of equal bargaining power and especially if the risks are being borne by insurance, the decision of the parties to apportion their risk should be respected.[238] In contrast to exemption clauses, limitation clauses are more openly accepted and may therefore be considered as valid if they are used by classification societies.

The third category of clauses finally relates to the limitation of damages which can be sought by the plaintiff.[239] The rules of classification societies often incorporate a clause which limits the damages to a certain amount which is based on a multiple of the costs of classification.[240] Such a disclaimer limits the liability for damages to a determinable sum. In relation to such a clause, Section 11 (4) of the Unfair Contract Terms Act 1977 states that

> 'Where by reference to a contract term or notice a person seeks to restrict liability to a specified sum of money, and the question arises (under this or any other Act) whether the term or notice satisfies the requirement of reasonableness, regard shall be had in particular (but without prejudice to subsection (2) above in the case of contract terms) to–
> (a) the resources which he could expect to be available to him for the purpose of meeting the liability should it arise; and
> (b) how far it was open to him to cover himself by insurance.'

There are not yet any verdicts which relate to such limitation clauses by classification societies. The number of cases which take this provision into account is in

---

[237] *Smith v. Eric S. Bush,* [1990] 1 A.C. 831, at 858–859 per Lord Griffiths; *compare Flamar Interocean v. Denmac (The Flamar Pride and the Flamar Progress)*, [1990] 1 Lloyd's Rep. 434 at 439; *Overseas Medical Supplies Ltd. v. Orient Transport Services Ltd.,* [1999] 2 Lloyd's Rep. 273, at 277.

[238] *Watford Electronics Ltd. v. Sanderson Cfl Ltd.*, [2002] F.S.R. 19, at 322 (C.A.(Civ. Div.)); *Photo Productions Ltd. v. Securicor Transport Ltd.,* [1980] A.C. 827 (H.L.), which does not relate to the UCTA, gives a similar statement.

[239] Chitty, *On Contracts* (2004), § 14–03.

[240] The CMI Draft Model Clauses also provide for such clause, *see* Kröger, *Presentation on Behalf of the German Shipowners' Association and of the Maritime Law Committee of ICS*, [1997] *CMI Yearbook* 185, at 187–188; Skou, *Presentation on Behalf of IACS to the Centenary Conference of the CMI*, [1997] *CMI Yearbook* 180, at 183–184.

general rather limited. It has been held that such clauses are valid if immense claims occur.[241] The claims against a classification society can be quite significant in comparison with the fee charged. The societies, however, may purchase insurance for these risks and for what in fact they insure themselves. Besides, whether or not the classification society actually acquires insurance is of no relevance.[242]

The aim of § 11 (4) UCTA is to protect small businesses and professional persons that do not have sufficient resources to meet unlimited liability or that may be exposed to claims that exceed sums for which insurance is available.[243] Classification societies are no small companies. One may only wonder whether their claims are insurable. It must, however, be taken for granted that the insurance market offers coverage for against classification societies.[244] Yet the costs of such insurance remain in doubt. What is rather difficult to answer in this circumstance is the question of whether the defendant has to purchase insurance totalling such an amount that it might be uneconomic in relation to the margin of profit achieved. Bearing in mind that limitation clauses aim to facilitate the exchange of services, one may strongly doubt such a requirement.

To summarise, limiting liability to a multiple of the fee charged must be deemed reasonable. In each and every case, however, one should consider whether the limitation, for instance to a maximum of seven times the fee of the classification, is too low, as insurance would be available for considerably higher amounts. Nevertheless, in circumstances with very large sums of money at stake, such limitation clauses will in most cases be reasonable and effective.

II. United States Law

1. The Applicable Law: Federal or State Law

A contractual liability of classification societies to their clients can theoretically be subject to federal law or state law. In the United States, every state has its own civil law, including a distinct set of precedents; the law could therefore differ according to the state law which applies to the contract. If a classification contract was, however, a maritime contract, federal maritime law would apply. The standing precedent says that, with regard to maritime contracts, federal maritime law controls the contract interpretation unless the dispute is inherently local.[245] For this reason, the first and foremost question which needs to be answered is whether federal maritime law or state law is to be applied. A maritime contract is one that

[241] *Heathmill Multimedia ASP Ltd. V. British Telecommunications Plc*, [2003] EWHC 690 (QBD) at para. 65 (6).

[242] *SAM Business Systems Limited v. Hedley & Co.*, [2002] WL 31784544 (QBD), at para. 65.

[243] Chitty, *On Contracts* (2004), § 14–087.

[244] *Compare also* Part 3 C II 1.

[245] *Kossick v. United Fruit Co.,* 365 U.S. 731, 735, 81 S.Ct. 886, 889, 6 L.Ed.2d 56 (1961); *Norfolk Southern Railway Co. v. Kirby*, 125 S.Ct. 385, 160 L.Ed.2d 283 (U.S.2004).

'relate[s] to a ship in its use as such, or to commerce or to navigation on navigable waters, or to transportation by sea or to maritime employment.'[246]

Therefore,

'[t]o ascertain whether a contract is a maritime one, [a court] cannot look to whether a ship or other vessel was involved in the dispute, as [it] would in a putative maritime tort case. Nor can [the court] simply look to the place of the contract's formation or performance. Instead, the answer "depends upon ... the nature and the character of the contract," and the true criterion is whether it has "reference to maritime service or maritime transactions".'[247]

A contract will be of a maritime nature if the

'matters performed or entered upon under it pertain to the fitment of [the] vessel for navigation.'[248]

The contract must be considered maritime in nature and character, meaning that it relates to a maritime service or a maritime transaction.[249] Both a contract to inspect a vessel for its compliance with the society's own rules and one which promises to analyse compliance with international safety rules are contracts which are unique to the world of seafaring, since the resulting certificates are required either legally or practically before a shipowner may ply navigable waters.[250] Such a contract is therefore of maritime nature, and federal maritime law applies to it.[251]

---

246 *CTI-Container Leasing Corp. v. Oceanic Operations Corp.*, 682 F.2d 377, 379 (2d Cir.1982). *See also Sundance Cruises Corp. v. The American Bureau of Shipping,* 7 F.3d 1077, 1080 (2d Cir.1993).

247 *Norfolk Southern Railway Co. v. Kirby*, 125 S.Ct. 385, 388 (U.S.2004), *references omitted.*

248 *Cox v. Murray*, 6 F.Cas. 681, 682 (S.D.N.Y.1848). *See* also Benedict, O*n Admiralty* (2002), § 183 at 11–6.

249 Benedict, *On Admiralty* (2002), § 181, at 12–2; Gruendel/Crain, 'The Maritime Contract and Admiralty Jurisdiction: Recent Developments Help Clarify and Inherently Confused Landscape', 77 *Tul.L.Rev.* 1235, at 1243 (2003); Mangone, *United States Admiralty Law* (1997), at 40–54.

250 *Sundance Cruises Corp. v. American Bureau of Shipping,* 799 F.Supp. 363, 369 (S.D.N.Y. 1992), *aff'd,* 7 F.3d 1077, 1081 (2d Cir.1993).

251 Similar: *Shipping Corporation of India v. American Bureau of Shipping*, 744 F.Supp. 447, at 449 (S.D.N.Y.1990): the court held that (at least) the classification society's pre-delivery and post-delivery services are maritime services, provided pursuant to a maritime contract. In *Inversiones Calmer, S.A. v. C.E. Heath & Co.,* 681 F.Supp. 100 (D.Puerto Rico 1988) it was held by a District Court that a contract for a classification decision for insurance purpose is not a maritime question, as it is not its aim to prepare to navigate or conduct marine commerce but to prepare the procurement of insurance. This decision is, however, based on a misunderstanding of the nature of a classification contract.

As the building of a vessel is not necessarily a maritime service or transaction, one may wonder about the nature of the contract of a classification society with a shipyard. The contract between the shipowner and the shipyard for the building of a new vessel has been considered not to be a maritime contract.[252] However, the services of a classification society at a shipyard are closely related to the issuance of the certificate at a later period of time as well as to subsequent surveys, which are carried out according to a maritime contract. Also, if it is not the shipyard but the shipowner that contracts with the classification society as from the beginning, the contract will have to be considered as maritime in nature because it shares the same legal nature before and after the vessel is put into service. The contract between the shipowner and the classification society is considered as a contract for service.[253] Therefore, the contract between the classification society and the shipyard should also be considered as maritime in nature.

2. *Breach of Contract, Warranty of Workmanlike Performance and Tort Law*

Due to the fact that United States law is also grounded in common law, its contract law is similar to English contract law. Someone who enters into a contract guarantees that he may perform the contractual duties. If the classification society breaches a contractual duty which it has expressly or impliedly warranted and thereby causes a foreseeable damage to the contracting party, it will be liable. Regarding the breach of contract, one differentiates between non-performance[254] and partial non-performance of the duty.[255] This differentiation is, however, only rele-

---

Even if the parties stipulated a choice-of-law clause that New York law governs the case, as is stipulated in the standard clauses of ABS, federal maritime law would govern. New York law requires the application of federal maritime law to maritime cases. (*Hess v. United States,* 361 U.S. 314, 318, 80 S.Ct. 341, 345, 4 L.Ed.2d 305 (1960); *Kermarec v. Compagnie Generale Transatlantique*, 358 U.S. 625, 628, 79 S.Ct. 406, 408, 3 L.Ed.2d 550 (1959); *Pope & Talbot, Inc. v. Hawn,* 346 U.S. 406, 409, 74 S.Ct. 202, 204, 98 L.Ed. 143 (1953); *Allied Chemical Int'l Corp. v. Companhia de Navegacao Lloyd Brasileiro,* 775 F.2d 476 (2d Cir.1985); *Sundance Cruises Corp. v. American Bureau of Shipping,* 7 F.3d 1077, 1081 (2d Cir.1993); *Lerner v. Karageorgis Lines, Inc.,* 66 N.Y.2d 479, 497 N.Y.S.2d 894, 895, 488 N.E.2d 824, 825 (1985)).

252 *People's Ferry Co. v. Beers,* 61 U.S. (20 How.) 393, 401–402 (1857). Gruendel/Crain, 'The Maritime Contract and Admiralty Jurisdiction', 77 *Tul. L. Rev.* 1235 fn. 50 (2003).

253 *Compare Carbotrade S.p.A. v. Bureau Veritas,* 99 F.3d 86 (2d Cir.1996), at 91; *Cargill, Inc. v. Bureau Veritas*, 902 F.Supp. 49, 1996 A.M.C. 577 (S.D.N.Y.1995), at 52; *Great American Insurance Co. v. Bureau Veritas*, 338 F.Supp. 999 (S.D.N.Y.1972), at 1009, 1012; *Sealord Marine Co., Ltd. v. American Bureau of Shipping,* 220 F.Supp.2d 260 (S.D.N.Y.2002), at 266; *Shipping Force Co., Ltd. v. American Bureau of Shipping,* 2004 WL 51233 (S.D.N.Y.2004), at 1; *Sundance Cruises Corp. v. American Bureau of Shipping,* 7 F.3d 1077 (2d Cir.1993), at 1077.

254 § 236 Restatement (Second) of Contracts.

255 Only full performance of a duty under a contract discharges the duty, §§ 235 (1), 241, 243 Restatement (Second) of Contracts.

vant to a repudiation of the contract, not to the question of liability. The scope of the contractual obligations is ascertained by interpreting the agreement.[256] The explicit warranties and conditions that are included in a contract with a classification society depend on the individual contract. The general scope of obligations has been developed and categorized *supra*[257] and is equally relevant under United States law.

A shipowner could also make a claim based on the *Ryan* warranty of workmanlike performance, as will be analysed in the following section, which relates to the leading precedents.[258] Further to this, he may have a cause of action in tort, based on the tort of negligence or the tort of negligent misrepresentation. Similar to the situation under English law, an action in contract may concur with an action in tort. The *East River* doctrine, however, bars a claim in tort under certain conditions, as the *Shipping Corporation of India II* case illustrates, which will also be commented on later.[259] In brief, according to the case law which will be analysed below, neither breach of contract, nor the *Ryan* warranty of workmanlike performance, or tort law provides the shipowner with a claim against a classification society.

3. *The Leading Precedents*

a. The Great American Insurance Case

aa. The Facts

The vessel TRADEWAYS II sank while on a voyage from Antwerp, Belgium, to the United States on 22 October 1965 with the loss of the entire cargo and the lives of 11 members of her crew.[260] The shipowners and their insurance compa-

---

[256] §§ 200–204 (–218) Restatement (Second) of Contracts: 'to determine the parties' intent in entering into the contract'. The interpretation of contracts is analysed in detail in Farnsworth, *On Contracts* (1998), §§ 7.7–7.14; Williston, *A Treatise on the Law of Contracts* (2001), §§ 32F:1–32F:10. The aim of interpretation is to find out the will of the parties. If in doubt, the usual meaning of a phrase applies, but usages and the course of dealing between the parties must be taken into account. The *contra preferentem* rule defines that uncertainties are to be construed against the party that has formulated the clause in doubt.

[257] *See* Part 2 A I 1.

[258] *See* Stuart/Caffrey, 'Liability of Marine Surveyors, Adjusters, and Claims Handlers', 22 *Tul.Mar.L.J.*, 1 (1997), at 39, 42.

[259] *East River S.S. Corp. v. Transamerica DeLaval, Inc.,* 476 U.S. 858, 106 S.Ct. 2295, 90 L.Ed.2d 865 (1986). *See also Sundance Cruises Corp. v. American Bureau of Shipping,* 799 F.Supp. 363, 383–384 (S.D.N.Y.1992).

[260] *Great American Insurance Co. v. Bureau Veritas*, 338 F.Supp. 999 (S.D.N.Y.1972), *aff'd*, 478 F.2d 235 (2d Cir.1973). Case comments: Bar-Lev, 'Liability of a Vessel Classification Society Cannot Be Based on Warranty of Seaworthiness', 4 *J.Mar.L.&Com.* 334 (1973), France, 'Classification societies: their liability–an American lawyer's point of view in light of recent judgments', 1 *I.J.S.L.* 67 (1996), at 73; Gordan, 'The Liability of Marine Surveyors and Ship Classification Societies', 19 *J.Mar.L.&Com.* 301 (1988); Leslie, 'Civil Liability Responsibilities of Vessel Owners

nies, which had settled the various claims asserted against their clients, sought indemnification from BV. The TRADEWAYS II had been built in 1944 and registered by BV in 1964, after a special survey was carried out. In September 1965, BV completed the annual survey of the vessel, including a survey of the hull. No deficiencies were discovered. Shortly after the annual survey, BV conducted an "On Hire" survey on behalf of the charterer. Since an "On Hire" survey should inform the charterer of the condition of the vessel and assure the charterer that it may safely make its voyage, such a survey is more thorough than an annual survey. Although it was carried out by the same surveyor who had also performed the annual survey, a number of serious deficiencies in the lower hold areas of the vessel were discovered. As a result, the class was suspended and the classification certificate removed. Following the suspension of the class, several repairs were carried out. However, the frames and deep tank tops in the No. 1 hold were not repaired. Some other repairs were allowed to be deferred until the next annual survey. On boarding the vessel, the new crew surveyed it and declared they were satisfied with the condition, even though repairs to some of the deficiencies had not been carried out.

From the beginning of her final voyage, the ship required pumping from the engine room, boiler room and tunnel bilges. After the ship encountered heavy weather, water entered the deep hold tank No. 1. Shortly thereafter water was discovered in holds No. 2 and No. 3. Not even two and a half hours after the discovery of water in the No. 1 hold, a distress signal was sent out. Lifeboats launched by members of the crew sank in the proximity of the TRADEWAYS. Some of the crew jumped overboard and attempted to swim to vessels which offered assistance. 11 crew members died during these operations. The master and the remaining crew constructed rafts out of dunnage, but were rescued by a life raft which an aircraft dropped in the vicinity of the vessel. The vessel finally sank with a total loss of the cargo.

bb. The Verdict

The plaintiffs submitted a theory of recovery that BV undertook to make inspections or surveys pertaining to the seaworthiness of the vessel and that such services were performed negligently and in breach of BV's warranties of workmanlike service.[261] The Federal District Court held that the plaintiffs had failed to establish evidence that the four wasted frames in the No. 1 hold failed and allowed initial entry of seawater. The plaintiffs could not prove that the deferred repairs

---

and Classification Societies', [1994] *CMI Yearbook* 256; Miller, 'Liability of Classification Societies from the Perspective of United States Law', 22 *Tul.Mar.L.J.* 75 (1997), at 88–93; O'Brien, 'The Potential Liability of Classification Societies to Marine Insurers Under United States Law', 7 *U.S.F.Mar.L.J.* 403 (1994–1995), at 410–413; Starer, 'Liability, is it Just Around the Corner? An Advocate's View of a Classification Society and its Duty', [1994] *CMI Yearbook* 259.

[261] *Great American Insurance Co. v. Bureau Veritas*, 338 F.Supp. 999 (S.D.N.Y.1972), at 1005.

constituted an unseaworthy condition and caused the vessel to sink. The lack of a causal link may, however, be substituted for by the presumption of unseaworthiness. Whenever a ship is lost under normal conditions with no other explanation, the law presumes that she was unseaworthy.[262] This presumption traditionally operates against the owner or demise charterer. However, it cannot be used against a classification society:

> 'Plaintiffs maintain that Bureau Veritas had control over the condition of the vessel in that the owner and charterer could not have sailed under their insurance policies without the classification certificate. While this might constitute control in some practical or economic sense, it is not sufficient to bring into play the presumption, for the owner and charterer could have either sailed without insurance or paid a higher premium. Accordingly, I find that the presumption of seaworthiness cannot be used against a classification society which did nothing more than to classify a ship that proved to be unseaworthy.'[263]

The District Court discussed whether a liability based on the *Ryan* doctrine[264] applies to classification societies. In *Ryan,* a stevedore was sued by the shipowner whose ship he had loaded. The Supreme Court held that in undertaking to load and unload the ship, and in assuming control of that operation, the stevedore had given the shipowner an implied warranty of workmanlike performance. The injury of the longshoremen, who had recovered from the shipowner damages for personal injuries, was the direct result of the stevedore's breach of that implied warranty.[265] The idea behind the *Ryan* doctrine is that even though the shipowner is under a non-delegable duty of seaworthiness, the stevedore is at the time of the loading or unloading of the vessel more capable than the shipowner of avoiding accidents. He acts without the supervision of the shipowner, and the shipowner would none-

---

262 *Great American Insurance Co. v. Bureau Veritas*, 338 F.Supp. 999 (S.D.N.Y.1972), at 1008. *See also* Beck, B., 'Liability of Marine Surveyors for Loss of Surveyed Vessel', 64 *Notre Dame L. Rev.* 246 (1989), at 255, *South Seas, Inc. v. Moran Towing & Transp. Co.,* 360 F.2d 1002 (2d Cir.1966).

263 Judge *Tyler, Great American Insurance Co. v. Bureau Veritas*, 338 F.Supp. 999 (S.D.N.Y.1972), at 1009.

264 *Ryan Stevedoring Co. Inc. v. Pan-Atlantic Steamship Corp.,* 350 U.S. 124, 76 S.Ct. 232, 100 L.Ed. 133 (1956). *See also* Beck, B., 'Liability of Marine Surveyors for Loss of Surveyed Vessel', 64 *Notre Dame L. Rev.* 246 (1989), at 263-265; Davis, 'The Illusive Warranty of Workmanlike Performance: Constructing a Conceptual Framework', 72 Neb. L. Rev. 981 (1993); Goldsmith, 'River Pilot, Marine Surveyor, and Third-Party Inspector Liability', 26 *Tul.Mar.L.J.* 463 (2002), at 502–505; O'Brien, 'The Potential Liability of Classification Societies to Marine Insurers Under United States Law', 7 *U.S.F.Mar.L.J.* 403 (1994–1995), at 408–410; Schoenbaum, *Admiralty and Maritime Law* (2004), § 5-8 at 190, 192-196; Stuart/Caffrey, 'Liability of Marine Surveyors, Adjusters, and Claims Handlers', 22 *Tul.Mar.L.J.*, 1 (1997), at 35–39.

265 *See Ryan Stevedoring Co. Inc. v. Pan-Atlantic Steamship Corp.,* 350 U.S. 124, at 133–134, 76 S.Ct. 232, at 237, 100 L.Ed. 133 (1956).

theless have to answer for his actions. A classification society, however, does not exercise a similar power over the ship.

> '[...] I conclude that no theories based on the *Ryan* doctrine can help plaintiffs recover here, principally because, as already discussed, the burden of insuring the seaworthiness of a vessel must ultimately rest upon the shipowner or charterer unless there is good reason to shift this burden to another party. Presumably one of the reasons that the Supreme Court decided in *Ryan* to shift the responsibility for the unseaworthy condition to the stevedore was the fact that the owner had little or no direct, immediate control over the stevedore or its services there provided. Recognizing this rationale, I note that the services and activities of a classification society differ markedly from those provided by a stevedore, carpenters, ship's cleaner, and the like. While an owner may have little or no direct control of the activities of a classification society aboard ship, the society rarely, if ever, would create hazards or defects by its functions and activities. Moreover, unlike a stevedore and other similar service contractors, a classification society is functionally incapable of repairing or rectifying defects or hazards, caused by itself or others. Virtually all a society can do is observe and report to the owner whatever its inspections reveal. In the light of these distinctions, to rule that a ship owner or operator can evade or pass off his historic primary duty to furnish a seaworthy vessel by strict application of the *Ryan* doctrine to a classification society, in my judgment, would work an unsound and unfair dilution of that legal duty.'[266]

In *Great American Insurance* it was still argued that it is also applicable to other persons in control over the condition of the vessel. This was based on the decision of the District Court *In re Marine Sulphur Transport Corp.*,[267] which extended it to a designer-converter who negligently rebuilt a ship in an unseaworthy manner. The Court of Appeals reversed this part of *In re Marine Sulphur Transport Corp.* and held that the presumption of unseaworthiness does not operate against the shipbuilder, as 'the duty of providing the crew with a seaworthy ship runs only to the owner, and the shipbuilder neither employs the crew nor can he control what happens to the ship once she leaves the yard.'[268] The reason for the discussion of the presumption of unseaworthiness in *Great American Insurance* is therefore no longer applicable.

Apart from the *Ryan* doctrine, the court mainly concentrated on issues of negligence and tort law. It made an interesting statement as to the duties a classification society generally owes in tort to its clients.

> 'Viewing the matter under theories of tort law, the obvious question is, what duties are owed by a classification society to its clientele? Although there is scant law on the subject, it can be reasoned that by undertaking to survey and classify a vessel, a classification society obligates itself to perform two duties with due care. The first duty, as already discussed, is to survey and classify vessels in accordance with rules and standards established and promulgated by the society for that purpose. The second duty of a clas-

---

[266] Judge Tyler, *Great American Insurance Co. v. Bureau Veritas*, 338 F.Supp. 999 (S.D.N.Y.1972), at 1015. *See also In the Matter of: Oil Spill by the Amoco Cadiz off the Coast in France on March 16, 1978,* 1986 A.M.C. 1945 (N.D.Ill.1986), at 1952.

[267] *In re Marine Sulphur Transport Corp.*, 312 F.Supp. 1081 (S.D.N.Y.1970), at 1098.

[268] *In re Marine Sulphur Queen,* 460 F.2d 89 (2d Cir.1972), at 101.

sification society is that of due care in detection of defects in the ship it surveys and the corollary of notification thereof to the owner and charterer.'[269]

The existence of a society's duty to survey and classify vessels in accordance with its rules was rejected by Justice Tyler by way of the following statement:

> 'The unstated policy underlying the decisions not to allow surveys and classifications to operate as defenses to the duty of providing a seaworthy ship is clearly to preserve the ancient, absolute responsibility of an owner for the condition of his ship. This is evidenced by the fact that, were such surveys and classifications allowed to constitute a due diligence defence, the accountability of owners for the seaworthiness of their vessel for all practical purposes would evaporate. This, in turn, would have the effect of leaving injured seamen and shippers with no effective remedy in most cases.
> In theory, recognition of a right of action against a classification society would confer benefit upon ship owners, ship operators and seamen. In practice, such a "new remedy" would produce several undesirable effects. One of these would be to place the ultimate responsibility for seaworthiness on an organization which has contact with the vessel for only brief annual periods, whereas the owner, who is always "present" in respect to this vessel, would elude liability in many cases. Second, this right of action would have the effect of making the classification society an absolute insurer of any vessel it surveys and certifies. Not only is this liability not commensurate with the amount of control that a classification society has over a vessel; it is also not in accord with the intent of the parties, the fees charged or the services performed. Further, by making classification societies the effective insurer of nearly all seagoing vessels, insurance companies such as those here involved, might be putting themselves out of business, a result they certainly did not contemplate by bringing this suit.'[270]

As regards the second possible duty to take due care in the detection of all perceptible defects in the ship it surveys and notification thereof to the owner, the District Court relied on *Skibs v. Hyman*.[271] Justice Tyler was convinced that such a

[269] *Great American Insurance Co. v. Bureau Veritas*, 338 F.Supp. 999 (S.D.N.Y.1972), at 1012.

[270] *Great American Insurance Co. v. Bureau Veritas*, 338 F.Supp. 999 (S.D.N.Y.1972), at 1012.

[271] In *Skibs v. Hyman*, several actions were brought against a cargo surveyor by the owner of the vessel GYDA, the owner of the cargo and its underwriters (*Skibs A/S Gylfe v. Hyman-Michaels Company et. al.*, 304 F.Supp. 1204 (E.D.Mich.1969), *aff'd,* 438 F.2d 803 (6th Cir.1971)). Due to spontaneous combustion, the cargo consisting of a certain type of scrap metal developed an excessive heat and several fires occurred when it was discharged, which caused substantial damage to both the ship and its cargo. The third-party defendant National Cargo Bureau had executed an "On Hire" survey and surveyed the vessel's cargo spaces on behalf of the seller of the steel turnings, as well as the cargo itself with regard to the U.S. Coast Guard's fire and safety regulations. The surveyor had controlled the temperature of the cargo on dock and the amount of debris present. But he did not control the temperature of the cargo on dock on a regular basis. Also, there was no surveyor present during the loading in order to advise the cargo owner whether the cargo was being stowed in a safe manner and the safety regulations were being complied with. When loading was finally completed, the surveyor did not

duty would provide a sounder basis for tort liability of a classification society, but in the case there was not sufficient factual support for such a theory.

> 'So far as I can determine, this theory of liability would not offend established case law in admiralty; indeed, it is supported by the holding of the only case which has heretofore dealt squarely with the question of a surveyor's liability. In *The Gyda,* [*Skibs A/S Gylfe v. Hyman-Michaels Company et. al.,* 304 F.Supp. 1204 (E.D.Mich.1969), *aff'd,* 438 F.2d 803 (6th Cir.1971)] the defendant classification society, the National Cargo Bureau, had expressly undertaken to perform an "on hire" survey, oversee the loading of dangerous cargo and advise the charterer regarding the safe or unsafe character or the stowage. [...] Although the facts and circumstances upon which *The Gyda,* [ibid.] was decided are different from those presented in this case, the ruling that a classification society may be liable for a failure to detect or warn of dangers on board a ship that it is surveying should theoretically apply to the case at hand. *The Gyda* holding was expressed in terms of a breach of an express undertaking; nonetheless, the district court's extensive use of negligence language and tort theories of causation suggests that its decision was based as much on a breach of duty of care as upon breach of contract. If so, the court's analysis seems sound; surely, a ship's surveyor or classification society should be charged in law with the reasonable duty of detecting all perceptible defects of the vessel encountered during the survey and notifying the owner and/or charterer thereof.'[272]

The Court of Appeals affirmed this judgment. In its view, the appellants had failed to establish a causal relationship between BV's negligence and the loss of the vessel.

---

inform the cargo owners that it was not safe to sail at that time due to the high temperature of the cargo. Based on these facts, the plaintiff alleged that the defendant had breached a contractual duty. The court concluded that the contractual obligations of the National Cargo Bureau extended only until the time the vessel set sail and that it did not undertake to perform additional duties as a volunteer. The only duties which were breached were the obligation to control the temperature of the cargo aboard and to be present at the time of the loading.
It was held that the breach of contract by the National Cargo Bureau was not a proximate cause to the fire since the Bureau had undertaken only to warn or advise. Once the master or the cargo owners became aware of the situation, they were obliged to decide which action to take (at 1220). As they became aware of the situation at the first port of call, at a time when no fires had yet started in the cargo hold, the responsibility shifted from the cargo surveyor to the master and the cargo owner at that time. Also, there was an intervening cause, as the fire had been directly caused by the Master's order to apply water to the cargo, thereby causing spontaneous combustion (at 1220). The court therefore concluded that no breach of duty or undertaking on the part of the cargo surveyor was a proximate cause of the fire.

[272] *Great American Insurance Co. v. Bureau Veritas*, 338 F.Supp. 999 (S.D.N.Y.1972), at 1012–1013.

cc. Case Comment

The *Great American Insurance* case was the first published one which related to the liability of classification societies from the point of view of United States law. It laid the ground for all subsequent decisions and has been referred to several times.[273] The first theory of the court is usually cited in order to answer the question of the liability of classification societies in the negative. It is, however, remarkable that the second theory of the District Court, which regards the duty to take due care in the detection of all perceptible defects in the ship it surveys and notification thereof to the owner,[274] has never been decisive in subsequent litigation against classification societies.[275] Presumably this occurred since the reference to this theory was very short and dismissed for lack of factual support. However, the court considered it to be a stronger theory than the first one. The advantage of it is that such a duty would not make a classification society the insurer of the vessel and would not place the ultimate responsibility on it.

The court, no doubt, is correct in its view that classification societies are not responsible for the seaworthiness of the vessel. The arguments employed, however, lead to the danger of further misunderstandings of the issues involved. That a classification society does not have to answer for the seaworthiness of the vessel is not due to the fact that the shipowner has the primary obligation to provide a seawor-

---

[273] *See i.e. Steamship Mutual Underwriting Association Ltd. v. Bureau Veritas*, 380 F.Supp. 482 (E.D.La. 1973), at 492 *et seq.*; *Sundance Cruises Corp. v. American Bureau of Shipping,* 799 F.Supp. 363 (S.D.N.Y.1992), at 385–386; *Cargill, Inc. v. Bureau Veritas*, 902 F.Supp. 49, 52 *et seq.* (S.D.N.Y.1995); *Otto Candies, L.L.C. v. Nippon Kaiji Kyokai Corp.*, 2002 WL 1798767 (E.D.La. 2002), 346 F.3d 530, 538, 2003 A.M.C. 2409, 2409 (5th Cir.(La.) 2003).

[274] *Great American Insurance Co. v. Bureau Veritas*, 338 F.Supp. 999 (S.D.N.Y.1972), at 1012. Despite the court's enlargement of the second duty to cover owners and charterers, this should not be misinterpreted as a statement of duties towards third parties in general. In this case there was a contract with both the shipowner and the charterer.

[275] It has apparently been referred to in *Psarianos v. Standard Marine, Ltd.*, 728 F.Supp. 438 (E.D.Tex. 1989), 790 F.Supp. 134 (E.D.Tex. 1989), 12 F3d 461 (5th Cir.(La.) 1994), cert. den. 114 SCt. 2164, 511 U.S. 1142, 128 L.Ed.2d 887 (1994). However, since the discussion on the merits has not been published, it is rather difficult to comment on this case. *Sundance* makes short reference to this case, but then largely relies on the argumentation in respect of the first duty as identified by *Great American Insurance, see Sundance Cruises Corp. v. American Bureau of Shipping,* 799 F.Supp. 363 (S.D.N.Y.1992), at 377. The theory has, however, been applied by a State Court in litigation against the individual marine surveyor of a recreational vessel, which carried out an insurance and financing survey on behalf of the purchaser before the purchase of the vessel. The surveyor was held liable, as he was considered to have breached the duty to use due care to detect and give notice of perceptible structural defects, which means that he will be held to a standard of good marine surveying practice, *i.e.*, what is customary and usual in practice, *see Krohnert v. Yacht Systems Hawaii, Inc.*, 664 P.2d 738 (Haw. Ct. App.1983), at 742.

thy vessel.[276] Also, the brief contact of the classification society with the ship is not the reason either. Nor is the reason the theoretical effect that the classification society would be an absolute insurer of the vessel contrary to the parties' intentions, however such an insurer may be defined. Neither is it the disparity between the fees charged and the services performed. The reason that the classification society does not have to answer for the vessel is simply that it does not undertake such a service. It does not control whether or not a vessel is seaworthy. It only controls whether the vessel corresponds to a certain number of rules that it has established, which aim at improving the safety of the vessel. No more and no less. These rules are, however, often mistaken as guaranteeing an absolute standard of safety and implying the seaworthiness of the vessel. That is not the fact.[277] They have been developed with hindsight, based on analysed occurrences and deficiencies, and are improved through mathematical calculations of marine engineering. But they do not guarantee the seaworthiness of the vessel. And since a classification society controls only according to its rules, it does not in any way guarantee the seaworthiness of the vessel. The classification society has to survey the vessel in a way which corresponds to the technical standard of surveys. This does not imply that it guarantees that the vessel does not sustain any deficiencies after the survey. It implies that the society has done its best to establish all deficiencies and requested their repair by way of a condition or recommendation or else it suspends or withdraws the vessel's class. A classification society should therefore be accountable if it discovers a serious deficiency, but retains a vessel in class.[278] A shipowner, by contrast, is obliged to answer for the seaworthiness of the vessel in any case. He cannot use a due diligence defence that he did all he could to ensure the seaworthiness of the ship. The fact that the shipowner employed a classification society to conduct a survey of his ship does not exonerate him from his duty.[279]

---

276 Apparently, the argumentation is also based on an analysis of the duties of the shipowner and the aim that the shipowner shall not be able to evade his duty to furnish a seaworthy vessel in any way (*see Federazione Italiana Dei Corsorzi Agrari v. Mandask Compania de Vapores, S.A., (The Perama)* 388 F.2d 434 (2d Cir.1968), cert. denied 393 U.S. 828, 89 S.Ct. 92, 21 L.Ed.2d 99 (1968)). But that is a problem which needs to be separated from the liability in question and which is not affected even if a classification society can be held liable.

277 *Compare supra* Part 1 A III 5.

278 Miller, 'Liability of Classification Societies', 22 *Tul.Mar.L.J.* 75 (1997), at 91.

279 *See Federazione Italiana Dei Corsorzi Agrari v. Mandask Compania de Vapores, S.A., (The Perama)* 388 F.2d 434 (2d Cir.1968), cert. denied 393 U.S. 828, 89 S.Ct. 92, 21 L.Ed.2d 99 (1968)).

The primary responsibility for the vessel has to rest with the shipowner, but there can be cases in which both he and the classification society may be held liable.[280]

The judge erred in holding the National Cargo Bureau for a classification society. Moreover, the argumentation is too restrictive in its view of the duties which correspond to the activities of a classification society.[281] It has been shown in Part 1 that a classification society undertakes more surveys these days than it used to in former times.[282] It no longer develops its rules only with hindsight, but also with the aid of highly developed marine engineering and mathematical calculations; moreover, it provides computer programmes for the design of a vessel and, of course, offers classification services.

There is another assumption which is misleading in this case. The shipowner would not be discouraged from taking effective measures to furnish a seaworthy vessel if he were a joint tortfeasor with a classification society.[283] If this were true, in every case involving two parties at fault only one of them would be held liable because otherwise one of them would be encouraged not to take effective measures against the occurrence of this tort in the future.[284]

Moreover, one may criticise the fact that the court did not mention the situation of the review of plans. When reviewing plans, a classification society can require that certain modifications are made and therefore directly influence the way the vessel is constructed. Contrary to the opinion of the court, such activity may cause the unseaworthiness of a vessel. Whenever these modifications do not attain the necessary standard of safety or even create additional hazards, a classification society may have a power similar to that of a stevedore, which was considered to be sufficient in *Ryan*. Also one should consider whether the statement is correct that classification societies do not have control over the vessel. The threat not to issue

---

280 Miller, 'Liability of Classification Societies from the Perspective of United States Law', 22 *Tul.Mar.L.J.* 75 (1997), at 90–91 further argues that the court misunderstands the impact if classification societies are held liable. The primary responsibility of the shipowner does not prohibit recovery from both when the negligent acts of both together produce a common harm, which is merely an application of the common law tort doctrine of joint and several liability. 'In short, no conceptual basis exists for insulating a negligent classification society from liability merely because the shipowner is also guilty of negligence with respect to the seaworthiness of the vessel' (at 92).

281 *Miller* also criticises the fact that the court chose a too restrictive definition of an only two-fold duty of classification societies (Miller, 'Liability of Classification Societies from the Perspective of United States Law', 22 *Tul.Mar.L.J.* 75 (1997), at 90 *et seq.*). It is argued that first the rules must be formulated, which should also lead to the imposition of liability if they are wrong. Secondly, liability should also be imposed if a serious defect is detected which poses an imminent danger and nevertheless the classification society fails to take measures that will remove the vessel from service.

282 *See supra* Part 1 A I, Part 1 A III 7, Part 1 B II.

283 *Compare Great American Insurance Co. v. Bureau Veritas*, 338 F.Supp. 999 (S.D.N.Y.1972), at 1012.

284 This is pointed out by Miller, 'Liability of Classification Societies from the Perspective of United States Law', 22 *Tul.Mar.L.J.* 75 (1997), at 92.

or endorse a certificate gives them a considerable amount of factual control over the vessel, as the shipowner is in need of these certificates. However, it must be admitted that this control is not precisely the same that a stevedore executes, who can change the whole situation by himself and does not need to make someone else change it, as is the case with a classification society. Apart from this case, the *Ryan* doctrine cannot be applied with respect to classification societies. These societies do not give an implied warranty of workmanlike performance.[285]

To sum up, the decision should solely have applied the duty to survey the vessel and take due care in the detection of defects, which it identified as a second duty, in a straightforward way. This would have saved a number of subsequent misunderstandings.

b. The Shipping Corporation of India II Case

The plaintiff had ordered four vessels from a Yugoslavian shipyard, which were built according to ABS rules.[286] The drawings of these vessels had been analysed by ABS and they had been inspected by its surveyors. The plaintiff, however, alleged that the ships were not suited for their intended use, because they were incapable of withstanding the normal stress incident to their operation in such a capacity. It therefore claimed damages to the value of USD 89 million and alleged

> 'fault, neglect, errors, omissions and breaches of or by ABS or those for whom it is responsible, in performance of its obligations with respect to
> A. ABS' formulation of its Rules and standards applicable to ABS' design review and approval, construction surveys and classification of OBO type vessels;
> B. ABS' application of its Rules and standards to the design review and approval, construction surveys and classifications of [the plaintiff's vessels];
> C. ABS' neglect or default in specifying and approving corrosion control procedures; and

[285] *Compare In the Matter of the Complaint of Eternity Shipping, Ltd.*, 2006 WL 2422705 (D.Md.2006), 10.

[286] *Shipping Corporation of India v. American Bureau of Shipping*, 744 F.Supp. 447 (S.D.N.Y.1990). In *Shipping Corporation of India I* (603 F.Supp. 801 (S.D.N.Y.1985)), a dismissal of the claims on *forum non conveniens* grounds was denied. *Shipping Corporation of India II* (744 F.Supp. 447 (S.D.N.Y.1990)) was a summary judgment in favour of the defendant, in which the tort cause of action was dismissed because of an application of the *East River* doctrine to maritime tort. In *Shipping Corporation of India III* (752 F.Supp. 173 (S.D.N.Y.1990)) this was affirmed and no interlocutory appeal certified. *Shipping Corporation of India II* was reaffirmed in *Sundance Cruises Corp. v. American Bureau of Shipping,* 799 F.Supp. 363 (S.D.N.Y.1992), at 383. With regard to forum selection clauses, *compare Holland America v. Wartsila North America, Inc.,* 2005 WL 1287993 (W.D.Wash.2005); *Hellenic Investment Fund, Inc. v. Det Norske Veritas,* 2006 WL 2567462 (5th Cir.(Tex)2006).

D. ABS' services, inspections, structural analyses, investigations and recommendations performed and made during construction and after delivery of [the plaintiff's vessels].'[287]

The litigation concentrated for a long time on procedural questions and did not expand on the relationship between the shipowner and the classification society or the duties imposed on the latter. Its main argumentation related to claims based on both contract and tort law. It applied the *East River* doctrine.[288] This doctrine bars tort claims whenever there are no large disparities in bargaining power between the parties if the claims deal with losses that are purely economic.[289] It relates not only to products, but also to services.[290] It was held that contract law provides adequate remedies in a commercial setting where parties have a bargaining power equal enough to allocate among themselves risks of defects, as was considered so in this case. The plaintiff admitted that for the time when there was no privity of contract during the building of the ships, he was an intended third-party beneficiary of the classification contracts between the shipyard and ABS, and therefore this doctrine applied all the same. Because of *East River*, the plaintiff's negligence claims were not cognisable in maritime tort. The verdict only related to this issue, and the contractual claim against ABS was later settled outside the courtroom.

c. The Sundance Case

aa. The Facts

On 14 June 1984, ABS issued a classification certificate and a number of statutory certificates regarding the passenger vessel SUNDANCER. On 29 June, the vessel ran aground due to a failure of the pilot and subsequently sank. The shipowner, *Sundance Cruises Corp.*, acknowledged responsibility for the grounding, but con-

287 *Shipping Corporation of India II did not provide the details of the case, these are contained in Shipping Corporation of India I*, 603 F.Supp. 801 (S.D.N.Y.1985), at 803.

288 *East River S.S. Corp. v. Transamerica DeLaval, Inc.*, 476 U.S. 858, 106 S.Ct. 2295, 90 L.Ed.2d 865 (1986).

289 This doctrine was developed in the context of product liability. There are no public policy concerns in a commercial contract which require the imposition of a duty in tort in addition to the protection by warranty or contract (*see Employers Ins. of Wausau v. Suwannee River Spa Lines, Inc.* 866 F.2d 752 (5th Cir.1989), at 753). In *East River* it was held that 'a manufacturer in a commercial relationship has no duty under either a negligence or a strict products-liability theory to prevent a product from injuring itself'. 'Contract law, and the law of warranty in particular, is well suited to commercial controversies [...] because the parties may set the terms of their own agreements'. The court in *Sundance* added that the parties could protect their claims by means of insurance, or otherwise allocate liability by contract (799 F.Supp. 363 (S.D.N.Y.1992), at 383).

290 *Employers Ins. of Wausau v. Suwannee River Spa Lines, Inc.* 866 F.2d 752 (5th Cir.1989), at 753. *Shipping Corporation of India v. American Bureau of Shipping,* 744 F.Supp. 447 (S.D.N.Y.1990), at 449 stated that there is no reason why it should matter whether the defendant is a manufacturer of goods or provider of services essential to such production.

tented that the ship would not have sunk but for the classification society's negligence, gross negligence, negligent misrepresentation, breach of contract and breach of implied warranty of workmanlike performance.[291]

The vessel suffered from two different kinds of deficiencies. The first one was a hole in a watertight bulkhead and an unsealed pipe fracture which allowed water to flow from one watertight compartment to the other. The second one was the defective grey-water piping system or starboard galley drain, which lacked non-return valves designed to prevent progressive flooding. Neither plan review nor surveys by the classification society had revealed these deficiencies, which had existed since the vessel was converted or since the time of its construction.

bb. The Verdict

Sundance is a landmark case which relates to four important issues. The first problem is whether the behaviour of the defendant amounted to gross negligence. The second one is whether it justified a claim for negligent misrepresentation. The third and fourth issues are whether the *East River* doctrine limits the plaintiff's action to contract remedies, and if so, whether or not the plaintiff could make out a contract claim under the *Ryan* doctrine. The importance of the *Sundance* case is that it specifies the different responsibilities between the shipowner and classification societies, and relates to the duties of a classification society. The judgment of the District Court has been affirmed by the Court of Appeals.[292]

The plaintiff alleged that the defendant had been grossly negligent in performing its services, inspections, structural analysis, investigations and recommendations during vessel conversion design review and approval, conversion surveys, statutory certification and classification of the vessel. The defendant had supposedly also been grossly negligent in the training, supervision and in the review of the surveyors who performed the functions, and in the review of the surveys performed. The plans were not provided in time, only one surveyor executed the sur-

---

[291] *Sundance Cruises Corp. v. American Bureau of Shipping,* 799 F.Supp. 363 (S.D.N.Y. 1992), *aff'd,* 7 F.3d 1077 (2d Cir.1993); for case comments *see* Cane, 'The Liability of classification societies', [1994] *L.M.C.L.Q.* 363; Clarke, 'Negligence–under control and under contract?', 53 *Cambridge L.J.* 220 (1994); Cochran, 'Otto Candies, L.L.C. v. Nippon Kaiji Kyokai Corp.' [Case comment], 28 *Tul.Mar.L.J.* 613 (2004), at 616; Hildebrandt, 'Personal Injury and Wrongful Death Remedies for Maritime Passengers', 68 *Tul.L.Rev.* 403 (1994), at 421; Honka, 'The Classification System and its Problems with Special Reference to the Liability of Classification Societies', 19 *Tul.Mar.L.J.* 1 (1994), at 13–25; Miller, 'Liability of Classification Societies from the Perspective of United States Law', 22 *Tul.Mar.L.J.* 75 (1997), at 96–98; O'Brien, 'The Potential Liability of Classification Societies to Marine Insurers Under United States Law', 7 *U.S.F.Mar.L.J.* 403 (1994–1995), at 406–409, 414–415; Starer, 'Liability, is it Just Around the Corner? An Advocate's View of a Classification Society and its Duty', [1994] *CMI Yearbook* 259, at 261–262.

[292] *Sundance Cruises Corp. v. American Bureau of Shipping,* 7 F.3d 1077 (2d Cir.1993), at 1082–1083 affirmed the judgment in all parts except for that which related to immunity for statutory surveys under Bahamian law. This issue will therefore not be analysed.

veys which were of an extensive scope. And even though the surveyor had exercised his profession for years, he had no experience in surveying passenger vessels, and he did not follow the schedule of a checklist. If the plaintiff proves a gross negligent behaviour by the defendant, he is entitled to punitive damages. According to the District Court for the Southern District of New York gross negligence has been defined

> 'as meaning that "defendant has not only acted carelessly in making a mistake, but that it was so extremely careless that it was equivalent to recklessness." *Hong Kong Export Credit Ins. v. Dun & Bradstreet* (S.D.N.Y.1975) 414 F.Supp. 153, 160. The Second Circuit has "drawn attention to the close affinity of the concepts, gross negligence and deliberate indifference," citing – in a footnote – the Massachusetts Supreme Judicial Court's definition of gross negligence as an 'indifference to present legal duty and utter forgetfulness of legal obligations, so far as other persons may be affected' *Doe v. N.Y.C. Dept. of Social Services* (2d Cir.1981) 649 F.2d 134, 143, n. 4, *quoting Burke v. Cook* (1923) 246 Mass. 518, 141 N.E. 585.'[293]

The court held that it found no act or omission on the part of the defendant or its employees that was 'so extremely careless that it was equivalent to recklessness'.[294] The claim for punitive damages based on a gross negligence was therefore dismissed.

With regard to the negligent misrepresentation cause of action,[295] the District Court reiterated that

> '[...] to prevail on a claim for this tort a plaintiff must establish that the defendant: (1) at plaintiff's request supplied information for it's guidance; (2) failed to use reasonable care in so doing; (3) knew plaintiff would rely on the information for particular purposes; and (4) plaintiff suffered an economic loss because it relied on the information. *See Coastal (Bermuda) Ltd. v. E.W. Saybolt & Co.* (5th Cir.1987) 826 F.2d 424, 428-29.'

The court was convinced that the plaintiff (the shipowner) had not asked the classification society to provide him with any information for its guidance and therefore rejected the negligent misrepresentation cause of action.[296]

The third problem relates to the application of the *East River* doctrine.[297] As has been shown, this doctrine has been developed with regard to product liability, but is also applied in the context of classification societies, as has been held in *Ship-*

---

[293] *Sundance Cruises Corp. v. American Bureau of Shipping,* 799 F.Supp. 363 (S.D.N.Y. 1992), at 378–379.

[294] *Sundance Cruises Corp. v. American Bureau of Shipping,* 799 F.Supp. 363 (S.D.N.Y. 1992), at 380 *et seq.*

[295] *See also* Part 2 B II 3 where this tort is analysed in detail.

[296] *Sundance Cruises Corp. v. American Bureau of Shipping,* 799 F.Supp. 363 (S.D.N.Y. 1992), at 382.

[297] *East River S.S. Corp. v. Transamerica DeLaval, Inc.*, 476 U.S. 858, 106 S.Ct. 2295, 90 L.Ed.2d 865 (1986). Regarding their application to classification societies, *see also Shipping Corporation of India v. American Bureau of Shipping*, 744 F.Supp. 447 (S.D.N.Y.1990).

ping Corp. of India v. American Bureau of Shipping.[298] *Sundance* reiterated this argumentation and held that those tort claims that relate to the loss of the vessel were of a purely economic kind and were barred by the *East River* doctrine. Claims which related to losses the plaintiff suffered as a result as being called upon to indemnify passenger injuries were, however, not affected.

The fourth question is whether the *Ryan* doctrine[299] applies to the case. After first stating the essential elements of *Ryan,*[300] the court referred to the *Great American Insurance* case.

> 'The 'unique' factors that permit indemnification liability under an implied warranty of workmanlike performance pertain especially to 'elements of expertise, control, supervision and ability to prevent accidents.' *Fairmont Ship Corp. v. Chevron Int'l Oil Co., Inc.* (2d Cir.1975) 511 F.2d 1252, 1257. In that case the Second Circuit specified those elements at 1258: the crucial elements of *Ryan* [are] as follows: a shipowner, relying on the expertise of another party [...] enters into a contract whereby the contractor agrees to perform services *without supervision or control by the shipowner;* the improper, unsafe or incompetent execution of such services would foreseeably render the vessel unseaworthy or bring into play a pre-existing unseaworthy condition; and the shipowner would thereby be exposed to liability regardless of fault.'[301]

In *Great American Insurance*, the court was of the opinion that a classification society has no control over the vessel and does not create its unseaworthiness by the execution of its services. In this respect the *Sundance* decision completely agrees with the *Great American Insurance* holding:

---

298 *Shipping Corporation of India v. American Bureau of Shipping,* 603 F.Supp. 801 (S.D.N.Y.1985), 744 F.Supp. 447 (S.D.N.Y.1990), 752 F.Supp. 173 (S.D.N.Y.1990). ABS classified four ships which were built in a Yugoslavian shipyard, but allegedly they were not suitable for their trade, *see* above. *Shipping Corporation of India II* was a summary judgment in favour of the defendant, in which the tort cause of action was dismissed because of an application of the *East River* doctrine to maritime tort. *East River* not only applies to products but also to services. It was held that contract law provides adequate remedies in a commercial setting where parties are of bargaining power equal enough to allocate among themselves risks of defects, which was considered to be the case in this instance. The plaintiff admitted that he was an intended third-party beneficiary of the Classification Contracts between the shipyard and ABS. Because of the application of *East River*, the plaintiff's negligence claims were not cognisable in maritime tort. In *Shipping Corporation of India III* this was affirmed and no interlocutory appeal certified. *Shipping Corporation of India II* has been reaffirmed in *Sundance Cruises Corp. v. American Bureau of Shipping,* 799 F.Supp. 363 (S.D.N.Y. 1992), at 383.

299 *Ryan Stevedoring Co. Inc. v. Pan-Atlantic Steamship Corp.,* 350 U.S. 124, 76 S.Ct. 232, 100 L.Ed. 133 (1956).

300 *See also Great American Insurance Co. v. Bureau Veritas*, 338 F.Supp. 999, 1015 (S.D.N.Y. 1972), *aff'd*, 478 F.2d 235 (2d Cir.1973).

301 *Sundance Cruises Corp. v. American Bureau of Shipping,* 799 F.Supp. 363 (S.D.N.Y. 1992), at 385.

'Presumably one of the reasons that the Supreme Court decided in *Ryan* to shift the responsibility for the unseaworthy condition to the stevedore was the fact that the owner had little or no direct, immediate control over the stevedore or its services there provided. Recognizing this rationale, I note that the services and activities of a classification society differ markedly from those provided by a stevedore, carpenters, ship's cleaner, and the like. While an owner may have little or no direct control of the activities of a classification society aboard ship, the society rarely, if ever, would create hazards or defects by its functions and activities. Moreover, unlike a stevedore and other similar service contractors, a classification society is functionally incapable of repairing or rectifying defects or hazards, caused by itself or others. Virtually all a society can do is observe and report to the owner whatever its inspections reveal. In the light of these distinctions, to rule that a ship owner or operator can evade or pass off his historic primary duty to furnish a seaworthy vessel by strict application of the *Ryan* doctrine to a classification society, in my judgment, would work an unsound and unfair dilution of that legal duty.'[302]

A shipowner, therefore, does not have an implied contractual right of indemnity against his classification society under the *Ryan* doctrine.[303]

The Court of Appeals affirmed the District Court's judgment in *Sundance* and largely agreed with its arguments. It further added that there are two main arguments against a liability in contract. The first one is the disparity between the fee charged and the damages sought. The second is the apportionment of responsibility between the shipowner and the classification society.

'We think this result [that Sundance has failed to show any damage caused by the issuance of the classification certificate] is sound, and it reflects our view that a shipowner is not entitled to rely on a classification certificate as a guarantee to the owner that the vessel is soundly constructed. First, the great disparity between the fee charged (USD 85,000) by ABS for its services and the damages sought by Sundance (USD 264,000,000) is strong evidence that such a result was not intended by the parties. We can only conclude that the small fees charged could not have been intended to cover the risk of such liability; the ship classification industry could not continue to exist under such terms. [...]
Second, and probably most significantly, the shipowner, not ABS, is ultimately responsible for and in control of the activities aboard ship. In the case of the SUNDANCER, for example, Sundance had full responsibility for the conversion, repairs, and maintenance of the vessel. This ongoing responsibility for the vessel is supplemented by the maritime-law requirement that the shipowner has a nondelegable duty to furnish a seaworthy vessel. [...] ABS can not be said to have taken over Sundance's obligations in this regard by agreeing to inspect and issue a classification certificate to Sundance.'[304]

Most important for cases involving third parties is the additional remark the court made with regard to third-party claims.

---

[302] *Sundance Cruises Corp. v. American Bureau of Shipping,* 799 F.Supp. 363 (S.D.N.Y. 1992), at 385–386.

[303] *See also In the Matter of: Oil Spill by the Amoco Cadiz off the Coast in France on March 16, 1978,* 1986 A.M.C. 1945 (N.D.Ill.1986), at 1952.

[304] *Sundance Cruises Corp. v. American Bureau of Shipping,* 7 F.3d 1077 (2d Cir.1993), at 1084.

> 'This case must be distinguished from a suit brought by an injured third party who relied on the classification or safety certificates.'[305]

It is, therefore, expressly left open how claims of third parties are to be treated.

The Court of Appeals also made a general remark as to the purpose of a classification certificate, which has subsequently been referred to by several courts.[306]

> 'Put simply, the purpose of the classification certificate is not to guarantee safety, but merely to permit Sundance to take advantage of the insurance rates available to a classed vessel.'[307]

In brief, the gist of *Sundance* can be seen in the following. *Sundance* only applies to the claims of a contracting party. The Court of Appeals has expressly stated that it does not give any indication as to how claims of third parties are to be treated. As regards the claims of a shipowner, it was held that a classification society is neither liable in contract nor in tort for a negligent survey regarding the seaworthiness of the vessel. The *East River* doctrine bars all claims in tort which relate to the loss of the vessel, but not those which relate to the compensation for injury of the passengers. However, no gross negligent behaviour could be established in that case. A claim for negligent misrepresentation was denied, because the court was convinced that the shipowner did not ask the classification society to provide it with any information for his guidance. Apparently, a classification certificate is not of any guidance to him.

The question whether the *Ryan* doctrine was to be applied, leading to an implied warranty of workmanlike performance, was answered in the negative. The District Court held that a classification society has no control over the vessel and does not create hazards on its own.

The Court of Appeals added that in any case there was such a great disparity between the fees paid by the shipowner and the damages claimed from the classification society that it could not be assumed from the contract that the classification society was to be held liable for its actions by the shipowner. It was also held that the classification society did not assume the non-delegable duty of the shipowner to provide a seaworthy ship only by issuing a classification certificate.

cc. Case Comment

Sundance is the established precedent for the liability of classification society to shipowners, and the most important case in this regard. However, several criticisms need to be made. First and foremost, *Sundance* is based on a too restrictive understanding of the duties and functions of a classification society and on a sim-

---

305 *Sundance Cruises Corp. v. American Bureau of Shipping,* 7 F.3d 1077 (2d Cir.1993), at 1084.

306 Similar: *Cargill, Inc. v. Bureau Veritas*, 902 F.Supp. 49 (S.D.N.Y.1995), at 52; *Otto Candies, L.L.C. v. Nippon Kaiji Kyokai Corp.*, 346 F.3d 530 (5th Cir.(La.) 2003), at 534.

307 *Sundance Cruises Corp. v. American Bureau of Shipping,* 7 F.3d 1077 (2d Cir.1993), at 1084.

plification of the purpose of classification. The topic is basically reduced to an insurance question, even though classification is of further relevance even to the owner. This is also illustrated by the fact that the same Court of Appeals later extended its argumentation from one to two major benefits for shipowners.[308] A classification is a precondition for the issuance of certain statutory certificates,[309] it is usually required by the cargo owners that the vessel has it, and additionally a non-classed vessel is more likely to be subject to close scrutiny by port State control than any other vessel. Even a self-insured shipowner has therefore several advantages if his vessel is classed. The question is not solely one of insurance matters. Also, it is not correct that a classification only allows the shipowner to save money on the insurance premium. On the contrary, it is generally not possible in most markets to insure a vessel at all if it does not possess a class. The only possibility is to be a self-insurer in such a case.

Secondly, the Court errs in stating that the shipowner had not asked the classification society to provide him with any kind of information, the argumentation by which the claim for negligent misrepresentation was rejected. The fact that a vessel is classed gives at least the information that it conforms with the society's rules and therefore corresponds to a certain standard of safety. It should be borne in mind how much a shipowner can actually know about his vessel. The more advanced the technical skills and mathematical formulations of a classification society are, as for example with regard to calculations of the stability of a vessel, the more the classification society has the advantage of superior knowledge over the shipowner. A shipowner can no longer precisely ascertain the condition of his vessel in the way a classification society can, be it for technical reasons or due to unreasonable cost. Major petroleum companies have already for some years been vetting their tonnage according to rigorous and comprehensive standards and employed their own surveyors.[310] Also, classification societies are unique in possessing the long-term experience of having monitored the performance of thousands of vessels over decades, thereby gaining a vast body of cumulative data, knowledge and experience unavailable to the individual members of the shipping industry.[311] And that is precisely why these technical advisors and survey organisations are of

---

308 *American Bureau of Shipping v. Tencara Shipyard S.P.A.,* 170 F.3d 349, at 351, 1999 A.M.C. 1858 (2nd Cir.1999): 'Vessel classifications provide two major benefits for shipowners. First, insurance is much less expensive for classed ships than for non-classed ships. Second, many governments-the French authorities in this case-require a vessel classification before they will allow a craft to sail under their national flag.'

309 SOLAS Ch II–1, Regulation 3–1 requires that the ship shall be designed, constructed and maintained in accordance with the structural, mechanical and electrical requirements of a recognised classification society. The SOLAS safety construction certificate will only be issued if these requirements are fulfilled.

310 France, 'Classification societies: their liability–an American lawyer's point of view in light of recent judgments', 1 *I.J.S.L.* 67 (1996), at 69.

311 *See also* Miller, 'Liability of Classification Societies from the Perspective of United States Law', 22 *Tul.Mar.L.J.* 75 (1997), at 79.

such importance to the maritime industry. *Sundance* is based on the belief that a shipowner knows everything about his vessel – and in fact more than a classification society. But only very big companies have the financial resources to acquire such knowledge themselves. Of course, a shipowner may be able to find out whether or not the machinery is properly maintained, whether or not there is sufficient life-saving equipment and the current status of wear and tear of the vessel. However, there are calculations or interpretations which he cannot perform and therefore will, of course, be interested in the society's representations in this regard. The court should rather have concentrated on the question of whether the deficiencies violated the rules, since they at least violated SOLAS.[312] However, the classification society was protected by the Bahamian immunity statute in this regard according to the District Court (this was later denied by the Court of Appeals). Another interesting issue in this regard would have been how such a case would have to be treated in which both statutory requirements and requirements of the rules are violated.[313]

Thirdly, the non-delegable duty of the shipowner to provide a seaworthy vessel to his contracting parties can only be of relevance in that actual relationship and not in order to define the duties of a classification society which is not party to such a contract. It should, therefore, not be referred to under these circumstances. Since the classification society does not even give any representation of the seaworthiness of the vessel, it cannot influence or deter the owner's duties to third parties either. Moreover, it needs to be borne in mind that whenever someone other than the shipowner (such as the shipyard, a purchaser or a charterer) contracts with a classification society, the non-delegable duty is definitely of no relevance. Such a case could therefore be distinguished and decided differently from *Sundance*.[314] Nonetheless, in such a case the disparity of fees illustrates that the parties did not mean to imply any liability. However, as the *Interore III* case shows (*see below*), a different approach might be taken in such a case.

Again, the disparity of the fees and the amount of liability imposed is only relevant to contract law; it is actually included in § 351 Restatement (Second) of Contracts, Comment f. It should, therefore, be strictly limited to contract law and not be applied to the tort of negligence, especially not in third-party cases. It would have been better if the court had avoided any language which might lead to such a misunderstanding. Also, as *Miller* criticises, the issue of the disparity between the fee and the alleged liability is overwrought.[315] Fees are usually low despite the possible liability. In the lifetime of a vessel, they add up to a considerable sum.

---

312 *Sundance Cruises Corp. v. American Bureau of Shipping,* 799 F.Supp. 363 (S.D.N.Y. 1992), at 371.

313 Regarding this question, *see also infra* Part 2 C IV.

314 Only the disparity between the fees and the amount of liability imposed could then prevent the imposition of a liability.

315 Miller, 'Liability of Classification Societies from the Perspective of United States Law', 22 *Tul.Mar.L.J.* 75 (1997), at 98. Similarly Cane, 'The Liability of classification societies', [1994] *L.M.C.L.Q.* 363, at 367–369.

Such an argument is never presented in a product-liability case where the product costs little money but the damages awarded are indeed high.

As regards the argumentation concerning the *Ryan* doctrine, *Sundance* expands on *Great American Insurance* and covers criticisms which have been made in the comments on that verdict.[316] The differences between the actions of classification societies and stevedores are more thoroughly defined, which makes the argumentation much more precise und convincing. Even though *Sundance* also lacks any reference to the possibility of incorrect advice on construction plans, a case in which a classification society has significant power, one may say that once again such a power is only an indirect one, as the societies only recommend certain modifications to be made, which need to be approved by the shipyard and the shipowner. As they cannot change the blueprint on their own, a difference remains, which is similar to the one which has been described by the *Sundance* court. However, also in these circumstances the reference to the non-delegable duty of the shipowner to provide a seaworthy vessel should be avoided, as it cannot be of reference to third parties such as a stevedore and a classification society.

The gist of the criticism of *Sundance* decision, therefore, is that it should not have been impaired by considering duties towards third parties which are not of relevance to the relationship between the classification society and the shipowner. It is sufficient to analyse the duties and functions of a classification society to come to a coherent decision, which is also valid when analysing its argumentation and outcome, bearing in mind the aspect of non-delegable duty. There is, in fact, no good reason (except for an exemption clause) why it should not be possible for a contracting party to hold a classification society liable for its representation if it is incorrect.[317] This decision is not applicable to a third party, as has been expressly stated and pointed out several times before. A clear distinction has to be made with such cases of third-party liability.

d. The Interore III Case

In this case, a shipper sued an inspector whom it had hired to check the cargo-hold of a vessel which was supposed to transport fertiliser products from Sweden to New Zealand. Even though the crew had failed to remove a substantial quantity of barley grains trapped in parts of the cargo-holds, the inspector certified the holds

---

316 *See supra* Part 2 A II 3 a cc.

317 *See also* Miller, 'Liability of Classification Societies from the Perspective of United States Law', 22 *Tul.Mar.L.J.* 75 (1997), at 97, who points out that the decision went too far in practically exempting classification societies from liability to the shipowner. There may be cases in which a shipowner poorly maintained his vessel and then the classification society must, of course, be exonerated from liability. But there may be quite different cases, in which a shipowner must have some kind of relief.

as clean, dry and suitable for loading.[318] On arrival of the vessel at its port of destination in New Zealand, officials of the New Zealand Ministry of Agriculture and Fisheries discovered that the fertiliser was contaminated with barley and barred its discharge. As all attempts failed to sell the fertiliser in Australia or South-East Asia, the fertiliser had to be brought to Belgium to be sold. The plaintiff incurred damages in cost and lost value of USD 959,375.44, which it wanted to recover from the inspector. The Court of Appeals held that any duty owed by the inspector to the shipper with regard to the inspection of the cargo was derived from the contract between the parties and could not be based in tort. The shipper and the inspector contemplated that the inspector would bear the risk of a negligent inspection. Thus, the inspector was liable for the shipper's damages when its negligent inspection of cargo resulted in the contamination of the shipper's cargo on grounds of breach of contract. Although there was a great disparity between the shipper's damages and the fee for inspection, the inspector was a professional organisation in the market for inspection services and the purpose of the inspection was to insure the preservation of the cargo. The plaintiff was therefore successful with its action.

Even though this case relates to a marine surveyor, those parts are relevant in which the Court of Appeals compares the *Interore III* case with issues which were relevant to the *Sundance* case. The Court of Appeals dismissed any recourse to the *Vitol*[319] reasoning that the disparity between the fees and the alleged damages shows that the defendant did not assume the liability, as this statement only represented the opinion of one judge.[320] *Vitol* was a claim against a cargo inspector who negligently carried out a test of naphtha shipments. As the plaintiff did not prove that the breach of duty of workmanlike performance was the direct and proximate cause of the shipper's lost profits, it did not succeed with its special damages claim. In contrast to *Interore III*, New York state law governed this case because it was not a maritime tort. In *Sundance* a similar argumentation had been applied, which had been based on *Vitol*, but at the same time on § 351 Restatement (Second) of Contracts, Comment f.[321]. However, the Court of Appeals reiterated its decision in *Sundance* and held that it was not to the contrary, despite the fact that *Sundance* relied on exactly the *Vitol* reasoning that the Court of Appeals for the Second Circuit dismissed this time as only representing the opinion of one

---

318 *International Ore and Fertilizer Corp. v. SGS Control Services, Inc.*, 38 F.3d 1279 (2d Cir.1994). Even though the District Court based its opinion on New York law, the Court of Appeals stated that the same argumentation applied under general federal maritime law (*ibid.*, at 1283–1284).

319 *Vitol Trading S.A. v. SGS Control Services*, 874 F.2d 76 (2d Cir. 1989), at 81–82.

320 *International Ore and Fertilizer Corp. v. SGS Control Services, Inc.*, 38 F.3d 1279 (2d Cir.1994), at 1284.

321 *Sundance Cruises Corp. v. American Bureau of Shipping*, 7 F.3d 1077 (2d Cir.1993), at 1084.

judge.[322] For this reason, the part of *Sundance* which relates to the disparity between the fees and the damages sought can only be based on § 351 of the *Restatements*, not on *Vitol*. As the disparity was not considered to be of any relevance in *Interore III*, one may argue that it should not have been of relevance in the *Sundance* case either. In *Interore III*, the inspector charged a seemingly low fee relative to the potential liability. This fact was considered to be of no relevance to the question of whether or not the inspector could be held liable. The court held:

> 'The fact that [the defendant] charged a seemingly low fee relative to potential liability hardly suggests that the parties failed to contemplate [the defendant's] bearing the risk of a negligent inspection. Indeed, the Certificate expressly "limited" [the defendant's] "responsibility [...] to the exercise of reasonable care." [The defendant] performs similar professional services on a frequently recurring basis and can insure against liability for inaccurate inspections which result in major damage to cargo. Then, [the defendant] can set its prices accordingly.'[323]

This argumentation applies to classification societies all the same; the allegation that low fees illustrate that the parties have not contemplated the risks (which is also stated in *Sundance*) is, therefore, not very convincing. The provision of professional services on a frequent basis applies just as well to classification societies, and similarly they can insure against liability for inaccurate inspections.

Interore III once again states that if both contractual liability and liability in tort exist, contractual liability prevails.[324] Also, it was held that the tort of negligent misrepresentation cannot be the basis of liability where the sole legal duties of the plaintiff arose entirely out of a contract.[325] Furthermore, it was held that in con-

---

[322] In *Sundance* the District Court held: 'First, the great disparity between the fee charged (USD 85,000) by ABS for its services and the damages sought by Sundance (USD 264,000,000) is strong evidence that such a result was not intended by the parties. We can only conclude that the small fees charged could not have been intended to cover the risk of such liability; the ship classification industry could not continue to exist under such terms. *See, e.g., Vitol Trading S.A. v. SGS Control Services*, 874 F.2d 76 (2d Cir. 1989), at 81–82 (quoting Restatement (Second) of Contracts § 351 cmt. f: 'fact that price [charged] is relatively small suggests that it was not intended to cover the risk of such liability')' (*Sundance Cruises Corp. v. American Bureau of Shipping,* 7 F.3d 1077 (2d Cir.1993), at 1084).

[323] *International Ore and Fertilizer Corp. v. SGS Control Services, Inc.,* 38 F.3d 1279 (2d Cir.1994), at 1284.

[324] *International Ore and Fertilizer Corp. v. SGS Control Services, Inc.,* 743 F.Supp. 250, 828 F.Supp. 1098 (S.D.N.Y.1994), 38 F.3d 1279, 1284 (2d Cir.1994) citing *East River S.S. Corp. v. Transamerica Delaval Inc.*, 476 U.S. 858, 106 S.Ct. 2295, 90 L.Ed.2d 865 (1986); New York law: *Clark-Fitzpatrick, Inc. v. Long Island R.R. Co.*, 70 N.Y.2d 382, 521 N.Y.S.2d 653, 516 N.E.2d 190 (1987).

[325] *International Ore and Fertilizer Corp. v. SGS Control Services, Inc.,* 38 F.3d 1279 (2d Cir.1994), at 1283, citing *East River S.S. Corp. v. Transamerica DeLaval, Inc.,* 476 U.S. 858, 106 S.Ct. 2295, 90 L.Ed.2d 865 (1986) and *Clark-Fitzpatrick, Inc. v. Long Island Rail Road Company,* 70 N.Y.2d 382, 516 N.E.2d 190 (N.Y.1987).

tractual relations the inspector is obliged by the Certificate and by an implied duty to perform the contract in a workmanlike fashion.[326]

The Court of Appeals distinguished the present case from *Sundance* in the following way:

> 'Our recent decision in *Sundance Cruises Corp. v. American Bureau of Shipping* [...] is not to the contrary. *Sundance* was an action for damages on a contract for the classification for insurance purposes of an ocean-going passenger vessel. The court held that the disparity between the fee charged on the contract and damages sought disclosed that the parties did not foresee the risk of such liability. However, the purpose of the contractual obligation of the ship classification society in *Sundance* contrasts markedly with that of the inspector in *Vitol* and in the present case. *Sundance* likened the suit against the classification society to a case in which "one who causes a vehicle accident [...] then sues the Motor Vehicle Bureau for damages to his car because it issued him a driver's licence that falsely represented his fitness to drive." 7 F.3d at 1084. In *Sundance*, the court therefore concluded that "the purpose of the classification certificate is not to guarantee safety but merely to permit [the ship owner] to take advantage of the insurance rates available to a classed vessel." *Id.* The purpose of the inspection in this case, however, was precisely to guarantee the condition of the hold so as to insure the preservation of the cargo. There is no other reason to perform such an inspection and no other reason to pay for one, whatever the amount.'[327]

The stated contrast between *Sundance* and the present decision is not as large as the court makes it appear to be. As has been criticised in the case comment on *Sundance*, the court simplified the duties and functions of a classification society. When re-phrasing the duties to cover the checking and survey of whether the vessel fulfils the rules of the society, the differences between these two decisions do not appear to be as remarkable as the court wants them to be. In one instance, the cargo surveyor checks whether the condition of the hold is such as to ensure the preservation of the cargo; in the other, the surveyor checks the whole vessel to see whether it complies with the rules. These two services differ in regard to the scope of the duties and their complexity. Also, the classification certificate is for the general use of the shipowner and he may show it to a large number of persons. By contrast, the specific inspection and certificate issued by the marine inspector in *Interore III* is only for the use of the contracting party and an additional third party which is known by or foreseeable to the inspector. However, one must criticise the fact that this does not distinguish this case so markedly from one of a classification certificate that its reasoning could not be applied. Moreover, whenever the classification society carries out Special Surveys on behalf of entities like the shipyard or the charterer, these Surveys do not involve the non-delegable duty of

---

[326] *International Ore and Fertilizer Corp. v. SGS Control Services, Inc.*, 38 F.3d 1279 (2d Cir.1994), at 1284; *Mayer Boat Works v. Bright Marine Basin,* 265 F.Supp. 352 (E.D.N.Y.1966), at 355; *Lunn v. Silfies*, 106 Misc.2d 41, 431 N.Y.S.2d 282, 284 (Spu.Ct.1980).

[327] The comparison with a Motor Vehicle Bureau is rejected by France, 'Classification societies: their liability–an American lawyer's point of view in light of recent judgments', 1 *I.J.S.L.* 67 (1996), at 70.

the shipowner and are more similar to the services performed by the cargo surveyor in *Interore III.* Based on its argumentation, liability for such services should be imposed on a classification society.

e. Conclusion

Under general federal maritime law, the shipowner cannot hold the classification society liable for its activities, as the precedents, first and foremost the *Sundance* case,[328] illustrate. They do not give an implied warranty of workmanlike performance, as the *Ryan* doctrine does not apply to them. Because of the *East River* doctrine, contractual liability prevails over liability in tort for pure economic loss. According to *Sundance*, classification societies are generally exempt from liability towards the shipowner.

One can definitely argue about this, and several points can be put forth against *Interore III.* In *Sundance*, liability was rejected since the main purpose of the classification certificate was considered to be lower insurance rates, because the disparity between the fees and the potential financial responsibility was interpreted as showing that the parties did not aim at covering such a risk and since the shipowner would otherwise be exempt from his non-delegable duty to provide a seaworthy vessel. As shown above, all three reasons are not convincing. The first one, the insurance issue, is simply incorrect and a simplification of the purpose of classification. The second one, the disparity between the fees and the amount of potential financial liability, was rejected in *Interore III*, even though it can generally be of relevance to the interpretation of contractual duties. The fact that the provision of this information is the professional service of the classification societies, which they do on a recurring basis and against whose risks they can insure themselves, speaks clearly against a rejection of a liability based purely on these grounds. And the third rationale, the non-delegable duty of a shipowner, should not be of relevance for two reasons.[329] On the one hand, it is a duty which the shipowner has towards third parties to the classification contract and which should therefore not be taken into account. On the other hand, the classification society does not exercise any kind of duty which actually interacts or conflicts with the

[328] A number of other cases shall only be shortly mentioned, in which a shipowner sued a classification society, but which did not make any statements on the legal theory or on the merits. These cases are *Gulf Tampa Drydock Co. v. Germanischer Lloyd*, 634 F.2d 874 (5th Cir.1981), at 878, which only gave indications on tort law that will be considered in Part 2 B II 2, 3, and moreover *In the Matter of the Complaint of Dann Marine Towing, LC et al.*, 2004 WL 744881 (E.D.La.2004), and *American Bureau of Shipping v. Société Jet Flint, S.A., et al.*, 1998 WL 273083 (S.D.N.Y.1998), *aff'd in part, reversed in part and remanded sub nom American Bureau of Shipping v. Tencara Shipyard S.P.A.*, 170 F.3d 349, 1999 A.M.C. 1858 (2nd Cir.1999).

[329] *See also* France, 'Classification societies: their liability–an American lawyer's point of view in light of recent judgments', 1 *I.J.S.L.* 67 (1996), at 69. *Miller* comes to the same conclusion (Miller, 'Liability of Classification Societies from the Perspective of United States Law', 22 *Tul.Mar.L.J.* 75 (1997), at 109–110).

shipowner's duty. The shipowner has to answer for the seaworthiness of his vessel; the classification society only checks whether or not certain safety measures are complied with. Whether or not the fact that the shipowner asks a classification society to survey his ship can be interpreted as a due diligence defence against the non-delegable duty to furnish a seaworthy vessel is a question which has to be answered only in the context of this duty, not in the context of the duty of a classification society to the shipowner.[330] But even if one had to take any indirect effects into account, this would not change anything. Since the classification society does not guarantee the seaworthiness of the vessel to anyone, the shipowner is not even indirectly relieved of his duty towards the third parties. A classification society can only be responsible for surveys which it has performed. And what good reason is there against a contractual liability of a classification society for undertakings and representations towards the shipowner? In fact, according to contract law there is none. Classification societies should therefore – contrary to current general federal maritime law – be liable for any breach of their contractual duty to survey the vessel according to their rules and notify the shipowner of any detectable deficiencies. Regarding Special Surveys on behalf of entities other than the shipowner, the precedents lead to the conclusion that liability is to be imposed. That the shipowner may have a cause of action against the classification society is also pointed out by *Miller*:

> 'While this reasoning is sound, it raises the interesting question of what result should be reached when the shipowner does not know of the defect. The proper resolution of that legal issue, it would seem, depends upon the shipowner's reasonable expectations and the explanation for its lack of knowledge. If, with the classification society's knowledge, the shipowner consciously relied upon the classification society to perform certain vessel-surveying and/or performance-monitoring tasks that the shipowner otherwise would have performed, the shipowner's detrimental reliance unquestionably should spawn a viable cause of action against the classification society.'[331]

The *Amoco Cadiz* case is based on a similar understanding:

> 'With respect to the surveys by ABS, this court notes that ABS will not be held liable for failing to disclose those defects and problems with the *Amoco Cadiz* about which Amoco knew. With respect to those problems, it cannot be said that Amoco relied upon ABS's undertaking. Moreover, to hold ABS liable in that situation would be contrary to public policy. A shipowner who has knowledge of problems with its vessel cannot escape liability for failing to correct those problems on the basis that a classification society hired to survey the ship did not detect those defects.'[332]

And further:

---

[330] Similarly, *Miller* also states that the shipowner's duty to make the vessel seaworthy would not be undermined, Miller, 'Liability of Classification Societies from the Perspective of United States Law', 22 *Tul.Mar.L.J.* 75 (1997), at 91–92.

[331] Miller, 'Liability of Classification Societies from the Perspective of United States Law', 22 *Tul.Mar.L.J.* 75 (1997), at 93.

[332] *In the Matter of Oil Spill by the Amoco Cadiz*, 1986 A.M.C. 1945 (N.D.Ill.1986), at 1954–1955.

> 'When a shipowner has prior knowledge of its vessel's defects, certification by a classification society does not establish the seaworthiness of a ship or the lack of negligence on the part of a shipowner. *See Complaint of Ta Chi Navigation (Panama) Corp. S.A.*, 574 F.Supp. 418, 428 (S.D.N.Y.1983); *Navegacion Castro Riva v. The M.S. Nordholm*, 178 F.Supp. 736, 741 (E.D.La.1959) [...], *aff'd*, 287 F.2d 398 (5th Cir.1961).'[333]

If the shipowner knows about defects or deficiencies, he does not reasonably rely on the representation and therefore there is no causation and no recovery on tort claims.[334] This consideration would have been a more profound basis of the *Sundance* decision.

However, this criticism does not strive to mislead that up until today, no classification society has been held liable towards a contracting party under United States law. It only seeks to demonstrate that the findings of the courts should be reconsidered and that there are good reasons to come to different conclusions in the future.

4. Exemption and Limitation Clauses

As it has been determined that classification societies should be held liable under United States contract law, it shall also be analysed whether these societies could effectively stipulate in their contracts a clause which aims at restricting their financial risk or their exposure to liability. United States law distinguishes between an impressive array of such provisions. The classification society may include disclaimers of warranty liability, which deny any claim for breach of warranty; clauses exculpating from negligence and other tort liability and seeking to reject any claim for lack of care; release clauses which try to avoid any claim to liability; clauses excluding consequential damages; provisions shortening the period during which notice must be given or suit must be brought; and indemnity clauses which aim at holding harmless the indemnitee, the classification society, by requiring an indemnitor to shoulder any liability of the indemnitee. Furthermore, all of these clauses can be used in combination.

Any such clause must be closely scrutinised, as it can be contrary to several theories of law. Generally, the autonomy of the parties is respected. Therefore, a commercial transaction between two business entities of equal bargaining power is normally held to be valid, and courts will refuse to rewrite the transaction in the absence of evidence that one party unfairly exploited its position of advantage.[335] Since the contracting parties are not consumers, issues of consumer protection are irrelevant. However, there are four different kinds of restrictions on what the classification society is allowed to stipulate. First of all, the public interest or public

---

333 *In the Matter of Oil Spill by the Amoco Cadiz*, 954 F.2d 1279 (7th Cir. 1992). See also *Great American Insurance*: The owner knew of the defects, and in permitting the vessel to sail simply took a calculated risk. (*Great American Insurance Co. v. Bureau Veritas*, 338 F.Supp. 999 (S.D.N.Y.1972), at 1011).

334 France, 'Classification societies: their liability–an American lawyer's point of view in light of recent judgments', 1 *I.J.S.L.* 67 (1996), at 74.

335 McCormack, 'Warranties and Disclaimers', 62 *Tul.L.Rev.* 549 (1988), at 553.

policy can draw a line. Clauses exculpating a classification society from liability for negligence can be unenforceable.[336] Protection will be afforded only to ordinary negligence, not to gross negligence or intentional or reckless torts.[337] Express agreements which aim only at limiting liabilities are usually not against public policy. However, a different solution may apply if one party is exonerated for damages for breach of contract.

Secondly, the doctrine of unconscionability limits the contractual stipulations possible. 'Unconscionability has generally been recognized to include an absence of meaningful choice on the part of one of the parties together with contract terms which are unreasonably favorable to the other party.'[338] Courts analyse whether there are "unreasonably favorable" terms (so-called "substantive unconscionability") and "an absence of meaningful choice" (which is usually referred to as "procedural" unconscionability, which is often present in cases of superior bargaining power of one party). Usually, the more either of these two kinds of unconscionability is present, the less the other one is required to make the clause unenforceable. However, the fact that only one of them is present does not suffice. The problem is, therefore, whether the bargaining power of one party is extremely restricted to the point where it becomes impossible for one party to reject the limitation clause. Otherwise the courts prefer to allow the parties to define their contractual circumstances.[339]

The third restriction on the autonomy of the parties relates to contradictions in drafting. Whenever the contract includes express warranties of a party, these warranties cannot be disclaimed.

Relating to the interpretation of the contract, the fourth limitation is that clauses are strictly construed in the case of ambiguity. Any disclaimer clause must contain "clear and unequivocal" language which contains the 'plainly expressed intention of the parties, manifested by language couched in unmistakable terms.'[340] Language is interpreted *contra preferentem,* which means against the person that has used it. Similarly, exculpatory clauses which are couched in general language are insufficient to bar claims for liability for negligence. Specific mention needs to be made of negligence, and the scope of activities and events covered by the limitation needs to be precisely defined.[341]

---

336 *See generally* Farnsworth, *On Contracts* (2004), § 5.2.

337 *Murphy v. North American River Runners*, 186 W.Va 310, 412 S.Ed.2d 504, 510 (1991); Restatement (Second) of Contract, § 195 (1).

338 *Williams v. Walker-Thomas*, 350 F.2d 445 (D.C.Cir.1965), at 449.

339 *Alcoa Steamship Co., Inc. v. Charles Ferran & Co., Inc.*, 251 F.Supp. 823 (D.C.La. 1966), at 826, *aff'd,* 383 F.2d 46 (5th Cir.(La.)1967), *cert. denied*, 393 U.S. 836, 89 S.Ct. 111 (U.S.1968).

340 *Hudson Waterways Corp. v. Coastal Marine Service*, 436 F.Supp. 597 (D.C.Tex.1977), at 605.

341 *See* Farnsworth, *On Contracts* (2004), § 4.29a with further references.

A more severe law applies to persons who perform a public service duty.[342] Such providers cannot effectively stipulate clauses which aim at exempting them from liability. Also, they are not allowed to impose indemnity clauses. Regarding classification societies, there is no case law on this question yet. The existing precedents are also quite ambiguous, since a common carrier,[343] hospital[344] or a house inspection service[345] have been considered as constituting a public service duty, whereas a ski resort[346] or a service providing recreational boats[347] has not. Generally, the following criteria are taken into consideration in order to ascertain whether a party performs a public service duty:

> '(1) whether the enterprise is a business of a type generally thought suitable for public regulation; (2) whether the service is of great importance to the public and which is often a matter of practical necessity for some members of the public; (3) whether the party performing the service holds itself out as willing to perform it for any member of the public who seeks it or, at least, for any member of the public within certain established standards; (4) whether the nature of the service and the economic setting give the provider a decisive advantage of bargaining strength against any member of the public who might seek the service; (5) whether the provider exercises its superior bargaining power through a standardized adhesion contract of exculpation and makes no provision to allow a purchaser to pay additional fees to obtain protection against negligence; (6) whether those who seek the service must be placed under the control of the provider thereby becoming subject to the risk of carelessness on the part of the provider.'[348]

The first five criteria should usually be satisfied as regards classification societies, the sixth, however, is not. The classification society only surveys the vessel and gives advice, but does not impose additional dangers. The shipowner (or the shipyard or ship repairer) is the one who remains in control of the vessel at all times.

To sum up, disclaimers by classification societies which exculpate them from any liability in survey reports and documents are not enforceable under United States law.[349] Such clauses are generally considered as being contrary to public

---

342 Murray, *On Contracts,* (2001), § 98, at 580.

343 *Lohman v. Morris,* 146 Ill.App.3d 457, 497 N.Ed.2d 143 (3d Dist.1986).

344 *Tunkl v. Regents of University of California,* 60 Cal.2d 92, 383 Pa.2d 441, 32 Cal.Rptr. 33 (1963).

345 *Mattegat v. Klopfenstein,* 50 Conn.App. 97, 717 A.2d 276 (1998).

346 *Szczotka v. Snowridge, Inc.,* 869 F.Supp. 247 (D.Vt.1994).

347 *Waggoner v. Nags Head Water Sports,* 1998 U.S. App. LEXIS 6792, at 18 (4th Cir.1998).

348 *Tunkl v. Regents of University of California,* 60 Cal.2d 92, 383 Pa.2d 441, 32 Cal.Rptr. 33 (1963), *Gardner v. Downtown Porsche Audi,* 180 Cal.App.3d 713, 225 Cal.Rptr. 757 (2d Cir.1986), *Szczotka v. Snowridge, Inc.,* 869 F.Supp. 247 (D.Vt.1994), Restatement (Second) of Contracts, § 195 (2).

349 *Dillingham Tug & Barge Corp. v. Collier Carbon & Chem. Corp.,* 548 F.Supp. 691 (N.D.Cal.1981), at 699, *aff'd in part, rev'd in part,* 707 F.2d 1086, 1984 A.M.C. 1990 (9th Cir.1983). Similar *Skibs A/S Gylfe v. Hyman-Michaels Company et. al.,* 304 F.Supp. 1204, at 1220 (E.D.Mich.1969), *aff'd,* 438 F.2d 803 (6th Cir.1971), *cert. de-*

policy.[350] Clauses which limit their liability are, by contrast, not usually contrary to public policy and enforceable unless they contradict any of the other aforementioned restrictions in the given case.[351]

III. German Law

1. The Legal Nature of the Contract

Under German law, classification societies have not yet been held liable towards a contracting party. However, in the sole decision of the Federal Court of Justice (*Bundesgerichtshof*) in this regard,[352] the claim against the classification society was statute-barred.[353] For this reason, the dismissal of a claim in this decision cannot be generalized. In the following, the legal principles which courts developed in different cases will therefore be applied to this yet unsolved question.

A classification society could be liable to its client if it commits a breach of contract. The concept of breach of contract (*Pflichtverletzung*) is a general concept in German contract law. However, as will be further elaborated in the next paragraph, the preconditions of such breach of contract differ from one kind of contract to the other, as they depend on what the contractual debtor has to do in order to discharge his duty. A classification contract could either be a contract for work or for service.[354] Unlike English and United States courts, which have always con-

---

nied sub nom. Hyman-Michaels Co. v. National Cargo Bureau, Inc., 404 U.S. 831 (1971).

[350] *See Bisso v. Inland Waterways Corp.*, 349 U.S. 85 (1955). *Sundance Cruises Corp. v. American Bureau of Shipping,* 799 F.Supp. 363 (S.D.N.Y.1992), at 378.

[351] Honka, 'The Classification System and its Problems with Special Reference to the Liability of Classification Societies', 19 *Tul.Mar.L.J.* 1 (1994), at 15–18. Indications on how such clause should be formulated gives Goldsmith, 'River Pilot, Marine Surveyor, and Third-Party Inspector Liability', 26 *Tul.Mar.L.J.* 463 (2002), at 512–513.

[352] BGH 3 March 1998, [1998] *NJW–RR* 1027.

[353] In LG Hamburg 18 January 1972, 10 O 176/70 (unpublished), the classification society was not in breach of contract.

[354] Both a contract for work and a contract for service could appear as a contract which aims at taking care of a matter (*Geschäftsbesorgungsvertrag*), § 675 (1) BGB. This contract is defined as an independent activity of an economic kind in the interest of someone else (BGH 25 April 1966, 45 BGHZ 223, at 228; BGH 12 November 1991, [1992] *NJW* 560). The activity concerns affairs which in principle the creditor has to look after himself (Larenz, *Lehrbuch des Schuldrechts*, vol. II/1 (1986), at § 56 V states examples of a contract in the sense of § 675 para. 1 BGB: the contract with a lawyer for the representation in court or as a consultant, with a tax adviser, a chartered accountant or an arbitrator). As neither the shipowner nor the shipyard nor the manufacturer may classify a vessel or certify a product, the contracts are not of such a legal nature. (Similar: Basedow/Wurmnest, *Third Party Liability of Classification Societies* (2005), 46; Basedow/Wurmnest, 'Klassifikationsverträge als Verträge mit Schutzwirkung zugunsten Dritter', [2005] *VersR* 328, at 330–331; contrary: Drobnig, *Tätigkeit und Haftung*

sidered the classification contract to be a contract for service, there is only one case under German law which relates to the activities of a classification society. That case related to a contract to supervise the building of a wooden yacht, which has a more limited scope than an ordinary classification contract. The *Bundesgerichtshof* has considered such a contract to be a contract for work.[355]

A contract for work differs from a contract for service as regards its limitation period, its preconditions of a breach, the extent of the obligations of the classification society as well as the place of performance. A claim based on a contract for work is subject to a limitation period of two years from acceptance of the completed work,[356] whereas claims from a contract for service are statute-barred three years after they arise, as long as the creditor knows or should know about their circumstances.[357] Also, these contracts differ in their consequences of the right to give notice. Contrary to a contract for service, there are statutory regulations concerning the consequences of the execution of the right to give notice in the law of contract for work. According to § 649 BGB, the customer has a right to give notice to terminate the contract at any time up until the completion of the work. When he gives such notice, the contractor may claim the remuneration that has been agreed upon. He must, however, deduct what he saves in expenses or what he acquires or maliciously neglects to acquire by a different application of his working capacity.[358]

Moreover, jurisdiction may differ according to the nature of the contract. § 29 ZPO offers a special venue relative to the place of performance of the contractual obligation. If it was a contract for service, the service is performed at the place of the survey, e.g. at the shipyard. In the case of a contract for work, the place of performance would be where the certificate or information was handed over, *e.g.*, at the headquarters of the shipowner. A German court would decide, according to the same provisions, whether it would affirm its jurisdiction if the cases pointed towards the jurisdictions of several different countries. From the point of view of German law, international jurisdiction follows domestic jurisdiction.[359]

Even more important is the question of what the classification society has to do in order to perform its contractual obligations and to acquire a right to remuneration. A contract for work obliges the classification society to achieve the stipulated

---

von Klassifikationsgesellschaften in der Bundesrepublik Deutschland am Beispiel des Germanischen Lloyd (1995), 104–105.

355 BGH 3 March 1998, [1998] *NJW–RR* 1027.

356 § 634 a para. 1 no. 1, para. 2 BGB. Only houses are constructions in the sense of § 634 a para. 1 no. 2, see Sprau in: Palandt, *Bürgerliches Gesetzbuch* (2006), § 634 a at no. 10; BGH 3 March 1998, [1998] *NJW–RR* 1027. As an exemption, in case of fraudulent concealment of defects, the claim becomes statute-barred after three years, §§ 634 a para. 3, 195.

357 §§ 195, 199 para. 1 no. 1, 2 BGB.

358 § 649 s. 2 BGB, translation by Forrester/Goren/Ilgen, *The German Civil Code* (1994).

359 §§ 12 *et seq.* ZPO; *see* Geimer, *Internationales Zivilprozeßrecht* (2005), at no. 946–950.

result. For a contract for service, no specific result has to be achieved; the classification society would only be obliged to perform the service regardless of whether any result is being achieved or not.

As it depends on the definition of the service or the work, the distinction between the two different kinds of contracts is often difficult. The classification society establishes whether the product or the vessel is in accordance with its rules and gives advice on how to achieve this. In general, German courts consider an expert opinion as a result.[360] That points to a contract for work. By contrast, the classification contract usually runs throughout the whole life of the vessel, which makes the single survey appear less important. A precise definition of the performance in contrast to a consecutive activity of a general character is considered to be an indication for a contract for work.[361] Considering the long-term relationship, this implies that it may be regarded as a contract for service.

The result which the classification society owes to its client because of the classification contract is not the granting of a class, as such a result would be contrary to the checking of safety; the class will only be granted if the standard of safety is met. The result which the society is obliged to achieve is to establish whether all rules are fulfilled by the vessel or what has to be done in order to fulfil them. The classification society therefore owes the issuance of an expert opinion. As all other individual contracts which have been mentioned above are expert opinions,[362] they also share the nature of a contract for work. The *Bundesgerichtshof* has compared an individual contract for the checking of blueprints and the supervision of the building of a yacht with the supervision of the building process of a house executed by an architect. Both are considered to be contracts for work.[363]

From the point of view of German law, the contract will even be considered as a contract for work if the General Conditions of the classification society include a reference to the fact that the society only provides a service, not a result.[364] The wording of the General Conditions is only an indication for its interpretation. More important are the general intentions of the contract and the behaviour of the parties. An interpretation of the contract depends on all details of the contractual relationship.[365] The wording of the general clauses is irrelevant if the contractual circumstances lead to a different conclusion.[366] The classification contract obliges the classification society to give an expert opinion on certain precisely defined

---

360 BGH 8 December 1966, [1967] *NJW* 719, at 720; BGH 10 June 1976, 67 BGHZ 1, at 4; BGH 10 November 1994, 127 BGHZ 378, at 384.

361 BGH 1 February 2000, [2000] *NJW* 1107 with further references.

362 *See supra* in this section .

363 BGH 3 March 1998, [1998] *NJW–RR* 1027, at 1028.

364 *E.g.* General Conditions of BV, Article 5.1; unlike BV, GL defines the contract in I Part 0 G 1 of its rules as a contract for work.

365 BGH 26 November 1959, 31 BGHZ 224; BGH 18 Mai 1972, [1972] *WM* 947.

366 Peters in: Staudinger, *Bürgerliches Gesetzbuch, §§ 631– 651* (2003), Vorbem zu § 631 at no. 23.

questions. The classification society owes specific duties to its contracting party. For this reason, its contracts are contracts for work.[367]

2. *Liability for Breach of Contract*

Norm de base for the liability of classification societies under principles of contract law is § 280 (1) BGB. This provision obliges the debtor to compensate the creditor for damage if the debtor breaches a contractual duty unless he acted without negligence.[368] In a contract for work, there is a different liability regime, depending on whether or not the work has been accepted. Before acceptance, the general regime of contractual liability of §§ 280 *seq.* BGB applies, which is based on the principle of fault.[369] After acceptance, the fault of the classification society is no longer relevant; all that is required is a defect (*Mangel*) in the performed work. As a classification contract consists of several activities which have to be performed, acceptance must be made of every obligation that is performed (*Teilleistung*). Whenever a survey is carried out, advice is given or blueprints are certified. These acts need to be accepted in an explicit or implicit way and the corresponding duties must be fully discharged.[370]

As has been enumerated *supra*,[371] a breach of contract may be constituted in several different ways. A classification society may directly cause damage at the time that it is performing its contractual duties. As an example, a surveyor might drop a torch in the engine room and thereby cause damage to the engine. In such a case, the classification society would have to answer for its surveyor as his vicarious agent (*Erfüllungsgehilfe*) with regard to the contractual obligation pursuant to § 278 BGB. Its liability would derive from the breach of a collateral duty (*Ne-*

---

367 *See also* Basedow/Wurmnest, *Third Party Liability of Classification Societies* (2005), 46. *Compare* LG Hamburg 18 January 1972, 10 O 176/70 (unpublished), at 12.

368 German law seeks to protect a person who gives advice gratuitously. In that spirit, § 675 (2) BGB stipulates that a person who gives advice, recommendation or information to another is not bound to compensate for any damage arising from following it. However, this provision only aims at such advice that is given without the intent to cause a binding contract (Wittmann in: Staudinger, *Bürgerliches Gesetzbuch, §§ 652-704* (1995), § 676 at no. 8). Classification societies act for commercial reasons and conclude binding contracts with their clients. § 675 (2) BGB does not exempt them from liability.

369 There was a major revision of the German law of contracts on 26 November 2001. Pursuant to § 5 of Art. 229 EGBGB, all contracts which have been concluded after 1 January 2002 fall under these new regulations. They apply to long-term contractual relations from 1 January 2003. In this thesis, reference is made solely to the revised law of contracts. For an introduction to the history of the revision and an introduction to the revised law of obligations, *see* Zimmermann, *The new German Law of Obligations* (2005).

370 For an analysis of the damages that can be awarded, *see* Brinkmann, 'German Law: Damage to Persons, Property and the Environment', 22 *Tul.Mar.L.J.* 545 (1998).

371 *See supra* Part 2 A I 1.

benpflichtverletzung) to protect the interests of the contracting party. The duty to take care of the property of the contracting party is an accessory consideration (*Nebenleistung*) which may impose liability according to §§ 282, 280 (1), 241 (2) BGB.[372]

Moreover, the work which the classification society has performed may also cause damage in an indirect way.[373] For example, the classification certificate that was issued showed no deficiencies, whereas the vessel did fail to meet the applicable rules of the society, and the society should have discovered such a mistake. If the shipowner consequently puts the vessel into ordinary service and damage is caused to the vessel, the classification society could also be liable. Such liability follows the principles of §§ 634 no. 4, 280 (1) BGB. It requires a defect (*Mangel*) and a behaviour of the debtor that is contrary to his duty (*Pflichtwidrigkeit*) which has caused the defect. In addition, the cause of this defect needs to be assigned to the debtor.[374]

As regards the defect (*Mangel*) which is required after the acceptance of the work, § 633 BGB distinguishes between a defect of title (*Rechtsmangel*) and a defect of substance (*Sachmangel*). A defect of title is present whenever third parties may exercise rights with regard to the work.[375] Regarding the work of classification societies, this may not happen. In contrast to its denomination, a defect of substance (*Sachmangel*) may also be present in intangible goods.[376] It is defined as a divergence in the actual condition of the work (*Istbeschaffenheit*) compared with the target condition (*Sollbeschaffenheit*).[377] However, this gives rise to the question of what precisely the target condition is as stipulated in the contracts with a classification society. The target condition may be established in accordance with the arrangements of the contractual parties or what they have commonly (even implicitly) assumed at the time of the conclusion of the contract.[378] There is every reason to believe that, in general, both parties assume that the survey, classification or certification – in short, the work – is carried out in accordance with acknowledged standards which are state of the art.[379] Whenever this is not explicitly laid down in the contract, one may interpret the contract as implicitly containing such an obligation.[380] It is further relevant whether the work is suitable for a com-

---

372 Such claims are subject to a prescription period of three years after the existence of the claim if the claimant knows or should without gross negligence know the circumstances of the claim and the person of the defendant, §§ 195, 199 BGB.

373 For a detailed analysis of such cases, *see supra* Part 2 A I 1.

374 §§ 276, 278 BGB, *compare* Peters in: Staudinger, *Bürgerliches Gesetzbuch, §§ 631-651* (2003), § 634 at no. 109–119.

375 § 633 (3) BGB.

376 Sprau in: Palandt, *Bürgerliches Gesetzbuch* (2006), § 633 at no. 5.

377 Sprau, *ibid.*

378 § 633 para. 2 s. 1 BGB.

379 BGH 7 July 1981, [1981] *WM* 1108; Peters in: Staudinger, *Bürgerliches Gesetzbuch, §§ 631-651* (2003), § 633 at no. 168.

380 § 633 para. 2 s. 2 no. 1 BGB.

mon usage and shows a condition customary to similar works which can be expected by the customer from the nature of the work.[381]

The customer of a classification society may expect that the work – for instance, the survey – performed is state of the art. This applies just as well to the rules which are relevant to each and every expert opinion of a classification society. To give but one example, the number of samples which are inspected aboard a vessel has to be sufficient from a technical point of view in order to show deficiencies at a high probability. The rules are state of the art if they correspond to technical regulations for the design and performance of the work which are recognised by scientists as theoretically verified and established and are especially known to the specialist circles relevant to their application. These technical regulations have to be recognised on reasons of continuing practical experience as suitable, adequate and necessary.[382] State-of-the-art are those technical regulations which are the most up-to-date ones at the time of acceptance.[383]

3. *Tort Law*

Under German law, contract law does not exclude the application of tort law to the same set of facts.[384] Tort law is considered to be the minimum standard of protection and is not overridden by contract law. However, as the tort law provisions of §§ 823 *seq.* BGB are more important in the context of liability towards third parties, they will be treated in detail when considering such liability (*see infra* Part 2 B).

4. *Exemption and Limitation Clauses*

Clauses which classification societies include in their contracts are most likely to be standard terms, as they are pre-formulated and likewise used in a number of contracts.[385] Their contracting party cannot influence them. As a consequence, classification societies cannot exclude or limit their liability for injury or death caused by a negligent breach of duty (*Pflichtverletzung*) by themselves or their agents or employees.[386] Moreover, a classification society cannot contractually

---

[381] § 633 para. 2, 2nd sentence no. 2 BGB.

[382] Busche in: Rebmann/Säcker/Rixecker, *Münchener Kommentar zum Bürgerlichen Gesetzbuch, §§ 611-704* (2005), § 633 at no. 17; Peters in: Staudinger, *Bürgerliches Gesetzbuch, §§ 631-651* (2003), § 633 at no. 169.

[383] Busche in: Rebmann/Säcker/Rixecker, *Münchener Kommentar zum Bürgerlichen Gesetzbuch, §§ 611-704* (2005), § 633 at no. 18–19.

[384] BGH 17 March 1987, [1987] *NJW* 2008, at 2010; Sprau in: Palandt, *Bürgerliches Gesetzbuch* (2006), Einf v § 823 at no. 5.

[385] *See* §§ 305 (1), 310 (1) 1 BGB.

[386] § 309 no. 7 lit. a BGB.

rule out liability for its own gross negligence or wilful behaviour or those of its agents or employees.[387]

IV. Conclusion

Under English law, liability is possibly based on a breach of contract, an implied contractual duty or on the tort of negligence. An exemption clause is most likely to be considered not to be reasonable, whereas a limitation clause which limits the liability to a multiple of the fees will be deemed valid. Under United States law, there is currently no liability of a classification society towards a shipowner. However, the argumentation on which these precedents are based is mostly not sound. In fact, the opposite is the case: it should be possible to hold a classification society liable under United States law as well. Under German law, a breach of contract may constitute a claim in contract against the classification society. If the preconditions of a liability in tort are fulfilled at the same time, an action in tort may lie as well. Classification societies cannot exclude or limit liability for injury or death nor for their own or their agents' or employees' gross negligent or wilful behaviour.

B. Private Functions: Liability Towards Third Parties

Whenever an accident happens, it is most likely that a third party who is not bound by the classification contract will sustain damage. Compensation for this damage by the shipowner is, however, not guaranteed and the party is not even likely to receive full compensation. Not only can the shipowner limit his liability, as will be further scrutinised in Part 3,[388] but there may not even be any compensation at all if the shipowner is not insured. Due to the limitation of liability or the lack of any compensation, third parties often seek to hold classification societies liable.

I. English Law

In English law, someone who receives information without having a contract with the person who gave the information can only be protected by tort law. Under common law, torts have developed parallel to the system of writs. At the beginning, there were a large number of nominate torts, such as trespass on land or chattel. It took until the end of the nineteenth century to establish the innominate

[387] *See* § 309 no. 7 lit. b BGB; *compare* Basedow in: Rebmann/Säcker/Rixecker, *Münchener Kommentar zum Bürgerlichen Gesetzbuch, §§ 241–432* (2003), § 309, especially at no. 8 *et seq.*

[388] *See infra* Part 3 A II–IV.

tort of negligence.[389] Its preconditions and definitions continue to be specified and extended by the courts, and there are still dissenting opinions.[390]

1. Contractual Protection of the Third Party

The Contracts (Rights of Third Parties) Act 1999 gives the possibility of contracting for the benefit of third parties. A third party can be granted certain rights, and would be protected against a breach of contract, based on the implied duty of workmanlike performance or against negligent behaviour. The same principles of contractual protection apply to such a party as has already been described in the section relating to the protection of contracting parties.[391] The third party on whom the right shall be conferred must, however, be expressly identified by name, as a member of a class or as answering a particular description.[392] In the contracts which are under discussion here, rights will rarely, if ever, be conferred on third parties.

2. Tort of Negligence

As Lord Steyn observed in the *Marc Rich* case,[393] 'the common law develops incrementally on the basis of a consideration of analogous cases where a duty has been recognized or desired.' As concerns the tort of negligence,[394] this implies that there is no precise definition of a duty of care which is applicable to all cases. One may, however, state that the tort of negligence requires a *duty of care*, which is owed by the defendant to the plaintiff, a *breach* of that duty by the defendant's failure to conform to the required standard[395] and a *loss* or *damage* which is in-

[389] Negligence as a tort cause of action is to be distinguished from the same term used as a form of wrongful conduct itself, which is an element of a large number of different tort causes of action.

[390] *Perrett v. Collins,* [1998] 2 Lloyd's Rep. 255 (C.A.).

[391] *See supra* Part 2 A I 1, 2.

[392] § 1 (3) of the Contracts (Rights of Third Parties) Act 1999.

[393] Lord Steyn in *Marc Rich & Co. AG v. Bishop Rock Marine Co. Ltd. (and ClassNK) ("The Nicholas H."),* [1995] 2 Lloyd's Rep. 299 (H.L.), at 313.

[394] The leading case is *Heaven v. Pender, Trading as West India Graving Dock Company,* [1883] 11 Q.B.D. 503 (C.A.), with the definition of negligence on page 507.

[395] There must be reasonable evidence of negligence and the damage must have been avoidable (*Lloyde v. West Midlands Gas Board,* [1971] 2 All E.R. 1240 (C.A.); *Pickford v. Imperial Chemical Industries plc*, [1998] 3 All E.R. 462 (H.L.); *Swan v. Salisbury Construction Co.Ltd.*, [1966] 2 All E.R. 138 (P.C.). The standard is a reasonable man: 'negligence is the omission to do something which a reasonable man, guided by those considerations which ordinarily regulate the conduct of human affairs, would do, or doing something which a prudent and reasonable man would not do', *Blyth v. Birmingham Waterworks Co.*, [1856] 11 Ex: 781, 784, 156 E.R. 1047 (Ex.), at 1049 per Alderson B.

curred by the plaintiff.[396] Whether or not these preconditions are met in a given case is, however, more difficult to ascertain. Damages will only be awarded if the consequential damage that has been suffered is recognised by the law and is considered not to be too remote. This requires that the plaintiff proves that the alleged damage was caused by the defendant's breach of duty and that there was a causal connection. Moreover, the damage needs to be a natural or probable consequence or one that could be reasonably foreseen.[397]

Further differentiations are made according to the kind of loss. Whenever the defendant directly injured the health of the plaintiff, a duty of care will be easily established. There is, however, only in very rare cases a duty of care for economic loss – especially indirect loss –, as in a competitive environment everyone has the right to enjoy the economic benefits of his actions which necessarily incur economic disadvantages for other people.[398] In order not to overstretch liability, financial loss requires sufficient cause. Since the decision in *Dorset Yacht Co. Ltd. v. Home Office*[399], a duty of care generally requires – whatever harm has been sustained – that the prerequisites of foreseeability and proximity,[400] as well as considerations of fairness, justice and reasonableness, are met.

---

396 *Hedley Byrne & Co. Ltd. v. Heller & Partners*, [1963] 2 All E.R. 575, [1964] A.C. 465 (H.L.); the decision of *Anns v. Merton London Borough Council*, [1978] A.C. 278 (H.L.) was overruled by the House of Lords in *Murphy v. Brentwood District Council*, [1991] 1 A.C. 398; [1990] 2 All E.R. 908; [1990] 2 Lloyd's Rep. 467 (H.L.). *See also Smith v. Eric S. Bush*, [1989] 2 All E.R. 514 (H.L.), at 536; *Caparo Industries plc v. Dickman*, [1990] 2 A.C. 605 (H.L.); [1989] 2 W.L.R. 316 (H.L.); regarding the protected interests: *Harris v. Evans and Another*, [1998] 3 All E.R. 522 (C.A.); as concerns the duty of care *Atwell v. Michael Perry & Co.*, [1998] 4 All E.R. 65 (Ch.D.).

397 *See* in general the *Wagon Mound* case (*Overseas Tankship (U.K.) Ltd. v. Morts Dock & Engineering Co. Ltd.*, [1961] A.C. 388 (P.C.)). *See* also *Jolley v. Sutton London Borough Council*, [1998] 3 All E.R. 559 (C.A.(Civ.Div.)); *Mullin v. Richards*, [1998] 1 All E.R. 920 (C.A.).

398 *See Home Office v. Dorset Yacht Co. Ltd.*, [1970] 1 Lloyd's Rep. 453 (H.L.), at 455, col. 2, *per* Lord Reid.

399 *Dorset Yacht Co. Ltd. v. Home Office,* [1970] A.C. 1004; [1970] 1 Lloyd's Rep. 453 (H.L.).

400 The leading case with regard to *proximity* is *Smith v. Eric S. Bush*: 'I would certainly wish to stress that in cases where the advice has not been given for the specific purpose of the recipient acting upon it, it should only be in cases where the adviser knows that there is a high degree of probability that some other identifiable person will act upon the advice that a duty of care should be imposed. It would impose an intolerable burden upon those who give advice in a professional or commercial context if they were to owe a duty not only to those to whom they give the advice but to any other person who might choose to act upon it.' (*Smith v. Eric S. Bush*, [1990] 1 A.C. 831 at 865 (H.L.)).

> '[...] The three so-called requirements for a duty of care are not to be treated as wholly separate and distinct requirements but rather as convenient and helpful approaches to the pragmatic question whether a duty should be imposed in any given case.'[401]

The establishment of a duty of care is the first and actually most difficult prerequisite of the tort of negligence.[402] 'Negligence must fail where duty is not estab-

---

401 *Dorset Yacht Co. Ltd. v. Home Office,* [1970] A.C. 1004, at 1077; [1970] 1 Lloyd's Rep. 453 (H.L.), at 496. *See also* Lord Steyn in *Marc Rich & Co. AG v. Bishop Rock Marine Co. Ltd. (and ClassNK) ("The Nicholas H."),* [1995] 2 Lloyd's Rep. 299 (H.L.), at 312–313.

402 Due to the fact that at that time the tort of negligence was not yet fully accepted by the courts (the first time it was fully accepted was in *Donoghue v. Stevenson,* [1932] A.C. 562 (H.L.)) and since its preconditions had not yet been developed, the decision of *Sir John Humphery v. Thomas A. Bowers*, (1929) 33 Ll.L. Rep. 167 (K.B.) is mainly of historical interest. Sir *John Humphery* claimed damages from the LR surveyor *Thomas A. Bowers* for alleged negligence and breach of duty in the examinations of the masts, spars and rigging of his yacht *Xenia.* Sir *Humphery* had applied for a special survey at LR in order to have his yacht classified. The surveyor Mr *Bowers* did not at all perform the survey, but reported to LR that the yacht was in a good and efficient state. LR classified the yacht and based its certificate on this report. The plaintiff allegedly relied on the certificate and engaged a crew, but in the course of fitting out the yacht for sea discovered that the mainmast was rotten in places and wholly unfit for use. The plaintiff claimed damages of a delay of three weeks due to the replacement of the mast, the loss of his crew's wages and the use of his vessel for that period of time. Since LR was protected by a contractual exemption clause, the plaintiff sued the surveyor. Mr. Justice Rowlatt held that the defendant surveyor was guilty of gross neglect of duty in this matter. However, he did not owe a duty of care to the plaintiff. The duty of the defendant (the surveyor) required only the use of care and skill to avoid the certificate being made injurious to the plaintiff by the defendant's report to Lloyd's Register: 'Now, no doubt, where one's person or property may be endangered by want of care and skill of another, there are many classes of circumstances in which a duty of care or skill does arise independently of contract on the part of the latter towards the former. For breach of such duty resulting in damage an action in tort will lie, damages being of the gist of the action. But it is not in every set of circumstances where the interest of one person depends really upon the care of another, that this duty arises. In all the well-known cases upon this subject (to most of which I have been referred) the question was whether the particular circumstances were such as to give rise to such duty.
What is contended for in the present case comes to this, that the mere knowledge on the part of a sub-contractor or employee that the contractee in the principal contract will suffer damage if the principal contract is not performed, gives rise to a duty on the part of the sub-contractor or employee to the principal contractee to take care that his contractual rights are not violated as the result of any default on his part, and that the damages for the breach of such duty are measured by the damages flowing from the breach of the principal contract. This would indeed be a far-reaching doctrine. But neither the circumstances as stated above, out of which the duty is said to arise, nor the subject-matter–namely the certificate–with reference to which care and skill is said to have

lished'.[403] Despite the character of the tort of negligence as an innominate and therefore widely applicable tort, there is not yet a general definition of duty. The efforts by judges and legal scholars to develop a general definition have not ultimately been crowned with success. One of the statements generally referred to was made by Lord Atkin in the House of Lords in *Donoghue v. Stevenson*:

> 'At present I content myself with pointing out that in English law there must be, and is, some general conception of relations giving rise to a duty of care, of which the particular cases found in the books are but instances. The liability for negligence, whether you style it such or treat it as in other systems as a species of "culpa," is no doubt based on a general public sentiment of moral wrongdoing for which the offender must pay. But acts or omissions which any moral code would censure cannot in a practical world be treated so as to give a right to every person injured by them to demand relief. In this way rules of law arise which limit the range of complainants and the extent of their remedy. The rule that you are to love your neighbour becomes in law, you must not injure your neighbour; and the lawyer's question, Who is my neighbour? receives a restricted reply. You must take reasonable care to avoid acts or omissions which you can reasonably foresee would be likely to injure your neighbour. Who, then, in law is my neighbour? The answer seems to be – persons who are so closely and directly affected by my act that I ought reasonably to have them in contemplation as being affected when I am directing my mind to the acts or omissions which are called in question.'[404]

If the person who provides information has a duty of care towards the recipient, he is liable towards this third party, even for financial loss, if he negligently breaks the duty of care and thereby causes damage to the third party.[405] In the words of Lord Morris:

---

been due, nor the damages, bear the slightest resemblance to the circumstances, the subject-matter or the damages in any of the cases in which claims have succeeded in this branch of the law.'

403 *Heaven v. Pender, Trading as West India Graving Dock Company*, [1883] 11 Q.B.D. 503, at 507 (C.A.).

404 *Donoughe v. Stevenson*, [1932] A.C. 562 (H.L.), at 580; *see also Afzal v. Ford Motor Co. Ltd.*, [1994] 4 All E.R.720 (C.A.(Civ.Div.)).

405 In the first cases, the courts did not accept such a duty of care towards a third party, *see Candler v. Crane, Christmas & Co.*, [1951] 2 K.B.164 (K.B.). But since *Hedley Byrne & Co. Ltd. v. Heller & Partners*, [1963] 2 All E.R. 575 (H.L.) everybody who gives advice or expert opinions in a business transaction has been subject to a duty of care if he employs professional knowledge and if he reasonably has to assume that other persons who learn about this information put trust in its correctness. According to *Hedley Byrne*, no distinction is to be made, in principle, between financial loss and physical loss (Charlesworth & Percy, *On Negligence* (2006), § 2–151; *Rookes v. Barnard*, [1964] A.C. 1129 (H.L.)). *See also Lancashire & Cheshire Association of Baptist Churches v. Howard & Seddon Partnership,* [1993] 3 All E.R. 467 (Q.B.D.(O.R.)); *Petch v. Commissioners of Customs and Excise*, [1993] .C.R. 789 (C.A.(Civ.Div.)); *Murphy v. Brentwood District Council*, [1991] 1 A.C. 398; [1990] 2 All E.R. 908; [1990] 2 Lloyd's Rep. 467 (H.L.); *White v. Jones*, [1995] 2 A.C. 207 (H.L.), *compare*

> '[...] it should now be regarded as settled that if someone possessed of a special skill undertakes, quite irrespective of contract, to apply that skill for the assistance of another person who relies upon such skill, a duty of care will arise. The fact that the service is to be given by means of or by the instrumentality of words can make no difference. Furthermore, if in a sphere in which a person is so placed that others could reasonably rely upon his judgment or his skill or upon his ability to make careful inquiry, a person takes it upon himself to give information or advice to, or allows his information or advice to be passed on to, another person who, as he knows or should know, will place reliance upon it, then a duty of care will arise.'[406]

The overriding principle is that the duty of care must be established by the plaintiff.[407] An essential fact which needs to be proven is whether the defendant (expressly or impliedly) *assumed liability* for the statement made. The question of this objective test is whether the claimant could reasonably rely on an assumption of personal responsibility by the individual. This has been described in the following way:

> 'It is sometimes said that there has to be an assumption of responsibility by the person concerned. That phrase can be misleading in that it can suggest that the professional person must knowingly and deliberately accept responsibility. It is however clear that the test is an objective one [...] The phrase means simply that the law recognises a duty of care. It is not so much that responsibility is assumed as that it is recognised or imposed by the law.'[408]

This requires that the adviser needs to carry out the profession of giving advice of the kind sought; otherwise there will not be an accepted standard of skill and care which the advisee can legitimately expect to be observed.[409]

Applying this to a classification society, which is a professional organisation of experts in the maritime field, the following conclusions can be drawn. The provision of information is its business. However, this does not answer the question of whether the relevant society also assumes liability towards a third party when issuing a certificate or other kind of information or expert opinion, notably in a case in which this information is handed out to its contracting party. Whether or not a classification society owes a duty of care in tort to third parties needs to be ascertained by analysing the leading precedents regarding classification societies. If the precedents cannot give an answer, one needs to call upon comparable precedents. In this regard, a decision relating to the survey of aircraft needs to be analysed.[410]

---

comment by Zimmermann, 'Erbfolge und Schadensersatz bei Anwaltsverschulden', [1996] *ZEuP* 672.

406 *Hedley Byrne & Co. Ltd. v. Heller & Partners*, [1964] A.C. 465 (H.L.), at 502–503, *per* Lord Morris.

407 Charlesworth & Percy, *On Negligence* (2006), § 2–156.

408 *Phelps v. London Borough of Hillingdon*, [2003] 3.W.L.R. 776 at 790 (H.L.), *per* Lord Slynn. *See also Williams v. Natural Life Health Foods Limited,* [1998] 1 W.L.R. 830 (H.L.), at 835, stressing that it is an objective test.

409 Charlesworth & Percy, *On Negligence* (2006), § 2–163.

410 *Perrett v. Collins,* [1998] 2 Lloyd's Rep. 255 (C.A.).

a. Mariola Marine Corporation v. Lloyd's Register of Shipping (The "Morning Watch")

The first time an English court considered the issue of whether a classification society owes a duty in tort towards a third party was in *The Morning Watch*.[411] In this case, the purchaser of a yacht sued a classification society for negligently misrepresenting its condition. To cut a long story short: at the request of the owners, who wanted to sell the yacht in the following season, Lloyd's Register (LR) carried out a Special Survey of the *Morning Watch*. Subsequently, an interim certificate was issued, stating that the yacht be credited with passing the Special Survey when certain listed repairs, mainly to localised areas of corrosion, had been carried out. On receipt of the interim certificate, the owners issued particulars, offering the *Morning Watch* for sale with a note that the yacht had passed the current Special Survey. The interim certificate was not shown to the purchasers of the yacht. LR allowed the remaining repairs to be deferred until the refitting of the yacht. The refitting was, however, not carried out by the seller of the yacht, but by the purchasers. When these modifications were undertaken by the plaintiffs, deck planking was removed and several areas of corrosion were discovered. According to the plaintiffs, these were serious defects which rendered the yacht unseaworthy, and which should have been detected by the surveyor. They claimed damages for economic loss suffered as a consequence of relying on the fact that the yacht had been surveyed and no significant defects had been found.

The main question of the decision of the Queen's Bench was whether the classification society owed a duty of care not to cause economic loss to persons other than the owners who were likely to rely upon the statement of LR regarding the survey of the yacht.[412] The court held that it was reasonably foreseeable by the classification society that a purchaser would be influenced by the results of the Special Survey when considering whether to buy the yacht.[413] The decision of the

---

411 *Mariola Marine Corporation v. Lloyd's Register of Shipping ("The Morning Watch")*, [1990] 1 Lloyd's Rep. 547 (Q.B.(Comm.)). For case comments, *see* East, 'The Duty of Care in a Marine Context–Is There Someone to Blame?', in: Rose, *Lex Mercatoria* (2000), 129, at 137–141; Ebenroth/Dillon, 'The International Rating Game: An Analysis of the Liability of Rating Agencies in Europe, England, and the United States', 24 *Law & Pol'y in Int'l Bus.* 783 (1993), at 794–795; Feehan, 'Liability of Classification Societies from the British Perspective: The Nicholas H', 22 *Tul.Mar.L.J.* 163 (1997), at 171–172; Lawson, 'Determining the Indeterminate Class: The Morning Watch', [1990] *L.M.C.L.Q.* 482.

412 *Mariola Marine Corporation v. Lloyd's Register of Shipping ("The Morning Watch")*, [1990] 1 Lloyd's Rep. 547 (Q.B.(Comm.)), at 555–563. Philipps, J. held at 556: 'A duty of care will only arise where (i) it is reasonably foreseeable to the defendant that the plaintiff is liable to rely upon his statement; (ii) there is the necessary proximity between the plaintiff and the defendant; (iii) it is just and reasonable in all the circumstances to impose a duty of care on the part of the defendant to the plaintiff.'

413 Phillips. J. considered that in all cases which do not involve economic loss, the criterion of foreseeabilty was sufficient; considerations of proximity and fairness, justice, and reasonableness were thought to be relevant only when compensation for economic loss

Queen's Bench was particularly influenced by a circular of LR to its surveyors. The circular stated that it was common practice for yacht brokers and owners to use the class as an indication of the condition and quality of the yacht, and since there had been several complaints by the purchasers, the surveyors should ascertain that all the prescribed requirements of LR's rules were met by the yacht.

As concerns the sufficient degree of *proximity* between the plaintiff and the defendant, the court rejected the general proposition that a classification society owed a duty of care to those foreseeably liable to suffer economic loss in consequence of reliance on the negligent classification of a yacht.[414] As there is no precise definition of *proximity,* the enquiry rather focused on the closeness and directness of the relationship between the parties.[415] Phillips, J. cited *Al Saudi Banque v. Clarke Pixley,*[416] which held that *Caparo*[417] marked the furthest limit to which the duty of care for negligent misstatement has so far been taken in England, and that it's reasoning did not encourage any further advance. In the view of the judge, it would be a substantial further advance in the law of negligence to accept such a general proposition as has just been described.

Additionally, even on the facts of the case there was no sufficient proximity between the classification society and the purchaser which could have given rise to a duty of care. The court analysed whether the knowledge of the society that the yacht was being sold resulted in proximity, as the plaintiff had argued. The Queen's Bench established that the case was not comparable to the leading precedent of *Smith v. Bush.*[418] It distinguished between the expert opinion given by the valuer in *Smith v. Bush,* who knew that it was going to be shown to the purchaser of the house, and an interim or classification certificate, whose main purpose was

---

was claimed. Even though *Dorset Yacht Co. Ltd. v. Home Office,* [1970] A.C. 1004; [1970] 1 Lloyd's Rep. 453 (H.L.) gave some first indications against this assumption, this question was settled in the negative only after *Marc Rich & Co. AG v. Bishop Rock Marine Co. Ltd. (and ClassNK) ("The Nicholas H."),* [1995] 2 Lloyd's Rep. 299 (H.L.), at 312–313.

414 *Mariola Marine Corporation v. Lloyd's Register of Shipping ("The Morning Watch"),* [1990] 1 Lloyd's Rep. 547 (Q.B.(Comm.)), at 560. Similarly, the House of Lords *per* Lord Lloyd (dissenting) agreed that a decision with regard to a duty of care towards cargo-owners has to be carefully limited, as there was no generalised duty of this kind, *see Marc Rich & Co. AG v. Bishop Rock Marine Co. Ltd. (and ClassNK) ("The Nicholas H."),* [1995] 2 Lloyd's Rep. 299 (H.L.); at 303. The leading opinion came to similar conclusions, at 316.

415 Lord Justice Bingham in *Caparo Industries Plc v. Dickman,* [1989] 2 W.L.R. 316 (H.L.), at 322. *Compare also* Lawson, 'Determining the Indeterminate Class: The Morning Watch', [1990] *L.M.C.L.Q.* 482, at 485–487.

416 *Al Saudi Banque v. Clarke Pixley,* [1990] 2 W.L.R. 344 (Ch.), at 356.

417 This decision related to the Court of Appeals, which was reversed by the House of Lords, *Caparo Industries Plc v. Dickman,* [1989] 2 W.L.R. 316 (C.A.), [1990] 2 A.C. 605 (H.L.), [1989] 2 W.L.R. 316 (H.L.).

418 *Smith v. Eric S. Bush,* [1990] 1 A.C. 831, [1989] 2 All E.R. 514 (H.L.).

to uphold the classification of the yacht.[419] At the time of the survey, no particular purchaser was under consideration and the special survey was not carried out for the purpose of a particular transaction.[420] The court made an interesting remark as concerns the value of a special survey:

> 'While it was possible that a purchaser would rely upon the special survey without independent inquiry this was not probable or highly probable.'

In brief, a duty of care in *The Morning Watch* was therefore rejected. Even though it was foreseeable that a purchaser was influenced by the results of the special survey when considering the purchase of the yacht, there was no sufficient proximity between the society and the purchaser. The argumentation with regard to foreseeability can easily be transferred to many other cases involving a classification society. The finding that there was no *proximity* between the classification society and those foreseeably liable to suffer economic loss in consequence of reliance on the negligent classification of a ship has been confirmed by the House of Lords in *Marc Rich* in an implicit way.[421] A sufficient *proximity* needs to be proven on the basis of the facts of the specific case.

It should be pointed out here that *The Morning Watch* was decided on the fact that the classification society did not know who exactly would be purchasing the yacht. Whenever the classification society knows from the outset that the survey is mainly being carried out for a (specific) purchaser of the yacht, *The Morning Watch* implies that *Smith v. Eric S. Bush* would apply. As a result, the classification society would owe a duty of care towards the purchaser.

b. The Marc Rich Case (The "Nicholas H.")

aa. The Facts

The *Marc Rich* case is the landmark case under English law as regards the liability of classification societies towards third parties. It will therefore be closely scrutinised. Its main issue is whether the third defendant, a classification society, owes a duty of care towards cargo-owners.[422] To give but a short summary of the facts,

---

419 *Mariola Marine Corporation v. Lloyd's Register of Shipping ("The Morning Watch"),* [1990] 1 Lloyd's Rep. 547 (Q.B.(Comm.)), at 561.

420 At 561 Phillips, J. held: 'But the survey was an incident in the regular schedule of inspections that were involved in keeping *Morning Watch* classed at Lloyd's and it cannot be suggested that the sole reason that the survey was carried out was for the purpose of selling the yacht. The survey was not carried out for the benefit of a specific individual purchaser. Mariola had not come on the scene when the survey was ordered. They were not intended to act on the result of the survey, they were merely one of an indeterminate class of persons who might do so.'

421 *See infra* Part 2 B I 2 b bb.

422 *Marc Rich & Co. AG v. Bishop Rock Marine Co. Ltd. (and ClassNK) ("The Nicholas H."),* [1992] 2 Lloyd's Rep. 481 (Q.B.(Comm.)), [1994] 1 Lloyd's Rep. 492 (C. A.), [1995] 2 Lloyd's Rep. 299 (H.L.). Case comments: Beck, A. 'Lord Lloyd probes the pragmatists: The Nicholas H', 9 (8) *Corporate Briefing* 23 (1995); Bonassies, 'Chambre des Lords, 6 juillet 1995, Navire "Nicholas H"' [case-comment], [1995] *DMF* 750;

Marc Rich owned the vessel *Nicholas H,* which had loaded the plaintiff's cargo of lead and zinc at Chile for carriage to Italy and the USSR. The vessel developed several cracks in the hull, which were surveyed by a surveyor of the vessel's classification society ClassNK. The surveyor recommended permanent repairs, for which facilities would have been available locally. The owners refused to have these repairs carried out, as they would have required unloading of the vessel and caused considerable delay. In order to avoid such delay, the owners ordered that only temporary repairs be carried out. These repairs were surveyed by the same surveyor of the defendant classification society and found to be sufficient for the journey. The vessel retained its class on condition that it carried out permanent repairs at the earliest opportunity after discharging the present cargo. The day after the vessel had sailed, the welding of the temporary repairs cracked and a week later it sank with all its cargo. The claim against the owner was settled for about USD 500,000, as the bills of loading included the Hague Rules. The balance of the alleged loss, about USD 5.5 million, was claimed against the classification society.

Cane, 'Classification Societies, Cargo Owners and the Basis of Tort Liability (The Nicholas H)', [1995] *L.M.C.L.Q.* 433; Cane, 'The Liability of classification societies', [1994] *L.M.C.L.Q.* 363; Convery, 'Standard Form Building Contracts and Duty of Care', 62 *Mod.L.Rev.* 766 (1999), at 771; East, 'The Duty of Care in a Marine Context–Is There Someone to Blame?', in: Rose, *Lex Mercatoria* (2000), 129; Feehan, 'Liability of Classification Societies from the British Perspective: The Nicholas H', 22 *Tul.Mar.L.J.* 163 (1997); France, 'Classification societies: their liability–an American lawyer's point of view in light of recent judgments', 1 *Int.J.Ship.L.* 67 (1996); Grime, 'Liability of Classification Societies', (1994) *All E.R. Annual Review* 376; Grime, 'Nicholas H in the House of Lords', (1995) *All E.R. Annual Review* 464; Herber, *Seehandelsrecht* (1999), 176; Hadley-Piggin, 'Duty of care: classification societies', 6 *I.C.C.L.R.* C204 (1995); Harling, 'The Liability of Classification Societies to Cargo Owners', [1993] *L.M.C.L.Q.* 1; Honka, 'The Classification System and its Problems with Special Reference to the Liability of Classification Societies', 19 *Tul.Mar.L.J.* 1 (1994), at 25–29; Kaye, 'Acts speak louder than statements, or nine into one will go', 58 *M.L.R.* 574 (1995); Lethwaite, 'Pure economic loss: a new perspective', 4 *Nott.L.J.* 224 (1995); Lopez de Gonzalo, 'La Responsabilità delle Società di Classifica', (1997) *Diritto del Commercio Internazionale* 651; MacDonald, 'Occasional survey by classification society', 2 *Int.Mar.L.* 202 (1995); Moriarty, 'Negligence in a commercial context', 1 *Comm.Law.* 11 (1995); Mullis, 'Torts in a commercial context are different: the tortious non–liability of classification societies', 7 *K.C.L.J.* 108 (1996-1997); Oats, 'Cargo Insurance–Liability for Negligence', 3 *Int.I.L.R.*. G209 (1995); Oliphant, 'Tort', 49 (Part I) *Current Legal Problems* 29 (1996), at 56–62; Reissner/Wood, 'Duty of care in English law: the tort of negligence v. the doctrine of binding precedent', 2 *Int.I.L.R.*. 351 (1994); Reissner/Wood, 'No duty of care owed by classification society', 4 *Int.I.L.R.*. 30 (1996), at 31.

bb. The Verdict

A number of assumptions were made on appeal to the House of Lords,[423] namely that it was foreseeable that a lack of care by the classification surveyor was likely to expose the cargo to the danger of physical damage, that the damage suffered was physical damage to the goods of the plaintiff, and that the loss of the vessel and cargo was a result of the carelessness of the surveyor. The sole question left was to establish whether in law the classification society owed a duty of care to the cargo-owners capable of giving rise to liability.[424] In this regard, the leading opinion of Lord Steyn assumed the existence of a sufficient degree of *proximity*, whereas the dissenting opinion found that *proximity* had been proven. Lord Steyn argued that even though it had no legal right to stop the ship from sailing, the classification society's *de facto* control was absolute.[425] Since there was a universal role in maritime law that cargo and ship are taking part in a joint venture, the master also acted in the interest of the cargo when he called upon the surveyor. Therefore, the duty of the classification society towards the ship extended to the cargo as well. The dissenting opinion considered the financial exposure of classification societies as being rather limited, since a relation to the cargo-owner comparable with a joint venture is relatively rare.[426] The leading opinion also advanced the argument that the flood-gates would be opened if the court established a duty of care, because such duty would otherwise extend to all kinds of surveys.[427] This assertion was rejected by the dissenting opinion in view of the precise definition of *proximity*.[428] As this criterion is only satisfied in rare cases, the flood-gates would not have been opened.[429]

However, the criterion of *proximity* was not the most relevant issue of *Marc Rich*. The main line of argumentation concentrated on the question of whether it is fair, just and reasonable to impose a duty of care on a classification society towards cargo-owners. The leading opinion rejected such a duty with several arguments, mostly related to policy considerations. It started off with more general reflections relating to criteria on which a duty of care had been based in other cases. Only in the end did it turn to fairness, justice and reasonableness. According to its

---

423 *See* 312.

424 Lord Steyn at 312.

425 At 306.

426 At 306.

427 At 316 col. 2.

428 Lord Lloyd at 308, col. 1. 'I would only add at this point that if concern is felt that a decision in favour of the cargo-owners would open a wide field of liability, I would reply "not so". There is an obvious, sensible and readily defensible line between the surveyor in the present case, where the cargo was on board, and the joint venture was in peril, and a surveyor called in to carry out a periodic survey.'

429 Interestingly, the United States Court of Appeals for the 5th Circuit advanced a similar argument when restricting the application of its tort theory, *see Otto Candies, LLC v. Nippon Kaija Kyokai Corp.*, 2002 WL 1798767 (E.D.La.2002), aff'd. 346 F.3d 530, 2003 A.M.C. 2409 (5th Cir.(La.)2003), cert. denied 72 USLW 3668, 72 USLW 3672 (U.S.2004).

arguments, classification societies were considered as acting in the public interest and fulfilling a role which in their absence would have to be fulfilled by States. Moreover, an additional layer of insurance would be required, whose costs would ultimately have to be borne by the shipowners. The Hague Rules allowed the shipowner to limit his liability, although he is primarily responsible for providing a seaworthy vessel. Such a system would not apply to classification societies. The leading opinion therefore considered it not to be fair, just and reasonable to impose on the classification society, without any such limitation, an identical duty to that imposed on shipowners.

A closer scrutiny of the arguments of the House of Lords reveals five different lines of argument. The basic difference between the approach of the leading and the dissenting opinion is that the leading opinion considered the case to be incomparable to any precedent and put much emphasis on policy considerations,[430] whereas the dissenting opinion argued in favour of a straightforward application of the principles which had been developed in *Donoghue v. Stevenson* in order to prevent a disintegration of the law of negligence.[431]

(1) Direct Physical Loss

The leading opinion first analyses whether there was a direct physical loss or a reliance of the cargo owners, *i.e.* criteria which have pointed towards a duty of care in other cases. With regard to the question of whether the physical loss was direct, this opinion seems to have been convinced *prima facie* that this question has to be answered in the negative. A comparison with *Clay v. Crump*,[432] in which an architect was considered to have directly caused the injury of a workman as he assured a demolition contractor that a wall could be safely left standing, was rejected. According to Lord Steyn, the architect was primarily responsible for leaving the wall in a dangerous condition, whereas in contrast to that it was the shipowner who was primarily responsible for the seaworthiness of a vessel, not the classification society.[433] The dissenting opinion elaborated on this argument of primary responsibility. In its view, it was uncertain what the statement that the shipowner is primarily responsible for taking care meant and why this militates against the need to impose a similar duty on a classification society. The existence of the contract of carriage does not militate against a duty of care owed by a third party in tort. Hence,

---

[430] 'In this area the common law develops incrementally on the basis of a consideration of analogous cases where a duty has been recognized or desired. But none of the cases cited provided any realistic analogy to be used as a springboard for a decision one way or the other in this case. The present case can only be decided on the basis of an intense and particular focus on all its distinctive features, and then applying established legal principles to it. No doubt those principles are capable of further development but, for present purposes, the applicable principles can readily be identified and require no reexamination' (at 313).

[431] At 309. *Donoghue v. Stevenson,* [1932] A.C. 562 (H.L.).

[432] *Clay v. A. J. Crump & Sons Ltd.,* [1964] 1 Q.B. 533 (Q.B.).

[433] At 314.

the dissenting opinion concluded that: 'The function of the law of tort is not limited to filling in gaps left by the law of contract.'[434]

(2) Voluntary Assumption of Responsibility

The next criterion to which the leading opinion refers is *reliance. Reliance* is an indication relevant to the doctrine of voluntary assumption of responsibility, which also may create a duty of care.[435] *Hedley Byrne* related to a person who seeks, in the ordinary course of business, advice or information from another who is not under any contractual or fiduciary obligation to give it, in circumstances where a reasonable man so asked would know that he was being trusted or that his skill or judgment was being relied on. If such a person, without clearly disclaiming responsibility for it, proceeds to give the advice or information sought, that person accepts a legal duty to exercise such care as the circumstances require in making his reply.[436] If that care is not exercised and if foreseeable loss or damage is the result, the victim will have an actionable claim in negligence. In *Marc Rich*, the cargo-owners did not even know that the classification society examined the ship; they simply relied on the representations of the shipowner. Since *reliance* requires a direct exchange between the plaintiff and the defendant, which was not present in this case, there was no voluntary assumption of responsibility by the classification society.[437]

(3) Policy Considerations: Insurance

Another line of argumentation of the leading opinion relates to policy considerations, specifically to insurance, the Hague Rules and the role of classification societies. With regard to insurance, the argument is threefold. First, it is assumed that classification societies would require an additional layer of insurance, the costs of which would be passed on to the shipowner. Secondly, the shipowner's premium reflects his limited liability; if he were to pay for the unlimited insurance of the classification society, the limitations of his liability would become pointless. As a result, the balance created by the Hague and the Hague-Visby Rules, as well as tonnage limitations, would be disturbed. Thirdly, there is a system of two insurers in existence which works and which is easier than a complex settlement system involving three parties.

---

434 *Per* Lord Llloyd, at 305.

435 *Henderson v. Merrett Syndicates Ltd.* (sub nom. *The Lloyd's Litigation*), [1994] 2 Lloyd's Rep. 468, at 489 and 493–495; [1994] 3 W.L.R. 761 (H.L.), at 773 D–H and 789C–791B.

436 *Hedley Byrne & Co. Ltd. v. Heller & Partners*, [1963] 2 All E.R. 575, [1964] A.C. 465 (H.L.). *See* also *Henderson v. Merrett Syndicates Ltd.* (sub nom. *The Lloyd's Litigation*), [1994] 2 Lloyd's Rep. 468; [1994] 3 W.L.R. 761 (H.L.); *White v. Jones*, [1995] 2 A.C. 207, [1995] 2 W.L.R. 187, [1995] 1 All E.R. 691 (H.L.).

437 *Marc Rich & Co. AG v. Bishop Rock Marine Co. Ltd.* (*and ClassNK*) (*"The Nicholas H."*), [1995] 2 Lloyd's Rep. 299 (H.L.), at 314, 317.

The dissenting opinion argues that whether or not classification societies pass on the costs for insurance is mere guess-work.[438] Also, it is uncertain whether or not classification societies do already insure; possibly no additional layer of insurance might be required.[439] According to the dissenting opinion the availability of insurance is irrelevant to the existence of a duty of care (and to its fairness, justice and reasonableness requirements)[440] although the dissenting opinion admits that this traditional view may have been gradually replaced. However, Lord Lloyd stated that if a court based its conclusions on the availability of insurance or the impact of imposing a fresh liability on the insurance market generally, these conclusions should be based on proper material and not mere guess-work.[441]

(4) Policy Considerations: the Role of Classification Societies

In the words of the leading opinion, classification societies are independent and non-profit-making entities created and operated for the sole purpose of promoting collective welfare, namely the safety of lives and ships at sea. They fulfil a role which in their absence would have to be fulfilled by States.[442] The dissenting opinion replies that the fact that they are charitable non-profit organisations does not alter their liability, as is the case with hospitals, for example.[443] Only a statutory exemption regulation can be relevant. The dissenting opinion cannot say anything against the fact that it is quite likely that classification societies would adopt a more defensive position if they owed a duty to a third party, as Lord Steyn points out.[444] Even more important, there is a danger that classification societies would no longer survey those vessels which most urgently required examination due to the risk of liability.[445]

(5) Policy Considerations: Regulations on the Limitation of Liability

The key argument of the leading opinion relates to the system of limitations of liability in shipping.[446] It cited the Court of Appeals, in which Lord Justice Saville stated:

> 'The Hague Rules (and their successor the Hague-Visby Rules) form an internationally recognized code adjusting the rights and duties existing between shipowners and those shipping goods under bills of lading. [...] The proposition by Mr Gross [plaintiff's representant] would add an identical or virtually identical duty owed by the classification

---

[438] At 305.

[439] At 308.

[440] Lord Lloyd at 308, citing Markesinis & Deakin, *Tort Law* (1994), 114.

[441] Lord Lloyd at 308, col. 2.

[442] *Marc Rich & Co. AG v. Bishop Rock Marine Co. Ltd. (and ClassNK) ("The Nicholas H.")*, [1995] 2 Lloyd's Rep. 299 (H.L.), at 316 col. 1 *per* Lord Steyn.

[443] At 308 col. 2.

[444] At 316 col. 1.

[445] At 316 col. 2.

[446] That this was the main argument has also been mentioned by Lord Justice Buxton, *Perrett v. Collins,* [1998] 2 Lloyd's Rep. 255 (C.A.), at 277.

society to that owed by the shipowners, but without any of these balancing factors, which are internationally recognised and accepted. I do not regard that as a just, fair or reasonable proposition.'[447]

'The question is not whether the classification society is covered by the [Hague] Rules, but whether in all the circumstances it is fair, just and reasonable to require them to shoulder a duty which by the Rules primarily lies on the shipowners, without the benefits of those Rules or other international conventions.'[448]

This argumentation is backed up by pointing out the effects of such duty of care on insurance and international trade. Lord Steyn argues that the limitation of liability of shipowners to cargo-owners would effectively be destroyed; shipowners are to be effectively protected from the costs of unlimited insurance. As otherwise such a duty of a classification society would disturb the balance of the system, the Law Lord argues that the international trade system tends to militate against the recognition of the claim in tort put forward by the cargo-owners against the classification society.[449]

Lord Lloyd counters this by submitting that the Hague Rules should only be considered if they apply to the parties.[450] In this case, they do not apply at all:

'With great respect, therefore, the 'intricate regime' of the Hague Rules to which all three Judges in the Court of Appeal referred has nothing to do with whether it is fair, just and reasonable that Mr. Ducat [the surveyor] and his employers should be liable to cargo for their assumed negligence. The irrelevance of the Hague Rules is underlined by the further consideration that the limitation provisions on which the shipowners relied to limit their liability, and which is said to contrast with the unlimited liability sought to be imposed on the N.K.K., is not derived from the Hague Rules at all, but from s. 503 of the Merchant Shipping Act, 1894, shortly to be re-enacted as s. 185 of and Schedule 7 to the Merchant Shipping Act, 1995.'

From his point of view, the balance of rights and liabilities between shipowners and cargo would not be upset by holding the classification society liable for its carelessness, as the Hague Rules had nothing to say on the issue of a duty of care towards classification societies.[451]

The Law Lord also identified the problem that the results would otherwise vary if the Hague Rules were either included in a contract of carriage or in a charter-

[447] *Marc Rich & Co. AG v. Bishop Rock Marine Co. Ltd.* (*and ClassNK*) (*"The Nicholas H."*), [1994] 1 Lloyd's Rep. 492 (C. A.), at 498 col. 2; [1995] 2 Lloyd's Rep. 299 (H.L.), at 314 col. 2.

[448] *Marc Rich & Co. AG v. Bishop Rock Marine Co. Ltd.* (*and ClassNK*) (*"The Nicholas H."*), [1994] 1 Lloyd's Rep. 492 (C. A.), at 499 col. 2; [1995] 2 Lloyd's Rep. 299 (H.L.), at 314 col. 2.

[449] At 315, col. 2.

[450] At 304.

[451] Lord Lloyd in *Marc Rich & Co. AG v. Bishop Rock Marine Co. Ltd.* (*and ClassNK*) (*"The Nicholas H."*), [1995] 2 Lloyd's Rep. 299 (H.L.), at 304 col. 2, 305 col. 1.

party. If they were only included in a charter-party, they could be irrelevant to the cargo-owner. Lord Lloyd considered this an unbearable solution:

> 'It would make nonsense of the law if a surveyor [...] owed duty of care towards cargo if the contract of carriage were contained in a charter-party, which does not incorporate the Hague Rules, but not if it were contained in a bill of lading which does.'[452]

Another argument of Lord Lloyd against this policy consideration is that in his view it has never before been acknowledged in similar cases. He cited case law regarding damage caused by a stevedore to cargo which fell under a bill of lading including the Hague Rules, where the stevedores were held liable, even though the shipowner could limit his liability and had the primary responsibility for discharging the cargo with due care.[453] He estimated that the position of a classification society was not different from that of a shipyard, which would be liable to an unlimited extent for damage to cargo on board caused by its negligence.[454]

Furthermore, if, in the view of Lord Lloyd, liability is limited, such protection must be granted by the legislator, not by judges. Citing the words of Lord Reid:

> 'I am bound to say that I have some sympathy with the respondents on the issue of limitation of liability. But a Court must go by the provisions which have been agreed and enacted. If the special position of salvors was unforeseen, then we must await alteration of those provisions if those concerned see fit to make some alteration.'[455]

(6) Conclusions

The main arguments are pointed out in the conclusions of both opinions. Lord Steyn concluded that

> 'the recognition of a duty would be unfair, unjust and unreasonable, as against the shipowners who would ultimately have to bear the costs of holding classification societies liable, such consequence being at variance with the bargain between shipowners and

---

452 *Marc Rich & Co. AG v. Bishop Rock Marine Co. Ltd.* (*and ClassNK*) (*"The Nicholas H."),* [1995] 2 Lloyd's Rep. 299 (H.L.), at 304 col. 2.

453 High Court of Australia in *Wilson v. Darling Island Stevedoring and Lighterage Co. Ltd.,* [1956] 1 Lloyd's Rep. 346 (H.C.(Aus.)).; *Midland Silicones Ltd. v. Scruttons Ltd.,* [1961] 2 Lloyd's Rep. 365; [1962] A.C. 446 (H.L.).

454 Lord Lloyd at 306 col. 2: 'How then does the position of a surveyor, called in by shipowners because the vessel is leaking, differ from that of the ship repairer? The answer is that it differs not at all. If it is fair, just and reasonable to hold a shiprepairer liable to an unlimited extent for damage to cargo on board caused by his negligence, even though the damage does not occur until after the vessel has sailed, why should it not be fair, just and reasonable in the case of a surveyor? Suppose in case of the inspection cover, the surveyor negligently tells the fitter that four bolts are sufficient to secure the cover, instead of the usual six, how could it be fair, just and reasonable that the surveyor should not be liable? On what principle would the fitter be liable in such circumstances, when he acts unadvised, but not the surveyor who advises him?'

455 *Bureau Wijsmuller N.V. v. Owners of the Tojo Maru (The "Tojo Maru"),* [1971] 1 Lloyd's Rep. 341 (H.L.), at 348; [1972] A.C. 242 (H.L.), at 270, *per* Lord Reid.

> cargo-owners based on an internationally agreed contractual structure. It would also be unfair, unjust and unreasonable towards classification societies, notably because they act for the collective welfare and unlike shipowners they would not have the benefit of any limitation provisions.'[456]

As regards cargo-owners, the leading opinion states that they may suffer a shortfall, which is already insurable under the existing system. Therefore 'lesser injustice was done by not recognizing a duty of care'.[457]

Lord Lloyd, on the other hand, argued that there were no special difficulties in this case. All it required was a straightforward application of the principles that had been articulated in *Donoghue v. Stevenson*.[458] And he expressed an important fear:

> 'Otherwise there is a risk that the law of negligence will disintegrate into a series of isolated decisions without any coherent principle at all, and the retreat from Anns [*Anns v. Merton London Borough Council*, [1978] A.C. 728] will turn into a rout.'[459]

cc. Case Comment

Despite the doctrine of *stare decisis*, scholarly research takes the liberty of commenting on and analysing the arguments that were presented by the court. The decision of the House of Lords is based, on the one hand, on reasonable reliance, which is a criterion that has been decisive in other cases, and, on the other hand, on policy considerations.

(1) Reasonable Reliance

In *Marc Rich*, there was no reliance of the victims on the statements made by the classification society. This criterion was therefore not of any guidance to the case. However, in a different context there may be such a direct exchange of a classification society with a third party. Even though the societies tend not to give information to third parties, such a case is at least theoretically possible. As a result of such *reliance*, the classification society would assume a duty of care towards the third party.[460] Even the leading opinion admits that such a possibility exists. Whether or not the injured party reasonably relied on the representations made by the classification society therefore needs to be analysed in any given case.

---

456 *Marc Rich & Co. AG v. Bishop Rock Marine Co. Ltd. (and ClassNK) ("The Nicholas H.")*, [1995] 2 Lloyd's Rep. 299 (H.L.), at 316–317, *per* Lord Steyn.

457 At. 317 col. 1.

458 *Donoghue v. Stevenson,* [1932] A.C. 562 (H.L.).

459 Lord Lloyd in *Marc Rich & Co. AG v. Bishop Rock Marine Co. Ltd. (and ClassNK) ("The Nicholas H.")*, [1995] 2 Lloyd's Rep. 299 (H.L.), at 309 col. 2.

460 *Hedley Byrne & Co. Ltd. v. Heller & Partners*, [1963] 2 All E.R. 575 (H.L.), [1964] A.C. 465 (H.L.). *See* also *Henderson v. Merrett Syndicates Ltd.* (sub nom. *The Lloyd's Litigation*), [1994] 2 Lloyd's Rep. 468 (H.L.), [1994] 3 W.L.R. 761 (H.L.); *White v. Jones*, [1995] 2 A.C. 207 (H.L.), [1995] 2 W.L.R. 187 (H.L.), [1995] 1 All E.R. 691 (H.L.); *Spring v. Guardian Assurance*, [1995] 2 A.C. 296 (H.L.), [1994] 3 W.L.R. 354 (H.L.), [1994] 3 All. E.R. 129 (H.L.).

(2) Policy Considerations

Even though one may be reluctant to accept policy considerations as a decisive factor for the law of torts, the notions of fairness, justice and reasonableness, that are preconditions for a duty of care under English law, essentially require such considerations. However, the reflections on insurance matters and on the role of classification societies of both Lord Steyn and Lord Lloyd should not be overestimated.

Insurance is not a decisive argument for several reasons. Classification societies already insure their risks. Of course, the premium would considerably change if the House of Lords affirmed a duty of care towards the cargo-owners.[461] Up until now, insurance companies have calculated the premium on a limited risk of litigation, as no classification society has yet been held liable towards a third party. Referring to insurance issues, the court seems to be of the opinion that the risk of loss or damage in the circumstances could not have been reduced; but there was a possibility.[462] Had the surveyor not been induced to change his mind, the vessel would not have sailed and no damage would have occurred. Insurance is the best method of distributing maritime risks.[463] However, the primary aim should be to minimise this risk rather than guess how a duty of a classification society towards cargo-owners might influence marine insurance.

Moreover, whether or not a classification society could pass on the costs of the insurance premium to the shipowner very much depends on the competition between classification societies as well as on the market for these services. As the member societies of IACS have a major position in this market, it is quite likely that they could pass on the costs, despite competing with one another.[464]

As for the argument that a third party would complicate the simple insurance system which is currently in existence, this argument appears to be irrelevant. One should make things as easy as possible, but not easier. If, for good reasons, the system is a complex one, there is no point in trying to simplify it.[465]

The reflections on the protection of the shipowner from the costs of insurance for an unlimited risk are based on the assumption that the shipowner shall not have to bear such costs. However, there is no hint in any international convention or national regulation and not even in their records that such a protection is the aim of

---

461 This is also pointed out by Honka, 'The Classification System', 19 *Tul. Mar. L. J.* 1 (1994), at 34.

462 France, 'Classification societies', 1 *Int.J.Ship.L.* 67 (1996) , at 70.

463 France, 'Classification societies', 1 *Int.J.Ship.L.* 67 (1996) , at 70.

464 However, despite a considerable increase in insurance premiums, surveying fees have not risen significantly within in past few years, *compare* Commission of the European Communities, Commission Working Document on the control of recognised organisations by the Commission, of 11 October 2006, COM(2006) 588 final, Annex at 3.6.

465 Similarly, France points out that the simplification of the settlement process hardly outweighs the incoherence which the reasoning of this judgment has introduced into maritime law (*ibid.*, at 72).

the contracting party or the legislator.[466] In brief, the dissenting opinion is not convincing in claiming that insurance is practically irrelevant to the question of a duty of care, as it is a question of fairness, justice and reasonableness. However, as has been pointed out before, insurance is not a criterion which should be attributed much importance to in this case.[467]

The same applies to the role of classification societies. The dissenting opinion remarks quite correctly that hospitals may be charitable non-profit organizations as well, but they can still be subject to liability. Either there are legal rules which protect classification societies in a way that they limit their liability or exempt the societies from liability at all, or there are not. With regard to classification societies, there are currently no such rules in existence,[468] so their role is of no concern. Lord Lloyd convincingly cited Lord Reid, who said that the establishment of limitation or exemption provisions is the duty of the lawmaker, not of the judge.[469]

The last and predominant line of argument of the leading opinion relates to the internationally established system of limitation provisions (like the Hague Rules or the LLMC). These arguments were the most important ones for their Lordships. However, there are several points which need to be made against the argumentation of the leading opinion as well as against the dissenting opinion.

To begin with the dissenting opinion, it makes some very strong remarks. At first, it criticises the fact that there are similar cases regarding stevedores, but that no-one has ever discussed an indirect effect of limitation provisions that exist with respect to shipowners. The same should therefore apply to classification societies. However, the decisions regarding stevedores cited by the dissenting opinion cannot be referred to as precedents, because in none of them was the duty of care at issue. All of these decisions are only related to the question of whether or not a contractual or statutory limitation or exemption provision could also be applied to a third party. This was answered in the negative. In those cases, considerations of fairness, justice and reasonableness were not yet considered to be relevant for the existence of a duty of care in cases of indirect infliction of economic loss.[470] Either

[466] This argument is further elaborated in Part 3 B I 1.

[467] Goldberg argues similarly that insurance should not be a decisive criterion as to whether or not liability is to be imposed, Goldberg, 'A Reexamination of Glanzer v. Shepard', 3 *Theoretical Inquries in Law*, 475 (2002), at 503.

[468] This will be further elaborated upon in Part 3 B I 1.

[469] Lord Lloyd at 308, col. 1.

[470] This precondition developed only after the decisions of *Smith v. Eric S. Bush,* [1990] 1 A.C. 831 (H.L.); *Van Oppen v. Clerk to the Bedford Charity Trustees*, [1990] 1 W.L.R. 235 (C.A.(Civ.Div.)), *per* Lord Justice Balcombe at 253 and Lord Justice Croom-Johnson at 265; *Caparo Industries Plc v. Dickman,* [1990] 2 A.C. 605, [1989] 2 W.L.R. 316(H.L.); *Spring v. Guardian Assurances plc.,* [1995] 2 A.C. 296 (H.L.); *Marc Rich & Co. AG v. Bishop Rock Marine Co. Ltd.* (*and ClassNK*) *("The Nicholas H."),* [1996] 1 A.C. 211, [1995] 2 Lloyd's Rep. 299 (H.L.). *See* Jackson & Powell, *On Negligence,* (1997), §§ 1–30 to 1–35.

the court answered the question of a duty of care in the affirmative[471] or the decision was only an interlocutory appeal limited to the application of the exemption clause to the stevedores as third parties to the contract.[472] Moreover, whether or not the stevedore owed a duty of care in tort to a third party and the precise definition of the preconditions of such a duty of care were of no relevance to all these decisions. In contrast, in *Marc Rich* the existence of a duty of care was the only question which mattered. The application of a contractual exemption clause to a third party was not at issue. The question of whether or not such an indirect application of an exemption or limitation provision would only arise after the existence of a duty of care has been affirmed.[473] For this reason, these decisions with regard to stevedores need to be distinguished.

As for the second criticism by Lord Lloyd, he stated that it would make 'nonsense of the law' if the existence of a duty of care depended on the contract in which the limitation clause was included. He thereby intends to say that similar cases are to be treated similarly. Nevertheless, one may wonder whether there is such a similarity. One could either add emphasis to the fact that in both cases the Hague Rules are of relevance or one may differentiate between the fact that in one case the Hague Rules protect the shipowner, whereas in others they do not. If one compares different cases, one always needs to bear in mind the premises of such a comparison. In this case, the differences seem to outweigh the similarities, because the Hague Rules are relevant for the definition of the carrier.

The holding of Lord Steyn can be criticised in several ways as well. Why should it be unfair for a classification society to be subject to unlimited liability[474] if at the same time they are expected to pass on the costs of insurance to the shipowners?[475] This appears to be a contradiction. Classification societies would only be in an awkward situation if it was impossible to insure such unlimited risks; but Lord Steyn does not argue in such a way.

Also, one may wonder why shipowners should be of any relevance to the case at all. At issue is whether it is fair, just and reasonable to impose a duty of care on the *classification society* towards the third party. This criticism is also included by Lord Steyn in his third line of argument, when he argued that the Hague Rules are

---

471 *Midland Silicones Ltd. v. Scruttons Ltd.*, [1961] 2 Lloyd's Rep. 365; [1962] A.C. 446 (H.L.); *Wilson v. Darling Island Stevedoring and Lighterage Co. Ltd.*, [1956] 1 Lloyd's Rep. 346 (H.C.(Aus.)).

472 *Adler v. Dickson,* [1954] 2 Lloyd's Rep. 267, [1955] 1 Q.B. 158 (C.A.).

473 However, one may argue that from a dogmatic point of view, the discussion of the effects of the limitation regulations should rather be carried out when analysing whether there are any exemption clauses in existence, as has been done in *Midland Silicones* and *Wilson v. Darling Island.*

474 At 317, col. 1.

475 At 316 col. 2.

irrelevant to third parties.[476] The House of Lords had to establish whether the relationship between the classification society and the third party is such that, in the circumstances of the case, a duty of care has to be imposed on the classification society. Solely the notion that the shipowner is *primarily responsible* for the safety of the vessel relates to the importance of the shipowner. It is, however, implicitly assumed that it would be unfair for the classification society to have to answer for something for which someone else is primarily responsible. But the leading opinion thereafter continues to treat the shipowner as if he were of relevance to the relationship between the classification society and the third party. As a consequence, this opinion twists and changes the argument, which intended to protect the classification society from a liability for which the shipowner has to answer, to the statement that the shipowner has to be protected from the costs of insurance for unlimited liability, even though he is not a party to the two-party relationship. In fact, this becomes the decisive argument of the *Marc Rich* decision. The liability imposed on the shipowner, however, should not be referred to when a duty of care of a classification society to cargo-owners is being discussed.[477] As a result, a duty of care might have to be considered fair, just and reasonable.

(3) Consequences: to Whom Are the Societies Liable?

Even though it is very tempting to apply the *Marc Rich* reasoning to all cases involving classification societies or even to all cases in which liability is limited for a primarily responsible person, the decision must be restricted on the facts to cases in which a classification society did not directly inflict physical loss but caused economic harm to another person in an indirect way. The term *indirect* depends on the fact that not the society but the shipowner is primarily responsible for the ship. Additionally, it only applies to cases in which the shipowner may limit his liability because of certain statutory limitation regulations.

Other cases may require different solutions. For instance, a direct contact between the classification society and the third party is likely to cause an assumption

[476] 'It follows that I cannot share the view of the Court of Appeal that the existence of a contract of carriage between the cargo-owners and the shipowners 'militates against' the liability of the surveyor in tort. To my mind the existence of the contract is as irrelevant as is the fact that in this particular case it happened to incorporate the Hague Rules.' (p. 306, col. 2, *per* Lord Lloyd). *Compare also* Cane, 'The Liability of classification societies', [1994] *L.M.C.L.Q.* 363, at 369, 373.

[477] One may already doubt whether the amount of financial liability incurred (in this case a theoretically unlimited one) may be of relevance to the question of a duty of care. This is rather a matter relevant to remedies than to the theory which allows compensation for damages at all.

of liability.[478] Whenever the facts are similar to a case which has been tried before, the reasoning of the leading case must be applied, as the doctrine of *stare decisis* states. Considerations of fairness, justice and reasonableness, which have to be considered in every new case, may then be irrelevant or decided in a different way.[479]

c. Reeman v. Department of Transport

aa. The Facts

The plaintiffs had bought a fishing vessel which carried a certificate from the Department of Transport (DOT) that certified that the vessel complied with various statutory regulations designed to ensure her seaworthiness.[480] The vessel had been built in Holland and surveyed by a DOT surveyor when she was brought to England by her seller. The surveyor made a negligent error when calculating the vessel's metacentric height, which led to the conclusion that she fulfilled the stability requirements, which in fact she did not. Subsequently, the DOT issued the statutory certificate, which was renewed at a later time. When the plaintiffs bought the vessel, she still had a valid certificate. A year after the purchase, the certificate had to be renewed, but when stability tests were carried out, the deficiencies of the vessel were discovered. The vessel's certificate was withdrawn, so that she could no longer put to sea. The plaintiffs suffered a financial disaster, as the vessel could not be modified at an economically sensible price to meet the DOT's minimum criteria.

bb. The Verdict

As the negligent act of the surveyor had occurred at a time when the plaintiffs were only third parties, they claimed against the DOT damages for breach of duty of care alleged to have been owed to them under the law of negligence. The approach of the House of Lords was the following, as Lord Justice Philips ascertained:

---

478 *Hedley Byrne & Co. Ltd. v. Heller & Partners*, [1963] 2 All E.R. 575 (H.L.), [1964] A.C. 465 (H.L.). *See* also *Henderson v. Merrett Syndicates Ltd.* (sub nom. *The Lloyd's Litigation*), [1994] 2 Lloyd's Rep. 468 (H.L.); [1994] 3 W.L.R. 761 (H.L.); *White v. Jones*, [1995] 2 A.C. 207 (H.L.), [1995] 2 W.L.R. 187 (H.L.), [1995] 1 All E.R. 691 (H.L.); *Spring v. Guardian Assurance*, [1995] 2 A.C. 296, [1994] 3 W.L.R. 354 (H.L.), [1994] 3 All. E.R. 129 (H.L.).

479 *Henderson v. Merrett Syndicates Ltd.* (sub nom. *The Lloyd's Litigation*), [1995] A.C. 145 (H.L.), at 181C–D. *See* also Jackson & Powell, *On Professional Negligence* (1997), § 1-41.

480 *Reeman and Another v. Department of Transport and Others,* [1997] 2 Lloyd's Rep. 648 (C.A.). For case comments *see* Burgin, 'Negligence–certification of fishing vessel by Department of Transport', 4 *Int.M.L.* 143 (1997); East, 'The Duty of Care in a Marine Context–Is There Someone to Blame?', in: Rose, *Lex Mercatoria* (2000), 129, at 152–154; Young, 'Classification Societies–a duty of care to buyers', 11 *P&I Int.* 254 (1997).

'When confronted with a novel situation, the Court does not, however, consider these matters [foreseeability, proximity of relationship and the question of whether it is fair, just and reasonable to impose a duty of care] in isolation. It does so by comparison with established categories of negligence to see whether the facts amount to no more than a small extension of a situation already covered by authority, or whether a finding of the existence of a duty of care would effect a significant extension of the law of negligence. Only in exceptional cases will the Court accept that the interests of justice justify such an extension of the law.'[481]

As the criterion of a reasonable foreseeability was not challenged by the DOT, the judgment concentrated on the issues of proximity and whether it would be fair, just and reasonable to impose such duty.[482] Future purchasers were not considered to form part of a class that was capable of definition and delimitation by identifiable characteristics; also, the certificate was not issued for the purpose of providing information to assist them in deciding whether or not to purchase the vessel; the alternative theory of an assumption of responsibility was therefore rejected.[483] Noteworthy is the following statement by Lord Bingham on the preconditions of the doctrine of voluntary assumption of responsibility:

'The cases show that before a plaintiff can recover compensation for financial loss caused by negligent mis-statement his claim must meet a number of conditions. Among these are three particularly relevant here. The statement (whether in the form of advice, and expression of opinion, a certificate or a factual statement) must be plaintiff-specific: that is, it must be given to the actual plaintiff or to a member of a group, identifiable at the time the statement is made, to which the actual plaintiff belongs. Secondly, the statement must be purpose-specific: the statement must be made for the very purpose for which the actual plaintiff has used it. Thirdly, and perhaps overlapping with the second condition, the statement must be transaction-specific: the statement must be made with reference to the very transaction into which the plaintiff has entered in reliance on it. If these conditions are met, it is necessary to turn to other conditions which the plaintiff must satisfy.'[484]

Turning to the precondition of a sufficient proximity, Lord Justice Philipps stated that if there was insufficient proximity of relationship to give rise to a duty of care in respect of death or injury to the skipper or crew of a certified vessel or in respect of economic loss directly caused to the owner of the vessel at the time of the certification, it was hard to imagine such proximity between the department and

---

481 *Per* Lord Justice Phillips, at 678, col. 1.

482 The knowledge by the DOT that the certificate would be communicated to others was considered not to be relevant for *proximity,* but for the *foreseeability*: 'So here knowledge by the department that the certificate and the statement in it would be communicated to a prospective purchaser specifically in connection with a transaction of a particular kind, viz. a purchase, and that a prospective purchaser such as the plaintiffs would be very likely to rely on the statement for the purposes of deciding whether or not to enter upon the purchase of the vessel should not have led the Judge to conclude that proximity was established' (at 684, col. 1, *per* Peter Gibson, L.J.).

483 At 684-685.

484 At 685, col. 2.

those who may rely on the existence of a certificate in relation to commercial transactions that anyway involve the risk of economic loss. As a proof that there was insufficient proximity in the first place, he relied on the one hand on *Murphy*, where it was expressly left open whether a local authority which had failed to take reasonable care to ensure compliance with building byelaws would be legally liable in respect of injury to persons resulting from such failure.[485] On the other hand, Lord Justice Philipps cited *Philcox v. Civil Aviation Authority,*[486] where it was similarly held that the Civil Aviation Authority's statutory duty to issue certificates of airworthiness involved no duty to the owner of the aircraft to exercise reasonable care to prevent him or his aircraft suffering injury as a result of taking off in an unairworthy condition. As the statutory framework in the *Reeman* case was one which was designed to promote safety at sea, these regulations do not intend to protect commercial interests, which may foreseeably be affected by the unseaworthiness of vessels.[487] *Proximity* only exists if the information given is being used for the same purpose for which it has been given. For this reason, it was absent in this case:

> 'When a British fishing vessel certificate is issued those who may in the future place reliance on that certificate when deciding whether to purchase the vessel do not form part of a class that is capable of definition and delimitation by identifiable characteristics.'[488]

Even though it was held that there was not a sufficient *proximity* for a duty of care, the judges also made some statements regarding the question of whether it would be fair, just and reasonable to impose such a duty. This was also rejected for three different reasons. First, such a duty would go further than the duty of a shipbuilder, who does not owe a duty towards subsequent purchasers of a yacht.[489] Secondly, an alternative remedy was possible. The purchaser could, *inter alia*, have the vessel surveyed or demand contractual warranties, which provide protection against the risk that the DOT certificate does not reflect the true condition of the vessel.[490] Thirdly, as it was held in *The Morning Watch* and in *Marc Rich* that classification societies did not owe a duty of care to the purchasers of a vessel or the owners of the cargo, as their purpose was furthering safety at sea rather than protecting commercial interests, it would neither be fair, just nor reasonable to impose a duty on the DOT, which carried out a similar task.[491]

---

485 In *Murphy v. Brentwood District Council*, [1990] 2 Lloyd's Rep. 467, [1991] 1 A.C. 398 (H.L.), *per* Lord Mackay at 470, 457 and Lord Keith at 474, 463.

486 *Philcox v. Civil Aviation Authority,* [1995] *The Times* 8 June 1995 (C.A.(Civ.Div.)), Transcript No. 821 of 1995, CA.

487 At 680, col. 2.

488 At 681, col. 1.

489 At 682, col. 2.

490 At 683, col. 1.

491 *Per* Lord Phillips, at 683, col. 1; Lord Bingham, at 685, col. 1.

cc. Case Comment

A distinct feature of the *Reeman* case is that it relates to public duties. Since in English law there is no special law of governmental liability, the ordinary rules of tort law apply.[492]

Reeman mainly refers to *Marc Rich*, even though from the point of view of the facts *The Morning Watch* would have been more similar. As it was an economic loss which had been caused indirectly, the reference to *Marc Rich* was, however, appropriate. The decision neither analyses nor directly applies the *Marc Rich* reasoning. There are no remarks on whether the loss was caused directly or indirectly, which is of relevance according to *Marc Rich*. The Court rather cited whether a duty of care was owed according to *Marc Rich*, then analysed the reasons why this duty of care was being imposed. It is therefore disappointing that the Court merely tries to apply *Marc Rich* and *The Morning Watch* in an analogous way, despite the fact that the main issue of *Reeman* was whether there was a sufficient *proximity*. In *Marc Rich*, by contrast, the sole issue was whether a duty of care would be fair, just and reasonable. The Court in *Reeman* expressly states that its reasoning merely extends to economic loss caused by misstatements. Its scope of application is, therefore, limited to this question.[493]

The first point of criticism is that the criterion of foreseeability is being phrased in a way that is too narrow. Even though it is absolutely correct that the courts phrase it in a way that it must be foreseeable which group of persons will be protected by the duty of care in order to provide some kind of delimitation of the liability and a foreseeability of the possible damages, this understanding appears to be too narrow in cases of the purchase of a vessel. If the damage is solely transferred from one person (the first purchaser and contracting party) to another, and this other person suffers from the same damage as the first person would have, there is no good reason why the second person should not be protected. This would not prove to be a kind of unlimited extension of liability towards an unlimited number of persons, but simply the occurrence of a similar damage not to the person where it was expected in the first place, but suffered by a second person.

Secondly, an argument has to be criticised that is solely made *obiter*. It is assumed that the DOT does not owe a duty of care in respect of death or injury to the skipper or the crew of a certified vessel. However, the cases referred to do not expressly say so or they solely relate to a duty of care towards the owner of an aircraft to prevent him from injuring himself (*Philcox*). Even though Lord Justice Phillips says that 'I consider it at least arguable that no duty of care is owed to the owner of a vessel in relation to the process of survey and certification,'[494] he con-

---

[492] *See* Eörsi, 'Governmental Liability in Tort', *Int.Enc.Comp.L.* XI-4, § 4-169, 4-173. Crown Proceedings Act, 1947, 10 & 11 Geo. 6, c. 44.

[493] 'It can readily be seen that negligence causing loss not connected with nor flowing from physical damage to property or person gives rise to problems of scope', at 683, col. 2. As a consequence, one can argue that there are no such problems when other damage is incurred.

[494] At 679, col. 2.

tinues as if such a duty was definitely not in existence, neither to the shipowner, nor to the crew:

> 'The relevance of these considerations is simply that, if there is insufficient proximity of relationship to give rise to a duty of care in respect of death or injury to the skipper or crew of a certificated vessel or in respect of economic loss directly caused to the owner of the vessel at the time of the certification, it is hard to accept that such proximity exists between the department and those who may rely on the existence of a certificate in relation to commercial transactions that involve the risk of economic loss.'[495]

As will be seen in *Perret v. Collins*, this is an unconvincing statement. The decision in *Reeman* seems to be led by the aim to protect the DOT from claims, and therefore should be strictly limited to its facts.

d. Perrett v. Collins and Others

aa. The Facts

The first defendant, Mr. *Collins*, purchased a kit aircraft and assembled it.[496] He changed the type B gearbox for a type C gearbox, which was said to give a better performance. However, he did not change the propeller for the one which was furnished with the alternative gearbox. The second defendant inspected the aircraft on behalf of the third defendants, the *Popular Flying Association (PFA)*, and issued certain documents required to obtain a certificate of airworthiness, and a certificate for fitness for flight, valid for one month. The second defendant knew and approved of the change of the gearbox. He did not object to the fact that the propeller was not exchanged. The inspector provided the certificate which authorised Mr. *Collins* to take the aircraft on test flights with one passenger on board. On the second test flight, the aircraft went out of control and hit the ground, with the result that the plaintiff, who was a passenger at that time, was injured. The plaintiff sued for personal injuries which were caused by the negligence of one or more of the defendants. At the time of the flight, he did not have any knowledge of how it had come about that the aircraft had been certified fit to fly. The preliminary issue for decision was restricted to whether the second or the third defendants owed a duty of care in tort to the plaintiff.

bb. The Verdict

The Court of Appeals distinguished this case from *Marc Rich* and held that in cases of personal injuries, considerations of fairness, justice and reasonableness did not matter, as they only applied to cases of indirectly inflicted economic loss. The damage was considered to be foreseeable; if the second and third defendants granted such a certificate, an accident was quite likely to occur. They ought rea-

---

495 *Ibid.*

496 *Perrett v. Collins,* [1998] 2 Lloyd's Rep. 255 (C.A.). For case comments *see* Brodie, 'The negligence liability of public authorities: a traditional solution', [1999] *L.M.C.L.Q.* 16; East, 'The Duty of Care in a Marine Context–Is There Someone to Blame?', in: Rose, *Lex Mercatoria* (2000), 129, at 154–155; Witting, 'Negligent Inspectors and Flying Machines', 59 *Cambridge L.J.* 544 (2000).

sonably to have had in mind that a passenger on the test flight might be affected in the way the plaintiff was affected. The surveyor was considered to execute a role which was not subsidiary to the one of the constructor of the aircraft. He had an independent and critical role in granting a certificate, without which the aircraft could not take off.[497]

Personal loss is considered to be the basic concept on which the law of negligence is founded. The Court argues for this reason that the difficulties which arise when an economic loss occurs are not relevant to such a case. Nonetheless, the three judges slightly differ in their approach to the case. Lord Justice Hobhouse chooses to take an approach which is based on whether or not there are authorities which regulate the case or which are comparable rather than applying the criteria of foreseeability, proximity and whether it is fair, just and reasonable to impose such a duty:[498]

> 'Thus where a case fits into a category where the existence of a duty of care and a potential liability in the tort of negligence has already been recognized, the more elusive criteria to which Lord Bridge [in *Caparo Industries Plc. v. Dickman,* [1990] 2 A.C. 605, at pp. 617-618] referred for dealing with the cases that go beyond the recognized category of proximity do not arise.'[499]

Lord Justice Swinton Thomas seems to accept that fairness, justice and reasonableness is a precondition on its own, but argues that in this case it is not of importance:

> 'One must consider the question of proximity and 'fair, just and reasonable' in the context of the case under consideration but on the facts of a case such as this the two can conveniently be considered together. [...] Accordingly, in this case, I prefer to consider

---

[497] *Perrett v. Collins,* [1998] 2 Lloyd's Rep. 255 (C.A.), at 259, col. 2.

[498] 'The over-arching formula does not affect the outcome. Established categories, with or without the assistance of 'common sense and justice', provide the answer. The certainty provided by the previous authorities is not undermined. Indeed it would be surprising if Lord Steyn had, by his decision of what he described a *novel* question relating to property or economic interests, intended to depart from or call into question established decisions and principles relating to personal injury. It is a truism to say that any case must be decided taking into account the circumstances of the case, but where those circumstances comply with established categories of liability, a defendant should not be allowed to seek to escape from liability by appealing to some vaguer concept of justice or fairness; *the law cannot be re-made for every case.* Indeed, the previous authorities have by necessary implication held that it is fair, just and reasonable that the plaintiff should recover in the situations falling within the principles they have applied. Accordingly, if the present case is covered by the decisions in or the principles recognized by previous authorities–and it is–*Marc Rich* does not require us to depart from them; indeed, we remain bound to follow them.' (at 263, col. 2, *per* Hobhouse, L.J., emphasis added.)

[499] *Perrett v. Collins,* [1998] 2 Lloyd's Rep. 255 (C.A.), at 261, col. 1.

> the questions of 'proximity' and whether it is 'fair, just and reasonable' to impose a liability on the second and third defendants together.'[500]

Lord Justice Buxton is apparently the only one who applies *Marc Rich* phrase by phrase, as he first ascertains in which way the loss was caused. Since he held that it was an indirectly caused loss, he made reference to all of the preconditions. The statement of Lord Oliver in *Murphy v. Brentwood District Council* only related to direct infliction of physical injury:

> 'In the straightforward case of direct infliction of physical injury by the act of the plaintiff there is, indeed, no need to look beyond the foreseeability by the defendant of the result in order to establish that he is in a 'proximate' relationship with the plaintiff. [...] The infliction of physical injury to the person or property of another universally requires to be justified.'[501]

According to Lord Justice Buxton, the most important differentiation consequently has to be made not between economic loss and personal injury, but between direct and indirect infliction of loss.[502] The definition of *directness* remains a very difficult issue:

> 'That notion is difficult to define, and is not defined in the cases that employ it; but at least one consideration seems to be that damage may be held not to be 'direct' if it is inflicted by an act of the tortfeasor that produces the damage without other human intervention.'[503]

Marc Rich has shown that cases in which a classification society did not directly inflict harm upon someone else, such as in the example of the lighted cigarette which is thrown into a cargo hold with combustible cargo thereby causing an explosion, any kind of injury is caused in an indirect way, due to the primary responsibility of the shipowner.

In *Perret v. Collins,* there was no such primary responsibility of the constructor.[504] There is no provision which is similar to the Hague Rules. As the third defendant, the PFA, was very closely involved in organisational terms with the constructor of the aircraft, Lord Justice Buxton considered it to be a directly inflicted harm.[505] Nonetheless, he added that even if the loss were considered to be indirect, the preconditions of a duty of care would be satisfied.

---

500 *Per* Swinton Thomas, L.J., at 268, col. 2.

501 *Murphy v. Brentwood District Council,* [1990] 2 Lloyd's Rep. 467, at 488, col. 2– 489, col. 1; [1991] A.C. 398 (H.L.), at 486H–487B.

502 '[...]where the physical damage is deemed to be indirect, the questions of proximity, justice, fairness and reasonableness remain wholly in issue and to be established by the plaintiff' (at 273, col. 2.)

503 *Per* Lord Justice Buxton, at 273, col. 2.

504 Lord Justice Hobhouse argued similarly at 259, col. 2: 'The role of the inspector is distinct and is independent of the role of the constructor. It is not secondary or ancillary to that of the constructor, although each has a responsibility for the safety and airworthiness of the aircraft.'

505 At 274, col. 2.

All three of the judges therefore focus on authorities of a direct infliction of loss. Only as an additional justification is reference made to considerations of fairness, justice and reasonableness.

The preconditions of *foreseeability* and *proximity*, which are relevant to cases of personal injury,[506] were satisfied according to the judges. Since the claim against the surveyor might be the injured person's sole remedy, matters of insurance could not be of any interest:

> 'It was thus argued, by analogy from the Marc Rich case, that there is no need or warrant to put another defendant into the loop because the injured party's right are adequately addressed by having regard to the liability of the constructor and the insurance carried by him. Whatever may have been the merits or demerits of that argument in the context of the Marc Rich case, they do not apply to the present case. An injured passenger's sole remedy may be against the person who has certified the aircraft fit to fly. The denial of a duty of care owed by such person in relation to the safety of the aircraft towards those who may suffer personal injuries, whether as passengers in the aircraft or upon the ground, would leave a gap in the law of tort notwithstanding that a plaintiff has suffered foreseeable personal injury as a result of the unsafety of the aircraft and the unreasonable and careless conduct of the defendant. It would be remarkable if that were the law.'[507]

Here, the regulations intend to improve safety in air transport, and therefore aim at the protection of passengers as well. From that point of view, *Philcox* could be distinguished as well, in which damages were claimed for an economic loss which is not protected by the relevant safety regulations.

As a result, it is held to be irrelevant what form the conduct takes: it may just as well occur in the form of a misstatement. Whenever proximity has been established, it ceases to be material what form the unreasonable conduct takes.[508]

cc. Case Comment: Fairness, Justice and Reasonableness to be Considered?

First, from a dogmatic point of view, the three dicta of their Lordships are somewhat inconsistent, as all three judges appear to emphasise different aspects. In brief, it emerges that in cases where there are no comparable precedents, it first has to be established whether the loss has been caused directly or indirectly. The notion of *directness* is quite difficult to define and several different aspects have to be taken into consideration. If the harm is caused in a direct way, precedents such as *Murphy v. Brentwood District Council* apply. As a result, only foreseeability

---

506 At 261, col. 2: 'In cases of personal injury, it suffices that the activity of the defendant has given rise to the situation which has caused the injury to the plaintiff. Where the defendant is involved in an activity which, if he is not careful, will create a foreseeable risk of personal injury to others, the defendant owes a duty of care to those others to act reasonably having regard to the existence of that risk. The limiting factors are the concepts of foreseeability and reasonableness (*e.g. Woods v. Duncan,* [1946] A.C. 401 [(H.L.)]).'

507 At 259, col. 2; 260, col. 1, *per* Hobhouse, L.J.

508 *Per* Hobhouse, L.J., at 262, col. 2.

and proximity is relevant. Otherwise, *Marc Rich* has to be applied whatever damage has occurred, resulting in the necessity of an additional criterion of fairness, justice and reasonableness. It was not the intention of the judges in *Marc Rich* to further advance the law of negligence in a way that fairness, justice and reasonableness has to be applied to all cases; existing precedents which do not relate to indirect loss are not altered. As a result, there already is a disintegration of the law of negligence into several small islands. This result can be illustrated by referring to several other decisions:

> '*Marc Rich* should not be regarded as an authority which has a relevance to cases of personal injuries or as adding any requirement that an injured plaintiff do more than bring his case within established principles. If a plaintiff is attempting to establish some novel principle of liability, then the situation would be different and the considerations discussed by Lord Steyn could be relevant.'[509]

> 'It follows that, once the case is identified as falling within the *Hedley Byrne* principle, there should be no need to embark upon any further enquiry whether it is 'fair, just and reasonable' to impose liability for economic loss – a point which is, I consider, of some importance in the present case.'[510]

> 'In the straightforward case of the direct infliction of physical injury by the act of the plaintiff there is, indeed, no need to look beyond the foreseeability by the defendant of the result in order to establish that he is in a 'proximate' relationship with the plaintiff [...] The infliction of physical injury to the person or property of another universally requires to be justified. [...] The causing of economic loss does not.'[511]

Secondly, *Reeman* is cited incorrectly by Lord Justice Swinton Thomas.[512] Lord Justice Phillips said exactly the opposite of what Lord Justice Swinton Thomas alleged, as Lord Justice Phillips rejected liability for personal injury. The following citation is therefore incorrect and should not be referred to:

> '[H]e rejected the argument that it was proper to reason from a liability of the department for loss of life or personal injury to those sailing on board an unsafe and negligently certified vessel to a conclusion that there was a liability to the owners for economic loss. His reasoning therefore confirms and supports the reasoning which I have developed in this judgment.'

Thirdly, *Marc Rich* depended on its own facts, as the shipowner was primarily responsible for the vessel sailing in a seaworthy condition and the role of the classification society was considered to be a subsidiary one; the system of limitations on which the insurance of international trade depends is a very distinct system as

---

509 Lord Justice Hobhouse in *Perrett v. Collins,* [1998] 2 Lloyd's Rep. 255 (C.A.), at 264, col. 2.

510 *Henderson v. Merrett Syndicates Ltd.* (sub nom. *The Lloyd's Litigation*), [1994] 2 568 Lloyd's Rep. 468; [1994] 3 W.L.R. 761 (H.L.), *per* Lord Goff.

511 Lord Oliver of Aylmerton in *Murphy v. Brentwood District Council,* [1990] 2 Lloyd's Rep. 467 at 488–489; [1991] A.C. 398 (H.L.), at 486H–487B.

512 At 265, col. 2.

well. However, the system already differs if one refers to statutory surveys, as there is no such system of double insurance. The question therefore remains how statutory surveys by classification societies are to be treated, and whether the *Perret* reasoning can be applied by analogy. One might argue that the shipowner is primarily responsible for his ship. Even so, in *Marc Rich* this kind of responsibility was established in view of the Hague Rules. Therefore, a different solution might apply with regard to the statutory provisions enacted to improve maritime safety. It can be argued that a classification society owes a duty of care to those persons whose life or health may be affected. The statement in *Philcox v. Civil Aviation Authority* is therefore somewhat similar:

> 'It is clear, to my mind, that the risk which the scheme of the legislation is designed to prevent is the risk that the owner or operator of an aircraft will fly the aircraft even when it is unfit to fly and that the persons for whose protection the scheme has been established are the passengers, the cargo owners, and other members of the public likely to be harmed if an aircraft is allowed to fly.
> The owners and operators of the aircraft are not within the class of persons for whose protection the scheme has been established; they are the persons against whose imprudent activities the scheme is designed to protect the public. They are not entitled to rely on the issue of the certificate to exonerate them from their own responsibilities to ensure the aircraft are fit to fly.'[513]

The same kind of protection is required in shipping. Furthermore, it does not make a difference to this question whether or not the shipowner has the means to ensure the safety of his vessel, a differentiation made in *Perret v. Collins* with regard to the question of a primary responsibility of the constructor of a kit aircraft. It is also not apparent why such differentiation should matter to third parties at all. The crew and the passengers, in addition to other parties of maritime trade, have to be protected from an irresponsible shipowner. It is therefore true in shipping just as well as in air transport that 'a passenger about to be taken up in an aircraft is entitled to assume that it has met the applicable safety requirements and that those involved have taken proper care, and to rely upon it.'[514]

e. Conclusion: Marc Rich Reasoning to be Applied to All Cases?

To sum up, *Marc Rich* has to be directly applied to all cases of cargo-owners who sue a classification society due to a negligent classification, whether or not the cargo was aboard at the time of the survey. Additionally, the liability of the shipowner has to be limited by statutory regulations.

Whenever a novel case has to be decided, strict adherence is to be paid to the principle that one primarily has to ascertain whether the loss has been caused in a direct or an indirect way. Even if a classification society is sued, this does not imply automatically that *Marc Rich* is to be applied, since this reasoning is limited to

---

513 *Philcox v. Civil Aviation Authority* ([1995] *The Times* 8 June 1995 (C.A.(Civ.Div.)), Transcript No. 821 of 1995, CA.) *per* Lord Justice Millet at 17, as cited *per* Swinton Thomas, L.J., *Perrett v. Collins,* [1998] 2 Lloyd's Rep. 255 (C.A.), at 271, col. 1.

514 *Perrett v. Collins,* [1998] 2 Lloyd's Rep. 255 (C.A.), at 264, col. 2.

cases of indirectly caused economic loss by the cargo-owners. The duty of care is subject to the directness and the kind of damage.

The first question is, therefore, whether it was a rare act in which a surveyor acted and thereby caused a physical loss without any further causative acts. Such is the example of the cigarette which is thrown by a surveyor in combustible cargo, thereby causing an explosion. No doubt, a duty of care is evident in such a case and does not require any discussion.

Whenever the damage is caused by the issuance of a certificate or other kind of expert opinion, the situation is more complex. In such a case, the duty of care depends on whether or not this act may be labelled as *directly* or *indirectly* causing the loss. The notion of *directness* depends on the relationship between the shipowner and the classification society. If the shipowner is primarily responsible for the vessel, the damage has been caused in an *indirect* way (as in *Marc Rich*). In such cases of indirect infliction, *Marc Rich* applies and there exists a duty only if the criteria of *foreseeability*, *proximity* and *fairness*, *justice and reasonableness* are satisfied. With regard to purchasers of a vessel, *The Morning Watch* is the relevant precedent. Whether or not *Marc Rich* can be extended to all cases in which there are limitation provisions in favour of the shipowner appears to be doubtful. On the one hand, the argumentation seems to point to such a conclusion, especially since the House of Lords differed on whether the limitations were actually included in the Hague Rules or the Merchant Shipping Act. On the other hand, such considerations relating to costs for limited or unlimited liability for economic loss are not likely to be extended to cases of personal loss, for example to crew or passengers. Even though there are limitation provisions in existence as well, such a case is likely to be distinguished because of the kind of injury:

> 'However, when one turns to the judgmental issues of justice, fairness, and reasonableness the importance of fact that what is put at risk is the plaintiff's body, and not just his goods, is, as Lord Justice Hobhouse has demonstrated, deeply embedded in the law of negligence.'[515]

It is therefore highly probable that even if limitation provisions exist in favour of the shipowner regarding the crew and the passengers, it is considered *fair*, *just* and *reasonable* that the classification society owes a duty of care towards them. Of course, in such a case it would first have to be ascertained whether on the basis of the facts it was *foreseeable* that the crew and the passengers sustained such a loss, and whether there was a sufficient degree of *proximity*. Especially the *proximity of relationship* will be very difficult to prove by a passenger.

In all cases of an indirect loss other than economic loss, the damage is likely to be *foreseeable* and proximate, according to *Perret v. Collins*. Loss in property is economic loss according to *Marc Rich*. The threefold criterion is irrelevant in such a case, and a duty of care most likely exists. *Perret v. Collins* therefore only applies to cases of personal injury or loss of life. However, in such a case it needs to

---

[515] *Perrett v. Collins,* [1998] 2 Lloyd's Rep. 255 (C.A.), *per* Lord Justice Buxton, at 275, col. 1.

be scrutinised whether an act of the classification society caused the personal injury or loss of life or contributed to it. It is not the classification society that is responsible for the vessel, but the shipowner. The classification society only controls the vessel and does not thereby assume any responsibility for it. If the society, however, makes certain recommendations, *e.g.* as regards repairs to the ship, requires that modifications of the vessel be carried out, defines its rules in a certain way which does not guarantee the safety of the vessel contrary to current know-how in marine engineering, its act may be part of the chain of causation, and it may be under a duty of care towards third parties.

An alternative theory in cases of direct contact of the classification society with the injured party is offered by the doctrine of *voluntary assumption of responsibility*. According to this doctrine, a duty of care may exist for economic loss as well.[516] It must be a situation equivalent to contract, and the advice must be, as held in *Reeman*,

> 'plaintiff-specific: that is, it must be given to the actual plaintiff or to a member of a group, identifiable at the time the statement is made, to which the actual plaintiff belongs. Secondly, the statement must be purpose-specific: the statement must be made for the very purpose for which the actual plaintiff has used it. Thirdly, and perhaps overlapping with the second condition, the statement must be transaction-specific: the statement must be made with reference to the very transaction into which the plaintiff has entered in reliance on it.'[517]

However, only in very rare cases will a classification society directly provide information to a third party which can be identified as being plaintiff-, purpose- and transaction-specific.

3. Tort of Deceit

In some rare cases a classification society may be held liable for *deceit*. This nominate tort, which is sometimes called *conversion* or *fraud*, has been developed by the leading cases *Pasley v. Freeman*[518] and *Derry v. Peek*[519]. Five preconditions need to be satisfied:[520] there has to be a false representation of fact by the defendant;[521] the defendant needs to know that it is untrue or has no belief in its truth or is reckless as to its truth; the defendant intends that the plaintiff should act in reliance on the representation; the plaintiff in fact does so; and thereby he sustains a loss. The advantages for the plaintiff in suing for fraud is that there is no need to

---

516 *Reeman and Another v. Department of Transport and Others,* [1997] 2 Lloyd's Rep. 648 (C.A.), at 684, col. 2.

517 *Reeman and Another v. Department of Transport and Others,* [1997] 2 Lloyd's Rep. 648 (C.A.), at 685, col. 2.

518 *Pasley v. Freeman*, (1789) 3 *T.R.* 51.

519 *Derry v. Peek*, [1889] 14 App.Cas. 337, 61 L. T. Rep. N. S. 265 (H.L.).

520 *See* Clerk & Lindsell, *On Torts* (2006), § 18–01 *et seq.*

521 A statement of opinion is always a statement of fact to the extent that it is an assertion that the maker does in fact hold that opinion, *per* Lord Evershed M.R. in *Brown v. Raphael,* [1958] Ch. 636 (C.A.), at 641.

show a special relationship, contributory negligence is not applicable, the damages are likely to be higher and it takes a longer period of time before the claim is statute-barred.[522] Only briefly shall it be mentioned that a principal is vicariously liable for a false statement of his agent made in the course of his employment.[523] The representation must be made in one way or the other to the plaintiff in order to induce him to act upon it. This does not require that the plaintiff is clearly identified:

> 'In order to enable a person injured by a false representation to sue for damages, it is not necessary that the representation should be made to the plaintiff directly; it is sufficient if the representation is made to a third person to be communicated to the plaintiff, or to be communicated to a class of persons of whom the plaintiff is one, or even if it is made to the public generally, with a view to its being acted on, and the plaintiff as one of the public acts on it and suffers damage thereby.'[524]

However, there needs to be an actual intention to deceive the claimant or the class to which the claimant belongs.[525] The practical test to identify whether the defendant had in interest is whether it was in the defendant's interest that the plaintiff should act so.

Section 2 (1) of the Misrepresentation Act 1967 extends the tort of deceit to cases in which fraud cannot be proved.[526] Since this provision only relates to a misrepresentation by a party of the disadvantageous contract that was being influenced,[527] it does not apply to classification societies. In brief, only on very rare occasions may a classification society be liable for the tort of deceit, as the following examples illustrate.

---

[522] Limitation Act 1980, s. 32(1): 'Where the action is based upon the fraud of the defendant [...] the period of limitation shall not begin to run until the plaintiff has discovered the fraud [...] or could with reasonable diligence have discovered it.'

[523] *Lloyd v. Grace, Smith and Co.*, [1912] A.C. 712 (H.L.), at 732–738; *Briess v. Woolley*, [1954] A.C. 333 (H.L.); *United Africa Co. v. Saka Owoade Ltd*, [1955] A.C. 130 (P.C.); *Credit Lyonnais Nederland NV (Now known as Generale Bank Nederland NV) v. Export Credits Guarantee Department*, [2000] 1 A.C. 486 (H.L.).

[524] *Per* Justice Quain in *Swift v. Winterbotham,* (1873) L.R. 8 Q.B. 244 (Q.B.), at 253; approved by Justice Blackburn in *Richardson v. Silvester,* (1873) L.R. 9 Q.B. 34 (Q.B.), at 36; *see also Gross v. Lewis Hillman*, [1970] Ch. 445 (C.A.).

[525] Clerk & Lindsell, *On Torts* (2006), § 18–29.

[526] 'Where a person has entered into a contract after a misrepresentation has been made to him by another party thereto and as a result thereof he has suffered loss, then, if the person making the representation would be liable to damages in respect thereof had the misrepresentation been made fraudulently, that person shall be so liable notwithstanding that the misrepresentation was not made fraudulently, unless he proves that he had reasonable ground to believe and did believe up to the time the contract was made that the facts represented were true.' *See* Clerk & Lindsell, *On Torts* (2006), § 18–02.

[527] *Resolute Maritime v. Nippon Karji Kyokai,* [1983] 1 Lloyd's Rep. 431 (Q.B.), *per* Mustill J.

a. Braginton v. Chapman and Others (The "Midas")

The plaintiff, the current owner of the vessel *Midas*, sued the trustees of Lloyd's Register of British and Foreign Ships (which was hereafter named LR) for the loss he sustained due to defects in the vessel which were discovered after the plaintiff had purchased it.[528] The plaintiff argued that he had relied on the statement contained in the certificate by LR as to the condition of the vessel. The classification contract was concluded between LR and the former owner who had sold the vessel. The plaintiff was not a subscriber to the Register Book, which was handed out only on subscription at that time. It was admitted for the purpose of the case that the survey had been carried out negligently, and that, but for such negligence, the defects in the vessel would have been discovered and the plaintiff saved from the loss he sustained. The sole question was whether the plaintiff was entitled to recover on the facts of the case.

The court held there was no contract, as the plaintiff had not contracted with LR, and the consultation of the certificate evidently did not suffice for the conclusion of a contract. At that time, the tort of negligence had not been developed.[529] The plaintiff could only base his case on fraudulent misrepresentation, which could not be proven, as LR had no intention to deceive. Judgment was therefore ordered for the defendants.

b. Thiodon v. Tindall (The "Ibex")

The plaintiff bought the sailing yacht *Ibex* from the then owner, who had contracted with LR for the classification of the yacht.[530] The classification certificate gave the information that the yacht had been built of materials ten and twelve years old and under special survey of LR, whereas in truth it was neither of the said material nor built under special survey. The condition of the yacht was unknown to the plaintiff and it could not be discovered by the use of ordinary care and means. The plaintiff allegedly paid a much higher price than he would otherwise have done, and had to pay great amounts of money for repairing her and putting her in a condition to be registered. The plaintiff had neither subscribed to the Register Book nor was he a member of the Society.

J.P. Aspinall, Q.C., gave a noteworthy statement for the plaintiff, which perfectly sums up the common-sense approach for which a classification society should be held liable:

> 'That principle, however, does not apply, but I base my claim upon this ground, that the defendants have taken upon themselves a duty to the public, that is, to the ship-buying public, have undertaken a duty which they have negligently performed, and for the negligent performance of that duty they are liable in damages to any person who buys a

---

[528] *Braginton v. Chapman and Others (Trustees of Lloyd's Register of Shipping) (The "Midas"),* [1878] 7 Asp. 77 (Q.B.).

[529] As has been said before, the first authority in which the tort of negligence was discussed as being a distinctive tort is *Donoghue v. Stevenson,* [1932] A.C. 562 (H.L.).

[530] *Thiodon v. Tindall and Others (the Committee of Lloyd's Register) (The "Ibex"),* [1891] 7 Asp. 76 (Q.B.).

> ship upon the faith of their representation as to the classification and character of that ship. The defendants are bound by the act of their servants or officers in making that survey and classification, and a breach of duty by such servants or officers is a breach of duty by the defendants themselves, for which the defendants would be liable.'[531]

The High Court of Justice nonetheless applied *Braginton v. Chapman*, because in its view *Thiodon v. Tindall* was not to be distinguished from it. A claim could only be based on deceit as had been established by the House of Lords in *Derry v. Peek*.[532] As there was neither a contract nor deceit, the claim was dismissed.

4. The Effect of Disclaimers of Liability

As regards clauses that seek to limit the liability of classification societies, the situation of third parties differs from those of contracting parties. By reason of the doctrine of privity of contract, an exemption clause contained in the classification contract will not be binding upon third parties.[533] It is a common law principle that two persons cannot contractually extend the effect of an exemption clause to a third party.[534] However, the situation differs if the third party is awarded a contractual right pursuant to the Contracts (Rights of Third Parties) Act 1999. In this situation, if such a right is contractually limited, the doctrine of privity of contract is not influenced, as only the extent of the right may be limited.

Notwithstanding this, the courts have accepted disclaimers of liability in cases in which advice was handed over to third parties. In *Smith v. Eric S. Bush*, the House of Lords held that the Unfair Contract Terms Act 1977 even applies to cases of duty of care in tort if the relationship of the parties is such that a duty of care would be found "but for" the disclaimer or liability.[535] In such a case, not the liability would be disclaimed, but the existence of a duty of care towards the third party would be denied. First of all, it has to be ascertained whether a duty of care exists without the disclaimer, and then the effect of that clause will be analysed. A classification society may therefore avoid a duty towards third parties in the first place by way of a suitable worded disclaimer: 'A man cannot be said voluntarily to be undertaking a responsibility if at the very moment when he is said to be accepting it he declares that in fact he is not'.[536] As a result, it is possible to include a contractual disclaimer which purports to prevent any duty of care arising. Such a contractual disclaimer is generally included in the classification certificate, which

---

531 *J.P. Aspinall, Q.C. in: Thiodon v. Tindall and Others (the Committee of Lloyd's Register) (The "Ibex")*, [1891] 7 Asp. 76 (Q.B.), at 80.

532 *Derry v. Peek*, [1889] 14 App.Cas. 337, 61 L. T. Rep. N. S. 265 (H.L.).

533 *Haseldine v. Daw & Son* [1941] 2 K.B. 343 (C.A.).

534 *Haseldine v. C.A. Daw & Son Ltd.* [1941] 2 K.B. 343 (C.A.); *Leigh and Sillavan Ltd v. Aliakmon Shipping Co. Ltd. (The "Aliakmon")*, [1986] A.C. 785 (H.L.), at 817.

535 *Smith v. Eric S. Bush,* [1990] 1 A.C. 831 (H.L.), at 856–857. The House of Lords main argument is the wording of §§ 11 (3), 13 (1) UCTA.

536 Per Lord Devlin, *Hedley Byrne & Co. Ltd. v. Heller & Partners*, [1964] A.C. 465 (H.L.), at 533, *see also* 493 per Lord Reid, 504 per Lord Morris, 511 per Lord Hodson, and 540 per Lord Pearce.

states that the information 'is for the use of the contracting party only'.[537] However, such a disclaimer must be *reasonable* according to the Unfair Contract Terms Act 1997. The criteria which are relevant to the test of reasonableness have already been elaborated.[538] Hence, it is of relevance whether the injured party could have easily purchased its own advice and whether it is a consumer or inexperienced person who needs to be protected or is it someone with considerable experience in this field of law. Liability for death or personal injury resulting from negligence cannot be disclaimed.[539] As a result, these disclaimers are mainly of relevance to cases of pure economic loss.

A duty of care exists towards passengers and crew regardless of any contractual disclaimer that the certificate may not be intended for their use. In fact, as the contractual duty does not derive from the issuance of the certificate but from the participation in the safety of the vessel, as has been argued before, the contractual disclaimer is of no relevance to that duty. Neither is it of any relevance whether or not the third party has seen the certificate and its disclaimer. Liability for death or personal injury cannot be disclaimed. What is more difficult is the legal situation in the case of physical damage. Here, the effect of the disclaimer depends on whether the plaintiff bases the classification society's duty on the certificate or on a specific aspect of its activities. In the first situation, a claim based on the negligently incorrect certificate, the plaintiff must accept the disclaimer even if he has not read it.[540] If the duty of care is, however, based on the service of the classification society which has an effect on the safety of the vessel, the disclaimer is irrelevant.

5. Conclusion

The tort of negligence protects third parties in several cases. If physical loss is directly caused by the classification society, for example if a surveyor directly causes damage to the cargo, the society owes a duty of care to the third party. Moreover, in all cases of direct advice to the injured party the doctrine of *voluntary assumption of responsibility* applies, according to which the classification society owes a duty of care to the recipient of the information.

In all other cases, notably those which relate to classification and certification, it needs to be established whether limitation provisions exist in favour of the shipowner and whether the plaintiff claimed damages for economic loss. If damages

---

537 *Compare* the classification certificates of LR, included in Lux, *Classification Societies* (1993), Appendix 2, at 88, 113, 121, 124, 126.

538 *See supra* Part 2 A I 4.

539 § 2 (1) UCTA.

540 *Harris v. Wyre Forest District Council*, [1990] 1 A.C. 831 (H.L.), at 861. The contrary argument in *Norwich City Council v. Harvey*, [1989] 1 W.L.R. 828 (C.A.(Civ.Div.)) should be distinguished on the facts and has been severely criticised as it leaves the doctrine of privity of contract (*British Telecommunications plc v. James Thomson & Sons (Engineers) Ltd.*, [1999] 1 W.L.R. 9 (H.L.); *see also* Clerk & Lindsell, *On Torts* (2006), § 3–111).

for economic loss are claimed, according to *Marc Rich* the classification society does not owe a duty of care towards the third party. Loss of property is also considered to be economic loss.

Whenever there are limitation provisions when the plaintiff sues for damages for personal injury, the case must be distinguished from *Marc Rich*, because personal injury is deeply embedded in the law of the tort of negligence. The classification society owes a duty of care to the victim if it proves a sufficient degree of *foreseeability* and *proximity*. Since passengers are not an easily identifiable group, they face difficulties in proving *proximity*. Nevertheless, it is evident that the vessel is used for the transport of passengers and how many of them. This is sufficient for the criterion of *proximity*.

If no limitation provisions apply or statutory surveys are carried out, and physical loss has been caused, only *foreseeability* and *proximity* have to be proven. In cases of economic loss, it additionally has to be *fair, just and reasonable* to impose a duty of care on the classification society.

The tort of deceit protects every victim from every damage caused by the deceit. A fraudulent representation is, however, quite unlikely to occur and its scope of application is rather limited.

II. United States Law

Under United States law a third party can base a claim against a classification society on four different theories. Not only can a contract theory in favour of a third party beneficiary be discussed, but the tort of negligence, as well as the tort of negligent misrepresentation, needs to be analysed. Furthermore, a reference to the (admittedly quite unlikely) tort of fraudulent misrepresentation shall be made.

As a main difference to the tort of negligence, the tort of negligent misrepresentation is a recognised category of tortious behaviour[541] which only allows claims for damage because of information that has been incorrectly given. In its alternative as promulgated by § 552 Restatement (Second) of Torts, it aims at economic loss, whereas the alternative of § 311 Restatement (Second) of Torts protects from physical harm caused by a negligent provision of false information.[542] The tort of negligence, by contrast, is applied more generally.

---

541 *Somarelf v. American Bureau of Shipping,* 720 F.Supp. 441, 453 (D.N.J.1989).

542 § 311 Restatement (Second) of Torts: Negligent Misrepresentation Involving Risk of Physical Harm

(1) One who negligently gives false information to another is subject to liability for physical harm caused by action taken by the other in reasonable reliance upon such information, where such harm results

(a) to the other, or

(b) to such third persons as the actor should expect to be put in peril by the action taken.

(2) Such negligence may consist of failure to exercise reasonable care:

1. *Contractual Right of Indemnity*

Regarding contractual rights, one could think of a protection of third parties in three different ways. As to the first one, it is evident that according to the principles of contract law, the issuance of a certificate does not establish a contractual relationship between the issuer and the party receiving the certificate.[543]

Also, the contractual parties may expressly stipulate a benefit for a third party. Whether the parties intended to benefit a third party is determined according to an analysis of the following factors:

> '(1) the existence of a legal relationship between the promisee and the third person involving an obligation owed by the promisee to the beneficiary which performance of

---

(a) in ascertaining the accuracy of the information, or
(b) in the manner in which it is communicated.

§ 552 Restatement (Second) of Torts: Information Negligently Supplied for the Guidance of Others

(1) One who, in the course of his business, profession or employment, or in any other transaction in which he has a pecuniary interest, supplies false information for the guidance of others in their business transactions, is subject to liability for pecuniary loss caused to them by their justifiable reliance upon the information, if he fails to exercise reasonable care or competence in obtaining or communicating the information.
(2) Except as stated in Subsection (3), the liability stated in Subsection (1) is limited to loss suffered
   (a) by the person or one of a limited group of persons for whose benefit and guidance he intends to supply the information or knows that the recipient intends to supply it; and
   (b) through reliance upon it in a transaction that he intends the information to influence or knows that the recipient so intends or in a substantially similar transaction.
(3) The liability of one who is under a public duty to give the information extends to loss suffered by any of the class of persons for whose benefit the duty is created, in any of the transactions in which it is intended to protect them.

543 Even though this has been argued by ABS when seeking to compel arbitration against the shipowners of a vessel which had not contracted with ABS. 'Conversely, in the instant case ABS issued all classification certificates to Tencara, the shipyard, and not to the owners of the TAG HEUER. More importantly, the Yacht Owners did not formally retain ABS. Quite the opposite, the Request for Class agreement was executed between ABS and Tencara. In *International Ore* and *Sundance Cruises*, the courts found a contractual relationship solely between the party issuing the certificate and the party in direct receipt. Thus, these cases do not compel the conclusion that issuance of a certificate contractually binds both the party in direct receipt of the certificate, Tencara, as well as a third-party, the Yacht Owners, to a relationship with the issuer. Accordingly, I decline to find a binding arbitration agreement between ABS and the Yacht Owners simply because the certificates issued by ABS to Tencara were ultimately provided to the Yacht Owners' (*American Bureau of Shipping v. Société Jet Flint, S.A.,* 1998 WL 273083 (S.D.N.Y.1998)).

the promise will discharge; (2) the existence of a factual relationship between the promisee and the third person, where (a) there is a possibility of future liability either personal or real on the part of the promisee to the beneficiary against which performance of the [...] [promisor] will protect the former; (b) securing an advantage for the third person may beneficially affect the promisee in a material way; (c) there are ties of kinship or other circumstances indicating that a benefit by way of gratuity was intended.'[544]

In a classification contract there are generally no express stipulations for the benefit of a third party. The only exemption can be the contract with the shipyard for the classification of a newly constructed ship, which can be for the benefit of the shipowner.

The other alternative, which has come up in several law suits, is the *Ryan* doctrine of an implied contractual right of indemnity based on an implied warranty of workmanlike performance.[545] *Ryan* was a case in which stevedores created a hazard aboard the ship. The rationale for imposing such an implied warranty of workmanlike performance is based on the belief that a stevedoring company which takes control of the vessel is more capable than the shipowner of avoiding accidents while unloading the vessel.[546] As has been discussed *supra*, however, classification societies are not responsible for a similar condition of a vessel.[547]. They only control the vessel. Neither may their control cause an unseaworthiness of the vessel nor may a pre-existing unseaworthy condition of the vessel re-occur because of their surveys:

> 'While an owner may have little or no direct control of the activities of a classification society aboard ship, the society rarely, if ever, would create hazards or defects by its functions and activities. Moreover, unlike a stevedore and other similar service contractors, a classification society is functionally incapable of repairing or rectifying defects or hazards, caused by itself or others. Virtually all a society can do is observe and report to the owner whatever its inspections reveal. In the light of these distinctions, to rule that a ship owner or operator can evade or pass off his historic primary duty to furnish a seaworthy vessel by strict application of the *Ryan* doctrine to a classification society, in my judgment, would work an unsound and unfair dilution of that legal duty.' [548]

---

544 *In the Matter of the Complaint of Dann Marine Towing, LC et al.*, 2004 WL 744881 (E.D.La.2004), at 6.

545 *Ryan Stevedoring Co. Inc. v. Pan-Atlantic Steamship Corp.,* 350 U.S. 124, 76 S.Ct. 232, 100 L.Ed. 133 (1956).

546 *Somarelf v. American Bureau of Shipping,* 704 F.Supp. 59 (D.N.J.1988), at 62 (*Somarelf I*), citing *Italia Societa per Azioni di Navigazione v. Oregon Stevedoring Co.,* 376 U.S. 315, 324, 84 S.Ct. 748, 754, 11 L.Ed.2d 732 (1964), *Maritime Overseas Corp. v. Northeast Pet. Indus.,* 706 F.2d 349, 353 (1st Cir. 1983).

547 *See supra* Part 2 A II 3 a bb, Part 2 A II 3 c bb.

548 *Great American Insurance Co. v. Bureau Veritas*, 338 F.Supp. 999 (S.D.N.Y.1972), at 1012. These considerations are quoted and adhered to in *Sundance Cruises Corp. v. American Bureau of Shipping,* 799 F.Supp. 363 (S.D.N.Y.1992), at 385–386. *See also In the Matter of: Oil Spill by the Amoco Cadiz off the Coast in France on March 16,*

The application of the *Ryan* doctrine to classification societies, therefore, must be generally rejected.[549]

2. *Tort of Negligence*

The tort of negligence is based on common law, but has developed distinct features and preconditions under United States law. There is no common tort law system in the United States, because the States possess their own distinct systems. Tort law is developed by judges in the context of resolving concrete disputes, and since there are no statutes in this regard, the courts may take different approaches.[550] This makes tort law in the United States a highly decentralized and dynamic field of law. However, cases which involve classification societies are generally cases of maritime tort, which is governed by federal maritime law. In most of these cases, reference is made not only to the leading precedents but also to the Restatements of the Law as issued by the American Law Institute (ALI).[551]

In an admiralty case, general maritime law applies, as developed by the judiciary.[552] With admiralty jurisdiction comes the application of substantive admiralty law.[553] Drawn from state and federal sources, the general maritime law is an amalgam of traditional common-law rules, modifications of those traditional rules and

---

1978, 1986 A.M.C. 1945, 1952 (N.D.Ill.1986), *aff'd* 954 F.2nd 1279 (7th Cir. 1992). and *Somarelf v. American Bureau of Shipping,* 704 F.Supp. 59 (D.N.J.1988), at 62 (*Somarelf I*). However, in *Skibs A/S Gylfe v. Hyman-Michaels Company et. al.,* 304 F.Supp. 1204 (E.D.Mich.1969), *aff'd,* 438 F.2d 803 (6th Cir.1971) the court held that the cargo surveyor which had contracted with shippers of steel turnings impliedly warranted to the shippers the performance of the obligations in a workmanlike fashion, and that the shipowner received the benefit of this warranty as a third party beneficiary in the sense of *Ryan.* As regards classification societies, however, this decision must be distinguished on the facts, as the aforementioned case law illustrates as well.

549 *Compare supra* Part 2 A II 3 a bb, Part 2 A II 3 c bb.

550 Law, 'Torts', in: Morrison, *Fundamentals of American Law* (1996), 239.

551 *See e.g. Otto Candies, L.L.C. v. Nippon Kaiji Kyokai Corp.*, 346 F.3d 530 (5th Cir.(La.) 2003), at 532: general maritime law 'cautiously recognizes the tort of negligent misrepresentation [in the sense of § 552 Restatement (Second) of Torts] as applied to classification societies' (adhered to by *In the Matter of the Complaint of Dann Marine Towing, LC et al.*, 2004 WL 744881 (E.D.La.2004)).

552 *East River S.S. Corp. v. Transamerica DeLaval, Inc.,* 476 U.S. 858, 106 S.Ct. 2295, 90 L.Ed.2d 865 (1986), *United States v. Reliable Transfer Co.,* 421 U.S. 397, 409, 95 S.Ct. 1708, at 1714, 44 L.Ed.2d 251 (1975); *Knickerbocker Ice Co. v. Stewart,* 253 U.S. 149, at 160–161, 40 S.Ct. 438, at 440, 64 L.Ed. 834 (1920)

553 *Executive Jet Aviation, Inc. v. City of Cleveland,* 409 U.S. 249, at 255, 93 S.Ct. 493, at 498. *See also* 28 U.S.C. § 1333(1): 'District courts shall have original jurisdiction, exclusive of the courts of the States, of: (1) Any civil case of admiralty or maritime jurisdiction [...].'

rules that are entirely new.[554] The landmark cases on the application of maritime law require that the committed wrong bears a significant relationship to traditional maritime activity. There also has to be a potential impact on maritime commerce, as this is the primary focus of admiralty jurisdiction.[555] Alleged negligence of a classification society when carrying out maritime activities such as formulating the rules, surveying a ship and issuing certificates have almost always been considered as bearing a significant relationship to a traditional maritime activity with a potential impact on maritime commerce.[556] The general maritime law therefore applies to the cases which are here in question.

---

554 See *Kermarec v. Compagnie Generale Transatlantique,* 358 U.S. 625, at 630, 79 S.Ct. 406, at 409, 3 L.Ed.2d 550 (1959); *Romero v. International Terminal Operating Co.,* 358 U.S. 354, 373–375, 79 S.Ct. 468, at 480–481, 3 L.Ed.2d 368 (1959).

555 *Executive Jet Aviation, Inc. v. City of Cleveland,* 409 U.S. 249, 253, 93 S.Ct. 493, 497, 34 L.Ed.2d 454 (1973); *Foremost Ins. Co., et al. v. Richardson, et al.,* 457 U.S. 668, 73 L.Ed. 300, 102 S.Ct. 2654 (1982). *See also* American Law Reports, 80 *ALR Federal* 105, 'Admiralty Jurisdiction: Maritime Nature of Tort', § 2.

556 *Coastal (Bermuda) Ltd. v. E.W. Saybolt & Co.*, 761 F.2d 198 (5th Cir.1985); 826 F.2d 424 (5th Cir.1987): general maritime law applies to the damage which a petroleum products surveyor caused to a cargo purchaser. *Royal Embassy v. Ioannis Martinos,* 1986 A.M.C. 769 (E.D.N.C.1984): maritime misrepresentation claim can be made in the context of maritime law. *Somarelf v. American Bureau of Shipping,* 704 F.Supp. 59 (D.N.J.1988) (*Somarelf I)*: the question whether general maritime law recognises a negligent misrepresentation cause of action in circumstances involving maritime services was answered in the positive. Not only does general federal maritime law apply, but the tort of negligent misrepresentation can also be called upon. *Shipping Corporation of India v. American Bureau of Shipping*, 744 F.Supp. 447 (S.D.N.Y.1990), at 449: the court held that (at least) the classification society's pre-delivery and post-delivery services are maritime services, provided pursuant to a maritime contract. Federal maritime law applies exclusively to a vessel purchaser's action against a classification society based on alleged negligent classification of the vessel (at 448) (citing *Pope & Talbot, Inc. v. Hawn,* 346 U.S. 406, 409, 74 S.Ct. 202, 204, 98 L.Ed. 143 (1953)). *American Bureau of Shipping v. Tencara Shipyard S.P.A.,* 170 F.3d 349, at 351, 1999 A.M.C. 1858 (2nd Cir.1999): Subject-matter jurisdiction in a suit in which the shipyard, the shipowners and the insurers claim damages from a classification society for the negligent issuance of an interim certificate of classification is grounded in admiralty, pursuant to 28 U.S.C. § 1333. *Sealord Marine Co., Ltd. v. American Bureau of Shipping,* 220 F.Supp.2d 260 (S.D.N.Y.2002), at 261: alleged negligent performance of inspections of the vessel and issuing improper certificates relating to the condition of the vessel is an alleged maritime tort, and so the substantive law to be applied is federal admiralty law (in the case then, according to federal maritime choice-of-law provisions, Greek law was to be applied). *Otto Candies, L.L.C. v. Nippon Kaiji Kyokai Corp.*, 346 F.3d 530 (5th Cir.(La.) 2003), at 532: general maritime law 'cautiously recognizes the tort of negligent misrepresentation as applied to classification societies' (adhered to by *In the Matter of the Complaint of Dann Marine Towing, LC et al.*, 2004 WL 744881 (E.D.La.2004)). *See also Toubaniaris v. American Bureau of Shipping*, 981 S.W.2d 858

In order to have an actionable claim in negligence, the plaintiff must prove that the defendant owed him a duty of care.[557] As an example, such duty of care might be not to engage in unreasonably risky conduct. In such a case, the defendant must have breached this duty by his unreasonably risky conduct and the defendant's conduct needs to have caused the harm to the plaintiff. Moreover, the defendant's conduct must have been a proximate cause of the plaintiff's harm, meaning that the defendant's conduct is perceived to have a significant relationship to the harm suffered by the plaintiff. Finally, the plaintiff has to prove the existence and amount of damage, based on actual harm of a legally recognised kind such as physical injury to person or property.[558] Negligent conduct is one that involves unreasonable risks.[559] In order to establish a definition of what is to be considered as an unreasonable risk, one needs to turn to case law. As a defence of the *prima facie* case, the defendant may plead contributory negligence, assumed risk and the statute of limitations.[560]

The main question, therefore, is to which third parties a classification society owes a duty of care.[561] Moreover, it also needs to be established whether the breach of that duty was also a proximate cause of the plaintiff's harm. There is neither a definition of a general standard of care nor a universal test for the question of whether a duty exists.[562] One might, however, describe the duty of care with the words of *Dobbs* as

(C.A.Tex.(1st Dis.)1998) which briefly referred to the maritime tort but concentrated on the limitation period for federal maritime torts and *forum non conveniens* considerations. The only case in which a misconception of the nature of classification services clearly occurred was *Inversiones Calmer, S.A. v. C.E. Heath & Co.,* 681 F.Supp. 100 (D.Puerto Rico 1988), at 106. Apparently the plaintiff did not illustrate the services of a classification society clearly enough, since the court held that the decision to withdraw the class (which was considered to be an implied contract) was only a prerequisite of the insurance of the vessel and not relevant to maritime affairs.

557 More accurately, the absence of any rule limiting the general duty of ordinary care.

558 For all these preconditions, *see* Dobbs, *The Law of Torts* (2000), § 114, at 269.

559 Negligence is defined by § 282 Restatement (Second) or Torts: 'Negligence is conduct which falls below the standard established by law for the protection of others against unreasonable risk of harm.'

560 Dobbs, *The Law of Torts* (2000), § 114, at 269.

561 The duty of care towards third parties has been expanded significantly by some State courts. For example, a psychotherapist was held liable due to the fact that he did not warn the subsequent victims of the possible threat from his patients, *Tarasoff v. The Regents of the University of California*, 17 Cal.3d 425, 551 P.2d 334, 131 Cal.Rptr. 14 (1976).

562 Mr. Justice Cardozo argued for the 'need for caution in framing standards of behavior that amount to rules of law. [...] Extraordinary situations may not wisely or fairly be subjected to tests or regulations that are fitting for the commonplace or normal' (*Pokora v. Wabash Ry.*, 292 U.S. 98 (1934)).

'the duty to exercise the care that would be exercised by a reasonable and prudent person under the same or similar circumstances to avoid or minimize risks of harm to others.'[563]

The court has to weigh several factors in order to decide whether or not a duty has to be imposed. The facts of the case will be discussed in the light of several considerations of policy which have first been stated by the California State Court:[564]

'1) the extent to which the transaction was intended to affect the plaintiff
2) the foreseeability of harm to him
3) the degree of certainty that the plaintiff suffered injury
4) the closeness of the connection between the defendant's conduct and the injury suffered
5) the moral blame attached to the defendant's conduct
6) the policy of preventing future harm by deterrence
7) administrative factors, including the feasibility of administering a rule that imposed a duty.'

It needs to be added that the first consideration is not relevant in cases of personal injury, as it was developed for a case of economic loss. In addition to these factors, the relationships of the parties and the customs to which they jointly subscribe have also to be taken into consideration.[565] Interestingly, in jury trials the jury bases its decision on whether or not the conduct was negligent on the same factors. These factors are neither cumulatively applied nor are they weighed in a certain distinctive manner. A distinction, however, needs to be made between cases of misfeasance and cases of nonfeasance. Whenever active misconduct causes an injury to others, the law provides protection against negligent acts in the interest of the person's security and every kind of interest in tangible property.[566] These interests are generally entitled to legal protection against the defendant's conduct. The protection from economic loss, however, requires further justification. Also, in cases of nonfeasance, the plaintiff has to prove some specific relation to the defendant. He must bring himself within the scope of a definite legal obligation. The defendant has no duty to act affirmatively for the benefit of others in the absence of any special relationship.[567]

The standard of reasonable conduct which is required not to breach that duty is determined by several factors. § 289 Restatement (Second) of Torts generally re-

563 Dobbs, *The Law of Torts* (2000), § 117, at 277 citing *Mansfield v. Circle K.Corp.*, 877 P.2d 1130 (Okla.1994); *Gossett v. Jackson*, 249 Va. 549, 457 S.Ed.2d 97 (Va.1995). *Compare Brown v. Kendall,* 60 Mass. 292 (1850).

564 *Amaya v. Home Ice, Fuel & Supply Co.,* 59 Cal.2d 295, 379 P.2d 513, 29 Cal. Rptr. 33 (1963) (overruled on its holding but not on its methodology in *Dillon v. Legg,* 68 Cal.2d 728, 441 P.2d 912, 69 Cal.Rptr. 72, 29 A.L.R.3d 1316 (1968)).

565 Dobbs, *The Law of Torts* (2000), § 229, at 582.

566 'In the usual run of cases, a general duty to avoid negligence is assumed, and there is no need for the court to undertake detailed analysis of precedent and policy' *Hamilton v. Accu-Tek*, 62 F.Supp.2d 802 (1999).

567 Dobbs, *The Law of Torts* (2000), § 227, at 579.

quires the objective standard of a reasonable man, despite the fact that superior knowledge of the person that causes the damage is also taken into account.[568] For this reason, reference is often made to the standard of care of a "prudent person" who is member of that class; in this case, the relevant standard of care would be that of a prudent classification society. In order to determine the risk which would be acceptable for a reasonable person, one first puts oneself in the position of the imaginary reasonable person and compares his conduct with the defendant's. Secondly, one takes into account specific regulations which specify certain general standards, such as in the case of classification societies' domestic technical regulations or safety standards. And finally one needs to weigh the risks involved with the costs and benefits of acting more safely.[569]

The rule of *stare decisis*, of course, obliges the judge to adhere to a decision of an appellate court, which prescribes a precedent for other cases in which the facts are identical or essentially the same. It shall therefore be analysed below whether there are precedents regarding the standard of reasonable conduct owed by a classification society, and cases in which a duty of care was established.

a. The Steamship Mutual Case

The SS PENSACOLA, which had been classified by BV, sank on 15 February 1966. Subsequently, the insurer of the vessel settled cargo and other claims, which it tried to recover by way of an action against the classification society.[570] The ship had been built under the supervision of ABS and was registered with BV in April 1964. In January 1966, BV had carried out a special survey of the vessel in a dry-dock. Only a visual inspection of the vessel was executed, with hammer-testing of suspect areas. No drilling or audio-gauging was performed. Certain repairs were carried out and the vessel was retained in class. On its first journey after the survey, water entered the vessel, and with the help of divers a circular crack was discovered at a spot where a keel block had been at the time of the dry-docking. Temporary repairs were carried out under the supervision of a BV inspector and the Class was confirmed on the condition of a re-examination of the temporary repairs and the execution of permanent repairs within thirty days. The vessel continued its journey and faced relatively rough weather for several days. Large quantities of water were discovered in holds No. 1 and 2, but the source of the inflow

[568] § 289. Recognizing Existence of Risk
The actor is required to recognize that his conduct involves a risk of causing an invasion of another's interest if a reasonable man would do so while exercising
(a) such attention, perception of the circumstances, memory, knowledge of other pertinent matters, intelligence, and judgment as a reasonable man would have; and
(b) such superior attention, perception of the circumstances, memory, knowledge of other pertinent matters, intelligence, and judgment as the actor himself has.

[569] *Compare* Dobbs, *The Law of Torts* (2000), §§ 117–147.

[570] *Steamship Mutual Underwriting Association Ltd. v. Bureau Veritas*, 380 F.Supp. 482 (E.D.La. 1973). Case comment: Miller, 'Liability of Classification Societies from the Perspective of United States Law', 22 *Tul.Mar.L.J.* 75 (1997), 93–94.

could not be detected. Fearing that the cargo of grain might swell and cause the vessel to break apart, the officers decided to abandon the vessel. The vessel sank two and a half hours after they had left the ship.

The plaintiff proved that BV conducted the inspection and testing of the vessel's shell plating in a negligent way, and that its surveyor violated BV's rules, which required gauging of shell plating. However, the plaintiff did not succeed in proving that the cause of the entering of the water could have been discovered by BV in a proper conduct of the survey. Even according to expert witnesses, it was uncertain what had actually caused the vessel to sink.

As there was no representation made by the classification society to the plaintiffs – the cargo owners had no knowledge of the certificates or of the ship's register – this was not a case of negligent misrepresentation. Since it related solely to the safety promoted by a classification society by way of its surveys, the court applied the tort of negligence. Not only may the certificates serve as guidance for the shipowner and third parties, but the surveys and controls also aim at the observance of a certain standard of safety. Whether or not the third party knows about it, the classification society controls the vessel and tries to ascertain this level of safety as laid down in its own rules. This *safety dimension* is important to all cases of loss of life or property, especially whenever the plaintiff has no knowledge of the certificates. In this regard, the verdict is an invitation to further reflections.

The *Steamship Mutual* case was decided against the plaintiff as he did not prove all the preconditions of the tort of negligence. The classification society had behaved negligently in failing to gauge the shell plating of the vessel, and in failing to inspect certain of the double bottom tanks, which it should have done according to its own rules. However, since the plaintiff did not show that the sinking was caused by some defect which could have been discovered by an adequate survey, this negligent behaviour did not justify an action in tort.[571] Only if there was a presumption of unseaworthiness because of the negligent inspection would the plaintiff not have to prove causation.[572] However, as the court reiterated, the presumption of unseaworthiness does not apply against classification societies. Citing the *Great American Insurance* case,[573] the court stated in the *Steamship Mutual* case that even though that case was one of contractual liability, its reasoning with regard to this presumption is also applicable to liability in tort. The issue of the presumption directly relates to the duty to provide a seaworthy vessel. 'Historically the presumption has been applied against those who are responsible for and in control of the vessel, thus owners or demise charterers.'[574] A similar argumenta-

---

[571] *Steamship Mutual Underwriting Association Ltd. v. Bureau Veritas*, 380 F.Supp. 482 (E.D.La. 1973), at 492.

[572] *Steamship Mutual Underwriting Association Ltd. v. Bureau Veritas*, 380 F.Supp. 482 (E.D.La. 1973), at 493.

[573] *See supra* Part 2 A II 3 a.

[574] *Steamship Mutual Underwriting Association Ltd. v. Bureau Veritas*, 380 F.Supp. 482 (E.D.La. 1973), at 493.

tion has been enacted in the *Marine Sulphur* case,[575] in the fact that the presumption only applies to those who are responsible for and in control of the vessel was emphasised. Even though a classification society can require modifications to be made or repairs to be carried out, which are likely to be carried out by the shipowner, as he has to adhere to these recommendations or conditions due to, *inter alia*, his insurance contracts, the classification society is not in control of the vessel. Someone who merely classifies a ship is not responsible for and in control of the vessel.[576] Only the shipowner continues to be the person in charge and in control of the vessel. Since there is no presumption of unseaworthiness against a classification society, suits against it are governed by traditional tort concepts and their consequential regulations regarding the burden of proof.

It needs to be realised that *Steamship Mutual* is a straightforward application of tort law. It is in no way affected by any policy considerations, insurance issues, the nondelegable duty of the shipowner to provide a seaworthy vessel, or the like.[577] In that regard, it differs from the approach that has been taken under English law.

Steamship Mutual implicitly recognises a cause of action against a classification society based on the tort of negligence, as it more or less applied it in a straightforward way.[578] At one point at the end of the verdict, reference was made to the *Great American Insurance* argumentation relating to the "first duty":

575 *In re Marine Sulphur Queen,* 460 F.2d 89, 101 (2d Cir.1972): 'The duty of providing the crew with a seaworthy ship runs only to the owner, and the shipbuilder neither employs the crew nor can he control what happens to the ship once she leaves the yard. Therefore, traditional tort concepts apply to the claim against [the shipbuilder] and, contrary to the trial court's conclusion, neither justice nor logic compel the application against it of the permissible inference rule from the unseaworthiness doctrine'; *Steamship Mutual Underwriting Association Ltd. v. Bureau Veritas*, 380 F.Supp. 482 (E.D.La. 1973), at 493.

576 *Steamship Mutual Underwriting Association Ltd. v. Bureau Veritas*, 380 F.Supp. 482 (E.D.La. 1973), at 493.

577 This is also pointed out by France, 'Classification societies', 1 *I.J.S.L.* 67 (1996), at 73.

578 'Thus it is apparent that what actually caused the vessel to take on water and sink is unknown. It may very well be that some hidden defect in the vessel's hull, which would not have been discoverable regardless of the diligence which the defendant exercised in the survey, caused a hole in the hull allowing water to enter. Plaintiff has not shown that the cause of the water entering was something which the defendant could have discovered from a proper conduct of his survey. [...] In summary then, plaintiff has not shown what caused the vessel to sink. True, the vessel is gone and plaintiff cannot inspect it to determine the exact cause. Nevertheless, as we have said, plaintiff has failed to show that the sinking was caused by some defect which was discoverable by a completely adequate survey.' (*Steamship Mutual Underwriting Association Ltd. v. Bureau Veritas*, 380 F.Supp. 482 (E.D.La. 1973), at 492). *See* also Miller, 'Liability of Classification Societies from the Perspective of United States Law', 22 *Tul.Mar.L.J.* 75 (1997), at 94.

'Admittedly, the result reached does place a heavy burden on the plaintiff since the vessel has sunk. However, to lessen the plaintiff's burden would be to place the defendant more in a position of an insurer of the vessel, a situation commensurate with neither the services rendered nor the fees charged.'[579]

The reasoning of the court would however have been more coherent without it. The reference was not only incomplete, as it only referred to the first one of the two duties defined by *Great American Insurance*. It also implied that even if causation had been proven, the classification society would not have been liable due to these considerations. That is a rather risky statement to make, since the court did not analyse the argumentation of *Great American Insurance*, nor did it fully analyse the legal situation by itself. The court only included these few lines as if they were the ultimate argumentation in this field of law, even though according to the court which pronounced them, they were not.

b. The Gulf Tampa Drydock Case

The CAP NORTE sustained a deck-plating fracture while en route to New York.[580] Having surveyed the damage, its classification society GL decided that repairs had to be carried out in order to keep the vessel in class. The owners disagreed, but after some discussion it became evident that GL's surveyor would not allow the vessel to remain in class unless at least temporary repairs were carried out. The shipowners selected Gulf Tampa Drydock to undertake these repairs and warned GL's surveyor of inflammable insulation materials in the area of the fracture. Without securing detailed diagrams of the ship's structure, the surveyor ordered Gulf Tampa Drydock to weld steel bars across the fracture without pointing out specific welding spots. The repair was carried out in that way, but Gulf Tampa Drydock erred in selecting the welding spots and welded the bars against inflammable material. The fire which was thereby brought about caused damage to both the ship and the cargo.

The shipowner consequently sued Gulf Tampa Drydock for damages.[581] Subsequently, Gulf Tampa Drydock brought this action against GL for contribution based on contributory negligence. It was claimed that GL was responsible for the negligence of its employee in ordering, supervising and inspecting the repairs of the vessel.

The District Court held GL liable in an unpublished decision. This verdict was vacated by the Court of Appeals and remanded to the lower court, as further findings on what duties a classification society owes to shipowners were necessary. Since it was an action for contribution, the plaintiff could only recover if the clas-

---

579 *Steamship Mutual Underwriting Association Ltd. v. Bureau Veritas*, 380 F.Supp. 482 (E.D.La. 1973), at 494.

580 *Gulf Tampa Drydock Co. v. Germanischer Lloyd*, 634 F.2d 874 (5th Cir.1981). *See also* Gordan, 'The Liability of Marine Surveyors and Ship Classification Societies', 19 *J.Mar.L.&Com.* 301 (1988).

581 *Hamburg-Suedamerikanische Dampfschiffahrts-Gesellschaft Eggert & Amsinck v. Gulf Tampa Drydock Co.,* No. 71335 (M.D.Fla.1973) (unpublished).

sification society was a joint tortfeasor, that meant either jointly or severally liable with the dry-dock company for the damage to the ship.[582] As a precondition for such tort liability, the classification society must owe a duty of care in tort to the shipowner. The plaintiff did not succeed in showing that the classification society owed the shipowner a duty to order specific repairs.[583] The second decision of the court below is again unpublished. Interesting are the remarks the Court of Appeals made regarding the duties a classification society owes to a shipowner in tort:

> 'A classification society owes certain duties to a shipowner. Those duties include the determination that a ship conforms to certain standards of seaworthiness set by the society. This was explained at the trial below by a general marine surveyor testifying for Tampa Drydock:
> '[T]he function of a classification society [is] to set rules and standards [...] such that [...] vessels be reasonably and solely operated in their respective societies.
> The classification societies then demand the ships be [...] subject to inspections [...], and that the rules and standards are still kept in force.'[...]
> An additional classification society duty is inspection of damaged ships to determine whether they continue to meet class standards, and if not, what must be undertaken to bring the ship back up to class standards.'[584]

This short reference is interesting with regard to the duties of care in tort towards contracting parties, but of limited value to third parties. Also, the definition remains rather vague, and the case was remanded to the court below in order to specify the duties. Noteworthy, however, is the fact that the court held that the classification society does not ensure absolute seaworthiness, but only the standard of safety as laid down in its rules.

Due to the fact that there was no representation to the owners of the cargo, only the tort of negligence was the relevant legal basis. The value of the case is limited, however, as the Court of Appeals did not expressly state whether or not a classification society owes a duty of care to third parties.

c. The Continental Insurance Case

On its maiden voyage, the AMERICAN NEW YORK sustained water damage to its cargo due to an unsealed watertight manhole cover on one of the vessel's ballast tanks.[585] The claims of the cargo owners were subrogated to their insurers, who brought action against the shipbuilder and ABS. Plaintiffs alleged that ABS owed the users of the vessel a duty to discover the defect which caused the leakage and that ABS had breached that duty. The shipbuilder had contracted with ABS to review specifications of the vessel, survey it and certify its compliance with the rules of ABS. The manhole cover had been surveyed and declared waterproof by an ABS surveyor, but it had subsequently been opened again by employ-

---

582 *Gulf Tampa Drydock Co. v. Germanischer Lloyd*, 634 F.2d 874 (5th Cir.1981), at 878.

583 *Gulf Tampa Drydock Co. v. Germanischer Lloyd*, 634 F.2d 874 (5th Cir.1981), at 875.

584 *Gulf Tampa Drydock Co. v. Germanischer Lloyd*, 634 F.2d 874 (5th Cir.1981), at 878.

585 *Continental Insurance Co. v. Daewoo Shipbuilding & Heavy Machinery Ltd.*, 707 F.Supp. 123 (S.D.N.Y.1988).

ees of the shipyard to complete the painting of the tank. Plaintiffs did not claim that there was negligence regarding the survey, but only that ABS failed to reinspect the manhole cover. The Federal District Court for the Southern District of New York held:

> 'ABS's duty is delimited by its contract with [the shipbuilder]. The terms of its contract required it only to exercise due care in reviewing design and surveying construction before certifying that the vessel met ABS standards. It was required to certify not to the absolute seaworthiness of the vessel, but only to the vessel's conformity to ABS Rules. *See Gulf Tampa Drydock Co. v. Germanischer Lloyd*, 634 F.2d 2874, 2878 (5th Cir.1981) (classification society's duty is to determine that ship conforms to standards set by society); *Steamship Mutual Underwriting Association Ltd. v. Bureau Veritas*, 380 F.Supp. 482, 488 (E.D.La. 1973) (negligence of classification society limited to failure to conform to its own rules).
> To extend a classification society's duty to the operational details of the vessel's management would both ignore the clear limits of its contractual duty and make it an absolute insurer of the vessel. *Great American Insurance Co. v. Bureau Veritas*, 338 F.Supp. 999, 1012 (S.D.N.Y.1972) (Tyler J.), *aff'd*, 478 F.2d 235 (2d Cir.1973). This the court declines to do.'[586]

The classification society therefore owed the shipyard (contracting party) no duty to ensure that the water-tight manhole cover was properly sealed after inspection of the vessel or even at the time of the vessel's sea trials.[587] This further illustrates that a classification society is not in charge of the safety of the vessel at all times, but is only a survey organisation which checks whether the vessel corresponds to a certain standard of safety at the time of its inspection.

The decision relates to the tort of negligence, as there was no representation of the classification society to the cargo owners. Just as in *Steamship Mutual* and *Gulf Tampa Drydock*, the safety dimension of the services of a classification society was at issue. In this case it is finally and expressly stated that the duty of care of the classification society is defined by the contract with the shipowner.[588] As a result, the classification society is not responsible for the operation of the vessel, since it has no such duty towards the shipyard. However, the verdict does not include comments on whether the duty of care towards the contracting party may at all extend to third parties, and if so, to what degree. This case should not be misinterpreted to suggest that the plaintiff always needs to ascertain which duties the classification society owes to its contracting party. It solely indicates that a classification society cannot be held liable for an action which it is not even obliged to do by the classification contract. This case is, therefore, only a small piece in the mosaic of the duty of care which is relevant to the tort of negligence.

---

[586] *Continental Insurance Co. v. Daewoo Shipbuilding & Heavy Machinery Ltd.*, 707 F.Supp. 123 (S.D.N.Y.1988), at 123-124.

[587] *Continental Insurance Co. v. Daewoo Shipbuilding & Heavy Machinery Ltd.*, 707 F.Supp. 123 (S.D.N.Y.1988), at 124.

[588] *Continental Insurance Co. v. Daewoo Shipbuilding & Heavy Machinery Ltd.*, 707 F.Supp. 123 (S.D.N.Y.1988), at 123.

d. The Psarianos Case

The THOMAS K sank on its last voyage with the loss of eight members of its crew, while the remaining seven members sustained varying degrees of injury.[589] Crew members and decedents' representatives brought claims *inter alia* against ABS on a general negligence theory and for punitive damages for wilful, wanton and grossly negligent conduct.

ABS had been contacted prior to the fatal voyage in order to restore the classification of the vessel. Its rules required dry-docking of the vessel every two and a half years. The shipowner was willing to dry-dock the vessel, if necessary. However, ABS suggested and subsequently performed an underwater divers' inspection of the hull and tail shaft instead of dry-docking. The dry-docking requirement was subsequently extended for six months.[590] When the vessel encountered pounding seas and heavy weather on its voyage, it suffered from a separation of the exterior shell (hull) plating and water entered. After five days' fighting with the elements, the vessel was in dire distress and imminent danger of sinking. The Japanese Coast Guard offered assistance, which, however, the master refused. Only a few hours later the vessel sank with the loss of eight lives.

A jury returned an unpublished verdict against both ABS and the shipowner in excess of USD 22 million, finding each of them fifty percent liable for the plaintiffs' injuries and damage sustained by the decedents' representatives. Punitive damages against both of them were assessed amounting to USD 3 million each. Since the decision on the merits has not been published nor is it accessible, it is not possible to comment on the argumentation of the jury.

e. Again: The Great American Insurance Case

The facts of this case have already been provided in the section concerning liability towards contracting parties.[591] However, this case is also of interest to the tort of negligence, as it is the only one which provides a definition of a classification society's duties of care in tort. The Court defined the duties which a classification society owes in tort in the following way:

> 'Viewing the matter under theories of tort law, the obvious question is, what duties are owed by a classification society to its clientele? Although there is scant law on the subject, it can be reasoned that by undertaking to survey and classify a vessel, a classification society obligates itself to perform two duties with due care. The first duty, as already discussed, is to survey and classify vessels in accordance with rules and standards established and promulgated by the society for that purpose. The second duty of a clas-

---

589 *Psarianos v. Standard Marine, Ltd.*, 728 F.Supp. 438 (E.D.Tex. 1989), 790 F.Supp. 134 (E.D.Tex. 1989), 12 F3d 461 (5th Cir.(La.)1994), *cert. den.'d* 114 SCt. 2164, 511 U.S. 1142, 128 L.Ed.2d 887 (1994). The part of the judgment which was published relates to questions of jurisdiction against the P&I Club and a waiver of an arbitration clause by the P&I Club as well as direct claims against the P&I Club.

590 *Psarianos v. Standard Marine, Ltd.*, 728 F.Supp. 438 (E.D.Tex. 1989), at 441.

591 *See supra* Part 2 A II 3 a. *Great American Insurance Co. v. Bureau Veritas*, 338 F.Supp. 999 (S.D.N.Y.1972), *aff'd*, 478 F.2d 235 (2d Cir.1973).

sification society is that of due care in detection of defects in the ship it surveys and the corollary of notification thereof to the owner and charterer.'[592]

The existence of the first duty, described as a duty to survey and classify vessels in accordance with its rules, was, however, rejected under these circumstances. In order to allow a close scrutiny, the precise wording of the Court shall be cited again:

'The unstated policy underlying the decisions not to allow surveys and classifications to operate as defenses to the duty of providing a seaworthy ship is clearly to preserve the ancient, absolute responsibility of an owner for the condition of his ship. This is evidenced by the fact that, were such surveys and classifications allowed to constitute a due diligence defence, the accountability of owners for the seaworthiness of their vessel for all practical purposes would evaporate. This, in turn, would have the effect of leaving injured seamen and shippers with no effective remedy in most cases.
In theory, recognition of a right of action against a classification society would confer benefit upon ship owners, ship operators and seamen. In practice, such a 'new remedy' would produce several undesirable effects. One of these would be to place the ultimate responsibility for seaworthiness on an organization which has contact with the vessel for only brief annual periods, whereas the owner, who is always "present" in respect to this vessel, would elude liability in many cases. Second, this right of action would have the effect of making the classification society an absolute insurer of any vessel it surveys and certifies. Not only is this liability not commensurate with the amount of control that a classification society has over a vessel; it is also not in accord with the intent of the parties, the fees charged or the services performed. Further, by making classification societies the effective insurer of nearly all seagoing vessels, insurance companies such as those here involved, might be putting themselves out of business, a result they certainly did not contemplate by bringing this suit.'[593]

From the language used, one might get the impression that the Court states that a classification society does not owe a duty of care in tort to any third party. This is not, however, true. The aim of the court was to ascertain that the duty to provide a seaworthy vessel remains a duty of the shipowner. Unfortunately, the court used a very general description of its so-called *first duty* as a duty relating to the survey and classification of the vessel in accordance with the society's rules. On closer scrutiny of the explanation why such duty was rejected, it becomes evident that the Court did not generally want to deny a duty of care for surveys. In other words: the duty should be defined that a classification society neither guarantees that the vessel is seaworthy nor does it assume such a duty of the shipowner. Otherwise a classification society would have to answer for all vessels which it classifies, as illustrated by the Court's statement that a classification society would otherwise be an 'effective insurer of nearly all seagoing vessels'. It is obvious that no classification society would be capable of taking over such a role. Moreover, the contracting parties do not intend to assign such a duty to a classification society.

---

592 *Great American Insurance Co. v. Bureau Veritas*, 338 F.Supp. 999 (S.D.N.Y.1972), at 1012.

593 *Great American Insurance Co. v. Bureau Veritas*, 338 F.Supp. 999 (S.D.N.Y.1972), at 1012.

Throughout the course of this thesis it has for these reasons always been made clear that the surveys by a classification society do not guarantee the seaworthiness of the vessels, since they only aim at checking the vessel in accordance with certain standards which have with hindsight proved to increase the safety of the vessel or which should increase it because of technical calculations. However, if these standards are not adhered to, the classification society has an obligation to inform its contracting party and to offer advice on how this situation may be changed. Rather than referring to the policy consideration that the shipowner has a nondelegable duty to provide a seaworthy ship,[594] the Court should have analysed what precisely a classification society does and what it represents. It would then have come to the same conclusion and it would have avoided misunderstandings which its *obiter dictum* may have caused, because it appears to be based on policy considerations.

Besides, the verdict expressly states that a classification society owes a duty in tort to use due care to detect and warn of hazards. Of course, the detection of a hazard is only possible if a survey is carried out. This illustrates that the definition of the so-called *first duty* to survey and classify the vessel in accordance with its rules is too broad. In the words of the judge, this *second duty* is described as follows:

> 'On the other hand, the duty to use due care to detect and warn of hazards appears to provide a sounder basis for tort liability of a ship classification society. So far as I can determine, this theory of liability would not offend established case law in admiralty; indeed, it is supported by the holding of the only case which has heretofore dealt squarely with the question of a surveyor's liability. In *The Gyda* [*Skibs A/S Gylfe v. Hyman-Michaels Company et. al.,* 304 F.Supp. 1204 (E.D.Mich.1969), *aff'd,* 438 F.2d 803 (6th Cir.1971)] the defendant classification society, the National Cargo Bureau, had expressly undertaken to perform an "on hire" survey, oversee the loading of dangerous cargo and advise the charterer regarding the safe or unsafe character or the stowage. [...] Although the facts and circumstances upon which *The Gyda, supra.,* was decided are different from those presented in this case, the ruling that a classification society may be liable for a failure to detect or warn of dangers on board a ship that it is surveying should theoretically apply to the case at hand. *The Gyda* holding was expressed in terms of a breach of an express undertaking; nonetheless, the district court's extensive use of negligence language and tort theories of causation suggests that its decision was based as much on a breach of duty of care as upon breach of contract. If so, the court's analysis seems sound; surely, a ship's surveyor or classification society should be charged in law with the reasonable duty of detecting all perceptible defects of the vessel encountered during the survey and notifying the owner and/or charterer thereof.'[595]

---

594 For the obligation to render the vessel seaworthy, see 46 USC § 192 Note 60, and 57.

595 *Great American Insurance Co. v. Bureau Veritas*, 338 F.Supp. 999 (S.D.N.Y.1972), at 1012–1013. This duty has, *e.g.*, thereafter been employed by a Panel arbitrating claims of IBAR Ltd. against ABS, *see In the Matter of the Arbitration v. Ibar Limited and Vincent Francis Barrett, Petitioners, and American Bureau of Shipping, Respondent,* 2003 WL 2012400, 2003 U.S. LEXIS 7386 (S.D.N.Y.2003), *aff'd.* 92 Fed. Appx. 820, 2004 U.S. App. LEXIS 4273 (2nd Cir.2004).

Since the court referred to whether or not the plaintiffs had argued that the defendant was negligent because it failed to detect all perceptible dangers on board a ship that it surveyed and to notify the owner and/or charterer thereof, these remarks are not made *obiter*. The plaintiffs could have argued that because the classification society discovered the four wasted frames, it should have warned of a danger if immediate repairs were not carried out and that its deferment of the repairs therefore resulted in negligence. Causation could not have been proven, since it was unknown what had caused the vessel to sink.

Unfortunately, the court did not expound on the parties or the interests which are protected by such a duty. This issue needs to be resolved with reference to general principles of tort law. Contrary to physical injury and personal harm, a duty in tort to protect someone from economic loss exists only in very rare cases, as such duty would strongly interfere with the powers of a free market and since no-one is protected against making a loss. Under United States law, one should not ask whether a duty of care exists, but whether there are reasons why it should not exist.[596] In cases of physical injury or personal harm, it is, however, very difficult to argue why such a duty should not exist.

It must be added that it remains uncertain why the court argued that a classification society owes only two different kinds of duties – one of which is not even owed to its clientele on closer scrutiny. At the exercise of each and every of its activities, a classification society is obliged to avoid personal damage or physical harm to third parties. However, a classification society does more than surveying a vessel, detecting deficiencies and warning of them. To name but a few activities, it also develops and continuously revises its own rules, it imposes and withdraws conditions, and it grants exemptions from obligations imposed by its rules. All these activities do not challenge the duty of the shipowner to provide a seaworthy vessel. For the same reasons, a duty of care in tort should correspond to each of these activities. Despite the fact that the court did not hold the classification society liable in this case, one will therefore come to a different conclusion if one applies its reasoning to other cases.

f. Conclusions

The cases have shown that generally classification societies do not owe a duty of care towards third parties for the safety of the vessel. The shipowner has to guarantee the seaworthiness of the vessel and answer for the consequences if that is not the case. However, when resolving situations which are not yet covered by case-law, one might establish a duty of care in some cases.

Everybody is under a general duty to avoid or minimise risks of harm to other persons if possible. This requires that classification societies do not cause additional dangers to third parties which have not been inherent in the vessel before. In practice, this should imply a duty of care whenever the classification society has influenced the deficiency which caused the accident, but not for the vessel in general. The classification society may influence the deficiency by way of its rules or

[596] Dobbs, *The Law of Torts* (2000), §§ 227–229, at 578–584.

if it gives recommendations to carry out repairs in a certain way or makes conditions. In such a case, the classification society has an influence on the safety and condition of the vessel, and is therefore required to avoid or minimise all risks which it might thereby cause. If it only surveys the vessel or checks the blueprints and requests that certain repairs are carried out or modifications made, it is only under a duty to make such requirements that are state-of- the-art in the eyes of a prudent classification society. The classification society is mainly under a duty towards the shipowner to check the vessel; it is not under such a duty towards third parties. If it, however, makes certain requirements, it should be under a general duty to avoid any risk of harm to third parties as well. Therefore, only if the classification society makes a certain requirement, recommendation or gives certain advice which influences the vessel in a way that it is not as safe as it should be if it were state-of-the-art, that society should be under a duty of care towards third parties to prevent any harm occurring to them. Another issue is which interests are protected by this duty. As the activity of a classification society is not directed towards protection from economic loss, and since a duty to protect from economic loss requires a specifically close relationship, the classification society is not under a duty towards third parties to prevent such damage from occurring.

Under certain circumstances, third parties may therefore base their claim on the tort of negligence. An application is not prohibited by *Great American Insurance*. This case solely relates to the shipowner. A classification society may not cause any personal harm to them; yet the duty does not extend to protect from economic loss. Whether or not a duty of care exists towards third parties has never been explicitly stated, but impliedly *Steamship Mutual* points in such a direction.[597] *Great American Insurance* provides for a duty in tort to detect and warn of deficiencies of the vessel. Such a duty gives an incentive to classification societies to detect deficiencies and not close their eyes if they find any indications. However, this does not imply that they guarantee the seaworthiness of the vessel or become some kind of insurer. If it is impossible to detect such deficiencies or if they are deficiencies only with hindsight but state-of-the-art at the time of the survey, classification societies do not owe such a duty. Nevertheless, there are several other duties corresponding to all activities of a classification society which may possibly cause physical harm to third parties if the society acts negligently. Whether or not the negligent behaviour of the society is a proximate cause needs to be ascertained according to the facts of the case. The fees which have been paid by the contractual party and a possible disparity in comparison with the liability to which the classification society is exposed should not be of relevance to these tort cases. It is evident that the classification society does not owe a duty of care for services which it does not provide to its contracting party. That is what *Continental Insurance* implies when stating that a classification society cannot owe any duty to a third party which it does not owe to the shipowner. For example, since the society does not supervise the navigation of the vessel, it cannot be held liable for negligent navigation.

---

597 Just as well as *Cargill* and *Carbotrade*, as will be shown in the following section.

Claims by third parties that relate to a negligent misrepresentation of the classification society will be analysed in the following section. The tort of negligence, by contrast, is mainly of relevance whenever no such representation is made to a third party. As examples, one may think of cases where the rules are negligently developed, revised or misinterpreted; exemptions are granted, even though there is no reason for such exemption; conditions are withdrawn; or whenever the society requests the shipyard to modify the blueprints, resulting in an insufficient standard of safety; and by each and every of these actions the classification society has caused or contributed to the deficiency of the vessel.

3. *Tort of Negligent Misrepresentation*

This tort aims at a liability for the negligent provision of false information and is for this reason especially relevant to classification societies. It is relevant in situations in which a classification society provides information which is inaccurate according to the files; states that a vessel complies with the rules, even though it does not, a fact which should and could have been discovered by the classification society; defers repairs even though the deferment may result in danger; or negligently withdraws a condition or fails to warn of deficiencies.

In the Restatement (Second) of Torts there are two different alternatives of the tort of negligent misrepresentation, § 311 and § 552.[598] This tort aims at the prevention of the supply of false information for the guidance of others, and protects the user of this commercial information from physical harm as well as economic loss[599]. In addition, any third party that the defendant should expect to be put in danger is protected from physical harm. If the defendant knows that the recipient will supply the information to a certain person or a limited group of persons, these third parties may sue for economic loss as well. This does not imply that there is a general protection of everyone who might reasonably and foreseeably consult a classification certificate. Practically the entire maritime industry comes into contact with the information contained in the classification certificate. This industry is not at all a limited group of persons.

As has been determined with regard to the tort of negligence,[600] the *Sundance* dictum does not prohibit liability towards third parties.[601] It will be shown that the

598 These provisions are reprinted in the introduction to this chapter *supra* at Part 2 B II.

599 § 552 Restatement (Second), comment a.

600 *See supra* Part 2 A II 3 c.

601 According to *Sundance*, the issuance of certificates which entitle the owner of the ship to procure insurance and operate his vessel, is not a kind of "guidance" in the sense of the tort of a negligent misrepresentation (*Sundance Cruises Corp. v. American Bureau of Shipping,* 799 F.Supp. 363 (S.D.N.Y.1992), at 377). But that does not give any indication as to whether such a certificate may be of guidance to a third party. Most important is the addendum which the court made with regard to third party claims: 'This case must be distinguished from a suit brought by an injured third party who relied on the classification or safety certificates' (*Sundance Cruises Corp. v. American Bureau of Shipping,* 7 F.3d 1077 (2d Cir.1993), at 1084).

opposite is true.[602] It has been affirmed in several decisions that the tort of negligent misrepresentation is applicable to classification societies under general federal maritime law. The first one was *Coastal (Bermuda),*[603] which did not involve a classification society but laid the foundation for the subsequent decisions regarding classification societies. The second were the *Somarelf* cases,[604] which were followed by *Cargill*[605] and *Otto Candies.*[606] As all of these cases only relate to the tort of negligent misrepresentation in cases of economic loss, and therefore § 552 Restatement (Second) of Torts, consideration will thereafter be given to the other alternative, *i.e.*, § 311 Restatement (Second) of Torts.

a. The Coastal (Bermuda) Case

As a purchaser of 60,000 tons of fuel oil No. 6, *Coastal (Bermuda)* sued the cargo inspection company Saybolt for its alleged negligence in failing to reveal that the quality analysis it had carried out on the cargo was the result of a composite sample of the various tanks of oil. Saybolt carried out the report for the first seller of the oil, and included neither a reference with regard to the fact that it related to a composite sample nor made reference to minimum or maximum viscosity of the products analysed. The performance of this final sample was, however, carried out as a composite sample according to industry practice. The report was neither consulted by the second seller nor by *Coastal (Bermuda)*, and none of them asked or was told whether the report stated that the test was composite. The final sample of the total oil cargo loaded on the vessel was taken from samples which were blended by hand from each tank of oil and weighed according to the amount of oil in each tank. As a result, a report was given that the viscosity of the oil corresponded with the requirements for No. 6 fuel oil.

---

602 The statement of *Cochran* is therefore absolutely correct: '[I]t cannot be ignored that classification societies are professional organizations that by definition fall directly within the type of establishments section 552 of the Restatements is meant to address' (Cochran, 'Otto Candies, L.L.C. v. Nippon Kaiji Kyokai Corp.', 28 *Tul.Mar.L.J.* 613 (2004), at 624). To a similar result regarding insurance companies, but based on a different argumentation comes O'Brien, 'The Potential Liability of Classification Societies to Marine Insurers Under United States Law', 7 *U. S. F. Mar. L. J.* 403 (1994–1995), at 415.

603 *Coastal (Bermuda) Ltd. v. E.W. Saybolt & Co.*, 826 F.2d 424 (5th Cir.1987), at 428.

604 The first *Somarelf* case was *Somarelf v. American Bureau of Shipping*, 704 F.Supp. 59 (D.N.J.1988), at 64. The Court found that ABS was not subject to an implied contractual duty of indemnity. As regards a tort-based indemnity payment, the summary judgment motion of ABS was denied because of remaining material issues of fact. Concerning the tort of negligent misrepresentation, this judgment is only of limited use. But the second *Somarelf* case (*Somarelf v. American Bureau of Shipping,* 720 F.Supp. 441 (D.N.J.1989)) provides further guidance on this question.

605 *Cargill, Inc. v. Bureau Veritas*, 902 F.Supp. 49 (S.D.N.Y.1995).

606 *Otto Candies, LLC v. Nippon Kaija Kyokai Corp.*, 346 F.3d 530 (5th Cir.(La.)2003), at 534.

Upon arrival of the vessel at its port of destination, the oil was too cold to discharge or even to test. It required twelve days of heating the vessel's holds before most of the oil could be discharged. 340 cubic metres of oil could not be discharged at all and remained on board the vessel. The United States Court of Appeals for the Fifth Circuit defined the requirements of a negligent misrepresentation in the following way:

> 'In order to state a cause of action for negligent misrepresentation under section 552 of the *Restatement (Second),* the plaintiff must allege that: (1) the defendant, in the course of its profession, supplied false information for the plaintiff's guidance in a business transaction; (2) the defendant failed to exercise reasonable care in gathering the information; (3) the plaintiff relied on the false information in a transaction that the defendant intended the information to influence; and (4) the plaintiff thereby suffered pecuniary loss. *Grass v. Credito Mexicano, S.A.,* 797 F.2d 220 (5th Cir.1986).'[607]

Due to the fact that the court found no evidence that Saybolt supplied false guidance for Coastal (Bermuda)'s guidance in this business transaction, nor that it failed to exercise reasonable care in obtaining or communicating the test results, and since no evidence was presented that Coastal justifiably relied on Saybolt's final ship report when it interpreted the report to indicate a pre-blended, uniform cargo of No. 6 oil, the court did not hold Saybolt liable for the provision of the report.[608]

The importance of this decision is that it recognised the tort of negligent misrepresentation in the context of maritime law and specified its preconditions.[609] This decision is only a precedent for an aspect of the services of classification societies, in particular the execution of special surveys, such as an On Hire Survey, with a precisely defined and limited scope of application. This decision solely relates specifically to the inspection of the viscosity of cargo oil. For this activity, the obligation of the shipowner to provide a seaworthy vessel, which otherwise clouds the issue, is not of any relevance. This decision, however, defined the preconditions of the tort of negligent misrepresentation under general maritime law which have been taken up and further developed in subsequent decisions.

b. The Somarelf II Case

aa. The Facts

The first American case against a classification society in which a claim was based on the tort of negligent misrepresentation is *Somarelf v. American Bureau of*

---

607 *Coastal (Bermuda) Ltd. v. E.W. Saybolt & Co.*, 826 F.2d 424 (5th Cir.1987), at 428 *et seq. See* also *Sundance Cruises Corp. v. American Bureau of Shipping,* 799 F.Supp. 363 (S.D.N.Y.1992), at 382.

608 *Coastal (Bermuda) Ltd. v. E.W. Saybolt & Co.*, 826 F.2d 424 (5th Cir.1987), at 429.

609 *See* Cochran, 'Otto Candies, L.L.C. v. Nippon Kaiji Kyokai Corp.', 28 *Tul.Mar.L.J.* 613 (2004), at 615; *Somarelf v. American Bureau of Shipping,* 704 F.Supp. 59 (D.N.J.1988), at 64 (*Somarelf I)*: 'This Court agrees with the Fifth Circuit and can find no persuasive authority or maritime law principles suggesting that a negligent misrepresentation cause of action should not be recognized under maritime law.'

Shipping.[610] This case is also rather special in kind as it did not involve the classification of a ship, but the issuance of a specific tonnage certificate. The plaintiff was Fairfield Maxwell Services Ltd., the managing agents of the owners and operators of two vessels, the HAPPY SPRITE and the JOLLY SPRITE. Somarelf had chartered the two motor tank vessels, which it employed for the carriage of crude oil and petroleum products. It chartered the vessels on four occasions, which gave rise to its claims against ABS (and also to claims against Fairfield Maxwell). Fairfield Maxwell had settled Somarelf's claims, which were based on the supply of incorrect tonnage information. Fairfield Maxwell therefore wanted to take recourse against ABS for these claims which had been subrogated by Somarelf.

The vessels had been classified by ABS from the time of their delivery. ABS had prepared and issued the Suez Canal Special Tonnage Certificates when the vessels were constructed. The certificates were for the benefit of the builders and the owners of the vessel. They reflect the measured or calculated volumes, not the actual weight, of the vessel's hull and superstructure. ABS used computations by the shipyard, which were based on the incorrect assumption that under deck water ballast spaces were to be subtracted from the under deck tonnage. As a result, the Suez Net tonnage certified by ABS showed a tonnage of 43,000 tons instead of the correct 57,000 tons. Since they were sister vessels, the certificates of both vessels reflected the same miscalculation.

When one of the vessels was transferred from the Liberian to the British flag, ABS additionally issued a British tonnage certificate, for which new computations were carried out. This new certificate showed the correct numbers according to the British formula. Since the British and Suez Canal procedures for performing the under deck tonnage calculation differ only slightly, the Suez Canal Authority noticed the discrepancy between the vessel's British tonnage certificate and the current Suez Canal certificate. The Suez Canal Authority subsequently sought supplemental dues from Somarelf for both vesse ls. Somarelf paid USD 166,185 for uncollected canal dues for both vessels for the sub-chartered journeys, which it could not recoup from the sub-charterers of the vessels. Since both Fairfield Maxwell and Somarelf were convinced that Somarelf could have charged higher freight rates under the time charters, they settled Somarelf's claims amounting to USD 200,000, which included claims for interest on the lost freight rates.

---

610 *Somarelf v. American Bureau of Shipping*, 720 F.Supp. 441 (D.N.J.1989). Yet there have been claims based on a negligence theory before, *see Steamship Mutual Underwriting Association Ltd. v. Bureau Veritas*, 380 F.Supp. 482 (E.D.La. 1973). *Somarelf I* was a summary motion by defendant ABS in the same affair which was dismissed as there were a number of unresolved issues of fact (*Somarelf v. American Bureau of Shipping,* 704 F.Supp. 59 (D.N.J.1988)). Case comments of *Somarelf II* are France, 'Classification societies', 1 *I.J.S.L.* 67 (1996), at 74–75; Miller, 'Liability of Classification Societies from the Perspective of United States Law', 22 *Tul.Mar.L.J.* 75 (1997), at 94–96.

bb. The Verdict

The District Court for the District of New Jersey held that in order to sustain the claim of negligent misrepresentation under § 552 Restatement (Second) of Torts, the plaintiff had to prove that

> '(1) ABS in the course of its profession, supplied false information for Somarelf's guidance in a business transaction; (2) ABS failed to exercise reasonable care in gathering the information; (3) Somarelf relied on the false information in a transaction that ABS knew the information would influence; and (4) Somarelf thereby suffered pecuniary loss.'[611]

All these prerequisites had been proven by the plaintiff. The court held that ABS supplied in the course of its profession incorrect Suez Canal tonnage figures for the vessel's owner's and Somarelf's guidance in a business transaction; and ABS also failed to use reasonable care in gathering the incorrect information.[612] The most critical part of the decision is the argumentation that the information was given also for the charterer's guidance and that ABS actually '*knew*' the information would influence a particular business transaction. In fact, ABS did not actually know that the certificate would be presented to the charterer. The court reasoned in the following way:

> 'ABS has an obligation to accurately satisfy requests for issuance of tonnage certificates. Such certificates are relied upon by governments and canal authorities, and are an indispensable part of the maritime industry. ABS knows the importance of their tonnage certificates to the maritime industry, and ABS officers and employees understand that many parties may properly rely on Suez Canal special tonnage certificates issued by ABS. Those Suez Canal certificates are not specifically addressed to any one party and there is no disclaimer of liability or accuracy on the certificate. The Court finds, therefore, that ABS understood that the Suez Canal special tonnage certificates for the HAPPY SPRITE and JOLLY SPRITE could be used for the benefit of other parties in the maritime industry with an obvious need to rely on such certificates; specifically, time charterers and voyage charterers, as well as owners.'[613]

The court confirmed this common-sense approach in the following way:

> 'What was required was proof that ABS, through its relevant employees, had knowledge and understanding of the importance of its [...] tonnage certificates [...] to the maritime industry and specifically that ABS, when issuing [its] certificates with no disclaimer and not specifically addressed to any single party, understood that parties such as time charterers and voyage charterers, as well as owners, would properly and foreseeably rely on the [...] tonnage certificates issued by American Bureau of Shipping.'[614]

---

[611] *Somarelf v. American Bureau of Shipping,* 720 F.Supp. 441 (D.N.J.1989), at 452.

[612] *Somarelf v. American Bureau of Shipping,* 704 F.Supp. 59 (D.N.J.1988), at 64 (*Somarelf I).* This was confirmed in *Somarelf II*, 720 F.Supp. 441 (D.N.J.1989), at 445, 452.

[613] *Somarelf v. American Bureau of Shipping,* 720 F.Supp. 441 (D.N.J.1989), at 445, No. 16.

[614] *Somarelf v. American Bureau of Shipping,* 720 F.Supp. 441 (D.N.J.1989), at 453.

As it was held that Somarelf could have charged a higher differential to its voyage charterers had the correct net tonnage been known, Somarelf also suffered financial loss as a result of ABS's negligence. ABS was therefore held liable for negligent misrepresentation.

cc. Case Comment

An analysis of the *Somarelf II* case shows that even though it is an important case, because it is one of the few in which a classification society has been held liable, it is of rather limited value to the question of the liability of classification societies for the issuance of classification certificates. One may apply its reasoning in an analogous way to the issuance of certificates of a public character with a specific scope of application. However, as the decision does not refer to the specific problems of the shipowner's responsibility according to international conventions, it offers no assistance on whether or not the nondelegable duty of the shipowner to provide a seaworthy ship or his limited liability needs to be taken into account. For these reasons, it has been distinguished on the facts in subsequent litigation relating to the liability for the issuance of a classification certificate.[615]

Even though the wording seems to apply to all kinds of certificates, including classification certificates, it should be realised that this case cannot be generally applied. The fact that § 552 of the Restatements (Second) of Torts requires that the information is provided for the guidance of a third party aims at a restriction of the application of this tort. This is clearly illustrated by its comment h, which includes the phrase:

> 'It is not enough that the maker merely knows of the ever-present possibility of repetition to anyone, and the possibility of action in reliance upon it, on the part of anyone to whom it may be repeated.'[616]

---

615 *Sundance Cruises Corp. v. American Bureau of Shipping,* 799 F.Supp. 363 (S.D.N.Y. 1992), at 377;

616 § 552 comment h:
'The rule stated in this Section subjects the negligent supplier of misinformation to liability only to those persons for whose benefit and guidance it is supplied. In this particular his liability is somewhat more narrowly restricted than that of the maker of a fraudulent misrepresentation (see § 531), which extends to any person whom the maker of the representation has reason to expect to act in reliance upon it.
Under this Section, as in the case of the fraudulent misrepresentation (see § 531), it is not necessary that the maker should have any particular person in mind as the intended, or even the probable, recipient of the information. In other words, it is not required that the person who is to become the plaintiff be identified or known to the defendant as an individual when the information is supplied. It is enough that the maker of the representation intends it to reach and influence either a particular person or persons, known to him, or a group or class of persons, distinct from the much larger class who might reasonably be expected sooner or later to have access to the information and foreseeably to take some action in reliance upon it. It is enough, likewise, that the maker of the representation knows that his recipient intends to transmit the information to a similar per-

That the shipowner showed the tonnage certificate to the charterer could also have been identified as such an 'ever-present possibility of repetition to anyone'. Only the fact that this particular shipowner never managed and operated his vessels, or that chartering of vessels is a very common business in shipping and most likely to occur throughout the life of most ships, would have allowed different conclusions. The way the court phrased the preconditions of the tort of negligent misrepresentation in this case does not allow a restriction of liability only to persons for whose guidance the information is provided. The argument that the certificates are important for practically the entire maritime industry does not allow the slightest limitation of the scope of application.[617] The analogous application of this reasoning to a liability for the issuance of other certificates, including classification certificates, should therefore be avoided.

Surprisingly, in *Somarelf* the question of the applicable law is not mentioned with a single word. The court applies Federal maritime law right away. Even though it was the American classification society which issued the tonnage certificate, the charterer Somarelf was a French corporation, the negligent miscalculations were carried out in New York and the damage occurred in Egypt, because of a certificate which was issued on behalf of the authorities of the Suez Canal. There could have been domestic Egyptian exemption regulations, such as those which led the courts in the *Sundancer* case to dismiss the claims based on misrepresentation as regards the statutory certificates.[618] At least a short reference to this question would have been fruitful.

c. Again: The Sundance Case

Sundance was a case which not only referred to contractual claims, but also to claims in tort.[619] Several courts have cited this verdict in cases of third-party liabil-

son, persons or group. It is sufficient, in other words, insofar as the plaintiff's identity is concerned, that the maker supplies the information for repetition to a certain group or class of persons and that the plaintiff proves to be one of them, even though the maker never had heard of him by name when the information was given. *It is not enough that the maker merely knows of the ever-present possibility of repetition to anyone, and the possibility of action in reliance upon it, on the part of anyone to whom it may be repeated'* (emphasis added).

617 That the duty of care not to issue false information therefore extended to all those who properly and foreseeably rely on the tonnage certificate, as stated by France, 'Classification societies', 1 *I.J.S.L.* 67 (1996), at 75, does not allow a precise definition of the scope of application either.

618 In the *Sundancer* case, the classification society issued the statutory certificates on behalf of the Bahamas, which have enacted legislation which exempts classification societies from liability when acting for the flag State.

619 *Sundance Cruises Corp. v. American Bureau of Shipping,* 799 F.Supp. 363 (S.D.N.Y. 1992), *aff'd,* 7 F.3d 1077 (2d Cir.1993).

ity, just as several scholars have paid reference to this case.[620] However, *Sundance* cannot simply be applied by analogy to third-party claims. Its reasoning is restricted to a claim that is made by the shipowner.

One should therefore not misinterpret the following statements, which out of their context appear to apply to the liability of classification societies in general, including liability to third parties. The court held that claims of the shipowner were barred even in tort, since

> 'A shipowner is not entitled to rely on a classification certificate as a guarantee [...] that the vessel is soundly constructed.'[621]

Reference is also often made to the court's comparison of a classification society with a Motor Vehicle Bureau.

> 'We agree with the district court that Sundance's posture in this lawsuit is somewhat similar to one who causes a vehicle accident and then sues the Motor Vehicle Bureau for damages to his car, because it issued him a driver's licence that falsely represented his fitness to drive. Or, another example, Sundance may be here likened to a truck owner seeking recovery from a truck inspection service because it issued a safety certificate shortly before the truck's negligently maintained brakes failed.'[622]

While it is evident that the Motor Vehicle Bureau has no responsibility towards the car driver to assure that he is fit to drive, the case has a different connotation and may be treated differently if third parties are involved. The following statement is misleading as well:

> 'Put simply, the purpose of the classification certificate is not to guarantee safety, but merely to permit Sundance to take advantage of the insurance rates available to a classed vessel.'[623]

---

620 *See for example Cargill, Inc. v. Bureau Veritas*, 902 F.Supp. 49, 1996 A.M.C. 577 (S.D.N.Y.1995); *Carbotrade v. Bureau Veritas,* 901 F.Supp. 737, 1996 A.M.C. 561 (S.D.N.Y.1995), *vacated on other grounds,* 99 F.3d 86, 1997 A.M.C. 98 (2d Cir.1996), *cert. denied sub. nom. Veritas v. Carbotrade S.p.A.,* 117 S.Ct. 2454 (1997). Cochran, 'Otto Candies, L.L.C. v. Nippon Kaiji Kyokai Corp.', 28 *Tul.Mar.L.J.* 613 (2004), at 616; Honka, 'The Classification System and its Problems with Special Reference to the Liability of Classification Societies', 19 *Tul.Mar.L.J.* 1 (1994), at 13–25; Miller, 'Liability of Classification Societies from the Perspective of United States Law', 22 *Tul.Mar.L.J.* 75 (1997), at 96–98; O'Brien, 'The Potential Liability of Classification Societies to Marine Insurers Under United States Law', 7 *U.S.F.Mar.L.J.* 403 (1994–1995), at 406–409, 414–415.

621 *Sundance Cruises Corp. v. American Bureau of Shipping,* 7 F.3d 1077 (2d Cir.1993), at 1084.

622 *Sundance Cruises Corp. v. American Bureau of Shipping,* 7 F.3d 1077 (2d Cir.1993), at 1084. This comparison is rejected by France, 'Classification societies', 1 *I.J.S.L.* 67 (1996), at 70, stating that a classification society is not a peripheral party because of its special knowledge of *inter alia* marine engineering.

623 *Sundance Cruises Corp. v. American Bureau of Shipping,* 7 F.3d 1077 (2d Cir.1993), at 1084.

As has been shown above,[624] the purpose of a classification certificate is not restricted to allowing a shipowner to take advantage of lower insurance rates. A vessel which does not possess a class cannot be insured at all. Besides, a classification certificate is also relevant to the shipowner as it shows that the vessel corresponds to the rules and because a vessel which is classed by a classification society of good standing will be less frequently checked by port State control.

In *Sundance*, the shipowner sued his classification society, arguing that even though he was responsible for the running aground of his vessel, the vessel would not have sunk but for, *inter alia*, the classification society's negligence in issuing the vessel's certificates even though the vessel lacked certain installations to prevent progressive flooding. As has been pointed out in the *Great American* Case, the shipowner has a non-delegable duty to provide a seaworthy vessel and shall not be able to escape this duty when having his ship surveyed by a classification society. The idea is that only the shipowner is responsible for his own behaviour (and therefore for the way he looks after his vessel as well). This is also implied by the comparison with a Motor Vehicle Bureau. The Court of Appeals however expressly excluded the application of these remarks to cases of liability towards third parties:[625]

> 'This case must be distinguished from a suit brought by an injured third party who relied on the classification or safety certificates.'[626]

The court continued to draw attention to cases of misrepresentation towards third parties in which the misrepresentor was held liable, showing that the statements with regard to the non-existence of such duty of care in tort to the shipowner does not imply the same result in third- party cases. Because of this inapplicability to third-party cases, the effects of the statement that 'put simply, the purpose of the classification certificate is not to guarantee safety, but merely to permit [the shipowner] to take advantage of the insurance rates available to a classed vessel'[627] need to be restricted to the shipowner. It may be argued that insurance matters are the main reason why a shipowner has his vessel classified and that to claim that insurance matters are of similar importance to third parties would be misleading, because the fact that a vessel is classed rather shows to these third parties that it fulfils a certain standard of safety and is likely to perform a certain voyage. Even

---

[624] *See supra* Part 1 A III 2, Part 1 B I 3.

[625] This is also remarked by Cochran, 'Otto Candies, L.L.C. v. Nippon Kaiji Kyokai Corp.', 28 *Tul.Mar.L.J.* 613 (2004), at 616: 'The Court was careful to distinguish a suit brought directly by a vessel owner for unseaworthiness from "a suit brought by an injured third party who relied on the classification or safety certificates".' Similar: O'Halloran, 'Otto Candies, L.L.C. v. Nippon Kaiji Kyokai Corp.', 78 *Tul.L.Rev.* 1389 (2003–2004), at 1392.

[626] *Sundance Cruises Corp. v. American Bureau of Shipping,* 7 F.3d 1077 (2d Cir.1993), at 1084.

[627] *Sundance Cruises Corp. v. American Bureau of Shipping,* 7 F.3d 1077 (2d Cir.1993), at 1084.

if the wording appears to be of a general kind, its application needs to be strictly restricted on the facts of the case to the shipowner, as is done by the Court of Appeals.

Similarly, the disparity between fees charged and liability of the classification society is solely of relevance to a contractual liability. The foundation of this argument is included in § 351 comment f Restatement (Second) of Contracts, which is also referred to in *Sundance.* However, under tort law principles, liability is even possible if the information which caused the damage has been given gratuitously, which is illustrated for instance by § 311 comment c Restatement (Second) of Torts; the disparity between the fees and the potential liability should therefore not be taken into account in tort law.[628]

The precise wording of the court only refers to a suit in which a third party relied on the classification or safety certificates. However, this should not be construed in such a way that the court meant to exclude the tort of negligence in third party cases. *Sundance* was a case in which the main question was whether the shipowner suffered damage by relying on the certificates issued by the classification society. As a result, the court concentrated on the situation that the shipowner relied on the certificates. It was therefore only necessary to state that third parties relying on certificates would not be excluded from the application of tort law. Moreover, there is no good reason why the court should exclude the application of § 311 Restatement (Second) of Torts, as it also applies to cases in which not the third party but someone else relied on the statement, but allow recovery whenever § 552 Restatement (Second) of Torts applies. § 552 only aims at economic loss, whereas § 311 envisages physical harm, which tort law considers to be more valuable, since it is protected under less strict preconditions than economic loss.

The gist of *Sundance* is that its reasoning only applies to the shipowner and does not exclude liability towards third parties based on tort. Quite the opposite, in fact: the court expressly states that such claims should be possible.

d. The Cargill Case

In *Cargill, Inc. v. Bureau Veritas*, the cargo owners, shippers and assignees of vegetable oil claimed damages for economic loss against BV. They argued that BV had negligently misrepresented to the owner that the vessel PACIFIC DAWN was fit for sailing.[629] BV had surveyed the vessel and issued several certificates which postponed the survey of certain overdue continuous survey items. Even though the vessel suffered repeated breakdowns and scavenge fires on its journeys, new certificates were handed out together with the specification that perma-

[628] *See also* Miller, 'Liability of Classification Societies from the Perspective of United States Law', 22 *Tul.Mar.L.J.* 75 (1997), at 97–98. Regarding the question of disparity, *see also* Goldberg, 'A Reexamination of Glanzer v. Shepard', 3 *Theoretical Inquries in Law*, 475 (2002), at 493–503.

[629] *Cargill, Inc. v. Bureau Veritas*, 902 F.Supp. 49 (S.D.N.Y.1995). *See also* Miller, 'Liability of Classification Societies from the Perspective of United States Law', 22 *Tul.Mar.L.J.* 75 (Winter 1997), at 99–112.

nent repairs had to be carried out to the diesel generator by a certain date. When the vessel departed for another journey, it sustained a machinery failure, which forced it to dock. On 8 April 1992, the vessel sailed again, although its last certificates had expired. When the ship docked in New Orleans between the 14th and 17th of April, the cargo at issue was loaded on board the vessel, even though the classification certificate for machinery items had expired. On 26 May 1992, a BV surveyor examined the portside generator and witnessed test runs and finally issued a "Detailed Report of Survey" indicating that all continuous survey machinery items had been put into satisfactory condition. Certificate No. 6 specified that permanent repairs had been dealt with, but certificate No. 7 required certain recommendations to be addressed at the vessel's next port of call.

Only hours after it departed from New Orleans on 1 June 1992, the vessel had to cast anchor due to smoke in the engine room. Repairs were made until June 4, which were not surveyed by BV, but characterised by the vessel's chief engineer as "major repairs". On 15 June, the main engine stopped because of fires in its scavenge spaces. It could not be re-started, purportedly due to problems with the portside generator. The vessel could not continue its journey and had to be towed to New York. On 21 August, BV suspended class for the vessel retroactively to June 1. The plaintiffs claim that BV owed them a duty to ensure the seaworthiness of the vessel which it breached by failing to revoke classification and by making several misrepresentations.

In the verdict, the court quoted *Great American Insurance* and *Sundance* and held that a classification society is not an insurer of the seaworthiness of a vessel:

> 'To deem a classification society as a warrantor of a vessel's seaworthiness would create a liability which is not commensurate with a classification society's limited control over a vessel, the intent of the parties, the fees charged for classification or the services performed. [...] The same rationale compels the conclusion that, by classifying a vessel, a classification society is also not liable as an insurer of a vessel's seaworthiness to third party cargo owners, such as the plaintiffs.'[630]

Since the classification society does not guarantee the seaworthiness of the vessel, it cannot be held liable for it. However, from the point of view of the District Court for the Southern District of New York, the classification society can be liable for representing something else. The court approved of the theory that a cause of action may exist for negligent misrepresentation if the classification society negligently inspects the vessel and fails to revoke its class, and as a result negligently misrepresents that the vessel is fit for sailing, thereby foreseeably causing damage to a third party. [631] As the plaintiffs did not establish that they actually and reasonably relied on the certificates issued by BV, they could not prevail on this theory. Neither did the plaintiffs consult the classification society's ship's register, nor did they have knowledge of any certificate. In addition to that, the plaintiffs hired their own marine surveyor to have the vessel surveyed one week after BV

[630] *Cargill, Inc. v. Bureau Veritas*, 902 F.Supp. 49 (S.D.N.Y.1995), at 52.
[631] *Cargill, Inc. v. Bureau Veritas*, 902 F.Supp. 49 (S.D.N.Y.1995), at 52.

last surveyed the ship, at a time when the ship had already undergone major repairs. The court also referred to the possibility for the plaintiffs to require a confirmation of class from the owners, which would have reflected current conditions and recommendations at the time of the journey. That the classification certificate for machinery items (alongside several statutory certificates) had expired at the time the plaintiffs loaded the vessel was not known to them, but in the eyes of the court of no concern either. For this reason, it was held that the plaintiffs had not asked BV to provide them with any information for their guidance, as would have been required by § 552 Restatement (Second) of Torts.

As a commentary on this case, one may add that the court correctly held in *Cargill* that the classification society does not give a representation as to the seaworthiness of the vessel, but that it may, however, be held liable for negligent misrepresentation by a third party. Once again after *Great American Insurance* and *Sundance* it is stated that such liability is possible. However, the decision is not precise in its reliance on *Great American Insurance*. That case related to the liability of a classification society towards a contracting party. Therefore, the argumentation of the District Court in *Cargill*, that the 'same rationale' applies to this case of third party liability is not convincing. The level of fees which are charged for the services performed are only of relevance in the case of contractual liability, but irrelevant to a liability in tort.[632]

Apart from that, the District Court erred in another aspect: it is quite unlikely that the plaintiffs would have received a confirmation of class if they had wanted to obtain additional information on the current conditions and recommendations at the time of the journey. The classification society may not give such information without approval of the shipowner. It is not usual that a shipowner grants such a certificate to cargo-owners.

e. The Otto Candies Case

aa. The Facts

Otto Candies L.L.C. bought the high-speed aluminium passenger vessel SPEEDER from a company called Diamond, which had operated it as a coastal passenger ferry from 1995 to 1998, on 22 December 1999. It was classed by the Japanese classification society ClassNK as "coastal (Japanese Government) passenger vessel". In 1998, the vessel was taken out of service and the classification lapsed. As a condition of sale, it was required that ClassNK restore and make current the vessel's coastal classification, free of any outstanding recommendations. A Class Maintenance Certificate was issued by ClassNK on 5 January 2000 which did not indicate any outstanding deficiencies. The company then transported the vessel to the United States, where it was surveyed by ABS. *Otto Candies* intended to transfer the vessel's classification to this classification society. The ABS surveyor discovered several significant deficiencies which required repair. The costs of these

[632] *See supra* the analysis of the Sundance case, Part 2 A II 3 c cc.

repairs added up to USD 328,096.43 for which Otto Candies sued ClassNK, based on the tort of negligent misrepresentation.[633]

bb. The Verdict

This is one of the rare cases in which a United States court held a classification society liable. Otto Candies had an actionable claim for USD 328,096.43 against ClassNK. The Court of Appeals for the 5th Circuit first referred to the difficulties of cases which concern classification certificates and the spheres of responsibilities of shipowners and classification societies.

> '[...] [W]e emphasize that a claim for negligent misrepresentation in connection with the work of maritime classification societies should be strictly and carefully limited. The societies' surveys and certificate system are essential to maintaining the safety of maritime commerce, yet their activities should not derogate from shipowners' and charterers' nondelegable duty to maintain seaworthy vessels. Imposition of undue liability on classification societies could be harmful in several ways. The societies could be deterred by the prospect of liability from performing work on old or damaged vessels that most need their advice. The spreading of liability could diminish owners' sense of responsibility for vessel safety even as it complicates liability determinations. Ultimately, broader imposition of liability upon classification societies would increase their risk management costs and rebound in higher fees charged to the societies' clients throughout the maritime industry. Whether such risk-spreading is cost-efficient in an industry with well-developed legal duties and insurance requirements is doubtful. The distinctions articulated in case law to date recognize the care with which claims against classification societies must be studied.'[634]

The court distinguished this case from one which involves a complex system of responsibilities between the shipowner and the classification society. *Otto Candies* was not the usual case of the classification of a vessel for a long period of time with subsequent surveys. At issue was only the thorough check of whether the vessel satisfied the rules and could be granted a classification once again. Even though ClassNK was required to re-class the vessel, it was evident from the beginning that the buyer would register the vessel with another classification society and that the re-classification was solely a condition precedent to the sale of the vessel. This was, therefore, not a case of the classification of a vessel for a long period of time. ClassNK was aware that its certification was directly related to the pending sale of the vessel to Otto Candies and that the certification would be used to guide Otto Candies' decision to buy the vessel, even though the certificate had

---

633 *Otto Candies, LLC v. Nippon Kaija Kyokai Corp.*, 2002 WL 1798767 (E.D.La.2002), *aff'd.* 346 F.3d 530, 2003 A.M.C. 2409 (5th Cir.(La.)2003), *cert. den.'d* 72 USLW 3668, 72 USLW 3672 (U.S.2004). For case comments, *see* Charvet/Waterman, 'Recent Developments in Maritime Law', 28 *Tul.Mar.L.J.* 375 (2004), at 445; Cochran, 'Otto Candies, L.L.C. v. Nippon Kaiji Kyokai Corp.', 28 *Tul.Mar.L.J.* 613 (2004); O'Halloran, 'Otto Candies, L.L.C. v. Nippon Kaiji Kyokai Corp.', 78 *Tul.L.Rev.* 1389 (2003–2004).

634 *Otto Candies, LLC v. Nippon Kaija Kyokai Corp.*, 346 F.3d 530 (5th Cir.(La.)2003), at 535.

to go through Diamond's hands and was not directly provided to Otto Candies by ClassNK.

First of all, the court held that the tort of maritime misrepresentation was cautiously recognised in maritime law.[635] In addition to the well-established preconditions of the tort of negligent misrepresentation, *i.e.*, false information, failure to exercise reasonable care, justifiable reliance of the third party, and pecuniary loss,[636] the Court of Appeals put forth two additional preconditions[637] which limit the scope of application to a

> '"person, or a member of a 'limited group' of persons, for whose benefit and guidance the defendant either intends to supply the information or knows that the recipient intends to supply it." [...] Thus Otto Candies must establish that NKK provided the class certificate to Diamond and knew that Diamond intended it for Otto Candies' guidance and benefit.
> This is because "[t]he Restatement expressly limits liability to a select group of nonclients who the misinformer *actually knows* will receive inaccurate information [...]" The fact that it was merely possible or foreseeable that a nonclient of the information supplier would rely on the information is insufficient. [...] Furthermore, the information supplier's liability under section 552 is limited to those persons whom the enagement is intended to benefit.'[638]

The first additional prerequisite, therefore, is that the third party was a member of the limited group of persons for whose benefit and guidance the information was intended. The second one is its actual knowledge that the third party would receive the inaccurate information.

Justifiable reliance consists of two elements, actual reliance and reasonable reliance.[639] 'The justifiableness of the reliance is judged in light of the plaintiff's intelligence and experience.'[640] Even though this is not a very precise definition, it allows for the restriction of the application of the tort of negligent misrepresentation whenever a liability would appear unfair to the judges.

---

635 *Otto Candies, LLC v. Nippon Kaija Kyokai Corp.*, 346 F.3d 530, at 535, 2003 A.M.C. 2409, at 2410 (5th Cir.(La.)2003).

636 At 535: 'To prevail on a cause of action for negligent misrepresentation under section 552 of the *Restatement (Second) of Torts,* Otto Candies had to establish that (1) NKK, in the course of its profession, supplied false information for Otto Candies' guidance in a business transaction; (2) NKK failed to exercise reasonable care in gathering the information; (3) Otto Candies justifiably relied on the false information that NKK intended to influence; and (4) Otto Candies thereby suffered pecuniary loss.'

637 As has been articulated in *Scottish Heritable Trust v. Peat Marwick Main & Co.,* 81 F.3d 606 (5th Cir.1996).

638 *Otto Candies, LLC v. Nippon Kaija Kyokai Corp.*, 346 F.3d 530 (5th Cir.(La.)2003), 535 *et seq.*

639 *Scottish Heritable Trust v. Peat Marwick Main & Co.,* 81 F.3d 606 (5th Cir.1996), at 615.

640 *Scottish Heritable Trust v. Peat Marwick Main & Co.,* 81 F.3d 606 (5th Cir.1996), at 615.

In *Otto Candies*, policy issues such as the limitation of liability of the shipowner or carrier were of no relevance to the case. The court, however, made important remarks *obiter* in which way it would restrict liability towards other third parties in the course of a regular long-term classification:

> 'Comments to section 552 make clear that even parties that customarily rely on certain information are not entitled to bring a section 552 claim unless the information supplier knew at the time it supplied the information that it was for their benefit and guidance. As the California Supreme Court notes:
> [b]y confining what might otherwise be unlimited liability to those persons whom the engagement is designed to benefit, the Restatement rule requires that the supplier of information receive notice of potential third party claims, thereby allowing it to ascertain the potential scope of its liability and make rational decisions regarding the undertaking.
> [...] Thus, in this context, we reject any implication that classification societies can be liable for negligent misrepresentation to parties, including without limitation seamen, longshoremen, passengers, cargo owners, and charterers that may rely upon a survey or class certificate, absent actual knowledge by the classification society that the certificate or survey report was being provided for the guidance and benefit of the party.'[641]
> 'The certificate or survey in no way guarantees a vessel's seaworthiness, however, but extends only as far as the nature of the survey performed.'[642]

Otto Candies therefore tries to restrict the liability of classification societies, and only allows it under certain conditions. The court explicitly recognises the policy issues which are involved, but does not consider that these policy issues forbid a liability of classification societies towards third parties.

cc. Case Comment

Otto Candies is a landmark case with regard to the liability of classification societies, because it finally defines the duty of care towards third parties in view of § 552 Restatement (Second) of Torts. Its reasoning is, however, restricted to § 552, because the claims were only made for economic loss, not for physical harm in the sense of § 311 of the Restatements. The importance of *Otto Candies* is not only that the preconditions of the tort of negligent misrepresentation have been further specified. What is most important is the fact that even though it referred to the policy issues such as the non-delegable duty of the shipowner to provide a seaworthy vessel or the limitations of liability in shipping, it did not refrain from imposing liability contrary to the approach taken by the English House of Lords. In this respect, the United States approach to the liability of classification societies significantly differs from the English precedent.

It is of further relevance that after *Great American Insurance* and *Sundance* the preconditions of a liability for negligent misrepresentation were finally specified and that a classification society was actually held liable for its performance of a

---

[641] *Otto Candies, LLC v. Nippon Kaija Kyokai Corp.*, 346 F.3d 530 (5th Cir.(La.)2003), at 536 *et seq.* (emphasis added).

[642] *Otto Candies, LLC v. Nippon Kaija Kyokai Corp.*, 346 F.3d 530 (5th Cir.(La.)2003), at 538.

re-classification survey. Especially after *Sundance,* many authors were of the opinion that a classification society could not be liable for its actions, which was also reflected in case law.[643] The remarks of the court that a classification society was not the insurer of the seaworthiness of the vessel and that the fees charged to their customers reflect that both parties assume that the classification society could not be held liable for its services have often been extended to cases in which tort law was the subject matter. The remarks of the court which distinguished a *second duty* to detect deficiencies and warn of them[644] or which referred to the different situation if not the shipowner but a third party was involved[645] have consistently been ignored. That these arguments cannot be ignored and that the provision of information to a third party may result in liability has been explicitly shown by *Otto Candies.*[646] The gist of the argumentation is that the certificate does not guarantee the seaworthiness of the vessel (just as was held in *Great American Insurance* and *Amoco Cadiz*),[647] but merely gives a statement that the vessel has been surveyed as to whether it conforms to the rules, which establish a certain standard of safety. However, in view of this certain standard, a classification society may be held liable, even by third parties. Claims for economic loss require a certain kind of foreseeability and need to be restricted in their application, as otherwise the financial exposure might be immense. This restriction is achieved by requiring that the information must be intended for the benefit and guidance of the third party.

It has been criticised that the court was very cautious in applying the principles of negligent misrepresentation.[648] According to that criticism, the court should rather have applied the principle in a straightforward way. The exposure would be restricted by case law such as *Scottish Heritable Trust, Carbotrade,* and *First Na-*

---

643 *Cargill, Inc. v. Bureau Veritas*, 902 F.Supp. 49 (S.D.N.Y.1995). Miller, 'Liability of Classification Societies from the Perspective of United States Law', 22 *Tul.Mar.L.J.* 75 (1997), at 96–98; O'Brien, 'The Potential Liability of Classification Societies to Marine Insurers Under United States Law', 7 *U.S.F.Mar.L.J.* 403 (1994–1995), at 406–409, 414–415.

644 *Great American Insurance Co. v. Bureau Veritas*, 338 F.Supp. 999 (S.D.N.Y.1972), at 1012–1013.

645 *Sundance Cruises Corp. v. American Bureau of Shipping,* 7 F.3d 1077 (2d Cir.1993), at 1084.

646 *See Otto Candies, LLC v. Nippon Kaija Kyokai Corp.*, 346 F.3d 530 (5th Cir.(La.)2003), at 534. O'Halloran comments on this in the following way: 'However, no matter how narrowly the court tailored the opinion, it has created a precedent that will be used to impose liability on classification societies' (O'Halloran, 'Otto Candies, L.L.C. v. Nippon Kaiji Kyokai Corp.', 78 *Tul.L.Rev.* 1389 (2003–2004), at 1398).

647 *Great American Insurance Co. v. Bureau Veritas*, 338 F.Supp. 999 (S.D.N.Y.1972), at 1012; *In the Matter of: Oil Spill by the Amoco Cadiz off the Coast in France on March 16, 1978,* 954 F.2nd 1279 (7th Cir. 1992), at 1300.

648 Cochran, 'Otto Candies, L.L.C. v. Nippon Kaiji Kyokai Corp.', 28 *Tul.Mar.L.J.* 613 (2004), at 622.

tional Bank anyway.[649] However, except for a *caveat* which described the problems and dangers involved and served as an introduction to the verdict, the court exactly did what its critics claimed it should have done. It applied the tort of negligent misrepresentation in a straightforward way.[650] Furthermore, its *caveat* is justified. The court held that 'a claim for negligent misrepresentation in connection with the work of maritime classification societies should be strictly and carefully limited'.[651] This only requires courts in subsequent proceedings to be aware of the scope of problems which this issue involves as described by the court. However, the precise way the court has limited its application does not differ from any other decision based on this theory. The court has applied exactly the same restrictions as have been defined in *Scottish Heritable Trust, Carbotrade,* and *First National Bank.* The *caveat* therefore does not introduce any further requirements, but solely summarises the necessity of classification societies for maritime safety, which is relevant to a general understanding of the topic.

The case does not establish a precedent for all cases which involve a classification certificate, as there are a number of details which make this case just as distinct and special as *Somarelf II.*[652] In *Otto Candies*, the vessel needed to be re-classified, which is evidently more than a confirmation of class or a usual classification. Unlike in the case of a confirmation of class, the vessel was surveyed as a whole, and the status of the certificate was therefore current (and not according to the files). After a re-classification, the shipowner and the third party have to be able to rely on the fact that the vessel really complies with the rules at the time of the inspection.

Another special aspect was the fact that the classification society knew exactly for which third party the certificate was intended.[653] Unlike a classification certificate which is handed out to the shipowner who might pass it on to third parties unknown to the classification society, the classification society in this case exactly

---

649 *Scottish Heritable Trust v. Peat Marwick Main & Co.,* 81 F.3d 606 (5th Cir.1996), at 615. In *Carbotrade* it was held that the tort of misrepresentation claims are 'only appropriate where there is a relationship approaching privity between the defendant and the third party' (*Carbotrade v. Bureau Veritas,* 901 F.Supp. 737, at 747, 1996 A.M.C. 561 (S.D.N.Y.1995)); *First National Bank of Commerce v. Monco Agency Inc.,* 911 F.2d 1053 (5th Cir.1990): not only must a classification society have actual knowledge that the third party would receive the inaccurate information, but also it must have actual knowledge that 'its client intends to use the accurate information to influence a particular business transaction, or a substantially similar transaction, to follow' (at 1061)]

650 This is also pointed out by O'Halloran, 'Otto Candies v. Nippon Kaiji Kyokai Corp', 78 *Tul. L. Rev.* 1389 (2003–2004), at 1395.

651 *Otto Candies, LLC v. Nippon Kaija Kyokai Corp.*, 346 F.3d 530 (5th Cir.(La.)2003), at 535.

652 In this regard O'Halloran errs, *compare* O'Halloran, 'Otto Candies v. Nippon Kaiji Kyokai Corp', 78 *Tul. L. Rev.* 1389 (2003–2004), at 1398–1399.

653 This is also pointed out by Block, 'No Class Act: A Bad Survey Lands a Classification Society in Hot Water', *Marine Digest and Transportation News*, 16 November 2003, 15, at 16.

knew that the information was to be provided to the purchaser of the vessel. The classification society knew that the certificate was of relevance to the third party, as the re-classification was carried out only on request of the third party. The shipowner was only interested in the certificate insofar as it was a condition precedent to the execution of the purchase of the vessel. Of course, the shipowner did not want to repair or modify the vessel, as this would involve further costs. For this reason, a re-classification is not comparable to a certificate of class, as in such a case the classification society does not know who will learn about the existence or contents of this certificate. Also, a re-classification survey is not comparable to an annual survey, as it has a much larger scope. A re-classification is more similar to the way the vessel is scrutinised at the time it is first entered in the Register of Ships. ClassNK therefore had to know precisely in what a condition the vessel was in.

To sum up, precisely the situation which was adjudicated by the court is not very likely to re-occur. However, the broad statements give some important indications as to how other cases of third-party liability would be solved by this court. A rather restrictive approach must be taken, as the classification society not only has to know that the certificate was intended for the benefit and guidance of a limited group of persons, but also that the third party would receive the inaccurate information. The society must be aware that it is performing a job for a third party apart from the shipowner that has hired it. This may be the case if it issues specialised documentation, *i.e.* for the charterer, or an attestation or confirmation for a certain person or group of persons.[654] Not everybody who has knowledge of the contents of a certificate by one way or the other will be protected. It has to be evident to the classification society that the claimant takes account of the information or that the information is for the use of the claimant. The main problem about this decision is that these passages are only made *obiter dictum*. The next time someone brings a suit against a classification society, the court in question might follow these remarks or might not. The doctrine of *stare decisis* does not apply to *obiter dicta*. Hence, the *Otto Candies* verdict gives important implications, although a court would not be bound to adhere to its findings. Despite the fact that this dictum correctly sums up the situation as regards the tort of negligent misrepresentation under § 552 Restatement (Second) of Torts, it remains interesting what approach other courts will take in the future.

f. § 311 Restatement (Second) of Torts

As has been stated before, an action in tort will be based on § 552 Restatement (Second) of Torts for cases of economic loss, and on § 311 if a physical harm was

[654] This reasonable reliance is therefore unjustifiably answered in the positive by Miller ('Liability of Classification Societies', 22 *Tul.Mar.L.J.* 75, at 107 (1997)) without a detailed analysis of how exactly the cargo-owner relied on the representation of the classification society and in which way this was reasonably foreseeable to the society.

caused by the alleged negligent misrepresentation.[655] Being a variant of the tort of negligent misrepresentation, the principles that are laid down in § 311 are accepted as part of general maritime law.[656] The preconditions of this tort are that (i) the defendant must negligently provide false information, (ii) the recipient of that information must have taken action as the result of relying on that information, (iii) physical harm must result from that action, and (iv) the injured person must be one whom the defendant knows or whom he should expect to be put in danger by the negligent misrepresentation. This tort is particularly applied if it is a part of the actor's business or profession to provide information on which the safety of the recipient or the third party depends.[657]

---

655 Section 311 Restatement (Second) of Torts: Misrepresentation Involving Risk of Physical Harm

(1) One who negligently gives false information to another is subject to liability for physical harm caused by action taken by the other in reasonable reliance upon such information, where such harm results
  (a) to the other, or
  (b) to such third persons as the actor should expect to be put in peril by the action taken.

(2) Such negligence may consist of failure to exercise reasonable care:
  (a) in ascertaining the accuracy of the information, or
  (b) in the manner in which it is communicated.

656 *See Coastal (Bermuda) Ltd. v. E.W. Saybolt & Co.*, 826 F.2d 424 (5th Cir.1987), at 428–429; *Royal Embassy v. Ioannis Martinos*, 1986 A.M.C. 769 (E.D.N.C.1984), at 786–787; *Somarelf v. American Bureau of Shipping,* 704 F.Supp. 59 (D.N.J.1988), at 63–64 (*Somarelf I*). Miller, 'Liability of Classification Societies', 22 *Tul.Mar.L.J.* 75 (1997), at 103 also points out that the tort of negligent misrepresentation has been recognised in several decisions as a part of general maritime law, and that this includes § 311. Federal courts have in the exercise of their admiralty jurisdiction repeatedly embraced the Restatements as a reliable and trusted source for formulating general maritime law in the absence of any clearly articulated jurisprudential rule (*see* Miller, 'Liability of Classification Societies', 22 *Tul.Mar.L.J.* 75 (1997), at 104 citing *Doxsee Sea Clam Co. v. Brown,* 13 F.3d 550, 1994 A.M.C. 305 (2d Cir.1994), *Texport Oil Co. v. M/V Amolyntos*, 11 F.3d 361, 1994 A.M.C. 815 (2d Cir.1993). *See also Jurgens v. Poling Transport Corp.,* 113 F.Supp.2d 388 (E.D.NY.2000).
It is however surprising that in the *Eternity Shipping*-Case, the District Court analysed § 522, and not § 311 Restatement (Second) of Torts, *see In the Matter of the Complaint of Eternity Shipping, Ltd.*, 2006 WL 2422705 (D.Md.2006), 9. The Third-Party-Plaintiffs, which consisted of the mother of a seaman who died as a result of the collapse of a crane which had been certified by ABS, and of the owner of a damaged shore crane, sued the classification society for damages. They argued that ABS had conducted a sub-standard inspection of the crane and had failed to identify alleged defects that ultimately contributed to the accident. The Court concluded that there was no evidence that the Third-Party Plaintiffs had relied on the representation by the classification society and therefore dismissed the claim.

657 § 311 Restatement (Second) of Torts, comment b.

As has been pointed out before,[658] the classification society is not an insurer and does not guarantee the seaworthiness of the vessel. It will behave negligently if it does not perform a survey with reasonable care, skill, diligence and ability, employs inexperienced surveyors, does not implement state-of-the-art requirements, or the like. § 311 only requires that information is provided to the recipient who takes action in reliance on that action; the injured party may be a third party different from the recipient of the information. If the shipowner, as the recipient of the information, puts the vessel to sea in reliance on that information and this causes a casualty of the vessel with physical harm to third parties, the classification society will be liable to those third parties that it knows or should expect to be put in danger by its negligent misrepresentation to the shipowner. However, as § 311 requires *reliance* on the information, the classification society's information must relate to the reason of the casualty. Additionally, it is once again an issue whom the classification *expects* or *should expect* to put in danger due to a reliance on its surveys and certificates. These are first of all those who can be identified as *aboard* the vessel, such as crew, passengers and cargo-owners with their property interest. Moreover, these can be persons *outside* the vessel as well who suffer physical injuries because of the fact that the vessel puts to sea due to a reliance of the shipowner on the classification certificate and the representations by the classification society. However, it always needs to be scrutinised whether the damage caused is physical harm, whereas any kind of economic loss can only be claimed under the stricter provisions of § 552 of the Restatement (Second) of Torts.

4. *Strict Liability?*

Present case law solely refers to theories of negligence and negligent misrepresentation. This does not necessarily have to be the end of the issue. As common law systems develop incrementally by way of what the courts hold what the law is, it must be considered whether policy considerations which have led to the imposition of strict liability under certain circumstances also apply to the activities of classification societies. If such conditions apply, classification societies will be strictly liable for their actions.

a. Abnormally Dangerous Activities

Strict liability for abnormally dangerous activities is grounded on the English case *Rylands v. Fletcher*.[659] In this case, the defendants had, with the permission of the adjacent landowner, constructed a water reservoir. The defendants took no part in the construction, but employed a competent engineer and contractor to construct it. Beneath the site which had been chosen were abandoned mine shafts, which had been filled with soil. Although the existence of these mine shafts was not disclosed to the defendants, the contractors became aware of them in the course of the excavation. When the defendants filled the reservoir with water, the soil which had been used to fill one of the abandoned mine shafts collapsed under the pres-

658 *See* for instance *supra* Part 1 A I, Part 1 A III 5, Part 1 B 1 2, 3.

659 *Rylands v. Fletcher,* (1868) L.R. 3 H.L. (E. & 1 App.) 330 (H.L.).

sure of the water, which flooded the plaintiff's working mine, that was situated under land close to the location of the reservoir. The defendants were held liable irrespective of the proof of negligence on their own part or on the part of anyone engaged by them to construct the reservoir.[660]

The principles of *Rylands v. Fletcher* have been re-phrased in §§ 519, 520 Restatement (Second) of Torts. § 519 establishes strict liability for such activities,[661] and § 520 lists factors which are to be taken in consideration when determining whether an activity is abnormally dangerous.[662] As an effect, under strict liability there is no test whether the defendant exercised reasonable care or skill.[663]

---

660 The chief opinion was delivered in the Court of Exchequer by Mr. Justice Blackburn (*Fletcher v. Rylands,* (1866) L.R. 1 Exch. 265, at 278): 'The person who for his own purpose brings on his lands and collects and keeps there anything likely to do mischief, if it escapes, must keep it in at his peril, and if he does not do so, is *prima facie* answerable for all the damage which is the natural consequence of its escape. He can excuse himself by showing that the escape was owing to the plaintiff's default; or, perhaps, that the escape was the consequence of *vis major*, or the act of God; but as nothing of this sort exists here, it is unnecessary to inquire what excuse would be sufficient. The general rule, as above stated, seems on principle just. The person whose grass or corn is eaten down by the escaping cattle of his neighbor, or whose cellar is invaded by the filth of his neighbor's privy, or whose habitation is made unhealthy by the fumes and noisome vapors of his neighbor's alkali works, is damnified without any fault of his own; and it seems but reasonable and just that the neighbor, who has brought something on his own property which was not naturally there, harmless to others so long as it is confined to his own property, but which he knows to be mischievous if it gets on his neighbor's, should be obliged to make good the damage which ensure, if he does not succeed in confining it to his own property. But for his act in bringing it there no mischief could have accrued, and it seems but just that he should at his peril keep it there, so that no mischief may accrue, or answer for the natural and anticipated consequences. And upon authority, this we think is established to be the law, whether the things so brought be beasts, or water, or filth, or stenches.' For a comprehensive analysis of *Rylands v. Fletcher, see* Bohlen, 'The Rule in Rylands v. Fletcher', 59 *U. Pa. L. Rev.* 298 (1911); *compare also* McLoughlin/Bellinger, *Environmental Pollution Control* (1993), at 108–109; Woolley/Pugh-Smith/Laugham/Upton, *Environmental Law* (2000), § 17:33–17:36.

661 § 519 General Principle.

(1) One who carries on an abnormally dangerous activity is subject to liability for harm to the person, land or chattels of another resulting from the activity, although he has exercised the utmost care to prevent the harm.

(2) This strict liability is limited to the kind of harm, the possibility of which makes the activity abnormally dangerous.

662 § 520 Abnormally Dangerous Activities

In determining whether an activity is abnormally dangerous, the following factors are to be considered:

(a) existence of a high degree of risk of some harm to the person, land or chattels of others;

It might be argued that the transportation of cargo such as oil and oil products constitutes an abnormally dangerous activity.[664] To refer to the preconditions of § 520, there is clearly a high degree of risk of great harm, which apparently cannot be eliminated by the use of care. And the transportation of oil is not conducted by many members of the community. One might even argue that oil transport is inappropriate in some locations, as illustrated by the immense damage from oil spills.[665] Even if one agrees with this argumentation, which has not been recognised by the courts,[666] it would only apply to shipping companies which transport oil, not to classification societies. It is not the classification society who is responsible for the transport of the oil. The survey of a vessel does not constitute such a risk in itself.[667] Quite the opposite, it actually aims at minimising existing risks. The checking of a vessel is not an activity which is dangerous to the public. Hence, §§ 519, 520 do not apply to the activities of classification societies.

b. Liability for Defective Products

A large body of law relates to products liability. An entire volume of the Restatements (Third) on Products Liability, which was published in 1998, covers this field of law. And there has been a substantial development throughout the years since the first decisions in the 1940s in which products liability was for the first time identified as an individual tort involving distinct considerations and special

(b) likelihood that the harm that results from it will be great;
(c) inability to eliminate the risk by the exercise of reasonable care;
(d) extent to which the activity is not a matter of common usage;
(e) inappropriateness of the activity to the place where it is carried on; and
(f) extent to which its value to the community is outweighed by its dangerous attributes.

See also Santos, *Limits and Scope of Environmental Law* (1995), at 94–97.

663 *Heritage v. Pioneer Brokerage & Sales, Inc.*, 604 P.2d 1059 (Alaska 1979), at 1061–1063; *accord, Garcia v. Sky Climber, Inc.*, 470 S.W.2d 261 (Tex.Civ.App.1971), at 267–269; *Ford Motor Co. v. Carter,* 239 Ga. 657, 661, 238 S.Ed.2d 361, 364–365 (1977).

664 A detailed analysis of the risks of different cargos, including chemicals, is provided by Kindt, 'Marine Pollution and Hydrocarbons: The Goal of Minimizing Damage to the Marine Environment', 14 *Cal.W.Int'l L.J.* 233 (1984).

665 Speiser/Krause/Gans, *The American Law of Torts*, (1990), vol. 7, § 19:11, at 40.

666 There are however more and more statutory provisions which impose strict liability, such as the Federal Water Quality Improvement Act of 1970, 33 U.S.C.S. § 1161(f), (g).

667 *Compare* Beck, B., 'Liability of Marine Surveyors for Loss of Surveyed Vessel: When Someone Other Than the Captain Goes Down With the Ship', 64 *Notre Dame L. Rev.* 246 (1989), at 268.

treatment.[668] There is also products liability in maritime law.[669] Bearing in mind the rapid developments in the law of products liability, and the amount of cases and literature in that respect, it is evident that coverage of this theory of law will necessarily be far from comprehensive here.

Products liability has been based on a rich variety of public policy considerations. First of all, there is the notion that the consumer needs to be protected from damage which dangerous products may cause. The right of physical integrity has a special value, as is illustrated by the quote that: '[t]he public interest in human life and health demands all the protection that law can give.'[670] As the manufacturer is the person who can most effectively prevent dangerous products from entering the market, he has an obligation to do so. Public policy requires that responsibility be fixed wherever it will most effectively reduce the hazards to life and health inherent in defective products that reach the market.[671] Even if the manufacturer is not negligent at the time he manufactures the product, he is responsible for the defective product reaching the market.[672] The same rationale is employed for holding all subsequent sellers in the chain of distribution of a defective product strictly liable under United States law.[673] In contrast to the European approach of an extensive system of public safety regulations, the United States has chosen to rely largely on the forces of the market to enforce product safety.[674] The threat of punitive private claims should motivate the manufacturers to improve the safety of their products. Another consideration is that the manufacturer may insure the risks incurred and enjoys the benefits of selling his products.

---

668 *Escola v. Coca-Cola Bottling Co.,* 24 Cal.2d 453, 461–462, 150 P.2d 436, 440–441 (1944), *per* Traynor, J., concurring. But at that time, Traynor, J. could not yet convince his fellow judges. The first identification of the new development as "strict liability to the consumer" was in Prosser, 'The Assault Upon the Citadel (Strict Liability to the Consumer)', 69 *Yale L.J.* 1099 (1960). The landmark cases which triggered the Products Liability revolution were *Henningsen v. Bloomfield Motors, Inc.,* 32 N.J. 358, 161 A.2d 69 (1960), *Greenman v. Yuba Power Products,* 59 Cal.2d 57, 377 P.2d 897, 27 Cal. Rptr. 697 (1963), and *Goldberg v. Kollsman Instrument Corp.,* 12 N.Y.2d 432, 191 N.E.2d 81, 240 N.Y.S.2d 592 (1963).

669 *East River S.S. Corp. v. Transamerica DeLaval, Inc.,* 476 U.S. 858, 106 S.Ct. 2295, 90 L.Ed.2d 865 (1986), Frumer/Friedman, *Products Liability* (2004), vol. 4, ch. 32.

670 *Suvada v. White Motor Co.,* 32 Ill. 2d 612, 619, 210 N.E.2d 182 (1965), at 186.

671 Shapo, *The Law of Products Liability* (1994), vol. 1, § 7–33.

672 *Escola v. Coca-Cola Bottling Co.,* 24 Cal.2d 453, 150 P.2d 436 (1944).

673 *Marko v. Stop and Shop, Inc.,* 169 Conn. 550, 556, 364 A.2d 217, 220 (1975), Frumer/Friedman, *Products Liability* (2004), vol. 1, ch. 6.

674 Reimann, 'Liability for Defective Products at the Beginning of the Twenty-First Century: Emergence of a Worldwide Standard?', 51 *Am. J. Comp. L.* 751 (2003), at 760.

A classification society offers a service.[675] It neither manufactures a product nor is it, despite its involvement in the construction of a vessel, comparable to a manufacturer or seller of a product. On the other hand, one may argue that it has an enormous influence on the design of the vessel because of its rules, especially if it provides software to aid stability calculations. The classification society can improve the technical aspect of a vessel, not the human one, because it possesses significant knowledge in marine engineering and thereby may prevent dangerous incidents from occurring. As the shipbuilder has an obligation *vis-à-vis* its client to build a vessel which is classed, the classification society may enforce the requirements of its rules by fact, not by law. However, the responsibility for the vessel remains the responsibility of the shipbuilder, not of the classification society. It is not the classification society that decides whether the vessel reaches the market and goes to sea (even if it might practically prevent the vessel from doing so), but the shipowner and the shipyard. One might argue that this constitutes a contributory fault, which is also relevant for cases of strict liability.[676] Against this it can be argued that the imposition of strict liability requires a situation and interests which are similar to those which exist in a products liability case. Without strict liability, there is no need to think about the apportionment of liability. Nevertheless, the provision of a service by a classification society is not comparable to the production or sale of a product.

Therefore, the situation of a classification society is not comparable to either that of a manufacturer or that of the seller of a defective product. Products liability is a very distinct field of law and cannot be applied by analogy. One might only argue that the same rationale applies which has led to the imposition of strict liability on the manufacturer of a defective product. Unlike a civil-law system, a common-law system allows and even encourages such argumentation. However, even such argumentation in its lines of thought and policy considerations is not convincing. The aforementioned quotation that '[t]he public interest in human life

---

[675] *Carbotrade S.p.A. v. Bureau Veritas,* 99 F.3d 86 (2d Cir.1996), at 91; *Cargill, Inc. v. Bureau Veritas*, 902 F.Supp. 49, 1996 A.M.C. 577 (S.D.N.Y.1995), at 52; *Great American Insurance Co. v. Bureau Veritas*, 338 F.Supp. 999 (S.D.N.Y.1972), at 1009, 1012; *Sealord Marine Co., Ltd. v. American Bureau of Shipping,* 220 F.Supp.2d 260 (S.D.N.Y.2002), at 266; *Shipping Force Co., Ltd. v. American Bureau of Shipping,* 2004 WL 51233 (S.D.N.Y.2004), at 1; *Sundance Cruises Corp. v. American Bureau of Shipping,* 7 F.3d 1077 (2d Cir.1993), at 1077. That Products Liability does not apply to services is the argumentation in cases concerning liability for the provision of contaminated blood conserves, which is determined as a service, *see Perlmutter v. Beth David Hospital*, 123 N.E.2d 792 (N.Y.1954), *Howell v. Spokane & Inland Empire Blood Bank,* 785 P.2d 815 (Wash.1990), Hermann/Schurgin, *Legal Aspects of Aids* (2004), § 3:09, Jenner, *Transfusion-Associated AIDS* (1995), 83.

[676] § 1 Uniform Comparative Fault Act, comment (a), which has been cited by the Supreme Court regarding the apportionment of damages in an admiralty case, *McDermott, Inc. v. Amdyde & River Don Casting, Ltd.,* 511 U.S. 202, 209, 114 S.Ct. 1461, 128 L.Ed.2d 148, 156 (1994). The Uniform Comparative Fault Act is included in Frumer/Friedman, *Products Liability* (2004), vol. 9, app. K.

and health demands all the protection that law can give'[677] appears to work in favour of an imposition of strict liability on everyone who may prevent such damage. However, this concept is not accepted throughout the law. Danger to life or health in itself does not determine a tort. Negligent behaviour which endangers these interests is required.[678]

There are also several other arguments against the application of the law of products liability to classification societies. Products liability is based on the concept that those who enjoy the benefits of selling the product shall have to bear the potential negative consequences. A classification society only benefits from the fees which it charges for a survey. Mainly the shipyard benefits from selling the vessel, and the shipowner from its operation. One might, of course, argue that there is no weighing of benefits and even the slightest benefit should suffice. In that sense, under the United States law of products liability, not only the manufacturer can be held liable, but also all those who have sold the product.[679] It is argued that all sellers of the product have a certain influence on the manufacturer, which may result in a higher standard of safety of the product, and that these subsequent sellers also benefit from selling the product. A classification society has, no doubt, a benefit and a considerable influence on whether or not the vessel enters the market, or rather in which state this happens.

However, to examine this point, reference has to be made to *Smith v. Mitlof.*[680] In this products liability case, *Norwalk Maritime* sold a pontoon boat to *Mitlof.* When the boat capsized causing injuries to plaintiffs, they sued *Norwalk* alleging breach of contract, breach of warranties, negligent repair and failure to warn, fraud and breach of statutory duties under the Federal Boat Safety Act. All causes of action were dismissed except for the negligent failure to warn. The products liability claim was rejected, as *Norwalk* had no ownership interest in the vessel at the time of the injuries. The company was not a manufacturer of recreational vessels and made no direct warranties or representations to plaintiffs. However, based on § 388 Restatement (Second) of Torts, the court held that '[i]f *Norwalk* knew or

677 *Suvada v. White Motor Co.,* 32 Ill. 2d 612, 619, 210 N.E.2d 182, 186 (1965).

678 The American tort law system has actually developed from a strict liability concept to the necessity of fault. In 1681, English law required someone who harmed another to compensate for the injury or damage irrespective of fault. In *Lambert v. Bessey,* T Raym 421, 83 Eng Reprint 220 it was held: 'In all civil acts the law doth not so much regard the intent of the actor, as the loss and damage of the party suffering.' Today, the situation is more precisely described by the majority of the California Supreme Court: 'Tort law has evolved from a legal obligation initially imposed without 'fault,' to recovery which, generally, was based on blameworthiness in a moral sense. For reasons of social policy and because of the unusual nature of defendant's acts, liability without fault continued to be prescribed in a certain restricted area [...].' (*Daly v. General Motors Corp.,* 20 Cal.3d 725, 144 Cal. Rptr. 380, 575 P.2d 1162, at 1165 (1978)).

679 This is an important difference to the European model, under which these entities are generally exempt from liability, as basically the manufacturer of the product shall shoulder its burdens.

680 *Smith v. Mitlof,* 198 F.Supp.2d 492 (S.D.N.Y.2002).

had reason to know that, as a result of the vessel's latent defects and limitations, the [vessel] would be dangerous for *Mitlof's* intended use, and had reason to believe that *Mitlof* would not discover these defects, it could be found liable to prospective passengers under section 388 for failure to warn of dangerous conditions.'[681] Just as in *Norwalk*, a classification society has neither an ownership interest in the vessel, nor is it a manufacturer of vessels or usually makes direct warranties or representations to the third parties. Such a duty to warn of dangerous conditions may have to be imposed on a classification society in a situation similar to that of *Norwalk*. A strict liability may not.

Moreover, there is another incompatibility with the law of products liability. Products liability aims at the protection of a consumer. Whereas some of the injured may be consumers, i.e. passengers, the largest part of potential plaintiffs cannot be identified as such. Members of the crew may be in severe need of protection, but they act in their capacity as employees. Cargo-owners similarly exercise a profession. Furthermore, it is hardly arguable that States which suffer the consequences of an oil spill do so as a consumer of any kind. A strict liability only towards passengers, however, would appear inconsistent. If that were the case, strict liability would only depend on the chances of an injury to a passenger. One should not forget that there is already a certain protection of the passenger, notably by the Athens Convention and its Protocol of 2002. It may not be perfect, but the international community has taken the decision that such protection should currently be sufficient for a passenger or siblings. It is at least not insufficient to such a degree that strict liability has to be imposed on classification societies only for reason of an adequate compensation for damage to passengers.

If the idea that liability shall provide a sufficient restitution does not necessarily require the imposition of strict liability on classification societies, the second theoretical aspect of liability, deterrence, might prove to do so.[682] Admittedly, strict liability would establish a strong incentive to employ all possible means of avoiding an occurrence. But is there such a strong need for deterrence that it has to be assured by way of strict liability? Products liability deals with the life and health of consumers. A strict liability imposed on classification societies would also deal with the life and health of passengers and crew as well as the protection of the marine environment. However, danger for life and health does not in itself justify the imposition of a strict liability; even if it is a danger to a large number of persons. Otherwise there would not be a need for a section of the Restatements on abnormally dangerous activities (in Restatement (First) it was even required that these were ultra-hazardous activities), if any kind of danger were sufficient. This would turn the law upside-down. Even if one argued that only a danger for a certain number of especially protected interests would require protection by strict liability, the question would then remain how to define a certain number.

Strict liability would significantly encourage litigation. On the one hand, classification societies may be in a better position to prove that they have no responsi-

---

[681] *Smith v. Mitlof*, 198 F.Supp.2d 492 (S.D.N.Y.2002), at 503.

[682] On deterrence, *see* Shapo, *The Law of Products Liability* (1994), vol. 1, 7-34.

bility for an incident than the plaintiff trying to prove their negligence. Under a regime of strict liability, it is of no relevance whether the classification society is responsible for damage, as liability is imposed irrespective of fault. Also, foreseeability is not a requirement for cases of strict liability.[683] To aid the plaintiff to enforce his claims, the procedural law already provides him with numerous discovery rights. Long before trial, a party can question witnesses under oath, request the defendant to give written responses to questions and demand the delivery of files.[684] Federal Rules of Civil Procedure, which apply to admiralty cases, even require the defendant to identify and hand over proof on his own motion.[685] Solely the greater simplicity of the proof of innocence by a classification society does not, therefore, justify the imposition of such a heavy burden on classification societies.

c. Conclusion

There is no strict liability imposed for the provision of classification services. Neither the considerations of a strict liability for abnormally dangerous activities nor for defective products apply to this case.

5. *Tort of Fraudulent Misrepresentation*

Whenever someone fraudulently makes a misrepresentation of fact, he will be liable to the third party for his deceit. This tort is based on the common-law tort of deceit as developed in the leading case *Derry v. Peek*,[686] which is widely followed by United States' courts.[687] In brief, it is required that a fraudulent misrepresentation of fact, opinion, or law is made, for the purpose of inducing justifiable reliance, thereby causing pecuniary loss.[688] This requires intent of the tortfeasor or in the words of Lord Herschell in *Derry v. Peek*:[689]

> 'Fraud is proved when it is shown that a false representation has been made (1) knowingly, or (2) without belief in its truth, or (3) recklessly, careless whether it be true or false.'

Conscious misrepresentation which involves the risk of physical harm may just as well lead to liability of the misrepresentor.[690] In the rare case that these preconditions can be proven, a classification society will be liable to the injured party.

---

683 *Newman v. Utility Trailer & Equip. Co.*, 278 Or. 395, 397, 564 P.2d 674, 675 (1977).

684 Reimann, 'Liability for Defective Products' 51 *Am J.Comp.L.* 751 (2003), at 817.

685 Federal Rules of Civil Procedure 26–37.

686 *Derry v. Peek*, [1889] 14 App.Cas. 337.

687 Dobbs, *The Law of Torts* (2000), § 471, at 1346; *see also* Restatement (Second) of Torts, §§ 525-549.

688 *See* § 525 Restatement (Second) of Torts.

689 *Derry v. Peek*, [1889] 14 App.Cas. 337, 61 L. T. Rep. N. S. 265 (H.L.).

690 *See* § 310 Restatement (Second) of Torts: An actor who makes a misrepresentation is subject to liability to another for physical harm which results from an act done by the other or a third person in reliance upon the truth of the representation, if the actor

6. The Effect of Disclaimers of Liability

Despite the fact that a contractual exemption or limitation clause, which has been analysed *supra*,[691] has no effect on third parties, classification societies may disclaim their liability to third parties by way of employing suitable disclaimers on their certificates. Such a disclaimer precludes the plaintiff's reasonable reliance on the certificate, which is required for stating a cause of action for negligent misrepresentation. Somewhat similar to the situation under English law, the classification society may prevent reliance and therefore liability. If the plaintiff nonetheless acts in reliance on that certificate, he assumes the risk.

Since most of the cases deal with the liability of public accountants for negligent misrepresentations to investors or shareholders which are not in privity of contract, the courts have predominantly dealt with the question of whether it is possible to disclaim reliance on such reports that have caused economic loss. Most disclaimers by these accountants state that the instructions which specified the requested audit or the data basis were limited and that the representation has been made to the best of their knowledge. Classification societies, by contrast, often incorporate a clause that specifies that the information is for the use of the contracting party only and does not represent the condition of the vessel to third parties. The idea behind such a clause is that third parties are acting at their own risk if they nevertheless rely on the certificate. There is no case-law on such a clause yet. As regards liability for pure economic loss pursuant to § 552 of the Restatement, the plaintiff cannot justifiably put reliance on the certificate if he knows that it is not for his use. However, the situation is different regarding § 311. In such a case the information is given to the shipowner, but a third party, which the classification society should expect to be put in peril by the action of the shipowner, sustains the harm. It is therefore the contracting party, the shipowner, who relies on the certificate and whose act puts the third party in peril.[692] The third party does not need to have knowledge of the existence of the certificate. Of relevance to § 311 is therefore not the representation of the condition of the vessel to the third party, but to the shipowner. Just as required by the certificate, it is only used by the contracting party. Based on such argumentation, one can argue that such a disclaimer does not operate against third parties which sustain physical harm and fulfil the preconditions of § 311.

(a) intends his statement to induce or should realize that it is likely to induce action by the other, or a third person, which involves an unreasonable risk of physical harm to the other, and

(b) knows

(i) that the statement is false, or

(ii) that he has not the knowledge which he professes.

691 *See supra* Part 2 A II 4.

692 *Compare supra* Part 2 B II 3 f.

7. Conclusion

First of all, there is no contract theory which protects third parties. Neither does the *Ryan* doctrine apply nor is there a kind of implied contractual right or an application of the doctrine of a third-party beneficiary. The liability towards third parties is essentially based on the tort of negligence and negligent misrepresentation. In some rare cases, the tort of fraudulent misrepresentation may apply.

The marine activities of a classification society are maritime in nature, and so tortious behaviour may cause a maritime tort, resulting in the application of federal maritime law. The tort of negligence is relevant to all cases in which the tortious behaviour is not a misrepresentation to the third party. An example of such tortious behaviour is the negligent formulation of rules which are not state-of-the-art. Moreover, it can also be of relevance if a requirement or advice of the classification society causes a deficiency or risk in the vessel. For most of the cases, however, only the tort of negligent misrepresentation applies. Whenever the plaintiff claims damages for physical harm, § 311 may be of relevance, irrespective of whether the victim knew of the representation or not; a negligent misrepresentation to the contracting party suffices if the classification society should expect thereby to put the third party in danger. This limits the financial exposure of the classification society to foreseeable plaintiffs. All those who suffer economic loss may try to recover on the basis of § 552 Restatement (Second) of Torts. But the preconditions of this are very difficult to satisfy: not only must there be false information, a failure to exercise reasonable care, justifiable reliance of the third party and pecuniary loss, but the injured party also has to be a member of a 'limited group' of persons for whose benefit and guidance the defendant either intends to supply the information or knows that the recipient intends to supply it. The classification society also needs to have actual knowledge that the third party would receive the inaccurate information. These preconditions will not be satisfied in the usual case of a classification certificate. They can, however, be satisfied in the case of a special survey which is carried out mainly for the benefit of the third party. The disparity between the fees and the liability incurred is of no relevance either to the tort of negligence or to the tort of negligent misrepresentation. The same applies to the policy considerations which are relevant under English law, such as the non-delegable duty of the shipowner to provide a seaworthy ship or the limitation of liability in shipping. As no classification society guarantees by way of the certificates that the vessel is seaworthy, its duties do not interfere with the non-delegable duty of the shipowner.

III. German Law

Under German law, a classification society which provides an expert opinion can be held liable by third parties under the principles of contract law or of tort law. As regards contract law, jurisprudence has chosen two different legal theories to expand the protection of the contract to third parties: an implied agreement to provide information (*konkludenter Abschluss eines Auskunftsvertrages*) and a contract with protective effects towards third parties (*Vertrag mit Schutzwirkung zugunsten*

Dritter). In addition to that, the institute of *culpa in contrahendo* may offer protection in some cases of provision of information. Moreover, a third party may also base an actionable claim on tort law, notably the provisions of §§ 823, 826 BGB. However, because the rule of vicarious liability under tort law pursuant to § 831 BGB is a rather weak one, since the master may avoid liability for the torts committed by his servants whenever he can prove that he selected and supervised them carefully.[693] Besides, under § 823 (1) BGB the injured party cannot recover in tort for pure economic loss which has been negligently inflicted.[694] In order to increase the protection of third parties, the courts have recourse to the aforementioned principles of contract law such as an implied agreement to provide information (*konkludenter Abschluss eines Auskunftsvertrages*) and the contract with protective effects towards third parties (*Vertrag mit Schutzwirkung zugunsten Dritter*). Despite the fact that a number of scholars have argued for a long time in favour of the establishment of a distinctive set of rules of professional liability ("*Berufshaftung*"),[695] there is no such regulation yet.

1. *Implied Agreement to Provide Information (Konkludenter Abschluss eines Auskunftsvertrages)*

Whenever someone provides information to someone else that gives reason for reliance, German courts have always applied the doctrine of an implied agreement to provide information.[696] Even though the provider and the recipient did not expressly conclude a contract, an agreement is assumed whenever the supplier of information was called into the negotiations as a neutral and competent man of confidence who directly furnished information to the recipient, which was, as the

---

693 *Compare* Markesinis, *The German Law of Obligations* (1997), vol. I, at 276.

694 Markesinis, *The German Law of Obligations* (1997), vol. I, at 276.

695 Hirte, *Berufshaftung* (1996), especially at 386 *et seq.*, 412 *et seq.*, 417 *et seq.*; Hopt, 'Nichtvertragliche Haftung außerhalb von Schadens- und Bereicherungsausgleich', 183 *AcP* 608 (1983); Baumbach/Hopt, *Handelsgesetzbuch* (2006), § 347 at no. 22; Hopt, 'Die Haftung des Wirtschaftsprüfers', in: Hofmann/Meyer-Cording/Wiedemann, *Festschrift für Klemens Pleyer* (1986), 341, at 359; Lammel, 'Zur Auskunftshaftung', 179 *AcP* 337 (1979); Lang, 'Einmal mehr: Berufsrecht, Berufspflichten und Berufshaftung', 201 *AcP* 451 (2001); Lorenz, W., 'Das Problem der Haftung für primäre Vermögensschäden bei der Erteilung einer unrichtigen Auskunft', in: Paulus/Diederichsen/Canaris, *Festschrift Larenz I* (1973), 575, at 591.

696 RG 27 October 1902, 52 RGZ 365; RG 9 February 1921, 101 RGZ 297; RG 2 February 1931, 131 RGZ 239; BGH 18 January 1972, [1972] *NJW* 678; BGH 18 January 1973, [1973] *WM* 165; BGH 30 March 1976, [1976] *WM* 498; BGH 4 March 1987, [1987] *ZIP* 500; BGH 6 July 1993, 123 BGHZ 126, at 128. *See* also Huber, 'Verkehrspflichten zum Schutz fremden Vermögens', in: Ficker/König/Kreuzer, *et al*, *Festschrift für Ernst von Caemmerer* (1978), 359, at 368 *et seq.* At first sight one might wonder that this liability is treated under the title of the protection of third parties, as this would be a contractual liability. This structure has been chosen to allow a comparability of the legal systems. The other two legal systems solve such cases by means of tort law doctrines.

supplier ought to have known, of substantial importance to the recipient and which was intended to lay the foundations for material measures in the economic, legal or factual domain.[697] Under German law, no consideration is required to conclude a contract.

Such contractual liability has for a long time been criticised by legal scholars as a liability not because of want, but because of must.[698] The conclusion of a contract by way of an implied agreement has often been considered as a fiction that has no basis in the will of the contracting parties.[699] It appears to be in conflict with § 675 (2) BGB, which stipulates that a person who gives advice, makes a recommendation or provides information to another person is not bound to compensate any damage arising from the use made of it. The intention of § 675 (2) BGB is to protect the provider of information, because the fathers of the BGB believed that such a person does not possess the will to conclude a contract. Whoever follows the advice or the recommendation is considered as acting at his own risk.[700] However, according to § 675 (2) BGB, this does not apply in cases of fraudulent behaviour or of an explicit or implied contract. An implied contract does not require a consideration; it is sufficient that the advice or recommendation is given by virtue of the profession or trade of the provider.[701] For this reason, § 675 (2) BGB is not contrary to the doctrine of an implied agreement to provide information.

As concerns the further argument that the supplier of the information has no will to give information relevant in law, the courts have refuted this criticism

[697] BGH 29 October 1952, 7 BGHZ 371, at 374; BGH 6 July 1970, [1970] *NJW* 1737; BGH 23 January 1985, [1986] *NJW-RR* 484, at 485; BGH 6 July 1993, 123 BGHZ 126, at 128; BGH 13 February 1992, [1992] *NJW* 2080, at 2082.

[698] Medicus, *Bürgerliches Recht* (2004), at no. 371.

[699] *See* Jost, F., *Vertragslose Auskunfts- und Beratungshaftung* (1991), at 47, 83 *et seq.*; Lorenz, W., 'Haftung für primäre Vermögensschäden bei unrichtiger Auskunft', in: Paulus/Diederichsen/Canaris, *Festschrift Larenz I* (1973), 575, at 681. For this reason, a number of scholars base such liability on trust claimed by the supplier and granted by the recipient (Canaris in: Staub, *Handelsgesetzbuch*, *Bankvertragsrecht* (2005), at no. 89; Ehmann in: Erman, *Bürgerliches Gesetzbuch* (2004), § 675 at no. 9, Lorenz, *ibid.*). They argue that it is a quasi-contractual liability, based not on will but on objective circumstances (Wittmann in: Staudinger, *Bürgerliches Gesetzbuch, §§ 652-704* (1995), § 676 at no. 7) therefore not a contractual but a statutory liability.

[700] *Motive zu dem Entwurfe eines Bürgerlichen Gesetzbuches für das Deutsche Reich* (1888), at 554.

[701] *Motive zu dem Entwurfe eines Bürgerlichen Gesetzbuches für das Deutsche Reich* (1888), at 555: 'Vorbehalten [eines Haftungsausschlusses] müssen aber die Fälle werden, in welchen die besonderen Umstände eine weitergehende Haftung begründen. Dahin gehört zunächst der Fall, wenn der Rath oder die Empfehlung auf Grund eines ausdrücklichen oder stillschweigenden Vertrages, vielleicht sogar gegen Entgelt ertheilt ist und eine umfassendere Haftung aus den für Verträge geltenden allgemeinen Grundsätzen sich ergiebt. Zu diesen Vertragsfällen gehören auch diejenigen, in welchen Rath und Empfehlung kraft Gewerbes oder Berufes ertheilt ist.'

through the assumption that the behaviour of the supplier as a neutral expert is to be considered as an indication of his will to give information relevant in law.[702] Classification societies would be considered as such neutral experts. It will be held that they therefore possessed the will to give information relevant in law if there are further indications that the classification society has an interest in concluding such an implied contract. Such an indication could be an economic interest in the realisation of another business transaction,[703] a personal engagement in the way of the acceptance of a guarantee,[704] the promise to check the statements made by the business partner of the recipient of the information or a further existing contractual relation with this person.

The doctrine of the implied agreement may only apply in cases in which the classification society directly supplies information to the third-party recipient. This, however, is in practice hardly ever the case.[705] Contacts and consultation between the classification society and the shipyard appear generally in the context of a contract between these two. If there is no such contract, the classification society acts on behalf of the person who ordered the ship and represents his interests towards the shipyard.[706] Even though the classification society directly furnished information of substantial importance to the shipyard in such a case, it is not called into the negotiations as a neutral, competent man of confidence. At the time of the provision of the information, it is clear to all participants that the classification society acts only in the interests of its contracting party.

Another example which occurs quite often is information sought by entities which consider buying a vessel. They tend to act upon the information given to a classification society in order to receive further details about the classed vessel or to have certain parts checked in accordance with the rules of the classification society. The societies react to such inquiries by stating that they only give information to their contractual party, the seller. They have to react in such a way in order to comply with their contractual obligations to keep strict secrecy; otherwise the seller may hold them liable for breach of a collateral duty (*Nebenpflicht*).[707]

---

702 BGH 5 December 1972, [1973] *NJW* 321; BGH 17 September 1985, [1986] *NJW* 180, at 181.

703 BGH 5 July 1962, [1962] *WM* 1110, at 1111.

704 BGH 29 October 1952, 7 BGHZ 371, at 377; BGH 13 June 1962, [1962] *NJW* 1500.

705 Basedow/Wurmnest, *Die Dritthaftung von Klassifikationsgesellschaften* (2004), at 34–35; Basedow/Wurmnest, *Third-Party Liability of Classification Societies* (2005), at 44. *Compare* Drobnig, *Tätigkeit und Haftung von Klassifikationsgesellschaften in der Bundesrepublik Deutschland am Beispiel des Germanischen Lloyd* (1995), at 152. Drobnig even discusses and denies at 153–158 a contractual guarantee of the classification society for the accuracy of the information. As such a guarantee would be purely fictitious, it is not discussed in this thesis.

706 *See also* Basedow/Wurmnest, *Die Dritthaftung von Klassifikationsgesellschaften* (2004), at 34–35; Basedow/Wurmnest, *Third-Party Liability of Classification Societies* (2005), at 44–45.

707 A liability which follows §§ 241 (2), 280 (1) BGB.

If, however, the classification society directly provides such information to the buyer or another third party, the prerequisites of an implied agreement to provide information are fulfilled. The classification society may then be liable according to the principles which have been discussed before under the section regarding contractual liability of classification societies.[708]

2. *Contract with Protective Effects Towards Third Parties (Vertrag mit Schutzwirkung zugunsten Dritter)*

A contract does not necessarily protect only the contractual party. It may also extend its protection towards third parties. Compared with a claim based on tort, such a contractual claim has several advantages for a third party: contract law is stricter in its application as regards liability for persons employed by the debtor in the performance of his obligation.[709] It protects against all sorts of injuries, even pure economic loss.[710] In addition, it is more favourable to the injured party as regards the burden of proof.[711] Each and every contract may protect third parties if that is stipulated by the contracting parties. However, neither the classification contract nor any individual contract with a classification society provides for a clause providing that certain third parties are protected by the contract.

In the absence of an express clause relating to third parties, a contract may have protective effects towards them under certain circumstances, which have been developed by jurisprudence.[712] According to this doctrine, there needs to be an especially close relationship between the third party and the performance by the promisor (contractual debtor), which is referred to as a proximity of performance (*Leistungsnähe*) of the third-party beneficiary (*Drittbegünstigter*). According to the terms of the contract, the third party needs to be affected by the contractual performance in a similar way as the creditor. Moreover, the contractual creditor, who is under these circumstances usually the shipowner, must have an interest in the protection of the injured third party (*Gläubigernähe*). Also, the contractual

---

[708] *See supra* Part 2 A III 2.

[709] § 278 BGB and not § 831 which is applicable to liability in tort.

[710] Whereas liability under § 823 (1) BGB only protects a limited number of interests, such as life, body, health, freedom, property (*Eigentum*), and certain other interests (defined by case law) but not against pure economic loss.

[711] For example, § 280 BGB as the *rule de base* of contractual liability requires the proof of a breach of duty (*Pflichtverletzung*), the incurring of a loss, and the causal connection between the breach of duty and the incurring of a loss. That it was not his fault is an objection the debtor has to prove, *see* § 280 (1) 2nd sentence BGB. When applying § 823 (1) BGB, the harmed party also has to prove the fault of the infringing party.

[712] For an introduction to the contract with protective effects towards third parties *see* Coester/Markesinis, 'Liability of Financial Experts in German and American Law', 51 *Am.J.Comp.L.* 275 (2003), at 281–289 with intresting remarks on the differences under German and United States law of the liability for the provision of information at 291–309. *See also* Markesinis/Lorenz, W./Dannemann, *The German Law of Obligations, vol. I* (1997), at 276–282.

debtor (the promisor), here the classification society, must have been able to foresee that his action could cause harm not only to his contracting party but also to the third party. Hence, the supplier ought to have known that the third party would be affected (*Erkennbarkeit*). And, last but not least, the third party has to be in need of protection (*Schutzbedürftigkeit des Dritten*). From a bird's eye perspective, one may position the contract with protective effects towards third parties between tort and contract. It is a contractual liability but it protects third parties who are not parties to the contract.[713] The difference between contract and tort should not be blurred.[714] However, it is slightly confusing to consider that it is neither strictly a contractual liability, because the courts impose liability even against the will of the contracting parties (as will be shown below), nor is it a liability in tort, since only contract law is being applied. The application of this doctrine therefore needs to be restricted to a limited and distinguishable group of persons in order to avoid the establishment of a quasi-tortious liability.[715]

The doctrine of a contract with protective effects towards third parties has two main fields of application. In the first one, the creditor himself is obliged to protect the third party. He has a special obligation to protect the third party and a duty to give assistance (*Schutz- und Fürsorgepflicht*). In the second one, the contractual parties want to create a duty of protection of the third party according to the court's finding. This group relates to the professional liability of lawyers,[716] ex-

[713] There is a learned controversy about the dogmatic foundation of the contract with protective effects towards third parties. It is either based on a complementary interpretation of the contract pursuant to § 157 BGB (*see* RG 7 June 1915, 87 RGZ 64; RG 18 November 1915, 87 RGZ 289, at 292; RG 5 October 1917, 91 RGZ 21, at 24; RG 3 June 1921, 102 RGZ 231; RG 10 February 1930, 127 RGZ 218, at 222; RG 4 April 1939, 160 RGZ 153; BGH 11 April 1951, 1 BGHZ 383, at 386; BGH 28 April 1952, 5 BGHZ 378, at 384; BGH 15 March 1954, [1954] *NJW* 874; BGH 25 April 1956, [1956] *NJW* 1193; BGH 15 May 1959, [1959] *NJW* 1676; BGH 27 November 1959, [1960] *VersR* 153, at 155 *et seq.*; BGH 23 June 1965, [1965] *NJW* 1757; BGH 10 January 1968, [1968] *JZ* 304. Critical: Hopt, 'Dritthaftung für Testate', [1987] *NJW* 1745, at 1746) or a statutory elaboration of the contractual relationship corresponding to § 242 BGB (*see* BGH 6 July 1965, [1965] *NJW* 1955). Nonetheless, as this doctrine is generally accepted, the controversy about the dogmatical foundation does not require further elaboration (*see* BGH 28 January 1976, 66 BGHZ 51, at 57; Flume, *Allgemeiner Teil des Bürgerlichen Rechts*, vol. 2, § 16 4 f; Larenz/Wolf, *Allgemeiner Teil des Bürgerlichen Rechts*, at no. 113).

[714] BGH 9 October 1968, [1969] *NJW* 41; BGH 11 January 1977, [1977] *NJW* 2073; Hadding in: Soergel/Siebert/Mertens, *Bürgerliches Gesetzbuch*, *§§ 241–432* (1990), Anh § 328 at no. 14; Jagmann in: Staudinger, *Bürgerliches Gesetzbuch*, *§§ 328–359* (2004), § 328 at no. 96.

[715] Unlike under French law (*see* Art. 1382, 1383 Code Civil), there is no general tort in German law.

[716] BGH 11 January 1977, [1977] *NJW* 2073; BGH 13 June 1995, [1995] *NJW* 2551; BGH 2 December 1999, [2000] *NJW* 725.

perts,[717] tax advisers[718] and chartered accountants.[719] All persons that possess a special knowledge which is recognised by the government are under a duty of protection towards the third party, whenever their performance of the contractual obligations is solely or partly intended for use towards a third party and shall be provided with a special probative value.[720] However, only as far as these professionals assume the responsibility for the correctness of their certificate will they be liable.[721] Their breach of duty must at least in part have caused the harm. As a result, they have to restore the *status quo ante* in which it would be if there had not been an incorrect expert opinion.[722]

Regarding classification societies, there may be cases in both of the main fields of application. First of all, if the vessel is operated by a crew that is employed by the shipowner himself or a bare-boat charterer or an operator, *e.g.*, a ship management company, a special duty of the shipowner, bare-boat charterer or operator to protect and give assistance to its crew stems from the employment. Depending on whether the shipowner is involved in the operation of the vessel at all, it is either the shipowner or the operator that concludes the classification contract with the classification society.

The main field of application, however, is the second one, relating to cases of professional liability. Classification societies are only called upon because of their special knowledge of marine engineering and their experience as surveyors. This special knowledge of classification societies is also recognised by governments. Any flag State which grants authority to a classification society recognises the classification society and its knowledge. The European Commission has the power to recognise those classification societies that are eligible for the assignment of such authority.[723] As this recognition only applies to the issuance of statutory sur-

---

717 BGH 10 November 1994, [1995] *NJW* 392; BGH 2 November 1983, [1984] *NJW* 355; BGH 14 November 2000, [2001] *NJW* 514.

718 BGH 26 November 1986, [1987] *NJW* 1758; BGH 19 December 1996, [1997] *NJW* 1235.

719 BGH 2 April 1998, 138 BGHZ 257; BGH 19 March 1986, [1986] *NJW-RR* 1307.

720 BGH 2 November 1983, [1984] *NJW* 355, at 356; BGH 23 January 1985, [1986] *NJW-RR* 484, at 485–486; BGH 26 November 1986, [1987] *NJW* 1758, at 1759; BGH 13 November 1997, [1998] *NJW* 1059; BGH 20 April 2004, [2004] *NJW* 3035, at 3036.

721 *Compare* BGH 18 October 1988, [1989] *NJW-RR* 696, at 697.

722 BGH 14 November 2000, [2001] *NJW* 514, at 515.

723 This follows the procedure set out in Directive 94/57/EC, OJ No. L 319 of 12.12.1994, p. 20, as amended by Directive 2001/105/EC of the European Parliament and of the Council of 19 December 2001, OJ No. L 19 of 22.1 2002, p. 9 and by Directive 2002/84/EC of the European Parliament and of the Council of 5 November 2002, OJ L 324 of 29.11.2002, p. 53. The Commission has recognised classification societies in its Decision 96/587/EC of 30 September 1996 (OJ L 257 of 10.10.1996, p. 43), last amended by Commission Decision 2002/315/EC of 29 April 2002 (OJ L 113 of 30.04.2002, p. 31) on the publication of the list of recognised organisations which have been notified by Member States in accordance with Council Directive 94/57/EC. *See also* Part 3 B I 2.

veys, it relates to public functions. One might therefore argue that public and private functions should not be confused, but the special knowledge of the classification society recognised by the government is the same as that which is relevant in the context of private classification functions.[724]

Regarding the intention of the shipowner or other contracting party to use the certificate *vis-à-vis* a third party, such a use is evident in the case of a confirmation of class. Its overriding purpose is to demonstrate to a third party the status of the vessel according to the files. A confirmation of class is of no other use for the contracting party, and it also has a special probative value, as it gives proof of this status. The same applies to the classification certificates. It is always the aim of a certificate to prove something and to allow the recipient to present it to other parties. In this context, the certificates that are issued by a classification society prove that the vessel or a specific item of it is in conformity with the rules of the society.

To sum up, the contract with protective effects towards third parties can generally apply to the services of a classification society. Therefore, it needs to be further ascertained whether its other preconditions are also fulfilled.[725]

a. Proximity of Performance (*Leistungsnähe*)

The prerequisite of proximity of performance has been developed to restrict liability to only those third parties who are in contact with the dangers imposed by the contract. The third party needs to be affected by the performance of the contractual duties in the same way as the promisee. This implies that the third party has to come into contact with the performance according to the terms of the contract.[726]

When analysing the obligations performed by classification societies, one will notice that these cases differ from the cases of expert opinions on the value of chattel or real estate.[727] First of all, the expert opinion of the classification society does not contain information about the value of the vessel. The advice given by a classification society during the construction of the vessel, as well as recommendations or conditions provided subsequent to surveys, illustrate that a classification is not merely an expert opinion on the safety of the ship. The classification of

[724] *Compare* OLG Hamburg 14 June 1990, [1990] *TranspR* 345, at 348; OLG Hamburg 27 March 2001, 9 U 364/99 (unpublished).

[725] Both the system of limitations in shipping and the solutions by other legal orders of the liability of classification societies are not preconditions of the contract with protective effects towards third parties. They are of relevance to the question of whether their liability should be limited by an international convention (*see* Part 3), but should not be taken into consideration when assessing whether these preconditions are fulfilled (contrary to Basedow/Wurmnest, *Die Dritthaftung von Klassifikationsgesellschaften* (2004), at 42–45; Basedow/Wurmnest, *Third-Party Liability of Classification Societies* (2005), at 52–56).

[726] BGH 2 July 1996, 133 BGHZ 168.

[727] *See* Basedow/Wurmnest, *Die Dritthaftung von Klassifikationsgesellschaften* (2004), at 39–41; Basedow/Wurmnest, *Third-Party Liability of Classification Societies* (2005), at 51–52.

a vessel is also part of the process to make it safe and seaworthy. Nevertheless, a classification certificate does not state that the vessel is safe or seaworthy. It only informs that the vessel conforms to the rules. It is implicitly stated that the rules are state-of-the-art. Moreover, a classification society does not only survey a ship and provides information as to whether or not this ship is safe. If the condition of the ship is held to be unsatisfactory, the classification society gives advice on what needs to be changed in order to achieve the necessary degree of safety for a classification. It is in this sense that the classification society takes part in the process of making the vessel safe. The shipowner, no doubt, can recognise certain deficiencies of his vessel, but the knowledge of the classification society is without doubt more advanced. These societies have eminent technical experts who have know-how in marine engineering and experience in the survey of marine technology that even some flag States do not possess. They are not only called upon to ascertain a neutral vetting process, but also because of their superior knowledge and experience.[728]

The contractual performance by the classification society is the survey of the vessel and the subsequent issue of the classification certificate. If the classification society breaches its obligation to survey the vessel as required by its rules, the certificate will be incorrect and the vessel may not be as safe as it should be. This may cause harm to the third party. It is evident to the classification society that a crew is needed to operate the vessel, as it is equally obvious that a certain number of passengers may be transported, which is specified in the certificate, and that a cargo vessel will likewise fulfil its task of transporting a certain quantity of bulk cargo or containers. Although these are different groups of persons, they all come under the category of third parties to the contract. For all these third parties it is evident that they may come into contact with the work of the classification society.[729] Everybody who takes notice of a classification certificate or consults the

[728] *Compare* BGH 2 November 1983, [1984] *NJW* 355, at 357, relating to the difference in the knowledge expected by the contracting party and the expert.

[729] Basedow/Wurmnest, *Die Dritthaftung von Klassifikationsgesellschaften* (2004), at 39–40; Basedow/Wurmnest, *Third-Party Liability of Classification Societies* (2005), at 51 argue that the number of persons is considerably larger than the number of parties in most professional liability cases. However, it may be doubted that it is possible to define the average number of persons that come into contact with an expert opinion. Different expert opinions may entail different numbers of parties. The precedents do not even provide a certain maximum number of third parties. They solely state that it needs to be possible to determine the third parties in an objective way, BGH 2 November 1983, [1984] *NJW* 355, at 356; BGH 23 January 1985, [1986] *NJW-RR* 484, at 485–486; BGH 26 November 1986, [1987] *NJW* 1758, at 1759. Even auditors cannot clearly foresee the number of persons that may consult their audits. Basedow/Wurmnest cite § 323 German Commercial Code (HGB) which excludes liability towards third parties that relied on audit records. However, this provision does not apply to classification societies and can therefore hardly be used as an argument that their liability is likewise limited. By contrast, this provision is only needed if otherwise an application of the contract with protective effects towards third parties is possible. One could, however,

society's Register of Ships and thereafter relies on the representations made therein is for these reasons affected by the performance of the contractual stipulations in a similar way as the contracting party.

A more difficult issue is whether States that have suffered from oil pollution are in proximity of performance. These States normally do not consult the information provided by the classification society. Nonetheless, if the classification society does not work properly, it may be part of the causal chain that causes the casualty; because a vessel may not put to sea without a valid classification, as it is neither insured nor can the shipowner fulfil his contractual duties to the cargo-owner. Classification societies require that vessels are built in a certain way in order to prevent casualties. However, this kind of influence does not suffice to bring these coastal States within the scope of application *according to the terms of the contract* (*bestimmungsgemäß*). Despite the fact that some classification societies expressly refer to the aim of the protection of the environment, which also includes the environment of coastal States,[730] it is not evident according to the terms of the contract that coastal States are in contact with the dangers imposed by the contract.

In brief, every third party who the classification society must expect to be influenced by the safety of the vessel is in proximity of performance, such as the crew, passengers, cargo- owners, the vessel's insurance company, the charterer of the vessel, the ship's financers, cruise lines, and purchasers of a vessel. Coastal States that have to bear the consequences of a casualty which pollutes their environment are not in proximity of performance.

---

argue that a similar provision would be needed in respect of classification societies as well, *see also* Part 3 C VI 3.

Besides, it is argued that the class is granted without restriction, as the shipowner would not accept any restraints (at 52). Nonetheless, that refers to factual problems of the classification society in their contractual relationship with the shipowner. If they have a problem with the shipowner to limit the use of the classification certificate only to certain third parties, the societies have to take care of it. To exclude all third parties does not solve that problem between the shipowner and the classification society. Moreover, the existence of the classification societies' Registers of Ships gives proof of the fact that they have an interest of their own in the information being publicly accessible. If they have such an interest, they also will have to bear the consequences.

730 *See for instance* GL Rules I–0–2 § 2.3 Scope: 'GL reserve the right to extend the scope of Classification to all equipment and machinery used in the operation of the ship, which by their character and/or arrangement may impair the safety of human life, of the ship and her cargo or of the environment.' CCS Rules, General, § 2 (9) 'to provide technical consultancy service and other related technical services for ensuring safety of operation and prevention of environmental pollution'.

b. Interest of the Contractual Creditor (*Gläubigernähe*)

The protection of the third party by the contract must be an interest of the contractual creditor which is worth being protected.[731] The courts used to specify that the creditor has to be responsible for the third party "for better or for worse" (*für Wohl und Wehe*).[732] This narrow definition only applied to cases of employment, family or other relationships which involve duties of care or giving assistance (*Fürsorge- und Obhutspflichten*), as for example a contract of employment. General contractual duties of care (*Sorgfaltspflichten*) of the promisee to the third party are not sufficient.[733] Nevertheless, an intensified duty of care which comes into play if the basis of the existence of the third party is endangered would suffice.[734] In a much-criticised decision, the Federal Court of Justice (*Bundesgerichtshof*) extended the definition towards all third parties in whose protection the contractual creditor is *objectively* interested by arguing that the parties are at liberty to define the scope of protection of the contract not only in an explicit way, but also implicitly.[735] Even without expressly referring to third parties, a contract could have such protective effects if it itself or the circumstances under which it was concluded can be interpreted in such a way. This decision has led to a significant expansion of the scope of application of the contract with protective effects. The interest of the contractual creditor is no longer defined in a subjective way that precisely analyses the interest of the contractual creditor, but in a so-called *objective* way by construing the terms of the contract and the contractual relationship.[736] Even in cases in which the interests of the promisee cannot be squared with the protection of the third party, the objective interest of the party may point to the inclusion of the third party in the scope of protection. If an officially recognised expert has given an expert opinion, the courts may infer from this that he has to deal with the conflicting interests in a neutral way, as it is often the case that expert opinions are

---

731 BGH 2 July 1996, 133 BGHZ 168, at 173: *Es muß ein schutzwürdiges Interesse des Gläubigers an der Einbeziehung des Dritten in den Schutzbereich des Vertrages hinzutreten.*

732 *See for instance* BGH 26 November 1968, 51 BGHZ 91, at 96; BGH 15 June 1971, [1971] *NJW* 1931; BGH 28 January 1976, 66 BGHZ 51, at 57; BGH 15 June 1971, [1971] *NJW* 1931; BGH 2 November 1983, [1984] *NJW* 355, at 355–356.

733 BGH 17 September 2002, [2002] *NJW* 3625, at 3626.

734 BGH 17 September 2002, [2002] *NJW* 3625, at 3626.

735 BGH 2 November 1983, [1984] *NJW* 355, at 355–356. *See also* BGH 23 January 1985, [1986] *NJW-RR* 484; BGH 14 November 2000, [2001] *NJW* 514, at 516. For criticism, *see* Littbarski, 'Die Berufshaftung–eine unerschöpfliche Quelle richterlicher Rechtsfortbildung', [1984] *NJW* 1667, at 1669; Canaris, 'Schutzwirkungen zugunsten Dritter bei "Gegenläufigkeit" der Interessen', [1995] *JZ* 441; Honsell, 'Anmerkung zum Urteil des BGH vom 23.1.1985–IVa ZR 66/83', [1985] *JZ* 952; Hübner, 'Die Berufshaftung–ein zumutbares Berufsrisiko?', [1989] *NJW* 5; Plötner, *Die Rechtsfigur des Vertrags mit Schutzwirkung zugunsten Dritter und die sogenannte Expertenhaftung* (2003), 48; Weber, 'Die Haftung des Abschlußprüfers gegenüber Dritten', [1999] *NZG* 1.

736 BGH 2 November 1983, [1984] *NJW* 355, at 356; BGH 23 January 1985, [1986] *NJW-RR* 484, at 485–486; BGH 26 November 1986, [1987] *NJW* 1758, at 1759.

commissioned in order to show them to third parties.[737] The probative force of the expert opinion is only warranted if its author compiles it to the best of his knowledge and belief and answers for that to third parties.[738] The expert is called upon or is presented as a neutral person and therefore has to mediate between the parties and take into consideration the interests of both of them. As an example, one can refer to a seller who shows an expert opinion to the buyer on the value of the item he wishes to sell. In order to achieve a high purchase price, the seller wants the expert opinion to state a high value of the item, whereas the buyer's interests are exactly the opposite. Nonetheless, according to the jurisprudence of the *Bundesgerichtshof*, the seller is considered as having an *objective* interest in protecting the buyer, even if he does not intend this personally. For this reason, even conflicting interests between the promisee and the third party do not prevent an application of the contract with protective effects towards third parties.

The promisor does not need to know the precise number or even the names of the protected third parties. It is solely required that the group of persons can be limited in an objective manner,[739] which means: according to the terms of the contract. Nonetheless, the courts state that the scope of protection shall not be enlarged in an unlimited way.[740] They aim to restrict it by construing whether it can be recognised in an objective way that the contracting parties intended to establish a duty of protection (*Schutzpflicht*) towards the third party. As regards expert opinions, it is of relevance whether the promisee has ordered the expert opinion in order to submit it to a group of third parties for whom it will serve as the basis of a specific decision.[741] All those third parties are included to whom the expert opinion shall be submitted according to the foreseeable purpose of the expert opinion.[742] When interpreting the contractual circumstances, all statements contained in the expert opinion regarding its function, its other contents and additional remarks made by the expert have to be taken into consideration.[743] There is no pro-

[737] BGH 2 November 1983, [1984] *NJW* 355; BGH 23 January 1985, [1986] *NJW-RR* 484, at 486; BGH 26 November 1986, [1987] *NJW* 1758, at 1759; BGH 18 October 1988, [1989] *NJW-RR* 696; BGH 10 November 1994, [1995] *NJW* 392; BGH 13 November 1997, [1998] *NJW* 1059.

[738] BGH 10 November 1994, [1995] *NJW* 392.

[739] BGH 20 February 1958, 26 BGHZ 365, at 371; BGH 7 November 1960, 33 BGHZ 247, at 249; BGH 2 November 1983, [1984] *NJW* 355; BGH 26 November 1986, [1987] *NJW* 1758, at 1760; BGH 10 November 1994, [1995] *NJW* 392.

[740] BGH 22 January 1968, 49 BGHZ 350, at 354; BGH 19 September 1973, 61 BGHZ 227, at 234; BGH 15 February 1978, [1978] *NJW* 883; BGH 26 November 1986, [1987] *NJW* 1758, at 1760 BGH 13 November 1997, [1998] *NJW* 1059, at 1062; BGH 20 April 2004, [2004] *NJW* 3035, at 3037.

[741] BGH 2 November 1983, [1984] *NJW* 355, at 356; BGH 23 January 1985, [1986] *NJW-RR* 484, at 485–486; BGH 26 November 1986, [1987] *NJW* 1758, at 1759.

[742] *Compare* BGH 13 November 1997, [1998] *NJW* 1059; BGH 20 April 2004, [2004] *NJW* 3035, at 3036.

[743] BGH 20 April 2004, [2004] *NJW* 3035.

tection of third parties if the expert opinion is solely for the internal relationship between the expert and the other contracting party.

It may be criticised that this development completely blurs the difference between a contractual liability and a liability in tort. It makes the aforementioned statutory restrictions of tort law pointless, such as the weakened vicarious liability, the lack of protection from pure economic loss and the shorter limitation period.[744] Moreover, such liability would be rather a statutory liability than a liability based on contract. In practically all cases in which the third party is in proximity of performance, there would be such an interest of the contractual creditor (*Gläubigernähe*). However, the courts apply the criterion in such a way and continue to do so despite all learned criticism. Since the aim of this thesis is to compare the law as it stands and is applied by the courts in all three jurisdictions, it will refrain from joining the concert of criticism and apply the principles that have been established by the courts.

Classification societies will try to argue that the classification of a vessel is only intended for its contracting party and not for any third party. Nonetheless, this argument can be rebutted. A classification includes the information whether or not a vessel is classed and which class notations are assigned in a register which it publishes on-line. It is therefore aware that large parts of the shipping industry are interested in this information. The classification society thereby implicitly accepts that this information, which is the result of the surveys, is not solely for the use of its contracting party.

With respect to the *crew*, it has already been established that the shipowner may be responsible for his crew "for better or for worse" (*für Wohl und Wehe*). If the crew are not employed by the shipowner (as is the case under a bare-boat charter), the shipowner will nonetheless have an objective interest to include them in the scope of protection. The same applies to *passengers*. The classification contract even expressly refers to the numbers of crew and of passengers. The shipowner has to provide details about the vessel in the application form for a classification. It is also evident from the submitted plans, which are part of the contractual circumstances, how many passengers the vessel may transport, and how many crew members are required to operate it. The possible number, but not the exact figure or even the identity, of the potential victims is known by the classification society.

As regards the *cargo* that is transported by the vessel, the picture is more complex. Damage that is caused to the cargo can be rather difficult to identify. Generally, claims for physical loss can fall under the contract with protective effects as well.[745] The basis for an objective interest in protection is that the shipowner wants to use the certificate towards third parties, which he may do, *e.g.*, *vis-à-vis* a potential purchaser or a bank that should give him credit. Or, the shipowner may have an interest in the third party being protected as well, since he has a special obligation for their well-being (as for example towards employees or members of

[744] *See supra* introduction to Part 2 B III.

[745] BGH 22 January 1968, 49 BGHZ 350, at 355.

his family). In such a case, the protected third party does not see the certificate, but will be likewise affected if the classification does not fully perform its obligations. Every shipowner, therefore, would wish that specifically these parties are protected – that is what is meant when the courts talk of an *objective* interpretation of the contract. Regarding cargo, the shipowner is not responsible *for better or for worse* for the cargo. But he may want to show the certificate to the cargo-owner or give him the opportunity to consult the classification society's ship's register, as has been argued before.[746] Nonetheless, this interest in showing the certificate to others does not necessarily imply an objective interest in the protection of these others. Expert opinions in a buyer-seller relationship differ from the situation of classification societies in that the group of third parties can be limited in an objective manner in a buyer-seller relationship. As regards cargo interests, there is a multitude of persons and interests involved which changes constantly. A limitation of the group of persons according to the terms of the contract is impossible in regard of cargo interests because of their constant change. The contracting parties do not intend to establish a duty of protection of the classification society towards the third party either. Cargo interests are therefore not in the scope of protection of the contract with protective effects towards third parties.

When it comes to the confirmation of class, it is in the objective interest of the shipowner that the purchaser of the vessel is protected as well. This has been affirmed in the *Hecht V* case.[747] One should keep in mind that the number of purchasers is limited. Even if the classification society does not know the identity of the purchaser or the group of purchasers, the damage that may be caused is di-

---

[746] *See supra* Part 1 A I, III 1.

[747] *See* OLG Hamburg 14 June 1990, [1990] *TranspR* 345, at 348 (“*Hecht V*”): “Für eine derartige Schutzwirkung spricht insbesondere, daß der Klasse eines Schiffes in Schiffahrtskreisen generell und gerade auch bei dem Kauf eines Schiffes eine große Bedeutung beigemessen wird, da die Klassifikationsgesellschaften über anerkannte Sachkunde auf dem Gebiet der Schiffstechnik verfügen und sogar in die Erfüllung staatlicher Aufgaben einbezogen sind. Eine Klassifikationsgesellschaft, die vom Eigentümer eines Schiffes um eine Klassebestätigung gebeten wird, muß daher damit rechnen, daß die von ihr ausgestellte Bescheinigung zur Vorlage bei einem Dritten, und zwar regelmäßig entweder einer Versicherungsgesellschaft oder einem Kaufinteressenten dient, der auf die Richtigkeit des Inhaltes der Bescheinigung vertraut. Weitergehend wird sie sogar damit rechnen müssen, daß der Dritte auch darauf vertraut, daß diejenigen Besichtigungen, die die Klassifikationsgesellschaft im Zusammenhang mit der Klassifizierung des Schiffes vorgenommen hat und die die Klassifikationsgesellschaft ihrer Bescheinigung zugrunde legt, sorgfältig und sachverständig durchgeführt worden sind. Da der Käufer selbst regelmäßig nicht ohne weiteres den technischen Zustand des Schiffes beurteilen kann, hat er ebenso wie der unmittelbare Vertragspartner der Klassifikationsgesellschaft ein schutzwürdiges Interesse daran, daß die Klassebescheinigung die Ergebnisse der durchgeführten Besichtigungen zutreffend wiedergibt. Aus diesen Gründen erscheint es gerechtfertigt, im Falle der Ausstellung einer Bescheinigung über den Lauf der Klasse einen Drittschutz zugunsten des Käufers, dem die Klassebestätigung vorgelegt werden soll, zu bejahen“ (*citations omitted*).

rectly linked to the vessel. The exposure of the classification society to liability is therefore limited. Moreover, as has already been observed at the beginning of this section, the expert needs to assume the responsibility for the correctness of his certificate.[748] The aim of the classification certificate, as well as of a confirmation of class, is to determine the safety of the vessel and whether certain measures which safeguard the protection of the environment, are enforced. The classification society does not intend to give a statement concerning the value of the vessel.[749] It does not assume responsibility for economic loss. As in the case of the confirmation of class only the risks are transferred from the shipowner to the purchaser, it does not increase the risk for the classification society.[750] The shipowner has an objective interest in the protection of the purchaser to whom he shows a confirmation of class, because such a document is only of value and authority if the expert has to answer for the consequences of default.

Last but not least, the shipowner does not have an objective interest in the inclusion of *coastal States* within the scope of protection of the classification contract. He neither wants to show them the certificate and thus might have such an objective interest nor is he under duties of care *vis-à-vis* coastal States or a duty to give assistance (*Fürsorge- und Obhutspflichten*) or under a special duty of protection (*Schutzpflicht*) which would make him responsible "for better or for worse" (*für Wohl und Wehe*). Even if the shipowner is under a statutory obligation to protect the marine environment, this duty is a general duty of all human beings and has no specific beneficiary other than mankind as a whole. It is therefore not sufficiently distinct to create a special duty of protection that would be required in view of a contract with protective effects towards third parties.

c. Foreseeability (*Erkennbarkeit*)

The interests of the classification society are only safeguarded if it is able to judge the consequences of its behaviour. It needs to be able to foresee that the third party will be affected in case of its default. It must be possible to describe this group of persons in an objective way.[751] The risk of liability must be comprehensible, cal-

---

748 *Compare* BGH 18 October 1988, [1989] *NJW-RR* 696, at 697.

749 *See supra* Part 1 A III 3, Part 1 A III 5, Part 2 A I 1. *Compare* Basedow/Wurmnest, *Die Dritthaftung von Klassifikationsgesellschaften* (2004), at 45; Basedow/Wurmnest, *Third-Party Liability of Classification Societies* (2005), at 57.

750 BGH 2 November 1983, [1984] *NJW* 355, at 356; BGH 20 April 2004, [2004] *NJW* 3035, at 3038.

751 BGH 2 November 1983, [1984] *NJW* 355; BGH 23 January 1985, [1986] *NJW-RR* 484, at 486: '[...] *sofern die zu schützende Personengruppe objektiv abgrenzbar ist*'.

culable and insurable.[752] But this does not imply that the classification society has to know in advance the exact number of protected persons, their names or the precise kind and amount of cargo. The courts only require general objective implications of the possible risk, not a precise knowledge of the items in peril at all times – a knowledge which would be practically impossible to have.[753]

A case in which it is argued that the contract between the shipowner and the classification society has protective effects towards third parties differs from the usual cases of expert opinions, which have been analysed by jurisprudence. Expert opinions are usually valid only for a short period of time. It is clear that an opinion on the value of a particular chattel or real estate can only give indications for a limited period of time. After a number of years, the market has completely changed. In contrast to this, classification societies check the vessel throughout its whole life from the time of its construction until it is scrapped. One could argue that this long-term character makes their expert opinions somewhat special, as it might expose classification societies to liability for a comparatively long period of time. There needs to be some kind of limitation of the time-frame, as it would otherwise be practically impossible to recognise at the time of the first inspection all third parties who might be affected throughout the life of a vessel. However, on closer scrutiny, the long time-frame does not cause a problem. It does not lead to an accumulation of risks. The certificate only runs for a period of five years and requires annual endorsements. Besides, the third parties and the risks change frequently. Only those passengers or goods that are on board may be injured. However, it does not make any difference if the injury occurred shortly after the initial survey or a long time thereafter. Throughout the time of a valid contract between the shipowner and the classification society there is no need for any limitation. The society surveys the vessel on a yearly basis. Only if the shipowner changes the classification society is a limitation regarding the period of liability of the old classification society required. After the classification society's change, the old classification society is no longer responsible for the survey of the vessel, but the new one, which has surveyed the vessel before accepting it for its register. Also, the former contract with the shipowner will no longer be valid. The contract does not extend its protection towards these parties after its expiry.

As the definition of foreseeability of the third party is rather broad, one has to apply it restrictively in order to avoid excessive liability. Otherwise this criterion would be of little importance if it excluded only those persons who were acciden-

---

752 BGH 26 November 1968, 51 BGHZ 91, at 96; BGH 18 June 1968, [1968] *NJW* 1929, at 1931; BGH 23 January 1985, [1986] *NJW-RR* 484; *Gottwald* in Rebmann/Säcker/Rixecker, *Münchener Kommentar zum Bürgerlichen Gesetzbuch, §§ 241–432* (2003), § 328 at no. 91; Hadding in: Soergel/Siebert/Mertens *Kommentar zum Bürgerlichen Gesetzbuch* (1990), Anh § 328 at no. 17; Jagmann in: Staudinger, *Kommentar zum Bürgerlichen Gesetzbuch, §§ 328–359* (2004), § 328 at no. 105.

753 BGH 20 February 1958, 26 BGHZ 365, at 371; BGH 7 November 1960, 33 BGHZ 247, at 249; BGH 2 November 1983, [1984] *NJW* 355; BGH 26 November 1986, [1987] *NJW* 1758, at 1760; BGH 10 November 1994, [1995] *NJW* 392.

tally injured. Liability would neither be calculable nor insurable. This is also illustrated in a number of cases in which the application of the contract with protective effects towards third parties has been rejected due to considerations of excessive, unpredictable damage. In cases of product liability, for example, it has been held that a contract between the manufacturer and the retailer does not extend towards the consumer.[754] Similarly, such protection does not exist towards all consumers of electricity whenever works are carried out to power cables, as these consumers are not foreseeable and the liability would reach too far.[755]

A large number of persons may be affected if the classification society does not exercise its duties, such as the checking of blueprints or surveys, in the way it should. The number of persons that are affected by a confirmation of class is not the problem, as only the buyer of the vessel may consult it. As regards the classification certificate, the situation is, however, completely different. The shipowner shows the certificate to a large number of persons, such as insurers, charterers, cargo-owners, ship's financers and/or cruise lines. In fact, he shows it to practically everyone who has an interest in the ship. One may therefore doubt whether it is foreseeable to the classification society that it may be liable to all these parties, and that such liability would be comprehensible, calculable and insurable. Bulk vessels may transport different kinds of cargo in bulk which also differ in value. Tankers may carry different chemicals, products or crude oil which largely all differ in value as well. It is even more difficult, if not impossible, to estimate the potential liability with regard to container vessels, as virtually everything can be transported in a container today. As a result, the potential risk exposure of damage to the cargo can be rather difficult to ascertain.

The potential risk is almost impossible to ascertain if one tries to determine the liability that may be caused by cargo *vis-à-vis* coastal States. The costs of preventive measures depend on the type of oil, on the vulnerability and specifications of the eco-system where the oil has been spilled,[756] and also on external factors such as the distance of the vessel to the shore, the weather and currents in the sea. It is therefore more or less impossible to estimate the potential liability. If the requirement of foreseeability is to make any sense and restrict the exposure to liability in any way, it cannot be interpreted in such a broad manner. The risks of coastal States are therefore not foreseeable to classification societies.

Despite these difficulties concerning the potential risk exposure and the necessity of a limitation of the exposure to liability, *foreseeability* should not be phrased

---

[754] BGH 26 November 1968, 51 BGHZ 91, at 96; BGH 14 May 1974, [1974] *NJW* 1503; BGH 11 October 1988, [1989] *NJW* 1029; LG Köln 23 November 1977, [1978] *NJW* 329, at 330; *Westermann* in: *Erman*, § 328 at no. 12a, 34; *Gottwald* in: Rebmann/Säcker/Rixecker, *Münchener Kommentar zum Bürgerlichen Gesetzbuch, §§ 241–432* (2003), § 328 at no. 116.

[755] BGH 3 November 1961, [1962] *VersR* 86, at 88; BGH 12 July 1977, [1977] *NJW* 2208, at 2209.

[756] The vulnerability of the Alaska eco-system is one of the reasons for the especially high costs of the preventive measures in the aftermath of the Exxon Valdez casualty.

too narrowly either. A sensible limitation of the exposure to risks can be found if one takes the aim of the activities of the classification society into account. Its duties relate solely to issues of safety and the protection of the marine environment, not to the protection of the contracting party or even third parties from economic loss. A classification society therefore does not assume liability for economic loss.[757]

Classification societies usually try to avoid liability towards such a large number of third parties by stating in their certificates that these are solely intended for the use of the contracting party. Such a clause may be interpreted as trying to exempt it from liability and will therefore be further analysed at a later point of this thesis.[758] It does not, however, influence foreseeability in the sense of the contract with protective effects towards third parties. Foreseeability is a question of fact, not of law.

To sum up, all those persons that the classification society must expect to have an interest in the classification of the vessel or to be put in danger are foreseeable to it. This includes the insurers, charterers, cargo-owners, ship's financers and cruise lines as well as the potential purchasers of the vessel. Seamen and passengers are also protected, despite the fact that they do not necessarily consult the classification certificate or the ship's register, since it is evident to the classification societies that their interests will be affected in the case of a negligent discharge of the society's duties. However, as the classification society only analyses the safety of the vessel and its compliance with regulations that protect the marine environment, it does not aim at the prevention of economic loss and cannot be held liable for such loss.

d. Third Party in Need of Protection (*Schutzbedürftigkeit des Dritten*)

If the third party is already protected by contractual claims, against whomever they may be directed, there is no need to include it in the protection of the contract and extend the liability of the classification society.[759] However, the contractual claims need to have the same or at least an equivalent extent as the claims which the third party would receive when protected by the contract.[760] Despite having a

757 *Compare* also *supra* Part 2 A I 1.

758 *See infra* Part 2 B III 7; *compare supra* Part 2 A III 4.

759 According to Kraft/Schlingmann, 'Die Dritthaftung von Klassifikationsgesellschaften', [2004] *VersR* 1095, at 1101 this precondition is no longer of value to these cases. Such argumentation has to be rejected. Jurisprudence has not abolished this precondition nor changed the law as it now stands. Even if there may be cases in which it has not expressly referred to whether the third party was in need of protection (Kraft/Schlingmann referred to BGH 10 November 1994, [1995] *NJW* 392 and BGH 13 November 1997, [1998] *NJW* 1059), the *Bundesgerichtshof* did not fully adjudicate these cases but remanded all them to the court below.

760 BGH 15 February 1978, [1978] *NJW* 883; BGH 2 July 1996, 133 BGHZ 168, at 173–174; BGH 2 July 1996, 133 BGHZ 168, at 173.

separate claim against another party, the third party is in need of protection if the limitation period of that claim differs,[761] if its extent differs or if the aims of the claims differ.[762] As regards those parties that may be affected by the classification certificate, there are considerable differences.[763]

aa. Recipients of a Confirmation of Class

Recipients of a confirmation of class that purchase the classed vessel may have contractual claims against the seller of the vessel. However, usually these claims will not have the same scope as a claim against the classification society.[764]

One could first think of the fact that the sales contract usually contains a clause which exempts the seller from liability. One might therefore think that if such a disclaimer applies, the third party will not have any rights and therefore is in need of protection.[765] Such argumentation must be contested, since the purchaser voluntarily waived his claims. There is no need to protect him if he does not consider himself in need of protection.[766] In addition to that, the claim against the classification society would largely depend on the fact that an exemption clause had been included in the contract and is valid.[767]

Secondly, the claims against the seller will most likely not be subject to German law. Under the Norwegian Saleform the parties often choose English law and London arbitration.[768] One could, of course, argue that the purchaser has voluntar-

---

For this reason, since the person who ordered a vessel from a shipyard may sue the shipyard in cases of misconstruction of the vessel, it does not have a claim against the classification society, *see* OLG Hamburg 27 March 2001, 9 U 364/99 (unpublished).

761 BGH 8 June 2004, [2004] *NJW* 3420, at 3421.

762 BGH 8 June 2004, [2004] *NJW* 3420, at 3421: the protection of investors is a different aim to that of the protection of confidence in the accuracy of expert opinions.

763 *Similarly* Basedow/Wurmnest, *Die Dritthaftung von Klassifikationsgesellschaften* (2004), at 36; Basedow/Wurmnest, *Third-Party Liability of Classification Societies* (2005), at 45–46. Therefore too general: Holtappels, 'Haftung von Klassifikationsgesellschaften in der Handelsschiffahrt', [2002] *TranspR* 278, at 279–280; Drobnig, *Tätigkeit und Haftung von Klassifikationsgesellschaften in der Bundesrepublik Deutschland am Beispiel des Germanischen Lloyd* (1995), at 171.

764 Contrary to Basedow/Wurmnest, *Die Dritthaftung von Klassifikationsgesellschaften* (2004), at 47–51; Basedow/Wurmnest, *Third-Party Liability of Classification Societies* (2005), at 45–46, 59–63.

765 Apparently Kraft/Schlingmann seem to think in such a way, *see* Kraft/Schlingmann, 'Die Dritthaftung von Klassifikationsgesellschaften', [2004] *VersR* 1095, at 1101.

766 *See also* Basedow/Wurmnest, *Die Dritthaftung von Klassifikationsgesellschaften* (2004), at 49–50. Basedow/Wurmnest, *Third-Party Liability of Classification Societies* (2005), at 62.

767 Kraft/Schlingmann realize that, *see* Kraft/Schlingmann, 'Die Dritthaftung von Klassifikationsgesellschaften', [2004] *VersR* 1095, at 1101.

768 Clause 16 offers a choice between arbitration London with English law applicable, arbitration New York with Title 9 of the United States Code and the Law of the State of New York applicable, and arbitration elsewhere as agreed between the parties.

ily accepted this venue and that he therefore needs to accept the consequences as well.[769] It may be difficult to determine for a German court whether the scope of the claim by the third party under English law is equivalent to the claim against the classification society under German law. The interpretation of the duties, functions and liabilities under the sales contract, which is subject to foreign law, should however not affect the liability of the classification society towards these third parties.

Moreover, and more important, such claims are not equivalent for yet another reason: they have different aims. Claims that are based on the sales contract shall protect the purchaser from defects of the vessel and damage that might be caused by the vessel. The idea is that the purchaser shall get what he reasonably expected and contracted for. The aim of claims based on the contract with protective effects towards third parties is, however, to protect the confidence in the accuracy of the expert opinion.[770] Since the aims differ, the third party is in need of protection.[771]

If German law applies to the claims against the seller as well, another argument can be added. A sales contract is subject to a different limitation period to that for a contract for work, such as the classification contract or the contract for a confirmation of class. Claims based on a sales contract are statute-barred two years after delivery.[772] Only if the seller was deceitful will the ordinary limitation period apply.[773] To a classification contract, which is a contract for work, the ordinary limitation period applies, unless the contracting parties have agreed upon a different limitation period.[774]

---

769 This seems to have been the opinion of the OLG Hamburg 14 June 1990, [1990] *TranspR* 345, at 349 as well.

770 *Compare* BGH 8 June 2004, [2004] *NJW* 3420, at 3421.

771 Similar result: Drobnig, *Tätigkeit und Haftung von Klassifikationsgesellschaften in der Bundesrepublik Deutschland am Beispiel des Germanischen Lloyd* (1995), at 169–170.

772 § 438 (1) no. 3 BGB.

773 §§ 438 (3), 195, 199 (1) BGB. The claim is statute-barred three years from the end of the year in which the claim came into existence and the claimant knew or should have known the facts on which the claim is based. Regardless of this knowledge, the claim is definitely statute-barred after thirty years in the case of personal injury or death or in ten years in other cases, § 199 (2), (3) BGB.

774 §§ 634a (1) Nr. 3, 195, 199 (1) BGB. The performance of a surveillance (*Überwachungsleistung*) in § 634a (1) Nr. 1, to which a two-year limitation period applies, only refers to the supervision of a construction, which is not the aim of the contract for a confirmation of class. That the confirmation of class is a contract for work by itself has been held by the OLG Hamburg 14 June 1990, [1990] *TranspR* 345, at 347. For an example of such a shorter limitation period, *compare* Rules of GL, I Part 0, Section 1 G (2).

To sum up, contractual claims of the recipients of a confirmation of class differ in their extent from a claim against the classification society. These entities are therefore in need of protection.[775]

bb. Passengers

Passengers might not be in need of protection as they may have contractual claims against their contracting party if not against the shipowner himself. One might again wonder whether such claims have the same aim as claims based on a false expert opinion.[776] Unlike the purchasers of a vessel, passengers do not voluntarily waive the liability of their carrier; there are statutory regulations such as the Athens Convention and the LLMC and their domestic implementations which limit the extent of their claims against the carrier. Hence, one cannot argue that they voluntarily waived their rights. A difficult question is whether these conventions or domestic regulations bar the recovery of damages that are higher than the limitations in all cases. In the third part of this thesis it will be shown that the societies do not come within the scope of application of these conventions and that an application by analogy is not possible.[777] Therefore, since these claims do not have the same extent as the claims against the classification society based on the contract with protective effects, the passengers are in need of protection.

The passengers may have purchased insurance which provides them with claims against an insurance company in the case of a casualty. These claims could therefore make the protection of these third parties unnecessary. However, such claims exist because the third party has purchased coverage, which was not done in order to exonerate the classification society.[778] The premium is also calculated on the basis that the insurance company might take recourse against the wrongdoer. It is not the intention of the insurance company to relieve the wrongdoer of the responsibility for his acts. Claims against insurance companies should there-

---

[775] OLG Hamburg 14 June 1990, [1990] *TranspR* 345, at 348 came to the same conclusion, but rejected that damage was caused by the confirmation of class, as the confirmation of class was correct according to the files. The classification society only has to answer for the *formal accuracy* of the confirmation of class, which means that it conforms to the data kept in the files, but not to the *material accuracy,* which would require a thorough re-survey of the vessel. OLG Hamburg 27 March 2001, 9 U 364/99 (unpublished), however, differed in a case in which the classification contract had been concluded with the shipyard. It held that the purchaser of the vessel was not in need of protection, as it had contractual claims against the shipyard at the time the contract was concluded. That was, however, a rare case in which both the claims against the shipyard and against the classification society aimed at the same interest. The claim was made for damages due to the fact that the vessel itself did not correspond to the rules of the classification society. Herber, *Seehandelsrecht* (1999), 176 also argues that the purchasers of a vessel are protected by the contract with protective effects towards third parties.

[776] *See also supra* Part 2 B III 2 d aa.

[777] *See infra* Part 3 B I.

[778] This idea is sometimes called attribution of benefits (*Vorteilsanrechnung*).

fore not be taken into consideration when estimating whether the third party is in need of protection.

cc. Crew Members

If German law applies to the contract between the shipowner and the crew member, the crew member will have a claim based on either §§ 618, 280 (1) or § 80 SeemG. Claims against the employer are, however, only possible if the harm was caused intentionally.[779] As such claims are barred by statutory law, they are not equivalent to the ones against the classification society. One may point out that the crew member will receive compensation from the compulsory accident insurance scheme provided by the *See-Berufsgenossenschaft* if a casualty occurs.[780] As this claim exists regardless of fault, one could argue that it favours the crew member, who is therefore not in need of protection. However, this claim is once again a claim against an insurance system, namely the system of compulsory insurance against accidents. Once again, the payment by the insurer, the *See-Berufsgenossenschaft*, depends on the participation of the crew member in the insurance scheme. The crew member finances this scheme by his contributions and the scheme only aims at the protection of the crew member himself and does not purport to relieve the classification society.

Moreover, the aims of the claims differ. The claim of the crew member against the shipowner seeks to protect him from harm incurred during employment. In a wider context, it aims at the implementation of reasonable working standards, whereas the aim of a claim against the classification society is to protect confidence in the accuracy of this expert opinion.

dd. Insurance Companies

Apart from the fact that the claims of insurance companies, such as hull underwriters, will be claims for economic loss and are therefore not in the scope of protection,[781] there is no need to protect these companies. If they indemnify the shipowner, they will be assigned the shipowner's claims (or the shipyard's claims if the incident occurs before the maiden voyage) against the classification society.[782]

---

779 §§ 104–107 Sozialgesetzbuch (SGB) VII.

780 Basedow/Wurmnest, *Die Dritthaftung von Klassifikationsgesellschaften* (2004), at 59; Basedow/Wurmnest, *Third-Party Liability of Classification Societies* (2005), at 71.

781 *See supra* Part 2 B III 2 a.

782 Pursuant to § 67 VVG or the appropriate clause in the insurance contract. *Compare* Basedow, 'Rechtsvergleich', in: Basedow/Fock, *Europäisches Versicherungsvertragsrecht* (2002), 1, at 110–115.

Hence, there is no need to include them in the scope of protection of the classification contract.[783]

e. Addendum: Incorrect Information by the Shipowner

The classification society has an obligation to check and survey the vessel. Whenever the crew members as employees of the shipowner provide incorrect information or suppress deficiencies, this may influence the classification certificate.[784] Under such circumstances, the shipowner will not have a claim against the classification society, since he has been responsible for the misrepresentation.

The *Bundesgerichtshof* has however held in a case that does not relate to classification societies that an expert must be aware of the fact that his expert opinion is likely to be shown to third parties who put specific confidence in the trustworthiness and experience of the expert if the expert opinion is destined for such use; it suffices that the expert must contemplate that his expert opinion will be shown to third parties and that the third party will use the expert opinion as a basis of its decisions.[785] Representations of the expert are more trustworthy than those made by the contracting party itself. There is an objective interest of the third party that the expert opinion is accurate, even if the inaccuracy has been caused by the contracting party. The classification society can exclude this risk of liability by expressly stating whether and to what extent it depended on information that was provided by the shipowner. If the classification society makes such representation, it indicates that it does not assume responsibility for the information provided by the shipowner.[786]

3. *Culpa in Contrahendo*

According to some German legal scholars, the purchaser of a vessel can claim damages from a classification society under the doctrine of *culpa in contrahendo*

---

[783] *Compare* Basedow/Wurmnest, *Die Dritthaftung von Klassifikationsgesellschaften* (2004), at 53–55; Basedow/Wurmnest, *Third-Party Liability of Classification Societies* (2005), at 66–67. Contrary: Drobnig, *Tätigkeit und Haftung von Klassifikationsgesellschaften in der Bundesrepublik Deutschland* (1995), at 165; Herber, *Seehandelsrecht* (1999), 176; Holtappels, 'Haftung von Klassifikationsgesellschaften in der Handelsschiffahrt', [2002] *TranspR* 278, at 279 *et seq.*

[784] *Compare also supra* Part 1 A VI 3.

[785] BGH 20 April 2004, [2004] *NJW* 3035, at 3036 with further reference; BGH 10 November 1994, [1995] *NJW* 392, at 393. § 334 BGB is therefore implicitly excluded.

[786] *Compare* BGH 13 November 1997, [1998] *NJW* 1059, at 1061.

pursuant to § 311 BGB if the vessel's certificates are incorrect.[787] *Culpa in contrahendo* mainly offers a quasi-contractual protection whenever either contractual negotiations have commenced or if one person submits his legal interests to dangers in view of a future contract. Neither of these alternatives applies here. Additionally, this doctrine also protects cases of a business contact that is similar to the aforementioned alternatives.[788]

For such a *similar business contact*, the courts require a somewhat close relationship.[789] The consultation of a certificate only provides the information that the vessel has fulfilled the requirements of the rules at the time of the survey but is not a business contact with the classification society. One might argue that the certificates or the ship's register give the impression that a certain legal situation exists (*Rechtsschein*). But this is not the fact. The classification certificate only gives a representation about a certain factual situation, not a legal situation. If the information contained in the certificates or the register is wrong, the third party will therefore rely on an incorrect factual situation, not on an incorrect legal situation. An incorrect factual situation cannot cause a liability for the ostensible existence of a legal situation (*Rechtsscheinshaftung*).[790] A *culpa in contrahendo* based on a *similar business contact*[791] does not exist for the consultation of certificates. Even

---

[787] Kraft/Schlingmann, 'Die Dritthaftung von Klassifikationsgesellschaften', [2004] *VersR* 1095, at 1102. Drobnig argues with the aims of prospectus liability, *Tätigkeit und Haftung von Klassifikationsgesellschaften in der Bundesrepublik Deutschland* (1995), at 178 *et seq*. The application of this doctrine was rejected by OLG Hamburg on 14 June 1990, [1990] *TranspR* 345 at 349. *See also* Basedow/Wurmnest, *Die Dritthaftung von Klassifikationsgesellschaften* (2004), at 60–61; Basedow/Wurmnest, *Third-Party Liability of Classification Societies* (2005), at 73–75.

[788] § 311 (2) no. 3 BGB.

[789] For example, if several people sell something together without any legal relationship between one another, they may be liable towards one another for culpa in contrahendo due to their business contact (*see* BGH 7 July 1980, [1980] *NJW* 2464).

[790] Canaris, *Die Vertrauenshaftung im deutschen Privatrecht* (1971), 496: 'Weiterhin ist zu unterscheiden, ob der Vertrauenstatbestand sich auf ein *Rechtsverhältnis* oder auf eine *natürliche Tatsache* bezieht. Auch das spielt vor allem für die Festlegung des Anwendungsbereichs der *Rechtsscheinhaftung* eine Rolle. Diese setzt nämlich, wie schon ihr Name sagt, voraus, daß der Schein einer bestimmten *Rechts*lage besteht, während entsprechende Regeln über die Einstandspflicht für einen *'Tatsachen*schein' dem geltenden Recht unbekannt sind.'

[791] As regards the wording, § 311 (3) BGB might also be applicable ((3) 'Ein Schuldverhältnis mit Pflichten nach § 241 Abs. 2 kann auch zu Personen entstehen, die nicht selbst Vertragspartei werden sollen. Ein solches Schuldverhältnis entsteht insbesondere, wenn der Dritte in besonderem Maße Vertrauen für sich in Anspruch nimmt und dadurch die Vertragsverhandlungen oder den Vertragsschluss erheblich beeinflusst.' Translation by Coester/Markesinis, 'Liability of Financial Experts in German and American Law', 51 *Am.J.Comp.L.* 275 (2003), at 290: 'An obligation involving duties according to § 241 (2) may also arise with regard to persons not party to the contract. Such obligation arises especially when the third party claims special trustworthiness for

if someone consults a certificate issued by a classification society, such a contact is not comparable to the other two possibilities.

In addition to these statutory categories, the *Bundesgerichtshof* employs the doctrine of *culpa in contrahendo* to cases of prospectus liability. Those who publish a prospectus or are responsible for the information that it contains may be held liable for incorrect or incomplete indications. This includes lawyers, chartered accountants, and tax advisers - in brief, everyone who creates some kind of trust on the part of the investor by participating in the prospectus.[792] Classification societies do not offer any kind of information included in a prospectus. However, since the *Bundesgerichtshof* bases prospectus liability on a general concept of law, that general concept has to be taken into consideration as well. The idea is that everyone has to answer for the consequences if he influences the free exercise of the will of investors.[793] For instance, whenever someone tolerates the use of his auditor's reports which do not conform with the prospectus, he causes or maintains trust which may lead to a *culpa in contrahendo*.[794] This case law only enlarges the concept of prospectus liability to a similar constellation involving a chartered accountant whose auditor's reports have not been included in the prospectus, but which are with his knowledge shown to the investor in a situation that is compara-

itself and thereby exerts substantial influence on the contractual negotiations or on the conclusion of the contract.' § 241 II BGB: 'Each party to the obligation may, according to the content of the obligation, be required to apply proper care as to the rights and interests of the other party', Coester/Markesinis, *ibid.*) The legislator made some statements in this direction as well, *see* Bundestags-Drucksache 14/6040, at 163; Bundestags-Drucksache 14/7052 at 190. And in fact, a number of scholars argue that this regulation includes the liability for expert opinions (Canaris, 'Die Reform des Rechts der Leistungsstörungen', [2001] *JZ* 499, at 520 *et seq.*; Huber/Faust, *Schuldrechtsmodernisierung* (2002), § 3, at no. 14). There is no case law on the application of § 311 (3) s. 2 BGB on expert opinions yet. But several legal scholars come to the opposite conclusion (Emmerich in: Rebmann/Säcker/Rixecker, *Münchener Kommentar zum Bürgerlichen Gesetzbuch, §§ 241–432* (2003), § 311 at no. 202–207, 227–232; Heinrichs in: Palandt, *Bürgerliches Gesetzbuch* (2006), § 311 at no. 60). The legislator has all the same included a statement that the aim was not to change the law as it is, but jurisprudence should think about changing its concept of professional liability based on the contract with protective effects towards third parties and base it on § 311 (3) s. 2 (*see* Bundestags-Drucksache 14/6040, at 163; Canaris, *Schuldrechtsreform 2002* (2002), at XIX). As there is no decision in this respect yet, the concept stays the same. Liability for the provision of expert opinions may not be based on § 311 (3) s. 2 BGB, but on a contract with protective effects towards third parties.

792 BGH 6 October 1980, 79 BGHZ 337, at 341, 342; BGH 31 May 1990, [1990] *NJW* 2461; BGH 1 December 1994, [1995] *NJW* 1025; BGH 31 March 1992, [1992] *NJW-RR* 879, at 883; Weimann, *Prospekthaftung* (1998), at 19.

793 BGH 6 October 1980, 79 BGHZ 337, at 341–342.

794 BGH 22 May 1980, [1980] *NJW* 1840; BGH 6 October 1980, 79 BGHZ 337, at 341–342; BGH 31 May 1990, [1990] *NJW* 2461, at 2462; BGH 8 June 2004, [2004] *NJW* 3420, at 3421.

ble to a prospectus. Besides, the *Bundesgerichtshof* did not mean to establish a general concept of liability for the provision of expert opinions under the doctrine of *culpa in contrahendo*; otherwise its comprehensive approach to the contract with protective effects towards third parties would be pointless.[795] As a classification society only provides information about the safety of the vessel and its observance of regulations that protect the marine environment but does not influence the free exercise of the will of investors, it cannot be held liable under the general principle on which prospectus liability is based nor under the theory of prospectus liability.[796]

Only for the sake of completeness will another category of *culpa in contrahendo* be mentioned to which the *Bundesgerichtshof* referred in a number of cases, but which has never been applied. Those who provide an expert opinion may expressly or impliedly state that they want to be liable for the information *to whom it may concern*. As the court itself puts it, this is almost never the case.[797] This is especially true with regard to classification societies, considering their disclaimers that information is only intended for the contractual party.[798]

4. § 823 (1) BGB

The German tort law provision of § 823 (1) BGB protects only an enumerated number of rights and interests, namely life, body, health, freedom, property or any "other right" (*sonstiges Recht*). Such "other right" in the sense defined by the courts envisages, *inter alia*, a delictual protection of family relationships, the right of an established and operating business (*Recht am eingerichteten und ausgeübten Gewerbebetrieb*) and the general right to one's personality (*allgemeines Persönlichkeitsrecht*). It does not include a protection of pure economic loss (*Vermögensschaden*).

In order to be liable pursuant to § 823 (1) BGB, it is required that the classification society has harmed any of these rights or interests. It must be possible to attribute the injury to actions or omissions of the classification society. The check-

---

795 For this reason not convincing: Drobnig, *Tätigkeit und Haftung von Klassifikationsgesellschaften in der Bundesrepublik Deutschland am Beispiel des Germanischen Lloyd* (1995), at 178–179. There is also no coherent argumentation in that Drobnig admits claims of Products Liability but denies a special professional liability only because this would overstretch the institute of *culpa in contrahendo* in the case of classification societies (at 182–186). If a professional liability based on *culpa in contrahendo* overstretched the basis of this institute, it does so always and not only in view of classification societies and therefore does not require such a lengthy analysis.

796 Similar Basedow/Wurmnest, *Die Dritthaftung von Klassifikationsgesellschaften* (2004), at 60–61; Basedow/Wurmnest, *Third-Party Liability of Classification Societies* (2005), at 73–74. Contrary: Drobnig, *Tätigkeit und Haftung von Klassifikationsgesellschaften in der Bundesrepublik Deutschland* (1995), at 178 *et seq.;* Kraft/Schlingmann, 'Die Dritthaftung von Klassifikationsgesellschaften', [2004] *VersR* 1095, at 1102, 1104.

797 BGH 6 July 1970, [1970] *NJW* 1737; BGH 5 December 1972, [1973] *NJW* 321, at 323.

798 These disclaimers will be further analysed *infra* Part 2 B III 7.

ing of blueprints or the survey of the vessel must, therefore, have caused the casualty that caused the harm. The checking or survey is only a remote contributing act in a long chain of causation. The checking is not sufficient to cause the harm; the vessel also needs to be put in service, and possibly several other acts are required as well. In addition to that, in many cases in which such casualties occur, the harm will rather have to be attributed to the nonfeasance of the classification society than to a misfeasance.[799] Since there is no general duty to provide assistance to the general public, it needs to be examined whether the acts of the classification society have contributed to the harm and whether the classification society had a duty to act even towards the injured third party. As a way of making such an analysis, German courts and scholars have developed the doctrine of *Verkehrspflichten,* which may be translated literally as *duties of securing intercourse.*[800] The idea behind this doctrine can be described as follows:

> 'Its meaning could be summarized by saying that whoever by his activity or through his property establishes in everyday life a source of potential danger which is likely to affect the interests and rights of others is obliged to ensure their protection against the risks thus created by him.'[801]

Verkehrspflichten are also relevant to cases of nonfeasance and whenever a long chain of causation caused the harm. Under the German law of causation, every act that has contributed to the harm in any way will be deemed as causative to it.[802] It is evident that the scope of application of this doctrine needs some kind of restric-

---

[799] For this reason undifferentiated: Drobnig, *Tätigkeit und Haftung von Klassifikationsgesellschaften in der Bundesrepublik Deutschland am Beispiel des Germanischen Lloyd* (1995), at 187.

[800] Translation used by Zepos/Christodoulou, 'Professional Liability', in: *Int.Enc.Comp.L., XI Torts* (1983) ch. 6 s. 8. Throughout this thesis the term *Verkehrspflichten*, not *Verkehrssicherungspflichten*, will be used. Sometimes these terms are used interchangeably. Most of the scholars, however, use the term *Verkehrssicherungspflicht* as regards streets, property and real estate and *Verkehrspflichten* with reference to all other sources of potential danger, *see* von Bar, *Verkehrspflichten* (1980), at 43 *et seq.*

[801] Markesinis, *The German Law of Torts, A Comparative Introduction* (2002), at 64; *see* RG 30 October 1902, 52 RGZ 373; RG 23 February 1903, 54 RGZ 53; RG 19 September 1921, 102 RGZ 372; BGH 28 April 1952, 5 BGHZ 378, at 380 *et seq.*; BGH 15 June 1954, 14 BGHZ 83, at 85; BGH 30 January 1961, 34 BGHZ 206, at 209; BGH 1 June 1970, 54 BGHZ 165, at 168; BGH 18 December 1972, 60 BGHZ 54, at 55; BGH 1 March 1988, 103 BGHZ 338, at 340; BGH 25 February 1993, 121 BGHZ 367, at 375; BGH 17 June 1997, 136 BGHZ 69, at 77; BGH 4 December 2001, [2002] *NJW-RR* 525, at 526; von Bar, *Verkehrspflichten* (1980), at 43 *et seq.*; von Caemmerer, 'Wandlungen des Deliktsrechts', in: von Caemmerer, *Festschrift zum 100jährigen Bestehen des Deutschen Juristentages* (1960), vol. II, 49, at 72 *et seq.*

[802] Oetker in: Rebmann/Säcker/Rixecker, *Münchener Kommentar zum Bürgerlichen Gesetzbuch, §§ 241–432* (2003), § 249 at no. 98–103 with further references; BGH 11 May 1951, [1951] *NJW* 711.

tion or limitation in order to avoid overexposure to indirect and remote claims for consequential damage (*mittelbare Verletzungen*).[803]

Classification societies provide expert opinions not on the value of the vessel, but only on its standard of safety, as has been argued before.[804] As it is not even their obligation to protect their contracting party from economic loss, they do not owe a *Verkehrspflicht* to a third party to protect it from economic loss.

No German court has yet determined whether a classification society owes a *Verkehrspflicht* to a third party. The few cases involving classification societies which have been decided mainly focus on the concept of a contract with protective effects towards third parties, not on tort.[805] This may be surprising, as in cases involving architects or technical experts the existence of a *Verkehrspflicht* has always been a matter of discussion. Such cases shall be analysed in the following section and it will be determined whether they are of value to the liability of classification societies under § 823 (1) BGB.

a. *Verkehrspflicht*: Surveying and Rule-making as a Potential Source of Danger

A *Verkehrspflicht* comes *inter alia* into existence whenever someone allows the public to come into contact with a specific danger or creates a new danger. In German legal terminology, that person "opens an intercourse" (*eröffnet einen Verkehr*). This may be apparent in all cases in which a person grants access to his premises, whether that access is granted by law or by fact. Additionally, those who manufacture products and sell them in a dangerous condition to the public are subject to a *Verkehrspflicht* to the buyers. All those who have the responsibility for dangerous goods owe a *Verkehrspflicht* to those persons that could be harmed. Those who can prevent the public from being hurt have to do so. However, that does not require unreasonable effort by the person that owes the *Verkehrspflicht*.

803 Hager in: Staudinger, *Kommentar zum Bürgerlichen Gesetzbuch, §§ 823- 825* (1999), § 823 at s. E 3; Larenz/Canaris, *Lehrbuch des Schuldrechts*, vol. II/2 (1994), § 76 III 1. Some scholars (such as Mertens, 'Deliktsrecht und Sonderprivatrecht–Zur Rechtsfortbildung des deliktischen Schutzes von Vermögensinteressen', 178 *AcP* 227 (1978); Huber, 'Verkehrspflichten zum Schutz fremden Vermögens', in: Ficker/König/Kreuzer, Festschrift für Ernst von Caemmerer (1978), at 359; von Bar, *Verkehrspflichten*, at 145 *et seq.*, 154 *et seq.*) argue that there are or should be *Verkehrspflichten* which protect from pure economic loss. And that they would give rise to a liability pursuant to § 823 (2) BGB, which protects all interests, not only an enumerated number. Until now the courts have turned a deaf ear to such argumentations.

804 *See supra* Part 1 A III 5, Part 2 A I 1.

805 Apart from the first one of 1907, which was based on § 826 BGB, *see* OLG Hamburg 26 October 1906, [1907] *Hanseatische Gerichtszeitung, Hauptblatt*, 37 (*Theodor Schiff, Heinecke & Co. und Bergeest & Siemers* v. *Bureau Veritas (Schoonergaliote "Industrie")*); *affirmed* RG 4 November 1907, [1908] Hanseatische Gerichtszeitung, Hauptblatt, at 163. The following decisions concentrate on a contract with protective effects towards third parties: OLG Hamburg 14 June 1990, [1990] *TranspR* 345 (*"Hecht V"*) and OLG Hamburg 27 March 2001, 9 U 364/99 (unpublished).

Those precautions are to be taken that are required according to the safety expectations of the group of persons that may be affected.[806] Within the scope of economically reasonable effort, it is required to prevent those dangers to third parties that are imminent in the destined use or even in an irregular use that could easily be foreseen.[807] A danger only gives rise to a *Verkehrspflicht* if a competent person would expect that it is likely that the interests of other persons could be injured.[808] Whether or not a *Verkehrspflicht* exists and to which interests it extends is influenced by the legitimate expectations of the third party that takes part in the intercourse.[809] A *Verkehrspflicht* depends on the situation and may change in time and according to its circumstances.[810] What is also relevant is the relation between the inherent danger and the costs of prevention.[811] Whenever life or health or similarly important interests are threatened, special efforts to minimise the danger are required.[812]

The courts generally reject a *Verkehrspflicht* that is only based on the exercise of a professional duty (*Berufspflicht*), i.e. on the fact that someone offers a service as part of his profession, and not on the danger of a certain activity to the public.[813] The starting point of this development was a decision by the *Reichsgericht*. It held that a veterinary surgeon who decided that a cow which suffered from anthrax be put down was liable towards a butcher for the reason of lack of information about

[806] BGH 11 December 1984, [1985] *NJW* 1076, at 1077.

[807] BGH 21 February 1978, [1978] *NJW* 1629.

[808] BGH 15 April 1975, [1975] *VersR* 812.

[809] BGH 11 December 1984, [1985] *NJW* 1076; BGH 4 February 1986, [1986] *NJW* 1863, at 1864; BGH 7 October 1986, [1987] *NJW* 372 *et seq.*; BGH 17 October 1989, [1990] *NJW* 906; BGH 20 September 1994, [1994] *NJW* 3348, at 3349.

[810] BGH 21 January 1965, [1965] *NJW* 815.

[811] Hager in: Staudinger, *Kommentar zum Bürgerlichen Gesetzbuch, §§ 823–825* (1999), § 823 at s. E 31.

[812] BGH 8 February 1972, 58 BGHZ 149, at 156; BGH 14 October 1964, [1965] *NJW* 197, at 199.

[813] That a professional liability as a dogmatic category of its own does not yet exist has been shown clearly by Wagner in: Rebmann/Säcker/Rixecker, *Münchener Kommentar zum Bürgerlichen Gesetzbuch, §§ 705–853* (2004), § 823 at no. 245. As concerns the scholars who are in favour of a *Berufspflicht*, including protection from pure economic loss, *see* Hirte, *Berufshaftung* (1996), at 389 *et seq.*; Huber, 'Verkehrspflichten zum Schutz fremden Vermögens', in: Ficker/König/Kreuzer, *Festschrift für Ernst von Caemmerer* (1978), 359 at 378; Ulmer, 'Die deliktische Haftung aus der Übernahme von Handlungspflichten', [1969] *JZ* 163, at 169 *et seq.* As the legislator has chosen not to include pure economic loss in the catalogue of interests included in § 823 (1) BGB, and since there are no criteria on how to restrict such liability, this concept shall not be followed in this thesis. However, it must be admitted that there is case law in which the courts based the liability on the fact that someone exercised a professional activity, *e.g.* BGH 28 April 1953, 9 BGHZ 301, at 307; BGH 16 June 1987, [1987] *NJW* 2510, at 2511; BGH 11 October 1990, [1991] *NJW* 562, at 563.

the risk of an infection.[814] It was held that even though there is no general duty to protect another person's health unless some kind of legal relationship existed, everybody who executes a profession that relates to a certain danger and offers his services to the public has a responsibility

> 'that wherever use was being made of his services, a proper state of affairs was being ensured. A professional activity or a commercial enterprise of this kind creates such general legal duties of a special kind, which one may in a comprehensive sense denominate *Verkehrspflichten.*'[815]

This duty does not only envisage the protection of life and health, but also of property.[816] And has been extended to a large number of professions, such as architects,[817] carriers,[818] physicians[819] and other medical staff.[820] When extending such *Verkehrspflicht* to other professions, one has to be very careful, as there is no general concept of professional liability based on a delictual *Verkehrspflicht.* Even though a number of learned scholars have argued for a "*Berufshaftung*" (professional liability), based on contract, quasi-contract, tort, or as a category of its own,[821] the courts have not yet recognised such a concept of liability. There only

---

[814] RG 19 September 1921, 102 RGZ 372; affirmed by BGH 16 December 1953, [1954] *VersR* 100.

[815] RG 19 September 1921, 102 RGZ 372, at 375: '[...] daß da, wo von seinen Diensten Gebrauch gemacht wird, ein geordneter Verlauf der Dinge gewährleistet ist. Durch eine Berufstätigkeit oder einen Gewerbebetrieb dieser Art werden solche besonders gearteten allgemeinen Rechtspflichten erzeugt, die man in einem umfassenden Sinn Verkehrspflichten nennen kann.'

[816] *See* RG 19 September 1921, 102 RGZ 372.

[817] BGH 10 March 1977, 68 BGHZ 169; BGH 20 October 1964, [1964] *VersR* 1250; BGH 30 January 1968, [1968] *VersR* 470; BGH 11 March 1971, [1971] *NJW* 1130; BGH 24 April 1975, [1975] *NJW* 1316; BGH 28 October 1986, [1987] *NJW* 1013; BGH 11 October 1990, [1991] *NJW* 562.

[818] BGH 28 April 1953, 9 BGHZ 301, at 307.

[819] BGH 7 November 1960, 33 BGHZ 251; BGH 22 April 1980, [1980] *NJW* 1905.

[820] BGH 10 November 1970, [1971] *NJW* 241, at 243.

[821] Of fundamental importance is Hopt, 'Nichtvertragliche Haftung außerhalb von Schadens- und Bereicherungsausgleich', 183 *AcP* 608 (1983), who identifies four different consequences of professional behaviour (as regards the contract, contractual consequences without a contract, professional obligations and professional duties of care). *Compare* also Hopt, 'Die Haftung des Wirtschaftsprüfers', in: Hofmann/Meyer-Cording/Wiedemann, *Festschrift für Klemens Pleyer* (1986), 341, at 359. Others such as *Lammel* argue for a liability for the provision of information based on a category between contract and tort, which he terms professional capacity, *see* Lammel, 'Zur Auskunftshaftung', 179 *AcP* 337 (1979), at 365. There are a number of different concepts with different denominations which try to establish a liability for professional behaviour, such as e.g. "*Selbstbindung ohne Vertrag*" (self-commitment without contract–Köndgen, Selbstbindung ohne Vertrag), "*Berufshaftung*" (professional liability–Hirte, *Berufshaftung* (1996), at 426: 'of a contractual rather than a tort nature'; Lang, 'Einmal

may be a *Verkehrspflicht* based on the exercise of a profession if the exercise of the profession entails a specific risk to third parties.[822]

As regards classification societies, the question whether they owe *Verkehrspflichten* towards the public and third parties is a rather complex one. None of the aforementioned constellations under which someone owes a *Verkehrspflicht* to other persons really fits. These societies do not manufacture a product. However, their opinion is of relevance to the shipyard, and they take part in the process of building the ship by analysing the blueprints and surveying it at the time of its construction. They are not comparable to an architect either, as an architect assumes the *Verkehrspflicht* of the owner of the building site by law, and may take measures to minimise damage to the public. Regarding architects, it has been held that the reason for their *Verkehrspflicht* is a risk that is grounded in the construction:

> 'In these cases the delictual liability of the architect finds its inner justification in the dangerous condition of the building made accessible to the intercourse by the owner, which may partly be blamed on the architect, that means in the circumstance that due to his poor performance there have directly been dangers to the interests of third persons which are imposed by the building itself.'[823]

A classification society, by contrast, cannot directly change the danger that is imminent in the vessel; it has to require that someone else does it, but cannot even give orders that it shall be done. Nevertheless, it should not be forgotten that the shipyard, for instance, is obliged to deliver a classed vessel and is therefore most likely to follow any requirements by the classification society. The shipyard and the future shipowner decide how the vessel is built, but the classification society has an enormous influence on safety issues. One could therefore argue that they indeed exercise a certain control over any dangers that are imminent to the vessel and whether these dangers are submitted to the public. As such, they would owe a

---

mehr: Berufsrecht, Berufspflichten und Berufshaftung', 201 *AcP* 451 (2001), at 577: a category of its own which influences both contract and tort); "*Haftung wegen wirtschaftlichen Eigeninteresses*" (Liability due to own economic interest–Wiegand, *Die Sachwalterhaftung als richterliche Rechtsfortbildung* (1991)), "*berufsbezogene Erklärung*" (declaration related to the profession–Jost, F., *Vertragslose Auskunfts- und Beratungshaftung* (1991)). *Compare* also Emmerich in: Rebmann/Säcker/Rixecker, *Münchener Kommentar zum Bürgerlichen Gesetzbuch, §§ 241–432* (2003), § 311 at no. 227 *et seq.*

822 RG 19 September 1921, 102 RGZ 372, at 375; Wagner in: Rebmann/Säcker/Rixecker, *Münchener Kommentar zum Bürgerlichen Gesetzbuch, §§ 705–853* (2004), § 823 at no. 245.

823 BGH 28 October 1986, [1987] *NJW* 1013: '*In diesen Fällen findet die deliktische Haftung des Architekten ihre innere Rechtfertigung in dem von ihm mit verursachten Gefahr bringenden Zustand des von dem Bauherrn dem Verkehr zugänglich gemachten Gebäude, das heißt in dem Umstand, daß sich infolge mangelhafter Architektenleistungen unmittelbar aus dem Bauwerk selbst Gefahren für die Schutzgüter dritter Personen ergeben haben.*'

Verkehrspflicht to the public not because of law, but because of fact. Just as the *Reichsgericht* pointed out, everybody who executes a profession that relates to a certain danger and offers his services to the public has a responsibility to ensure a proper state of affairs not only in view of his contracting party but also towards the general public wherever use is being made of his services.[824] However, one should not be too hasty with the decision, as the shipowner remains responsible for the vessel. By only analysing and trying to minimise the vessel's dangers, the classification society does not assume responsibility for it, despite a possible reliance of the shipyard or the shipowner.[825]

The classification of a vessel in itself is not a dangerous activity. No third party will be hurt if a classification society analyses blueprints or surveys the vessel. The process of classification comprises activities that are in themselves not dangerous; it is the vessel that incurs by its nature a certain danger. In all adjudicated cases, the person that owed a *Verkehrspflicht* to a third party had a sphere of responsibility in which it could decide independently and in which originated the dangers leading to the imposition of a *Verkehrspflicht*. In the case of classification societies, there is no such sphere of responsibility. It is not the activity of the classification society that creates dangers to the public, but the operation of the vessel. A vessel that is put in service incurs several risks and may cause injuries to both persons or cargo aboard, property ashore and the marine environment. The shipowner (and in the same way the shipyard and the manufacturer of parts)[826] has to eliminate or at least minimise these risks. As the operation of the vessel is a potentially hazardous activity, the shipowner owes a *Verkehrspflicht* to those third parties who may be possibly affected.[827] This applies even if the ship possesses the certificates of safety and marine environment compliance, because they only intend to protect third parties from the risks incurred, but do not envisage exoneration of the tortfeasor. Moreover, the relevant regulations define only a minimum standard and not a final duty of care.[828] The only way to minimise such a risk is to

[824] RG 19 September 1921, 102 RGZ 372, at 375; affirmed by BGH 16 December 1953, [1954] *VersR* 100.

[825] Contrary to Kraft/Schlingmann, 'Die Dritthaftung von Klassifikationsgesellschaften', [2004] *VersR* 1095, at 1103.

[826] Products Liability (*Produkt- und Produzentenhaftung*) is the liability of the manufacturer of a product. Even though classification societies review blueprints, give advice and develop rules which are relevant to the vessel's architects and engineers, they are not a producer of the vessel, particularly not in the sense of § 4 (1) s. 1 Produkthaftungsgesetz. For the same reason, there is no product liability pursuant to § 823 (1) BGB as liability of the manufacturer for breach of an organisational duty (*Organisationspflicht*). The particularities of product liability (such as the reversal of the burden of proof) do not apply to classification societies.

[827] *See* BGH 28 February 1969, [1969] *VersR* 439; Edye, *Die Haftung des Reeders für Dritt- und Umweltschäden beim Seetransport gefährlicher Güter* (1993), at 115.

[828] BGH 9 December 1986, 99 BGHZ 167, at 176; BGH 16 March 1976, [1976] *VersR* 776, at 778; BGH 7 October 1986, [1987] *NJW* 372, at 373; Larenz/Canaris, *Lehrbuch des Schuldrechts* (1994), vol. II/2, § 76 III 3 f.

have it surveyed and checked, which is done by the classification society. As the shipowner does not in all cases have the knowledge to establish whether his vessel fulfils all standards which may contribute to its safety, he has to rely upon the knowledge of classification societies and their recommendations. If construction works are supervised by an architect, the architect has a sphere of responsibility of his own which he oversees and in which certain dangers may originate. It is up to him to decide whether a wall shall be torn down or not, and he has to answer for the consequences if he decides that the wall shall be left there standing and it then collapses over a construction worker.[829] Classification societies have no such responsibility.

Despite the fact that the advertisements of classification societies sometimes might give the impression that they protect the general public from any king of danger, such slogans are not sufficient to create a *Verkehrspflicht*. It is evident that they are only meant to create a positive image of the company, but shall not create a duty to answer for any kind of damage that occurs to third parties. If the opposite were the case, advertisements would not be possible at all.

With respect to classification societies, this implies that they generally do not have a *Verkehrspflicht* towards the public or third parties. If they only survey the vessel but do not make certain recommendations, conditions or requirements, they do not owe such a *Verkehrspflicht*. Nonetheless, if they require that something is done in a certain way, they have a duty towards the public that what they require does not create a new danger. They exercise sufficient control that a *Verkehrspflicht* can be assigned. As a result, if the classification society does not make any specific requirements at all, despite the fact that the vessel does not correspond to its rules, it only breaches a contractual duty which may give rise to recourse by the contracting party. If it does not act, the classification society does not change the inherent danger of the vessel, for which the shipyard or the shipowner is responsible, and therefore does not assume a *Verkehrspflicht*. The survey does not create a danger, but it should minimise it. If it, however, acts, it has an impact on the dangers which the vessel poses to the public and is for this reason required not to increase these dangers or create additional dangers, to minimise existing dangers appropriately and to act in a way that is state-of-the-art. If the classification society makes certain requirements, it has a responsibility that these requirements do not cause dangers to the public or, if they seek to minimise existing dangers, that these dangers are completely minimised. The logic of the *Reichsgericht*, which has been confirmed by the *Bundesgerichtshof*, is that those who offer surveys have to ascertain a proper state of affairs. A classification society only checks whether a vessel conforms to certain safety regulations; in general, it is therefore not responsible for the vessel. However, if the classification society requests that certain specific modifications be made to the vessel and gives instructions on how that is to be done, and these changes are carried out in that way, it exercises control over the vessel which must be reflected in terms of responsibility as well.

---

[829] BGH 28 October 1986, [1987] *NJW* 1013.

The classification society also owes a *Verkehrspflicht* to the public if it first grants the certificate under conditions that aim at protection of the public and later renounces these conditions due to pressure by the shipowner, despite the fact that the initial situation which gave rise to the condition has not changed. If the classification society orders something that protects the public and minimises dangers caused by the vessel, it may only renounce them if that is safe for the public; otherwise it exercises control over the danger that gives rise to a *Verkehrspflicht*.

These considerations can be applied to the rules as well. If the classification society made requirements that are unsafe and endanger the public, there could be a *Verkehrspflicht*. Such cases, however, need to be considered thoroughly and most carefully. The classification society needs to weigh the interests in the safety of the vessel with economic interests relating to the costs of safety requirements. Unlike surveys, the rules define a certain standard and therefore influence the imminent danger of the vessel under all circumstances. This may not be misinterpreted so that the classification society generally assumes responsibility for the vessel. The classification society has a power of discretion to determine how the standard of safety that is state-of-the-art may be achieved; if that standard is clearly not met, one may consider the imposition of a *Verkehrspflicht*, especially for life and health. Only if the rules are evidently no longer state-of-the-art or clearly inappropriate to minimising the dangers of the vessel and the requirements that should have been made would be reasonable in economic terms will such a *Verkehrspflicht* exist. For instance, if several incidents with sister vessels have proven that a certain rule does not sufficiently guarantee the standard of safety, the classification society has an obligation to change it. Such cases will be rare, but they may exist.[830]

A classification society might argue against such imposition of a *Verkehrspflicht* that it only acts for its customer and not for the public. Just as the employee of a manufacturer is not responsible for the product and therefore does not owe a *Verkehrspflicht* to the public,[831] the classification society might claim that it was not responsible for the vessel either. Such argumentation would not convince. The employee does not owe a *Verkehrspflicht* because he has no power of decision:

> 'Whoever has engaged towards someone else in undertaking a damage prevention can be called upon by a third party for damages in tort due to the non-performance of this obligation only as far as he has assumed a duty his contracting party owes to the public. [...] One may speak of such general legal duties, whose breach as such may lead to liability for damages even outside contractual relations, only with regard to persons who by profession or in their commercial life have gained a certain independent position or

---

830 For an example of such a case, see Holtappels, 'Haftung von Klassifikationsgesellschaften in der Handelsschiffahrt', [2002] *TranspR* 278, at 281 lit. b), who refers to the construction of the engine in a way that no crew member is harmed. If the construction proves to be insecure, the classification society is subject to a *Verkehrspflicht* to change the applicable rule.

831 *See* von Bar, *Verkehrspflichten* (1980), at 122.

who offer their professional or commercial services to the public and who have by virtue of their profession or trade assumed a certain responsibility towards the public.'[832]

The employee is part of the process of making the product. He cannot decide in which way the product is constructed or produced. As regards a classification society, the situation differs from the aforementioned cases. Whenever it makes distinct recommendations which are subsequently carried out, it has a power of decision over the vessel. Even if a classification society may claim that it only acts in the interest of the shipowner, the fact that the changes it requested were carried out shows that it has a somewhat neutral position and a limited (but original) power which is subject to the circumstances. As it is a matter of standing and relationship between the persons in question, the classification society cannot be compared with an employee, since it has a power of decision the employee does not have.

b. Two *Verkehrspflichten* of a Similar Kind – Exoneration of One of the Tortfeasors?

As has been elaborated in the previous section, under certain circumstances the classification society may owe a *Verkehrspflicht* to the public. Nonetheless, the shipyard or shipowner is also obliged to protect the public from any dangers that are inherent in the vessel. It therefore needs to be determined how these *Verkehrspflichten* interact. Is the classification society primarily responsible or does it share the *Verkehrspflicht* with the shipyard or shipowner?

The responsibility of the shipowner or shipyard is not affected by the acts of a classification society. Otherwise, the responsibility for the vessels would be completely shifted to the classification society. Such a result would clearly contradict the primary responsibility of the shipowner for his vessel, for which there is a good reason as well, which is the control of the shipowner over the vessel and the submission of the dangers to the public.

In similar cases, both parties owe a *Verkehrspflicht*, even if one of them has its own sphere of responsibility or is controlled by the other party. The *Verkehrs-*

[832] Translation by the author of BGH 17 December 1953, [1954] *VersR* 173: 'Wer sich einem anderen gegenüber verpflichtet hat, eine schadenverhütende Handlung vorzunehmen, kann von einem Dritten wegen Nichterfüllung dieser Verpflichtung auf Schadensersatz aus unerlaubter Handlung nur in Anspruch genommen werden, soweit er damit eine seinem Vertragspartner der Allgemeinheit gegenüber obliegende Pflicht übernommen hat. [...] Von derartigen allgemeinen Rechtspflichten, deren Verletzung als solche auch außerhalb vertraglicher Beziehungen zum Schadensersatz verpflichtet, läßt sich jedoch nur bei Personen sprechen, die beruflich oder im gewerblichen Leben eine gewisse selbständige Stellung erlangt haben oder kraft ihres Berufs oder Gewerbes eine besondere Verantwortlichkeit der Allgemeinheit gegenüber übernommen haben.'

pflicht of the second party adds to the one of the first.[833] As a consequence of such a composite *Verkehrspflicht*, the party which compensates for the loss has to bear the risk of insolvency of the other party when taking recourse. However, in these cases the classification society could choose its contracting party and *vice versa*. Also, this effect is common to all cases involving a multiple number of tortfeasors, as § 840 BGB orders that they are liable jointly and severally. The first one has a right to recourse pursuant to §§ 840 (1), 426 (1) s. 1 BGB or according to their contract.

c. Technical Standards as the Relevant Standard of Care

The standard of care that needs to be fulfilled in order not to be liable if one owes a *Verkehrspflicht* to third parties is to be established by analysing the function of the *Verkehrspflicht*[834] and customary practice. Administrative definitions and private technical standards have to be taken into consideration as well.[835] When carrying out surveys, a classification society has to follow the technical standards which define the state of the art, such as those defined by IACS regulations. However, a *Verkehrspflicht* may go further than statutory or administrative orders and prohibitions or private regulations.[836] The reason for this is that those orders and prohibitions shall protect the injured party and not the discharge of the person subject to a *Verkehrspflicht*.[837] Even so, their aims may differ.[838]

A *Verkehrspflicht* does not require that everything which is possible to cause the damage is done, but to ascertain that every *reasonable* step is taken in order to avoid the danger. What is reasonable from this point of view depends on the interest in danger – it is obvious that life and health require much more intensive efforts than property - and on the difficulty and costs of the measures. It will hardly

---

833 *See e.g.* BGH 10 March 1977, 68 BGHZ 169, at 175 *et seq.*; BGH 11 October 1990, [1991] *NJW* 562, at 563: 'The liability of the architect does not bar the builder from being responsible for the building in the first place. This defence has already been contested by the Senate as far as the Verkehrssicherungspflicht of the architect for the construction site was concerned [...].'

834 Wagner in: Rebmann/Säcker/Rixecker, *Münchener Kommentar zum Bürgerlichen Gesetzbuch, §§ 705–853* (2004), § 823 at no. 248, 277, 282.

835 BGH 1 March 1988, 103 BGHZ 338, at 341 *et seq.*; BGH 19 April 1991, 114 BGHZ 273, at 277; BGH 12 November 1996, [1997] *NJW* 582, at 583.

836 BGH 9 December 1986, 99 BGHZ 167, at 176; BGH 26 November 1974, [1975] *NJW* 533; BGH 11 March 1980, [1980] *NJW* 1745, at 1746; BGH 29 November 1983, [1984] *NJW* 801, at 802; BGH 23 October 1984, [1985] *NJW* 620, at 621; BGH 7 October 1986, [1987] *NJW* 372, at 373; BGH 28 April 1987, [1988] *NJW* 48, at 49; BGH 19 December 1989, [1990] *NJW* 1236, at 1237; BGH 12 November 1996, [1997] *NJW* 582, at 583; BGH 26 May 1998, [1998] *NJW* 2436.

837 Larenz/Canaris, *Lehrbuch des Schuldrechts* (1994), vol. II/2, § 76 III 4 f.

838 BGH 7 October 1986, [1987] *NJW* 372, at 373; BGH 19 December 1989, [1990] *NJW* 1236, at 1237.

be possible to put into place protection that is absolutely perfect and effective.[839] This is relevant especially if the *Verkehrspflicht* is due to insufficient standards of the rules. The rules shall reflect the state of the art, which is a compromise between technically achievable standards of security and reasonable expenditure. Whether this balance between the technical standards and economic considerations has been met must be decided on a case-by-case basis.

d. Other Prerequisites of § 823 (1) BGB

Harm to one of the interests that are protected by § 823 (1) BGB[840] must have been caused by the unlawful behaviour of the classification society, a causal nexus that is called "*haftungsbegründende Kausalität*", which could be translated as 'causation constituting liability', and the classification society must also have been at fault. According to the courts, unlawfulness (*Rechtswidrigkeit*) is defined from the point of view of the loss caused; every act which causes harm to any of the interests protected by § 823 (1) BGB is unlawful unless there is a justification for the action.[841] A classification society violates its *Verkehrspflicht* whenever it makes incorrect requirements that make the vessel unsafe or, in rare cases, if the standard laid down in its rules does not suffice. In order to be liable in such a case, this violation must not only have been causative for the injury or harm of the plaintiff, but the classification society must have been at fault as well. That requires that the classification society can be blamed for its act. As the classification society is civilly responsible (*zurechnungsfähig*), there must have been wilful conduct or negligence, and there must not have been a legal excuse of the classification society (*Schuldausschließungsgrund*). A compensation of the injured party also requires that there is a causal nexus between the breach of duty and the alleged damage (*haftungsausfüllende Kausalität*). All these preconditions depend on the individual case, as determined by the court.[842]

[839] BGH 1 October 1959, 31 BGHZ 73, at 74; BGH 13 July 1989, 108 BGHZ 273, at 274; BGH 21 January 1965, [1965] *NJW* 815; BGH 7 July 1970, [1971] *JZ* 63, at 64; BGH 25 April 1978, [1978] *NJW* 1626, at 1627; BGH 29 January 1980, [1980] *NJW* 1159, at 1160; BGH 29 November 1983, [1984] *NJW* 801, at 802; BGH 20 September 1994, [1994] *NJW* 3348.

[840] Life, body, health, freedom, property or other rights which are *inter alia* familiy relationships, the right of an established and operating business *(Recht am eingerichteten und ausgeübten Gewerbebetrieb)*, and the general right to one's personality *(Allgemeines Persönlichkeitsrecht)*.

[841] Wagner in: Rebmann/Säcker/Rixecker, *Münchener Kommentar zum Bürgerlichen Gesetzbuch, §§ 705–853* (2004), § 823 at no. 304; Hager in: Staudinger, *Kommentar zum Bürgerlichen Gesetzbuch, §§ 823- 825* (1999), § 823 at no. A3.

[842] The damages that may be awarded follow §§ 249–252 BGB and are discussed by Brinkmann, 'German Law: Damage to Persons, Property and the Environment', 22 *Tul.Mar.L.J.* 545 (1998).

5. § 823 (2) BGB

For the sake of completeness, reference will be briefly made to § 823 (2) BGB as well. This provision compensates also for economic loss, but requires the violation of a statutory provision that purports to protect others (*Schutzgesetz*). As there is no such statutory provision regarding the classification of a vessel, a classification society may not be liable pursuant to § 823 (2) BGB.[843]

6. § 826 BGB

A person who wilfully causes damage to another in a manner contrary to public policy is bound to compensate the other for the damage.[844] § 826 BGB covers a multitude of wrongs which are actionable as separate torts under common law, such as deceit, passing off, intimidation, procuring a breach of contract, unfair competition, malicious prosecution and the like.[845] It includes misstatements as well.[846] Under German law, all these wrongs are included in one formula which refers to an activity *contra bonos mores*. Public policy (*gute Sitten*) is defined as 'the sense of propriety of all good and right-thinking members of society.'[847] Since the content of such a definition is rather difficult to determine, and as morality

---

[843] *See also* Basedow/Wurmnest, *Third-Party Liability of Classification Societies* (2005), at 76–77.

[844] Such is the wording of § 826 BGB (translation by Forrester/Goren/Ilgen, *The German Civil Code* (1994)).

[845] Markesinis, *The German Law of Torts* (2002), at 658.

[846] Theoretically, in the case of misstatements which cause damage to the property of others one can also think of a liability pursuant to § 823 (2) BGB, § 263 StGB. But there should be very few cases in which the behaviour of the classification society fulfils the conditions of the criminal law provision of a fraud. Another statute for the protection of public safety (*Schutzgesetz*) might be the national implementation of a proposed EU directive. This proposed Directive on ship-source pollution and the introduction of sanctions, including criminal sanctions, for pollution offences (COM (2003) 92, not published in the OJ but accessible on the homepage of the EU) states the following: 'Art. 6 Criminal Offences and Sanctions (1) Member States shall ensure that the illegal discharge of polluting substances, the participation in and instigation of such discharge are regarded as criminal offences, when committed intentionally or by gross negligence.
(2) Any person (i.e. not only the shipowner but also the owner of the cargo, the classification society or any other person involved), who has been found by a court of law responsible within the meaning of parargraph 1, shall be subject to sanctions, including, where appropriate, criminal sanctions.' Apart from the fact that this Directive is not yet in force, it appears doubtful whether any individual is included within its protective ambit (which would be a prerequisite of such a liability, *see* Markesinis, *The German Law of Torts* (2002), at 655; Sprau in: Palandt, *Bürgerliches Gesetzbuch* (2006), § 823 at no. 57). The wording and the intention of the legislator rather point to the protection of the environment and the public than to that of an individual person.

[847] BGH 25 May 1955, 17 BGHZ 327, at 332.

changes in the course of time, whenever the German lawyer pleads § 826 BGB, he bases his case rather on jurisprudence than on the prerequisites of this provision.

The first impression when reading this provision is that it may practically never apply. The plaintiff must prove that the defendant acted wilfully, and his intention must have been directed to the damage, although the full extent of the damage and the way it was brought about does not need to have been specifically anticipated.[848] The defendant either has to know the consequences of his conduct and wishes to bring them about or must have been aware of the consequences of his conduct which he accepts as inevitable even though he may not specifically desire them.[849] The courts have considerably expanded the application of this provision by defining its terms in a broad sense. A positive knowledge of the consequences of the conduct is not required; it is sufficient not to know that something is contrary to public policy if the defendant wilfully closes his eyes to such knowledge.[850] Also, the wrongdoer does not have to know that his behaviour is actually contrary to public policy, but only needs to be aware of the relevant circumstances.[851] As a result, § 826 BGB has become a provision that is important for cases in which someone supplies incorrect information. A wilful misrepresentation which has caused the injured party to carry out the harmful act is contrary to public policy.[852] Similarly, a grossly negligent misrepresentation or reckless provision of an expert opinion by someone who bears in mind the possible harm to the other party is contrary to public policy if the provider of information can recognise that the information is of importance for the decision of the receiving party.[853] This is especially the case if the provider has claimed to be in possession of certain expertise.[854] If someone gives false information in good faith and subsequently becomes aware of its falsity, that person is under a duty to correct the false information. If he refrains from doing so, that person will be liable under § 826 BGB.[855] If a person gives recklessly false information about the credit of a third person, he may be liable to the recipient of this information under § 826 BGB.[856]

---

[848] BGH 14 June 2000, [2000] *NJW* 2896; Markesinis, *The German Law of Torts* (2002), at 658.

[849] BGH 26 November 1986, [1987] *NJW* 1758; BGH 14 June 2000, [2000] *NJW* 2896; BGH 24 April 2001, [2001] *WM* 1454; Markesinis, *The German Law of Torts* (2002), at 657.

[850] BGH 27 January 1994, [1994] *NJW* 2289.

[851] BGH 26 March 1962, [1962] *WM* 579.

[852] BGH 20 February 1979, [1979] *NJW* 1599.

[853] BGH 26 November 1986, [1987] *NJW* 1758.

[854] BGH 24 September 1991, [1991] *NJW* 3282.

[855] RG 27 May 1911, 76 RGZ 316, at 318; BGH 15 May 1979, [1979] *JZ* 725.

[856] BGH 13 July 1956, [1956] *WM* 1229.

To sum up, in all cases in which a classification society wilfully provides incorrect information or notices later on that information has been incorrect but avoids changing it, it may be liable to third parties pursuant to § 826 BGB.[857]

7. *The Effect of Disclaimers*

Contractual limitations that are incorporated in the classification contract are also applicable in respect of third parties if they are protected by the contract with protective effects towards third parties. Generally, the third party will not be granted rights which go further than those rights that are granted to the contracting party.[858] The contracting party may not only protect the third party, but may also limit the scope of protection that is offered.[859]

The certificates by the classification society usually contain a clause that they are only for the use of the contracting party. As has been elaborated before,[860] such a clause does not necessarily exempt the classification society from any liability towards the third party. All the circumstances, such as the contents of the expert opinion, the contract, the situation under which the order to survey the vessel was placed, as well as the certificate itself, need to be scrutinised.[861] When taking into account all circumstances, such as the existence of the ship's register that can be accessed by the public as well, classification societies expect that their certificates are consulted and taken into account by third parties. Therefore, they cannot rely on an exemption from liability by merely stating that the certificate is solely for the use of the contracting party. If the classification society, however, expressly

857 *See also* OLG Hamburg 26 October 1906, [1907] *Hanseatische Gerichtszeitung, Hauptblatt*, 37 *(Theodor Schiff, Heinecke & Co. und Bergeest & Siemers* v. *Bureau Veritas (Schoonergaliote "Industrie"));* RG 4 November 1907, [1908] Hanseatische Gerichtszeitung, Hauptblatt, at 163; Basedow/Wurmnest, *Die Dritthaftung von Klassifikationsgesellschaften* (2004), at 63–64; Basedow/Wurmnest, *Third-Party Liability of Classification Societies* (2005), at 77; Drobnig, *Tätigkeit und Haftung von Klassifikationsgesellschaften in der Bundesrepublik Deutschland am Beispiel des Germanischen Lloyd* (1995), at 192; Kraft/Schlingmann, 'Die Dritthaftung von Klassifikationsgesellschaften', [2004] *VersR* 1095, at 1103.

858 BGH 15 June 1971, [1971] *NJW* 1931, at 1932; BGH 10 November 1994, [1995] *NJW* 392, at 393; OLG Oldenburg 9 September 1997, [1998] *NJW-RR* 1746.

859 § 334 BGB, *see* LG Hamburg 18 January 1972, 10 O 176/70 (unpublished) at 8–9. BGH 10 November 1994, [1995] *NJW* 392 which has been mentioned *supra* Part 2 B III 2 e, does not show the contrary. It solely relates to the analysis of the third parties in an objective way and the obligation of the expert to indicate clearly if he relies on representations of the contracting party. In such a case, it may be possible that the third party is better protected than the contracting party. The reason for that protection is, however, the neutral character of the expert and his opinion. This decision cannot be interpreted in a way that it is not possible to limit the liability towards the third party as well. The limitation towards both the contracting party and the third party is the rule; the decision in BGH 10 November 1994, [1995] *NJW* 392 is an exception.

860 *See supra* Part 2 A III 4.

861 BGH 20 April 2004, [2004] *NJW* 3035, at 3039.

excludes in its rules that it is liable to third parties or limits its liability in that regard, the effectiveness of such a clause is limited by § 138 and § 307 BGB.[862] These provisions prohibit exemption clauses that are either *contra bones mores* or are included in general conditions and are in breach of good faith. § 826 BGB protects fundamental interests against behaviour *contra bones mores*. A limitation of or exemption from liability therefore contradicts § 138 BGB and is not possible.

Theoretically, an exemption or limitation can even be made implicitly. However, the low amount of the fees is not a sufficient indication of such an implied limitation or exemption as such,[863] since the provision of expert opinions is part of the business operations of the classification society. The society can insure its risks and has to calculate its fees accordingly.

Whether such exemption or limitation clauses can also protect the classification society against claims that are made pursuant to § 823 (1) is a more difficult question. Generally, it is not possible to exclude or limit liability in tort towards third parties, as tort law is a minimum standard of protection, regardless of the existence of a contract; otherwise such contract would be an illicit contract to the detriment of the third party (*Vertrag zu Lasten Dritter*). Two parties cannot decide that a third party shall have fewer rights than it naturally has. They can only limit or exclude those rights that their contract offers to a third party, but have no right to limit or exclude the general standard of protection which tort law offers.

Under German law, liability in contract and in tort may co-exist. In a two-party relationship consisting of the contracting parties, a limitation or exemption clause is usually construed to cover liabilities both in contract and in tort as well if both seek to protect the same interests.[864] If the contractual limitation clause seeks to limit delictual claims as well, it needs to be applied to such claims. Otherwise, an incident that gives rise to both liability in contract and in tort would give rise to a claim in tort despite the fact that the contracting parties wanted to limit or exclude all liability.

Three-party relationships are more complex. First of all, if the third party is assigned a certain right by the contract between the other parties, these parties may not only grant the right, but are also at liberty to limit it in a certain way. A contractual limitation clause between the contracting parties must be applied to claims by the third party that are based on the contract; such is the case for a claim based on the contract with protective effects towards third parties.[865] Moreover, the *Bun-*

---

[862] For comments on § 307, *see* Basedow in: Rebmann/Säcker/Rixecker, *Münchener Kommentar zum Bürgerlichen Gesetzbuch, §§ 241–432* (2003), § 307.

[863] BGH 13 November 1997, [1998] *NJW* 1059.

[864] *See for instance* BGH 24 November 1976, 67 BGHZ 359; BGH 7 April 1992, [1992] *NJW* 1820 with further references. However, *see by contrast* BGH 24 November 1976, 67 BGHZ 359, at 366–367: if the claim in tort protects a different interest from the one in contract, the contractual provisions cannot be applied.

[865] BGH 15 June 1971, [1971] *NJW* 1931, at 1932; BGH 2 April 1998, 138 BGHZ 257, at 260–262; OLG Oldenburg 9 September 1997, [1998] *NJW-RR* 1746. *See also* Herber, *Seehandelsrecht* (1999), 176.

desgerichtshof applies limitation provisions in contracts of carriage between the shipper and the carrier also to the relationship of the shipper with the performing carrier; if the shipper knows or has to expect that the carriage is performed by another, contractual limitations are also valid in that relationship.[866] Nonetheless, contractual limitations only apply in general to claims in contract, not in tort, that are made by the owner of the cargo.[867]

However, the relationship between the third party and the classification society cannot be compared with the relationship between the third party and the carrier or the performing carrier. The equivalent relationship to the one between the shipper and the performing carrier under a contract of carriage would be between the classification society and the third party. The precedents only relate to the situation that the contract has in effect been carried out by the performing carrier; limitations in regard to the carrier are valid with respect to the performing carrier as well, since the shipper is expecting such limitations throughout the time of the carriage. The classification society, by contrast, does not perform the obligation of the shipyard or shipowner towards the third party. Such a case therefore needs to be distinguished on the facts from those cases that relate to a contract of carriage.

If contractual limitation clauses even limited claims made by third parties in tort, the contract with protective effects towards third parties would not protect the third party but deprive it of its rights under § 823 (1) BGB. By effect, it would work to the detriment of the third party. However, the courts have chosen a contractual solution in order to protect the third party more efficiently than tort law would do, but not to limit the rights of the third party. As a result, a limitation clause that is contained in the contract with protective effects towards third parties does not limit or exclude liability pursuant to § 823 (1) BGB, as it would otherwise be a contract to the detriment of the third party.[868] Therefore, clauses which are contained in the classification contract between the classification society and the shipyard or shipowner do not limit their liability in tort towards third parties.[869]

8. Conclusion

Under German law, a classification society may be liable on the basis of a contract with protective effects towards third parties for harm other than economic loss that is sustained by recipients of a confirmation of class, passengers and members of the crew. If it makes recommendations which create a danger on the vessel, it may

---

866 BGH 12 July 1974, [1974] *NJW* 2177.

867 BGH 21 December 1993, [1994] *NJW* 852, at 855 (*obiter*).

868 For this reason incorrect: OLG Köln 4 June 1986, [1988] *NJW-RR* 157. This is also held by OLG Koblenz 5 October 1995, [1997] *NJWE-VHR* 69 at 70; *compare also* Klein, 'Haftungsbeschränkungen zugunsten und zu Lasten Dritter und ihre Behandlung in der Schuldrechtsreform', [1997] *JZ* 390, at 396.

869 Drobnig, *Tätigkeit und Haftung von Klassifikationsgesellschaften in der Bundesrepublik Deutschland am Beispiel des Germanischen Lloyd* (1995) at 224–226, however, does not differentiate between claims in contract and in tort. He concludes that the contracting parties may not limit claims by third parties at all.

also be liable for injury or loss of life or damage to property it thereby causes pursuant to § 823 (1) BGB. It may limit the rights of third parties that are granted by the contract with protective effects towards third parties, but cannot do so regarding claims based on § 823 (1) BGB. Whenever the classification society wilfully provides incorrect information or notices that information has been incorrect and does not change it, it may be liable according to § 826 BGB.

IV. Application of the Conclusions to Claims by Different Parties

In this section, the conclusions of the legal analysis will be applied to claims by different parties. As only a small number of the possible claims are covered by case-law, it should be noted that some parts of this section are based on jurisprudence which relates to cases that are comparable to those of classification societies.[870]

1. Claims by Recipients of a Confirmation of Class

A confirmation of class as a statement of the current status of the vessel according to the classification records provides some indications on the safety of the vessel. But it cannot replace a full survey of the vessel.[871] If one needs entirely new information about the vessel, a re-classification or re-survey of the vessel is required. Only if there are recommendations or conditions made by the classification society will the vessel be subjected to a limited survey in view of them. A confirmation of class is not an opinion on the value of the vessel nor does it require a re-examination of the entire ship; the information contained in the files is possibly outdated. Its value is therefore limited and should not be overestimated.

The shipowner may show such a certificate to potential purchasers of the vessel and to insurance companies as well. The shipowner may only have to prove that the vessel fulfils the requirements of the class to a hull insurer or a P&I Club if he concludes a new contract. However, under such circumstances the vessel is usually surveyed by a surveyor who is appointed by the insurer. Because of these surveys by the appointed surveyor, the insurer does not rely on the confirmation of class. Even if he could, his claims would be most probably for economic loss, which is not in the scope of protection of the classification society and accordingly not protected.

Often, the purchaser of the vessel will not be able or allowed to survey the vessel or have it surveyed by someone else. In such a case, the classification society is an important mediator for him.[872] Despite the danger that some information con-

870 Please consult in detail the applicable sections of Part 2 B in order to determine the existing case-law.

871 *See supra* Part 1 B I 3.

872 Regarding the importance of the confirmation of class under the Norwegian Saleform *see supra* Part 1 A III 3.

tained in the files is outdated, so that the confirmation of class does not represent the current status of the vessel, the purchaser will usually rely on that certificate.

The purchaser of the vessel is not protected under *English law*. The House of Lords held in *Marc Rich* that the tort of negligence bars any claim for economic loss and even a claim by a cargo-owner was considered to be economic loss; *Reeman* and *Perret v. Collins* solely relate to the protection of life and health. Although the latter decisions enlarged the scope of protection tremendously, they are of little help to the purchaser of the vessel. He could, however, argue that one of the main arguments on which *Marc Rich* was based does not apply under the given circumstances. As the shipowner cannot limit his liability under any of the international conventions when he sells the vessel, the sale does not touch upon the system of limitations.[873] Hence it could be fair to submit the classification society to a duty of care if the shipowner himself were not protected by an international convention. The fact that the shipowner is usually exempted by the sale contract is not of relevance to that argument, which only relates to the possible impact on the international system of limitations. Notwithstanding this, it is not very probable that a court would deviate from *Marc Rich*. First of all, a court might refer to the other arguments contained in *Marc Rich*, such as the possibility of insuring such unlimited liability and the role assumed by classification societies. Secondly, it could consider the *Morning Watch* as a precedent and deny liability, despite the fact that this decision did not relate to a confirmation of class but only to a classification certificate. And thirdly, as the classification society only aims at protecting the safety of the ship and life at sea and the marine environment, the confirmation of class does not provide information that could be relevant to the tort of negligence for economic loss. Only the tort of deceit would offer such protection, but it is not very likely that a confirmation of class might give rise to such claim.

Under *United States* law, the tort of negligent misrepresentation is relevant. § 552 Restatement (Second) of Torts applies to cases of economic loss, while § 311 is applicable if physical harm occurs. *Otto Candies* was one of the rare cases in which the purchaser was protected against economic loss. However, it cannot serve as a precedent in the usual case of a confirmation of class. In *Otto Candies*, the classification society was required to carry out a re-classification of the vessel knowing that the vessel was going to be sold and transferred to another classification society. The society actually knew that the purchaser relied on its certificates and that it would directly cause economic loss to the third party if it incorrectly performed the classification of the vessel. Under these circumstances, the classification was not intended to put the vessel in service but only to sell it, which was known to the classification society. Due to these unusual circumstances, the classification society had to be aware of the economic loss it would cause to the purchaser and was therefore held liable. Therefore, *Otto Candies* must be distinguished on the facts from general cases. Generally, there will not be protection of the purchaser of the vessel against economic loss pursuant to the tort of negligent

[873] *Compare supra* Part 2 B I 2 b bb (5), Part 2 B I 2 b cc (2).

misrepresentation. However, similarly to English law, the tort of fraudulent misrepresentation might apply and protect against such loss. There is however no case-law on this question as yet.

Under *German* law, the purchaser of the vessel who receives a confirmation of class will generally not be protected against economic loss either. A court has to analyse the contract with protective effects towards third parties and would most probably hold that the purchaser is in proximity of performance (*Leistungsnähe)*. There is also an objective interest of the contractual creditor (*Gläubigernähe*), since the confirmation of class is intended for the information of the purchaser and therefore must be accurate as an expert opinion. The purchaser also has to be foreseeable (*erkennbar*) to the classification society. It does not need to know its identity or whether it is a single purchaser or a group of investors. The risk has to be foreseeable in order to be insurable. Since the risk in this case is closely affiliated with the vessel, and as it is not even increased if a group of investors buy the vessel, there is such *foreseeability*. Whether the shipowner or the purchaser of the vessel suffers the harm does not make a difference regarding the risk of the classification society. One may wonder, however, whether the purchaser is really in need of protection (*schutzbedürftig*), because he may have contractual claims against the seller of the vessel. Nevertheless, as such contractual claims differ in their extent, the purchaser is also in need of protection. Yet, as has been argued before, he is most likely to sustain economic loss, against which not even the shipowner himself is protected, because such protection is not the aim of the activity of the classification society. The purchaser, therefore, cannot claim damages based on a contract with protective effects towards third parties nor on § 823 (1) BGB, as this tort provision does not protect against economic loss at all. Here again, a protection would only be available under § 826 BGB, which relates to wilfully caused damage to another in a manner contrary to public policy.

2. *Claims by Persons Which have Consulted the Classification Certificate or the Ship's Register*

In international shipping practice, large parts of the shipping industry rely on the information provided by classification societies in their certificates or their ship's register. The group that consults this information comprises the vessel's insurers, its charterer, cargo-owner and freight forwarders, its financers[874] and agents, and cruise lines, as well as potential purchasers of a ship who have not received a confirmation of class. This group has three things in common: first of all, its members reasonably rely on the document that they consult. Nevertheless, their relationship with the classification society is never so close that it effectively acts for the third party (as was the case in *Otto Candies*). Secondly, the damage they sustain in relying on the information will be economic loss. Thirdly, for the foregoing reason, it is generally assumed that none of them has a claim against a classification society.

[874] Regarding the importance of classification societies to the financing bank, *see* Goldrein/Turner, *Ship Sale and Purchase* (2003), 2-3.

As the tort of negligence under *English law* only protects life and health, the consultation of the certificate or the ship's register does not give an actionable claim for economic loss. If the cargo-owner loses his property, he will sustain economic loss and therefore does not have a claim against the classification society.[875] The tort of deceit could grant an actionable claim, but will rarely, if ever, apply. The situation under *United States* law is somewhat similar. Despite the fact that the tort of negligent misrepresentation in its form laid down in § 552 of the Restatements also protects against economic loss, there will never be a sufficiently close relationship between the third party and the classification society in these cases. § 311 of the Restatements could apply, but this provision does not protect from economic loss. Only the tort of fraudulent misrepresentation might offer protection against economic loss. Under *German law*, the contract with protective effects does not under the circumstances of a safety opinion protect against economic loss either. Regarding insurance companies, they would not even be in need of protection, as they dispose of the claims of the insured after their compensation.[876] The contract with protective effects does not protect cargo-owners who lose their property. Cargo-owners could only base their claims for loss of property on those rare cases that have been elaborated *supra* on § 823 (1) BGB. Here again, § 826 BGB should hardly ever provide a claim.

3. *Claims by Legal Subjects Which Have not Received Information*

a. Persons that Have Been Affected in Their Life or Health

Seamen and passengers may not have any information regarding the vessel's class or even know about the existence, let alone the duties and functions, of a classification society. Despite the lack of their reliance on a representation of the classification society, they may suffer harm to their interests that are valued higher than economic loss in most legal systems.

Under *English law*, the tort of negligence does not require a consultation of the certificate or information about the vessel. It solely protects life and health, but not the interests of the cargo-owner in his property, as *Marc Rich* shows. Under *United States law*, the tort of negligent misrepresentation pursuant to § 311 of the Restatements solely requires a representation to the shipowner or shipyard who thereupon acts and causes the damage. All physical harm is protected. The German contract with protective effects towards third parties protects both seamen and passengers.[877] § 823 (1) BGB also protects these interests, but will only apply in rare instances. There is however no case-law with regard to classification societies in any of these three legal orders on this question as yet.

---

875 *Compare* the *Marc Rich* case, *see supra* Part 2 B I 2 b.

876 § 67 VVG. *Compare* Basedow/Wurmnest, *Die Dritthaftung von Klassifikationsgesellschaften* (2004), at 53–55; Basedow/Wurmnest, *Third-Party Liability of Classification Societies* (2005), at 66.

877 *See supra* Part 2 B III 2 d bb, cc.

b. Legal Subjects that Have Sustained Other Damage

Last but not least, other persons such as cargo-owners who have not received information about the classification of the vessel, coastal States and their nationals,[878] or the International Oil Pollution Compensation Funds may sustain harm if the classification society does not perform its obligations properly. Such claims may be for loss of or damage to property or for economic loss. As there is no protection against economic loss if there is no specific reliance on the representations made by the classification society under any of the legal systems, only damage to property is of interest.[879] There is no jurisprudence in any of the three legal orders with regard to this question. The legal analysis therefore does not provide the law as it stands but tries to predict the way courts would probably apply it.

Damage to property can be caused to cargo-owners, to States as regards their coasts or related interests, and even to their inhabitants, as for instance if fishing gear can no longer be used after an oil spill. These property interests are not protected under English law, but they are envisaged by § 311 of the Restatements under United States law. Under German law, the contract with protective effects does not protect cargo owners. Neither is the damage suffered by coastal States from oil pollution protected, as these coastal States are not in proximity of performance and their protection is neither in the interest of the contractual creditor in the sense of the definition (the shipowner neither wants to show the classification certificate to a coastal State nor is he under a special duty of care towards it implying a responsibility for it) nor is this risk foreseeable to the classification society. Apart from the contract with protective effects, the classification society may be liable under § 823 (1) BGB. Last but not least, if there is a statement by the classification society to the shipowner that fulfils the requirements of a deceit, fraudulent misrepresentation or § 826 BGB, the society has to answer for all damage it thereby causes, which is even damage to third parties that do not know of the representation but suffer injuries as a result.

C. Public Functions

Due to the financial and personal constraints of the flag State and difficulties with the control of vessels in foreign ports, a classification society exercises public functions if it controls a vessel on behalf of its flag State and analyses whether the vessel conforms with the domestic statutory requirements, including regulations that implement international conventions for the safety of life at sea and the pro-

[878] Regarding an analysis of the losses to commercial fishermen due to alleged price decreases, *see* Grigalunas *et al.*, 'Liability for Oil Spill Damages: Issues, Methods, and Examples', 26 *Coastal Mgmt.* 61 (1998), at 66–67, 70–71.

[879] Moreover, since the International Oil Pollution Funds are assigned the claims of those whose damage they compensate, there is no need to offer them a direct action against the classification society.

tection of the marine environment, or if the society elaborates expert opinions which serve as a basis for a decision of the marine administration. It is evident that the same mistakes may occur during the exercise of public functions as during the carrying out of private functions. A ship may be negligently surveyed and certified, which is part of the causal link that leads to the incident.

The exercise of public functions may be organised in two different ways. In the first alternative, the classification society largely substitutes the flag State. The flag State only provides for interpretations of the international conventions or statutory requirements and supervises the activities of the classification society in a general way. Nevertheless, the flag State does not intervene in the activities that are carried out by the society. In the second alternative, the flag State does not fully grant such powers of authority. The flag State merely tries to make use of the experience and knowledge in marine engineering of the classification societies. The society is not authorised to issue the certificates itself, but only surveys the vessel and subsequently issues a report or attestation whether it is in conformity with the statutory regulations. Based on this statement, the maritime administration of the flag State thereafter issues the certificate.

In both alternatives, a plaintiff will be interested whether he can sue the classification society or the flag State, and whether the flag State or the classification society enjoys any immunities. These questions, as well as the recourse by the flag State against the classification society, will be analysed in the following sections from the point of view of the three legal systems.

I. Liability under English Law

1. Claims by Private Parties

In the United Kingdom, the Secretary of State has authorised certain classification societies[880] to issue a number of statutory certificates[881] in relation to cargo ships. Excepted are certificates relating to their radio installations and safety equipment. The surveys of passenger ships, other than Ro-Ro passenger ferries, may also be carried out by a surveyor appointed by a classification society if that society is specifically authorised for this purpose by the Secretary of State.[882] The Maritime and Coastguard Agency retains the right to issue the SOLAS Passenger Ship Safety Certificate if the ship is engaged in international trade, and the United

[880] LR, the British Committee of BV, the British Committee of DNV, the British Committee of GL, and the British Technical Committee of ABS, Merchant Shipping (Survey and Certification) Regulations 1995/1210, Regulation 1 (2) (b).

[881] Cargo Ship Safety Construction Certificate, Cargo Ship Safety Certificate, if authorised, Cargo Ship Safety Radio Certificate.

[882] Merchant Shipping (Survey and Certification) Regulations 1995/1210, Regulation 3 (2) (c).

Kingdom Cargo Ship Safety Construction Certificate.[883] Some classification societies[884] may also issue the International Certificate of Fitness for the Carriage of Dangerous Chemicals in Bulk and the International Pollution Prevention Certificate for the Carriage of Noxious Liquid Substances in Bulk pursuant to MARPOL Annex II,[885] as well as the International Oil Pollution Prevention Certificate issued in accordance with MARPOL Annex I.[886] Besides, they may also issue Load Lines[887] and Tonnage Measurement Certificates.[888]

a. Liability of the Classification Society

Under English law, employees of the Crown, as well as independent contractors[889] acting on its behalf, can be sued in a personal capacity.[890] It is part of the constitutional arrangements that there is a civil action of the injured party against public servants for the exercise of public duties.[891] As there is no distinctive set of rules

---

883 Merchant Shipping (Survey and Certification) Regulations 1995/1210, Regulations 10, 11.

884 LR, the British Committee of BV, the British Committee of DNV, the British Committee of GL, and the British Technical Committee of ABS, and the British Committee of Rina, Merchant Shipping (Dangerous or Noxious Liquid Substances in Bulk) Regulations 1996/3010, Regulation 2 (1).

885 Merchant Shipping (Dangerous or Noxious Liquid Substances in Bulk) Regulations 1996/3010, Regulations 2 (1), 9. Which of these Certificates are delegated depends on the authority granted.

886 Merchant Shipping (Prevention of Oil Pollution) Regulations 1996/2154, Part I Regulation 1 (2), Part II Regulation 6.

887 Merchant Shipping (Load Lines) Regulations 1998/2241 Part II Regulation 9.

888 Merchant Shipping (Tonnage) Regulations 1997/1510 Part I Regulation 2, Part II Regulation 9.

889 The distinction between *employee* (who is an agent or servant) and *independent contractor* is not of relevance at this point. It will be analysed in the following section relating to the liability of the Crown for the actions of the classification society.

890 *See* for instance *Reeman v. Department of Transport and Others*, [1997] 2 Lloyd's Rep. 648 (action against surveyors was not pursued as they went into liquidation); *Perrett v. Collins,* [1998] 2 Lloyd's Rep. 255, at 255.

891 Dicey, *Introduction to the Study of the Law of the Constitution*, 10th ed. (1959), at 193-194: 'We mean in the second place, when speaking of the 'rule of law' as a characteristic of our country, not only that with us no man is above the law, but (what is a different thing) that here every man, whatever be his rank or condition, is subject to the ordinary law of the realm and amenable to the jurisdiction of the ordinary tribunals.

for state liability, general civil law, notably tort law in a case of tortious behaviour, applies. The same principles therefore apply as have been set forth above.[892] The courts do not understand careless performance of a duty as a separate tort but apply the tort of negligence.[893] Likewise, it must be ascertained whether it is fair, just and reasonable to impose such duty of care.[894] If the classification society is under a duty towards the shipowner or third parties, the breach of this duty may lead to an actionable claim. Even if there is a contract with the shipowner, his damage will not be caused by a breach of contract but by the breach of duty, as that was the relevant tortious behaviour.[895]

The statutory provisions, under which a classification society acts, aim to increase the safety of ships and to protect the marine environment.[896] As a result, a duty of care may only exist in respect of these aims. There is no duty to prevent economic loss; the prevention of economic loss is not the aim of these regulations.[897]

It is, therefore, of interest whether the *Marc Rich* dictum can be directly applied to these cases of the breach of duty. This case referred to the internationally harmonised system of limitations of liability in shipping which cover the shipowner but not the classification society. As one of its main arguments, it was held not to be fair, just and reasonable to impose a duty of care on the classification society if that made this society liable to an unlimited extent, despite the primary responsibility of the shipowner - a person who may limit his exposure to liability – for the vessel. Although it deals with private classification, the *Marc Rich* reasoning would also apply to a duty of care for the exercise of public functions. This is also illustrated by the precedents of *Reeman v. DOT* and *Perrett v. Collins*, which both

In England, the idea of legal equality, or of the universal subjection of all classes to one law administered by the ordinary courts, has been pushed to its utmost limit. Every official, from the Prime Minister down to a constable or a collector of taxes, is under the same responsibility for every act done without legal justification as any other citizen. The Reports abound with cases in which officials have been brought before the courts, and made, in their personal capacity, liable to punishment, or to the payment of damages, for acts done in their official character but in excess of their lawful authority. A colonial governor, a secretary of state, a military officer, and all subordinates, though carrying out the commands of their official superiors, are as responsible for any act which the law does not authorise as is any private and unofficial person.'

892 *See supra* Part 2 B I 2.

893 *X v. Bedfordshire C.C.* [1995] 2 A.C. 633; *see* also Stanton/Skidmore, *et al.*, *Statutory Torts* (2003), § 1.012.

894 *Reeman v. Department of Transport and Others*, [1997] 2 Lloyd's Rep. 648, at 676.

895 *Compare Reeman v. Department of Transport and Others*, [1997] 2 Lloyd's Rep. 648.

896 *See also supra* Part 1 A IV.

897 *See also Reeman v. Department of Transport and Others*, [1997] 2 Lloyd's Rep. 648, at 680–681.

analyse the *Marc Rich* dictum.[898] The House of Lords considered in *Marc Rich* that the checks and balances of the system of limitations would otherwise be considerably undermined. Any other court which decides on the liability for the breach of duty will have to respect this precedent. In brief, the classification society will be liable in the same way that has been explained in the preceding sections.[899] Following the precedent of *Perrett v. Collins*, an actionable claim in tort would especially lie in cases of personal injury.[900]

b. Liability of the Crown for the Acts of the Classification Society

As the Secretary of State has granted authority to issue statutory certificates to certain classification societies, an injured party might also try to sue the Crown for any tortious acts committed by the classification society when acting on the Crown's behalf. The Crown Proceedings Act 1947 suspended the immunity of the Crown for its acts. Section 2(1) establishes the vicarious liability of the Crown for its employees in the course of their employment.[901] The Crown has to answer for the negligence of independent contractors if committed in circumstances that would render a private employer liable.[902]

First of all, one has to determine whether the classification society is an employee or an independent contractor in the sense of the English law when undertaking these activities. Whether someone is an employee or an independent contractor used to be decided in respect of the different amounts of control over the manner in which the work is to be done. If the employer had a right to control the method of performing the work, the other person was an employee.[903] In this case, the relationship as a whole needs to be considered. The maritime authorities supervise classification societies, as is also required by the European Directive 94/57/EC. However, they do not control the method of working of the classification society or check each and every survey that is carried out or certificate that is issued. The classical approach, therefore, would define them as independent contractors. Due to shortcomings in this classical approach, especially in view of per-

---

898 *Reeman v. Department of Transport and Others*, [1997] 2 Lloyd's Rep. 648, *per* Lord Phillips, at 683, col. 1; Lord Bingham, at 685, col. 1; *Perrett v. Collins,* [1998] 2 Lloyd's Rep. 255 (C.A.), at 259, col. 2.

899 *See supra* Part 2 B I 2.

900 *See supra* Part 2 B I 2 d.

901 Crown Proceedings Act 1947, § 2:

(1) Subject to the provisions of this Act, the Crown shall be subject to all those liabilities in tort to which, if it were a private person of full age and capacity, it would be subject:--

(a) in respect of torts committed by its servants or agents; […]

902 For instance *Darling v. Attorney-General*, [1950] 2 All. E.R. 793, Clerk & Lindsell, *On Torts* (2006), § 5–04.

903 Clerk & Lindsell, *On Torts* (2006), § 6–06; *Market Investigations Ltd. v. Minister of Social Security* [1969] 2 Q.B. 173 (Q.B.), at 186, *per* Cooke J.; *Global Plant Ltd. v. Secretary of State for Social Services* [1972] 1 Q.B. 139 at 151, *per* Widgery C.J.

sons that are employees but work in a rather independent and self-determined way, such as hospital medical staff, this approach has been modified to become a *multiple test*. The judges need to analyse all aspects of the relationship, considering notably control, ownership of the tools, and chance of profit and risk of loss.[904] Just like the issue of control that has already been referred to, the other factors illustrate that the classification society is an independent contractor. It owns its tools, and has a chance of profit and risk of loss concerning the surveys. Despite the supervision by the flag State, the classification society may therefore be regarded an independent contractor.

However, the Crown is only liable for an independent contractor to the degree that a private employer would be liable for an independent contractor. In principle, there is no such liability of the employer for an independent contractor. Of course, the employer can be liable for a breach of his own duties which he owes to the injured party. He will, therefore, be liable if he negligently selects the independent contractor, employs an insufficient number of men, or if he interferes in the work of the independent contractor in a way that damage occurs or if he authorises a tort that is committed by the independent contractor.[905] The employer also breaches a duty towards the plaintiff if he delegates a non-delegable duty to the independent contractor. The same applies to statutory obligations.[906] The statutory regulations oblige the Secretary of State to implement measures that ascertain the vessels and their conformity to marine environmental regulations. The Secretary of State, therefore, is under a duty to enforce these requirements. He cannot simply dispose of these duties by delegating them to the classification society. In effect he – or, to be more precise, the Crown – will be liable for the exercise of statutory obligations by the classification society.

2. *Recourse of the Flag State*

The recourse of the flag State against the classification society will be based on the agreement between these two parties. As has been shown in the section relating to the protection of contracting parties, a classification society owes a number of contractual duties to its parties. It notably has to carry out the surveys in the way the flag State requests and according to the standards that have been laid

---

[904] *Ready Mixed Concrete (South East) Ltd. v. Minister of Pensions and National Insurance* [1968] 2 Q.B. 497, at 524, *per* MacKenna J.: it is a contract of service [and therefore employee] if '(i) the servant agrees that, in consideration of a wage or other remuneration, he will provide his own work and skill in the performance of some service for his master, (ii) he agrees, expressly or impliedly, that in the performance of that service he will be subject to the other's control in a sufficient degree to make that other the master, (iii) the other provisions of the contract are consistent with a contract of service.'

[905] Clerk & Lindsell, *On Torts* (2006), § 6–52.

[906] *E.g. Darling v. Attorney-General*, [1950] 2 All. E.R. 793.

down by the flag State; furthermore, it must have sufficient knowledge and choose only suitably educated and experienced staff.[907]

II. Liability under United States Law

1. *Claims by Private Parties*

a. Choosing the Plaintiff: Whether to Sue the Classification Society or the U.S. Government

The Coast Guard Alternate Compliance Program (ACP)[908] allows owners, operators and builders of United States flag vessels to comply with United States Coast Guard (USCG) design and inspection regulations through the aid of recognised classification societies.[909] As it is a voluntary programme, the maritime industry may continue to call upon the USCG to carry out these tasks. The USCG will accept plan reviews and surveys performed by a recognised classifications society as equivalent to tests and examinations required for initial and periodic inspections for certification, re-examination, and dry-dock examinations.[910] There are additional ACP supplements, which, in addition to the international codes and conventions and the requirements laid down by the classification society's rules, determine the applicable standard of safety under United States law. Vessels under the United States flag need to have a Certificate of Inspection[911] and valid international convention certificates, as well as a classification by a recognised classification society. The Coast Guard issues the Certificates of Inspection, the Certificate of Documentation, and the Certificate of Financial Responsibility. If authorised, the classification society may issue the Stability Letter. Depending on the agreement with the Coast Guard, the classification society may also issue certain other international certificates. When carrying out plan review under the ACP, the classification society stamps the submitted plans on behalf of the USCG to indicate whether they are approved, examined or whether re-submission is required.[912] The United States Coast Guard Commandant may delegate authority to classification societies to review and approve commercial vessel plans and conduct commercial

---

907 *See also supra* Part 1 B II 2, Part 2 A I 1, 2.

908 For further information on ACP, *see* <http://www.uscg.mil/hq/gm/mse/acp/acp.htm>, last accessed 19 March 2007.

909 USCG Navigation and Vessel Inspection Circular No. 2–95, Change 1, Revision 1 August 1997 (accessible at <http://www.uscg.mil/hq/g-m/nvic/2_95/n2-95.htm>, last accessed 19 March 2007).

910 USCG Navigation and Vessel Inspection Circular No. 2–95, Change 1, at no. 6 and Enclosure (2). S*ee also* United States Department of Transportation, United States Coast Guard, Navigation and Vessel Inspection Circular No. 8–86 (accessible at <http://www.uscg.mil/hq/g-m/nvic/8_86/n8-86.htm>, last accessed 19 March 2007).

911 46 U.S.C. Chapter 33.

912 USCG Navigation and Vessel Inspection Circular No. 2–95, Change 1, Enclosure (2).

vessel inspections and examinations.[913] ABS, LR and DNV are accepted as ACP classification societies and have the authority to issue most international certificates.[914] ABS has been assigned the most duties,[915] whereas the other societies may undertake many but not all statutory surveys.[916] The Coast Guard has also authorised BV and GL to issue certain international certificates.[917] USCG Officers in Charge of Marine Inspection will generally accept the classification society's

---

913 46 U.S.C. 3316, 61 Federal Regulations 67952–02: Rules and Regulations, Department of Transportation, 49 CFR Part 1, Organization and Delegation of Powers and Duties; Delegation to the Commandant; United States Coast Guard of 26 December 1996.

914 International Load Line Certificate, International Tonnage Certificate, SOLAS Cargo Ship Safety Construction Certificate, SOLAS Cargo Ship Safety Equipment Certificate, SOLAS Certificate of Fitness for the Carriage of Dangerous Chemicals in Bulk, SOLAS Certificate of Fitness for the Carriage of Liquefied Gasses in Bulk, SOLAS Mobile Offshore Drilling Unit Safety Certificate, MARPOL 73/78 International Oil Pollution Prevention Certificates (Annex I – III, V full authorisation), MARPOL 73/78 International Oil Pollution Prevention Certificate for the Carriage of Noxious Liquid Substances in Bulk, ISM Document of Compliance (Procedures to be developed).

915 Memorandum of Understanding between the United States Coast Guard and the American Bureau of Shipping Concerning Delegation of Vessel Inspections and Examinations, and Tonnage Measurement, and Acceptance of Plan Review and Approval, of 12 January 1995, accessible at <http://www.uscg.mil/hq/g-m/mse/acp/uscgabs.pdf>, last accessed 19 March 2007.

916 DNV and LR may not issue the MARPOL Annex III Prevention of Pollution by Packaged Harmful Substances and Annex V Prevention of Pollution by Garbage Certificates as well as the SOLAS Mobile Offshore Drilling Unit Safety Certificate. LR may not issue the International Safety Management Certificate and Document Compliance either (Annex to the Memorandum of Agreement between the United States and Det Norske Veritas Governing Participation in the Alternate Compliance Program and the Delegation of certain Survey and Certification Services for United States of America Flagged Vessels, <http://www.uscg.mil/hq/gm/mse/acp/dnv.pdf>, last accessed 19 March 2007; Annex to the Memorandum of Agreement between the United States Coast Guard and Lloyd's Register Governing Participation in the Alternate Compliance Program and the Delegation of certain Survey and Certification Services for United States of America Flagged Vessels, <http://www.uscg.mil/hq/gm/mse/acp/lloyds.pdf>, last accessed 19 March 2007).

917 BV: International Load Line Certificate, International Tonnage Certificate, (Annex to the Memorandum of Agreement between the United States Coast Guard and Bureau Veritas Governing Delegation of certain Survey and Certification Services for United States of America Flagged Vessels of 10 September 2003, <http://www.uscg.mil/hq/gm/mse/acp/bv.pdf>, last accessed 19 March 2007); GL: International Load Line Certificate, International Tonnage Certificate, SOLAS Cargo Ship Safety Construction Certificate, MARPOL 73/78 Annex I; International Oil Pollution Prevention Certificate, International Safety Management Certificate (Annex to the Agreement Governing the Delegation of Certain Surveys and Certification Services for United States of America Flagged Vessels between the United States Coast Guard and Germanischer Lloyd, <http://www.uscg.mil/hq/gm/mse/acp/gl.pdf>, last accessed 19 March 2007).

approval of recommended repairs in non-reportable marine casualties. The Officers retain the ultimate authority to review and approve temporary repairs whenever a pollution incident is likely to result or the vessel might pose a hazard to the safety of a United States navigable waterway.[918]

According to 46 U.S.C.A. § 3316, each department, agency and instrumentality of the United States Government shall recognise ABS as its agent in classifying vessels owned by the Government and in matters related to classification.[919] When performing the plan reviews or surveys, or issuing the certificates, ABS therefore acts as an agent of the United States. When it acts as an agent in an official capacity, the principle of sovereign immunity bars suits against ABS.[920] As long as the agent is acting in conformity with its contract with the United States, he will be immune from liability. It is not the agent, but the United States that is the real party in interest. This has been interpreted in *Shaw v. Grumman Aerospace* in a wider sense: 'since the action of the agent is the act of the government, the contractor could be deemed to share in Federal sovereign immunity'.[921]

All other classification societies (including ABS when not performing classification services for vessels owned by the Unites States Government) are independent contractors, not agents of the Government. As regards independent contractors, the situation is more complex. They are not generally protected by immunity, but can be immune under certain circumstances. Congress has been reluctant to state unambiguously an independent basis of immunity for government contractors.[922] Generally, a contractor with the United States has no immunity from liability to third parties only because of this contract.[923] Nevertheless, the leading precedents illustrate that an independent contractor benefits from immunity if he performs work for the Federal Government whenever it is in an area of uniquely Federal interests.[924] In *Yearsley*, the Supreme Court held that 'if [the] authority to carry out the project was validly conferred, that is, if what was done was within

918 USCG Navigation and Vessel Inspection Circular No. 2–95, Change 1, at no. 6 c) (5).

919 A similar phrase is included in the MOU between the USCG and ABS, see No. III A of the Memorandum of Understanding between the United States Coast Guard and the American Bureau of Shipping Concerning Delegation of Vessel Inspections and Examinations, and Tonnage Measurement, and Acceptance of Plan Review and Approval, <http://www.uscg.mil/hq/g-m/mse/acp/uscgabs.pdf> last accessed 19 March 2007.

920 *Compare United States v. Shaw*, 309 U.S. 495, 60 S. Ct. 659, 84 L. Ed. 888 (1940).

921 *Shaw v. Grumman Aerospace Corp.*, 778 F.2d 736 (11th Cir.1985).

922 None of the following bills was ever passed: H.R. 4765, 99th Cong., 2d Session (1986) (limitations on civil liability of government contractors), S. 2441, 99th Cong., 2d Session (1986) (limitations on civil liability of government contractors), H.R. 2378, 100th Cong., 1st Sess. (1987) (indemnification of civil liability for government contractors), for further examples, *see* Hanash, *Environmental Liability of Government Contractors* (1992), at 27 footnote 10.

923 *Yuba Consol. Gold Fields v. Kilkeary*, 102 F. Supp. 999 (N.D. Cal. 1952).

924 *Yearsley v. W.A. Ross Construction Co.*, 309 U.S. 18 (U.S.1940); *Boyle v. United Technologies Corp.*, 487 U.S. 500, 108 S.Ct. 2510 (U.S.1988). *See also* Hanash, *Environmental Liability of Government Contractors* (1992), at 26–27, 34–35.

the constitutional power of Congress, there is no liability on the part of the contractor for executing its will.'[925] If the action is not personally against the contractor but in fact against the United States, the principle of immunity rules the case. Whether or not the United States is the real party in interest must be determined from the effect the judgment would have. If relief sought against the contractor in fact operates against the United States, the principle of immunity takes effect.[926] Such is the case if the relief sought would spread out onto the public treasury or domain, or if it obstructed public administration or hindered the government from acting or obliged it to act in a certain way.[927] The execution of statutory surveys has to be carried out by the maritime authority. Even if they are delegated to a classification society, it remains an obligation of the United States to ascertain the safety of the vessel. When acting as independent contractors, the classification societies therefore perform work for the Federal Government, and act in an area of uniquely Federal interests. If injury results from the act that the classification society is required to do by the maritime administration, they are shielded by immunity for such actions. A plaintiff has to sue the United States in such a case, not the classification society. If the classification society exceeds its authority or its authority was not validly conferred, it will be personally liable. Moreover, the principle of immunity does not protect the classification society if the claim is based on the negligent exercise of the authority that was granted to the classification society.[928] In any given case, one therefore needs to distinguish whether the injury was caused by the classification society's conforming to the requirements of the United States Coast Guard or whether it was caused by the negligent performance of the duties of the classification society. In the first case, the classification society will be protected by government immunity, in the second it will not.

b. The Concept of Immunity

"The king can do no wrong."[929] This theory in law stems from the idea that the sovereign authority derives directly from God, under whom it served. As governmental authority is no longer based on Christian theories today, this principle no longer applies in general either. However, the concept of sovereignty still requires that the State has consented to withhold immunity and to be subject to liability. The doctrine of sovereign immunity prohibits suits against governmental entities without their consent.[930] For such a claim, a waiver of immunity is necessary.

---

925 *Yearsley v. W.A. Ross Construction Co.,* 309 U.S. 18, at 20–21 (U.S.1940).

926 *State of Hawaii v. Gordon*, 373 U.S. 57, 83 S. Ct. 1052, 10 L. Ed. 2d 191 (U.S.1963).

927 *Pennhurst State School & Hospital v. Halderman*, 465 U.S. 89, 104 S.Ct. 900 (U.S.1984).

928 *Compare Brady v. Roosevelt Steamship Co.*, 317 U.S. 575 at 583, 63 S.Ct. 425 at 439 (U.S. 1943); Korpela, *American Law Reports*, 'Right of Contractor with Federal, State, or Local Public Body to Latter's Immunity from Tort Liability' (2004), § 2 [a].

929 Blackstone, *Commentaries on the Laws of England* (1765), 238.

930 Craig, *Civil Actions against the United States, Its Agencies, Officers, and Employees* (2005), vol. 1, § 1–1.

Both the Federal Tort Claims Act (FTCA)[931] and the Suits in Admiralty Act (SIAA)[932] provide a waiver for the liability of the United States for its agencies, officers and employees. These waiver statutes do not provide any substantive cause of action; they merely waive sovereign immunity for claims over which there is admiralty jurisdiction.[933] Whilst the FTCA covers all torts committed by governmental entities,[934] the SIAA applies to all claims in admiralty. Despite only relating to vessels at the beginning, the scope of application of the SIAA has been significantly expanded. The *Supreme Court* has held that the SIAA provides a uniform system which applies exclusively[935] to maritime-related causes of action that arise from Federal participation in merchant-shipping activities.[936] Before 1960 this act required either a government vessel or cargo; in 1960, Congress enlarged its scope of application to all admiralty claims against the United States in which a private person or property was involved.[937] If the act of the classification society is an act on behalf of the United States and constitutes an action in admiralty, the SIAA therefore applies.

---

[931] 28 U.S.C. §§ 1346(b), 2671–2680, *see* Craig, *Civil Actions against the United States* (2005), vol. 1, chapter 2.

[932] 46 U.S.C. App. §§ 741–752. Moreover, there is also the Public Vessels Act (46 U.S.C. §§ 781–790), which relates to all governmental vessels which are not employed in maritime commerce but in all other trades.

[933] *Trautman v. Buck Steber, Inc.*, 693 F.2d 440 (5th Cir.1982), Schoenbaum, *Admiralty and Maritime Law* (2004), § 20–1.

[934] The only limitation is that the claim must be made against the responsible federal agency and that the tort does not fall under the provision of 46 U.S.C. § 2680.

[935] *See* 46 U.S.C. App. 745; 28 U.S.C. § 2680(d), *Anderson v. United States,* 317 F.3d 1235, 2003 A.M.C. 94 (11th Cir.2003), *McCormick v. United States,* 680 F.2d 345, 1984 A.M.C. 1799 (5th Cir.1982), *Williams v. United States,* 711 F.2d 893 (9th Cir.1983), *Szyka v. United States Secretary of Defense,* 525 F.2d 62, 1975 A.M.C. 2504 (2d Cir.1975). In 1960, Congress amended the SAA with the intention to extend it to "the full range of admiralty cases" against the government, Session Report No. 92–1079, [1972] U.S. Code Cong. & Adm. News 3129, 3134.

[936] *United States Shipping Board Emergency Fleet Corp. V. Rosenberg Bros. & Co.*, 276 U.S. 202, 72 L.Ed. 531, 48 S.Ct. 256 (U.S.1928).

[937] 46 U.S.C. App. 742: 'In cases where if such vessel were privately owned or operated, or if such cargo were privately owned or possessed, or if a private person or property were involved, a proceeding in admiralty could be maintained, any appropriate nonjury proceeding in personam may be brought against the United States or against any corporation mentioned in section 741 of this title.' Congress Session Report No. 92–1079, [1972] U.S.Code Cong. & Adm. News 3129, 3134. *See also Kelly v. United States,* 531 F.2d 1144 (2d.Cir.1976); Carter Watson, 'The Suits in Admiralty Act', 17 *J.Mar.L.&Com.* 175, at 181 (1986); Conner, 'Maritime Tort Liability of the United States', 11 *J.Mar.L.&Com.* 271, at 274 (1979–1980); Helferich, 'Suits Against the United States Pursuant to the SIAA, PVA, EAA, FTCA and FECA', 26 *Trial Lawyer's Guide*, 121, at 133–134 (1982).

As has been explained before, a claim lies in admiralty if the subject matter relates to traditional maritime activity. It has been shown that a contract for classification is maritime in nature, as is a tort which is committed in connection with the survey of a vessel and the issue of classification certificates.[938] The survey and statutory certification of a vessel is likewise an activity which relates to the traditional maritime activity of operating a vessel. The claim lies therefore in admiralty, and the SIAA applies and provides a waiver for the sovereign immunity of the United States in such a case.[939] If the classification society shall be held liable for the statutory survey of a vessel which flies the flag of the United States, the law of the United States applies, and recourse is to be made to the same theories as for the issuance of classification certificates.[940]

c. The Discretionary Function Exemption

Under the Federal Tort Claims Act (FTCA)[941], the waiver of immunity does not apply to cases of a *discretionary function*.[942] Discretionary conduct involves an element of judgement or choice.[943] This exception to the FTCA provides that there shall be no liability for

---

[938] *See supra* Part 2 A II 1.

[939] Unfortunately, *Reino de Espana v. American Bureau of Shipping,* 328 F.Supp.2d 489 (S.D.N.Y.2004) only relates to the issue of whether the Foreign Sovereign Immunities Act applies to counterclaims of ABS against the Kingdom of Spain, and not to the question which is here at issue.

[940] *Sundance Cruises Corp. v. American Bureau of Shipping,* 799 F.Supp. 363, 386 *et seq.* (S.D.N.Y.1992), *aff'd,* 7 F.3d 1077 (2d Cir.1993), *Marine Coal Transport Corp., et al. v. United States of America and American Bureau of Shipping,* 1985 WL 1443 (S.D.N.Y.1985). *Compare Somarelf v. American Bureau of Shipping*, 720 F.Supp. 441 (D.N.J.1989). *See also* Force/Norris, *The Law of Maritime Personal Injuries* (2005), § 14:5.

[941] 28 U.S.C. §§ 1346, 2671–2678, 2680.

[942] The landmark cases are *Dalehite v. United States*, 346 U.S. 15, 73 S.Ct. 956, 97 L.Ed. 1427 (U.S.1953), *Indian Towing v. United States,* 350 U.S. 61, 76 S.Ct. 122, 100 L.Ed. 48 (U.S.1955), and *United States v. Varig Airlines*, 467 U.S. 797, 104 S.Ct. 2755, 81 L.Ed.2d 660 (U.S.1984); *Berkovitz by Berkovitz v. United States*, 486 U.S. 531, 108 S. Ct. 1954, 100 L. Ed. 2d 531 (1988). *See also* Force/Norris, *The Law of Maritime Personal Injuries* (2005), § 14:7; Barash, 'The Discretionary Function Exception and Mandatory Regulations', 54 *U.Chi.L.Rev.* 1300 (1987); Dombroff, 'Certification and Inspection: An Overview of Government Liability', 47 *J.Air L.&Com.* 229 (1982), at 246–251; McClure, 'Liability of Administrative Officials', 53 *Geo.Wash.L.Rev.* 206 (1984), at 206–214.

[943] *Berkovitz by Berkovitz v. United States*, 486 U.S. 531, 108 S. Ct. 1954, 100 L. Ed. 2d 531 (1988).

> "any claim [...] based upon the exercise or performance or the failure to exercise or perform a discretionary function or duty on the part of a federal agency or an employee of the Government, whether or not the discretion involved be abused."[944]

In *Varig Airlines*, the Supreme Court interpreted the *discretionary function* in a broad sense, despite arguing that it was impossible to determine precisely every contour of the discretionary function exemption.[945] It laid down certain factors that are useful for determining whether the acts of a Government employee are protected from liability by the discretionary function exemption. First, there is the nature of the conduct. It is not the status of the employee that is of relevance, but whether or not he exercised an act that in nature and quality Congress intended to shield from tort liability.[946] Secondly, discretionary acts of the Government when acting as a regulator of the conduct of private individuals are always shielded, as the Government shall be protected from liability that might hinder efficient government operation.[947]

Varig Airlines involved the negligent certification of a Boeing 707 aircraft, in which a waste receptacle was not constructed of fire-resistant material in violation of air safety regulations. A fire broke out in one of the lavatories, killing 124 of the 135 people on board. The Supreme Court held that Federal Aviation Agency (FAA) inspections cannot give rise to Federal liability under the FTCA because of the discretionary nature of the certification process. This certification process is quite similar to the certification of vessels. Despite the inspection of the aircraft by government authorities, the air carriers retain certain responsibilities, which are the duty to perform their services with the highest possible degree of safety, the duty to make or cause to be made every inspection required by the Secretary, and the duty to observe and comply with all other administrative requirements that are established by the Secretary.[948] Similarly, the FAA may delegate certain inspection and certification responsibilities to designated engineering representatives that assist in the certification process.[949] These representatives act as surrogates of the FAA in examining, testing and inspecting, and are guided by the same requirements, instructions and procedures as FAA employees.[950]

> "The FAA's implementation of a mechanism for compliance review is plainly discretionary activity of the "nature and quality" protected by § 2680 (a). When an agency determines the extent to which it will supervise the safety procedures of private individuals, it is exercising discretionary regulatory authority of the most basic kind. Decisions as to the manner of enforcing regulations directly affect the feasibility and practicality of the Government's regulatory program; such decisions require the agency to establish

944 28 U.S.C. § 2680 (a).

945 *United States v. Varig Airlines*, 467 U.S. 797, at 813 (U.S.1984).

946 *United States v. Varig Airlines*, 467 U.S. 797, at 813 (U.S.1984).

947 *United States v. Varig Airlines*, 467 U.S. 797, at 813–814 (U.S.1984).

948 *United States v. Varig Airlines*, 467 U.S. 797, at 804 (U.S.1984).

949 49 U.S.C. § 1355, 14 C.F.R. § 183.29.

950 14 C.F.R § 183.1; *United States v. Varig Airlines*, 467 U.S. 797, at 807 (U.S.1984).

> priorities for the accomplishment of its policy objectives by balancing the objectives sought to be obtained against such practical considerations as staffing and funding."[951]

Employees that conduct compliance reviews were specifically empowered to make policy judgments and therefore fall under the discretionary function exemption:

> "The FAA employees who conducted compliance reviews of the aircraft involved in this case were specifically empowered to make policy judgments regarding the degree of confidence that might reasonably be placed in a given manufacturer, the need to maximize compliance with FAA regulations, and the efficient allocation of agency resources. In administering the 'spot-check' program, these FAA engineers and inspectors necessarily took certain calculated risks, but those risks were encountered for the advancement of a governmental purpose and pursuant to the specific grant of authority in the regulations and operating manuals. Under such circumstances, the FAA's alleged negligence in failing to check certain specific items in the course of certificating a particular aircraft falls squarely within the discretionary function exception of § 2680 (a)."[952]

The Supreme Court also held that Congress did not intend to make the FAA an insurer of the safety of air transport and to impose liability for the regulatory enforcement of these safety provisions. As a result, actions against the FAA for its alleged negligence in certification of an aircraft are barred by the discretionary function exemption.

As has been said, statutory certification by a classification society is similar in kind and would also be covered by such discretionary function exemption. However, unlike the FTCA, the SIAA does not contain an explicit discretionary function exemption. Nonetheless, there is case law which establishes an implied discretionary function in the SIAA.[953] Despite the fact that the SIAA is not ambiguous, it was held that because of separation-of-powers principles there is such an implied function. The Judicial Branch would otherwise control tasks which are genuinely accomplished by legislation and administration.[954] The ability

---

951 *United States v. Varig Airlines*, 467 U.S. 797, at 819–820 (U.S.1984).

952 *United States v. Varig Airlines*, 467 U.S. 797, at 820 (U.S.1984).

953 *Gercey v. United States*, 540 F.2d 536, at 539 (1st Cir.1976), *cert. denied*, 430 U.S. 954 (U.S.1977); *Bearce v. United States*, 614 F.2d 556, at 560 (7th Cir.1980); *Canadian Transport Co. v. United States*, 663 F.2d 1081, at 1085 (D.C.Cir.1980); *Gemp v. United States*, 684 F.2d 404, at 408 (6th Cir.1982); *Williams v. United States*, 747 F.2d 700 (11th Cir.1984); *Robinson v. United States (In re Joint E. & S. Distributors Asbestos Litigation)*, 891 F.2d 31, at 34–35 (2d Cir.1989); *Sea-Land Service, Inc. v. United States*, 919 F.2d 888, 893 (3d Cir.1990); *Earles v. United States*, 935 F.2d 1028, at 1032 (9th Cir.1991); *Tew v. United States*, 86 F.3d 1003, at 1005 (10th Cir.1996); *McMellon v. United States*, 387 F.3d 329, at 338–342 (4th Cir.2004). *See also* Ingraham, 'The Suits in Admiralty Act and the Implied Discretionary Function', 1982 *Duke L.J.* 146 (1982); Ramsey & Monachino, 'Admiralty Claims against the United States', 5 *Mar. Lawyer* 31, at 40–42 (1980).

954 *McMellon v. United States*, 387 F.3d 329, at 341 (4th Cir.2004)

of the executive branch to faithfully administer the law would otherwise be substantially impaired.[955]

To sum up, the SIAA contains an implied discretionary function exemption, which bars the waiving of immunity for classification societies acting on behalf of the United States when performing statutory surveys.[956]

2. *Recourse of the Flag State*

As the United States are protected by the SIAA implied *discretionary function exemption*, they cannot be held liable. There is therefore no situation of recourse against the classification society.

III. Liability under German Law

1. *Claims by Private Parties*

a. Civil Liability or State Liability for the Survey of Vessels

In Germany, the maritime administration itself issues all statutory certificates which are required for a ship that is flying the German flag. Germany has not granted the authority to issue a statutory certificate to any classification society. It has, however, assigned classification societies the function to survey vessels. The results of these surveys are the basis for the decision by the maritime administration.

Anlage 2, Part B to § 9 (2) of the German *Schiffssicherheitsverordnung* (*SchSV*)[957] specifies the duties and functions of classification societies when carrying out surveys and issuing expert opinions that are the basis of the decision of the maritime authority which finally issues the certificate. The provision does not assign all surveys for statutory certificates to classification societies, but only those mentioned in Part B § 3.1 of Anlage 2 SchSV. In order to get a statutory certificate within the scope of this provision, a shipowner needs to contract with a recognised classification society for an attestation which certifies that his vessel fulfils the standards of safety as required by the applicable regulations.[958] Some of the certificates are issued by the *Seeberufsgenossenschaft* (*SeeBG*) and others by the

[955] *McMellon v. United States*, 387 F.3d 329, at 342 (4th Cir.2004)

[956] As the classification society was not acting on behalf of the United States, the discretionary function exemption was not of relevance to the *Somarelf II* case (*Somarelf v. American Bureau of Shipping*, 720 F.Supp. 441 (D.N.J.1989)).

[957] *Schiffssicherheitsverordnung* of 18 September 1998 (BGBl. I p. 3013), last amended by *Verordnung* of 18 February 2004 (BGBl. I p. 300).

[958] Such a classification does not only have to be recognised by the European Commission. It is also necessary to have concluded an agreement with the maritime administration that is approved by the Federal Ministry of Transport, Building and Housing (*Bundesministerium für Verkehr, Bau- und Wohnungswesen*), *see* §§ 3.1, 3.3 of Part B of Anlage B to § 9 of the SchSV. Such an agreement is also referred to in Art. 6 of the EC Directive 94/57 of 22 November 1994.

Bundesamt für Seeschifffahrt und Hydographie (*BSH*).[959] All a classification society may do is to survey the vessel and issue an attestation for the use of the maritime administration that the vessel conforms to the rules. The applicable standard of safety and the standard of care which the classification society has to apply when carrying out these surveys are both defined by the authorities.[960] The shipowner may also directly apply for a survey of his vessel by the maritime administration.[961] This is, however, an option that is hardly ever chosen.

A plaintiff who suffers injury or damage from the operation of the ship may argue that this damage has been caused by a negligent survey of the vessel in respect of a certain statutory requirement. He could, for example, purport that the classification society should have discovered a certain defect in the vessel which contributed to its sinking. The plaintiff could, therefore, have a claim either against the classification society or against the State, depending on whether the survey and issuance of the attestation by the classification society is solely governed by civil law or can be attributed to the State.

Under German law, State liability follows its own distinct rules and principles. One of the most important principles is that it is not the person who acts for the administration that will be liable, but rather the administrative body which has employed him.[962] Therefore, it has to be ascertained whether state liability is applicable if the classification society at the request of the shipowner surveys the vessel and analyses whether it corresponds to statutory requirements and thereafter issues an attestation for the use of the maritime administration, or whether this is a case of civil liability to which those theories apply that have been scrutinised *supra*.[963]

Public authorities are only liable for their officials. However, the definition of an "official" for the use of State liability is surprisingly wide. In addition to each and every person that is in public service, it also includes those persons that are not employed by the administration but who have been awarded (*beliehen*) a certain public function, and even includes aides of the administration (*Verwaltungshelfer*). A classification society is not part of the public service and therefore not a public servant in the sense of civil service law. Its surveys and attestations appear to be only a matter of private law. Nonetheless, there is a significant body of case law which illustrates that such a case might be subject to State liability. These cases relate to technical experts, notably motor-vehicle experts, who carry out technical surveys that the administration is required to perform according to the laws. If an expert is significantly involved in the function of the administration, his surveys and expert opinions can be a meaningful part of the surveillance of dangerous activities by the administration, and therefore may be identified as an

959 A list showing which authority is responsible for which certification is enclosed in Part A of Anlage 2 to § 9 SchSV.

960 § 3.4 of Anlage B to § 9 SchSV.

961 § 3.8 of Anlage B to § 9 SchSV.

962 Art. 34, 1 GG.

963 Part 2 A III 2, Part 2 B III 2, 4, 6.

administrative function.[964] Despite the fact that the expert has not the power to grant or deny the permission or certificate, in such a case the decision whether or not it will be granted is actually taken at the time the expert gives his opinion, issues his attestation or refuses it. What is relevant is not the status of the technical expert, and whether he is part of the public service or not, but whether he exercises a function that is assigned to the administration.[965] The courts differentiate between the situation in which there is a preventive prohibition without prejudice to permission (*präventives Verbot mit Erlaubnisvorbehalt*), which implies that the activity is in principle not allowed but permission may be granted. The other possible situation is one in which the activity is generally allowed but may be forbidden by the administration. Despite being divided between the administration and the private body, the legal unity of the entire process will not be destroyed even if the administration issues all certificates and enforces all sanctions, whilst the private body carries out all surveys.[966] One of the main criteria for deciding whether the survey is a public or a private function has to do with the character of the activity. If one is in general not allowed to exercise the activity and therefore needs permission to do so, the administration will otherwise be obliged to exercise the control that is undertaken by the private body. Due to the fact that the State shall not be allowed to escape from liability for activities which it is obliged to undertake, state liability applies all the same, even if the survey is carried out by a private body. Once the private expert issues his opinion, the decision whether or not the permission will be granted is practically taken in such a case. If, however, it is not prohibited to exercise the activity, the expert opinion is solely a preparatory opinion for the administration, but cannot be deemed part of the public function. In such a case, state liability does not apply.

The main example of the first situation, in which permission is mandatory in order to exercise a certain activity, is the registration of cars. In order to be registered, a vehicle needs to be checked whether it complies with certain safety regulations. In Germany, this is mainly carried out by licensed motor-vehicle experts (*amtlich anerkannter Kfz-Sachverständiger*). The owner shows them his car and they will thereafter issue an expert opinion on its condition and may put a sticker on the number plate if the car corresponds with the regulations. However, the administrative deed (*Verwaltungsakt*) of registering the car and granting permission to use it remains in the hands of the traffic administration. But since one is prohibited from using one's car without permission for the reason of public safety, and since the activity of the licensed motor-vehicle expert is so closely related to the administrative function to ensure the safety of traffic, it is the law that these ex-

[964] BGH 30 November 1967, 49 BGHZ 108, at 112–114; BGH 11 January 1973, [1973] *NJW* 458; BGH 2 November 2000, [2001] *NZV* 76, at 77; BGH 10 April 2003, [2003] *NVwZ-RR* 543.

[965] Ossenbühl, *Staatshaftungsrecht* (1998), at 17; *compare* Steiner, *Öffentliche Verwaltung durch Private* (1975), at 124–125, 131–132.

[966] Steiner, *Öffentliche Verwaltung durch Private* (1975), at 125.

perts are so closely integrated in the administrative functions that one can assign their activities to the administration.[967]

On the other hand, there are also examples of the second situation, in which an activity is considered not to be of relevance to state liability. If, for example, an institute which has been accepted by the administration as a testing laboratory for domestic appliances issues an attestation to the producer that his product complies with certain safety regulations, and the administration therefore abstains from its own examination of that product, the activity of the institute, however, is not considered an administrative function.[968] A licence or expert opinion granted or accepted by the administration is not sufficient for his survey and attestation to be deemed a public function.[969] Neither is it required that the actual request to survey the item will be made by the administration.[970] At least in a case in which the function and duties of the expert are defined by regulations, there is no necessity for such a request by the administration.[971] The main difference is that it is not prohibited to produce and sell products. It can only be forbidden to sell them if they prove to be dangerous.

As regards classification societies, it needs to be remembered that a vessel may not sail without registration. That registration can only proceed if the vessel has all statutory certificates. It is prohibited to operate a vessel without being in possession of such certificates. The surveys that are needed for these certificates are in effect carried out by the classification society. The supervision of maritime safety is a duty of the administration. The standard of safety that has to be attained by the vessel has been defined by the legislator, as well as the role of the classification society in this process.[972]

There are, however, a few differences between a classification society and licensed motor- vehicle experts. First of all, classification societies do not attach any kind of sticker to a public document. However, this does not fundamentally change their position, as that position needs to be analysed functionally in regard to the activities which they actually exercise. Secondly, a shipowner may also call upon the *SeeBG* with regard to the surveys; he is, therefore, not obliged to employ a classification society.[973] There is no such option as regards the survey of cars.

---

[967] BGH 11 January 1973, [1973] *NJW* 458, at 460; BGH 4 June 1992, 118 BGHZ 304, at 305; BGH NZV 2001, 343; *compare* also BGH 25 March 1993, [1993] *NJW* 1784, at 1785.

[968] BGH 9 February 1978, [1978] *NJW* 1978, 2548; OLG Hamm 27 June 1990, [1990] *NVwZ* 1105.

[969] BGH 27 May 1963, 39 BGHZ 358, at 361; BGH 2 November 2000, [2001] *NZV* 343, at 344.

[970] BGH 27 May 1963, 39 BGHZ 358, at 362; BGH 2 November 2000, [2001] *NZV* 343, at 344.

[971] BGH 30 November 1967, 49 BGHZ 108, at 116–117; BGH 2 November 2000, [2001] *NZV* 343, at 344.

[972] §§ 3.1, 3.4, 3.5 of Anlage B to § 9 SchSV.

[973] § 3.8 of Anlage B to § 9 SchSV.

However, this option does not fundamentally change the situation either, as it does not influence the function of the classification society in the administrative proceedings. And in fact these surveys are hardly ever undertaken by the *SeeBG.* Last but not least, the regulations that relate to licensed motor-vehicle experts include a provision which defines the recourse of the state against these experts. State liability law protects the person who acts for the state, and as a basic principle only allows recourse to be taken if the person caused grossly negligent or wilful injury or damage.[974] Therefore, recourse which is based on negligence must be regulated accordingly. However, there is no such regulation with respect to classification societies. The existence of such express law on recourse is, however, not of relevance to determining whether or not the survey and control that is exercised by classification societies has to be considered as part of the administrative proceedings.[975] The classification society is therefore so closely integrated in the administrative proceedings when issuing attestations that it must be deemed to be an official in the sense of the law of State liability.[976]

b. Preconditions of § 839 BGB

When it acts on behalf of the government, the activity of the classification society may provide the claimant with an actionable claim in tort against the administrative body on whose behalf it is acting pursuant to § 839 BGB in conjunction with Article 34 of the Grundgesetz (GG), the Basic Law of Germany.[977] It requires that an official duty has not been performed, that this official duty exists not only towards the general public, but also for the protection of the injured party, and the actual fault of the official with regard to the fact that the duty has not been performed, not the damage that arises therefrom.

An "official duty" is a duty of the administration which has to be performed by the official. If he undertakes an illicit misfeasance or fails to carry out an activity which he is obliged to do, the official is in breach of that duty. There are an almost limitless number of official duties. An official, for instance, has to ascertain the relevant facts, must give advice and must refrain from causing damage to third parties; he also has to act in accordance with the applicable regulations. A classification society, when acting on behalf of the German maritime administration, therefore has to carry out the surveys as required by § 3.4 of the Anlage B to § 9 SchSV. It must not thereby cause any damage to third parties. When analysing

---

974 Art. 34 sentence 2 GG.

975 This has been held in a case which relates to the survey of the airworthiness of BGH 2 November 2000, [2001] *NZV* 343, at 345.

976 Similar result: Drobnig, *Tätigkeit und Haftung von Klassifikationsgesellschaften in der Bundesrepublik Deutschland am Beispiel des Germanischen Lloyd* (1995), at 127; Herber, *Seehandelsrecht* (1999), 176.

977 § 839 BGB: (1) If an official wilfully or negligently commits a breach of official duty incumbent upon him against a third party, he shall compensate the third party for any damage arising therefrom. If only negligence is imputable to the official, he may be held liable only if the injured party is unable to obtain compensation elsewhere.

whether a certain party is a "protected third party" in the sense of § 839 BGB, one needs to scrutinise whether the affected interest shall be protected from the point of view of the intended purpose and the legal character of the official functions. The main issue is whether the administration has to take into consideration the interests of circumscribable third parties which deserve protection.[978] The official duty must, not necessarily solely but at least in part, aim at the protection of the interests of the injured third party.

There is generally no official duty to refrain from any activity which might cause economic loss. Economic loss is not in the scope of protection of such official duties.[979] An obligatory survey of the safety of a car not only protects the general public, but also each and every third party which may be affected by an unsafe car that is nonetheless allowed to drive on the roads.[980] A similar official duty must be recognised with regard to classification societies as well. Statutory surveys are carried out in order to ensure the safety of the vessel. Yet the different conventions strive to achieve differing aims. LL aims at safeguarding life and property at sea.[981] The official duty when carrying out LL calculations therefore relates to both the protection of crew and passengers, as well as cargo interests. SOLAS by contrast only seeks to protect safety of life at sea.[982] Its provisions indicate that it seeks to protect those persons who are on board the vessel, but also persons who may also be affected by a collision.[983] Mistakes which occur when a SOLAS survey is carried out are therefore relevant in all cases of personal injury thereby caused. MARPOL shall preserve the human environment in general and the marine environment in particular, which includes the preservation of the seas and coastal environment from pollution.[984] MARPOL, therefore, does not envisage the protection of individual third parties; one may only consider whether it seeks to protect the coastal state, as it intends to protect the coastal environment from pollution. An official duty extends towards third parties if the maritime administration or the classification society has to take into account the interests of the coastal State when undertaking the official act.[985] For instance, Article 8 (3) (b) as well as Article V of Protocol I, and Annex I Regulation 11 (c) to MARPOL illustrate that this convention not only tries to protect the marine environment, but also the State which may be harmed by a case of oil pollution.

The large number of controlled vessels and surveys which makes it impossible to guarantee the safety of each and every vessel does not eliminate such a duty.[986]

---

978 BGH 6 July 1989, [1990] *NJW* 381; BGH 1 February 2001, [2001] *NVwZ* 1074.

979 *See* for example BGH 27 May 1963, 39 BGHZ 358, at 364–365; BGH 11 January 1973, [1973] *NJW* 458.

980 OLG Koblenz 2 September 2002, [2003] *NJW* 297, at 298.

981 *See* LL, Preamble.

982 SOLAS, Preamble. The ISPS Code also aims at security.

983 For example Art. V, Annex I, Part A, Regulation 7 *et seq.*

984 MARPOL, Preamble.

985 *See* BGH 6 July 1989, [1990] *NJW* 381.

986 *See* OLG Koblenz 2 September 2002, [2003] *NJW* 297, at 298.

There is no freedom to act without responsibility or liability; every other solution would contradict the protection of the general public. The attestation that the vessel complies with the statutory regulations does not guarantee that the vessel is free of defects or even constitutes a liability regardless of negligence or fault. It solely declares that at the time of the inspection the vessel was free of deficiencies which would have debarred the vessel's seaworthiness. Within these limits there will, however, be a state liability if it turns out that there was a deficiency at the time of the survey which was overlooked contrary to duty and culpably and which was the cause of the casualty.[987] Despite the fact that a theoretically unlimited number of persons would be protected, such a duty exists. The claim is to be made against the body which recognised the classification society - in this case, the Federation (*Bund*).[988]

c. State Liability as a Subsidiary Liability

Whenever the surveyor of the classification society acts wilfully or grossly negligently, the administration will be liable for his behaviour. For behaviour which is only negligent, § 839 (1) 2 BGB lays down that the administration is merely liable on a subsidiary level. It only steps in if the plaintiff is unable to obtain compensation from someone else. However, it is irrelevant if some kind of insurance provides support for the plaintiff, as insurance claims are based on the achievement of the insured and do not exist for reasons of tortious behaviour by the insurance company.[989] A claim can only be subsidiary if it is based on the same factual allegations as the secondary claim.[990] The classification society usually performs classification and statutory surveys at the same time. For both kinds of surveys, a number of items need to be checked in the same or similar way. If the classification survey has been carried out negligently, the statutory survey may have to be qualified in the same way. The SOLAS safety construction certificate pursuant to Chapter II–1, Regulation 3–1, will also be issued if the vessel is in possession of a classification by a recognised classification society.

If the liability of the classification society for the classification surveys were limited, the principle of subsidiarity would not be of any relevance. From the outset, the claims against the classification society would most probably not meet the damage that has been caused. In view of such insufficient claims, the administration is not subsidiarily liable.[991] The current situation, however, is more complex, as there is no such limitation. As regards negligent behaviour which occurred at a class survey, a claim against the administration for incorrect surveys relating to the SOLAS safety construction certificate is based on the same factual circum-

---

987 *See also* OLG Koblenz 2 September 2002, [2003] *NJW* 297, at 298–299.

988 *Compare* Ossenbühl, Staatshaftungsrecht (1998), at 17.

989 Hüber, 'Haftungsprobleme der technischen Kontrolle', [1988] *NJW* 441, at 442; Ossenbühl, *Staatshaftungsrecht* (1998), at 83 with further references.

990 BGH 9 November 1959, 31 BGHZ 148, at 150 BGH 16 January 1997, [1997] *WM* 375, at 390.

991 *Compare* BGH 10 May 1976, [1976] *WM* 873, at 874.

stances as the classification certificate itself. It is, therefore, subsidiary to the claim against the classification society. Regarding other claims, a plaintiff has to ascertain whether they relate to the same factual circumstances as a negligent classification, despite the fact that the aims of the statutory surveys and of the classification survey are not necessarily the same, as is also illustrated by the different aims of statutory certificates that have been described *supra.*[992]

Such a solution involves a number of problems. First and foremost, two litigations at the same time always carry the risk of differing judgments. If the factual circumstances of the statutory survey and the classification survey actually differ, differing judgments can be justified; otherwise they would cause severe confusion. Also, if it turns out during the litigation that the statutory survey was identical to a part of the classification survey, the plaintiff would lose. However, the plaintiff may not know all the facts and the precise way the surveys were carried out. In fact, not even the classification society may at all times be able to distinguish between a survey which was carried out for statutory purposes and one that was only due for classification. Especially if the surveys were carried out at the same time, it may be rather difficult, if not even impossible, to identify which part of the survey was of relevance for the classification and which one for the statutory certificate, and, in the same vein, whether the negligence only existed with regard to the one or the other activity. On the other hand, if one was to deny state liability in all cases relating to surveys by a classification society for the reason of factual difficulty, one would eliminate the possibility of the control of this activity on behalf of the maritime administration. In brief, the plaintiff should try to establish whether or not the presumably negligent survey was the basis for both the statutory and the classification certificate. If that was the case, he has only a claim against the classification society for the negligent classification. In doubt, the plaintiff should claim damages from both the classification society for the classification survey and the administration for the statutory survey.

2. *Recourse of the Flag State*

The legal basis of the recourse against the classification society is a breach of the agreement between the administration and the classification society.[993] It is a matter of contract law, and therefore similar to the liability in contract that has been addressed *supra.* The administration is not obliged to take recourse; it is only an option.[994] Article 34, 2nd Sentence GG, however, limits the recourse against the official in the sense of state liability to cases of wilful and gross negligent behav-

---

992 *See supra* Part 1 A IV, Part 1 B II 2.

993 § 280 (1) BGB in connection with the agreement. BGH 14 October 2004, [2005] *NJW* 286; *see also* Herschel, 'Die Haftung der technischen Überwachungs-Vereine', [1969] *NJW* 817, at 820; Ossenbühl, *Staatshaftungsrecht* (1998), 119. Different: Drobnig, *Tätigkeit und Haftung von Klassifikationsgesellschaften in der Bundesrepublik Deutschland am Beispiel des Germanischen Lloyd* (1995), at 128.

994 Stelkens, 'Amtshaftung und Regress bei Schädigungen durch Verwaltungshelfer', [2004] *JZ* 656, at 660.

iour. It is therefore an issue whether this provision applies to the case in which a private person is carrying out surveys for the use of the maritime administration.

The Federal Court of Justice (*Bundesgerichtshof*) has recently held that Article 34, 2nd Sentence GG does not apply to an independent private business which has been assigned to a limited extent the exercise of certain official functions.[995] The aim of this provision is to protect the official's freedom to come to a decision and the effectiveness of public administration.[996] This reasoning, however, does not apply to an independent private business, which has the liberty to take its own decisions. The business can decide the extent and the manner of undertaking the assignment, and whether it is worth taking over the risks of liability, which usually can be insured. It may include these costs in the calculation of its prices or else abstain from the activity if the risk is too high.[997] According to the *Bundesgerichtshof*, there is no justification to exempt even partially the contractor, which is the classification society, from its contractual liability to the administration.[998] The maritime administration can, therefore, in all cases take recourse against the classification society for liability which is inflicted upon it by a negligent act of the society.

Pursuant to Article 6 (2) (b) lit. ii, iii of the Council Directive 94/57/EC of 22 November 1994, the Member States may decide to limit the liability of the classification society to recourse by the maritime administration if the classification society undertakes fully or in part the mandatory inspections and surveys. Germany has not yet opted to set up such a limitation. There are neither any statutory limitations, nor do the agreements with the classification societies contain such a clause.

IV. Excursus: Damage Caused by Both a Classification and Statutory Survey

Theoretically, damage can be caused by both a classification and a statutory survey. Especially in those cases in which the classification society exercises these surveys at the same time or if the existence of a classification is sufficient proof to show that the requirements are fulfilled, such as in the case of the SOLAS Cargo Ship Safety Certificate,[999] a single activity may be relevant both to liability for the

---

[995] BGH 14 October 2004, [2005] *NJW* 286, at 287.

[996] BGH 14 October 2004, [2005] *NJW* 286, at 288.

[997] BGH 14 October 2004, [2005] *NJW* 286, at 288. Similarly Stelkens, 'Amtshaftung und Regress bei Schädigungen durch Verwaltungshelfer', [2004] *JZ* 656, at 660; Quantz, 'Die Rückgriffsbeschränkung des Art. 34 S. 2 GG im Innenregress gegen Private', [2004] *VersR* 1244, at 1247.

[998] BGH 14 October 2004, [2005] *NJW* 286, at 288. *See also* Stelkens, 'Amtshaftung und Regress bei Schädigungen durch Verwaltungshelfer', [2004] *JZ* 656, at 660–661; Quantz, 'Die Rückgriffsbeschränkung des Art. 34 S. 2 GG im Innenregress gegen Private', [2004] *VersR* 1244, at 1247–1248.

[999] SOLAS Rule I/12.

exercise of private as well as public functions. However, despite the fact that the shipowner is obliged by the regulations to possess a certain number of statutory certificates, but not necessarily of a private classification, neither of these two kinds of liability prevails. There is no principle that the liability for the exercise of a statutory survey could pre-empt the liability for a classification survey. There is no reason for such pre-emption either, since these are two acts from a legal point of view. The fact that these two functions may actually be exercised at the same time or based on the same act does not change their legal character.

Of course, the disadvantage is that this could require two different proceedings which may result in two different verdicts. However, at the same time the defendants are not necessarily the same (in the case of statutory surveys, it may also be the maritime administration, which has granted authority to the classification society, as the preceding sections illustrate). Also, the standard of care is first determined by international or domestic regulations and secondly by the classification society's rules. If damage is caused by the exercise of both a private and a public function, the injured party may claim damages based on both functions.

Part 3 [A Convention on the Limitation of Liability of Classification Societies]

In order to facilitate the discussion of a convention which limits the liability of classification societies, the system of limitations will initially be analysed, and it will be scrutinised whether classification societies are protected by these regulations when performing their private duties such as issuing classification certificates. The limitation of liability in shipping generally applies only to the exercise of private activities, not of public ones. Furthermore, it shall be discussed whether a convention that would limit the liability of classification societies for the performance of private duties could be justified, and its principles will be determined. Sections A to D mainly relate to the private functions of a classification society. In section E, it will finally be considered whether such a convention should relate only to private classification or also to a society's public functions, *i.e.*, the performance of statutory surveys.

A. The Limitation of Liability in Shipping

There is a distinct system of limitations of liability in shipping, which channels the liability on the shipowner while exempting other members of the shipping industry from liability. This concept of channelling of liability on one person reflects the fact that it is primarily the shipowner who manages and controls his ship and derives revenue from its operation. Accordingly, it is also he who is legally responsible for the operation of his ship. The shipowner has to make sure that the applicable laws and international rules and regulations are observed. Therefore, the concept of channelling the liability on the shipowner mirrors his responsibility for the ship.

Channelling liability implies that only one (or a small number) of responsible persons are held accountable.[1000] Such channelling that is provided by law, as in shipping law, is called '*legal channelling*'. Channelling liability saves several lay-

---

[1000] Faure/Hui, 'The International Regimes for the Compensation of Oil-Pollution Damage; Are they Effective?', 12 *RECIEL* 242, at 250 (2003); Lammers, 'International Responsibility and Liability for Damage Caused by Environmental Interferences', 31 *Envtl. Pol'y & L.* 94, at 100 (2001).

ers of insurance of the same risk.[1001] There are also advantages relating to subsequent litigation. In the case of an effective channelling, all claims can be treated in one single proceeding. For the victim it has the advantage that he knows the person against whom he may claim damages and that there is only one hearing of evidence required.

In contrast to '*legal channelling*', one talks of '*economic channelling*' whenever the injured party for economic reasons prefers to sue a person other than the one who shall be primarily liable under the law. Not the shipowner but other members of the shipping business such as shipyards, which do not benefit from a limitation of their liability, may be sued because of low levels of compensation or even the lack of insurance of the shipowner in some instances.

I. The History of Limitations

Limitations of liability in shipping are the result of a long historical development. Their origins are, however, not entirely clear.[1002] Some authors trace them back to the Roman law principle of *noxae deditio*[1003], under which an owner could protect himself from liability. If the owner gave up the instrument which caused the harm, for example, for the acts of a slave by turning over the slave to the injured party,[1004] he could discharge himself from liability. Others refer to the Amalfian Table, which was the commercial code of the Italian republic of Amalfi.[1005] Some scholars have identified the *Consolato del Mare*, which was promulgated in the fourteenth century by the Aragonian kings and allowed a shipowner to limit his liability to the value of his share in the ship.[1006] In 1625, *Hugo Grotius* phrased a public need for a limitation of liability of the shipowner:

[1001] Rémond-Gouilloud, 'The Future of the Compensation System as Established by International Convention' in De La Rue, *Liability for Damage to the Marine Environment* (1993), at 95.

[1002] Abecassis/Jarashow, *Oil Pollution from Ships* (1985), § 9–29, at 185; Benedict, *On Admiralty* (2002), vol. 3, at 1–31; Donovan, 'The origins and development of limitation of shipowner's liability', 53 *Tul.L.Rev.* 999, at 1000 (1979); Eyer, 'Shipowner's Limitation of Liability–New Directions for an Old Doctrine', 16 *Stan.L.Rev.* 370, at 370 (1964); Gauci, *Oil Pollution at Sea, Civil Liability and Compensation for Damage* (1997), at 157; Özçayir, *Liability for Oil Pollution and Collisions* (1998), 299; *The Main v. Williams*, 152 U.S. 122, 14 S.Ct. 488, 38 L.Ed. 381 (1894).

[1003] Holmes, *The Common Law*, at 16 (1881); Marsden/Gault, *Marsden on collisions at sea* (2003). para. 172.

[1004] Holmes, *The Common Law*, at 10–16 (1881).

[1005] Özçayir, *Liability for Oil Pollution and Collisions* (1998), 299–300.

[1006] *The Main v. Williams,* 152 U.S. 122, at 126 (1894); Putnam, 'The Limited Liability of Ship-Owners for Master's Faults', 17 *Am.L.Rev.* 1 (1883).

> '[M]en would be deterred from employing ships, if they lay under the perpetual fear of being answerable for the acts of their masters to an unlimited extent… [This would not be] conducive to the public good.'[1007]

At that time, the shipowner had virtually no influence on the ship after it left port. He had no control over the vessel, its master or crew for months, sometimes even for years. It was therefore criticised that the principle of *respondeat superior* would be unfair because of the lack of control.[1008] Owners of ships could find themselves ruined without any fault on their part or any kind of influence.[1009] Moreover, shipping was a risky business, which made it necessary to limit the liability at stake to what the shipowner voluntarily puts at risk.[1010] In public opinion, holding the shipowner liable for an unlimited amount was considered to be unfair, especially since there was neither protection in the form of a limited liability company or in a generally available system of marine insurance.[1011] Many countries also feared that unlimited liability might be contrary to their needs for a strong national merchant marine.[1012]

Similar systems of limitation were developed almost simultaneously under different domestic laws.[1013] One can differentiate between the German, French and English systems, which came into existence by the middle of the nineteenth century.[1014] The German system did not place liability on the shipowner even if he

---

[1007] Grotius, *De Jure Belli ac Pacis libri tres* (1646/1995), at 139.

[1008] Schoenbaum, *Admiralty and Maritime Law* (2004), § 15–1, at 136.

[1009] Lord Mustill, 'Ships are different–or are they?', [1993] *L.M.C.L.Q.* 490, at 492.

[1010] Holmes, *The Common Law* (1881), 9.

[1011] Eyer, 'Shipowners' Limitation of Liability', 16 *Stan.L.Rev.* 370, at 372 (1964); Gilmore/Black, *The Law of Admiralty* (1975), 818; Lord Mustill, 'Ships are different–or are they?', [1993] *L.M.C.L.Q.* 490, at 492; Seward, 'The Insurance Viewpoint' in: Institute of Maritime Law, The University of Southampton, *The Limitation of Shipowners' Liability: The New Law* (1986), 161–162. Some authors appear to argue that the limitation of liability was established due to the fact that shipping was so dangerous in nature that incidents were most likely to happen. Tetley, 'Shipowners' Limitation of Liability and Conflicts of Law: The Properly Applicable Law', 23 *J.M.L.C.* 585 (1992): 'Limitation of shipowners' liability is a universal concept amongst shipping nations and recognizes the potentially perilous nature of maritime transport.' Similarly Seward, *ibid.*, 166.

[1012] *See* Eyer, 'Shipowners' Limitation of Liability', 16 *Stan.L.Rev.* 370, at 371 (1964) with further references; Killingbeck, 'Limitation of Liability for Maritime Claims and Its Place In the Past, Present and Future', *3 SCU L.R.* 1 (1999).

[1013] In *The Main v. Williams*, 152 U.S. 122, at 126 (1894) Mr Justice Brown referred to the following Codes which were in force at the time of the decision: Argentine Code, Art. 1039; Belgian Code, Art. 216; Brazilian Code, Art. 494; Chilean Code, Art. 879; Code de Commerce (French), Art. 216; German Maritime Code, Art. 452; Italian Code, Art. 311; Code of the Netherlands, Art. 321; Portuguese Code, Art. 1345; Russian Code, Art. 649; Spanish Code, Art. 621, 622.

[1014] *Eyer,* 'Shipowners' Limitation of Liability', 16 *Stan.L.Rev.* 370, at 371 (1964); Özçayir, *Liability for Oil Pollution and Collisions* (1998), 301–302.

was at fault, but submitted the ship to an *in rem* action.[1015] The French system of *abandon,* as incorporated in the French Ordinance of 1681,[1016] allowed the owner to discharge his obligations by handing over the ship and its cargo to the claimants, despite the fact that he was personally liable in principle. Only the English system limited the claims against the shipowner to the value of the ship *before* the incident took place.[1017] English law required that a shipowner had no 'privity and knowledge'.[1018] It granted limitation only for claims arising out of wrongful acts committed by the owner's servants in the course of their service to the ship.[1019] This was laid down in the English *Responsibility of Shipowners Act* of 1733.[1020] Moreover, the English system established different liability rules for personal claims. Under the 1854 Merchant Shipping Act, the limitation fund had to be at least 15 pounds sterling per ton in the case of a death or personal injury claim.[1021] The preamble to the *Responsibility of Shipowners Act* of 1734 clearly stated the intentions of the lawmaker:

> 'Whereas it is of the greatest consequence and importance to this kingdom, to promote the increase of the number of ships and vessels, and to prevent any discouragement to merchants and others from being interested and concerned therein; and whereas it has been held, that in many cases owners of ships or vessels are answerable for goods and merchandise shipped or put aboard the same, although the said goods and merchandise, after the same have been so put on board, should be made away with by the masters or mariners of the said ships or vessels, without knowledge or privity of the owner or owners by means whereof merchants and others are greatly discouraged from adventuring their fortunes, as owners of ships or vessels, which will necessarily tend to the prejudice of trade and navigation of this kingdom.'[1022]

1015 Tetley, *International Maritime and Admiralty Law* (2002), 274.

1016 The French Ordinance of 1681 served as a model of most of the modern maritime codes, *see The Main v. Williams*, 152 U.S. 122, at 126 (1894).

1017 Selvig, 'An Introduction to the 1976 Convention' in Institute of Maritime Law, The University of Southampton (ed.), *The Limitation of Shipowners' Liability: The New Law* (1986), at 4; Tetley, *International Maritime and Admiralty Law* (2002), 273.

1018 *Putnam*, 'The Limited Liability of Ship-Owners for Master's Faults', 17 *Am.L.Rev.* 1, at 5–13 (1883).

1019 Özçayir, *Liability for Oil Pollution and Collisions* (1998), 303.

1020 For the historical development of this Act *see* Lord Mustill, 'Ships are different–or are they?', [1993] *L.M.C.L.Q.* 490, at 496–497; Özçayir, *Liability for Oil Pollution and Collisions* (1998), 313–316.

1021 *See* Lord Mustill, 'Ships are different–or are they?', [1993] *L.M.C.L.Q.* 490, at 498; Özçayir, *Liability for Oil Pollution and Collisions* (1998), 304.

1022 Quoted in Lord Mustill, 'Ships are different–or are they?', [1993] *L.M.C.L.Q.* 490, at 496–497; *compare* Eyer, 'Shipowners' Limitation of Liability', 16 *Stan.L.Rev.* 370, at 371 fn. 9 (1964); Steel, 'Ships are different: the case for limitation of liability', [1995] *L.M.C.L.Q.* 77, at 79.

In the United States, it took until 1851 to develop a *Limitation of Liability Act.*[1023] Under United States law, liability was initially limited to the value of the vessel after the incident took place.[1024] This limitation was valid whether it was a claim in tort or in contract by seamen, passengers, shippers or stevedores.[1025] Similarly to the English system, a fund of at least USD 60 per gross ton for each distinct occasion had to be established for personal claims.[1026]

The shipping industry had to wait until 1924 for an international harmonisation of these limitations to take place, when both the Hague Rules[1027] and the International Convention for the Unification of Certain Rules Relating to the Limitation of the Liability of Owners of Sea-Going Vessels[1028] were adopted. Unlike the aforementioned national limitations, these two conventions distinguish between claims by parties of a contract of carriage and claims by other parties. The Hague Rules define contractual liability. The Brussels Convention of 1924, by contrast, limits the liability of the shipowner for all kinds of maritime claims, including those of third parties.

II. Cargo Limitations

The Hague Rules of 1924 were established at a time when carriers tended to exclude in their contracts all liability towards the shipper. It was thought to be against public interest if the carrier was completely exempt from any liability towards his contracting party. With regard to third parties, however, a different solution was chosen. For this reason, there was one convention regarding contractual parties, the Hague Rules, and another convention dealing with third parties, the Brussels Convention of 1924. While the Brussels Convention was still based on the traditional concept of limitation, the aim of the Hague Rules was not so much to protect the carrier, who is the shipowner or the charterer, but to protect the shipper. The carrier could no longer exclude his liability for damages which occur

---

[1023] Currently codified at 46 U.S.C. §§ 181–189. Initial to this Act was the decision in *New Jersey Steam Navigation Company v. Merchant's Bank (The Lexington),* 47 U.S. 344 (1848). Therein a shipowner who was unaware of the nature of his cargo was held fully liable for the loss of USD 18,000 in gold coins.

[1024] *See* the inter*pretation* of this Act by the Supreme Court in *Norwich Co. v. Wright,* 80 U.S. 104 (1871).

[1025] For further details on the different limitation provisions *see* Benedict, *On Admiralty* (2002), vol. 3, at § 4 and 21; Gilmore/Black, *The Law of Admiralty* (1975), ch. X.

[1026] 46 U.S.C. § 183 (b).

[1027] International Convention for the Unification of Certain Rules of Law relating to Bills of Lading (Hague Rules). Brussels, 25 August 1924, entry into force: 2 June 1931, 120 LNTS 155; 2 Bevans 430.

[1028] International Convention for the Unification of Certain Rules Relating to the Limitation of the Liability of Owners of Sea-Going Vessels, Brussels, 25 August 1924, entry into force: 2 June 1931, 120 LNTS 123. It is only in force in respect of Brazil, the Dominican Republic and Hungary.

at the time of the journey of the vessel. The carrier was only allowed to stipulate an exemption for the time of custody and care and handling of goods prior to the loading on and subsequent to the discharge from the ship.[1029] The limitations which were included in the Hague Rules were only meant to bar compensation for unforeseeably high damage. Despite the fact that most legal orders already require damages to be reasonable, the intention was to set out an internationally harmonised level of liability that the shipowner might possibly incur. As a result, the limits were quite high in the value of that time, also because the size of the packages was quite small. Each and every item had to be stowed by hand and therefore needed to be limited in size and weight. The carrier's liability should be limited to a level which he could reasonably foresee. He should be fully liable in almost all cases; only those few incidents of unexpectedly high damage, such as the loss of a package of precious stones and other valuables, should be excluded. Valuables should be declared separately. However, since such a declaration involved higher costs than additional self-insurance by the cargo-owner, this instrument never became of any relevance to the shipping industry.[1030]

The reason for the channelling of the liability on the carrier is the contractual relationship with the shipper. The carrier is not liable for loss or damage resulting under several different circumstances.[1031] In any case, neither the carrier nor the ship is liable in connection with goods for an amount exceeding 100 pounds sterling per package or unit unless the shipper declared the value of the goods before the shipment.[1032] In 1979, the definition in pounds sterling was replaced by the Special Drawing Right (SDR) as defined by the International Monetary Fund.[1033] The maximum liability was then set at SDR 667.67 per package or SDR 2 per kilogramme of gross weight of the goods lost or damaged, whichever is the higher.

Nowadays the limitation appears to be rather low. The reasons are the devaluation of the defined amounts of money and an increase in the size of the packages

---

[1029] Article 7 of the Hague Rules.

[1030] Herber, *Seehandelsrecht* (1999), 332. *Compare also* Basedow, *Der Transportvertrag* (1987), 410, 494.

[1031] Article 4 of the Hague Rules specifies that neither the carrier nor the ship is liable for loss or damage resulting from unseaworthiness of the vessel, unless it is caused by want of due diligence on the part of the carrier to make the ship seaworthy (para.1). Likewise, he is not liable for act, neglect or default of the master, mariner, pilot, or the servants of the carrier in the navigation or the management of the ship (para. 2 (a)), for fire, unless caused by the actual fault or privity of the carrier (para. 2 (b)), for perils of the sea (para. 2 (c)), act of god, war or public enemies (para. 2 (d–e)), and several other incidents.

[1032] Art. 4 (5) of the Hague Rules.

[1033] Protocol (SDR Protocol) amending the International Convention for the Unification of Certain Rules of Law relating to Bills of Lading of 25 August 1924 (The Hague Rules), as amended by the Protocol of 23 February 1968 (Visby Rules), Brussels, 21 December 1979, entry into force 14 February 1984, ATS 1993 No. 23; UKTS 1984 No. 28 (Cmnd. 9197).

in the age of containers. The importance of the Hague Rules is restricted to the definition of a minimum level of compensation for matters of insurance of both the carrier and the shipper. The shipper is no longer protected by the liability regime. He has to ensure his own protection by way of insurance of the cargo. The entire system of several layers of insurance has adapted to the rather extensive limitations set by the Hague Rules and their successors.[1034] Despite the fact that the Hague Rules used to aim at holding the carrier primarily responsible, the decrease in the value of the compensation has changed it into a system which motivates self-protection by the injured party against any possible damage. The channelling of liability on the shipowner is no longer effective.

III. Global Limitations

In contrast to the Cargo Limitations of the Hague Rules, under which the contractual partner knows exactly what amount he will receive as compensation, the global limitations of liability also relate to third parties who may not know that their rights and interests are limited. Global limitations of liability limit the shipowner's liability for all claims which arise on a certain occasion and during a certain time or in connection with a certain venture. The Hague Rules at least intended to give the shipper the opportunity to influence the liability regime by the declaration of the value of the goods; the third party, however, cannot influence the liability regime under the Brussels Convention or the LLMC. Global limitations of liability therefore have the effect that the victim will not get full compensation, regardless of his behaviour or influence.

Before these conventions were enacted, domestic regulations generally awarded compensation to the injured party only up to a maximum of the value of the vessel, either before or after the incident.[1035] At the time the conventions were concluded, there was no unlimited liability of the shipowner; on the contrary, his liability was strictly limited. The new conventions established higher limits, thereby improving the position of the injured party. Gradually the limits changed to these higher levels, which still may not be sufficient today. A complete abolition of all limits would, however, be unthinkable. Unless the entire world abolished its limi-

[1034] Amended by the Protocol to amend the International Convention for the Unification of certain Rules of Law relating to Bills of Lading (Visby Protocol), Brussels, 23 February 1968, entry into force: 23 June 1977, 1412 UNTS 127. Amended by the Protocol of 1979 to amend the International Convention for the Unification of certain Rules of Law Relating to Bills of Lading, 1924, as amended by the Protocol of 1968 (SDR Protocol), Brussels, 21 December 1979, entry into force 14 February 1984, ATS 1993 No. 23. United Nations Convention on the Carriage of Goods by Sea, Hamburg, 31 March 1978, entry into force: 1 November 1992 (The Hamburg Rules), 17 ILM 608, *see* Basedow, 'Seefrachtrecht: Die Hamburger Regeln sind in Kraft', (1993) *ZEuP* 100; Puttfarken, *Seehandelsrecht* (1997), at 126–130.

[1035] *See also supra* Part 3 A I.

tations, an abrogation by only a number of countries would result in significant competitive disadvantages for shipowners who operate under a flag which has abrogated the limitation provisions and established unlimited liability. As shipping has always been a global market, and is considered to be important not only for the national economy but also for the strategic value to each country, countries refrain from any action which is likely to penalise and destabilise their domestic merchant fleet.

The first of the Global Limitation Conventions, the 1924 Convention,[1036] relates to claims of third parties against the shipowner and limits his liability for damage caused by the master, crew, pilot or any other person in the service of the vessel to the value of the vessel and its freight after the incident unless the owner was at fault.[1037] For death or bodily injury, the maximum liability a shipowner incurred was 8 pounds sterling per ton of the vessel's tonnage.[1038] As the level of compensation was considered to be insufficient, the 1924 Convention was followed by the International Convention Relating to the Limitation of the Liability of Owners of Sea-Going Ships of 1957.[1039] The Brussels Convention of 1957 aimed at harmonising the limitations of the liability of the shipowner and the ship[1040] and at increasing the level of compensation. It only relates to claims for loss of life or personal injury,[1041] claims for damage to property on board the ship and to claims for wreck removal.[1042] In order to benefit from the limitation, the owner has to set up a fund which represents an equivalent of 1,000 gold francs for each ton of the ship's tonnage if the occurrence has only given rise to property claims or 3,100 gold francs if only personal claims have been caused.[1043] If both personal and property claims are caused, 2,100 gold francs per ton are reserved for personal claims and 1,000 gold francs per ton for property claims. The shipowner cannot limit his liability if the claim resulted from his actual fault or privity. The channelling clause included in Article 6 exempts the charterer, manager and operator as well as the master, members of the crew and other servants if the shipowner or any of them

[1036] International Convention for the Unification of Certain Rules Relating to the Limitation of the Liability of Owners of Sea-Going Vessels, Brussels, 25 August 1924, came into force on 2 June 1931, 120 LNTS 123. It only applies in Brazil, the Dominican Republic and Hungary.

[1037] Art. 1–3 of the Convention.

[1038] Art. 7 of the Convention.

[1039] International Convention Relating to the Limitation of the Liability of Owners of Sea-Going Ships of 1957, Brussels, 10 October 1057, came into force on 31 May 1968, RMC II.2.310. It applies in Belize, the Democratic Republic of Congo, Dominica, Fiji, Ghana, Grenada, Iceland, Iran, Israel, Kiribati, Luxembourg, Monaco, Papua New Guinea, Portugal, St. Vincent and the Grenadines, Seychelles, Syrian Arab Republic and Tuvalu.

[1040] *See* the Preamble to the Convention.

[1041] There is no limitation towards crew members if the contract of service does not allow the shipowner to limit his liability or if it provides for higher levels, Article 1 (4) (a).

[1042] Article 1 of the Convention.

[1043] Article 3 (1).

sets up such a fund. Even if the master or crew members are at actual fault, they can limit their liability.[1044] As a result, there is no channelling on only one person; the regulation rather envisages everyone that may have been responsible for the damage. Only if one of these persons sets up a fund will the clause exempt the others and channel liability on this person.

However, despite the fact that the United States took part in the Brussels Conference, they did not sign the Convention of 1957 on the grounds that they considered its limits to be too low. It may, however, be surprising that the limitations which are contained in the United States *Limitation of Liability Act* grant the shipowner the right to limit his liability to the value of the ship and her freight after the incident, and therefore to a much lower limit.[1045]

In 1976, the Convention on Limitation of Liability for Maritime Claims was signed in London. Levels of limitations were once again increased and a global limitation of liability for maritime claims was established, which has been ratified by 47 countries accounting for 46.11 percent of the world's tonnage.[1046] The LLMC not only envisages shipowners, but also allows salvors to limit their liability. In the same way, the charterer, manager or operator of a ship may call upon limitation provisions, as well as any person for whose act, neglect or default they or the owner are responsible. Liability for claims in respect of loss of life or personal injury is limited, as well as loss or damage to property occurring on board or in direct connection with the operation of the ship. Claims for delay in the carriage of cargo or passengers are also covered, as is loss resulting from the infringement of non-contractual rights and claims relating to wrecks. The shipowner's liability is limited to a certain amount per ton, which has subsequently been increased.[1047]

[1044] Article 6 (3).

[1045] 46 U.S.C. § 183 (a), *see* Schoenbaum, *Admiralty and Maritime Law* (2002), § 15–7, at 155; Chen, *Limitation of Liability for Maritime Claims* (2001), at 94–102. That the limitations were too low was also criticised in *In re Barracuda Tanker Corp. (S/T Torrey Canyon)*, 281 F.Supp. 228 (S.D.N.Y.1968), remanded 409 F.2d 1013 (2d Cir.1969). As an illustration for the discussions of that time, *see* Gilmore/Black, *The Law of Admiralty* (1975), § 10–4(a), at 823–824.

[1046] It has been directly transposed into domestic law by six more countries. Convention on Limitation of Liability for Maritime Claims, 1976 (LLMC 1976), London, 19 November 1976, entry into force: 1 December 1986, UNTS I–24635, 1456 UNTS 221; 16 ILM 606; ATS 1991 No. 12; UKTS 1990 No. 13 (Cm 955). As amended by the Protocol Amending the Convention on Limitation of Liability for Maritime Claims, London, 2 May 1996, entry into force: 13 May 2004, 35 ILM 1433; IMO Doc. LEG/CONF.10/8 of 9 May 1996. The Protocol has been ratified by 17 States accounting for 13.87 percent of the world's tonnage. Information on the percentage of the world's tonnage is based on national statistics as at 31 August 2005 and can be accessed online at <www.imo.org>, last accessed on 19 March 2007. On statistics of maritime transportation services *compare* Parameswaran, *The Liberalization of Maritime Transport Services* (2004), at 17–22.

[1047] Under the 1976 Convention the limits of liability are for loss of life and personal injury (respectively other damage) 333,000 (167,000) Special Drawing Rights (SDR) of the

The LLMC has significantly been revised by the Protocol of 1996, which came into force on 13 May 2004. The Protocol increased nearly twenty-fold the financial expenditure and dropped the ceiling of 25 million Special Drawing Rights per ship with regard to loss of life or personal injury of passengers, which had existed before.[1048] The salvor's liability does not depend on the tonnage of the vessel which he saves, but on the tonnage of his own vessel. If he works on the ship in respect of which he is rendering salvage services or does not operate from a ship (but for example from a helicopter), the salvor's liability is calculated as if he was operating from a vessel with a tonnage of 1,500.[1049] Hence his liability is, in most cases, considerably lower than the shipowner's. These differences in the level of compensation illustrate the fact that even during salvage operations the shipowner shall be primarily responsible for the ship, not the salvor. The LLMC also incorporates a different wording to that of the Brussels Convention regarding the clause which relates to the conduct which bars limitation. A person shall not be entitled to limit his liability only if it is proven that the loss resulted from the personal act or omission of this person, committed with the intent to cause such loss, or recklessly and with knowledge that such loss would probably result.[1050] However, until today this Protocol is only in force in 17 countries accounting for 13.87% of the world's tonnage.

Liability is not channelled on one person by the LLMC. Not only can the shipowner be held liable, but also the charterer, manager or operator of the ship, who are also included in the definition of *shipowner*, as well as all persons for whose act, neglect or default these persons are responsible. However, if any of those persons who can be held liable sets up a fund, all the others benefit and are exempt from liability to third parties as well. They can only be subject to recourse of the person who set up the fund. Because of the often limited financial capacity of the servants and agents of the owner, usually the shipowner or the charterer or man-

---

International Monetary Fund for up to 500 tons of tonnage, for each ton from 501 to 3,000 tons an additional SDR 500 (167), for each ton from 3,001 to 30,000 tons SDR 333 (167), for each ton from 30,001 to 70,000 tons an additional SDR 250 (167), and in excess of 70,000 tons SDR 167 (83). Passenger claims were limited to SDR 46,666, multiplied by the number of passengers which the ship is authorised to carry. However, a ceiling of SDR 25 million exists for passenger claims. Under the 1996 Protocol, this ceiling has been abandoned. Passenger claims are thereafter limited to SDR 175,000 multiplied by the number of passengers the vessel is authorised to carry. Claims for loss of life or personal injury of persons other than passengers (or any other claims) are limited to SDR 2 (1) million for a ship of up to 2,000 tons, for each ton from 2,001 to 30,000 tons there is an additional SDR 800 (400), for each ton from 30,0001 to 70,000 tons SDR 600 (300), and for each ton in excess of 70,000 tons SDR 400 (200).

[1048] See Article 7 (1) of the LLMC in the version before the amendements of the 1996 Protocol.

[1049] Article 6 (4), (1). Under the 1976 Convention it is fixed at SDR 833,000 in case of personal injury or SDR 164,000 in case of other claims. This has been revised in the 1996 Protocol to SDR 2 million for personal injury and SDR 1 million for other claims.

[1050] Article 5 LLMC.

ager will set up such a fund. The LLMC therefore channels the liability on the shipowner, charterer, manager or the operator who is responsible for the ship, but does not do so in an exclusive way unless and until any one of them sets up a fund.

IV. Limitations as Regards Passengers

The Athens Convention Relating to the Carriage of Passengers and Their Luggage by Sea (PAL 1974) was signed in 1974.[1051] Its aim was to harmonise the regulations relating to passengers and their luggage and to increase the levels of liability.[1052] The Athens Convention relates to both the contract of carriage between the passenger and the carrier and the liability in tort of the person who actually performs the carriage, the *performing carrier*.[1053] In its first dimension, the Athens Convention defines a minimum liability for contracts of carriage and prohibits more restrictive exemption or limitation clauses in the contract of carriage. Furthermore, it defines that the carrier is legally responsible for the performing carrier. In addition to that, the Athens Convention also defines the levels of compensation up to which the performing carrier can be held liable in tort. The convention

1051 Athens Convention Relating to the Carriage of Passengers and Their Luggage by Sea, 1974, Athens, 13 December 1974, entry into force: 28 April 1987 (PAL 1974), 1463 UNTS 20, 14 ILM 945, RMC I.5.190, II.5.190; Protocol (of 1976) to the Athens Convention relating to the Carriage of Passengers and their Luggage by Sea, 1974 (PAL PROT 1976), Athens, 13 December 1974, entry into force: 30 April 1989, 16 ILM 625, RMC I.5.200, II.5.200; UKTS 43 (1989); Protocol of 1990 to amend the Athens Convention relating to the Carriage of Passengers and their Luggage by Sea, 1974 (PAL PROT 1990), adopted: 29 March 1990, not yet entered into force, IMO document(s): LEG/CONF 8/10 of 29 March 1990, RMC I .5.201, II.5.201; Protocol of 2002 to amend the Athens Convention relating to the Carriage of Passengers and their Luggage by Sea, 1974 (PAL PROT 2002), adopted: 1 November 2002, not yet in force, IMO document(s): LEG/CONF.13/20 of 19 November 2002, RMC I .5.202, II.5.202. PAL 1974 is in force in 32 contracting States, which represent 38.64% of the world's tonnage. The Protocol of 1990 has been ratified by 5 countries representing 0.82% of the world's tonnage, and the Protocol of 2002 by only 4 countries accounting for 0.13% of the world's tonnage. It appears that the leading shipping nations consider the limitations included in these Protocols as being too high.

1052 The levels of limitation are the following (with amendments by the 1976 Protocol in brackets): The liability for the death or personal injury of the passenger shall in no case exceed 700,000 gold francs (SDR 46,666) per carriage, for cabin luggage 12,500 gold francs (SDR 833) per passenger, for loss or damage to vehicles 50,000 gold francs per vehicle (SDR 3,333), and a maximum of 18,000 gold francs (SDR 1,200) for loss or damage to luggage which is not cabin luggage. The 1990 and 2002 Protocol, which establish considerably higher limits, have not yet come into force.

1053 This is the shipowner, charterer or operator who actually performed the carriage, Article 1 lit. 1 (b) PAL 1974.

harmonises and increases the levels of compensation with the intent to fix them at insurable levels. The limitations shall improve the situation of the passenger, since the liability of the shipowner was originally limited to the value of the vessel before or after the incident.

The Athens Convention reverses the burden of proof if the death or personal injury of the passenger or the loss or damage to cabin luggage arose from or in connection with the shipwreck, collision, stranding, explosion or fire, or defect in the ship.[1054] With regard to luggage which is not cabin luggage, the burden of proof lies with the carrier.[1055] For an incident, not only is the carrier liable, but also the performing carrier, who is also protected by the limitation provisions.[1056] The carrier is responsible for the acts and omissions of the performing carrier and his servants and agents.[1057] These servants and agents are not exempt from liability, but may also limit their liability in the same way as the carrier and the performing carrier.[1058] Once the passenger has received compensation from one party, he has no claim against the others.[1059] If both the carrier and the performing carrier are liable, their liability is joint and several[1060] and it results in a claim for contribution by the other. The limitations can only be exceeded if the damage resulted from an act or omission of the carrier or performing carrier done with the intent to cause such damage, or recklessly and with knowledge that such damage would probably result.[1061] If the damage resulted from such behaviour of the carrier's or performing carrier's servants or agents, they may nonetheless limit their liability. Only the servants and agents themselves are not entitled to limitation in such a case.[1062]

Under the Athens Convention, liability is not channelled on only one person. Both carrier and performing carrier, as well as their servants and agents, can be held liable. There is no provision which establishes directly or indirectly that one of them shall be primarily liable for the damage. The passenger can claim damages from all of them. Of course, the passenger is likely to sue only those persons who are financially the most capable or who insure their risks. In the Athens Convention, there is to date no compulsory insurance. Rather than requiring one person (such as the carrier) to purchase mandatory insurance, the convention offers the passenger a choice of persons he could sue, ranging from their contractual partner, the carrier, to a third party, the performing carrier, or their servants and agents. As a result, there is practically no legal channelling under the convention, but only a weak economic one. The agents and servants of the carrier or the performing carrier are, for example, the members of the crew, who are not able to pay

[1054] Article 3 (3) PAL 1974.
[1055] *Ibid.*
[1056] Article 4 (1) PAL 1974.
[1057] Article 4 (2) PAL 1974.
[1058] Article 11 PAL 1974.
[1059] Article 12 PAL 1974.
[1060] Article 4 (4) PAL 1974.
[1061] Articles 13 (1), 4 (1) PAL 1974.
[1062] Article 13 (2) PAL 1974.

high damages. As a result, it is quite improbable that an injured passenger will sue them. Compensation by the performing carrier faces similar problems. On the one hand, his identity may be unknown; on the other hand, the passenger has contractual claims against the carrier, but only claims in tort against the performing carrier. For these reasons, liability under the convention is to some degree channelled on the carrier.

Regarding the limits, two remarks shall be added. First, the level of limitation for personal injury or death can be lower than that of the LLMC. In the LLMC, the maximum liability of the shipowner is calculated by multiplying the number of passengers the ship is authorised to carry by 46,666 SDR.[1063] If there are fewer passengers aboard at the time of the incident, each of them may claim damages which are higher than 46,666 SDR. The Athens Convention, however, establishes a fixed amount of 46,666 SDR per passenger, which relates to the number of passengers that are actually aboard.[1064] As a result, in no case will a passenger get more than those 46,666 SDR, unless the carrier behaved in a way that the limitations of his liability do not apply. Secondly, the international community apparently considers this level of compensation to be satisfactory. The Protocol of 1990, which nearly quadruples the level of compensation,[1065] has been ratified by only 5 countries, accounting for 0.82% of the world's tonnage; and the 2002 Protocol, which establishes levels of compensation that are nearly nine times[1066] as high as the 1976 Protocol and obliges the carrier to purchase insurance for the ship, has so far been ratified by only 4 countries, accounting for 0.13% of the world's tonnage (all percentages as at 31 August 2005).[1067]

To sum up, the Athens Convention sets up a rather weak system of channelling. Due to inflation and a rise in living standards, the level of 46,666 SDR per passenger for claims of death or personal injury is rather low. Since there is no compulsory insurance yet, the passenger may not receive any compensation at all if the carrier is insolvent.

V. Limitations of Civil Liability for Oil Pollution Damage

The Torrey Canyon disaster in 1967 was the starting point of the development of a different kind of convention.[1068] Under United States law, the *Limitation of Liability Act 1851* limited the liability of the shipowner for an oil spill to the value of the

[1063] Article 7 (1) LLMC.

[1064] Article 7 (1) PAL 1974.

[1065] Level of limitation for personal injury or death: 175,000 SDR per passenger, cabin luggage: 1,800 SDR, vehicle: 10,000 SDR, and other luggage: 2,700.

[1066] Limitation for personal injury or death: 400,000 SDR per passenger, cabin luggage: 2,250 SDR, vehicle: 12,700 SDR, other luggage: 3,375 SDR per passenger.

[1067] IMO, *Summary Status of Conventions as at 31 August 2005*, accessible at <http://www.imo.org/home.asp?topic_id=161>, last accessed 19 March 2007.

[1068] Abecassis/Jarashow, *Oil Pollution from Ships* (1985), § 10–04, at 194.

vessel after the incident. The Torrey Canyon was destroyed and had no longer any value. It was gone. The only thing that was left was one lifeboat, with a value of 48 USD.[1069] It became evident that such compensation was insufficient, especially for the enormous damage that a harmful substance such as oil may cause.[1070] The consequence was the development of a new convention, the International Convention on Civil Liability for Oil Pollution Damage (CLC), which was the nucleus of an innovative system of compensation.[1071] It included a new principle:[1072] the strict liability of the shipowner for the damage which is caused by oil spills. However, in order to make this strict liability insurable, the shipowner's liability is limited to

[1069] *In re Barracuda Tanker Corp. (S/T Torrey Canyon)*, 281 F.Supp. 228 (S.D.N.Y.1968), *remanded* 409 F.2d 1013 (2d Cir.1969); Gilmore/Black, *The Law of Admiralty* (1975), § 10–4(a), at 823.

[1070] A detailed analysis of the different kinds of dangerous cargos, including chemicals, is provided by Kindt, 'Marine Pollution and Hydrocarbons: The Goal of Minimizing Damage to the Marine Environment', 14 *Cal.W.Int'l L.J.* 233 (1984).

[1071] The CLC has not been enacted in the United States. The Oil Pollution Act 1990 set up a somewhat similar system, *see infra.* The transnational environmental accountability of this compensation system is discussed by Mason, 'Transnational Compensation for Oil Pollution Damage: Examining Spatialities of Environmental Liability', LSE Research Papers in Environmental and Spatial Analysis, Department of Geography and Environment, LSE 69 (2002), accessible at <http://www.lse.ac.uk/collections/geographyAndEnvironment/research/Researchpapers/rp69.pdf>, last accessed 19 March 2007.
The CLC has been a model for other conventions that are accompanied by an international fund which guarantees compensation of damage that exceeds the liability of the shipowner. Contributions to such an international fund are made by those who benefit from receiving the harmful substances. The International Convention on Liability and Compensation for Damage in Connection with the Carriage of Hazardous and Noxious Substances by Sea (HNS), also establishes such a dual system of a strict liability which is limited and a fund which covers excessive damages (*see* Article 13–36, 39–41 of the HNS Convention). The International Convention on Civil Liability for Bunker Oil Pollution Damage, however, does not require an international fund (this convention is analysed by Zhu, *Compulsory Insurance and Compensation for Bunker Oil Pollution* (2006)). Both the HNS Convention and the International Convention on Civil Liability for Bunker Oil Pollution Damage are not yet in force. The HNS Convention has been ratified by 8 countries, accounting for 4.83% of the world's tonnage, and the Bunkers Convention by 7 countries, accounting for 3.9%. The HNS Convention will come into force after ratification by at least 12 States, each of which has registered gross tonnage of at least 2 million, and contributors in those ratifying States must have received during the preceding calender year a minimum of 40 million tons of cargo consisting of bulk solids and other HNS liable for contributions to the general account. The Bunkers Convention will come into force 12 months after the ratification by 18 States, 5 of which have a combined gross tonnage of at least 1 million each. Since their channelling clauses are similar to the one of the CLC, only the provisions of the CLC will be analysed.

[1072] Abecassis/Jarashow, *Oil Pollution from Ships* (1985), § 10–05, at 194.

a certain amount per ton. There is a maximum liability, a 'ceiling', for each and every vessel, regardless of tonnage. At the same time, the shipowner is obliged to purchase insurance for the amount up to which he may be held liable. In order to minimise the negative economic effects of several layers of insurance at high cost, the channelling of the liability on the shipowner is much stronger than in conventions relating to cargo limitations or global limitations. The shipowner is the person who is primarily responsible for the vessel and he is the one who shall primarily answer for the damage.

The International Convention on Civil Liability for Oil Pollution Damage (CLC) was signed in 1969 and came into force in 1975.[1073] The CLC is a very successful convention[1074] and has, in combination with the Fund Conventions, set up an effective system of compensation.[1075] The person who owns the ship at the time of the incident is liable for any pollution damage caused by oil which has escaped

---

[1073] International Convention on Civil Liability for Oil Pollution Damage (CLC). Brussels, 29 November 1969, entry into force 19 June 1975, UNTS I–14097, 973 UNTS 3; 9 ILM 45. As amended by the Protocol to the International Convention on Civil Liability for Oil Pollution Damage, 1969, London, 19 November 1976, entry into force: 8 April 1981, 1225 UNTS 356; 16 ILM 617; ATS 1984 No. 3; BGBl. 1980 II 721; UKTS 1981 No. 26 (Cmnd. 8238). And the Protocol of 1992 to amend the International Convention on Civil Liability for Oil Pollution Damage of 29 November 1969 (with annex and final act). London, 27 November 1992, entry into Force: 30 May 1996, UNTS A–14097, 1956 UNTS 255; IMO Doc. LEG/CONF.9/15 of 2 December 1992; ATS 1996, No. 2; UKTS 1996 No. 86 (Cmnd. 3432). 2000 Amendments (Limitation Amounts in the Protocol of 1992 to amend the International Convention on Civil Liability for Oil Pollution Damage, 1969), London, 18 October 2000, entry into force: 1 November 2003, IMO Doc. Res. LEG.1(82), in: Annex 2 of IMO Doc. LEG 82/12 of 6 November 2000; IOPCF Doc. RMCI.7.52, II.7.52.

[1074] The CLC in the form of its 1992 Protocol has been ratified by 110 countries, representing 94.27% percent of the world's tonnage. The Fund Protocol 1976 has been ratified by 33 States, accounting for 47.71% of the world's tonnage; its 1992 Protocol by 95 countries which represent 88.89% of the world's tonnage. Its 2003 Protocol has currently been ratified by only 11 countries, which have 11.06% of the world's tonnage (<http://www.imo.org>, data as per 31 August 2005, last accessed 19 March 2007).

[1075] For a detailed analysis of the CLC, *see* Abecassis/Jarashow, *Oil Pollution from Ships* (1985), §§ 10–01 to 10–164; Gauci, *Oil Pollution at Sea* (1997), 149–196; 153; Göransson, 'The 1984 and 1992 Protocols to the Civil Liability Convention, 1969 and the Fund Convention, 1971', in De La Rue (ed.), *Liability for Damage to the Marine Environment* (1993), 71; Jacobsson, Måns, 'Compensation for Oil Pollution Damage Caused by Oil Spills from Ships and the International Oil Pollution Compensation Fund', 29 *Mar.Pol.Bull.* 378 (1994); Jacobsson, Måns, 'Le regime international d'indemnisation des victims des marées noires en pleine évolution', [2004] *DMF* 793; Jacobsson, Måns, 'The International Conventions on Liability and Compensation for Oil Pollution Damage and the Activities of the International Oil Pollution Compensation Fund' in De La Rue, *ibid.*, 39; Wu, *Pollution from the Carriage of Oil by Sea* (1996), 37–76, 129–192, 388–395.

or been discharged by the ship as a result of the incident; he has to purchase insurance to the value of his potential exposure to claims.[1076] The CLC only applies to ships which carry oil as their cargo and damage which is caused by oil that is carried as cargo or in the bunkers of such a ship.[1077] For those countries which have ratified the subsequent protocols, including the 2000 Amendments, the level of liability is limited between a minimum of SDR 4.51 million for a ship not exceeding 5,000 gross tonnage and a maximum of SDR 89.77 million for a ship of over 140,000 gross tonnage.[1078] The shipowner is not liable if he proves that the incident resulted from exceptional circumstances, such as acts of war or hostilities or an exceptional natural phenomenon, from an act or omission of a third party done with the intent to cause damage or by a governmental deficiency in maintaining navigational aids.[1079] The International Funds established by the 1971[1080] and 1992 Fund Conventions guarantee a compensation of up to a maximum of SDR 203 million per incident. However, this amount includes the compensation paid by the shipowner and his insurer.[1081] Since 2005 there has been a Supplementary Fund, set up by the 11 countries that have so far ratified the Supplementary Fund Protocol of 2003,[1082] which has a limit of SDR 750 million. Every person in a Member State of the Fund Conventions who has received crude oil or heavy fuel oil in excess of 150,000 tons, has to pay a contribution which is fixed by the Assembly of the IPOC Funds.[1083]

In its 1969 version, the CLC still provided that the shipowner is not entitled to avail himself of the limitation if the incident occurred as a result of the actual fault or privity of the owner.[1084] The 1992 Protocol made it more difficult to exceed the

[1076] Article III (1) CLC.

[1077] Article I Nr. 1, 5 CLC.

[1078] For a ship between 5,000 and 140,000 gross tonnage, liability is limited to 4.51 million SDR plus 631 SDR for each additional gross tonne over 5,000. Under the 1992 Protocol, the figures were 3 million SDR, 3 million plus 420 SDR per gross tonne and 59.7 million SDR respectively. The International Monetary Fund publishes the daily conversion rates for Special Drawing rights on its website (<http://www.imf.org>, last accessed 19 March 2007).

[1079] Article III (2) CLC.

[1080] The 1971 Fund Convention ceased to be in force in 2002. *See* Protocol of 2000 to the International Convention on the Establishment of an International Fund for Compensation of Oil Pollution Damage, 1971, adopted 27 September 2000, entry into force: 27 June 2001, RMC II.7.112, LEG/CONF.11/6 of 27 September 2000 (Resolution on the Termination of the 1971 Fund Convention and Accession to the 1992 Protocols: IMO document(s) LEG/CONF 11/8 of 27.9.2000.

[1081] Art. 4.4 of the 1992 Fund Convention.

[1082] Protocol of 2003 to the International Convention on the Establishment of an International Fund for Compensation for Oil Pollution Damage, London, 16 May 2003, entry into force: 3 March 2005, IMO Doc. LEG/CONF.14/20, RMC II.7.115.

[1083] International Oil Pollution Compensation Funds, *Annual Report 2004*, 30.

[1084] Article V (2) CLC.

limitations of liability.[1085] According to this protocol, the shipowner is not entitled to limit his liability if it has been proved that the pollution damage resulted from his personal act or omission, committed with the intent to cause such damage or recklessly and with knowledge that such damage would probably result.[1086]

The 1992 Protocol extends the channelling clause. In the past, the CLC used to exclude only the liability of the servants and agents of the owner. Article III (4), as revised by the 1992 Protocol, exempts the servants or agents of the owner or the members of the crew, the pilot or any other person who, without being a member of the crew, performs services for the ship, any charterer, manager or operator of the ship, any person performing salvage operations with the consent of the owner or on the instructions of a competent public authority, any person taking preventive measures as well as the charterers, salvors or the servants or agents of the person taking preventive measures. However, there is no exemption of classification societies nor of other legal subjects such as shipyards.[1087] Similar to the wording of the clause pursuant to which the limitation of the shipowner can be exceeded, these subjects are not exempt if the damage resulted from their personal act or omission or was committed with the intent to cause such damage or recklessly and with knowledge that such damage would probably result.[1088]

There are several justifications for the CLC. In the preamble to the CLC, the purpose of the convention was '[...] to ensure that adequate compensation is available to persons who suffer damage caused by pollution resulting from the escape or discharge of oil from ships, and to adopt uniform international rules and procedures for determining questions of liability and providing adequate compensation in such cases.' Oil pollution can cause claims which are so enormous that hardly anyone can compensate them. For example, claims after the "*Braer*" incident of 1993 in the United Kingdom were settled by the IOPC for GBP 51.9 million.[1089] This figure does not necessarily include all damage, as the IOPC Funds only pays compensation for damage which it acknowledges according to its

[1085] Protocol of 1992 to amend the International Convention on Civil Liability for Oil Pollution Damage of 29 November 1969 (with annex and final act). London, 27 November 1992, entry into Force: 30 May 1996, UNTS A–14097.

[1086] Article 6 (2) of the Protocol which amends Article V (2) of the 1969 version of the CLC.

[1087] Or Ship managers, bareboat charterers, *see* Abecassis/Jarashow (ed.), *Oil Pollution from Ships* (1985), § 10–23, 200.

[1088] Article III (4) of the CLC as amended by the 1992 Protocol.

[1089] IPOC, *Annual Report 2004*, at 50. For an analysis of the sources of oil spills, *see* Lentz/Felleman, 'Oil Spill Prevention: A Proactive Approach', (2003) *Int. Oil Spill Conf.* 1; a similar analysis under the United States O.P.A. provide Ketkar, 'The Oil Pollution Act of 1990: A Decade Later', 7 *Spill Science & Tech.Bull.* 45 (2002) and Kim, 'Ten years after the enactment of the Oil Pollution Act of 1990: a success or a failure', 26 *Mar. Pol'y* 197 (2002). Cleanup costs are analysed by Schmidt Etkin, 'Estimating Cleanup Costs for Oil Spills', (1999) *Int. Oil Spill Conf.* 165.

Claims Manual.[1090] The sinking of the "*Nakhodka*" in Japanese waters resulted in the settlement of claims against the IOPC Funds amounting to GBP 110.7 million.[1091] And both the "*Erika*" and the "*Prestige*" catastrophes resulted in claims which largely exceed the limits of the 1992 Fund Convention to the value of SDR 135 million. In the *Erika* case, the claims against the shipowner's limitation fund total EUR 484 million.[1092] Regarding the *Prestige*, the potential claims exposure of the IOPC was EUR 1,038 million according to the IOPC Funds.[1093] Even if the persons who are responsible for these incidents were liable for an unlimited amount, this does not necessarily mean that shipowners are financially capable of paying for the damage. Thus, they will try to seek limitation of their liability by way of company law, and will set up various separate limited liability companies.

Moreover, it can be very difficult to prove what actually caused a maritime casualty. If liability is based on fault, the injured party may not be able to hold the responsible person liable if it cannot prove his fault. Strict liability, by contrast, would be in the interest of the injured party. The contracting States considered oil to be such a harmful substance that the shipowner is to be held strictly liable for any damage which arises at the time of the transport.[1094] Concurrently, it was held that strict liability could only be imposed if it was limited.[1095] It was deemed to be impossible to insure the risk of an oil spill if liability were not limited. The limitation was, therefore, the other side of the coin of strict liability. The combination of this regime with compulsory insurance and international funds ensures that there is in most cases effective compensation for the damage. The underlying concept of the funds is that those who enjoy the benefits shall also bear the consequences of the inherent risk. At the same time, liability was intended to be channelled on the shipowner in order to avoid insurance of this high risk by numerous parties. The existence of several layers of insurance for one high risk was considered to be inefficient from an economic point of view. In addition, there is not as great a need for prevention, which is also a justification for the existence of liability. The inherent danger of bad news and a negative public opinion in the aftermath of an oil spill motivates not only a shipowner but especially the cargo-owners, which are oil companies whose business is highly affected by public opinion, to act respon-

---

[1090] Accessible at <http://www.iopcfund.org/publications.htm>, last accessed 19 March 2007.

[1091] *Ibid.*, at 44–45.

[1092] *Ibid.*, at 81. For an analysis of this case, *see* Harrison, 'The Accountability of Classification Societies, The Role of Classification and Market-oriented Policy Issues (The "Erika"), [2000] *J.I.M.L.* 299; Brans, 'The 1999 *Erika* Oil Spill in France', 2 *Inter.L.For.du droit intern.* 66 (2000).

[1093] *Ibid.*, at 95.

[1094] Inter-Governmental Maritime Consultative Organization, *Official Records of the International Legal Conference of Marine Pollution Damage, 1969* (London: 1973), 625–660, of 42 delegations which were present and voted at the Conference, 22 voted in favour of strict liability, 17 against and there were 3 abstentions, 665–666.

[1095] *Ibid.*, at 727–738.

sibly. Cargo-owners are already motivated to ascertain the safety of the vessels, as the careful vetting which large oil companies conduct when chartering a vessel illustrate. Furthermore, after the establishment of the 2005 Supplementary Fund, international funds guarantee compensation for the damage. Even a higher level of liability may not necessarily increase the existing motivation. For all these reasons, the CLC, in combination with the Fund Conventions, have been quite successful and effective as regards compensation for the oil pollution damage.

B. Limitation of Liability under the Current System of Limitations

I. On the Application of Existing Limitation Regulations to Classification Societies

The second part of this thesis has established that classification societies can be liable for their actions under certain circumstances. It has, however, not been analysed whether such liability would be limited or not. In this section, the conventions that limit liability in shipping, as well as regional and national limitation provisions, will therefore be scrutinised and the relevant provisions construed.

1. *International Conventions*

a. Cargo Limitations: The Hague/Visby and Hamburg Rules

aa. Interpretation of Servant, Agent and Independent Contractor in the Hague/Visby Rules

As concerns their legal character, the Hague Rules, Hague/Visby and Hamburg Rules standardise the private stipulations of liability as incorporated in the Bills of Lading. They solely relate to the contractual relationship between the carrier and the shipper. However, the protection of the shipper is extended to certain other persons. The Hague/Visby Rules include in Article IV *bis* the following clause:

> '(2) If such an action is brought against a servant or agent of the carrier (such servant or agent not being an independent contractor), such servant or agent shall be entitled to avail himself of the defences and limits of liability which the carrier is entitled to invoke under this Convention.
>
> (3) The aggregate of the amounts recoverable from the carrier, and such servants and agents, shall in no case exceed the limit provided for in this Convention.
>
> (4) Nevertheless, a servant or agent of the carrier shall not be entitled to avail himself of the provisions of this Article, if it is proved that the damage resulted from an act or omission of the servant or agent done with intent to cause damage or recklessly and with knowledge that damage would probably result.'

If the classification society is a servant or agent of the carrier, it will benefit from the limitations of liability of these regulations. Whether or not a classification society has the position of a servant or agent of the carrier is subject to interpretation. As there is no definition of a servant, agent or independent contractor in the convention, these terms need to be construed. The interpretation of international law, such as the Hague/Visby Rules, follows its own distinct rules, which are based on the sovereignty and sovereign equality of States, a basis not found in any other legal order.[1096] Articles 31 and 32 of the Vienna Convention on the Law of the Treaties[1097] have for the first time codified rules on treaty interpretation. These rules are binding for the parties to the Vienna Convention, but a large number of scholars consider them to be an expression of customary international law.[1098]

First, one has to scrutinise the ordinary meaning that is to be given to the terms of the treaty in its context, including the preamble and its annexes and all agreements that were made between the parties or declaration by one party that was accepted by all the others which relate to the treaty.[1099] This *grammatical* interpretation has already been recognised by the Permanent Court of International Justice

---

[1096] Bernhardt, 'Interpretation in International Law' in Bernhardt (ed.), *Encyclopaedia of Public International Law* (EPIL) (1995), vol. II, 1416.

[1097] Of 23 May 1969, entry into force 27 January 1980, UNTS I–18232. Article 31. General rule of interpretation

(1) A treaty shall be interpreted in good faith in accordance with the ordinary meaning to be given to the terms of the treaty in their context and in the light of its object and purpose.

(2) The context for the purpose of the interpretation of a treaty shall comprise, in addition to the text, including its preamble and annexes:

(a) any agreement relation to the treaty which was made between all the parties in connexion with the conclusion of the treaty;

(b) any instrument which was made by one or more parties in connexion with the conclusion of the treaty and accepted by the other parties as an instrument related to the treaty.

(3) There shall be taken into account, together with the context:

(a) any subsequent agreement between the parties regarding the interpretation of the treaty or the application of its provisions;

(b) any subsequent practice in the application of the treaty which establishes the agreement of the parties regarding its interpretation;

(c) any relevant rules of international law applicable in the relations between the parties.

(4) A special meaning shall be given to a term if it is established that the parties so intended.

Article 32. Supplementary means of interpretation

Recourse may be had to supplementary means of interpretation, including the preparatory work of the treaty and the circumstances of its conclusion, in order to confirm the meaning resulting from the application of article 31, or to determine the meaning when the interpretation according to article 31:

(a) leaves the meaning ambiguous or obscure; or

(b) leads to a result which is manifestly absurd or unreasonable.

[1098] Bernhardt, 'Interpretation in International Law' in Bernhardt (ed.), *EPIL* (1995), vol. II, 1416, at 1419; Ipsen, *Völkerrecht* (2004), § 11, no. 14; Verdross/Simma, *Universelles Völkerrecht* (1984), § 775.

[1099] *Compare* Schwarzenberger, *A Manual of International Law* (1960), 69.

(PCIJ) in 1925[1100] and continued to be applied by the International Court of Justice (I.C.J.).[1101] Since words can hardly be understood correctly in isolation, but have to be seen in the wider context of the relevant text, a *systematic* interpretation seems to be universally recognised.[1102] A systematic interpretation requires the adjustment of various parts of the treaties to one another by construing some of them extensively, others restrictively.[1103] If such an interpretation does not produce the required results, one may employ a *functional* interpretation, which determines the functions which the treaty or the relevant provision in the treaty was intended to fulfil.[1104] Whenever the object and purpose of a treaty is clearly indicated in its text, an interpretation which matches these two is to be preferred. However, such a functional interpretation does not imply that the widest meaning is used, as this might be contrary to the intentions of the contracting parties.[1105] Article 31 of the Vienna Convention on the Law of the Treaties speaks of the 'ordinary meaning to be given in the light of the object and purpose of the regulation'. Moreover, as a supplementary means of interpretation which is subsidiary to the other methods, a *historical* interpretation analyses the preparatory work and the circumstances in which the treaty was negotiated and concluded, Article 32 of the convention. Such a historical interpretation may either be used to affirm the meaning that has been determined by the other means of interpretation or to shed light on an ambiguous wording or to re-interpret it if the other means of interpretation established an unreasonable meaning.[1106]

[1100] P.C.I.J., *Polish Postal Service in Danzig* (*Advisory Opinion*), *Publications of the P.C.I.J.,* Series B, No. 11, at 39: 'It is a cardinal principle of interpretation that words must be interpreted in the sense which they would normally have in their context, unless such interpretation would lead to something unreasonable or absurd.'

[1101] I.C.J., *Competence of the General Assembly for the Admission of a State to Membership in United Nations* (*Advisory Opinion*), *I.C.J. Reports* 1950, 4, at 8: 'The Court considers it necessary to say that the first duty of a tribunal which is called upon to interpret and apply the provisions of a treaty, is to endeavour to give effect to them in their natural and ordinary meaning in the context in which they occur. If the relevant words in their natural and ordinary meaning make sense in their context, that is an end of the matter.'

[1102] Bernhardt, 'Interpretation in International Law' in Bernhardt (ed.) *EPIL*, vol. II, 1416, at 1420; Schwarzenberger, *A Manual of International Law* (1960), 69.

[1103] I.C.J., *Case Concerning Right of Passage over Indian Territory (Portugal v. India), I.C.J. Reports* 1960, 158.

[1104] *Compare* I.C.J., *Reservations to the Convention on the Prevention and Punishment of the Crime of Genocide, I.C.J. Reports* 1951, 15, at 24; I.C.J., *Case Concerning rights of Nationals of the USA in Morocco (France v. USA), I.C.J. Reports* 1950, 4, at 197 *et seq.*

[1105] *See* I.C.J., *Interpretation of Peace Treaties with Bulgaria, Hungary and Romania* (*Order*), *I.C.J. Reports* 1950, at 229: 'The principle of interpretation expressed in the maxim: *Ut res magis valeat quam pereat*, often referred to as the rule of effectiveness, cannot justify the Court in attributing to the provisions for the settlement of disputes in the Peace Treaties a meaning which [...] would be contrary to their letter and spirit.'

[1106] Verdross/Simma, *Universelles Völkerrecht* (1984), § 779.

(1) Grammatical Interpretation

Generally, a *servant* is a person who acts in the service of a master and who has to obey the orders of his superior.[1107] The master may give orders which work has to be done, which means shall be employed and how the work shall be accomplished. A classification society is requested to carry out the classification of a certain vessel, but is free in its choice of its means. Once the classification has been ordered, the shipowner cannot influence the way the classification is carried out. The shipowner does not exercise control and direction over it. A classification society is therefore not a servant of the shipowner.

An *agent* is usually defined as someone who acts on behalf of another person and who does the actual work for this other person.[1108] The express or implied authority of the *agent* allows him to act for the principal.[1109] A classification society has a contract with the shipowner, but acts independently of him. The classification society cannot act on behalf of the shipowner. It is therefore neither a *servant* nor an *agent*, but an *independent contractor*.

(2) Systematic Interpretation

This conclusion is also affirmed by a systematic interpretation. According to Article 4 (2) a), neither the carrier nor the ship is liable for loss or damage arising or resulting from act, neglect or default of his *servants* in the navigation or in the management of the ship. Article 6 allows the carrier and the shipper to enter into a separate agreement that relates to the care or diligence of the carrier's *servants* or *agents* with regard to the 'loading, handling, stowage, carriage, custody, care and discharge of the goods'. And the *agent* is mentioned several times as a representative of the carrier, notably when concluding the contract of carriage or other agreements or issuing the bill of lading.[1110] A *servant* is therefore a person who supports the carrier in the navigation or management of the vessel, whereas an *agent* acts on its behalf in certain regards. A classification society is neither of these. From the point of view of a systematic interpretation, Article IV *bis* of the Hague/Visby Rules does not envisage classification societies.

[1107] *The Oxford English Dictionary* (1933/1978): 'A person of either sex who is in the service of a master or a mistress; one who is under obligation to work for the benefit of a superior, and to obey his (or her) commands. [...] 2. In a wider sense: One who is under the obligation to render certain services to, and to obey the orders of, a person or a body of persons, esp. in return for wages or salary.' *Compare* Jowitt/Walsh/Burke, *Jowitt's Dictionary of English Law* (1977), vol. 1, 'Master and Servant'; Black/Nolan/Connolly, *Black's Law Dictionary* (1979), under 'Servant'.

[1108] *The Oxford English Dictionary* (1933/1978), under 'Agent'; Black/Nolan/Connolly, *Black's Law Dictionary* (1979), under 'Agent'.

[1109] Jowitt/Walsh/Burke, *Jowitt's Dictionary of English Law* (1977), vol. 1, 'Agent'.

[1110] Article 3 (3) lit. c), (6), (7), 4 (2) lit. q), (5).

(3) Functional Interpretation

The object and purpose of Article IV *bis* is to extend the scope of application to those persons for whom the carrier might have to answer for. Generally, one has to answer for one's *servants* and *agents* towards a contracting party. This provision therefore seeks to prevent the limitations in favour of the carrier being rendered inoperative through the back door. Otherwise the limitation of the liability of the carrier would be ineffective.

Since a classification society does not act on behalf of the carrier, he would not have to answer for it and its liability would not affect him. A functional interpretation of Article IV *bis* therefore reaffirms that classification societies are neither employees nor are they *agents* of the carrier, they are *independent contractors*. Their liability is not limited under the Hague/Visby Rules.

bb. The Hamburg Rules

The Hamburg Rules would also protect classification societies if they were *servants* or *agents* of the carrier.[1111] However, just as the grammatical interpretation of the Hague/Visby Rules establishes, classification societies are neither *servants* nor *agents* of the carrier. A *servant* or *agent* has to be a person who is acting for the carrier with regard to the performance of the contract of carriage by sea, as Article 5 (1) of the Hamburg Rules illustrates.[1112] A classification society helps to make the ship seaworthy, but does not act with regard to the performance of the contract of carriage. Also, generally it does not survey the vessel at the time it loads cargo, except if damage surveys are necessary. Hence, a classification society is neither a *servant* nor an *agent* in the sense of Article 7 (2) of the Hamburg Rules.

[1111] 'Article 7 of the Hamburg Rules

(1) The defences and limits of liability provided for in this Convention apply in any action against the carrier in respect of loss or damage to the goods covered by the contract of carriage by sea, as well as of delay in delivery whether the action is founded in contract, in tort or otherwise.

(2) If such action is brought against a servant or agent of the carrier, such servant or agent, if he proves that he acted within the scope of his employment, is entitled to avail himself of the defences and limits of liability which the carrier is entitled to invoke under this Convention.

(3) Except as provided in Article 8, the aggregate of the amounts recoverable from the carrier and from any persons referred to in paragraph 2 of this Article shall not exceed the limits of liability provided for in this Convention.'

[1112] 'Article 5 of the Hamburg Rules

(1) The carrier is liable for loss resulting from loss of or damage to the goods, as well as from delay in delivery, if the occurrence which caused the loss, damage or delay took place while the goods were in his charge as defined in Article 4, unless the carrier proves that he, his servants or agents took all measures that could reasonably be required to avoid the occurrence and its consequences.'

cc. Private Limitations under the Bills of Lading: Himalaya Clauses

Himalaya clauses extend the scope of a contractual protection to third parties who have not entered into the contract.[1113] They have been developed under *English law*, but have similar effects under the laws of various shipping countries. Such a stipulation is added to Bills of Lading in order to permit notably stevedores, terminal operators and dry-dock companies to benefit from certain terms of the Bill of Lading, such as the limitation provisions and the short prescription period. Theoretically, such a clause could also protect classification societies and allow them the protection of conventions which limit the liability in regard to cargo. These clauses have been named after the vessel *Himalaya*, by which the passengers were transported in the English case *Adler v. Dickson*.[1114] In that case, an injured passenger claimed damages against the master and the boatswain on a tort law theory, as there was no privity of contract between the claimant and these two. The shipowner was protected by an exclusion clause in the passenger ticket, which, however, did not indicate that the master and the boatswain were to be granted the benefit of the exclusion clause as well. The House of Lords expressly stated that the parties to the contract could have excluded the liability of these persons as well. This decision was therefore subsequently interpreted that if it was expressly stipulated in a *Himalaya clause* that the servants and agents and even certain independent contractors were protected, these persons would also benefit from the limitation provisions. Such clauses are accepted under *English* and *United States law*, and constitute a *pactum de non petendo* in favour of the third party under *German law*.[1115]

[1113] Barnett, 'The validity of Himalaya clauses–privity of contract on the brink of collapse?', 3 *I.J.S.L.* 178 (1998); Cook, 'Privity of contract and the function and scope of the Himalaya clauses', 7 *K.C.L.J.* 127 (1996–1997); Crowley, 'The Limited Scope of the Cargo Liability Regime covering Carriage of Goods by Sea: the Multimodal Problem', 79 *Tul.L.Rev.* 1461 (2005); Denniston/Gunn/Yudes, 'Liabilities of Multimodal Operators and Parties other than Carriers and Shippers', 64 *Tul.L.Rev.* 517, at 521 (1989); Doak, 'Liabilities of Stevedores, Terminal Operators, and Other Handlers in Relation to Cargo', 45 *Tul.L.Rev.* 752 (1971); Girvin, 'Contracting carriers, Himalaya clauses and tort in the House of Lords, [2003] 3 *L.M.C.L.Q.* 311; Healy, 'Carriage of Goods by Sea: Application of the Himalaya Clause to Subdelegees of the Carrier', 2 *Mar. Law.* 91 (1976–1977); Hill, *Maritime Law* (2003), 264–269; Schoenbaum, *Admiralty and Maritime Law* (2004), § 10–8; Tetley, 'The Himalaya Clause–Heresy or Genius?', 9 *J. Mar. L. & Com.* 111 (1977–1978); Tetley, 'The Himalaya clause – revisited', 9 *J.I.M.L.* 40 (2003); Todd, *Modern Bills of Lading* (1990), 215–223; Zawitoski, 'Limitation of Liability for Stevedores and Terminal Operators Under the Carrier's Bill of Lading and COGSA', 16 *J. Mar. L. & Com.* 337 (1985); Zeller, *Die Umgehung der Haager Regeln durch die Ladungsbeteiligten und die Himalaya–Klausel im Seefrachtrecht* (1966).

[1114] *Adler v. Dickson (the Himalaya)* [1955] 1 Q.B. 158.

[1115] The first decision under *English law* in this regard was *Midland Silicone v. Scrutton Ltd.* [1961] 2 Lloyd's Rep. 365 (H.L.), in which the House of Lords rejected the extension of the limitation provisions of the Bill of Lading to stevedores. There was no express term in the Bill of Lading that included the stevedores in the definition of carrier. Also, there was no evidence that the carrier was contracting as the stevedore's agent, which might otherwise have included them in the protection of the contract. Next followed *The Eurymedon* [1974] 1 Lloyd's Rep. 534, in which the Privy Council held that the Bill of Lading gave rise to a unilateral bargain that became a full contract when the stevedore discharged the goods. The discharge was interpreted as the consideration for the agreement that the stevedores should benefit from the exemptions and limitations in the Bill of Lading. In the *New York Star* [1980] 2 Lloyd's Rep. 317, the jurisdiction of the *Eurymedon* was confirmed and extended to the time after the discharge of the shipment. Similarly, *The Rigoletto (Lotus Cars Ltd. and others v. Southampton Cargo Handling Plc and others and Associated British Ports (The "Rigoletto"),* [2002] 2 Lloyd's Rep. 532) established that the Himalaya clause has no application prior to and outside the scope of the adventure for which the carrier itself has responsibility, i.e. the period of carriage.

Under *United States law*, there is also a long history of Himalaya clauses. The Supreme Court argued in *Herd v. Krawill* that it was neither the intention of the contracting parties of the Hague Rules nor of the United States Congress to extend the limitations to stevedores, but included an equivocal phrase, on which the legitimacy of Himalaya clauses was thereafter based ('No statute has limited its liability, and it was not a party to *nor a beneficiary of* the contract of carriage between the shipper and the carrier, and hence its liability was not limited by that contract' (emphasis added), *Robert C. Herd & Co. V. Krawill Machinery Corp.,* 359 U.S. 297 (1959), at 308, 79 S.Ct. 766, at 772, 1959 A.M.C. 879, at 888). This clause has been interpreted in the sense that the parties to a contract of carriage may express in a carrier's Bill of Lading or charter party the will to limit the liability of a stevedore, terminal operator or other independent contractor (Schoenbaum, *Admiralty and Maritime Law* (2004), § 10–8, at 614 with further references. In order to extend the limitation provision, a Himalaya clause, a period of responsibility clause and a clause paramount are required, *see* Schoenbaum, *ibid.,* Denniston/Gunn/Yudes, 'Liabilities of Multimodal Operators and Parties other than Carriers and Shippers', 64 *Tul.L.Rev.* 517, at 521 (1989)). In a recent decision, the United States Supreme Court even applied a Himalaya clause that was incorporated in Bills of Lading to a railroad, which was the intended beneficiary thereof. The cargo-owner was bound by the limitation of liability clause negotiated between an intermediary and the shipper, as the contract aimed at a door-to-door transportation of the goods (*Norfolk Southern Railway Co. v. Kirby*, 125 S.Ct. 385, 160 L.Ed.2d 283, 2004 A.M.C. 2705 (U.S.2004)). These clauses must, however, be strictly construed. They are to be limited to their intended beneficiaries and to the contract language or the intent of the parties (*Robert C. Herd & Co. v. Krawill Machinery Corp.,* 359 U.S. 297, at 305 (1959); *Norfolk Southern Railway Co. v. Kirby*, 125 S.Ct. 385, at 397 (U.S.2004)). Until today there has been no decision which has construed a Bill of Lading in favour of a classification society.

Under *German law*, the Himalaya clause is construed by the courts as a *pactum de non petendo*, as the preconditions of a contract in favour of third parties are not satisfied. The promisor does not promise to undertake something and does not give a claim to the third party. The third party that benefits from the Himalaya clause can only put in a plea against the action (BGH 7 July 1960, [1960] *VersR* 727. Contrary: Rabe, *Seehan-*

Whether or not a *Himalaya clause* protects classification societies depends on the wording of the individual clause.[1116] In general, such clauses only protect services which relate to the contract that incorporates the limitation provision, *i.e.* the Bill of Lading. The person that is to be protected, *e.g.* the stevedore, materially assists the carrier in the successful performance of the contract of carriage.

The services of the classification society are to check the vessel, but not to take part in the transport of the cargo. The shipper and the carrier could expressly state a protection of classification societies in the Bill of Lading, but they will most probably have no interest in doing so. One of the broadest Himalaya clauses favours 'any servant, agent or other person (including any independent contractor) whose services contribute to performing the contract.'[1117] Regarding the inclusion of independent contractors, the wording of the Himalaya clause differs from Article 4 *bis* of the Hague/Visby Rules and Article 7 of the Hamburg Rules. However, it is required that even these independent contractors 'contribute to performing the contract'. Since classification societies are neither directly involved in the carriage of goods nor act within the scope of the contract of carriage, it will be rather difficult if not impossible to construe a Himalaya clause in a way to limit their liability as well.

b. Limitations by the LLMC

The Convention on Limitation of Liability for Maritime Claims neither expressly extends limitation provisions to classification societies nor exempts them from li-

---

delsrecht (2000), § 607a, no. 12 who argues in favour of a direct protection of the third party through applying § 328 by analogy (similar Gottwald in: Rebmann/Säcker/Rixecker, *Münchener Kommentar zum Bürgerlichen Gesetzbuch* (2003), § 328, at no. 170)).

1116 An example of such a clause can be found in *Lotus Cars Ltd. and others v. Southampton Cargo Handling PLC and others and Associated British Ports (the Rigoletto)* [2002] 2 Lloyd's Rep. 532: 'It is hereby expressly agreed that no servant or agent of the carrier (including every independent contractor from time to time employed by the carrier) shall in any circumstances whatsoever be under any liability whatsoever to the merchant for any loss, damage or delay arising or resulting directly or indirectly from any act, neglect or default on his part while acting in the course of or in connection with his employment and, but without prejudice to the generality of the foregoing provisions in the clause, every exception, limitation, condition and liberty herein contained at every right, exemption from liability, defence and immunity of whatsoever nature acceptable to the carrier or to which the carrier is entitled hereunder shall also be available and shall extend to protect every such servant or agent of the carrier acting as aforesaid and for the purpose of all the foregoing provisions of this clause the carrier is or shall be deemed to be acting as agent or trustee on behalf of and for the benefit of all persons who are or might be his servants or agents from time to time (including independent contractors as aforesaid) and all such persons shall to this extent be or be deemed to be parties to the contract evidence by the Bill of Lading.'

1117 *Norfolk Southern Railway Co. v. Kirby*, 125 S.Ct. 385, at 397 (U.S.2004).

ability. Article 1 (4)[1118] and Article 9 (1) (a)[1119] of the LLMC include classification societies if the shipowner is responsible for their act, neglect or default. "Responsible" is generally defined as 'liable, legally accountable or answerable. [...]'[1120] or similarly 'answerable, accountable (*to* another *for* something); liable to be called to account.'[1121] The grammatical interpretation does not determine for whom the shipowner is precisely responsible, as this is not a question of fact but of law. There is no legal rule in the LLMC which defines who the shipowner has to answer for. However, at the International Conference on the Limitation of Liability for Maritime Claims, the contracting States put much emphasis on the inclusion of pilots in Article 1 (4) and that the limitations applied only to a limited number of persons.[1122] The question of who the shipowner is responsible for was expressly left open to be dealt with by domestic laws.[1123]

1118 'Article 1. Persons entitled to limit liability

(4) If any claims set out in Article 2 are made against any person for whose act, neglect or default the shipowner or salvor is responsible, such person shall be entitled to avail himself of the limitation of liability provided for in this Convention.'

1119 'Article 9. Aggregation of claims

(1) The limits of liability determined in accordance with Article 6 shall apply to the aggregate of all claims which arise on any distinct occasion:

(a) against the person or persons mentioned in paragraph 2 of Article 1 and any person for whose act, neglect or default he or they are responsible; [...]'

1120 Black/Nolan/Connolly, *Black's Law Dictionary* (1979).

1121 *The Oxford English Dictionary.*

1122 IMCO, *Official Records of the International Legal Conference of Marine Pollution Damage, 1969* (1973), at 228 (CONF.5/C.1/SR.3): 'Mr. BURSLEY (United States) introduced his delegation's amendment to Article 1 (4) (LEG/CONF.5/C.1/WP8). The proposal was to delete the word "responsible" and substitute the phrase "legally liable at law in the absence of contract". The aim was to limit as far as possible extension of the right to invoke limitation of liability. The present text of paragraph 4 would appear to permit shipowners entitled to limitation to extend that right to other persons by contract. [...]

Mr. SELVIG (Norway) thought that, on the contrary, a question of substance was involved. Paragraph 4 was designed to establish that all persons for whom the shipowner had civil responsibility were entitled to invoke limitation. The scope of that principle was normally determined by national law. The United States proposal might be interpreted as inadvertently excluding such civil responsibility, which was certainly not the intention. He thought it unnecessary to make the paragraph more specific, for it already seemed to him perfectly clear.

Mr. BURSLEY (United States) thanked the representative of Norway, and confirmed that his delegation's intention was indeed to reduce the categories of persons entitled to invoke limitation. If Article 1 (4) was understood in that way and if the Committee as a whole agreed to that interpretation, he was prepared to withdraw his proposal.

Mr. LYON (Canada) agreed with the Norwegian representative that the proposal could also be considered a substantive one. He shared the concern which had led the United States delegation to submit its amendment, but thought a recommendation that the

Under *English law*, an employer is liable for his employee, but according to general common law not for an independent contractor.[1124] An independent contractor carries on a business independently on his own account and contracts to do certain work, which he can decide for himself how to do.[1125] Whilst he may be subject to the directions of the employer, in no sense is he either under any contract of service to or under the control of the employer.[1126] An employee, by contrast, is bound to obey any lawful orders given by the employer as to the manner in which his work shall be done.[1127] Classification societies carry out their business independently and on their own account. They are independent contractors, not employees of the shipowner.

The same applies under *United States law*. A classification society is an independent contractor, which is defined as

> 'any person who does work for another under conditions which are not sufficient to make him a servant of the other. It is immaterial whether the work is done gratuitously or is done for pay, or, indeed, if the latter, whether it is done under a specific contract or under a general contract of employment.'[1128]

Drafting Committee should replace "responsible" by "liable" (which had a slightly narrower meaning) might suffice.
Lord DIPLOCK (United Kingdom) saw no reason to doubt the interpretation of paragraph 4, which seemed to him quite clear. The choice of the word "responsible" was, in his view, legally correct in the present context, and he feared that the new version proposed by the United States might, as the Norwegian representative had said, cast doubt on the applicability of the Convention in cases where civil responsibility arose in connection with the execution of a contract. [...]
Mr. BURSLEY (United States) agreed to withdraw the United States proposal [...]'.

[1123] *See expressly* IMCO, *Official Records of the International Legal Conference of Marine Pollution Damage, 1969* (1973), at 228 (CONF.5/C.1/SR.3): 'Mr. SELVIG (Norway) thought that, on the contrary, a question of substance was involved. Paragraph 4 was designed to establish that all persons for whom the shipowner had civil responsibility were entitled to invoke limitation. The scope of that principle was normally determined by national law.' The other parties agreed.

[1124] 'Unquestionably, no one can be made liable for an act or breach of duty, unless it be traceable to himself or his servant or servants in the course of his or their employment. Consequently, if an independent contractor is employed to do a lawful act, and in the course of the work he or his servants commit some casual act of wrong or negligence, the employer is not answerable.' (*Pickard v. Smith* (1861) 10 C.B.(N.S.) 470 (C.B.), *per* Williams J.) *See also Allen v. Hayward* (1845) 7 Q.B. 960 (Q.B). Clerk & Lindsell, *On Torts* (2006), § 6–52.

[1125] *Allen v. Hayward* (1845) 7 Q.B. 960 (Q.B.). Cooke J. in: *Market Investigations Ltd. v. Minister of Social Security* [1969] 2 Q.B. 773, at 784–785.

[1126] *Hardaker v. Idle District Council,* [1896] 1 Q.B. 335.

[1127] Definition by Charlesworth/Percy, *On Negligence* (2006), § 2–291.

[1128] Restatement (Second) of Torts, § 409, 370.

Also, none of the exceptions to the general common law rule that are laid down in §§ 410-429 Restatement (Second) of Torts applies. A shipowner is not responsible for a classification society.

As concerns *German law*, someone has to answer for the act, neglect or default of another if that person is either a person instructed by the debtor to perform his obligation to the creditor (*Erfüllungsgehilfe*) in contractual relations, or an employee entrusted with the execution of tasks allotted to him (*Verrichtungsgehilfe*) if the claim is based on tort. A *Verrichtungsgehilfe* is defined as a person who is assigned an activity by someone else which is to a certain degree dependent on the other person. The other person retains the right to decide at all times, restrict, prohibit, or fix the time or the extent of the activity of the *Verrichtungsgehilfe*. The opposite of a *Verrichtungsgehilfe* is a person who can at all times freely decide about the time and extent of his activity.

A classification society is not a *Verrichtungsgehilfe* of the shipowner or carrier with respect to the vessel. The aim of a classification society is to ensure the safety and seaworthiness of the ship, not its operation or management day by day. In comparison with pilots, who lead the vessel through difficult waters and ensure its safe arrival, classification societies do not participate in the operation of the vessel. It is one thing to advise the master of the ship in its navigation and another to survey at times its conformity with safety standards. That means that pilotage relates to the operation of the ship, whereas classification societies' surveys merely to its conformity with standards. For this reason, a classification society is not an *Erfüllungsgehilfe* of a contract of the shipowner either. Under *German law*, there is no civil responsibility of the shipowner for the classification society.

To sum up, the shipowner is not responsible for the classification society under the mentioned legal orders. The limitation clauses of the LLMC do not apply to classification societies.

c. Limitations by the Athens Convention

The Athens Convention[1129] also makes reference to *servants* or *agents* of the carrier, but requires for a limitation of their liability that the person has acted within his employment.[1130] Just as in the case of the Hague/Visby Rules, a classification society is neither a *servant* nor an *agent* of the shipowner. The Athens Convention does not limit the liability of classification societies either.

[1129] Athens Convention Relating to the Carriage of Passengers and their Luggage by Sea, 1974 (PAL 1974), as amended by the Protocols of 1976 and 2002 (not yet come into force).

[1130] 'Article 11. Defences and limits for carriers' servants
If an action is brought against a servant or agent of the carrier or of the performing carrier arising out of damage covered by this Convention, such servant or agent, if he proves that he acted within the scope of his employment, shall be entitled to avail himself of the defences and limits of liability which the carrier or the performing carrier is entitled to invoke under this Convention.'

d. Special Limitations: CLC and HNS Convention

aa. The CLC

Art. III (4) of CLC 1969[1131] as amended by the 1992 Protocol has a slightly broader wording than the aforementioned cargo limitations or global limitations.[1132] A classification society could be 'any other person who, without being a member of the crew, performs services for the ship.' From the point of view of a grammatical interpretation, this Article includes everyone who performs services for the ship without being a member of the crew. The classification society is not a member of the crew and only performs periodical surveys as well as repair surveys of the vessel. One might therefore argue that they perform some kind of service for the ship as well. For this reason, *Siccardi* argues that classification societies are protected by the CLC. [1133]

A systematic interpretation, however, puts emphasis on the context. The fact that the paragraph expressly mentions 'a pilot or any other person [...]' indicates that the character of the services performed for the ship has to be somewhat similar to the services of a pilot. The business of a classification society mainly relates to the safety of the vessel, as has been described in the last section, and is therefore different to the character of the services of a pilot.

As has been established, a functional interpretation is also of considerable weight in public international law.[1134] The Preamble to the CLC states that the main objects of the convention are to ensure adequate compensation for persons who suffer damage caused by pollution resulting from the escape or discharge of oil from ships and to adopt uniform international rules and procedures for deter-

---

[1131] With regard to this channelling clause *see* Altfuldisch, *Haftung und Entschädigung nach Tankerunfällen auf See* (forthcoming), Chapter 1, A II 5 a.

[1132] 'Art. III of CLC 1969

(4) No claim for compensation for pollution damage may be made against the owner otherwise than in accordance with this Convention. Subject to paragraph 5 of this Article, no claim for pollution damage under this Convention or otherwise may be made against:

(a) the servants or agents of the owner or the members of the crew;

(b) the pilot or any other person who, without being a member of the crew, performs services for the ship; [...]

(f) all servants or agents of persons mentioned in subparagraphs (c), (d) and (e);

unless the damage resulting from their personal act or omission, committed with the intent to cause such damage, or recklessly and with knowledge that such damage would probably result.'

Before the 1984 Protocol, Article III (4) of the CLC read: 'No claim for pollution damage under this Convention or otherwise may be made against the servants or agents of the owner.' The old versio of this Article must be constured in the same way as the Hamburg Rules and the Athens Convention. It does not envisage classification societies.

[1133] Siccardi, 'Pollution Liability and Classification Societies, Is the System a Fair One?', [2005] *Il Diritto Marittimo* 691, at 707.

[1134] *See supra* Part 3 B I 1 a aa (3).

mining questions of liability and providing adequate compensation in such cases. These objects do not give an answer to the question of whether or not classification societies are taken into account and thus protected by its channelling clause.

A historical argument may be put forth against the inclusion of classification societies in the scope of application of Article III (4) CLC. The International Conference of 1969 wanted to hold the owner primarily responsible for the damage as opposed to requests by some States that the cargo owner or the shipper should be liable for the damage.[1135] Due to the fact that the ownership could change and that both the identity of the cargo owner and the shipper might be relatively difficult to ascertain, it was decided that liability should rest with the shipowner. The question is whether this implied a liability with respect to third parties *exclusively* of the shipowner or *at least* of the shipowner.[1136] Article III (5) might be interpreted as an *exclusive* liability of the shipowner, stating that he is primarily responsible, but recourse is open against third parties.[1137] The 1992 revision changed the legal situation and rephrased the channelling clause. It was extended to pilots, charterers, managers and ships operators, as well as to salvors and persons that take preventive measures. The main question is whether Article III (4) is to be understood in a broad way as a general channelling clause including all third parties or in a narrow way relating only to those persons who are expressly mentioned.

An answer to this question may be found once again by having recourse to a systematic interpretation. If Article III (4) were to include all third parties that perform some kind of service for the ship or was intended to be a complete channelling of liability on the shipowner, it could have been phrased in a much simpler way. Yet the contracting parties have chosen to enumerate precisely which persons are envisaged. This clearly shows that the clause does not introduce a legal

---

1135 For this reason, the 1969 version of Article III CLC reads:

'(1) Except as provided in paragraphs 2 and 3 of this Article, the owner of a ship at the time of an incident, or where the incident consists of a series of occurrences at the time of the first such occurrence, shall be liable for any pollution damage caused by oil which has escaped or been discharged from the ship as a result of the incident. [...]

(4) No claim for compensation for pollution damage shall be made against the owner otherwise than in accordance with this Convention. No claim for pollution damage under this Convention or otherwise may be made against the servants or agents of the owner.'

1136 IMCO, *Official Records of the International Legal Conference on Marine Pollution Damage, 1969* (1973), 623–700.

1137 Article III (5) of CLC:

'Nothing in this Convention shall prejudice any right of recourse of the owner against third parties.'

channelling of all liability on the shipowner,[1138] but solely aims to protect those persons who are mentioned. The clause 'any other person who, without being a member of the crew, performs services for the ship' therefore only refers to persons who exercise services similar to those of a pilot. The services of classification societies aim at the safety of the ship and not at the navigation of it, as those of the pilot do, as has been established before. As a result, classification societies are not protected by Article III (4) CLC.[1139]

This view is affirmed by some authors, who understand the list of Article III (4) as being exhaustive. They argue that it is to be interpreted in a narrow way and should include only those persons whom it mentions.[1140] According to this view, shipbuilders or ship repairers or the owner or operator of a colliding ship, for example, are not included in the channelling clause of Article III (4) of the CLC.[1141] Some authors even clearly state that this clause does not envisage and protect classification societies.[1142]

bb. The HNS Convention

Due to the fact that the HNS Convention has been modelled upon the example of the CLC, its Art. 7 (5) contains a clause which has a very similar wording to the channelling clause of the CLC.[1143] As this clause enumerates in the same way as

---

[1138] As is the case in the law of nuclear installations, *see* the Paris Convention on Third Party Liability in the Field of Nuclear Energy of 1960, which was linked with the Vienna Convention on Civil Liability for Nuclear Damage of 1963 by the Joint Protocol adopted in 1988.

[1139] Contrary: Siccardi, 'Pollution Liability and Classification Societies, Is the System a Fair One?', [2005] *Il Diritto Marittimo* 691, at 707.

[1140] Bates/Benson, *Marine Environment Law* (1993), § 4.76; Wu, *Pollution from the Carriage of Oil by Sea* (1996), 170; De La Rue/Anderson, *Shipping and the Environment* (1998), 97.

[1141] Wu, *Pollution from the Carriage of Oil by Sea* (1996), 170.

[1142] Abecassis/Jarashow, *Oil Pollution from Ships* (1985) § 10–126, at 233; De La Rue/Anderson, *Shipping and the Environment* (1998), 98. This is also stated by Rémond-Gouilloud, 'The Future of the Compensation System as established by International Convention' in De La Rue, (ed.), *Liability for Damage to the Marine Environment* (1993), at 95.

[1143] Art. 7 (5) of the HNS-Convention

'Subject to paragraph 6, no claim for compensation for damage under this Convention or otherwise may be made against:

(a) the servants or agents of the owner or the members of the crew;
(b) the pilot or any other person who, without being a member of the crew, performs services for the ship;
(c) any charterer (howsoever described, including a bareboat charterer), manager or operator of the ship;
(d) any person performing salvage operations with the consent of the owner or on the instructions of a competent public authority;
(e) any person taking preventive measures; and

the CLC the persons that it protects, the intent of the contracting States was also not to limit the liability of all third parties, but only of those who are mentioned. 'Any other person who, without being a member of the crew, performs services for the ship' is only a person that helps with navigation or the like, as for example a pilot does. Classification societies are not protected by this clause.

2. *Regional Regulation: Directive 94/57/EC*

Directive 94/57/EC on common rules and standards for ship inspection and survey organisations and for the relevant activities of maritime administrations[1144] relates solely to classification societies and aims at removing all substandard vessels from Community waters by way of strict enforcement of international conventions with regard to maritime safety and marine pollution. All recognised classification societies[1145] are subject to certain minimum criteria[1146] and a monitoring scheme. The agreement between a flag State and a classification society has to include a clause concerning financial liability and must allow recourse of the flag State against the

(f) the servants or agents of persons mentioned in (c), (d) and (e);
unless the damage resulted from their personal act or omission, committed with the intent to cause such damage, or recklessly and with knowledge that such damage would probably result.'

[1144] Of 22 November 1994, OJ L 0057/2 of 29 November 2002. For a detailed analysis of this Directive *see* Pulido Begines, 'The EU Law on Classification Societies: Scope and Liability Issues', 36 *J.Mar.L.&Com.* 487 (2005); Pulido Begines, 'The Implementation of the EU Community Directive 94/57/EC: Degree of Harmonisation Achieved', [2005] *Il Diritto Marittimo* 1234. *Compare also* Comenale Pinto, 'La Responsabiltà delle Società di Classificazione di Navi', [2003] *Il Diritto Marittimo* 3; Martín Osante, 'La Normativa Comunitaria en Materia de Seguridad Marítima–Sociedades de Clasificación y Transporte de Petróleo', 11 *Anuario de Derecho Marítimo* 163 (2001). The European Commission proposes a revision of this Directive in order to strengthen the control systems, harmonize the system of recognition, improve on the recognition criteria and reform the system of penalties. *See* Commission of the European Communities, Proposal for a Directive on common rules and standards for ship inspection and survey organizations and for the relevant activities of the maritime administration, COM(2005) 587 final. The evaluation of the current Directive is reported in Commission of the European Communities, Commission Working Document on the control of recognised organisations by the Commission, COM(2006) 588 final.

[1145] The European Commission recognised in its Decision 96/587/EC (OJ 1996 D 0587 of 15 March 2002) of 30 September 1996 on the publication of the list of recognised organisations which have been notified by Member States in accordance with Council Directive 94/57/EC on the basis of Art. 4(1) of the Directive ABS, BV, CCS, DNV, GL, KR, LR, ClassNK, RINA and RS. The Hellenic Register of Shipping (HR) is recognised with effects limited to Greece and Registro Internacional Naval, SA (RINAVE) with effects limited to Portugal.

[1146] As defined in the Annex to Article 3 of the Directive.

classification society.[1147] The flag State may limit the liability for services that classification societies perform on its behalf either by way of the agreement with the classification society or through any kind of domestic regulation. The minimum liability must at least be equal to EUR 4 million in the case of a personal injury or death caused by a negligent or reckless act or omission of the classification society or its employees. For loss or damage to property caused by such a negligent or reckless act, it has to be at least equal to EUR 2 million. The Directive does not harmonise the legal basis of responsibility and liability of classification societies in the laws of the member States.[1148] It has also been transposed in different ways. Some Member States have limited the liability of classification societies,[1149] others have not.[1150] This Directive only applies to the public functions of classification societies for the flag States, not to private classification. Furthermore, it only aims at the recourse of the flag State against the classification society if the flag State is held liable by a competent court. Therefore, it does neither touch upon the question of liability of classification societies for private classification nor on the direct liability of these societies to third parties for the performance of statutory surveys.

3. *National Regulation: USA*

a. Cargo Limitations

Both the *Carriage of Goods by Sea Act (COGSA)*[1151] and the *Harter Act*[1152] limit the amount of recovery the cargo owner may receive to a certain amount per package or customary freight unit.[1153] The COGSA is the national implementation of the Hague Rules and protects both the shipowner and the charterer.[1154] As the

---

[1147] Art. 6 (2) lit. b Directive 94/57/EC as amended by Directive 2001/105/EC of 19 December 2001, OJ L 19/9 of 22 January 2002.

[1148] Directive 95/57/EC has been adopted on the basis of Article 80 (2) EC (ex Article 84 (2)).

[1149] Commission of the European Communities, Commission Working Document on the control of recognised organisations by the Commission, COM(2006) 588 final, Annex at 3.1: Cyprus, Hungary, Latvia, Lithuania, Poland, Slovenia, Sweden, UK: 4/2 million Euros for Art. 6.2(b)(ii)/(iii) respectively. Belgiuim, Denmark, Greece, Malta, Portugal, Norway: 5/2.5 million Euros. Finland, Ireland, the Netherlands: 5/2.5 milllion US dollars.

[1150] France, Germany, Italy, Luxemburg and Spain, *see* Commission of the European Communities, Commission Working Document on the control of recognised organisations by the Commission, COM(2006) 588 final, Annex at 3.1.

[1151] The Carriage of Goods by Sea Act, 46 USC App. § 1300–1315.

[1152] Section 3 of the Harter Act, 46 USC §§ 190–196, at § 192.

[1153] 46 USC App. § 1304: USD 500; this limit per package has been accepted by the Courts under the Harter Act as well, *see Gold Medal Trading Corp. v. Atlantic Overseas Corp.*, 580 F.Supp. 610, 1984 A.M.C. 2052 (S.D.N.Y.1984); Schoenbaum, *Admiralty and Maritime Law* (2004), § 10–34, at 716.

[1154] 46 USC § 1301 (a).

COGSA only implements these rules, it does not protect classification societies. Neither does the Harter Act include a clause that might be applicable to classification societies.

b. Global Limitations

Although they are not a party to the LLMC or its predecessors, the United States have had for a long time a somewhat similar system in the *Limitation of Shipowner's Liability Act* of 1851.[1155] The liability of the shipowner is limited to the value of the vessel and pending freight (which is the total earnings of the shipowner for the voyage),[1156] provided that the accident occurred without his privity or knowledge.[1157] The value of the vessel is determined at the termination of the voyage or the marine casualty. In the case of a total loss, the value of the vessel is zero. Insurance proceeds which the shipowner receives in respect of the casualty are not included in the limitation fund.[1158] If a loss of life or personal injury occurs and this sum is insufficient to cover the damages, the owner of a seagoing vessel is required to set up an additional fund.[1159] Classification societies are not protected by this Act.

c. Special Limitations: OPA 1990 and CERCLA

Even though the United States have adopted most international conventions that protect the marine environment, they have not signed the CLC and the Fund Conventions and are not likely to sign the HNS or the Bunker Oil Convention either.[1160] Instead, the United States have enacted the *Federal Water Pollution Control Act*, as amended by the *Clean Water Act*, which was partly superseded or modified by the *Oil Pollution Act* of 1990 *(OPA)*.[1161] The OPA was introduced in

---

[1155] 46 USC § 181–189. 46 USC § 183c provides that a carrier may not contract out of his liability for negligent acts that result in personal injury or death of passengers. To a limited extent, a carrier may limit his liability in cases of emotional distress, mental suffering or psychological injury except when such injury occurs in specified circumstances (46 USC § 183c (b)). *See* also Benedict, *On Admiralty* (2002), vol. 3 §§ 1–71; McCauley, 'Limitations of Liability and Recreational Vessels', 16 *Tul.Mar.L.J.* 289 (1992); Chen, *Limitation of Liability for Maritime Claims* (2001), 18–24, 30–54; Schoenbaum, *Admiralty and Maritime Law* (2004), § 15, 136–162; Schoenfeld/Butterworth, 'Limitation of Liability: The Defense Perspective', 28 *Tul.Mar.L.J.* 219 (2004).

[1156] *The Main v. Williams,* 152 US 122 (1894).

[1157] 46 USC § 183 (a).

[1158] *Place v. Norwich & NY Transp. Co. v. Wright*, 118 US 468 (1886).

[1159] 46 USC § 183 (b).

[1160] Force, 'United States', in: Huybrechts, *International Encyclopaedia of Laws, Vol. 3, Transport Law* (1998), § 296.

[1161] OPA is codified in 33 USC §§ 2701–2761. Anonymous, 'Anatomy of an oil spill: Exxon Valdez and the Oil Pollution Act of 1990. Note', *Seton Hall Legis.J.* 331 (1993); Rodriguez/Jaffe, 'Oil Pollution Act of 1990', 15 *Tul.Mar.L.J.* 1 (1990); Kopec/Peterson, 'Crude legislation: Liability and compensation under the Oil Pollution Act of 1990', 23 *Rutgers L.J.* 597 (1992); Schmuck, *Der US-Oil Pollution Act* (1996).

the aftermath of the "*Exxon Valdez*" oil spill, which was the largest spill in the US, but is not even under the top 20 oil spills world-wide.[1162] As concerns pollution from hazardous substances other than oil, the Clean Water Act has been supplemented by the *Comprehensive Environmental Response, Compensation, and Liability Act (CERCLA).*[1163] Both OPA and CERCLA provide for a strict liability and include provisions on the limitation of liability.[1164] In comparison with the CLC, the OPA is much stricter as regards the limitations of liability,[1165] the accepted age of tankers and their construction, as it does not admit single-hull tankers.[1166] Similarly, it is easier to exceed the limits of liability included in CERCLA, *e.g.* if the primary cause of the release was a violation (within the privity or knowledge of such person) of applicable safety, construction or operating standards or regulations.[1167] Damage which exceeds the limits of OPA and CERCLA are compensated for by a '*Superfund*'.[1168] The maximum amount which may be paid by the Oil Spill Liability Trust Fund for a single incident shall not exceed USD 1,000 million.[1169]

For precise observations on the relationship between these different legal regimes, *see* Rodgers, *Environmental Law* (1994), § 4.1. Additionally, an action may be brought under common law principles or special legislation enacted by some states, *see* Beaver/Butler/Myster, 'Stormy Seas? Analysis of new oil pollution laws in the west states', 34 *Santa Clara L.Rev.* 791 (1994); Harrington, 'Oil Pollution Act's delegation of admiralty power to the states', 48 *Case Western Reserve L.R.* 1 (1997); Mullahy, 'State's rights and the Oil Pollution Act of 1990', 25 *Hofstra L.R.* 607 (1996); Lipeles, 'State Control of Oil Pollution: Legislating in the Twilight Zone', 1 *Harv. Envt'l. Rev.* 431 (1976).

1162 *Özçayir,* 'The "Erika" and its Aftermath', 7 *Int.M.L.*, 230 (2000), at 234.

1163 CERCLA is codified in 42 USC § 9601–9675. For further information on OPA and CERCLA, please refer to Bagwell, 'Liability under United States Law for Spills of Oil or Chemicals from Vessels', [1987] *L.M.C.L.Q.* 496.

1164 OPA: 33 USC §§ 2702 (a), 2704; CERCLA 42 USC § 9607(a), (c).

1165 The total of liability incurred by the responsible party with respect to an incident is USD 1,200 per gross ton or, in the case of a vessel greater than 3,000 gross tons, USD 10,000,000, *see* 33 USC § 2704 (a) (1). Evidence of financial responsibility sufficient to meet the maximum amount of liability is required if the vessel uses any place subject to the jurisdiction of the United States or enters the exclusive economic zone in order to transship or lighter oil which is destined for a place subject to the jurisdiction of the United States, 33 USC § 2716 (a).

1166 For this reason, the European Commission fears that these tankers will be operated in EU waters from 2005, when they have to be phased out according to OPA, *see Özçayir,* 'The "Erika" and its Aftermath', 7 *Int.M.L.* 230, at 234 (2000).

1167 42 USC § 9607 (c) (2) (A) (ii).

1168 Hazardous Substances Superfund: 26 USC § 9507; Oil Spill Liability Trust Fund: 26 USC § 9509.

1169 26 USC § 9509 (c) (2). *See* also Özçayir, 'The "Erika" and its Aftermath', 7 *Int.M.L.* 230 (2000), at 237.

One could consider whether classification societies are covered by the definition of the person that is strictly liable under CERCLA. The Act envisages notably the owner and operator of a vessel or a facility, under certain circumstances the owner of hazardous substances, and the person who transports such hazardous substances.[1170] A classification society is not included. Despite the fact that CERCLA provides for an exemption of the responsible parties if the damage was caused solely by a third party, such a third party is neither strictly liable for the damage nor can it limit its liability pursuant to CERCLA.[1171] These regulations do not envisage classification societies.

OPA, by contrast, could possibly provide for a strict liability of classification societies and limit this liability at the same time. According to 33 USC § 2702 (a), the person who is responsible for a vessel is strictly liable for removal costs and

---

[1170] 42 USCA § 9607 (a): Notwithstanding any other provision or rule of law, and subject only to the defenses set forth in subsection (b) of this section--

(1) the owner and operator of a vessel or a facility,
(2) any person who at the time of disposal of any hazardous substance owned or operated any facility at which such hazardous substances were disposed of,
(3) any person who by contract, agreement, or otherwise arranged for disposal or treatment, or arranged with a transporter for transport for disposal or treatment, of hazardous substances owned or possessed by such person, by any other party or entity, at any facility or incineration vessel owned or operated by another party or entity and containing such hazardous substances, and
(4) any person who accepts or accepted any hazardous substances for transport to disposal or treatment facilities, incineration vessels or sites selected by such person, from which there is a release, or a threatened release which causes the incurrence of response costs, of a hazardous substance, shall be liable for-- […]

[1171] 42 USC § 9607 (b): There shall be no liability under subsection (a) of this section for a person otherwise liable who can establish by a preponderance of the evidence that the release or threat of release of a hazardous substance and the damages resulting therefrom were caused solely by-- […]

(3) an act or omission of a third party other than an employee or agent of the defendant, or than one whose act or omission occurs in connection with a contractual relationship, existing directly or indirectly, with the defendant (except where the sole contractual arrangement arises from a published tariff and acceptance for carriage by a common carrier by rail), if the defendant establishes by a preponderance of the evidence that (a) he exercised due care with respect to the hazardous substance concerned, taking into consideration the characteristics of such hazardous substance, in light of all relevant facts and circumstances, and (b) he took precautions against foreseeable acts or omissions of any such third party and the consequences that could foreseeably result from such acts or omissions; […]

certain other damages.[1172] More generally speaking, a "responsible party" is defined as any person that owns, operates or demise-charters the vessel.[1173] Only if a third party is solely responsible for the discharge of oil will it be treated as the responsible person. That third party will therefore be strictly liable for the discharge pursuant to 33 USC § 2702 (d), but may limit its liability in the same way as the shipowner could.[1174] As a prerequisite, however, the third party must fulfil the description of 33 USC § 2703 (a) (3), which requires that third party to be a 'third party, other than an employee or agent of the responsible party or a third party whose act or omission occurs in connection with any contractual relationship with the responsible party (except where the sole contractual arrangement arises in connection with carriage by a common carrier by rail).' The acts which might lead

---

[1172] 33 USC § 2702 (a): Notwithstanding any other provision or rule of law, and subject to the provisions of this Act, each responsible party for a vessel or a facility from which oil is discharged, or which poses the substantial threat of a discharge of oil, into or upon the navigable waters or adjoining shorelines or the exclusive economic zone is liable for the removal costs and damages specified in subsection (b) of this section that result from such incident.

[1173] 33 USC § 2701 (32) (A).

[1174] (d) Liability of third parties

(1) In general

(A) Third party treated as responsible party

Except as provided in subparagraph (B), in any case in which a responsible party establishes that a discharge or threat of a discharge and the resulting removal costs and damages were caused solely by an act or omission of one or more third parties described in section 2703 (a) (3) of this title (or solely by such an act or omission in combination with an act of God or an act of war), the third party or parties shall be treated as the responsible party or parties for purposes of determining liability under this subchapter.

(B) Subrogation of responsible party

If the responsible party alleges that the discharge or threat of a discharge was caused solely by an act or omission of a third party, the responsible party--

(i) in accordance with section 2713 of this title, shall pay removal costs and damages to any claimant; and

(ii) shall be entitled by subrogation to all rights of the United States Government and the claimant to recover removal costs or damages from the third party or the Fund paid under this subsection.

(2) Limitation applied

(A) Owner or operator of vessel or facility

If the act or omission of a third party that causes an incident occurs in connection with a vessel of facility owned or operated by the third party, the liability of the third party shall be subject to the limits provided in section 2704 of this title as applied with respect to the vessel or facility.

(B) Other cases

In any other case, the liability of a third party or parties shall not exceed the limitation which would have been applicable to the responsible party of the vessel or facility from which the discharge actually occurred if the responsible party were liable.

to a liability of classification societies may only occur in a contractual relationship with the shipowner.[1175] A classification society is, therefore, not a third party in the sense of 33 USC §§ 2702 (d) (1) (A), 2703 (a) (3). Hence, OPA does not apply to classification societies.

The last statute that determines a special limitation is the *Clean Water Act (CWA)*. This Act, which has amended the *Federal Water Pollution Control Act*, relates to the discharge of both oil and hazardous substances. Its regulations regarding liability for the discharge of oil have been expressly superseded by OPA.[1176] With regard to the discharge of hazardous substances, which is also covered by CERCLA, there is no such provision. Other than CERCLA, CWA holds a third party liable which solely causes the discharge of the hazardous substance by its act or omission, regardless of the relationship between the third party and the shipowner.[1177] Under the CWA, a classification society could therefore be liable

---

[1175] *See* also *United Sates v. J.R. Nelson Vessel Ltd.*, 1 F.Supp.2d 172, 1998 A.M.C. 2249 (E.D.NY.1998), aff'd, 173 F.3d 847 (2d.Cir.1999).

[1176] Section 2002 (a) of United States Public Laws 101–380 of 18 August 1990, 104 Stat. 484, provides that: 'Subsections (f), (g), (h), and (i) of section 311 of the Federal Water Pollution Control Act (33 USC 1321) shall not apply with respect to any incident for which liability is established under section 1002 of this Act [33 USC 2702].'

[1177] 33 USC § 1321 (g): Third party liability
Where the owner or operator of a vessel (other than an inland oil barge) carrying oil or hazardous substances as cargo or an onshore or offshore facility which handles or stores oil or hazardous substances in bulk, from which oil or a hazardous substance is discharged in violation of subsection (b) of this section, alleges that such discharge was caused solely by an act or omission of a third party, such owner or operator shall pay to the United States Government the actual costs incurred under subsection (c) of this section for removal of such oil or substance and shall be entitled by subrogation to all rights of the United States Government to recover such costs from such third party under this subsection. In any case where an owner or operator of a vessel, of an onshore facility, or of an offshore facility, from which oil or a hazardous substance is discharged in violation of subsection (b) (3) of this section, proves that such discharge of oil or hazardous substance was caused solely by an act or omission of a third party, or was caused solely by such an act or omission in combination with an act of God, an act of war or negligence on the part of the United States Government, such third party shall, notwithstanding any other provision of law, be liable to the United States Government for the actual costs incurred under subsection (c) of this section for removal of such oil or substance by the United States Government, except where such third party can prove that such discharge was caused solely by (A) an act of God, (B) an act of war, (C) negligence on the part of the United States Government, or (D) an act or omission of another party without regard to whether such act or omission was or was not negligent, or any combination of the foregoing clauses. If such third party was the owner or operator of a vessel which caused the discharge of oil or a hazardous substance in violation of subsection (b) (3) of this section, the liability of such third party under this subsection shall not exceed, in the case of an inland oil barge $125 per gross ton of such barge, or $125,000, whichever is greater, and in the case of any other vessel, $150 per gross ton

and benefit from the limitation provisions if it were solely responsible for the discharge. The Courts, however, construe this provision in a narrow way. A "third party" in the sense of this provision is only a party which is neither an agent nor an independent contractor of the shipowner.[1178] As a classification society is an independent contractor, it is not a "third party" pursuant to the CWA. It can neither be held liable under these provisions nor does it benefit from its limitations.

In conclusion, the United States system of limitations of liability in shipping does not protect classification societies either.

4. CMI Model Contractual Clauses and Principles of Conduct

In order to provide a complete picture of the regulations on the limitation of liability and on classification societies, the Model Contractual Clauses and the Princi-

---

of such vessel (or, for a vessel carrying oil or hazardous substances as cargo, $250,000), whichever is greater. In any other case the liability of such third party shall not exceed the limitation which would have been applicable to the owner or operator of the vessel or the onshore or offshore facility from which the discharge actually occurred if such owner or operator were liable. If the United States can show that the discharge of oil or a hazardous substance in violation of subsection (b) (3) of this section was the result of willful negligence or willful misconduct within the privity and knowledge of such third party, such third party shall be liable to the United States Government for the full amount of such removal costs. The United States may bring an action against the third party in any court of competent jurisdiction to recover such removal costs.

1178 *Burgess v. M/V Tamano*, 564 F.2d 964, at 982 (C.A.Me.1977): 'There appears to be no specifically significant legislative history, other than a change from a House version based on fault to a Senate version in the direction of strict liability. H.R.Rep. No. 127, 91st Cong., 1st Sess. (1969); S.Rep. No. 351, 91st Cong., 1st Sess. (1969); Conf.Rep. No. 940, 91st Cong., 2d Sess. (1970), but this change itself indicates that unless the exceptions are narrowly construed, the legislative purpose would be largely vitiated. The first three exceptions, "(A) an act of God, (B) an act of war, (C) negligence on the part of the United States Government," (which, individually or collectively, must be "solely" responsible) are manifestly addressed to actions entirely outside the ship, or in the case of actors, to strangers. We read the final exception, "(D) an act or omission of a third party without regard to whether such an act or omission was or was not negligent," correspondingly. To take a simple example, if a vandal opened a ship's valve, this would be an act of a third party. However, if the valve failed because of an act of the installer, the owners should not be permitted to avoid liability by claiming that the installer was a third party because he was an independent contractor rather than an employee. The installer acts for the ship.' This interpretation is confirmed by *United States of America v. LeBeouf Brothers Towing Co.*, 621 F.2d 787 (C.A.La.1980); *United States of America v. Hollywood Marine, Inc., et al.*, 625 F.2d 524, 1981 A.M.C. 2646 (C.A.Tex.1980), *cert. denied, Hollywood Marine, Inc., et al. v. United States of America*, 451 U.S. 994 101 S.Ct. 2336, 68 L.Ed.2d 855 (U.S.1981). Justice Rehnquist dissented and argued that such interpretation does not correspond with the plain language of the statute, which expressly provides a defense whenever the discharge is the result of an act of a "third party" (*ibid.*, at 995).

ples of Conduct for classification societies issued by the Comité Maritime International (CMI) shall be briefly mentioned.[1179] A Joint Working Group discussed these provisions from 1992 until 1999. As it was considered that a convention on the limitation of the liability of classification societies, possibly as an amendment to the LLMC, would take at least 8 to 10 years before it could become effective, the way of private regulation was chosen.[1180] Attention was focused on both the agreements between the classification societies and the flag States (public functions) and those with shipowners (private functions). However, as the classification societies and the shipowners could not agree on a maximum limit of liability to be inserted in the Clauses, the respective spaces were left blank in the Model Clauses. No coherent limitation of liability was introduced. The Model Clauses are intended to provide a uniform system of contractual liability, but as neither limitation based on a fixed sum nor one based on a fee basis could be enacted, they only serve as a guideline for the classification societies when drafting their General Conditions. A more relevant issue, however, is third-party liability, which has not even been tackled by the initiative. The Principles of Conduct set a good example of the rights and duties of classification societies and may serve to define their standard of care. The Model Contractual Clauses, however, did not succeed in their aim of harmonising the limitation of liability.

5. Conclusion

A number of international conventions and national legislation by the United States limit liability in shipping. None of these regulations applies to classification societies. There is no limitation of liability as concerns the exercise of private or public functions. Only the Member States of the European Union may introduce, as flag States in the agreement with a classification society, a limitation of recourse against these societies because of their exercise of public functions.

[1179] [1995] *CMI Yearbook* 1995, 100–106; also reprinted in Annex A & B to Wiswall, 'Classification societies: issues considered by the Joint Working Group', 2 *I.J.S.L.* 171 (1997), at 183, 185; Wiswall, 'Report and Panel Discussion concerning the Joint Working Group on a Study of Issues Re Classification Societies', [1995] *Il Diritto Marittimo* 66, at 274, 277.

[1180] Wiswall, 'Classification societies: issues considered by the Joint Working Group', 2 *I.J.S.L.* 171 (1997), at 172; Wiswall, 'Report and Panel Discussion concerning the Joint Working Group on a Study of Issues Re Classification Societies', [1994], *CMI Yearbook 1994*, 228, at 229. *Compare also* Wiswall, 'Report and Panel Discussion concerning the Joint Working Group on a Study of Issues Re Classification Societies', [1995] *Il Diritto Marittimo* 66.

II. The "Estonia" Case – an Example of the Effects of the Current System

On 28 September 1994, *en route* from Tallinn to Stockholm, the ro-ro passenger ferry "*Estonia*" sank in international waters in the Baltic Sea with the loss of 852 lives.[1181] The ship had been built in Germany in 1979 by *Jos. L. Meyer Werft GmbH* and had been operated by the Swedish-Estonian company *EstLine Marine Company* since January 1993. Half of the company was owned by the Estonian Government, the other by the Swedish company *Nordström & Thulin*. The cause of the sinking continues to be the subject of numerous speculations,[1182] especially because Estonia, Finland and Sweden concluded an agreement by which they designated the *Estonia* as a maritime grave instead of diving for remains and salvaging the wreck.[1183] Under the agreement, citizens of the contracting States[1184] are penalised if they approach the wreck.

The Athens Convention does not apply to this case, because neither Estonia nor Sweden has ratified it.[1185] Yet that does not mean that the shipowner is liable to an unlimited amount. Instead, the shipowner can resort to the global limitation included in the London Convention of 1976. The LLMC was in force in Sweden at the time of the tragedy in its status before the 1996 Protocol. Estonia, however, has not ratified the LLMC. Accordingly, the shipowner could only seek to limit his liability before a Swedish court.[1186]

[1181] The official report on the capsizing is accessible at <http://www.onnettomuustutkinta.fi/estonia/>, last accessed on 19 March 2007. Technical Details are enclosed in IMO Doc. FSI 4/Inf.2. The report is also published by The Joint Accident Investigation Commission, *Final report on the capsizing on 28 September 1994 in the Baltic Sea on the ro-ro passenger vessel MV Estonia* (1997). There is also an unofficial report by "The German Group of Experts", which was financed by the shipyard Jos. L. Meyer GmbH. It can be accessed at <http://www.estoniaferrydisaster.net>, last accessed on 19 March 2007. *See* also Jacobsson, Marie/Klabbers, 'Rest in Peace? New Developments Concerning the Wreck of the *M/S Estonia*', 69 *Nor.J.I.L.* 317 (2000).

[1182] *See* for example LL 30 November 1996, 20 August 1997, 26 September 1997, and 6 December 2004.

[1183] The text of the agreement is attached to Jacobsson, Marie/Klabbers, 'Rest in Peace? New Developments Concerning the Wreck of the *M/S Estonia*', 69 *Nor.J.I.L.* 317, at 330 (2000).

[1184] Subsequently Denmark, Latvia, Russia and the United Kingdom have acceded to the Agreement.

[1185] In general, the Convention applies if (a) the ship is flying the flag of or is registered in a State Party to this Convention, or (b) the contract of carriage has been made in a State Party to this Convention, or (c) the place of departure or destination, according to the contract of carriage, is in a State Party to this Convention.

[1186] Article 15 LLMC. There are no reports about litigation in Estonia. The reasons why there was no litigation of at least the domestic claimants, to whom no limitation would have applied (unless the Estonian domestic law limits the shipowner's liability), remains unknown.

The *Estonia* was authorised to carry 2,000 passengers. Under Swedish law, the level of limitation of the LLMC of SDR 46,666 per passenger has been increased to SDR 100,000 per passenger.[1187] According to Swedish law, the liability should therefore be limited to SDR 200 million for the 2,000 passengers with a limitation of SDR 100,000 per passenger.[1188] However, in this case the Swedish regulation does not increase the compensation for the victims. Article 7 of the LLMC limits the liability of the shipowner to a maximum of SDR 25 million (approximately USD 36.6 million). The overall limit in Article 7 LLMC therefore has the effect of a substantial limitation of the liability.

The shipowner's insurance company offered compensation to the victims of the casualty totalling USD 75 million in exchange for a contract disclaiming their rights to sue the company.[1189] In order to avoid litigation in both the countries of domicile of the claimants and in the United States, the offer has been higher than what the claimants would have received under the LLMC. More than 90% of all claimants have accepted the offer.[1190] In the aftermath of this tragic incident, approximately 1,200 claimants, victims and families from 14 countries claimed damages in the Court of Nanterre, France, against the Swedish maritime administration as well as against the vessel's shipyard, *Jos. L. Meyer Werft GmbH*, and the classification society BV. The case is still pending.[1191] A small number of claimants also seized a Swedish court in Stockholm.[1192]

As the example of the *Estonia* illustrates, even though the victim may theoretically sue several different persons, from an economic point of view it makes the most sense to sue a particular one, in this case both the shipyard and the classification society. The main reason why the plaintiff takes the effort to sue them, is the comparatively low amount of compensation which he receives from the shipowner. Especially in cases of cargo damage, the levels of limitation in favour of the carrier are so low that there is a good reason to sue the classification society, in particular as their liability is not limited at the moment. Because of the limited compensation by the shipowner, the claimants are likely to try to sue a classification society even if the chances of winning might not be very high. Nevertheless, the prospect of a very high reward in the case of winning their suits motivates the claimants to take the risk. The existing legal uncertainty as to whether or not classification societies can be held liable, in which cases and whether the limitations

---

1187 Dent/Roe, 'Liability, conventions, classification societies and safety in the Baltic–a case study of the Estonia' in: Roe (ed.): *Developments in the Baltic Maritime Marketplace* (1997), 83, at 91.

1188 SDR 200 million is approximately USD 293 million. For the daily conversion rate of the Special Drawing Rights, please consult <http://www.imf.org>, last accessed 19 March 2007.

1189 The offer is more precisely described in: Dent/Roe, *ibid.*, at 91–98.

1190 Dent/Roe, *ibid.*, at 96; *LL*, 1 April 1995.

1191 Case numbers: RG 0412238 and RG 0311275 (<http://www.elaestonia.org/>, last accessed 19 March 2007).

1192 LL 14 August 1996, 27 October 1998, 5 June 1998.

in shipping have any effect on classification societies intensifies such motivation. As long as it is not certain to which degree classification societies can be held liable, there will always be plaintiffs who will try to explore the possibilities of their liability and initiate proceedings against them.

There may also be a psychological motivation to sue a classification society. Injured parties, especially if they are private persons, often search for someone who can be made responsible for the incident. If the injured parties have made a deal with the insurance company of the shipowner, as was the case for most claimants in the *Estonia* case, proceedings against the classification society may determine the person by judicial order who was responsible for the incident and what had caused the vessel to sink. The classification society may therefore be sued, even if it is not at fault. If the plaintiffs find lawyers who work on a contingency-fee basis, the plaintiffs' initial costs may be rather low. This further stimulates an action. As it is very difficult to prove what exactly caused the casualty and whether the classification society did not perform as it should have done, tedious trials unfold. Such trials are mostly quite inefficient and they are likely to increase the costs for the entire shipping industry – and consequently for the customers as well. The ones who benefit the most from this situation are the lawyers who are involved.[1193]

From a general point of view, the plaintiff in such cases is often the insurance company of the cargo-owner, which tries to take recourse against the classification society. Such companies usually have sufficient financial means to resort to legal remedies. Unlike oil pollution damage, cargo claims are claims for property damage and not for economic loss. Under such circumstances, it is easier to state one's case, as is illustrated by the fact that in most cases against classification societies, claims were made for cargo damage.[1194]

Moreover, classification societies are considered to be wealthy. Plaintiffs perceive big classification societies as "deep pockets" because of their steady income through classification and other services and the possibility to insure their risks. If a plaintiff wins a case, there is a high probability that he will be able to enforce his

---

1193 There is a similar economic channelling on the others who do not profit from a limitation in air transport. The injured person will most likely call on these persons, *see* Schneider, *Haftung und Haftungsbeschränkung bei Personenschäden im internationalen Lufttransport* (1999), 194. There are thoughts of a system which includes them, *see* Schweickhardt, *Die Kanalisierung der Luftfrachtführerhaftung*, [1979] 2 *Association Suisse de Droit Aérien et Spatiale–Bulletin* 5, at 17.

1194 English Law: *Marc Rich & Co. AG v. Bishop Rock Marine Co. Ltd. (and ClassNK) ("The Nicholas H."),* [1992] 2 Lloyd's Rep. 481 (Q.B.D.); (C. A.) [1994] 1 Lloyd's Rep. 492; (H.L.) [1995] 2 Lloyd's Rep. 299. United States Law: *Steamship Mutual Underwriting Association Ltd. v. Bureau Veritas*, 380 F.Supp. 482 (E.D.La. 1973); *Continental Insurance Co. v. Daewoo Shipbuilding & Heavy Machinery Ltd.*, 707 F.Supp. 123 (S.D.N.Y.1988); *Carbotrade v. Bureau Veritas,* 901 F.Supp. 737, 1996 A.M.C. 561 (S.D.N.Y.1995), *vacated on other grounds,* 99 F.3d 86, 1997 A.M.C. 98 (2d Cir.1996), *cert. denied sub. nom. Veritas v. Carbotrade S.p.A.,* 117 S.Ct. 2454 (1997); *Cargill, Inc. v. Bureau Veritas*, 902 F.Supp. 49 (S.D.N.Y.1995).

claims. This high probability of compensation is also part of the motivation to sue a classification society.

It is uncertain whether the system will change in the future. The higher limitations that are laid down in the Protocols to the LLMC and the Athens Convention have so far been ratified by only a small number of countries. A higher or an even unlimited liability of the shipowner does not seem to be on the agenda for the moment. Only the liability for oil pollution has been considerably increased by the 1992 Protocol, which is now in force in 110 countries, representing 94.27% of the world's tonnage according to the IMO.[1195] In brief, it is not very likely that the economic channelling of liability on classification societies will change within the near future.

III. Conclusion

It is an equitable principle of law that the person who is primarily responsible for the danger shall have to bear the consequences, not a person who is remote and does not possess similar means to control the risk. Notwithstanding this, because of economic channelling it is rather the classification society which has to answer for the damage. It even has to answer for an unlimited amount.

If classification societies are liable to an unlimited amount in contrast to the shipowner, who may limit his liability, the system is not in balance. It contradicts the role the classification society plays, in particular the fact that it has only a limited control over the vessel as has been described *supra*.[1196] The shipowner shall be primarily responsible and liable for his ship, corresponding to his duty to secure the seaworthiness of the ship. The classification society has no such duty, but nonetheless cannot limit its liability. The perception that classification societies are "deep pockets" further increases the pressure on them. The liability of classification societies is only limited in the sense that they solely have to stand in for a negligent performance of their activities. If, however, a claim arises, their liability goes further than that of the shipowner, despite the fact that classification societies are no more responsible for the vessel than is the shipowner. In this regard, their liability does not correspond to their responsibility.

[1195] Summary of Status of Conventions as at 31 August 2005, accessible at <http://www.imo.org/>, last accessed 19 March 2007.

[1196] *See supra* Part 1 A I, Part 1 A VI 3 and Part 2 A I 1.

C. Justifications of a New Convention on the Limitation of Liability

I. Classification Societies as a Part of the Maritime Safety System

With respect to their particular classification services and statutory services, classification societies are of such relevance to the operation of the vessels that they cannot be compared with any kind of land-based institution of technical experts. There are several advantages in a system of maritime safety that calls upon the help of classification societies and of the system of classification. From an economic point of view, it is much more efficient to have a few companies which possess the necessary technical knowledge and means to exercise such surveys world-wide than to require each flag State to have sufficient surveyors to check its vessels. This is also illustrated by the fact that national marine safety agencies concentrate on the exercise of only those statutory surveys which generate the largest revenue, and delegate others to classification societies.[1197] Classification societies are also required because of the international character of shipping. A ship is today in one port and tomorrow in another port of call, and will hardly ever be in its port of registry. If the flag States had to send surveyors to other countries, it would have to face a problem of diplomacy and international law, and a considerable amount of bureaucracy and high costs would be incurred. If one society can conduct several surveys at the same time, be they classification or statutory, the layover time of the vessel is reduced. In short, classification societies act for the benefit of the entire maritime system. Due to limited capacity, governments tend to assign them even more duties, *e.g.*, regarding the checking of security as required by the ISPS Code. The system of maritime safety would be less secure and more expensive without them than it is with them. As an integral part of the system of maritime safety, classification societies should therefore benefit from similar limitations to those affecting most of the shipping industry.

II. Insurance and Compensation

1. Insurability of Unlimited Claims Against Classification Societies

One of the main reasons for the limitations is the necessity of insurance for very high claims.[1198] It is, therefore, of interest whether or not classification societies could insure an unlimited liability or whether a limitation of their liability is needed because otherwise the risks could not be insured. The person who is responsible should always have the possibility of insuring himself against the poten-

---

1197 'Marine Safety in Switch to Agency', *LL* 13 November 1992, at 1.

1198 As Basedow points out, economic considerations have always had a dominating influence on the limitations of liability, Basedow, *Der Transportvertrag* (1987), 463.

tially disastrous effects of liability. The International Legal Conference on Marine Pollution Damage, for example, which took place in Brussels in 1969, was very much concerned about the insurability of the risks of transporting oil.[1199] The members of the Conference were convinced that the insurance market could not cover all risks caused by the transport of such cargo and that the maximum exposure of the shipowner to liability should correspond to the maximum cover offered by insurance companies. The limits were therefore fixed at a level that was thought to be sustainable by the insurance market.

There is hardly any information available on whether or not the insurance market today could cover unlimited liability of classification societies or to which amount it could provide cover.[1200] Classification societies currently insure their risks, but not to an unlimited amount.[1201] Their risk is, however, calculated with regard to the fact that there are only a few cases in which they have been held liable so far. There are no companies which insure unlimited claims for oil pollution or personal injuries of passengers against the shipowner.[1202] Accordingly, it appears to be highly probable that hardly any insurance company will offer insurance for such claims against classification societies, which may also face considerably high passenger claims, especially if their liability is unlimited. In the existing insurance contracts, insurance companies have included ceilings beyond which they do not pay.

Only an institution similar to a P&I Club could offer a higher coverage. The extremely high insurance coverage, which is offered to vessels trading in United States waters, can only be assured because of the P&I system with a large basis of contributors. However, sharing the risk mutually between classification societies will not be possible. The ten international societies associated in the IACS vary significantly in the structure of their classed fleets, as some of them specialise in container vessels, others in bulk or passenger vessels. Different vessels have a different risk structure, which contradicts effective risk segregation. The more different the risk structure, the more difficult it is to establish a consistent premium which is accepted by all members of the club. Apart from this, it would be practi-

---

1199 *See e.g.* IMCO, *Official Records of the International Legal Conference of Marine Pollution Damage, 1969* (1973), 727 *et seq.*

1200 *See* Commission of the European Communities, Commission Working Document on the control of recognised organisations by the Commission of 11 October 2006, COM(2006) 588 final, Annex at 3.6. Similarly, the available capacity of the insurance market regarding oil pollution claims is also unknown, Colton, 'The Underwriting of Oil Pollution Risks' in De La Rue (ed.), *Liability for Damage to the Marine Environment* (1993), 153.

1201 Their professional indemnity cover generally spans between 10 and 100 million US dollars on an aggregate basis rather than a "per incident" cap, *see* Commission of the European Communities, Commission Working Document on the control of recognised organisations by the Commission, of 11 October 2006, COM(2006) 588 final, Annex at 3.6.

1202 Gauci, *Oil Pollution at Sea* (1997), 154.

cally impossible to include both national and international classification societies in the same club. It is highly unlikely that classification societies could be convinced to answer for each other, especially for national societies which international ones often consider to be substandard. If the parties in the pool do not accept to share the risk, because they do not consider one another equal, a pool solution will not work.[1203] Even within the IACS, the differences between the societies are so great that this association has several times been in danger of breaking apart.[1204] Another difficulty is that the number of classification societies is not large enough for an effective spreading of risk. As they invest most of their revenue in research and development, their capital base is too low to share the risks among themselves. Also, such an institution similar to a P&I Club would need to buy reinsurance for most of the risks it insures. However, reinsurance also introduces a ceiling beyond which it does not offer coverage. As a result, it is highly improbable that classification societies could insure an unlimited risk, be it with an insurance company or through a structure similar to a P&I Club.

2. Should the Shipowner be Protected from Additional Insurance Costs?

In England and the United States, it has been argued that the limitations in favour of shipowners and carriers aim at protecting them from the costs of insurance against unlimited liability.[1205] In the same vein, it is argued that classification societies should not be held liable to an unlimited amount, because they are likely to make up for their own costs by increasing the costs of their services. However, neither the preambles nor the texts of international conventions support such argumentation. In the official documents, one can indeed find the argument that the limitations of the shipowner correspond to the levels which the market can insure.[1206] Yet it is not mentioned anywhere that the shipowner should be protected from paying the premium for an unlimited liability or for any additional premium in an indirect way by paying the costs of classification of a vessel. Apart from that, it is not certain whether or not the costs of classification will increase. It is uncertain whether classification societies can charge higher prices in order to make good any changes in the insurance premium because the market for classifi-

---

[1203] *Compare* Faure/Skogh, *The Economic Analysis of Environmental Policy and Law* (2003), 273.

[1204] *See supra* Part 1 A V.

[1205] *See also* Lord *Steyn* in *Marc Rich & Co. AG v. Bishop Rock Marine Co. Ltd. (and Class NK) ("The Nicholas H.")*, [1995] 2 Lloyd's Rep. 299 (H.L.), at 315.

[1206] *See e.g.* IMCO, *Official Records of the International Legal Conference of Marine Pollution Damage, 1969* (1973), 727 *et seq.*

cation is a highly competitive one.[1207] Moreover, it is not certain that classification societies need to increase their prices at all, since they already pay for insurance today. Besides, even if the classification society can charge higher prices, it is not necessarily the shipowner who pays for these additional costs in the end, but rather the consumer. The shipowner will try to pass on such costs to his own clients. The argumentation that the shipowner should be protected from additional costs is, therefore, not reflected in the relevant conventions and not convincing.[1208]

III. Existence of a System of Compensation for Oil Pollution Damage

Moreover, as regards oil pollution damage, there is a comprehensive system which aims at a socialisation of the risks of the transport of oil. As has been analysed *supra*, the limitations of the liability of the shipowner are accompanied by several international funds that seek to offer effective compensation for the damage whilst being financed by a broad base of contributors.[1209] The channelling provisions in the CLC and the Bunker Oil Convention also show that this system is supposed to be an integrated one. There is no single legal entity that should have to shoulder all consequences of a casualty even if it was responsible for the incident. The existence of such a consistent and comprehensive system clearly indicates that the contracting parties did not wish to leave loop-holes in the CLC which would make someone liable to an unlimited amount even if his responsibility for the incident was proven. To sum up, the extent and the scope of these regulations indicate that classification societies should be able to limit their liability, if not even be exempt from liability just as all those parties that are enumerated in Article III (4) of CLC 1969 as amended by the 1992 Protocol.[1210]

IV. Self-Protection of Classification Societies by Company Law

Even if classification societies can be held liable to an unlimited amount, the injured party will not necessarily receive full compensation. The insurance company generally includes ceilings on its compensation in the insurance contract. If the

---

1207 Despite a considerable increase in insurance premiums (up to threefold), there has not been a rise in the surveying fees, *see* Commission of the European Communities, Commission Working Document on the control of recognised organisations by the Commission, of 11 October 2006, COM(2006) 588 final, Annex at 3.6.*See also supra* Part 1 A VI 2.

1208 Also not convinced: Basedow, *Der Transportvertrag* (1987), 464-465.

1209 *See supra* Part 3 A V.

1210 *See supra* Part 3 B I 1 d aa. *Compare also* Siccardi, 'Pollution Liability and Classification Societies, Is the System a Fair One?', [2005] *Il Diritto Marittimo* 691, at 707–708, 710.

damage is higher, the classification society has to compensate above the ceiling. However, the society will try to protect itself from the detrimental effects of insolvency by way of company law. The classification services are usually offered by limited liability companies, which are separate from other maritime services, in order to avoid the knock-on effects of insolvency. As an example, LR has divided its classification services into four different units, serving the different parts of the world.[1211] Hence, unlimited liability does not guarantee effective compensation unless each and every company has sufficient funds for compensation, or the corporate veil can be pierced. Instead, limited liability combined with mandatory insurance guarantees that at least this level is compensated for.[1212] However, in order to provide effective compensation, it is necessary for these levels to be sufficiently high.

V. Liability and the Control of Old Vessels

In the *Marc Rich* case, the House of Lords argued that if they were not exempt from liability, classification societies could be deterred by liability from acting on ships which need their aid the most. This argumentation, however, is not fully convincing. Old ships which are no longer safe or which are for other reasons a danger to the public should no longer be kept in service. There is a certain risk that such ships are put in service in local markets, where safety enforcement is lax. Yet even such local markets have only a limited capacity for old ships which could no longer make long journeys on the oceans. The aim should be to get such ships out of all markets; prolonging their life means increasing the risk of maritime casualties.

VI. How Should the Interests be Balanced?

The question of whether or not classification societies should be fully liable or only liable to a limited amount or even exempt from liability affects two conflicting aims. The first one is the concept that the aim of liability is to prevent damage

[1211] For the group structure, *see* <http://www.lr.org/About+Us/Our+structure.htm>, last accessed 19 March 2007.

[1212] An economic model for the consideration whether insurance shall be made compulsory in any given case is discussed and the advantages of a mandatory insurance are pointed out in Richardson, 'Mandating Environmental Liability Insurance', 12 *Duke Entl. L. & Pol'y F.* 293 (2002), at 308–321. Possible negative effects are however described in Organisation for Economic Co-operation and Development (OECD), *Policy Issues in Insurance: Environmental Risks and Insurance* (2003), at 50–51.

from occurring and to compensate if it cannot be prevented.[1213] The risk of being liable is a facet in the prevention of such damage. If, nonetheless, damage occurs, the consequences should be borne by the person best suited to providing compensation, i.e. the person that has caused the damage and that could have prevented it.[1214] Prevention and compensation require that the person who has caused damage has to answer for it. From this point of view, it appears to be appropriate to require the classification societies to compensate for the loss, and, if not for the entire damage, then at least up to a limited amount.

The other aim is to maximise welfare through economic efficiency. From that perspective, it is inefficient if the same or a similar risk is insured several times. If both the classification society and the shipowner insure a risk which could be described as being somewhat similar, the additional insurance premium ties up capital which could otherwise be used. From the point of view of economic efficiency, it might be most reasonable to exempt a classification society from any liability in order to economise on the additional insurance premium which a classification society would have to pay. However, how can these two conflicting aims be reconciled?

1213 Shapiro, 'Symposium on the economics of liability', 5 *J. Econ. Persp.* 3–10 (1991); Wüstendörfer, 'Zur Haftung für Feuerschaden an Bord von Seeschiffen nach den Haager Regeln', [1949] *MDR* 450, 515.

1214 *See* Mataja, *Das Recht des Schadensersatzes vom Standpunkt der Nationalökonomie*, (1888), at 19: 'Keine Gesetzgebung der Welt kann einen einmal eingetretenen Schaden beseitigen, das Recht steht demselben machtlos als einer vollendeten Thatsache gegenüber. Die Gesetzgebung kann daher in Beziehung auf die Schadensgefahr nur zweierlei Zwecke verfolgen: sie kann darnach trachten

(1) möglichst vorbeugend zu wirken und
(2) den gleichwohl eingetretenen Schaden jenen Personen zuzuwenden, welche nach den *Forderungen der Gerechtigkeit* und der *volkswirtschaftlichen Interessen* als die geeignetsten Träger der Last erscheinen.'

Basedow, *Der Transportvertrag* (1987), 490; Koller, *Die Risikozurechnung bei Vertragsstörungen in Austauschverträgen* (1979), 78 *et seq.*, 100 *et seq.*; Kötz, 'Haftungsausschlußklauseln', in: *25 Jahre Karlsruher Forum – Beilage*, [1983] *VersR* 145, at 147–148.

1. Prevention and Compensation

The aim of effective prevention and compensation is in the interest of three parties: first and foremost of the injured person.[1215] The victim wants to receive full compensation for the losses suffered in order to return as closely as possible to the situation in which he was before the incident took place. Apart from this *resitutio in integrum*, he may also want the person who caused the damage to pay for it. This can be described as a kind of moral compensation.[1216] Liability can be a settlement for the injustice done to the interests of the injured party. Liability in this sense is not meant as a punishment for wrongful behaviour. It is rather the price the offender has to pay for his freedom of commercial activity. He may only exercise commercial activities as long as they do not interfere with the freedom and protected rights of other persons. Anyone who makes use of his freedom, and thereby negligently causes damage to the interests of another person, has to make good for this behaviour. Financial compensation is required as an adjustment of any mischief which was incurred. Whenever someone sustains a loss, his main interest is to be compensated and to prevent a further intensification and extension of the damage.

The second party whose interests need to be considered is the person that is responsible for the damage, in this case a classification society. Ideally, such a person should be interested in compensation if he wishes to preserve a certain standing and credibility or if he wants to continue certain business relations with an injured client. The shipping industry will only put trust in classification societies as long as it considers that classification societies know more than all the other actors on the market and that they are independent and exercise their job correctly. Classification societies depend on the trust and confidence others put in them.[1217] They should, therefore, have a strong interest of their own in being accountable for any damage they cause.[1218] Their expert opinions would be of little value if their mistakes had no impact. However, this does not necessarily imply that the classification society should be held liable by third parties; a liability towards their contracting parties may well be sufficient. If a classification society has to compensate for damage, it will also be interested in minimising the possibility of any

---

[1215] For an analysis of the aims of liability especially with regard to the increase of efficiency, the deterrence of environmental damage and risk or loss spreading, *see* Bergkamp, *Liability and the Environment* (2001), at 70–119. *Compare also* Baker Röben, 'Civil Liability as a Control Mechanism for Environmental Protection at the International Level', in: Morrison/Wolfrum, *International, Regional and National Environmental* Law (2000), 821, at 825–827; Organisation for Economic Co-operation and Development (OECD), *Policy Issues in Insurance: Environmental Risks and Insurance* (2003), at 23–28.

[1216] Pound, *An Introduction to the Philosophy of Law* (1930), 151.

[1217] *See* Skou, 'Presentation on Behalf of IACS to the Centenary Conference of the CMI', [1997] *CMI Yearbook* , 182, para. 6.

[1218] Kröger, 'Presentation on Behalf of the German Shipowners' Association and of the Maritime Law Committee of ICS', [1997] *CMI Yearbook*, 185.

further extension of damage which has already occurred in order to prevent additional costs from accumulating.

The general public is the third and last party whose interests need to be taken into account when discussing prevention of and compensation for damage. The general public should seek to prevent any damage in order to maximise public wealth. Apart from that, it is also concerned about the impression which uncompensated damage might make on others. Prevention is necessary to avoid carelessness, which might lead to further incidents. If irresponsible and negligent behaviour has no consequences, such behaviour will be likely to spread. Compensation is necessary, as otherwise the general public itself might have to answer for the damage in the end, be it through social security systems in cases of personal injury or indirectly because of injured parties which become insolvent. The costs for the person responsible would not be internalised and included in the prices, but remain externalised and left to be paid by the general public.

Nonetheless, the question remains whether liability really motivates anyone to prevent casualties. Is there deterrence and therefore prevention if the tortfeasor is insured? If there is insurance, the tortfeasor does not have to bear any costs unless insurance has some kind of bonus/malus scheme or introduces deductibles. Insurance is, therefore, usually subject to the suspicion of *moral hazard*, namely that any person who is insured will behave less prudently and that mostly persons insure activities which are more dangerous than average. Prevention works especially well if the casualty has some adverse effect on the insured person, in this case the classification society.[1219] Otherwise, insurance has great advantages in that it guarantees compensation, but may contradict the aim of effective prevention. However, even if there is no such bonus/malus scheme or the like, there may be a motivation to prevent damage. There is no guarantee that one gets insurance or stays insured for all time. If too many casualties occur, an insurance company will rescind the insurance contract or will not renew it.

Apart from that, what generally motivates a company the most is a decline in its own reputation. As casualties involving oil pollution or a passenger vessel are always in the spotlight, there is already a considerable motivation for classification societies to prevent such incidents, be there liability or not. Whenever there is only the threat of damage to cargo, there is not such a strong motivation to prevent casualties. Nevertheless, if a classification society can be held liable for damage to

---

[1219] *Compare* Basedow, *Der Transportvertrag* (1987), 490–491 with further references. Bolin, however, argues that if liability is limited, the incentives for taking care are limited as well. Damages above the limit are not internalised in the firm's decisions unless the limit is higher than the injurer's total assets (Bolin, 'The Ownership of Funds and Systems for Reparation of very large Accidents', Department of Economics, Lund University, at 5, accessible at <http://www.nek.lu.se/publications/workpap/Papers/wp99_6.pdf>, last accessed on 19 March 2007. *See also* Richardson, 'Mandating Environmental Liability Insurance', 12 *Duke Entl. L. & Pol'y F.* 293 (2002), at 303; Bennett, 'Governing environmental risk: regulation, insurance and moral economy', 23 *Progress in Human Geography* 189 (1999), at 200–201.

cargo and has to pay partly for such damage because of the conditions of the insurance contract, liability will be a motivation to prevent such damage.

2. Economic Efficiency

On the other hand, the international community has an interest in having a system which is as efficient as possible, because economic efficiency helps to maximise public wealth. But in which way can the liability of classification societies be efficient or inefficient?

It is efficient to allocate liability to those who have caused the damage. These persons are generally in the best position of avoiding such a casualty in the future and achieving that at the lowest costs.[1220] It is evident that a passenger cannot check the safety of his cruise vessel; a classification society, by contrast, can. A classification society, as well as a knowledgeable shipowner, can prevent damage at the least cost. For this reason, it is efficient to oblige the classification society to do so. An incentive can only be given if the classification society is under the threat of being liable for its actions unless it performs in a way which is likely to prevent any damage from occurring.

Economic theory aims at obliging businesses to internalise externalities. Risks, damage and the use of external goods (which are usually common goods, such as nature) should be priced and included in the calculation of the costs of a product or service. Everyone should have to pay what the product or service really costs; no costs should be deferred to the general public. In that way, risks should be efficiently allocated to those who are responsible for them. Each and every person should have to answer for his own risks, as otherwise the person who pays for it in the end has to increase his prices. If the cost of such a risk is too high, it makes no sense to continue it. It has to be substituted by another service or needs to be abolished. Looking at the shipping market, the classification, for example, of old passenger vessels on a one-year survey cycle may incur a risk which is too high for a classification society, as the condition of such vessels can deteriorate within a shorter period of time. The society can react in three ways: it can shorten the period of time between two survey cycles, stop classifying such vessels or increase the costs of their classification in order to reflect the increased risk of liability. All three measures may have the effect that there are fewer unsafe old vessels trading on the seas.

To hold a classification society liable may be economically inefficient. The society will try to insure its risks. It has been argued that this would introduce an additional layer of insurance, which is inefficient, because the shipowner already insures the risks of his vessels. An additional insurance would bind more capital than necessary, which could otherwise be used. This argumentation is not fully convincing, as it is not exactly the same risk which is insured. The shipowner has to insure the manifold navigational dangers that a ship incurs and, regarding some damage, even strict liability. The classification society has to insure a different

[1220] *Compare* Basedow, *Der Transportvertrag* (1987), 490 with further references; Bergkamp, *Liability and the Environment* (2001), at 73–82.

risk; it insures that its employees do not negligently cause any harm to others. Despite the fact that an interaction by the ship is needed to cause such harm, which brings about the general liability of the shipowner as well, this risk is a different one. Also, a classification society would not have to buy insurance for each and every ship, but only insure the risk in general that his employees do not act properly. Such insurance incurs additional costs, but allows at the same time a more precise co-ordination of risks and costs. Apart from that, insurance has positive consequences regarding the accountability of the insured, as it directly tries to minimise the risk.

Who can insure at the lowest prices? The cheapest insurance is an insurance of the victims themselves. It is for several reasons cheaper than third-party insurance for liabilities towards third parties.[1221] In first-party insurance, the insurers have a direct contractual relationship with the victim, which allows them to control adverse effects that might negatively affect the policy and clearly assess the risk of insurance. An insurance company can reject potential victims with an increased risk or charge them a higher premium. They can minimise effects of *adverse selection*, which results from ineffective segregation of persons representing different risks.[1222] Also, in a first-party insurance context, the insurance companies can introduce incentives for the insured such as deductibles, co-insurance, caps, exclusions, premium differentiation and bonus/malus mechanisms to fight against *moral hazards*. Such hazards result from the fact that an insured party is likely to be less careful and thereby cause greater damage than it would if it were not insured.[1223]

Third-party liability is much more difficult to insure. First of all, the insurance company cannot control who the victim will be. It cannot reject potential victims who pose an increased risk, as it only has control over the insured persons. *Risk segregation* is therefore impossible, and consequently there may be *adverse selection* of persons who represent different risks. Apart from that, the insurance company does not have any means to control moral hazards either, because such hazards are provoked by the victims, on whom the insurance company has no influence. Moreover, the conditions of the insurance policy are not so much defined by the insurance contract in a third-party context, but are determined by the courts. Courts may construe liability standards and thereby considerably expand the scope of insurance coverage.

An additional problem of third-party insurance lies in the problem of excessive coverage. Tort law allows compensation of damage, which is rarely if ever insured in a first-party insurance context. For instance, in first-party contexts, pain and

---

1221 *See generally* Bergkamp, 'Environmental Risk Spreading and Insurance', 12 *RECIEL* 269 (2003), at 272–274; Richardson, 'Mandating Environmental Liability Insurance', 12 *Duke Entl. L. & Pol'y F.* 293 (2002), at 294, 322.

1222 Richardson, 'Mandating Environmental Liability Insurance', 12 *Duke Entl. L. & Pol'y F.* 293 (2002), at 323.

1223 Basedow, *Der Transportvertrag* (1987), 490–491; Bergkamp, 'Environmental Risk Spreading and Insurance', 12 *RECIEL*, 269 (2003), at 272–274.

suffering are usually not insured or only at very low fixed sum levels. Last but not least, the administrative costs of third-party insurance are much higher than first-party insurance, as it is generally estimated at 50% of the claims, in contrast to the 10% ratio which first-party insurance usually requires.[1224]

The current system is not entirely based on first-party insurance. Moreover, a complete exemption of all tortfeasors from any liability will not be enacted, mainly because of issues of prevention, but also because of issues of efficiency. If there was only first-party insurance, no-one would care any more about damaging others. As a result, the number of casualties would almost certainly rise and the costs of first-party insurance would increase accordingly.

The international community has preferred to try to minimise the costs of insurance by requiring third-party insurance of the shipowner which is limited in a certain way. Insurance companies can calculate the premium accordingly. Since only certain compensation can be due, differences in the level of damage are irrelevant. It is not the full amount of damage which will be compensated, but only a limited amount. A system of liability and both first- and third-party insurance, which are combined with deductibles or similar rewards of persons who cause only few claims, therefore prevents casualties in a better way and is more efficient.

If a classification society were liable to an unlimited amount, its insurance coverage would need a very high safety margin if it were to cover all losses. If it was, however, liable to an extent which was clearly limited, there would be no need for a high safety margin and as a result this inefficiency could be reduced. At the same time, the prevention of damage would be better than if a classification society was exempt from any liability. If there is some liability, there are positive effects regarding prevention of damage if insurance companies introduce reward schemes. It is obvious that the prevention of losses has an economic benefit as well.

It should not be forgotten that classification societies already insure their risks.[1225] Even if an international convention exempted them from any liability, they would not be very likely to stop insuring themselves unless all countries ratified this convention. Otherwise there would be a risk that they could be held liable. As a result, there is a layer of insurance in addition to self-insurance of victims and insurance by the shipowner. Even if one exempted classification societies from liability by way of an international convention, this would not necessarily in-

---

[1224] Bergkamp, 'Environmental Risk Spreading and Insurance', 12 *RECIEL*, 269, at 274 (2003).

[1225] Kröger, 'Presentation on Behalf of the German Shipowners' Association and of the Maritime Law Committee of ICS', [1997] *CMI Yearbook* 185, at 188: insurance of about 25 to 100 million USD per incident. Commission of the European Communities, Commission Working Document on the control of recognised organisations by the Commission, of 11 October 2006, COM(2006) 588 final, Annex at 3.6: insurance of 10 to 100 million on an aggregate basis with a total liability cap rather than a "per incident" cap.

crease economic efficiency. Unlimited liability would not be very efficient either, as it would need high insurance with a large safety margin. Limited liability for classification societies would be most efficient from an economic point of view.

3. *Conclusion: Exemption, Limitation or Unlimited Liability?*

One needs to make a choice between either a full exemption of classification societies from any liability, a limitation of their liability or unlimited liability. As has been shown, there are good arguments in favour of and against each and every of these possibilities.

A complete exemption could be most efficient because classification societies would no longer need to insure their risks. On the other hand, if there was no liability, there would be only a limited prevention of damage to cargo and an insufficient compensation in cases of loss of life or damage to passengers or crew, whenever such risk is not insured by the shipowner.[1226] Furthermore, an exemption would most probably cause a lack of accountability and credibility of these societies.[1227]

Unlimited liability would solve this deficiency concerning prevention, but would be quite inefficient. If the unlimited liability were insured, the insurance premium of classification societies would need to be calculated with a large safety margin, which would make such insurance very expensive. Moreover, unlimited liability would be fair to the injured party, but unfair to classification societies. They are an integral part of the maritime industry and only have a limited influence on the vessel, whereas the shipowner is responsible for the vessel, but may limit his liability.

Besides, the current limitations in shipping already show that the international community considers the interests of the injured party to be less relevant than those of the shipowner. The contracting States have decided that the shipowner should be liable only up to a limited amount; if the injured third party does not receive full compensation, it is because of this decision. There are critics who argue against this perception.[1228] These critics state that circumstances have changed over the years and that the shipowner's interests are no longer to be weighed higher than those of the injured party. Moreover, they say that the aims of a strong

---

[1226] *See supra* Part 3 A IV.

[1227] Similarly, classification societies did not ask for immunity in the Joint Working Group on a Study of Issues regarding Classification Societies, *see* Skou, 'Presentation on Behalf of IACS to the Centenary Conference of the CMI', [1997] *CMI Yearbook* 180, at 182, para. 6.

[1228] Altfuldisch, *Haftung und Entschädigung nach Tankerunfällen auf See* (forthcoming), Chapter 5 C I 3; Basedow, *Der Transportvertrag* (1987), 504–510; Eyer, 'Shipowners' Limitation of Liability', 16 *Stan.L.Rev.* 370, at 389 (1964); Gauci, *Oil Pollution at Sea* (1997), 153; Gauci, 'Limitation of liability in maritime law: an anachronism?', 19 *Mar. Pol'y* 65, 66–69; Justice Black in *Maryland Casualty Co. v. Cushing*, 98 L.Ed. 806, at 826 (1954); *Pettus v. Jones & Laughlin Steel Corp.,* 322 F.Supp. 1078, at 1082 (W.D.Pa.1971).

merchant fleet and of fairer competition between shipowners are satisfied. However, despite such argumentation, the limits are not very likely to be abolished soon, as is illustrated by the fact that there is currently no lobby for the abolition of these regulations on the international scene.

The most reasonable decision is, therefore, to limit the liability of classification societies. Economic efficiency cannot outweigh the necessity of a prevention of casualties. Apart from the fact that prevention also has an economic value, the interests of those who are in danger of sustaining a loss are otherwise not at all taken into consideration. Limited liability would motivate classification societies to prevent casualties. Moreover, it would not require a large safety margin in the calculation of the premium and would only have limited inefficiency due to several layers of insurance.

D. Principles of a Convention on the Limitation of Liability

A convention on the limitation of liability of classification societies would give rise to a number of questions. A primarily one is that of the form in which a regulation on the limitation of liability of classification societies should be introduced. If one takes the CLC into consideration, one might think of introducing strict liability or of basing liability on an internationally harmonised regulation of fault-based liability. A further question would be whether or not a reversal of the burden of proof should be introduced in favour of the victims. Most important is the level of limitation, which shall be granted to the societies, and the question whether it should be calculated on the basis of tonnage of the vessel or respectively on the number of passengers and crew the vessel is licensed to transport or of fees of the classification society. Finally, such a convention should interrelate with the existing systems of limitation in shipping. Would there be an aggregation of claims or should the victim be compensated by both the shipowner and the classification society, but in every case up to a limited amount? These questions shall be dealt with in the following.

I. European or International Law?

One could think of a regulation developed under the auspices of IMO. This organization has the competence to provide for the drafting of conventions and convene such conferences as may be necessary (Article 2 lit. b Convention on the IMO) on any matters concerning shipping (Article 1 lit. d Convention on the IMO).[1229] On the regional level the European Community could take up the matter

[1229] Convention on the International Maritime Organisation, Geneva, 6 March 1948, came into force on 17 March 1958, 298 UNTS 4.

on the basis of its competence for sea transport (Article 80 (2) EC) and adopt a regulation pursuant to Article 249 EC.

The adoption of an international convention is a complex legal and political process, which may take a considerable time. Occasionally, conventions which are hailed at their adoption in a conference never come into force due to a reluctance of the national parliaments, a change in the political climate or for other reasons. Law-making in the European Community is also a lengthy process. But once a regulation or directive has been adopted, it is binding for the Member States. There are only 25 parties on the regional level, and the interests are more coherent than in the IMO, where the commercial interests of the open shipping registers could easily lead to different views on the issue. No doubt, it is easier to find a solution on the European level, which may later become a model for national shipping laws of third countries or even for an international convention.

On the other hand, a European solution may amount to unilateralism. A regulation which may be appropriate in Europe might not meet the various interests on the international level. Besides that, the liability of classification societies is genuinely a global issue. The societies offer their services in almost every port of the world and the damage may occur virtually anywhere. The victim may sue the classification society in several countries. Shipping is not limited to the European continent, whether or not the shipowner is European, the ship flies a European flag or the classification society has its headquarters in Europe or has carried out a survey in a European port. Therefore, solving the issue of the limitation of liability of classification societies requires an international convention and not a regional European solution.

One formal question remains: what kind of international regulation should be enacted? One might, for example, consider a protocol on the liability of classification societies to the LLMC. But, the LLMC is not ratified by all countries in which classification societies could be sued, despite it has been enacted in their national laws by a number of others which have not ratified the convention.[1230] Moreover, in the discussion concerning such a new protocol other issues may come up, such as the level of limitations or a compulsory insurance of the liability, which have nothing to do with the liability of classification societies. Consequently such a project may become blurred. One should, therefore, start with a clean slate and envisage a new international convention which is confined to the liability of classification societies.

[1230] The LLMC is ratified by 47 countries accounting for 46.11% of the world's tonnage. Another 38 have enacted it without ratification. Its 1996 Protocol has been ratified by 17 States accounting for 13.87% of the world's tonnage. Source: <http://www.imo.org>, last accessed 19 March 2007.

II. Strict Liability?

One of the main problems for the plaintiffs in a case against a classification society is to prove negligent behaviour by the society. Even if the classification society is responsible for the casualty, it could be almost impossible to prove its negligence. Besides this, strict liability allows compensation even in difficult causative situations. Someone who is strictly liable has to stand in for any kind of damage which occurs.

Because of such difficulties of a fault-based liability, the CLC and the HNS Convention provide for strict liability of the shipowner for damage caused by the respective cargo. Some authors argue that the limitation of liability was required in order to countervail strict liability introduced by the conventions.[1231] However, if one analyses not only the documents to the CLC, but also the other existing conventions which limit the liability of the shipowner, strict liability is not a necessary precondition to the limitation of liability. It is only an additional feature of such a limitation convention. This is also illustrated by those cargo limitations and global limitations which do not require strict liability of the shipowner or carrier. During the drafting of the CLC, there was some discussion on whether or not strict liability could be justified and imposed on the shipowner.[1232]

[1231] Wu, *Pollution from the Carriage of Oil by Sea* (1996), at 62.

[1232] The Preliminary Report made by the Chairman of the International Subcommittee "Torrey Canyon" (Lord Devlin) argued in favour of a strict liability (*CMI Documents 1968*, vol. 1, at 78). The results of a subsequent CMI questionnaire, however, were somewhat ambiguous. Associations which were against strict liability: The Belgian Maritime Law Association (*CMI Documents 1968*, vol. 3, at 102, 104), The British Maritime Law Association (*CMI Documents 1969*, vol. 3, at 140), The Danish Maritime Law Association (*ibid.*, at 46), The Finnish Maritime Law Association (*ibid.*, at 14), The Hellenic Maritime Law Association (*ibid.*, at 80), The Netherlands Maritime Law Association (*ibid.*, at 62), The Norwegian Maritime Law Association (*ibid.*, at 6), and the Maritime Law Association of the United States (*ibid.*, at 136). The Japanese Maritime Law Association (*ibid.*, at 86) was against strict liability, but in favour of a reversal of the burden of proof as were The German Maritime Law Association (*ibid.*, at 34) and The Swiss Maritime Law Association (*ibid.*, at 30).
The French Maritime Law Association (*ibid.*, at 92, 94) argued for the introduction of strict liability in favour of individuals, but not of States. The Italian Maritime Law Association (*ibid.*, at 68) asked for strict liability for either all cases of the carriage of dangerous cargo or none. The Argentine Maritime Law Association (*ibid.*, at 122) was in favour of strict liability, as were the Irish Maritime Law Association (*CMI Documents 1969*, vol. 3, at 164), The Spanish Maritime Law Association (*ibid.*, at 108), and The Yugoslav Maritime Law Association (*ibid.*, at 112).

Strict liability can be justified for especially dangerous activities. The transport of oil is an ultra-hazardous activity.[1233] Not the oil itself, but its transport can have exceptional consequences if the hazard materialises. Casualties involving loaded tankers are likely to be disastrous. Despite the fact that classification societies check vessels which transport such substances, their activity is not inherently dangerous. Neither classification as such is dangerous; it is the operation of the vessel which implies the danger. Classification even aims at making the vessel safer, it does not add perils to the existing dangers of the vessel.

Moreover, the role of the classification society with respect to the dangerous activity does not justify the imposition of strict liability. The shipowner (or the charterer) has control over the vessel at all times, whereas the classification society surveys the ship only once a year. The shipowner, however, is only strictly liable for oil-pollution damage. If the classification society were generally subject to strict liability, it might be held liable for something over which it had no control and for which it was not responsible.[1234] It would be liable for each and every of its registered vessels. Although the protection of victims is a just and equitable goal – this would be unjust for the classification society.[1235]

The Preliminary Draft of the CLC of 10th July 1968 therefore included a liability based on fault with a reversal of the burden of proof (*CMI Documents 1968*, vol. 3, at 132, Doc. TC-22/8-68, Article 2), as did the Draft of International Convention on Civil Liability for Oil Pollution Damage, 1969 (*CMI Documents 1969*, vol. 3, at 44). The IMCO Report to the Legal Committee of the CMI came to the same conclusion (*CMI Documents 1969*, vol. 3, at 106, Article II). It was only at the IMCO–Brussels International Legal Conference on Maritime Pollution Damage, 1969, that strict liability was introduced in such cases. It took until the final days of the Conference before it was decided to adopt a principle of strict liability of the shipowner (*IMCO Official Records of the International Legal Conference on Marine Pollution Damage, 1969*, LEG/CONF/C.2./WP.35, 24 November 1969, at 596–597).

1233 Preliminary Report made by the Chairman of the International Subcommittee "Torrey Canyon" (Lord Devlin), *CMI Documents 1968*, vol. 1, at 74. One might only wonder whether liability should have been assigned to the owner or rather the person who is responsible for the vessel, *i.e.* the charterer. The international community chooses the person who can be identified because of the registry of the vessel. Despite not having control over the vessel at the time that it is chartered, the shipowner knows that it is being used for the transport of oil and has to insure for the potential liability. For justifications of strict liability in general, *see* Bergkamp, *Liability and the Environment* (2001), at 119–150.

1234 Basedow also points out that because the *culpa* of the defendant is not of relevance, the preventive effects of a strict liability are limited (Basedow, *Der Transportvertrag* (1987), 498).

1235 Same conclusion with regard to United States law: Beck, B., 'Liability of Marine Surveyors for Loss of Surveyed Vessel', 64 *Notre Dame L. Rev.* 246 (1989), at 265–269.

III. Harmonised Basis of Fault Liability?

If one does not establish strict liability for the classification society, one could consider a harmonisation of the legal basis of liability, which requires fault. As shown above in Part 2 of this thesis, English, German and United States law differs in its approach and in its results regarding the liability of classification societies. An international convention that provides for fault-based liability would have the advantage of minimizing these differences in the interest of both the classification societies and the plaintiffs.

The relationship between classification societies and their contracting parties are governed by their contracts. These contracts are the legal basis for liability. Accordingly, there is no need for an additional theory of fault-based liability vis-à-vis contracting parties.

Third parties are, however, not protected in the same way. Hence, they would benefit from the inclusion of a basis of liability in an international convention regarding classification societies. This legal basis should be based on negligence. If a classification society which owes a duty of care to a third party breaches that duty, and the third party incurs a loss or damage, this party should have a claim for compensation, provided that there is a causal connection between the alleged loss or damage and the breach of duty. However, the loss or damage must be foreseeable for the classification society.

In order to harmonize the law, it should also be determined that the classification society owes a duty of care towards the passengers and the crew. The activities of a classification society are by nature likely to affect these persons as well, and it is therefore the duty of the classification society to protect their health and life.[1236] Moreover, as has been elaborated *supra,* the level of compensation may be insufficient in such a case.[1237] That the passengers and the crew would be affected in their life and health by its negligent behaviour is also foreseeable for the classification society. There should consequently be a fault-based liability of the classification society for such instances.

Whether or not a duty of care exists towards cargo owners has to be determined on a case-by-case basis.[1238] A duty of care exists whenever the classification society has affected the deficiency which caused the accident. Such influence may have been exercised by way of the classification society's rules or if it recom-

[1236] *Compare supra* Part 1 B I 2, Part 3 C I.

[1237] *See supra* Part 3 A IV, Part 3 B II.

[1238] It should not be stated that the classification society owes a duty of care in every given case. A duty of care of the classification society towards cargo interests could otherwise infringe the system of first party insurance as it exists today and could establish an economical channelling of the liability on the classification society. Unless the claim were equally limited as the claim against the shipowner, there would be a strong incentive for the cargo to claim damages from the classification society. Whether or not such duty exists needs to be scrutinized and determined on a case-by-case basis.

mends carrying out repairs in a certain way or makes conditions.[1239] In such a case, the classification society affects the safety of the vessel, and is therefore required to avoid or minimise all risks which it might thereby cause. If it only surveys the vessel or checks the blueprints and requests that certain repairs are carried out or modifications are made, it is only under a duty to make such requirements that are state-of-the-art in the eyes of a prudent classification society. The classification society is under a duty towards the shipowner to check the vessel; there is no such duty towards third parties. Nevertheless, if it makes certain requirements, it should be under a general duty to avoid any risk of harm to third parties as well. Therefore, only if the classification society makes a certain requirement or recommendation or if it gives certain advice which influences the vessel in a way that it is not as safe as it should be if it were state-of-the-art, that society should be under a duty of care towards third parties to prevent any harm occurring to them. These standards should be set forth in the convention.

Nonetheless, it may be difficult to foresee the precise amount of damages. Everything can be carried in a container today, therefore it is almost impossible to calculate damages in advance if an incident to a container vessel occurs. In contrast, if a classification society conducts a repair survey of a bulker, and the cargo of *e.g.* iron is already aboard the vessel, the classification society may estimate its potential liability.

The precondition of foreseeability of the possible damage strives to limit claims to only those which the classification society must expect to occur, as the classification society should be able to insure for such claims. If the claims were, however, limited for instance to a certain amount per vessels' tonnage, the potential liability would be calculable. The classification society could estimate its exposure to liability and insure its risks accordingly. In the case of a limitation of liability, one could therefore argue that, regardless of the value of the cargo, the damage is foreseeable.

Contrary to damage *to* the cargo, damage which is caused *by* the cargo will hardly ever be foreseeable for the classification society. Consequently no duty of care should be determined in this regard. The extent of the damage which is caused for instance by a cargo of oil or HNS depends on the region in which it occurs and the specifics of the product. A spill of crude oil in a sensitive ecosystem causes a considerably higher damage than a casualty involving HNS on the high seas. Regarding the damage caused *by* cargo, the classification society therefore cannot estimate the potential liability it might face. One could solely argue in the same strand as in the preceding paragraph that if the liability is limited, the damage might however be foreseeable. In such a case, the classification society could calculate its risks and insure them.

In addition to that, under the laws of those countries which have ratified the CLC and the convention establishing the International Oil Pollution Compensation Funds or its Protocol of 2003 there is a comprehensive system which seeks to guarantee compensation. A similar system may well be established in the future

[1239] *See supra* Part 2 B II 2 f.

with respect to HNS. From the point of view of compensation, there is no need in such situations to grant third parties a claim against a classification society, as has been elaborated *supra*.[1240] Concerning prevention a classification society will already do as much as it can to prevent casualties in order to avoid the bad press that would go along with such casualties.[1241] For these reasons, it should be stated in the convention that a classification society is not liable for the respective damage whenever a system of compensation funds steps in.

IV. Reversal of the Burden of Proof?

A reversal of the burden of proof regarding the negligence of the classification society brings liability closer to a strict liability of the classification society. Such a reversal could be a considerable benefit to the victim. He or she may not only face considerable difficulties in proving what has caused the vessel to sink; it can be even more difficult to establish negligent behaviour on the part of the classification society due to the victim's lack of insight and information. A classification society, by contrast, has to document all its activities. Hence, it is more in the position to prove that it did everything right than the victim, who should prove that it did something wrong. Classification societies are, no doubt, likely to document precisely their activities.

Keeping in mind that the general division of the burden of proof means that the plaintiff has to prove all facts which benefit him and make his case, and considering the large number of vessels that are surveyed by classification societies, such a burden of proof might be hard to bear by these societies. On the other hand, if it remains the plaintiff's duty to prove the existence of a duty of care of the classification society as well as a breach of this duty, the classification society should be in a better position than the plaintiff to prove that it did not act negligently. Whenever the classification society proves that it did not act negligently it is not liable. If it proves that it did not act grossly negligent, it will benefit of the limitation of liability. In all other cases its liability will not be limited.

In the light of the fact that it will already be very difficult for the plaintiff to prove the existence of the duty of care and the breach of this duty, and taking the documentation of its activities by the classification society into account, a reversal of the burden of proof concerning negligence should be contained in the convention.

V. Basis of Limitation: Tonnage or Fees?

When drafting the Model Contractual Clauses, which relate to the liability of the classification society towards its contracting party, the CMI Joint Working Group

[1240] *See supra* Part 3 C III, Part 3 C VI 1.

[1241] *See supra* Part 3 C VI 1.

went through long discussions on whether tonnage or fees charged by the classification society should be the determining criteria for the calculation of the maximum amount of their liability. The classification societies argued in favour of a system based on fees. For them, only the fees are relevant, because they do not necessarily distinguish between a large and a small ship. In contradistinction, a tonnage-based calculation would imply that they are insurers of the vessel or that they are somewhat similar to shipowners.[1242] On the other hand, the shipowners were convinced that, because of its objectivity, the system should be based on tonnage.[1243]

Furthermore, the liability towards third parties should not be based on the considerations of the contracting parties, but on the perception and protection of the respective third party. For such a party, the fee structure is completely irrelevant and not comprehensible. The same service could cost a different amount of money, depending on the place where it was carried out. Classification societies include different factors in their calculations which relate to their own costs. They differ from country to country and depend upon the competition between the societies in the local markets. Thus, it may be more expensive to classify the same vessel in one country than in another. Moreover, classification societies may grant rebates to large fleets in order to offer them especially competitive prices. It does not make any difference to the injured party whether the negligent service has been carried out in a domestic port or overseas. Differences in market conditions, market power of the client or the like should not affect the compensation of the victim. A system based on tonnage or respectively the number of passengers the vessel is registered to carry is therefore a transparent system and preferable to one based on fees of the societies.

VI. Level of Limitations

The most critical and difficult factor which is crucial for the acceptance and implementation of the envisaged convention is the definition of a reasonable level of limitations.[1244] The fact that the CMI Joint Working Group, which developed the Model Contractual Clauses for classification societies, could not find a compromise on the level of contractual limitations illustrates the differences in perception between classification societies, shipowners and other actors on the market.[1245]

[1242] Skou, 'Presentation on Behalf of IACS to the Centenary Conference of the CMI', [1997] *CMI Yearbook,* 180, at 182–183.

[1243] Kröger, 'Presentation on Behalf of the German Shipowners' Association and of the Maritime Law Committee of ICS', [1997] *CMI Yearbook,* 185, at 188.

[1244] For an economist's approach to the question of optimum levels of liability for marine transport, *see* Jin/Kite-Powell, 'On the optimal environmental liability limit for marine oil transport', *Transportation Research Part E*, 77 (1999).

[1245] Wiswall, 'Classification societies: issues considered by the Joint Working Group', 2 *I.J.S.L.* 171 (1997), at 180–183.

With respect to the said convention, the situation is even more complex. Not only the limits of contractual liability should be defined, but also a reasonable amount of liability for all cases, including those of third-party liability, should be established. But what would be a reasonable amount? A classification society will present a much lower figure than a shipowner or a maritime authority. During the deliberations at the CMI Joint Working Group, the representatives of IACS considered a cap of USD 2 million or ten times the fee of the classification, whichever is *lower*, to be an acceptable level of contractual liability.[1246] A preliminary recommendation of the CMI, by contrast, mentioned a figure of USD 4 million or ten times the fee, whichever is *higher*.[1247] And the representative of the Maritime Law Committee of the International Chamber of Shipping (ICS) even proposed a double-digit million US dollars sum, as classification societies insure for liability claims of USD 25 to 100 million per incident anyway. He argued that such a level would not even increase the costs of classification.[1248]

The level of limitations also depends on the amount of liability which classification societies may insure. In this regard one differentiates between *technical* and *commercial* insurance. *Technical* insurance relates to the maximum amount which is theoretically insurable and for which the insurance market offers protection. It is obvious that if one has to guarantee compensation, one cannot set a limit which is higher than what is technically insurable. *Commercial* insurance, by contrast, is defined as the insurance which the insured persons can reasonably afford and include in the price of their products or services. The amount of liability which can be imposed from the point of view of *commercial* insurance is therefore much lower than what is *technically* insurable. Victims, of course, will argue that the amount of liability should be chosen on the basis of what is *technically* insurable. However, commercially this would not be sensible. Classification societies should only have to bear a level of liability which is *commercially* insurable. To define such a level in precise numbers is a very difficult task. It requires a study of the levels up to which classification societies currently insure, the costs of such insurance and possible reactions of the market for classification services to an increase in the price of insurance for the societies. However, until now such data is not available. *Technically*, a very large amount of damage can be insured; the level which is *commercially* insurable for classification societies, however, remains uncertain.

In Article 6 (2) lit. b of the Council Directive 94/57/EC, the European Union provided for the recourse of the flag State against the classification society. This rule defines that if the flag State limits the recourse, the classification society has to be liable for *at least* EUR 4 million in cases of personal injury and death, and

---

[1246] Skou, 'Presentation on Behalf of IACS to the Centenary Conference of the CMI', [1997] *CMI Yearbook,* 180, at 184.

[1247] Skou, 'Presentation on Behalf of IACS to the Centenary Conference of the CMI', [1997] *CMI Yearbook,* 180, at 183–184.

[1248] Kröger, 'Presentation on Behalf of the German Shipowners' Association and of the Maritime Law Committee of ICS', [1997] *CMI Yearbook,* 185, at 188.

EUR 2 million for any other damage. The Directive, however, does not explain on which basis these figures were chosen. The minimum limits included in the Directive 94/57/EC do not reflect the maximum liability which could possibly be borne by a classification society. Accordingly, they are obviously the result of a political compromise between the Member States and the Commission. There are quite a few Member States which have not included a limitation in their law implementing the Directive,[1249] whilst others have not defined any limits at all.[1250] The fact that some Member States of the European Union have introduced higher levels than those provided in the Directive illustrates that the levels laid down in the Directive are too low. It is not known which level of liability may be *commercially* insured.

The levels of limitation do not only depend on the aspect of insurability. They are also influenced by other factors. On the one hand, it has been argued that the aim of liability is compensation of the victim, especially in cases in which there is no insurance and an insolvent shipowner. This aspect requires a limitation which is as high as possible. On the other hand, there is the aspect of prevention. Liability should motivate classification societies to perform their services properly. And besides this, an economic channelling of liability on classification societies should be prevented.[1251] Such channelling is effectively prevented if the levels of liability are similar or less than the liability of the shipowner.

The current system of limitations in shipping, however, should not be transferred in its entire extent to classification societies. On the one hand, such a convention would be too complex, as it would require differentiating between the tonnage of the vessel, the victim and the kind of damage. Moreover, because there is not a similar level of limitations in all States, as some have ratified a large number of conventions and their protocols whilst others have not. It would, therefore, be almost impossible to determine a consistent level which could be accepted by all of them. A convention on the limitation of liability of classification societies should, therefore, adopt the minimum standard of limitations which are laid down in the LLMC – however without its protocols, as these protocols have only been accepted by a small number of countries until today. The large number of ratifications of the LLMC[1252] illustrates that this international convention has been largely accepted as a minimum standard of liability.

As regards cargo claims, the considerably lower claims of the Hague/Visby Rules should be imitated. Otherwise, this balanced system would be deterred by a

[1249] *E.g.* Denmark, Finland, Greece, Ireland, Portugal, Sweden and the United Kingdom in their agreements with the classification societies.

[1250] *E.g.* France, Germany, Italy and Spain.

[1251] *Compare* the example *supra* Part 3 B II.

[1252] It has been ratified by 47 countries accounting for 46.11% of the world's tonnage and has been directly transposed into national law by 7 more countries (Denmark, Finland, Germany, Japan, Sweden, the United Kingdom and the Faroe Islands) accounting for and additional 6.4% of the world's tonnage (source: Institute of Shipping Economics and Logistics, *ISL Shipping Statistics Yearbook 2004* (2004)).

strong economic motivation to sue classification societies. The low levels of compensation have led to first-party insurance of the risks, which is more efficient from an economic point of view, as it can more precisely determine the risk and calculate the premium and has fewer adverse effects, such as moral hazards.[1253] This system, which works quite effectively, would only be distorted by a higher liability of classification societies.

The effects of such a convention shall be illustrated by two examples: Even in the case of the world's largest passenger vessel, the *Freedom of the Seas*, liability would be fixed at the ceiling that is incorporated in the LLMC, i.e. a maximum of SDR 25 million, which is approximately USD 35 million. Considering the fact that the size of the fees of classification societies varied in 1997 within a range of USD 1,000 to 1 million or more,[1254] such a number would correspond to the level of limitation which was included in the preliminary recommendation of the CMI. A reason why this figure was rejected by classification societies can be seen in the *Marc Rich* decision. At that time, the classification societies felt they were in a strong position, because the House of Lords had just ruled that they did not owe a duty of care to cargo owners, which sounded as if they could not be held liable at all under English law. This was before the decision of *Perrett v. Collins*, which provided for a different solution regarding personal injury,[1255] and the decision of *Otto Candies*, which held a classification society liable for its negligent misrepresentation.[1256]

The second example is one of damage *to* the cargo.[1257] The world's largest tanker is currently the "Knock Nevis" (formerly "Jahre Viking"), with a gross tonnage of 260,851 tons.[1258] If an incident were caused by the classification society, it would be liable up to an amount of SDR 26 million, which is approximately USD 36.7 million.[1259] Such an amount should be technically as well as commercially insurable.

1253 *Compare supra* Part 3 C VI 2.

1254 Skou, 'Presentation on Behalf of IACS to the Centenary Conference of the CMI', [1997] *CMI Yearbook,* 180, at 182.

1255 *See supra* Part 2 B I 2 d, *Perrett v. Collins,* (C.A.) [1998] 2 Lloyd's Rep. 255.

1256 *See supra* Part 2 B II 3 e, *Otto Candies, L.L.C. v. Nippon Kaiji Kyokai Corp.*, 2002 WL 1798767 (E.D.La. 2002), 346 F.3d 530, 2003 A.M.C. 2409 (5th Cir.(La.) 2003), 2004 WL 179442, 72 USLW 3668, 72 USLW 3672 (S.Ct. 2004).

1257 As has been argued *supra,* a damage caused *by* the cargo will not be foreseeable and contradicts the compensation system offered by the International Oil Pollution Compensation Funds, *see* Part 3 C III.

1258 <http://www.globalsecurity.org/military/systems/ship/jahre-viking.htm>; <http://www.guinnessworldrecords.com>, both last accessed on 19 March 2007.

1259 For each ton from 501 to 30,000 tons, 167 Units of Account (29,499 GT x SDR/GT 167 = SDR 4,926,333); for each ton from 30,001 to 70,000 tons, 125 Units of Account (GT 39,999 x SDR/GT 125 = SDR 4,999,875); and for each ton in excess of 70,000 tons, 83 Units of Account (GT 190,851 x SDT/GT 83 = SDR 15,840,633) = SDR 25,766,841 (USD 36,709,761).

VII. Interrelation with the Limitation of Liability of the Shipowner

Finally the relationship of the liability of a classification society under such a convention with the liability of the shipowner has to be considered. There are indeed some instances in which the victim may claim damages against both the shipowner and the classification society. The first alternative is to allow the victim to claim damages against both, but to receive compensation only up to the amount which it may claim as a maximum against one of them. In such a case, the claims against both would be aggregated. The second alternative is not to allow such aggregation of these two different kinds of claims, but to enable the victim to claim damages against both the shipowner and the classification society, in each case up to the maximum amount which they can be held liable for.

For example, in the LLMC, all claims against the shipowner and his servants and agents are aggregated. Similarly, claims against the salvor and his servants and agents are aggregated as well.[1260] However, there is no such aggregation in case of claims against both the shipowner and the salvor. If the salvage operation of a vessel has caused damage to a third party, that party may not only sue the shipowner for the amount which he can be held liable for, but also the salvor for the amount for which the salvor can be held liable. Hence, the third party will be compensated by both of them up to the maximum amount of their liability.

Similarly, the claims against the classification society and the shipowner should not be aggregated. Evidently, if there is no aggregation, the victim is better protected, as he may claim damages against both of them. Just as in the example of salvors and shipowners, claims against classification societies and shipowners are based on different activities and a different risk. The shipowner is responsible for the operation of the ship. He has to stand in for the risks which it incurs while at operation. The classification society, by contrast, solely has a duty to control the vessel with regard to its own rules. It can only be liable if it has exercised its activities in a negligent way; activities such as surveys of the vessel or checking of the blueprints. Operational risks are not assigned to the classification society. If the casualty was however not solely caused by an operational risk, but by a negligent behaviour of the classification society, the injured party should be able to claim damages against both the classification society and the shipowner whenever operational risks contributed to the incident. An aggregation of claims would otherwise confer the impression that the shipowner and the classification society are in the same position and are responsible for the same risk, which they are not.

There should, however, be an aggregation of claims against the servants and agents of classification societies, and claims against the classification society itself. Such claims are based on the same risk. There is no reason why a classification society should have to answer for the behaviour of its employees because of the principle of *respondeat superior*, and why employees should be required to compensate the victim. In that regard, the same approach should be applied as in view of the shipowner or salvor and their servants and agents.

[1260] Article 9 LLMC.

E. The Limitation of Liability for Public Functions

As has been elaborated above (*see* Part 2 Section C), a classification society may be sued directly under English law if it issues a statutory certificate. The classification society will generally carry out the statutory surveys at the same time as its classification activities in order to reduce layover time and minimise the number of surveys. Some of these surveys may actually be required for both private and public functions. The same deficiency could, therefore, cause liability both for the exercise of a private function as well as for the public function. Unless domestic law limits the liability of the classification society for a public function, there is the risk that limitations, which are granted for the exercise of private functions, could be made ineffective by a claim that is based on the exercise of a public function which is based on the same behaviour.

Hence, despite the similarity regarding the way the surveys are exercised, it is nonetheless necessary to distinguish clearly between the private and public functions of classification societies. When exercising private functions, the classification society acts on behalf of the shipyard or shipowner. On the other hand, public functions are conducted on behalf of the flag State. Several of the considerations that have been advanced in favour of a limitation of liability for private functions do not apply to public functions. Due to the fact that the liability of the flag State for the control of the vessels is unlimited, the liability of the flag State interrelates with the liability of the classification society for the exercise of a public function. There is no economic channelling on the classification society either. However, the aspect that unlimited liability of classification societies could not effectively be insured, as has been pointed out before,[1261] again applies to its public functions. Already the aspect of insurance could justify a limitation of liability, as has been shown before.[1262] In addition to that, there are also several other aspects which require a limitation of the liability of a classification society for the exercise of public functions.

First of all, the requirements for private classification and statutory certification will often overlap. Certain safety measures are required both by public regulations, such as SOLAS, and the private rules of the classification societies. As it is in the interest of all parties to reduce the number of surveys of a vessel for economic reasons, the classification society will carry out statutory surveys and classification surveys simultaneously. The same survey may, therefore, be the basis for the decision under the private and the public vetting process. It may not even be possible after the event to determine which part of a survey was carried out in order to check statutory requirements and which part was solely necessary for exercising private functions. If in contradistinction to public functions the liability for the exercise of private functions is limited, one and the same act could lead to a limited liability for private functions, but to an unlimited one for public func-

[1261] *See supra* Part 3 C II 1.
[1262] *See supra* Part 3 C II 1.

tions. The limitation concerning the private function would therefore be without effect. Accordingly, the considerations which have led to the limitation of the liability for private functions would be rendered futile.

Secondly, as the classification society is acting on behalf of the flag State, there is no necessity to submit it to liability. Depending on domestic law, the flag State will usually be liable for the exercise of public functions.[1263] The plaintiff could sue the flag State, which then might take recourse against the classification society. The direct claim against the classification society turns out to be a claim against the flag State, which is obliged to provide for the safety of its registered vessels. For this reason, in cases of statutory surveys, classification societies should be exempted from direct actions of third parties and only be submitted to the recourse of the flag State on whose behalf they are acting. If a flag State decides to make use of a classification society, it should have to answer for the consequences of this decision and bear the risk that it cannot make full recourse to the society if it is insolvent. It is, however, not necessary to grant the victim an additional right to sue the classification society if it can claim damages against the flag State on whose behalf the classification society is acting. The classification society should, therefore, be exempt from liability based on a direct action of a victim and only be subject to the recourse of the flag State.

F. Conclusion

Taking everything into consideration, one can say that it is necessary to limit the liability of classification societies for several reasons. The societies cannot effectively insure unlimited risks at all or only to a ceiling that is introduced by the insurance company. Both would result in an insufficient protection of the injured party and in competitive advantages of classification societies that insure their risks to a more limited amount than others. Classification societies might otherwise seek protection by way of company law, which would leave injured parties without any or a merely insufficient compensation as well. Moreover, a limitation of their liability would be more efficient from an economic point of view, as third-party insurance of hardly calculable risks is the most expensive one. As preventive aspects are, of course, to be taken into account: these societies should not be exempted from liability, but be subject to a limited one. Therefore, an international convention should be developed which does not establish a strict liability of the classification societies but defines a harmonised legal basis, and reverses the burden of proof with regard to the negligence of the classification society. The plaintiff has to prove the breach of duty, whereas the classification society itself has to prove that it did not act (gross) negligently. If it acted without negligence, it will

[1263] Once again, due to the large differences in the legal systems, a harmonisation of the legal basis of the claim does not seem possible and is likely to be a source of irritation in domestic law.

not be liable. If its acts amount to negligence but not gross negligence, it will benefit from the limitations granted in the convention. The basis of the limitation should be tonnage or the number of passengers and crew the vessel is registered to carry, and not the fees of the classification society. The fees are neither objective nor consistent, nor even intelligible to the injured party. There should not be an aggregation of claims against the shipowner and those against the classification society, as they are not liable for the same risks. An aggregation of claims against the classification society and its servants and agents should, by contrast, be possible. Last but not least, the society should be exempt from liability for the exercise of public functions towards third parties and only be subject to the recourse of the flag State. Otherwise, the limitations would be ineffective and could be overcome if the public and the private function are conducted at the same time by the same act.

Bibliography

Abecassis, David W., and Jarashow, Richard L. (eds.), *Oil Pollution from Ships, International, United Kingdom and United States Law and Practice*, 2nd ed. (London: Stevens & Sons, 1985).

Altfuldisch, Rainer, *Haftung und Entschädigung nach Tankerunfällen auf See– Bestandsaufnahme, Rechtsvergleich und Vorschläge de lege ferenda* (Berlin, Heidelberg, New York: Springer, forthcoming).

American Bureau of Shipping, *Annual Review 2005* (accessible at <http://www.eagle.org/news/pubs/pdfs/AR05.pdf>, last accessed 19 March 2007.

American Law Reports (St. Paul (Min.): Thompson/West, 2005).

Anderson, Philip, *ISM Code–A Practical Guide to the Legal and Insurance Implications* (London, Hong Kong: LLP, 1998).

Anonymous, 'Anatomy of an oil spill: Exxon Valdez and the Oil Pollution Act of 1990. Note', *Seton Hall Legislative Journal*, p. 331 (1993).

Antapassis, Anthony, 'Classification Societies' Liability: A Comparison with Emphasis to Greek Law', in: Huybrechts, Marc (ed.), *Marine Insurance at the Turn of the Milennium*, Vol. 2 (Antwerp: Intersentia, 2000), p. 57.

Bagwell, David Ashley, 'Liability under United States law for spills of oil or chemicals from vessels', [1987] *Lloyd's Maritime and Commercial Law Quaterly*, p. 496.

Baker Röben, Betsy, 'Civil Liability as a Control Mechanism for Environmental Protection at the International Level', in: Morrison, Fred L., and Wolfrum, Rüdiger (eds.), *International, Regional and National Environmental Law* (The Hague, London, Boston: Kluwer, 2000), p. 821.

Ballin, Carl Wilhelm, *Die Verantwortlichkeit des Verfrachters für Seetüchtigkeit unter der Einbeziehung der anglo-amerikanischen Rechtsprechung* (Hamburg: Stehle, 1965).

Bar, Christian von, *Verkehrspflichten, Richterliche Gefahrsteuerungsgebote im deutschen Deliktsrecht* (Köln, Berlin, Bonn, München: Heymann, 1980).

——, *The Common European Law of Torts*, vol. 2 (Oxford, New York: Clarendon Press, 2000).

Barash, D. Scott, 'The Discretionary Function Exception and Mandatory Regulations', *The University of Chicago Law Review*, vol. 54, p. 1300 (1987).

Barber, John, 'Ramsgate Walkway Collapse: Legal Ramifications', *Construction Law Journal*, vol. 17, p. 25 (2001).

Bar-Lev, Joshua, 'Liability of a Vessel Classification Society Cannot Be Based on Warranty of Seaworthiness', *Journal of Maritime Law and Commerce*, vol. 4, p. 334 (1973).

Barnett, Richard, 'The validity of Himalaya clauses–privity of contract on the brink of collapse?', *International Journal of Shipping Law*, vol. 3, p. 178 (1998).

Basedow, Jürgen, *Der Transportvertrag, Studien zur Privatrechtsangleichung auf regulierten Märkten* (Tübingen: Mohr, 1987).

——, 'Haftungshöchstsummen im internationalen Lufttransport', [1988] *Transportrecht*, p. 353.

——, 'Landgericht München I 21.2.1984' [case comment], [1985] *Juristenzeitung*, p. 141.

——, 'Passagierschiffahrt–zur Novellierung des See- und Binnenschiffahrtsrechts', *Zeitschrift für das gesamte Handelsrecht und Wirtschaftsrecht*, vol. 148, p. 238 (1984).

——, 'Rechtsvergleich', in: Basedow, Jürgen, and Fock, Till, *Europäisches Versicherungsvertragsrecht* (Tübingen: Mohr Siebeck, 2002), p. 1.

——, 'Seefrachtrecht: Die Hamburger Regeln sind in Kraft', [1993] *Zeitschrift für europäisches Privatrecht*, p. 100.

——, and Fock, Till, *Europäisches Versicherungsvertragsrecht* (Tübingen: Mohr Siebeck, 2002).

——, and Wurmnest, Wolfgang, *Die Dritthaftung von Klassifikationsgesellschaften* (Tübingen: Mohr Siebeck, 2004).

——, and Wurmnest, Wolfgang, 'Klassifikationsverträge als Verträge mit Schutzwirkung zugunsten Dritter', [2005] *Zeitschrift für Versicherungsrecht*, p. 328.

——, and Wurmnest, Wolfgang, *Third-Party Liability of Classification Societies* (Berlin, Heidelberg: Springer, 2005).

Bates, John H., and Benson, Charles, *Marine Environment Law* (London, Hong Kong: LLP, 1993).

Baumbach, Adolf, Hopt, Klaus J., and Merkt, Hanno, *Handelsgesetzbuch mit GmbH & Co., Handelsklauseln, Bank- und Börsenrecht, Transportrecht (ohne Seerecht),* 32nd ed. (München: Beck, 2006).

Beale, H.G. (gen. ed.), *Chitty on Contracts*, vol. 1, 29th ed. (London: Sweet & Maxwell, 2004).

Beaver, James E., Butler, James N., III., and Myster, Susan E., 'Stormy Seas? Analysis of new oil pollution laws in the west states', *Santa Clara Law Review*, vol. 34, p. 791 (1994).

Beck, Anthony, 'Lord Lloyd probes the pragmatists: The Nicholas H', *Corporate Briefing*, vol. 9 (8), p. 23 (1995).

Beck, Brian J., 'Liability of Marine Surveyors for Loss of Surveyed Vessel: When Someone Other Than the Captain Goes Down With the Ship', *Notre Dame Law Review*, vol. 64, p. 246 (1989).

Beever, Allan, 'All at Sea in the Law of Negligent Misrepresentation', *New Zealand Business Law Quaterly*, vol. 9, p. 101 (2003).

Benedict, Erastus Cornelius, *On Admiralty*, 7th ed. (New York: Matthew Bender, 2002).

Bennett, Paul, 'Governing environmental risk: regulation, insurance and moral economy', *Progress in Human Geography*, vol. 23, p. 189 (1999).

——, 'Mutual Risk: P&I Insurance Clubs and Maritime Safety and Environmental Performance', *Marine Policy*, vol. 25, p. 13 (2001).

Bergkamp, Lucas, *Liability and the Environment, Private and Public Law Aspects of Civil Liability for Environmental Harm in an International Context* (The Hague, London, New York: Kluwer, 2001).

——, 'Environmental Risk Spreading and Insurance', *Review of European Community and International Environmental Law*, vol. 12, p. 269 (2003).

Bernhardt, Rudolf, 'Interpretation in International Law', in: Bernhardt, Rudolf (ed.), *Encyclopaedia of Public International Law*, vol. II (Amsterdam, Lausanne, New York, Oxford, Shannon, Tokyo: North-Holland Publ. Co., 1995), p. 1416.

Black, Henry Campbell, Nolan, Joseph R., and Connolly, M.J., *Black's Law Dictionary, Definitions of the Terms and Phrases of American and English Jurisprudence, Ancient and Modern*, 5th ed. (St. Paul (Minn.): West, 1979).

Black Sea Memorandum of Understanding on Port State Control, *Annual Report for 2005* (accessible at <http://www.bsmou.org/PDF/2005ANNUALREPORT.pdf>, last accessed 19 March 2007).

Block, Stephen W., 'No Class Act: A Bad Survey Lands a Classification Society in Hot Water', *Marine Digest and Transportation News*, 16 November 2003, p. 15.

Bohlen, Francis H., 'The Rule in Rylands v. Fletcher', *University of Pennsylvania Law Review*, vol. 59, p. 298 (1911).

Boisson, Philippe, 'The Liability of Classification Societies in the Marine Industry Context', in: Lux, Jonathan (ed.), *Classification Societies*, (London, New York, Hamburg, Hong Kong: Lloyd's of London Press, Ltd., 1993), p. 3.

——, 'Classification societies and safety at sea–Back to basics to prepare for the future', *Marine Policy*, vol. 18 (5), p. 363 (1994).

——, 'Classification Society Liability: Maritime Law Principles Must be Requestion (sic !)?', [1994] *CMI Yearbook*, p. 235.

——, 'Responsabilité des sociétés de classification: Faut-il remettre en cause les principes du droit maritime?', [1995] *Le droit maritime français*, p. 109.

——, 'Classification Society Cooperation with Port State Control: a Move Towards the End of Substandard Practices', *International Business Lawyer*, vol. 24, p. 352 (1996).

Bolin, Kristian, 'The Ownership of Funds and Systems for Reparation of very large Accidents', Department of Economics Paper, Lund University (accessible at <http://www.nek.lu.se/publications/workpap/Papers/wp99_6.pdf>, last accessed 19 March 2007).

Bonassies, Pierre, 'Chambre des Lords, 6 juillet 1995, Navire "Nicholas H" ' [case-comment], [1995] *Le droit maritime français*, p. 750.

——, 'Observations' [case comment of Cour de Cassation (1ère Chambre civile) 11 May 1999, [2000] *Le droit maritime français*, p. 39], [2000] *Le droit maritime français*, p. 41.

Bowstead, William, and Reynolds, Francis M.B., *Bowstead and Reynolds on agency*, 17th ed. (London: Sweet & Maxwell, 2001).

Brans, Edward H.P., 'The 1999 *Erika* Oil Spill in France', *International Law FORUM du droit international*, vol. 2, p. 66 (2000).

Breitzke, Christian, *Die Norwegian Saleform, Probleme der freiwilligen Seeschiffsveräußerung dargestellt am Standardformular der Norwegian Saleform*, (Hamburg: Juristische Dissertation, 1970).

Brinkmann, Thomas, 'German Law: Damage to Persons, Property and the Environment', *Tulane Maritime Law Journal, vol.* 22, p. 545 (1998).

Brodie, Douglas, 'The negligence liability of public authorities: a traditional solution', [1999] *Lloyd's Maritime and Commercial Law Quaterly*, p. 16.

Brown, Anthony, *300 years of Lloyds-A Lloyd's List Special Supplement* (Colchester: Lloyd's of London Press, 1988).

Brown, Robert H. and Novitt, John J., *Marine Insurance, Vol. 2: Cargo Practices*, 5th ed. (London: Witherby, 1985).

Burgin, Catherine, 'Negligence–certification of fishing vessel by Department of Transport', *International Maritime Law*, vol. 4, p. 143 (1997).

Caemmerer, Ernst von, *Wandlungen des Deliktsrechts,* in: Caemmerer, Ernst von (ed.), *Hundert Jahre Deutsches Rechtsleben: Festschrift zum 100jährigen Bestehen des Deutschen Juristentages 1860-1960* (Karlsruhe, C.F. Müller 1960), vol. 2, p. 49.

Canaris, Claus-Wilhelm, *Die Vertrauenshaftung im deutschen Privatrecht* (München: Beck, 1971).

——, in: Staub, Hermann, ——, *et al., Handelsgesetzbuch, Großkommentar, Bankvertragsrecht*, 4th ed. (Berlin: de Gruyter, 2005).

——, 'Schutzwirkungen zugunsten Dritter bei "Gegenläufigkeit" der Interessen', [1995] *Juristenzeitung*, p. 441.

——, 'Die Reform des Rechts der Leistungsstörungen', [2001] *Juristenzeitung*, p. 499.

—— (ed.), *Schuldrechtsreform 2002* (München: Beck, 2002).

Cane, Peter F., 'The Liability of classification societies', [1994] *Lloyd's Maritime and Commercial Law Quaterly*, p. 363.

——, 'Classification Societies, Cargo Owners and the Basis of Tort Liability (The Nicholas H)', [1995] *Lloyd's Maritime and Commercial Law Quaterly*, p. 433.

Capelle, K.-H., 'Die Frachtcharter in rechtsvergleichender Darstellung', *Übersee-Studien Heft 17* (Rostock: Hinstorff, 1940).

Carter Watson, Sue, 'The Suits in Admiralty Act', *Journal of Maritime Law and Commerce*, vol. 17, p. 175 (1986).

Carver, Thomas Gilbert, and Colinvaux, Raoul, *Carriage by Sea*, 13th ed. (London: Stevens, 1982).

Charlesworth, J., Percy, R.A. (*founders*), Walton, C.T., *Charlesworth and Percy on Negligence*, 11th ed. (London: Sweet & Maxwell, 2006).

Charvet, Kathleen K. and Waterman, Heather A., 'Recent Developments in Maritime Law', *Tulane Maritime Law Journal*, vol. 28, p. 375 (2004).

Chen, Xia, *Limitation of Liability for Maritime Claims, A Study of United States Law, Chinese Law and International Conventions* (The Hague, London, Boston: Kluwer Law International, 2001).

Chitty, J. (founder), Beale, H.G. (gen. ed.), *Chitty on Contracts*, vol. 1, 29th ed. (London: Sweet & Maxwell, 2004).

Clarke, Malcolm A., (ed.), *Shipbuilding Contracts–A Comparative Analysis of Contracts in the Major Maritime Jurisdictions*, 2nd ed. (London, New York, Hamburg, Hong Kong: Lloyd's of London Press, 1992).

——, 'Negligence–under control and under contract?', *Cambridge Law Journal*, vol. 53, p. 220 (1994).

Clerk, J. F., Lindsell, W. H. B. (founders), Dugdale, Anthony M., and Jones, Michael A. (gen. eds.), *Clerk & Lindsell On Torts*, 19th ed. (London: Sweet & Maxwell, 2006).

CMI Code of Conduct for Classification Societies, [1995] CMI Yearbook, p. 100.

Cochran, Courtney P., 'Otto Candies, L.L.C. v. Nippon Kaiji Kyokai Corp.: Further Extending Negligent Misrepresentation to Protect Third-Party Buyers that Rely on Erroneous Certificates Issued by Vessel Classification Societies', *Tulane Maritime Law Journal*, vol. 28, p. 613 (2004).

Coester, Michael, and Markesinis, Basil, 'Liability of Financial Experts in German and American Law: An Exercise in Comparative Methodology', *American Journal of Comparative Law*, vol. 51, p. 275 (2003).

Coffi, Christian Rodrigue, *Les sociétés de classification à l'épreuve de la sécurité maritime* (2001), Mémoire de la Faculté de Droit et de Sciences Politiques d'Aix-Marseille, Centre de Droit Maritime et des Transports (accessible at <http://www.cdmt.droit.u-3mrs.fr/memoires/2001/m01coch.doc>, last accessed 19 March 2007).

Colton, N.J., 'The Underwriting of Oil Pollution Risks' in De La Rue, Colin M. (ed.), *Liability for Damage to the Marine Environment* (London, New York, Hamburg, Hong Kong: Lloyd's of London Press, 1993), p. 149.

Comenale Pinto, Michele M., 'La Responsabiltà delle Società di Classificazione di Navi', [2003] *Il Diritto Marittimo*, p. 3.

Conner, M. Timothy, 'Maritime Tort Liability of the United States', *Journal of Maritime Law and Commerce*, vol. 11, p. 271 (1979–1980).

Convery, Jane, 'Standard Form Building Contracts and Duty of Care', *Modern Law Review*, vol. 62, p. 766 (1999).

Cook, Catriona, 'Privity of contract and the function and scope of the Himalaya clauses', *Kings College Law Journal*, vol. 7, 127 (1996–1997).

Corbin, Arthur Linton, *Corbin on Contracts, A Comprehensive Treatise on the Working Rules of Contract Law*, (St. Paul (Minn.): West, 1964).

Coste, Bertrand, 'Observations' [case-comment Cour d'Appel de Paris 9 June 1999, [2000] *Le droit maritime français,* p. 326 – "Mamer"], [2000] *Le droit maritime français,* p. 332.

Craig, Jon L. (ed.), *Civil Actions against the United States, Its Agencies, Officers, and Employees*, 2nd ed. (St. Paul (Minn.): West, 2005).

Crowley, Michael E., 'The Limited Scope of the Cargo Liability Regime covering Carriage of Goods by Sea: the Multimodal Problem', *Tulane Law Review*, vol. 79, p. 1461 (2005).

David, René, *et al.,* International Encyclopedia of Comparative Law, vol. XI, chap. 8 (Tübingen, The Hague, Paris, New York: Mohr 1972 *et seq.*).

Davis, Timothy, 'The Illusive Warranty of Workmanlike Performance: Constructing a Conceptual Framework', *Nebraska Law Review,* vol. 72, p. 981 (1993).

De La Rue, Colin M. (ed.), *Liability for Damage to the Marine Environment* (London, New York, Hamburg, Hong Kong: Lloyd's of London Press, 1993).

——, and Anderson, Charles B., *Shipping and the Environment* (London, Hong Kong: LLP, 1998).

Delebecque, Philippe, 'Observations–La responsabilité extra-contractuelle des sociétés de classification: quel régime juridique?', [2005] *Le droit maritime français,* p. 318.

Denniston, Thomas R., Gunn, Carter T., and Yudes, Alfred E., 'Liabilities of Multimodal Operators and Parties other than Carriers and Shippers', *Tulane Law Review*, vol. 64, p. 517 (1989).

Dent, Chris, and Roe, Michael, 'Liability, conventions, classification societies and safety in the Baltic–a case study of the Estonia', in: M. Roe (ed.): *Developments in the Baltic Maritime Marketplace* (Aldershot, Brookfield, U.S.A., Singapore, Sydney: Ashgate, 1997), p. 83.

Dicey, A.V., *Introduction to the Study of the Law of the Constitution*, 10th ed. (London and Basingstoke: Macmillian Press Ltd., 1959).

Doak, James B., 'Liabilities of Stevedores, Terminal Operators, and Other Handlers in Relation to Cargo', *Tulane Law Review*, vol. 45, p. 752 (1971).

Dobbs, Dan B., *The Law of Torts*, (St. Paul (Minn.): West, 2000).

Dombroff, Mark A., 'Certification and Inspection: An Overview of Government Liability', *Journal of Air Law and Commerce*, vol. 47, p. 229 (1982).

Lord Donaldson of Lymington, ' "Safer Ships; Cleaner Seas"–full spead ahead or dead slow?' [1998] *Lloyd's Maritime and Commercial Law Quaterly*, p. 170.

Donovan, James J., 'The origins and development of limitation of shipowner's liability', *Tulane Law Review*, vol. 53, p. 999 (1979).

Drobnig, Albrecht, *Tätigkeit und Haftung von Klassifikationsgesellschaften in der Bundesrepublik Deutschland am Beispiel des Germanischen Lloyd* (Münster, Hamburg: Lit, 1995).

Dugdale, Anthony M., and Jones, Michael A. (gen. eds.), *Clerk & Lindsell On Torts*, 19th ed. (London: Sweet & Maxwell, 2006).

Durr, Sean Diederich, *An Analysis of the Potential Liability of Classification Societies: Developing Role, Current Disorder & Future Prospects* (accessible at <http://www.uctshiplaw.com/theses/durr.htm>, last accessed 19 March 2007).

East, Lindsay, 'The Duty of Care in a Marine Context–Is There Someone to Blame?', in: Rose, Francis (ed.), *Lex Mercatoria: Essays on International Commercial Law in Honour of Francis Reynolds* (London: LLP, 2000), p. 129.

Ebenroth, Carsten Thomas, and Dillon, Thomas J., 'The International Rating Game: An Analysis of the Liability of Rating Agencies in Europe, England, and the United States', *Law & Policy in International Business,* vol. 24, p. 783 (1993).

Ebke, Werner F., and Finkin, Matthew W. (eds.), *Introduction to German law* (The Hague, London, Boston: Kluwer, 1996).

Edye, Christian E., *Die Haftung des Reeders für Dritt- und Umweltschäden beim Seetransport gefährlicher Güter* (Kehl am Rhein, Strasbourg, Arlington: Engel, 1993).

Eörsi, Gyula, 'Governmental Liability in Tort', in: David, René, Tunc, André, *et al.* (eds.), International Encyclopedia of Comparative Law, vol. XI, *Torts* (Tübingen, The Hague, Boston, London: Mohr, 1983) chap. 4.

Erman, Walter, Westermann, Harm Peter and Aderholz, Lutz (eds.), *Bürgerliches Gesetzbuch*, 11th ed. (Münster: Aschendorff, 2004).

Exxon Valdez Trustee Council, <http://www.evostc.state.ak.us/facts/qanda.html> (last accessed 19 March 2007).

Eyer, W.W., 'Shipowner's Limitation of Liability–New Directions for an Old Doctrine', *Stanford Law Review*, vol. 16, p. 370 (1964).

Farnsworth, E. Allan, *On Contracts*, 2nd ed. (New York: Aspen, 1998).

Faure, Michael, and Skogh, Göran, *The Economic Analysis of Environmental Policy and Law* (Cheltenham, Northampton (MA.): Edward Elgar, 2003).

Faure, Michael, and Hui, Wang, 'The International Regimes for the Compensation of Oil-Pollution Damage; Are they Effective?', *Review of European Community & International Environmental Law*, vol. 12, p. 242 (2003).

Feehan, Colin E., 'Liability of Classification Societies from the British Perspective: The Nicholas H', *Tulane Maritime Law Journal*, vol. 22, p. 163 (1997).

Ferrer, Michel, *La Responsabilité des Sociétés de Classification* (Aix-en-Provence: Presses Universitaires d'Aix-Marseille, 2004).

Ficker, Hans Claudius, König, Detlef, Kreuzer, Karl F. *et al.* (eds.), *Festschrift für Ernst von Caemmerer* (Tübingen: Mohr, 1978).

Flume, Werner, *Allgemeiner Teil des Bürgerlichen Rechts, Band 2: Das Rechtsgeschäft*, 4th ed. (Berlin, Heidelberg, New York: Springer, 1992).

Force, Robert, 'United States', in: Huybrechts, M. (ed.), *International Encyclopaedia of Laws, Vol. 3, Transport Law* (The Hague: Kluwer Law and Taxation Publ., 1998 et seq.).

——, and Norris, Martin J., *The Law of Maritime Personal Injuries*, 5th ed. (St. Paul (Minn.): Thomson/West, 2005).

Forrester, Ian S., Goren, Simon L., and Ilgen, Hans-Michael, *The German Civil Code* (Littleton (Colorado): Rothman, 1994).

France, William N., 'Classification societies: their liability–an American lawyer's point of view in light of recent judgments', *The International Journal of Shipping Law*, vol. 1, p. 67 (1996).

Frumer, Louis R., and Friedman, Melvin I., *Products Liability* (Newark, San Francisco: Bender, 2004).

Furger, Franco, 'Accountability and Systems of Self-Governance: The Case of the Maritime Industry', *Law & Policy*, vol. 19, p. 445 (1997).

Garcia, Iciar Patricia, 'Comment: "Nunca Mais!" How Current European Environmental Liability and Compensation Regimes are Addressing the Prestige Oil Spill of 2002',

University of Pennsylvania Journal of International Economic Law, vol. 25, p. 1395 (2004).

Gauci, Gotthard, 'Limitation of liability in maritime law: an anachronism?', *Marine Policy*, vol. 19, p. 65 (1995).

——, *Oil Pollution at Sea, Civil Liability and Compensation for Damage* (Chichester, New York, Weinheim, Brisbane, Singapore, Toronto: Wiley, 1997).

Geimer, Reinhold, *Internationales Zivilprozessrecht*, 5th ed. (Köln: Verlag Dr. Otto Schmidt, 2005).

Germanischer Lloyd, *Annual Report 2005* (accessible at <http://www.gl-group.com/images/glgroup/Annual_Report_2005_E.pdf>, last accessed 19 March 2007).

—— (ed.), Germanischer Lloyd-Internationales Register, 1867-1992, 2nd ed. (Hamburg: Germanischer Lloyd, 1992).

Gilmore, Grant, and Black, Charles L. Jr., *The Law of Admiralty*, 2nd ed. (Mineola, N.Y.: The Foundation Press, 1975).

Girvin, Stephen, 'Contracting carriers, Himalaya clauses and tort in the House of Lords, [2003] *Lloyd's Maritime and Commercial Law Quaterly*, p. 311.

Gold, Edgar, Chircop, Aldo E., and Kindred, Hugh M., *Maritime Law* (Toronto: Irwin Law, 2003).

Goldberg, Victor P., 'A Reexamination of Glanzer v. Shepard: Surveyors on the Tort-Contract Boundary', *Theoretical Inquiries in Law*, vol. 3, p. 475 (2002).

Goldrein, Iain, and Turner, Paul, *Ship Sale and Purchase*, 4th ed. (London, Hong Kong: LLP, 2003).

Goldsmith, Frederick B., 'River Pilot, Marine Surveyor, and Third-Party Inspector Liability', *Tulane Maritime Law Journal*, vol. 26, p. 463 (2002).

Gómez Prieto, María Teresa, 'Las sociedades de clasificación de buques', *Anuario de Derecho Marítimo*, vol. 11, p. 257 (1994).

Gooding, Nicholas, *Institute Classification Clause Revision* (2000) (accessible at <www.iumi.com/conferences/2000_london/docs/NickGooding.doc>, last accessed 19 March 2007).

Gordan, John D., III., 'The Liability of Marine Surveyors and Ship Classification Societies', *Journal of Maritime Law and Commerce*, vol. 19, p. 301 (1988).

Gorton, Lars, Hillenius, Patrick, Ihre, Rolf, and Sandevärn, Arne, *Shipbroking and Chartering Practice*, 6th ed. (London, Hong Kong: LLP, 2004).

Goss, Richard, 'Maritime Insurance and Economic Welfare', *Maritime Pollution Management*, vol. 30, p. 357 (2003).

Govare, James Paul, 'Le Bureau Véritas', in: Associazione Italiana di Diritto Marittimo, *Studi in Onore di Francesco Berlingieri* (Roma: Pubblicazione dell' Associazione Italiana di Diritto Marittimo, 1933), p. 250.

Grey, Michael, 'Classification societies under renewed scrutiny', *BIMCO Bulletin, vol.* 96, p. 44 (2001).

Grigalunas, Thomas A., Opaluch, James J., Diamantides, Jerry, and Mazzotta, Marisa, 'Liability for Oil Spill Damages: Issues, Methods, and Examples', *Coastal Management*, vol. 26, p. 61 (1998).

Grime, Robert P., 'Liability of Classification Societies', [1994] *All England Law Reports Annual Review*, p. 376.

——, 'Nicholas H in the House of Lords', [1995] *All England Law Reports Annual Review*, p. 464.

Grotius, Hugo, *De Jure Belli ac Pacis libri tres* (Washington: Carnegie Institute, 1646/1911, reprinted : 1995).

Hadley-Piggin, Jonathan, 'Duty of care: classification societies', *International Company and Commercial Law Review*, vol. 6, p. C204 (1995).

Hanash, Rami S., *Environmental Liability of Government Contractors: a practice guide for the corporate counselor* (Washington: Bureau of National Affairs, 1992).

Harling, Russel, 'The Liability of Classification Societies to Cargo Owners', [1993] *Lloyd's Maritime and Commercial Law Quaterly*, p. 1.

Harrington, Matthew P., 'Oil Pollution Act's delegation of admiralty power to the states', *Case Western Reserve Law Review*, vol. 48, p. 1 (1997).

Harrison, Jim, 'The Accountability of Classification Societies, The Role of Classification and Market-oriented Policy Issues (The "Erika"), [2000] *Journal of International Maritime Law*, p. 299.

Hart, H.L.A. and Honoré, Tony, *Causation in the Law*, 2nd ed. (Oxford: Clarendon Press, 1985).

Hayashi, Moritaka, 'Toward the Elimination of Substandard Shipping: The Report of the International Commission on Shipping', *International Journal of Marine and Coastal Law*, vol. 16, p. 501 (2003).

Hazelwood, Steven J., *P & I Clubs, Law and Practice*, 3rd ed. (London, Hong Kong: LLP, 2000).

Healy, Marie, 'Carriage of Goods by Sea: Application of the Himalaya Clause to Subdelegees of the Carrier', *The Maritime Lawyer*, vol. 2, p. 91 (1976–1977).

Helferich, James C., 'Suits Against the United States Pursuant to the SIAA, PVA, EAA, FTCA and FECA', *Trial Lawyer's Guide*, vol. 26, p. 121 (1982).

Herber, Rolf, 'Haftungsbegrenzungen und deren Durchbrechung im deutschen und internationalen Transportrecht', [2004] *Transportrecht*, p. 93.

——, *Seehandelsrecht, Systematische Darstellung* (Berlin: de Gruyter, 1999).

Hermann, Donald H.J. and Schurgin, William P., *Legal Aspects of Aids*, (St. Paul (Minn.): West, 2004).

Herschel, Wilhelm, 'Die Haftung der technischen Überwachungs-Vereine', [1969] *Neue Juristische Wochenschau*, p. 817.

Hildebrandt, Karen C., 'Personal Injury and Wrongful Death Remedies for Maritime Passengers', *Tulane Law Review*, vol. 68, p. 403 (1994)

Hill, Christopher, *Maritime Law*, 6th ed. (London, Hong Kong: LLP, 2003).

Hirte, Heribert, *Berufshaftung, Ein Beitrag zur Entwicklung eines einheitlichen Haftungsmodells für Dienstleistungen* (München: Beck, 1996).

Hodges, Susan, and Hill, Christopher, *Principles of Maritime Law* (London, Hong Kong: LLP, 2001).

Holmes, Oliver Wendell, Jr., *The Common Law* (1881) (Reprint, London, Melbourne: Macmillian, 1968).

Holtappels, Peter, 'Haftung von Klassifikationsgesellschaften in der Handelsschiffahrt', [2002] *Transportrecht*, p. 278.

Honka, Hannu, 'The Classification System and its Problems with Special Reference to the Liability of Classification Societies', *Tulane Maritime Law Journal*, vol. 19, p. 1 (1994).

Honsell, Heinrich, 'Anmerkung zum Urteil des BGH vom 23.1.1985–IVa ZR 66/83', [1985] *Juristenzeitung*, p. 952.

Hopt, Klaus J., 'Nichtvertragliche Haftung außerhalb von Schadens- und Bereicherungsausgleich', *Archiv für die civilistische Praxis*, vol. 183 (1983), p. 608.

——, 'Die Haftung des Wirtschaftsprüfers–Rechtsprobleme zu § 323 HGB (§ 168 AktG a.F.) und zur Prospekt und Auskunftshaftung', in: Hofmann, Paul, Meyer-Cording, Ulrich, and Wiedemann, Herbert, *Festschrift für Klemens Pleyer* (Köln, Berlin, Bonn, München: Heymann, 1986), p. 341.

——, 'Dritthaftung für Testate', [1987] *Neue Juristische Wochenschau*, p. 1745.
——, Baumbach, Adolf, ——, and Merkt, Hanno, *Handelsgesetzbuch mit GmbH & Co., Handelsklauseln, Bank- und Börsenrecht, Transportrecht (ohne Seerecht),* 32nd ed. (München: Beck, 2006).
Howard, Tim, and Davenport, Brian, 'English Maritime Law Update 1994/95', *Journal of Maritime Law and Commerce*, vol. 27, p. 427 (1996).
Huber, Konrad, 'Verkehrspflichten zum Schutz fremden Vermögens', in: Ficker, Hans Claudius, König, Detlef, and Kreuzer, Karl F. et al. (eds.), *Festschrift für Ernst von Caemmerer* (Tübingen; Mohr, 1978), p. 359.
Huber, Peter, and Faust, Florian, *Schuldrechtsmodernisierung* (München: Beck, 2002).
Hübner, Ulrich, 'Haftungsprobleme der technischen Kontrolle', [1988] *Neue Juristische Wochenschau*, p. 441.
——, 'Die Berufshaftung–ein zumutbares Berufsrisiko?', [1989] *Neue Juristische Wochenschau*, p. 5.
Hudson, N. Geoffrey, *The Institute Clauses* (London, Hong Kong: LLP, 1999).
Hutchison, John B., 'Practical and Political Considerations', in: Lux, Jonathan (ed.), *Classification Societies*, (London, New York, Hamburg, Hong Kong: Lloyd's of London Press, Ltd., 1993), p. 27.
Huybrechts, M. (ed.), *International Encyclopaedia of Laws, Vol. 3, Transport Law* (The Hague: Kluwer Law and Taxation Publ., 1998 et seq.).

IACS, Recommendation No. 82 of July 2003 'Surveyor's Glossary, Hull Terms and Hull Service Terms' (accessible at <http://www.iacs.org.uk/guidesandrecs.htm>, last accessed 19 March 2007).
——, Unified Requirement No. Z3.1.1 (Corr. Feb. 2004) 'Periodical Survey of the Outside of the Ship's Bottom and Related Items' (accessible at <http://www.iacs.org.uk/ureqs/main.htm>, last accessed 19 March 2007).
——, 'What are classification societies?' (accessible at <www.iacs.org.uk/_pdf/Class%20 monograph.pdf>, last accessed 19 March 2007).
——, Procedural Requirement No. 3, 'Transparency of Classification and Statutory Information' (accessible at <http://www.iacs.org.uk/preqs/main.htm>, last accessed 19 March 2007).
——, Procedural Requirement No. 1A, 'Procedures for Changing Classification Status' (accessible at <http://www.iacs.org.uk/preqs/main.htm>, last accessed 19 March 2007).
——, *Classification Societies–What, Why and How?* (2005) (accessible at <http://www.iacs.org.uk/_pdf/Class_WhatWhy&How.PDF>, last accessed 19 March 2007).
IMO, *Summary Status of Conventions as at 31 August 2005* (accessible at <http://www.imo.org/home.asp?topic_id=161>, last accessed 19 March 2007).
——, *Survey Guidelines Under the Harmonized System of Survey and Certification*, Resolution A.746(18) (accessible at <http://www.iacs.org.uk>, last accessed 19 March 2007).
——, *Guidelines for the authorization of organizations acting on behalf of the Administration*, Resolution A.739(18).
——, *Specifications on the survey and certification functions of recognized organizations acting on behalf of the Administration,* Resolution A.789(19).
——, *Guidelines under the Harmonized System of Survey and Certification,* Resolution A.948(23).
——, Sub-Committee on Flag State Implementation in its 11th Session on 3 January 2003 (FSI 11/7/1) (accessible at <http://www.iacs.org.uk/submissions.htm>, last accessed 19 March 2007).

Indian Ocean Memorandum of Understanding on Port State Control, *Annual Report 2005* (accessible at < http://www.iomou.org/annrep05.pdf>, last accessed 19 March 2007).

Ingraham, Donald S., 'The Suits in Admiralty Act and the Implied Discretionary Function', *Duke Law Journal*, vol. 1982, p. 146 (1982).

The Institute of London Underwriters in collaboration with Lloyd's in *Reference Book of Marine Insurance Clauses*, 75th ed. (London: Witherby, 2004).

Institute of Maritime Law, The University of Southampton (ed.), *The Limitation of Shipowners' Liability: The New Law* (London: Sweet & Maxwell, 1986).

Institute of Shipping Economics and Logistics, *ISL Shipping Statistics Yearbook 2004* (Bremen: Institute of Shipping Economics and Logistics, 2004).

Inter-Governmental Maritime Consultative Organization (IMCO), *Official Records of the International Legal Conference of Marine Pollution Damage, 1969* (London, IMCO: 1973).

International Oil Pollution Compensation Funds, *Report on the Activities of the International Oil Pollution Compensation Funds in 2004* (accessible at <http://www.iopcfund.org/npdf/AR2004English.pdf>, last accessed 19 March 2007).

——, *Report on the Activities of the International Oil Pollution Compensation Funds in 2005* (accessible at <http://en.iopcfund.org/npdf/AR05_E.pdf>, last accessed 19 March 2007).

Ipsen, Knut (ed.), *Völkerrecht,* 5th ed. (München: Beck, 2004).

Jackson, Rupert M., and Powell, John L., *On Professional Negligence*, 4th ed. (London: Sweet & Maxwell, 1997).

Jacobsson, Måns, 'The International Conventions on Liability and Compensation for Oil Pollution Damage and the Activities of the International Oil Pollution Compensation Fund', in: De La Rue, Colin M. (ed.), *Liability for Damage to the Marine Environment* (London, New York, Hamburg, Hong Kong: Lloyd's of London Press, 1993), p. 39.

——, 'Compensation for Oil Pollution Damage Caused by Oil Spills from Ships and the International Oil Pollution Compensation Fund', *Marine Pollution Bulletin* vol. 29, p. 378 (1994).

——, 'Le regime international d'indemnisation des victims des marées noires en pleine évolution', [2004] *Le droit maritime français*, p. 793.

Jacobsson, Marie, and Klabbers, Jan, 'Rest in Peace? New Developments Concerning the Wreck of the M/S Estonia', *Nordic Journal of International Law*, vol. 69, p. 317 (2000).

Jenner, Robert K., *Transfusion-Associated AIDS* (Tucson (AZ): Lawyers & Judges Pub. Co., 1995).

Jin, Di, and Kite-Powell, Hauke L., 'On the optimal environmental liability limit for marine oil transport', *Transportation Research,* Part E, p. 77 (1999).

The Joint Accident Investigation Commission, *Final report on the capsizing on 28 September 1994 in the Baltic Sea on the ro-ro passenger vessel MV Estonia* (Helsinki: Joint Accident Investigation Commission and Edita Ltd., 1997; also accessible at <http://www.onnettomuustutkinta.fi/estonia/>, last accessed 19 March 2007).

Jost, Fritz, *Vertragslose Auskunfts- und Beratungshaftung* (Baden-Baden: Nomos Verl.-Ges., 1991).

Jowitt, Earl, Walsh, Clifford, and Burke, John, *Jowitt's Dictionary of English Law*, vol. 1, 2nd ed. (London: Sweet & Maxwell, 1977).

Kaye, Tim, 'Acts speak louder than statements, or nine into one will go', *Modern Law Review*, vol. 58, p. 574 (1995).

Keeton, W. Page, and Keeton, Robert E., *Cases and Materials On the Law of Torts*, 2nd ed. (St. Paul (Minn.): West, 1977).

Ketkar, Kusum W., 'The Oil Pollution Act of 1990: A Decade Later', *Spill Science and Technologie Bulletin*, vol. 7, p. 45 (2002).

Killingbeck, Serge, 'Limitation of Liability for Maritime Claims and Its Place In the Past, Present and Future-How Can It Survive?', *SCU Law review*, vol. 3, p. 1 (1999).

Kim, Inho, 'Ten years after the enactment of the Oil Pollution Act of 1990: a success or a failure', *Marine Policy*, vol. 26, p. 197 (2002).

Kindt, John Warren, 'Marine Pollution and Hydrocarbons: The Goal of Minimizing Damage to the Marine Environment', *California Western International Law Journal*, vol. 14, p. 233 (1984).

Klein, Andreas, 'Haftungsbeschränkungen zugunsten und zu Lasten Dritter und ihre Behandlung in der Schuldrechtsreform', [1997] *Juristenzeitung*, p. 390.

Koller, Ingo, *Die Risikozurechnung bei Vertragsstörungen in Austauschverträgen* (München: Beck, 1979).

Köndgen, Johannes, *Selbstbindung ohne Vertrag: Zur Haftung aus geschäftsbezogenem Handeln* (Tübingen: Mohr, 1981).

Kopec, Daniel, and Peterson, Philip, 'Crude legislation: Liability and compensation under the Oil Pollution Act of 1990', *Rutgers Law Journal*, vol. 23, p. 597 (1992).

Kötz, Hein, 'Haftungsausschlußklauseln', in: *25 Jahre Karlsruher Forum – Beilage*, [1983] *Zeitschrift für Versicherungsrecht*, p. 145.

Korpela, A.E., 'Right of Contractor with Federal, State, or Local Public Body to Latter's Immunity from Tort Liability', in: *American Law Reports*, 3rd ed. (St. Paul (Min.): West, 2004).

Kraft, Holger, and Schlingmann, Matthias, 'Die Dritthaftung von Klassifikationsgesellschaften', [2004] *Zeitschrift für Versicherungsrecht*, p. 1095.

Kröger, Bernd, 'Presentation on Behalf of the German Shipowners' Association and of the Maritime Law Committee of ICS', [1997] *CMI Yearbook*, p. 185.

Kronke, Herbert, 'Seefrachtvertragliche Gehilfenhaftung', [1988] *Transportrecht*, p. 89.

Krüger, Kai, 'Fault Liability for Classification Societies Towards Third Parties?', in: Gorton, Lars, et. al. (eds.), *Festskrift till Kurt Grönfors* (Stockholm: Norstedt, 1991), p. 271.

Lambert, LeRoy, 'Damages Arising from Breach of Contract, Loss of Revenue, and "Indirect Damages" ', *Tulane Law Review*, vol. 72, p. 759 (1997).

Lammel, Siegbert, 'Zur Auskunftshaftung', *Archiv für die civilistische Praxis*, vol. 179, p. 337 (1979).

Lammers, Johan G., 'International Responsibility and Liability for Damage Caused by Environmental Interferences', *Environmental Policy and Law*, vol. 31, p. 94 (2001).

Lang, Volker, 'Einmal mehr: Berufsrecht, Berufspflichten und Berufshaftung', *Archiv für die civilistische Praxis*, vol. 201, p. 451 (2001).

Langavant, Emmanuel, and Boisson, Philippe, 'L'affaire du naufrage de la drague « Cap-de-la-Hague » et le problème de la responsabilité des sociétés de classification', [1981] *Le droit maritime français*, p. 131.

Lange, Hermann, and Schiemann, Gottfried, *Schadensersatz*, 3rd ed. (Tübingen: Mohr, 2003).

Larenz, Karl, *Lehrbuch des Schuldrechts*, Zweiter Band, Besonderer Teil, 1. Halbband, 13th ed. (München: Beck, 1986).

——, and Canaris, Claus-Wilhelm, *Lehrbuch des Schuldrechts*, Zweiter Band, Besonderer Teil, 2. Halbband, 13th ed. (München: Beck, 1994).

——, and Wolf, Manfred, *Allgemeiner Teil des Bürgerlichen Rechts*, 9th ed. (München: Beck, 2004).

Latin American Agreement on Port State Control of Vessels [Viña del Mar Agreement], *Summary of Annual Report 2003* (accessible at <http://200.45.69.62/PDF/Informe%20Anual%202003_i.pdf>, last accessed 19 March 2007).

Law, Sylvia A., 'Torts', in: Morrison, Alan B., *Fundamentals of American Law* (Oxford: Oxford University Press, 1996), p. 239.

Lawson, Mark, 'Determining the Indeterminate Class: The Morning Watch', [1990] *Lloyd's Maritime and Commercial Law Quaterly*, p. 482.

Lay, H.G., *Marine Insurance–A Text Book of the History of Marine Insurance including the Functions of Lloyd's Register of Shipping* (London: Post Magazine, 1925).

Lehmann, Eike, and Mau, Reinhard, *Geprüfte Sicherheit–Der Germanische Lloyd im Wandel der Zeiten*, 2nd ed. (Bremerhaven: NWD-Verlag, 1997).

Lentz, Sally Ann, and Felleman, Fred, 'Oil Spill Prevention: A Proactive Approach', [2003] *International Oil Spill Conference,* p. 1.

Leslie, Richard M., 'Civil Liability Responsibilities of Vessel Owners and Classification Societies', [1994] *CMI Yearbook,* p. 256.

Lethwaite, John, 'Pure economic loss: a new perspective', *Nottingham Law Journal*, vol. 4, p. 224 (1995).

Liesecke, Rudolf, 'Die Seetüchtigkeit des Schiffs beim Frachtvertrag in der Rechtsprechung, insbesondere des Bundesgerichtshofes', in: Baumann, Horst, Schirmer, Helmut, and Schmidt, Reimer, *Festschrift für Sieg* (Karlsruhe: Versicherungswirtschaft, 1976), p. 345.

Lipeles, Maxine, 'State Control of Oil Pollution: Legislating in the Twilight Zone', *Harvard Environmental Law Review*, vol. 1, p. 431 (1976).

Littbarski, Sigurd, 'Die Berufshaftung–eine unerschöpfliche Quelle richterlicher Rechtsfortbildung', [1984] *Neue Juristische Wochenschau,* p. 1667.

Lopez de Gonzalo, Marco, 'La Responsabilità delle Società di Classifica', *Diritto del Commercio Internazionale,* p. 651 (1997).

Lorenz, Werner, 'Haftung für primäre Vermögensschäden bei unrichtiger Auskunft', in: Paulus, Gotthard, Diederichsen, and Canaris, Claus-Wilhelm, *Festschrift Larenz I* (München: Beck, 1973), p. 575.

Lux, Jonathan (ed.), *Classification Societies*, (London, New York, Hamburg, Hong Kong: Lloyd's of London Press, Ltd., 1993).

MacDonald, Charles, 'Occasional survey by classification society', *International Maritime Law*, vol. 2, p. 202 (1995).

Mangone, Gerard J., *United States Admiralty Law* (The Hague, London, Boston: Kluwer, 1997).

Markesinis, Basil S., Lorenz, W., and Dannemann, G., *The German Law of Obligations, vol. I The Law of Contracts and Restitution: A Comparative Introduction* (Oxford: Clarendon Press, 1997).

——, and Deakin, Simon, F., *Tort Law*, 4th ed. (Oxford: Clarendon Press, 1999).

——, and Unberath, Hannes, *The German Law of Torts, A Comparative Treatise*, 4th ed. (Oxford: Clarendon Press, 2002).

Marsden, Reginald G., and Gault, Simon, *Marsden on collisions at sea*, 13th ed. (London: Sweet & Maxwell, 2003).

Martin, Frederick, *The History of Lloyd's and of Marine Insurance in Great Britain* (London: Macmillan and Co., 1876).

Martín Osante, José Manuel, 'La Normativa Comunitaria en Materia de Seguridad Marítima–Sociedades de Clasificación y Transporte de Petróleo', *Anuario de Derecho Marítimo*, vol. 11, p. 163 (2001).

Martowski, David W., 'Vetting Clauses', *Tulane Maritime Law Journal*, vol. 26, p. 123 (2001).

Mason, Michael, 'Transnational Compensation for Oil Pollution Damage: Examining Spatialities of Environmental Liability', LSE Research Papers in Environmental and Spatial Analysis, Department of Geography and Environment, LSE 69 (2002) (accessible at <http://www.lse.ac.uk/collections/geographyAndEnvironment/pdf/rp69.pdf>, last accessed 19 March 2007).

McCauley, Michael B., 'Limitations of Liability and Recreational Vessels', *Tulane Maritime Law Journal*, vol. 16, p. 289 (1992).

McClure, Helen P., 'Liability of Administrative Officials', *George Washington Law Review,* vol. 53, p. 206 (1984).

McCormack, Howard M., 'Warranties and Disclaimers', *Tulane Law Review*, vol. 62, p. 549 (1988).

McLoughlin, James, and Bellinger, E.G., *Environmental Pollution Control, An Introduction to Principles and Practice of Administration* (London, Dordrecht, Boston: Graham & Trotman/M. Nijhoff, 1993).

Medicus, Dieter, *Bürgerliches Recht*, 20th ed. (Köln, Berlin, München: Heymann, 2004).

Mertens, Hans-Joachim, 'Deliktsrecht und Sonderprivatrecht–Zur Rechtsfortbildung des deliktischen Schutzes von Vermögensinteressen', *Archiv für die civilistische Praxis,* vol. 178, p. 227 (1978).

Miller, Machale A., 'Liability of Classification Societies from the Perspective of United States Law', *Tulane Maritime Law Journal,* vol. 22, p. 75 (Winter 1997).

Mommsen, Friedrich, *Beiträge zum Obligationenrecht* (Braunschweig: Schwetschke, 1853-1855).

Moriarty, Stephen, 'Negligence in a commercial context', *Commercial Lawyer*, vol. 1, p. 11 (1995).

Morin, Michel, 'Observations' [case-comment Cour de Cassation (Chambre criminelle) 7 July 1998, [1999] *Le droit maritime français,* p. 106 – "Snekkar Arctic"], [1999] *Le droit maritime français,* p. 118.

Morrison, Alan B., *Fundamentals of American Law* (Oxford: Oxford University Press, 1996).

Morrison, Fred L., and Wolfrum, Rüdiger (eds.), *International, Regional and National Environmental Law* (The Hague, London, Boston: Kluwer Law International, 2000).

Motive zu dem Entwurfe eines Bürgerlichen Gesetzbuches für das Deutsche Reich, Amtliche Ausgabe, Band II Recht der Schuldverhältnisse (Berlin, Leipzig: Guttentag, 1888, re-print: Frankfurt/Main: Keip, 1983).

Mullahy, Michael P., 'State's rights and the Oil Pollution Act of 1990', *Hofstra Law Review*, vol. 25, p. 607 (1996).

Müller, Walter, 'Internationale Regelung der Haftung für Schäden bei der Beförderung gefährlicher Güter auf Binnenwasserstraßen', in: Thume, Karl-Heinz (ed.), *Transport- und Vertriebsrecht 2000, Festgabe für Rolf Herber* (Neuwied: Luchterhand, 1999), p. 280.

Mullis, Alastair, 'Torts in a commercial context are different: the tortious non–liability of classification societies', *Kings College Law Journal*, vol. 7, p. 108 (1996-1997).

Murray, James A.H., *The Oxford English Dictionary, Being a corrected Re-Issue with an introduction, supplement, and Bibliography of a New English Dictionary on historical Principles, founded mainly on the materials collected by the Philiogical Society* (Oxford: Clarendon Press, 1933 (Reprinted 1978)).

Murray, John Edward, *Murray on Contracts*, 4th ed. (New York: Lexis Nexis, 2001).

Lord Mustill, 'Ships are different–or are they?', [1993] *Lloyd's Maritime and Commercial Law Quaterly*, p. 490.

Myburgh, Paul, 'Review: Shipping Law', [2003] *New Zealand Law Review,* p. 287.

Oats, Maria, 'Cargo Insurance–Liability for Negligence', *International Insurance Law Review* vol. 3 (10), p. G209 (1995).

O'Brien, Damien L., 'The Potential Liability of Classification Societies to Marine Insurers Under United States Law', *University of San Francisco Maritime Law Journal*, vol. 7, p. 403 (1994–1995).

O'Gray, William, 'Why don't classification societies admit liability?', [1998] *BIMCO Review* 109.

Organisation for Economic Co-operation and Development (OECD), *Competitive Advantages Obtained by Some Shipowners as a Result of Non-Observance of Applicable International Rules and Standards* (Paris: OECD, 1996), Publication OECD/GD(96)4.

——, Directorate for Science, Technology and Industry, *The Costs to Users of Substandard Shipping* (Paris: OECD, 2001).

——, Directorate for Science, Technology and Industry, Maritime Transport Committee, *Report on the Removal of Insurance from Substandard Shipping*, June 2004 (unpublished).

——, Maritime Transport Committee, *Cost Savings Stemming from Non-Compliance with International Environmental Regulations in the Maritime Sector* (Paris: OECD, 2003), Publication DSTI/DOT/MTC(2002)8/FINAL.

——, Maritime Transport Committee, *Ownership and Control of Ships* (Paris: OECD, 2003).

——, *Policy Issues in Insurance: Environmental Risks and Insurance, A comparative Analysis of the Role of Insurance in the Management of Environment-Related Risks* (Paris: OECD, 2003).

Oliphant, Ken, 'Tort', *Current Legal Problems*, vol. 49 (Part I), p. 29 (1996).

Ossenbühl, Fritz, *Staatshaftungsrecht*, 5th ed. (München: Beck, 1998).

O'Halloran, Rory B., 'Otto Candies, L.L.C. v. Nippon Kaiji Kyokai Corp.: In a Novel Decision, the Fifth Circuit Recognizes the Tort of Negligent Misrepresentation in Connection with Maritime Classification Societies and Third-Party Plaintiffs', *Tulane Law Review*, vol. 78, p. 1389 (2003–2004).

Özçayir, Z. Oya, *Liability for Oil Pollution and Collisions* (London, Hong Kong: LLP, 1998).

——, 'The "Erika" and its Aftermath', *International Maritime Lawyer*, vol. 7, p. 230 (2000).

——, *Port State Control*, 2nd ed. (London, Singapore: LLP, 2004).

Palandt, *Bürgerliches Gesetzbuch*, 65th ed. (München: Beck, 2006).

Pappenheim, Max, *Handbuch des Seerechts, Schuldverhältnisse des Seerechts*, vol. 3 (München, Leipzig: Duncker & Humblot, 1918).

Parameswaran, Benjamin, *The Liberalization of Maritime Transport Services* (Berlin, Heidelberg: Springer, 2004).

Paris Memorandum of Understanding on Port State Control, *The year detention rate per Classification Society (2003-2005)* (accessible at <http://www.parismou.org/upload/anrep/RO%20performance%20list%202005.pdf>, last accessed 19 March 2007).

——, *Annual Report 2005* (accessible at <http://www.parismou.org/upload/anrep/Paris%20MOU%20JV%202004-LR.pdf>, last accessed 19 March 2007).

Paulus, Gotthard, Diederichsen, Uwe, and Canaris, Claus-Wilhelm (eds.), *Festschrift für Karl Larenz zum 70. Geburtstag,* (München: Beck, 1973).
Perillo, Joseph M., *Calamari and Perillo on Contracts*, 5th ed. (St. Paul (Minn.): West, 2003).
Plötner, Michael, *Die Rechtsfigur des Vertrags mit Schutzwirkung zugunsten Dritter und die sogenannte Expertenhaftung* (Berlin: Duncker & Humblot, 2003).
Pound, Roscoe, *An Introduction to the Philosophy of Law*, 4th ed. (New Haven: Yale University Press, 1930).
Prosser, William L., 'The Assault Upon the Citadel (Strict Liability to the Consumer)', *Yale Law Journal*, vol. 69, p. 1099 (1960).
——, and Keeton, W. Page, *The Law of Torts*, 5th ed. (St. Paul (Minn.): West, 1984, with addendum 1988).
Proutière-Maulion, Gwenaële, 'Observations' [case comment Tribunal correctionnel de Saint-Nazaire 18 March 2003, [2003] *Le droit maritime français*, p. 1068], [2003] *Le droit maritime français*, p. 1088.
Pulido Begines, Juan L., *La responsabilidad frente a terceros de las sociedades de clasificación de buques* (Vitoria-Gasteiz: Eusko Jaurlaritzka, 2006)
——, 'The EU Law on Classification Societies: Scope and Liability Issues', *Journal of Maritime Law and Commerce*, vol. 36, p. 487 (2005).
——, 'The Implementation of the EU Community Directive 94/57/EC: Degree of Harmonisation Achieved', [2005] *Il Diritto Marittimo*, p. 1234.
Putnam, Henry Ware, 'The Limited Liability of Ship-Owners for Master's Faults', *American Law Review*, vol. 17, p. 1 (1883).
Puttfarken, Hans-Jürgen, *Seehandelsrecht* (Heidelberg: Verlag Recht und Wirtschaft, 1997).

Quantz, Tobias, 'Die Rückgriffsbeschränkung des Art. 34 S. 2 GG im Innenregress gegen Private', [2004] *Zeitschrift für Versicherungsrecht*, p. 1244.

Rabe, Dieter, *Seehandelsrecht*, 4th ed. (München: Beck, 2000).
Rabel, Ernst, *Recht des Warenkaufs,* vol. 1 (Berlin & Leipzig: de Gruyter, 1936, re-print: 1957).
Ramsey, Clayton G., and Monachino, Vivienne, 'Admiralty Claims against the United States', *Maritime Lawyer*, vol. 5, p. 31 (1980).
Rebmann, Kurt, Säcker, Franz Jürgen, and Rixecker, Roland (eds.), *Münchener Kommentar zum Bürgerlichen Gesetzbuch, vol. 2a, Schuldrecht, Allgemeiner Teil, §§ 241–432,* 4th ed. (2003)*; vol. 4, Schuldrecht, Besonderer Teil II, §§ 611–704*, 4th ed. (2005); *vol. 5, Schuldrecht, Besonderer Teil III, §§ 705–853,* 4th ed. (München: Beck, 2004).
Reimann, Mathias, 'Liability for Defective Products at the Beginning of the Twenty-First Century: Emergence of a Worldwide Standard?', *American Journal of Comparative Law*, vol. 51, 751 (2003).
Reissner, David H., and Wood, Michael, 'Duty of care in English law: the tort of negligence v. the doctrine of binding precedent', *International Insurance Law Review*, vol. 2, p. 351 (1994).
——, 'No duty of care owed by classification society', *International Insurance Law Review*, vol. 4, p. 30 (1996).
Rémond-Gouilloud, M., 'The Future of the Compensation System as established by International Convention' in De La Rue, Colin M. (ed.), *Liability for Damage to the Marine Environment* (London, New York, Hamburg, Hong Kong: Lloyd's of London Press, 1993), p. 83.

Richardson, Benjamin J., 'Mandating Environmental Liability Insurance', *Duke Environmental Law and Policy Forum*, vol. 12, p. 293 (2002).
Rittmeister, Sabine, *Das Seerechtliche Haftungsbeschränkungsverfahren nach neuem Recht* (Kehl/Rhein, Strasbourg, Arlington: Engel, 1995).
Rodgers, William H., *Environmental Law*, 2nd ed. (St. Paul (Minn.): West, 1994).
Rodriguez, Antonio J., and Jaffe, Paul A.C., 'Oil Pollution Act of 1990', *Tulane Maritime Law Journal*, vol. 15, p. 1 (1990).
Roe, Michael (ed.), *Developments in the Baltic Maritime Marketplace* (Aldershot, Brookfield, U.S.A., Singapore, Sydney: Ashgate, 1997).
Rose, Francis (ed.), *Lex Mercatoria: Essays on International Commercial Law in Honour of Francis Reynolds* (London: LLP, 2000).

Salmond, John (found.), Heuston, Robert F.V., and Buckley, Richard A., *Salmond and Heuston On the Law of Torts*, 21st ed. (London: Sweet & Maxwell, 1996).
Santos, Miguel A., *Limits and Scope of Environmental Law* (Springfield (Ill.): C.C. Thomas, 1995).
Saunière, Yvette, *Le Buréau Véritas, Société Internationale de Classification de Navires et d'Aéronefs, et sa Responsabilité*, (Paris: Sirey, 1932).
Schaps, Georg, and Abraham, Hans Jürgen, *Das Seerecht in der Bundesrepublik Deutschland*, 4th ed. (Berlin, New York: de Gruyter, 1978).
Schmertz, John R., and Meier, Mike, 'In Dispute after Sinking of Cargo Vessel, Second Circuit Relies on Lauritzen Triad and Applies Law of Place with Predominant Interests Rather than Law of Flag', *International Law Update*, p. 140 (December 1996).
Schmidt Etkin, Dagmar, 'Estimating Cleanup Costs for Oil Spills', [1999] International Oil Spill Conference, No. 165.
Schmuck, Thomas, *Der US-Oil Pollution Act* (Neuwied: Luchterhand, 1996).
Schneider, Laurenz, *Haftung und Haftungsbeschränkung bei Personenschäden im internationalen Lufttransport* (Basel: Helbing & Lichtenhahn, 1999).
Schoenbaum, Thomas J., *Admiralty and Maritime Law*, 4th ed. (St. Paul (Minn.): West, 2004).
Schoenfeld, Jason A., and Butterworth, Michael M., 'Limitation of Liability: The Defense Perspective', *Tulane Maritime Law Journal*, vol. 28, p. 219 (2004).
Schwarzenberger, Georg, *A Manual of International Law*, 4th ed. (London: Stevens, 1960).
Schweickhardt, Armin, 'Die Kanalisierung der Luftfrachtführerhaftung', [1979] *Association Suisse de Droit Aérien et Spatiale-Bulletin*, vol. 2, p. 5.
Scrutton, Thomas E., and Boyd, Steward C., et al (eds.), *Scrutton On charterparties and bills of Lading*, 20th ed. (London: Sweet & Maxwell, 1996).
Selb, Walter, *Schadensbegriff und Regreßmethoden, Eine Studie zur Wandlung der Denkformen des Regresses bei Schuldnermehrheiten mit der Veränderung des Schadensbegriffes* (Heidelberg: Winter, 1963).
Selvig, Erling, 'An Introduction to the 1976 Convention', in: Institute of Maritime Law, The University of Southampton (ed.), *The Limitation of Shipowners' Liability: The New Law* (London: Sweet & Maxwell, 1986), p. 3.
Seward, R.C., 'The Insurance Viewpoint', in: Institute of Maritime Law, The University of Southampton (ed.), *The Limitation of Shipowners' Liability: The New Law* (London: Sweet & Maxwell, 1986), p. 161.
Shapiro, C., 'Symposium on the economics of liability', *Journal of Economic Perspectives*, vol. 3 (1991).
Shapo, Marshall S., *The Law of Products Liability*, 3rd ed. (Salem (New Hampshire): Butterworth, 1994, with suppl. 1999).

Siccardi, Francesco, 'Pollution Liability and Classification Societies, Is the System a Fair One?', [2005] *Il Diritto Marittimo,* p. 691.

Simpson, M.T.A., 'Die Klassifikationsgesellschaften heute, Ihre Funktionen im Interesse der Sicherheit auf See, Teil I', [1980] *Hansa*, p. 1726.

Skou, A.W., 'Presentation on Behalf of IACS to the Centenary Conference of the CMI', [1997] *CMI Yearbook*, p. 180.

Smith, J.R.G., 'The role of classification societies in the regulatory regime', *BIMCO Bulletin*, vol. 95, p. 18 (2000).

Soergel, Hans Th. (found.), Siebert, Wolfgang (ed.), and Mertens, Hans-Joachim, *Kommentar zum Bürgerlichen Gesetzbuch, Band 2, Schuldrecht I (§§ 241–432)*, 12th ed. (Stuttgart, Berlin, Köln: Kohlhammer, 1990).

Speiser, Stuart M., Krause, Charles F., and Gans, Alfred W., *The American Law of Torts*, (Deerfield (Ill.): Clark Boardman Callaghan, 2003).

Stahl, Ulrich H., *Die Zeitcharter nach englischem Recht* (Kehl am Rhein, Strasbourg, Arlington: Engel, 1989).

Stanton, Keith, Skidmore, Paul, Harris, Michael, and Wright, Jane, *Statutory Torts* (London: Sweet & Maxwell, 2003).

Starer, Brian D., 'Liability, is it Just Around the Corner? An Advocate's View of a Classification Society and its Duty', [1994] *CMI Yearbook*, p. 259.

Staub, Hermann, Canaris, Claus-Wilhelm, *et al., Handelsgesetzbuch, Großkommentar, Bankvertragsrecht*, 4th ed. (Berlin: de Gruyter, 2005).

Staudinger, Julius von, *Kommentar zum Bürgerlichen Gesetzbuch mit Einführungsgesetz und Nebengesetzen, §§ 249–254,* 13th ed. (2005); *§§ 328–359,* 13th ed. (2004); *§§ 652–704,* 13th ed. (1995); *§§ 823–825*, 13th ed. (Berlin: Sellier–de Gruyter, 1999).

Steel, David, 'Ships are different: the case for limitation of liability', [1995] *Lloyd's Maritime and Commercial Law Quaterly*, p. 77.

Steiner, Udo, *Öffentliche Verwaltung durch Private* (Hamburg: Hansischer Gildenverlag, 1975).

Stelkens, Ulrich, 'Amtshaftung und Regress bei Schädigungen durch Verwaltungshelfer', [2004] *Juristenzeitung*, p. 656.

Stoiber, Carlton, Baer, Alec, Pelzer, Norbert, and Tonhause, Wolfgang, *Handbook on Nuclear Law*, (Vienna: IAEA Publications, 2003) (accessible at <http://www.milieuom .nl/IAEA.pdf>, last accessed 19 March 2007).

Stoll, Hans, 'Consequences of Liability: Remedies', in: David, René, and Tunc, André, International Encyclopedia of Comparative Law, vol. XI, chapter 8 (Tübingen, The Hague, Paris, New York: Mohr 1972 *et seq.*).

Strong, Malcolm, and Herring, Paul, *Sale of Ships. The Norwegian Saleform* (London: Sweet & Maxwell, 2004).

Stuart, III, Claude L., and Caffrey, Evan T., 'Liability of Marine Surveyors, Adjusters, and Claims Handlers', *Tulane Maritime Law Journal*, vol. 22, p. 1 (1997).

Sullivan, Eric, *The Marine Encyclopaedic Dictionary*, 6th ed. (London, New York, Hamburg, Hong Kong: LLP, 1999).

Templeman, Frederick, and Lambeth, R.J., *On Marine Insurance*, 6th ed. (London: Pitman, 1986).

Tetley, William, 'The Himalaya Clause–Heresy or Genius?', *Journal of Maritime Law and Commerce*, vol. 9, p. 111 (1977–1978).

——, 'Shipowners' Limitation of Liability and Conflicts of Law: The Properly Applicable Law', *Journal of Maritime Law and Commerce*, vol. 23, p. 585 (1992).

——, *International Maritime and Admiralty Law* (Cowansville: Éditions Yvon Blais, 2002).

——, 'The Himalaya Clause–revisited', *Journal of International Maritime Law*, vol. 9, p. 40 (2003).

Thomas, D. Rhidian, *The Modern Law of Marine Insurance*, vol. 1 (London, New York, Hong Kong: LLP, 1996).

Thume, Karl-Heinz (ed.), *Transport- und Vertriebsrecht 2000, Festgabe für Rolf Herber* (Neuwied: Luchterhand, 1999).

Todd, Paul, *Modern Bills of Lading*, 2nd ed. (Oxford, London, Edinburgh, Boston, Melbourne: Blackwell Law, 1990).

Tokyo Memorandum of Understanding (MoU) on Port State Control, *Annual Report on Port State Control in the Asia-Pacific Region 2005* (accessible at <http://www.tokyo-mou.org/ANN05.pdf>, last accessed 19 March 2007).

Trotz, Norbert, *Die Revision der Konventionen über die zivilrechtliche Haftung für Schäden aus der Ölverschmutzung des Meeres und über die Errichtung eines Entschädigungsfonds* (Potsdam-Babelsberg: Akademie für Staats- und Rechtswissenschaften der DDR, Institut für Ausländisches Recht und Rechtsvergleichung, 1987).

Ulmer, Peter, 'Die deliktische Haftung aus der Übernahme von Handlungspflichten', [1969] *Juristenzeitung*, p. 163.

Ulrik, Anders, 'The Underwriter's Perspective', in: Lux, Jonathan (ed.), *Classification Societies* (London, New York, Hamburg, Hong Kong: Lloyd's of London Press, Ltd., 1993), p. 37.

Underdown, Michael, 'Surveys and Negligence', *The Maritime Law Association of Australia & New Zealand Journal,* vol. 18, p. 24 (2004) (accessible at <http://esvc000873.wic005u.server-web.com/docs/MLAANZ_Vol_18_2004_FINAL1.pdf>, last accessed 19 March 2007).

United States Coast Guard, *Classification Society Performance* (2004) (accessible at <http://www.uscg.mil/hq/g-m/pscweb/2004_Classification_Society.pdf>, last accessed 19 March 2007).

Verdross, Alfred, and Simma, Bruno, *Universelles Völkerrecht, Theorie und Praxis,* 3rd ed. (Berlin: Dunker & Humblot, 1984).

Vorbach, Joseph E., 'The Vital Role of Non-Flag State Actors in the Pursuit of Safer Shipping', *Ocean Development & International Law*, vol. 32, p. 27 (2001).

Walton, C.T., *Charlesworth and Percy on Negligence*, 11th ed. (London: Sweet & Maxwell, 2006).

Watson, Sue Carter, 'The Suits in Admiralty Act', *Journal of Maritime Law and Commerce*, vol. 17, p. 175 (1986).

Weber, Martin, 'Die Haftung des Abschlußprüfers gegenüber Dritten', [1999] *Neue Zeitschrift für Gesellschaftsrecht,* p. 1.

Weimann, Martin, *Prospekthaftung* (Bonn: Deutscher Anwaltverlag, 1998).

Welsch, H., 'Zur Haftung von Klassifikationsgesellschaften' [case comment OLG Hamburg 14 June 1990, [1990] *Transportrecht,* p. 345], [1991] *Transportrecht*, p. 230.

Wiegand, Annette, *Die Sachwalterhaftung als richterliche Rechtsfortbildung* (Berlin: Duncker & Humblot, 1991).

Wilford, Michael, Coghlin, Terence, and Kimball, John D., *Time Charters*, 5th ed. (London: LLP, 2003).

Williams, Harvey, *Chartering Documents*, 4th ed. (London, Hong Kong: Lloyd's of London Press, 1999).

Williston, Samuel, *A Treatise on the Law of Contracts*, 4th ed. (Rochester, N.Y.: West, 2001 *et seq.*).

Wiswall, Frank L. Jr., 'Report and Panel Discussion concerning the Joint Working Group on a Study of Issues Re Classification Societies', [1994] *CMI Yearbook*, p. 228.

——, 'Report and Panel Discussion concerning the Joint Working Group on a Study of Issues Re Classification Societies', [1995] *Il Diritto Marittimo,* p. 66.

——, 'Classification societies: issues considered by the Joint Working Group', *International Journal of Shipping Law*, vol. 2, p. 171 (1997).

Witting, Christian, 'Negligent Inspectors and Flying Machines', *Cambridge Law Journal*, vol. 59, p. 544 (2000).

Wolfensberger, Hans Rudolf, *Die summenmäßige Beschränkung der Haftung für Personenschäden* (Zürich: Keller, 1966).

Woolley, David, Pugh-Smith, John, Laugham, Richard, and Upton, William (eds.), *Environmental Law* (Oxford: Oxford University Press, 2000).

Wu, Chao, *Pollution from the Carriage of Oil by Sea: Liability and Compensation* (London, The Hague, Boston: Kluwer Law International, 1996).

Wurmb, Leopold von, *Die Haftung des Verfrachters für das Verschulden selbständiger Hilfspersonen* (Hamburg: Rodenbusch in Bamberg, 1966).

Wüstendörfer, Hans, *Studien zur modernen Entwicklung des Seefrachtvertrags, vol. I* (Dresden: Bömert, 1905–1909).

——, 'Zur Haftung für Feuerschaden an Bord von Seeschiffen nach den Haager Regeln', [1949] *Monatsschrift für deutsches Recht,* p. 450 (part I), p. 515 (part II).

——, *Neuzeitliches Seehandelsrecht mit besonderer Berücksichtigung des angloamerikanischen und des internationalen Rechts*, 2nd ed. (Tübingen: Mohr, 1950).

Young, Philip G., 'Classification Societies–a duty of care to buyers', *P&I International*, vol. 11, p. 254 (1997).

Zawitoski, Joanne, 'Limitation of Liability for Stevedores and Terminal Operators Under the Carrier's Bill of Lading and COGSA', *Journal of Maritime Law and Commerce*, vol. 16, p. 337 (1985).

Zeller, Rudolf, *Die Umgehung der Haager Regeln durch die Ladungsbeteiligten und die Himalaya-Klausel im Seefrachtrecht* (München: Bauknecht, 1966).

Zepos, Panayotis, and Christodoulou, Phoebus, *Professional Liability,* in: David, René, Tunc, André, *et al.* (eds.), International Encyclopedia of Comparative Law, vol. XI, *Torts* (Tübingen, The Hague, Boston, London: Mohr, 1983) chap. 6.

Zimmermann, Reinhard, 'Erbfolge und Schadensersatz bei Anwaltsverschulden', [1996] *Zeitschrift für europäisches Privatrecht*, p. 672.

——, *The new German Law of Obligations, Historical and Comparative Perspectives* (Oxford: Oxford University Press, 2005)

——, and Verse, Dirk, in: Falk, Ulrich, *Das Bürgerliche Gesetzbuch und seine Richter: zur Reaktion der Rechtsprechung auf die Kodifikation des deutschen Privatrechts (1896–1914)* (Frankfurt/Main: Klostermann, 2000).

Zhu, Ling, Compulsory Insurance and Compensation for Bunker Oil Pollution (Berlin: Springer, 2006).

Table of Cases

International

P.C.I.J., *Polish Postal Service in Gdansk* (*Advisory Opinion*), *Publications of the P.C.I.J.*, Series B, No. 11.
I.C.J., *Competence of the General Assembly for the Admission of a State to Membership in United Nations* (*Advisory Opinion*), *I.C.J. Reports* 1950, 4.
I.C.J., *Case Concerning rights of Nationals of the USA in Morocco (France v. USA)*, *I.C.J. Reports* 1950, 4.
I.C.J., *Interpretation of Peace Treaties with Bulgaria, Hungary and Romania* (*Order*), *I.C.J. Reports* 1950, 229.
I.C.J., *Reservations to the Convention on the Prevention and Punishment of the Crime of Genocide,* ICJ Rep. 1951, 15.
I.C.J., *Case Concerning Right of Passage over Indian Territory (Portugal v. India)*, *I.C.J. Reports* 1960, 158.
I.T.L.O.S., *MV Saiga (No. 2) Case*, 1 July 1999.

Australia

High Court of Australia in *Wilson v. Darling Island Stevedoring and Lighterage Co. Ltd.*, [1956] 1 Lloyd's Rep. 346.
Natcraft Pty & Henlock Party Ltd. v. Det Norske Veritas & Peter Colley, [2001] Q.S.C. 348 (file No. SC No. 7976/2000), *accessible at* <http://www.courts.qld.gov.au>, last accessed 19 March 2007.

England

Adler v. Dickson, [1954] 2 Lloyd's Rep. 267, [1955] 1 Q.B. 158 (C.A.).
Afzal v. Ford Motor Co. Ltd., [1994] 4 All E.R. 720 (C.A.(Civ.Div.)).
Alexandra Towing Co. Ltd. v. Owners of Dumb Barge Millet (The "Bramley Moore"), [1964] 1 All E.R. 105 (C.A.).
Allen v. Hayward, [1845] 7 Q.B. 960 (Q.B.).
W. Angliss and Co. (Australia) Property Ltd. v. Peninsular and Oriental Steam Navigation Co. Ltd., [1927] 28 Ll.L.Rep. 202; [1927] 2 K.B. 456 (K.B.).
Anns v. Merton London Borough Council, [1978] A.C. 728 (H.L.).
Atwell v. Michael Perry & Co., [1998] 4 All E.R. 65 (Ch.D.).
Blyth v. Birmingham Waterworks Co., [1856] 11 Ex. 781; 156 E.R. 1047 (Ex.).

Bolam v. Friern Hospital Management Committee, [1957] 1 W.L.R. 582 (Q.B.).
Braginton v. Chapman and Others (Trustees of Lloyd's Register of Shipping) (The "Midas"), [1878] 7 *Asp.* 77 (Q.B.).
Briess v. Woolley, [1954] A.C. 333 (H.L.).
British Telecommunications plc. v. James Thomson & Sons (Engineers) Ltd., [1999] 1 W.L.R. 9 (H.L.).
Brown v. Gould & Swayne, [1996] P.N.L.R. 130 (C.A. (Civ.Div.)).
Brown v. Raphael, [1958] Ch. 636 (C.A.).
Bureau Wijsmuller N.V. v. Owners of the Tojo Maru (The "Tojo Maru"), [1971] 1 Lloyd's Rep. 341; [1972] A.C. 242 (H.L.).
Candler v. Crane, Christmas & Co., [1951] 2 K.B.164 (C.A.).
Caparo Industries Plc v. Dickman, (C.A.) [1989] 2 W.L.R. 316; [1990] 2 A.C. 605; [1989] 2 W.L.R. 316 (H.L.).
Clay v. A. J. Crump & Sons Ltd., [1964] 1 Q.B. 533 (C.A.).
Compania de Navegación Pohling S.A. v. Sea Tanker Shipping (Pte.) Ltd. (The Buena Trader), [1978] 2 Lloyd's Rep. 325 (C.A. (Civ.Div.)).
Corisand Investments Ltd. v. Druce & Co., [1978] 248 E.G. 315.
Credit Lyonnais Nederland NV (now known as Generale Bank Nederland NV) v. Export Credits Guarantee Department, [2000] 1 A.C. 486 (H.L.).
Crofter Hand Woven Harris Tweed v. Veitch, [1942] A.C. 435 (H.L.).
Daisley v. B.S. Hall & Co., [1972] 225 E.G. 1553.
Dalton v. Angus, [1881] 6 App.Cas. 740 (H.L.).
Derry v. Peek, [1889] 14 App.Cas. 337 (H.L.).
Donoghue v. Stevenson, [1932] A.C. 562 (H.L.).
Dorset Yacht Co. Ltd. v. Home Office, [1970] A.C. 1004; [1970] 1 Lloyd's Rep. 453 (H.L.).
Eckersley v. Binnie, [1988] 18 Con. L.R. 1 (C.A.(Civ.Div)).
Flamar Interocean v. Denmac (The Flamar Pride and the Flamar Progress), [1990] 1 Lloyd's Rep. 434 (Q.B.D.(Comm.)).
Fletcher v. Rylands, (1866) L.R. 1 Exch. 265 (Exch.).
Ford v. Compagnie Furness, [1922] 2. K.B. 797 (K.B.).
Grant v. Australian Knitting Mills, [1936] A.C.85 (P.C.).
Greaves & Co. (Contractors) Ltd. v. Baynham Meikle & Partners, [1975] 1 W.L.R. 1095 (C.A.(Civ.Div.)).
Gross v. Lewis Hillman, [1970] Ch. 445 (C.A.).
Hacker v. Thomas Deal & Co., [1991] 2 E.G.L.R. 161.
Hardaker v. Idle District Council, [1896] 1 Q.B. 335 (C.A.).
Harmer v. Cornelius, (1858) 5 C.B.(N.S.) 236 (C.B.).
Harris v. Evans and Another, [1998] 3 All E.R. 522 (C.A.).
Harris v. Wyre Forest District Council, [1990] 1 A.C. 831; [1989] 2 W.L.R. 790 (H.L.).
Haseldine v. C.A. Daw & Son Ltd. [1941] 2 K.B. 343 (C.A.).
Health and Safety Executive v. Port Ramsgate Ltd. (and Lloyd's Register) (Unreported, 1997) (Central Crim.Ct.).
Heathmill Multimedia ASP Ltd. v. British Telecommunications Plc, [2003] EWHC 690 (Q.B.).
Heaven v. Pender, Trading as West India Graving Dock Company, [1883] 11 Q.B.D. 503 (C.A.).
Hedley Byrne & Co. Ltd. v. Heller & Partners, [1963] 2 All E.R. 575; [1964] A.C. 465 (H.L.).
Henderson v. Merrett Syndicates Ltd. (sub nom. *The Lloyd's Litigation*), [1995] A.C. 145, [1994] 2 Lloyd's Rep. 468; [1994] 3 W.L.R. 761 (H.L.).
Hewitt v. Bonvin, [1940] 1 K.B. 188 (C.A.).

Home Office v. Dorset Yacht Co. Ltd., [1970] 1 Lloyd's Rep. 453; [1970] A.C. 1004 (H.L.).
Honeywill & Stein Ltd. v. Larkin Bros. Ltd., [1934] 1 K.B. 191 (C.A.).
Hughes v. Percival, (1883) 8 App.Cas. 443 (H.L.).
Sir John Humphery v. Thomas A. Bowers, [1929] 33 Ll.L. Rep. 167 (K.B.).
Jolley v. Sutton London Borough Council, [1998] 3 All E.R. 559 (C.A.(Civ.Div.).
Lancashire & Cheshire Association of Baptist Churches v. Howard & Seddon Partnership, [1993] 3 All E.R. 467 (Q.B.D.(O.R.)).
Leigh and Sillavan Ltd. v. Aliakmon Shipping Co. Ltd. (The "Aliakmon"), [1986] A.C. 785 (H.L.).
Lloyd v. Grace, Smith and Co., [1912] A.C. 716 (H.L.).
Lloyds v. West Midlands Gas Board, [1971] 2 All E.R. 1240 (C.A.)
Marc Rich & Co. AG v. Bishop Rock Marine Co. Ltd. (*and ClassNK*) (*"The Nicholas H."),* [1992] 2 Lloyd's Rep. 481 (Q.B.D.); [1994] 1 Lloyd's Rep. 492 (C.A.); [1996] 1 A.C. 211; [1995] 2 Lloyd's Rep. 299 (H.L.).
Mariola Marine Corporation v. Lloyd's Register of Shipping ("The Morning Watch"), [1990] 1 Lloyd's Rep. 547 (Q.B.(Comm.)).
Market Investigations Ltd. v. Minister of Social Security, [1969] 2 Q.B. 173 (Q.B.).
Midland Bank Trust Co. Ltd. v. Hett, Stubbs & Kemp, [1979] 1 Ch. 384 (Ch.).
Midland Silicones Ltd. v. Scruttons Ltd., [1961] 2 Lloyd's Rep. 365; [1962] A.C. 446 (H.L.).
Mogul Steamship Co. Ltd. v. McGregor Gow & Co. Ltd., [1892] A.C. 25 (H.L.).
Murphy v. Brentwood District Council, [1991] 1 A.C. 398; [1990] 2 All E.R. 908; [1990] 2 Lloyd's Rep. 467 (H.L.).
Mutual Life & Citizens Assurance Co. Ltd. v. Evatt, [1971] A.C. 793 (P.C.(Aus.)).
Niobe Maritime Corporation v. Tradax Ocean Transportation S.A., [1993] 2 Lloyd's Rep. 52 (Com.Ct.); [1994] 1 Lloyd's Rep. 487 (C.A.); [1995] 1 Lloyd's Rep. 579 (H.L).
Norwich City Council v. Harvey, [1989] 1 W.L.R. 828 (C.A.(Civ.Div.)).
Overseas Medical Supplies Ltd. v. Orient Transport Services Ltd., [1999] 2 Lloyd's Rep. 273 (C.A.(Civ.Div.)).
Overseas Tankship (U.K.) Ltd. v. Morts Dock & Engineering Co. Ltd., ("The Wagon Mound"), [1961] A.C. 388 (P.C.).
Pasley v. Freeman, (1789) 3 T.R. 51.
Perrett v. Collins, [1998] 2 Lloyd's Rep. 255 (C.A.).
Petch v. Commissioners of Customs and Excise, [1993] I.C.R. 789 (C.A.(Civ.Div.)).
Phelps v. London Borough of Hillingdon, [2003] 3.W.L.R. 776 (H.L.).
Philcox v. Civil Aviation Authority, [1995] *The Times* 8 June 1995 (C.A.(Civ.Div.)), Transcript No. 821 of 1995, C.A.
Photo Productions Ltd. v. Securicor Transport Ltd., [1980] A.C. 827 (H.L.).
Pickard v. Smith, (1861) 10 C.B.(N.S.) 470 (C.B.).
Pickford v. Imperial Chemical Industries plc., [1998] 3 All E.R. 462 (H.L.).
Raineri v. Miles, [1981] A.C. 1050 (H.L.).
Ready Mixed Concrete (South East) Ltd. v. Minister of Pensions and National Insurance, [1968] 2 Q.B. 497 (Q.B.).
Reeman and Another v. Department of Transport and Others, [1997] 2 Lloyd's Rep. 648 (C.A.).
Resolute Maritime v. Nippon Karji Kyokai, [1983] 1 Lloyd's Rep. 431 (Q.B.).
Richardson v. Silvester, (1873) L.R. 9 Q.B. 34 (Q.B.).
Riverstone Meat Co. Pty. Ltd. v. Lancashire Shipping Co. Ltd. ("The Muncaster Castle"), [1961] 1 Lloyd's Rep. 57; [1961] A.C. 807 (H.L.).
Roberts v. J. Hampson & Co., [1990] 1 W.L.R. 94 (Q.B.D.).
Rookes v. Barnard, [1964] A.C. 1129 (H.L.).

Rutter v. Palmer, [1922] 2 K.B. 87 (C.A.).
Rylands v. Fletcher, (1868) L.R. 3 H.L. (E. & 1 App.) 330 (H.L.).
SAM Business Systems Limited v. Hedley & Co., [2002] WL 31784544 (Q.B.).
Smith v. Eric S. Bush, [1990] 1 A.C. 831; [1989] 2 All E.R. 514 (H.L.).
Sonicare International Ltd. v. East Anglia Freight Terminal Ltd., [1997] 2 Lloyd's Rep. 48.
Spring v. Guardian Assurance plc., [1995] 2 A.C. 296; [1994] 3 W.L.R. 354; [1994] 3 All E.R. 129 (H.L.).
Stewart Gill Ltd. v. Horatio Myer and Co. Ltd., [1992] Q.B. 600 (C.A.(Civ.Div.)).
Suisse Atlantique Société d'Armement Maritime S.A. v. N.V. Rotterdamsche Kolen Centrale [1967] 1 A.C. 361 (H.L.).
Swan v. Salisbury Construction Co. Ltd., [1966] 2 All E.R. 138 (P.C.).
Swift v. Winterbotham, (1873) L.R. 8 Q.B. 244 (Q.B.).
Tarry v. Ashton, (1876) 1 Q.B.D. 314 (Q.B.).
Thiodon v. Tindall and Others (the Committee of Lloyd's Register) (The "Ibex"), [1891] 7 Asp. 76 (Q.B.).
Bureau Wijsmuller N.V. v. Owners of the Tojo Maru (The "Tojo Maru"), [1971] 1 Lloyd's Rep. 341; [1972] A.C. 242 (H.L.).
Tor Line A.B. v. Alltrans Group of Canada Ltd., [1984] 1 W.L.R. 48 (H.L.).
Union of India v. N.V. Rederij, [1963] 2 Lloyd's Rep. 223 (H.L.).
United Africa Co. v. Saka Owoade Ltd., [1955] A.C. 130 (P.C.).
The Wagon Mound, Overseas Tankship (U.K.) Ltd. v. Morts Dock & Engineering Co. Ltd., [1961] A.C. 388 (P.C.).
Watford Electronics Ltd. v. Sanderson Cfl Ltd., [2002] F.S.R. 19 (C.A.(Civ.Div.)).
Whalley v. Roberts & Roberts, [1990] 1 E.G.L.R. 164.
White v. Jones, [1995] 2 A.C. 207; [1995] 2 W.L.R. 187; [1995] 1 All E.R. 691 (H.L.).
Bureau Wijsmuller N.V. v. Owners of the Tojo Maru (The "Tojo Maru"), [1971] 1 Lloyd's Rep. 341; [1972] A.C. 242 (H.L.).
Williams v. Natural Life Health Foods Limited, [1998] 1 W.L.R. 830 (H.L.).
Wilson v. Darling Island Stevedoring and Lighterage Co. Ltd., [1956] 1 Lloyd's Rep. 346 (H.C.(Aus.)).
World Horizon, [1993] 2 Lloyd's Rep. 56 (C.A.).
Woods v. Duncan, [1946] A.C. 401 (H.L.).
X v. Bedfordshire C.C., [1995] 2 A.C. 633 (H.L.).

France

Cour de Cassation (Chambre de requêtes) 15 May 1923, *Revue de droit maritime comparé*, vol. 3 (1923), p. 384.
Cour de Cassation (Chambre criminelle) 30 May 1980, [1981] *DMF* 146 – "*Cap-de-la-Hague"*.
Cour de Cassation (Chambre criminelle) 8 October 1985 – "Compass Rose III" (unpublished).
Cour de Cassation (Chambre criminelle) 7 July 1998, [1999] *DMF* 106 – "Snekkar Arctic".
Cour de Cassation (1ère Chambre civile) 11 May 1999, [2000] *DMF* 39.
Cour de Cassation (Chambre criminelle) 29 March 2001, [2002] *DMF* 14.

Cour d'Appel de Tunis 23 February 1955, [1956] *DMF* 87
Cour d'Appel de Douai 6 July 1978, [1981] *DMF* 153, –"*Cap-de-la-Hague"*.
Cour d'Appel de Caen 12 January 1983 – "Compass Rose III" (unpublished).

Cour d'Appel de Versailles 21 March 1996, [1996] *DMF* 721 – *"Elodie II"*.
Cour d'Appel de Paris 9 June 1999, [2000] *DMF* 326 – "Mamer".
Cour d'Appel de Versailles 9 December 2004, [2005] *DMF* 313 – *"Wellborn"*.

Tribunal de commerce de Marseille 6 January 1978, [1978] DMF 510.
Tribunal de Grande Instance d'Avrances 12 January 1982 – "Compass Rose III" (unpublished).
Tribunal correctionnel de Saint-Nazaire 18 March 2003, [2003] *DMF* 1068.

Chambre Arbitrale Maritime de Paris, Sentence n° 115 du 5 April 1974 , [1974] *DMF* 635.

Germany

RG 27 October 1902, 52 RGZ 365.
RG 30 October 1902, 52 RGZ 373.
RG 23 February 1903, 54 RGZ 53.
RG 4 November 1907, [1908] Hanseatische Gerichtszeitung, Hauptblatt, 163.
RG 27 May 1911, 76 RGZ 316.
RG 7 June 1915, 87 RGZ 64.
RG 18 November 1915, 87 RGZ 289.
RG 5 October 1917, 91 RGZ 21.
RG 9 February 1921, 101 RGZ 297.
RG 23 March 1921, 102 RGZ 38.
RG 3 June 1921, 102 RGZ 231.
RG 19 September 1921, 102 RGZ 372.
RG 10 February 1930, 127 RGZ 218.
RG 2 February 1931, 131 RGZ 239.
RG 4 April 1939, 160 RGZ 153.

BGH 11 April 1951, 1 BGHZ 383.
BGH 11 May 1951, [1951] *NJW* 711.
BGH 28 April 1952, 5 BGHZ 378.
BGH 29 October 1952, 7 BGHZ 371.
BGH 28 April 1953, 9 BGHZ 301.
BGH 16 December 1953, [1954] *VersR* 100.
BGH 17 December 1953, [1954] *VersR* 173.
BGH 15 March 1954, [1954] *NJW* 874.
BGH 15 June 1954, 14 BGHZ 83.
BGH 25 May 1955, 17 BGHZ 327.
BGH 25 April 1956, [1956] *NJW* 1193.
BGH 13 July 1956, [1956] *WM* 1229.
BGH 20 February 1958, 26 BGHZ 365.
BGH 15 May 1959, [1959] *NJW* 1676.
BGH 1 October 1959, 31 BGHZ 73.
BGH 9 November 1959, 31 BGHZ 148.
BGH 26 November 1959, 31 BGHZ 224.
BGH 27 November 1959, [1960] *VersR* 153.
BGH 7 July 1960, [1960] *VersR* 727.
BGH 7 November 1960, 33 BGHZ 247.

BGH 7 November 1960, 33 BGHZ 251.
BGH 30 January 1961, 34 BGHZ 206.
BGH 3 November 1961, [1962] *VersR* 86.
BGH 26 March 1962, [1962] *WM* 579.
BGH 13 June 1962, [1962] *NJW* 1500.
BGH 5 July 1962, [1962] *WM* 1110.
BGH 27 May 1963, 39 BGHZ 358.
BGH 14 October 1964, [1965] *NJW* 197.
BGH 20 October 1964, [1964] *VersR* 1250.
BGH 21 January 1965, [1965] *NJW* 815.
BGH 23 June 1965, [1965] *NJW* 1757.
BGH 6 July 1965, [1965] *NJW* 1955.
BGH 25 April 1966, 45 BGHZ 223.
BGH 8 December 1966, [1967] *NJW* 719.
BGH 30 November 1967, 49 BGHZ 108.
BGH 10 January 1968, [1968] *JZ* 304.
BGH 22 January 1968, 49 BGHZ 350.
BGH 30 January 1968, [1968] *VersR* 470.
BGH 18 June 1968, [1968] *NJW* 1929.
BGH 9 October 1968, [1969] *NJW* 41.
BGH 26 November 1968, 51 BGHZ 91.
BGH 28 February 1969, [1969] *VersR* 439.
BGH 1 June 1970, 54 BGHZ 165.
BGH 6 July 1970, [1970] *NJW* 1737.
BGH 7 July 1970, [1971] *JZ* 63.
BGH 10 November 1970, [1971] *NJW* 241.
BGH 11 March 1971, [1971] *NJW* 1130.
BGH 15 June 1971, [1971] *NJW* 1931.
BGH 18 January 1972, [1972] *NJW* 678.
BGH 8 February 1972, 58 BGHZ 149.
BGH 18 Mai 1972, [1972] *WM* 947.
BGH 5 December 1972, [1973] *NJW* 321.
BGH 18 December 1972, 60 BGHZ 54.
BGH 11 January 1973, [1973] *NJW* 458.
BGH 18 January 1973, [1973] *WM* 165.
BGH 19 September 1973, 61 BGHZ 227.
BGH 14 May 1974, [1974] *NJW* 1503.
BGH 12 July 1974, [1974] *NJW* 2177.
BGH 26 November 1974, [1975] *NJW* 533.
BGH 15 April 1975, [1975] *VersR* 812.
BGH 24 April 1975, [1975] *NJW* 1316.
BGH 28 January 1976, 66 BGHZ 51.
BGH 16 March 1976, [1976] *VersR* 776.
BGH 30 March 1976, [1976] *WM* 498.
BGH 10 May 1976, [1976] *WM* 873.
BGH 10 June 1976, 67 BGHZ 1.
BGH 24 November 1976, 67 BGHZ 359.
BGH 11 January 1977, [1977] *NJW* 2073.
BGH 10 March 1977, 68 BGHZ 169.
BGH 12 July 1977, [1977] *NJW* 2208.
BGH 9 February 1978, [1978] *NJW* 2548.

BGH 15 February 1978, [1978] *NJW* 883.
BGH 21 February 1978, [1978] *NJW* 1629.
BGH 25 April 1978, [1978] *NJW* 1626.
BGH 20 February 1979, [1979] *NJW* 1599.
BGH 15 May 1979, [1979] *JZ* 725.
BGH 29 January 1980, [1980] *NJW* 1159.
BGH 11 March 1980, [1980] *NJW* 1745.
BGH 22 April 1980, [1980] *NJW* 1905.
BGH 22 May 1980, [1980] *NJW* 1840.
BGH 7 July 1980, [1980] *NJW* 2464.
BGH 6 October 1980, 79 BGHZ 337.
BGH 7 July 1981, [1981] *WM* 1108.
BGH 2 November 1983, [1984] *NJW* 355.
BGH 29 November 1983, [1984] *NJW* 801.
BGH 23 October 1984, [1985] *NJW* 620.
BGH 11 December 1984, [1985] *NJW* 1076.
BGH 23 January 1985, [1986] *NJW-RR* 484.
BGH 17 September 1985, [1986] *NJW* 180.
BGH 4 February 1986, [1986] *NJW* 1863.
BGH 19 March 1986, [1986] *NJW-RR* 1307.
BGH 7 October 1986, [1987] *NJW* 372.
BGH 28 October 1986, [1987] *NJW* 1013.
BGH 26 November 1986, [1987] *NJW* 1758.
BGH 9 December 1986, 99 BGHZ 167.
BGH 4 March 1987, [1987] *ZIP* 500.
BGH 17 March 1987, [1987] *NJW* 2008.
BGH 28 April 1987, [1988] *NJW* 48.
BGH 16 June 1987, [1987] *NJW* 2510.
BGH 1 March 1988, 103 BGHZ 338.
BGH 11 October 1988, [1989] *NJW* 1029.
BGH 18 October 1988, [1989] *NJW-RR* 696.
BGH 6 July 1989, [1990] *NJW* 381.
BGH 13 July 1989, 108 BGHZ 273.
BGH 17 October 1989, [1990] *NJW* 906.
BGH 19 December 1989, [1990] *NJW* 1236.
BGH 31 May 1990, [1990] *NJW* 2461.
BGH 11 October 1990, [1991] *NJW* 562.
BGH 19 April 1991, 114 BGHZ 273.
BGH 24 September 1991, [1991] *NJW* 3282.
BGH 12 November 1991, [1992] *NJW* 560.
BGH 13 February 1992, [1992] *NJW* 2080.
BGH 31 March 1992, [1992] *NJW-RR* 879.
BGH 7 April 1992, [1992] *NJW* 1820.
BGH 4 June 1992, 118 BGHZ 304.
BGH 25 February 1993, 121 BGHZ 367.
BGH 25 March 1993, [1993] *NJW* 1784.
BGH 6 July 1993, 123 BGHZ 126.
BGH 21 December 1993, [1994] *NJW* 852.
BGH 27 January 1994, [1994] *NJW* 2289.
BGH 20 September 1994, [1994] *NJW* 3348.
BGH 10 November 1994, [1995] *NJW* 392.

BGH 1 December 1994, [1995] *NJW* 1025.
BGH 13 June 1995, [1995] *NJW* 2551.
BGH 2 July 1996, 133 BGHZ 168.
BGH 12 November 1996, [1997] *NJW* 582.
BGH 19 December 1996, [1997] *NJW* 1235.
BGH 16 January 1997, [1997] *WM* 375.
BGH 17 June 1997, 136 BGHZ 69.
BGH 13 November 1997, [1998] *NJW* 1059.
BGH 3 March 1998, [1998] *NJW-RR* 1027.
BGH 2 April 1998, 138 BGHZ 257.
BGH 26 May 1998, [1998] *NJW* 2436.
BGH 2 December 1999, [2000] *NJW* 725.
BGH 1 February 2000, [2000] *NJW* 1107.
BGH 14 June 2000, [2000] *NJW* 2896.
BGH 2 November 2000, [2001] *NZV* 76.
BGH 14 November 2000, [2001] *NJW* 514.
BGH 1 February 2001, [2001] *NVwZ* 1074.
BGH 22 March 2001, [2001] *NZV* 343.
BGH 24 April 2001, [2001] *WM* 1454.
BGH 4 December 2001, [2002] *NJW-RR* 525.
BGH 17 September 2002, [2002] *NJW* 3625.
BGH 10 April 2003, [2003] *NVwZ-RR* 543.
BGH 20 April 2004, [2004] *NJW* 3035.
BGH 8 June 2004, [2004] *NJW* 3420.
BGH 14 October 2004, [2005] *NJW* 286.

OLG Hamburg 26 October 1906, [1907] *Hanseatische Gerichtszeitung, Hauptblatt*, 37 (*Theodor Schiff, Heinecke & Co. und Bergeest & Siemers* v. *Bureau Veritas (Schoonergaliote "Industrie")).*
OLG Köln 4 June 1986, [1988] *NJW-RR* 157.
OLG Hamburg 14 June 1990, [1990] *TranspR* 345, [1991] *VersR* 476, ("*Hecht V*")
OLG Hamm 27 June 1990, [1990] *NVwZ* 1105
OLG Koblenz 5 October 1995, [1997] *NJWE-VHR* 69.
OLG Oldenburg 9 September 1997, [1998] *NJW-RR* 1746.
OLG Hamburg 27 March 2001, 9 U 364/99 (unpublished).
OLG Koblenz 2 September 2002, [2003] *NJW* 297.

LG Hamburg 18 January 1972, 10 O 176/70 (unpublished).
LG Köln 23 November 1977, [1978] *NJW* 329.
LG Hamburg 11 June 1999, 308 O 382/98 (unpublished).

Greece

Court of the First Instance of Athens 8909/1985, Hellenic Justice Review (*Elleniki Dikaiosini*) 26, 1409, 1415.

Italy

Tribunale di Savona 29 October 1990, "Tito Campanella", [1991] *Il Diritto Marittimo* 423.

New Zealand

The Attorney-General v. Wright & ORS, [2003] *N.Z.C.A.* 48, [2003] *N.Z.L.R.* 160, *accessible* at <http://www.austlii.edu.au>, last accessed 19 March 2007.

United States

Alcoa Steamship Co., Inc. v. Charles Ferran & Co., Inc., 251 F.Supp. 823 (D.C.La.1966), *aff'd*, 383 F.2d 46 (5th Cir.(La.)1967), *cert. denied*, 393 U.S. 836, 89 S.Ct. 111 (U.S.1968).

Allied Chemical Int'l Corp. v. Companhia de Navegacao Lloyd Brasileiro, 775 F.2d 476 (2d Cir.1985).

Alvarez v. J. Ray McDermott & Co., Inc., 674 F.2d 1037, 1984 A.M.C. 302 (5th Cir.1982).

American Bureau of Shipping v. Société Jet Flint, S.A., et al., 1998 WL 273083 (S.D.N.Y.1998), *aff'd in part, reversed in part and remanded sub nom American Bureau of Shipping v. Tencara Shipyard S.P.A.*, 170 F.3d 349, 1999 A.M.C. 1858 (2d Cir.1999).

Anderson v. United States, 317 F.3d 1235, 2003 A.M.C. 94 (11th Cir.2003).

In re Barracuda Tanker Corp. (S/T Torrey Canyon), 281 F.Supp. 228, 1968 A.M.C. 1711 (S.D.N.Y.1968), remanded 409 F.2d 1013 (2d Cir.1969).

Bearce v. United States, 614 F.2d 556 (7th Cir.1980).

Berkovitz by Berkovitz v. United States, 486 U.S. 531, 108 S.Ct. 1954, 100 L.Ed. 2d 531 (1988).

Robert R. Billy v. Arthur Young & Co., et al., 3 Cal.4th 370, 11 Cal.Rptr.2d 51, 834 P.2d 745 at 769 (Cal.1992).

Bivens v. Six Unknown Named Agents of Federal Bureau of Narcotics, 403 U.S. 388, 91 S.Ct. 1999 (U.S.1971).

Boyle v. United Technologies Corp., 487 U.S. 500, 108 S.Ct. 2510 (U.S.1988).

Canadian Transport Co. v. United States, 663 F.2d 1081 (D.C.Cir.1980).

Cargill, Inc. v. Bureau Veritas, 902 F.Supp. 49, 1996 A.M.C. 577 (S.D.N.Y.1995).

Carbotrade S.p.A. v. Bureau Veritas, 901 F.Supp. 737, 1996 A.M.C. 561 (S.D.N.Y.1995) (*Carbotrade I*), *vacated on other grounds*, 99 F.3d 86, 1997 A.M.C. 98 (2d Cir.1996) (*Carbotrade II*), *cert. denied sub. nom. Veritas v. Carbotrade S.p.A.*, 117 S.Ct. 2454 (1997), *on remand to Carbotrade S.p.A. v. Bureau Veritas*, 1998 WL 397847 (S.D.N.Y.1998) (*Carbotrade III*), *on remand to Carbotrade S.p.A. v. Bureau Veritas*, 1999 WL 714126 (*Carbotrade IV*), *aff'd Carbotrade S.p.A. v. Bureau Veritas*, 216 F.3d 1071, 2000 WL 821853 (2d Cir.(N.Y.)2000) (*Carbotrade V*).

Clark-Fitzpatrick, Inc. v. Long Island Rail Road Company, 70 N.Y.2d 382, 516 N.E.2d 190 (N.Y.1987).

Carrol Towing Co. v. United States, 159 F.2d 169 (1947).

Coastal (Bermuda) Ltd. v. E.W. Saybolt & Co., 761 F.2d 198 (5th Cir.1985); 826 F.2d 424, 1988 A.M.C. 207 (5th Cir.1987).

Commercial Melasses Corp. v. New York Tank Barge Corp., 114 F.2d 248 (2d Cir.1940), *aff'd* 314 U.S. 104, 62 S.Ct. 156, 86 L.Ed. 89 (1941).
Continental Insurance Co. v. Daewoo Shipbuilding & Heavy Machinery Ltd., 707 F.Supp. 123 (S.D.N.Y.1988).
Cox v. Murray, 6 F.Cas. 681 (S.D.N.Y. 1848).
Credit Alliance Corp. et al. v. Arthur Anderson & Co., 65 N.Y.2d 536, 493 N.Y.S.2d 435, 483 N.E.2d 110 (1985), *modified,* 66 N.Y.2d 812, 498 N.Y.S.2d 362, 489 N.E.2d 249 (1985).
CTI-Container Leasing Corp. v. Oceanic Operations Corp., 682 F.2d 377 (2d Cir.1982).
Dalehite v. United States, 346 U.S. 15, 73 S.Ct. 956, 97 L.Ed. 1427 (U.S.1953).
Daly v. General Motors Corp., 20 Cal.3d 725, 144 Cal. Rptr. 380, 575 P.2d 1162 (1978).
Dann Marine Towing, LC et al., In the Matter of the Complaint of, 2004 WL 744881 (E.D.La.2004).
Earles v. United States, 935 F.2d 1028 (9th Cir.1991).
East River S.S. Corp. v. Transamerica DeLaval, Inc., 476 U.S. 858, 106 S.Ct. 2295, 90 L.Ed.2d 865 (1986).
Employers Ins. of Wausau v. Suwannee River Spa Lines, Inc. 866 F.2d 752, 753 (5th Cir.1989).
Escola v. Coca-Cola Bottling Co., 24 Cal.2d 453, 150 P.2d 436 (1944).
In the Matter of the Complaint of Eternity Shipping, Ltd., 2006 WL 2422705 (D.Md.2006).
Executive Jet Aviation, Inc. v. City of Cleveland, 409 U.S. 249, 93 S.Ct. 493, 34 L.Ed.2d 454 (1973).
Fairmont Ship Corp. v. Chevron Int'l Oil Co., Inc., 511 F.2d 1252 (2d Cir.1975).
Federazione Italiana Dei Corsorzi Agrari v. Mandask Compania de Vapores, S.A., (The Perama) 388 F.2d 434 (2d Cir.1968), *cert. denied* 393 U.S. 828, 89 S.Ct. 92, 21 L.Ed.2d 99 (1968).
First National Bank of Commerce v. Monco Agency Inc., 911 F.2d 1053 (5th Cir.1990).
Ford Motor Co. v. Carter, 239 Ga. 657, 238 S.Ed.2d 361 (1977).
Garcia v. Sky Climber, Inc., 470 S.W.2d 261 (Tex.Civ.App.1971).
Gemp v. United States, 684 F.2d 404 (6th Cir.1982).
Glanzer v. Shepard, 233 N.Y. 236, 135 N.E. 275 (1922).
Goldberg v. Kollsman Instrument Corp., 12 N.Y.2d 432, 191 N.E.2d 81, 240 N.Y.S.2d 592 (1963).
Gold Medal Trading Corp. v. Atlantic Overseas Corp., 580 F.Supp. 610, 1984 A.M.C. 2052 (S.D.N.Y.1984).
Grass v. Credito Mexicano, S.A., 797 F.2d 220 (5th Cir.1986).
Great American Insurance Co. v. Bureau Veritas, 338 F.Supp. 999 (S.D.N.Y.1972), *aff'd,* 478 F.2d 235 (2d Cir.1973).
Greenman v. Yuba Power Products, 59 Cal.2d 57, 377 P.2d 897, 27 Cal. Rptr. 697 (1963).
Gulf Tampa Drydock Co. v. Germanischer Lloyd, 634 F.2d 874 (5th Cir.1981).
Hamilton v. Accu-Tek, 62 F.Supp.2d 802 (E.D.N.Y.1999).
Hellenic Investment Fund, Inc. v. Det Norske Veritas, 2006 WL 2567462 (5th Cir.(Tex)2006).
Hellenic Lines Ltd. v. Rhoditis, 398 U.S. 306, 90 S.Ct. 1731, 26 L.Ed.2d 252 (1970).
Henningsen v. Bloomfield Motors, Inc., 32 N.J. 358, 161 A.2d 69 (1960).
Robert C. Herd & Co. v. Krawill Machinery Corp., 256 F.2d 947 (4th Cir.1958), *aff'd* 359 U.S. 297, 79 S.Ct. 766, 3 L.Ed.2d 820, 1959 A.M.C. 879 (1959).
Heritage v. Pioneer Brokerage & Sales, Inc., 604 P.2d 1059 (Alaska 1979).
Hess v. United States, 361 U.S. 314, 80 S.Ct. 341, 4 L.Ed.2d 305 (1960).
Holland America v. Wartsila North America, Inc., 2005 WL 1287993 (W.D.Wash.2005).

Hudson Waterways Corp. v. Coastal Marine Service, 436 F.Supp. 597, at 605 (D.C.Tex.1977).
Ibar Limited and Vincent Francis Barrett, Petitioners, In the Matter of the Arbitration v. American Bureau of Shipping, Respondent, 2003 WL 2012400, 2003 U.S. LEXIS 7386 (S.D.N.Y.2003), *aff'd.* 92 Fed. App. 820; 2004 U.S. App. LEXIS 4273 (2d Cir.2004).
Indian Towing v. United States, 350 U.S. 61, 76 S.Ct. 122, 100 L.Ed. 48 (U.S.1955).
In re Barracuda Tanker Corp. (S/T Torrey Canyon), 281 F.Supp. 228, 1968 A.M.C. 1711 (S.D.N.Y.1968), remanded 409 F.2d 1013 (2d Cir.1969).
In the Matter of the Complaint of Dann Marine Towing, LC et al., 2004 WL 744881 (E.D.La.2004).
In the Matter of the Complaint of Eternity Shipping, Ltd., 2006 WL 2422705 (D.Md.2006).
In the Matter of the Arbitration v. Ibar Limited and Vincent Francis Barrett, Petitioners, and American Bureau of Shipping, Respondent, 2003 WL 2012400 (S.D.N.Y.2003).
In re Joint Eastern and Southern Districts Asbestos Litigation, 891 F.2d 31 (2d Cir.1989).
In re Marine Sulphur Transport Corp., 312 F.Supp. 1081 (S.D.N.Y.1970), *aff'd in part, rev'd in part on other grounds, sub. nom. In re Marine Sulphur Queen,* 460 F.2d 89 (2d Cir.1972), *cert. denied,* 409 U.S. 982, 93 S.Ct. 318, 34 L.Ed.2d 246 (1972).
In the Matter of: Oil Spill by the Amoco Cadiz off the Coast in France on March 16, 1978, 1986 A.M.C. 1945 (N.D.Ill.1986), *aff'd* 954 F.2nd 1279 (7th Cir. 1992).
International Ore and Fertilizer Corp. v. SGS Control Services, Inc., 743 F.Supp. 250, 1991 A.M.C. 25 (S.D.N.Y.1994) (*Interore I*), 828 F.Supp. 1098 (S.D.N.Y.1994) (*Interore II*), *aff'd on other grounds,* 38 F.3d 1279, 1995 A.M.C. 944 (2d Cir.1994) (*Interore III).*
Inversiones Calmer, S.A. v. C.E. Heath & Co., 681 F.Supp. 100 (D.Puerto Rico 1988).
Italia Societa per Azioni di Navigazione v. Oregon Stevedoring Co., 376 U.S. 315, 84 S.Ct. 748, 11 L.Ed.2d 732 (1964).
In re Joint Eastern and Southern Districts Asbestos Litigation, 891 F.2d 31 (2d Cir.1989).
Jordan v. United States Lines, Inc., 738 F.2d 48 (1st Cir.1984).
Keifer & Keifer v. Reconstruction Finance Corp., 306 U.S. 381 (1939).
Kelly v. United States, 531 F.2d 1144 (2d.Cir.1976).
Kermarec v. Compagnie Generale Transatlantique, 358 U.S. 625, 79 S.Ct. 406, 3 L.Ed.2d 550 (1959).
Knickerbocker Ice Co. v. Stewart, 253 U.S. 149; 40 S.Ct. 438; 64 L.Ed. 834 (1920).
Krohnert v. Yacht Systems Hawaii, Inc., 664 P.2d 738 (Haw. Ct. App.1983).
Lauritzen v. Larsen, 345 U.S. 571, 73 S.Ct. 921, 97 L.Ed. 1254 (1953).
Neederlandsche Amerikaansche Stoomvaart Maatschappij v. Mediterranean & General Traders, Inc. (The "Leerdam"), 17 F.2d 586, 1927 A.M.C. 509 (5th Cir.[La.] 1927).
Leka & Drivas, Inc. v. Goulandris, 306 F.2d 426 (2d Cir. 1962).
Lerner v. Karageorgis Lines, Inc., 66 N.Y.2d 479, 497 N.Y.S.2d 894, 488 N.E.2d 824 (1985).
Limar Shipping Ltd., et al. v. United States, 324 F.3d 1, 2003 A.M.C. 775 (1st Cir.2003).
Lunn v. Silfies, 106 Misc.2d 41; 431 N.Y.S.2d 282 (N.Y.Sup.1980).
Mahnich v. Southern S.S. Co., 321 U.S. 96, 64 S.Ct. 455; 88 L.Ed. 561; 1944 AMC 1 (1944).
The Main v. Williams, 152 U.S. 122; 14 S.Ct. 488; 38 L.Ed. 381 (1894).
In re Marine Sulphur Transport Corp., 312 F.Supp. 1081 (S.D.N.Y.1970), *aff'd in part, rev'd in part on other grounds, sub. nom. In re Marine Sulphur Queen,* 460 F.2d 89 (2d Cir.1972), *cert. denied,* 409 U.S. 982, 93 S.Ct. 318, 34 L.Ed.2d 246 (1972).
Maritime Overseas Corp. v. Northeast Pet. Indus., 706 F.2d 349 (1st Cir. 1983).
Marko v. Stop and Shop, Inc., 169 Conn. 550, 364 A.2d 217 (1975).

Maryland Casualty Co. v. Cushing, 98 L.Ed. 806 (1954).
Matthews v. United States, 150 F.Supp.2d 406 (E.D.N.Y.2001).
Mayer Boat Works v. Bright Marine Basin, 265 F.Supp. 352, 355 (E.D.N.Y.1966).
McClow v. Warrior & Gulf Navigation Co., 842 F.2d 1250 (11th Cir.1988).
McCormick v. United States, 680 F.2d 345, 1984 A.M.C. 1799 (5th Cir.1982).
McDermott, Inc. v. Amdyde & River Don Casting, Ltd., 511 U.S. 202, 114 S.Ct. 1461, 128 L.Ed.2d 148 (1994).
McMellon v. United States, 387 F.3d 329 (4th Cir.2004).
McPherson v. Union Oil Company of California, 628 F.Supp. 265, 1986 A.M.C. 425 (S.D.Tex.1985).
Miller v. American Bureau of Shipping, 168 E.3d 500, 1998 WL 879674 (9th Cir.(Cal.)).
Mitchell v. Trawler Racer, Inc., 362 U.S. 539, 80 S.Ct. 926, 4 L.Ed.2d 941 (1960).
New Jersey Steam Navigation Company v. Merchant's Bank (*The Lexington),* 47 U.S. 344 (1848).
Newman v. Utility Trailer & Equip. Co., 278 Or. 395, 564 P.2d 674 (1977).
Norfolk Southern Railway Co. v. Kirby, 125 S.Ct. 385, 160 L.Ed.2d 283, 2004 A.M.C. 2705 (U.S.2004).
Norwich Co. v. Wright, 80 U.S. 104 (1871).
The Osceola, 189 U.S. 158, 23 S.Ct. 483, 47 L.Ed. 760 (1903).
Otto Candies, L.L.C. v. Nippon Kaiji Kyokai Corp., 2002 WL 1798767 (E.D.La. 2002), 346 F.3d 530, 2003 A.M.C. 2409 (5th Cir.(La.) 2003), 2004 WL 179442, 72 USLW 3668, 72 USLW 3672 (S.Ct. 2004).
Pennhurst State School & Hospital v. Halderman, 465 U.S. 89, 104 S.Ct. 900 (U.S.1984).
Perlmutter v. Beth David Hospital, 123 N.E.2d 792 (N.Y.1954).
Pettus v. Jones & Laughlin Steel Corp., 322 F.Supp. 1078 (W.D.Pa.1971).
Philipps v. Western Company of North America, 953 F.2d 923, 1993 A.M.C. 1815 (5th Cir.1992).
The Plymouth, 70 U.S. 20 (Wall 1866), 18 L.Ed. 125.
Pokora v. Wabash Ry., 292 U.S. 98 (1934).
Pope & Talbot, Inc. v. Hawn, 346 U.S. 406, 74 S.Ct. 202, 98 L.Ed. 143 (1953).
Psarianos v. Standard Marine, Ltd., 728 F.Supp. 438 (E.D.Tex. 1989), 790 F.Supp. 134 (E.D.Tex. 1989), 12 F.3d 461 (5th Cir.(La.)1994), *cert. denied* 114 S.Ct. 2164, 511 U.S. 1142, 128 L.Ed.2d 887 (1994).
Reino de Espana v. American Bureau of Shipping, 328 F.Supp.2d 489 (S.D.N.Y.2004).
Robert C. Herd & Co. v. Krawill Machinery Corp., 256 F.2d 947 (4th Cir.1958), *aff'd* 359 U.S. 297, 79 S.Ct. 766, 3 L.Ed.2d 820, 1959 A.M.C. 879 (1959).
Robinson v. United States (In re Joint E. & S. Distributors Asbestos Litigation), 891 F.2d 31 (2d Cir.1989).
Romero v. International Terminal Operating Co., 358 U.S. 354, 79 S.Ct. 468, 3 L.Ed.2d 368 (1959).
Royal Embassy v. S.S. Ioannis Martinos, 1986 A.M.C. 769 (E.D.N.C.1984).
Ryan Stevedoring Co. Inc. v. Pan-Atlantic Steamship Corp., 350 U.S. 124, 76 S.Ct. 232, 100 L.Ed. 133 (1956).
Scottish Heritable Trust v. Peat Marwick Main & Co., 81 F.3d 606 (5th Cir.1996).
Sea-Land Service, Inc. v. United States, 919 F.2d 888 (3d Cir.1990).
Sealord Marine Co., Ltd. v. American Bureau of Shipping, 220 F.Supp.2d 260 (S.D.N.Y.2002).
Shaw v. Grumman Aerospace Corp., 778 F.2d 736 (11th Cir.1985).
Shipping Corp. of India v. American Bureau of Shipping, 603 F.Supp. 801 (S.D.N.Y.1985); 744 F.Supp. 447 (S.D.N.Y.1990); 752 F.Supp. 173 (S.D.N.Y.1990).

Skibs A/S Gylfe v. Hyman-Michaels Company et. al., 304 F.Supp. 1204, 1971 A.M.C. 2041 (E.D.Mich.1969), *aff'd*, 438 F.2d 803, 1971 A.M.C. 2032 (6th Cir.1971), *cert. denied sub nom. Hyman-Michaels Co. v. National Cargo Bureau, Inc.*, 404 U.S. 831 (1971).
Smith v. Mitlof, 198 F.Supp.2d 492 (S.D.N.Y.2002).
Smith v. Trans-World Drilling Co., 772 F.2d 157 (5th Cir.1985).
Somarelf v. American Bureau of Shipping, 704 F.Supp. 59, 1989 A.M.C. 1061 (D.N.J.1988) (*Somarelf I*), *Somarelf v. American Bureau of Shipping*, 720 F.Supp. 441 (D.N.J.1989) (*Somarelf II*).
South Seas, Inc. v. Moran Towing and Transportation Co., 360 F.2d 1002 (2d Cir.1966).
State of Hawaii v. Gordon, 373 U.S. 57, 83 S. Ct. 1052, 10 L.Ed.2d 191 (U.S.1963).
Steamship Mutual Underwriting Association Ltd. v. Bureau Veritas, 380 F.Supp. 482 (E.D.La.1973).
Sundance Cruises Corp. v. American Bureau of Shipping, 799 F.Supp. 363 (S.D.N.Y.1992), *aff'd*, 7 F.3d 1077 (2d Cir.1993).
Suvada v. White Motor Co., 32 Ill. 2d 612, 210 N.E.2d 182 (1965).
Szyka v. United States Secretary of Defense, 525 F.2d 62, 1975 A.M.C. 2504 (2d Cir.1975).
Tarasoff v. The Regents of the University of California, 17 Cal.3d 425, 551 P.2d 334, 131 Cal.Rptr. 14 (1976).
Tew v. United States, 86 F.3d 1003 (10th Cir.1996).
Thames Shipyard and Repair Co. v. United States, 350 F.3d 247, 2004 A.M.C. 112 (1st Cir.2004).
In re Barracuda Tanker Corp. (S/T Torrey Canyon), 281 F.Supp. 228, 1968 A.M.C. 1711 (S.D.N.Y.1968), remanded 409 F.2d 1013 (2d Cir.1969).
Toubaniaris v. American Bureau of Shipping, 981 S.W.2d 858 (C.A.Tex.(1st Dist.)1998).
Trautman v. Buck Steber, Inc., 693 F.2d 440 (5th Cir.1982).
Ultramares Corp. v. Touche et al., 255 N.Y. 170, 174 N.E. 441 (1931).
United States v. Carrol Towing Co., 159 F.2d 169 (1947).
United States v. J.R. Nelson Vessel Ltd., 1 F.Supp.2d 172, 1998 A.M.C. 2249 (E.D.N.Y.1998), aff'd, 173 F.3d 847 (2d.Cir.1999).
United States v. Reliable Transfer Co., 421 U.S. 397, 409, 95 S.Ct. 1708, 1714, 44 L.Ed.2d 251 (1975).
United States v. Shaw, 309 U.S. 495, 60 S.Ct. 659, 84 L.Ed. 888 (1940).
United States v. United Scottish Insurance Co., 467 U.S. 797, 104 S.Ct. 2755, 81 L.Ed.2d 660 (U.S.1984).
United States v. S.A. Empresa de Viacao Aerea Rio Grandense (Varig Airlines), 467 U.S. 797, 104 S.Ct. 2755, 81 L.Ed.2d 660 (U.S.1984).
United States Fire Insurance Co. v. United States, 806 F.2d 1529 (11th Cir.1986).
Usner v. Luckenbach Overseas Corp., 400 U.S. 494, 91 S.Ct. 514, 27 L.Ed.2d 562, 1971 A.M.C. 277 (1971).
Vitol Trading S.A. v. SGS Control Services, 680 F.Supp. 559 (S.D.N.Y.1987), *aff'd*, 874 F.2d 76 (2d Cir. 1989).
Williams v. United States, 747 F.2d 700 (11th Cir.1984).
Yearsley v. W.A. Ross Construction Co., 309 U.S. 18 (U.S.1940).
Yuba Consol. Gold Fields v. Kilkeary, 102 F.Supp. 999 (N.D.Cal.1952).

Table of International Conventions

Maritime Safety

International Convention for the Safety of Life at Sea, 1948 (SOLAS 1948). London, 10 June 1948, entry into force: 19 November 1952, 164 UNTS 113; 3 UST 3450; TIAS 2495; UKTS 1 (1953); Cmnd. 8720; Cmnd. 7492.

International Convention for the Safety of Life at Sea, 1960 (SOLAS 1960). London, 17 June 1960, entry into force: 26 May 1965, superseded by SOLAS 1974.

International Convention for the Safety of Life at Sea, 1974 (SOLAS 1974). London, 1 November 1974, entry into force: 25 May 1980, 1184 UNTS 278; 14 ILM 959; 32 UST 47; TIAS 9700; ATS 1983 No. 22; UKTS 46 (1980), Cmnd. 7874. Procès-verbal of rectification to the International Convention for the Safety of Life at Sea, 1974, London, 22 December 1982, TIAS 10626.

Protocol of 1978 relating to the International Convention for the Safety of Life at Sea, 1974 (with annex, appendix and final act). London, 17 February 1978, entry into force: 1 May 1981, UNTS A-18961, 1226 UNTS 237; 32 UST 5577, 5579, 5616; TIAS 10009; 17 ILM 579; ATS 1983 No. 28; UKTS 1981 No. 40 (Cmnd. 8277) and 1987 No. 36 (Cmnd. 196) p. 17.

Protocol of 1988 relating to the International Convention for the Safety of Life at Sea, 1974 (SOLAS PROT (HSSC) 1988), with annex. London, 11 November 1988, entry into force: 3 February 2000, IMO Doc. HSSC/CONF/11; US Treaty Doc. 102-2, p. 1; ATS 2000 No. 3; International Ship and Port Facility Security Code (ISPS Code), December 2002 Amendment to SOLAS, adopted on 12 December 2002, Entry into force: 1 July 2004 (tacit acceptance), SOLAS/CONF.5/32, SOLAS/CONF.5/33, SOLAS/CONF.5/34, RMC II.3.47.

International Convention on Load Lines, (LL 1966) (with annexes). London, 5 April 1966, entry into force: 21 July 1968, 640 UNTS 133; 18 UST 1857; TIAS 6331; ATS 1968 No. 23; UKTS 58 (1968), Cmnd. 3708.

Procès-verbal of rectification of the International Convention on Load Lines, 1966. London, 30 January 1969, 20 UST 17; TIAS 6629; London, 5 May 1969, 20 UST 2577; TIAS 6720.

Protocol of 1988 relating to the International Convention on Load Lines, 1966 (LL PROT 1988), with annexes, London, 11 November 1988, entry into force: 3 February 2000, IMO Doc.: HSSC/CONF/12; ATS 2000 No. 3; US Treaty Doc. 102-2, p. 83.

Amendments to the 1988 Load Lines Protocol, 5 June 2003, entry into force: 1 January 2005; IMO Doc.: Res. MSC.143(77).

2004 Amendments, adopted 9 December 2004, entry into force: 1 July 2006, IMO Doc.: Res. MSC.172(79).

Special Trade Passenger Ships Agreement, 1971 (STP) (with annex and final act). London, 6 October 1971, entry into force: 2 January 1974, 910 UNTS 61.

Protocol on Space Requirements for Special Trade Passenger Ships. London, 13 July 1973, entry into force: 2 June 1977, 1046 UNTS 317; UKTS 7 (1980), Cmnd. 7761.

International Regulations for Preventing Collisions at Sea, 1960 (COLREG 1960), adopted: 17 June 1960, entry into force: 1 September 1965, TIAS 5813; UKTS 23 (1966), Cmnd. 2956.

Convention on the International Regulations for Preventing Collisions at Sea, 1972 (COLREG), (with final act, procès verbal of rectification, resolutions and International Regulations). London, 20 October 1972, entry into force: 15 July 1977, 1050 UNTS 16; 1143 UNTS 346 (rectification); 28 UST 3459; TIAS 8587; ATS 1980 No. 5; UKTS 1977 No. 77 (Cmnd. 6962); NZTS 1976 No. 26; CTS 1977 No. 45.

International Convention for Safe Containers, 1972 (CSC 1972), (with annexes and protocol of signature). Geneva, 2 December 1972, entry into force: 6 September 1977, 1064 UNTS 3; TIAS 9037; ATS 1981 No. 3; 29 UST 3709; UKTS 40 (1979), Cmnd. 7535.

Convention on the International Maritime Satellite Organization (INMARSAT) (with annex and agreement). London, 3 September 1976, entry into force: 16 July 1979, 1143 UNTS 213; 15 ILM 233, 1075; UKTS 94 (1979), Cmnd. 7722; 31 UST 1; TIAS 9605; ATS 1979 No. 10.

Operating Agreement on the International Maritime Satellite Organization (INMARSAT), as amended (INMARSAT OA), adopted: 3 September 1976, entry into force: 16 July 1979, 1142 UNTS 213; 31 UST 135, 147; TIAS 9605; UKTS 94 (1979), Cmnd. 7722; ATS 1979/10; RMC II.3.270.

International Convention on standards of training, certification and watchkeeping for seafarers, 1978 (STCW 1978) (with annex and procès-verbaux of rectifications). London, 7 July 1978, entry into force: 28 April 1984, 1361 UNTS 190; ATS 1984 No. 7; UKTS 1984 No. 50 (Cmnd. 9266); CTS 1988 No. 36; NZTS 1986 No. 18.

International Convention on maritime search and rescue, 1979 (SAR) (with annexes). Hamburg, 27 April 1979, entry into force: 22 June 1985, 1405 UNTS 97; TIAS 11093; ATS 1986 No. 29; UKTS 1986 No. 59 (Cmnd. 12); NZTS 1985 No. 3; CTS 1985 No. 27.

Marine Pollution

International Convention for the Prevention of Pollution of the Sea by Oil, 1954 (OILPOL), adopted: 12 May 1954, entry into force: 26 July 1958, 327 UNTS 3; 9 ILM 1; UKTS 54 (1958), Cmnd. 595, as amended of 11 April 1962 (entry into force: 18 May/28 June 1967), 600 UNTS 332, as amended of 21 October 1969 (entry into force: 20 January 1978), 1140 UNTS 340; superseded as between the Contracting Parties to the MARPOL 1978 Protocol.

International Convention Relating to Intervention on the High Seas in Cases of Oil Pollution Casualties, 1969, with annex (INTERVENTION), Brussels, 29 November 1969, entry into force: 6 May 1975, 970 UNTS 211; 26 UST 765; TIAS 8068; 9 ILM 25; 64 AJIL 471; ATS 1984 No. 4; UKTS 1975 No. 77 (Cmnd. 6056); NZTS 1975 No. 17.

Protocol Relating to Intervention on the High Seas in Cases of Pollution by Substances other than Oil, 1973, as amended, London, 2 November 1973, entry into force: 30 March 1983, 1313 UNTS 3; 13 ILM 605; TIAS 10561; 68 AJIL 577; ATS 1984 No. 5; UKTS 1983 No. 27 (Cmnd. 8924).

4 July 1991 Amendments, entry into force: 24 July 1992 (IMO Doc.: Res. MEPC.49(31)).

10 July 1996 Amendments, entry into force: 19 December 1997 (IMO Doc. Res. MEPC.72(38)).

11 October 2002 Amendments, entry into force 22 June 2004 (IMO Doc.: Res. MEPC.100(48)).

International Convention for the Prevention of Pollution from Ships, 1973, (MARPOL 73/78), 2 November 1973, entry into force: 10 February 1983, not intended to enter into force without the 1978 Protocol, 1340 UNTS 184; 12 ILM 1319 (1973).

Protocol of 1978 relating to the International Convention for the prevention of pollution from ships, 1973, with annexes and protocol, London, 17 February 1978, entry into force: 2 October 1983, 1340 UNTS 61, 62; 17 ILM 546; ATS 1988 No. 29; UKTS 1981 No. 40, Cmnd. 827.

Protocol of 1997 to amend the International Convention for the Prevention of Pollution from Ships, 1973, as modified by the Protocol of 1978 relating thereto (MARPOL PROT 1997) (Annex VI on the Prevention of Air Pollution from Ships), adopted 26 September 1997, entry into force 19 May 2005, MEPC.78 (43); RMC II.7.180.

Convention on the prevention of marine pollution by dumping of wastes and other matter (LDC) (with annexes and procès-verbal of rectification). London, Mexico City, Moscow, Washington 29 December 1972, entry into force: 30 August 1975, 1046 UNTS 120; 26 UST 2403; 11 ILM 1294; RMC II.7.150; UKTS 43 (1976), Cmnd. 6486; TIAS 8165.

1996 Protocol to the Convention on the prevention of marine pollution by dumping of wastes and other matter, 1972, London, 7 November 1996, not yet entered into force, IMO Doc.: LC/SM 1/6; 36 ILM 1.

International Convention on Oil Pollution Preparedness, Response and Co-operation, 1990 (OPRC 1990) (with annex). London, 30 November 1990, entry into force: 13 May 1995, 503 UNTS 51; 30 ILM 735; US Treaty Doc. 102-11; ATS 1995 No. 12; RMC II.7.230.

Protocol on Preparedness, Response and Co-operation to pollution Incidents by Hazardous and Noxious Substances (HNS Protocol). London, 14 March 2000, not yet in force, IMO Doc.: HNS-OPRC/CONF/11/Rev.1 of 15 March 2000.

International Convention on the Control of Harmful Anti-fouling Systems on Ships. London, 5 October 2001, not yet in force, IMO Doc.: AFS/CONF/26.

International Convention for the Control and Management of Ships' Ballast Water and Sediments. London, 13 February 2004, not yet in force, IMO Doc.: BWM/CONF/36.

Carriage of Goods and Passengers

International Convention for the Unification of Certain Rules of Law Relating to Bills of Lading (Hague Rules). Brussels, 25 August 1924, entry into force: 2 June 1931, 120 LNTS 155; 2 Bevans 430.

Amended by the Protocol to amend the International Convention for the Unification of certain Rules of Law relating to Bills of Lading (Visby Protocol). Brussels, 23 February 1968, entry into force: 23 June 1977, 1412 UNTS 127; UKTS 1977 No. 83 (Cmnd. 6944).

Amended by the Protocol of 1979 to amend the International Convention for the Unification of certain Rules of Law Relating to Bills of Lading, 1924, as amended by the Protocol of 1968 (SDR Protocol). Brussels, 21 December 1979, entry into force: 14 February 1984, ATS 1993 No. 23; UKTS 1984 No. 28 (Cmnd. 9197).

Athens Convention Relating to the Carriage of Passengers and Their Luggage by Sea, 1974. Athens, 13 December 1974, entry into force: 28 April 1987 (PAL 1974), 1463 UNTS 20; 14 ILM 945; RMC I.5.190, II.5.190.

Protocol (of 1976) to the Athens Convention relating to the Carriage of Passengers and their Luggage by Sea, 1974 (PAL PROT 1976). London, 19 November 1976, entry into force: 30 April 1989, 16 ILM 625; RMC I.5.200, II.5.200; UKTS 43 (1989).

Protocol of 1990 to amend the Athens Convention relating to the Carriage of Passengers and their Luggage by Sea, 1974 (PAL PROT 1990). London, 29 March 1990, not yet entered into force, IMO Doc.: LEG/CONF.8/10 of 29 March 1990; RMC I .5.201, II.5.201;

Protocol of 2002 to amend the Athens Convention relating to the Carriage of Passengers and their Luggage by Sea, 1974 (PAL PROT 2002). London, 1 November 2002, not yet in force, IMO Doc.: LEG/CONF.13/20 of 19 November 2002; RMC I .5.202, II.5.202.

United Nations Convention on the Carriage of Goods by Sea. Hamburg, 31 March 1978, entry into force: 1 November 1992 (The Hamburg Rules), UN Doc. A/CONF.89/13; 17 ILM 608.

Limitation of Liability

International Convention on Civil Liability for Oil Pollution Damage (CLC). Brussels, 29 November 1969, entry into force, 19 June 1975, 973 UNTS 3; 9 ILM 45; UKTS 106 (1975), Cmnd. 6183; RMC II.70.30.

Protocol [of 1976] to the International Convention on Civil Liability for Oil Pollution Damage, 1969, London, 19 November 1976, entry into force: 8 April 1981, 1225 UNTS 356; 16 ILM 617; ATS 1984 No. 3; BGBl. 1980 II 721; UKTS 1981 No. 26 (Cmnd. 8238).

Protocol of 1992 to amend the International Convention on Civil Liability for Oil Pollution Damage of 29 November 1969 (with annex and final act). London, 27 November 1992, entry into Force: 30 May 1996, UNTS A-14097, 1956 UNTS 255; IMO Doc.: LEG/CONF.9/15 of 2 December 1992; ATS 1996, No. 2; UKTS 1996 No. 86 (Cmnd. 3432).

2000 Amendments (Limitation Amounts in the Protocol of 1992 to amend the International Convention on Civil Liability for Oil Pollution Damage, 1969), London, 18 October 2000, entry into force: 1 November 2003, IMO Doc.: Res. LEG.1(82), in: Annex 2 of IMO Doc.: LEG 82/12 of 6 November 2000; IOPCF Doc.: RMCI.7.52, II.7.52.

International Convention on the Establishment of an International Fund for Compensation for Oil Pollution Damage, 1971 (FUND 1971), Brussels, 18 December 1971, entry into force: 16 October 1978, cessation of the Convention: 24 May 2002, replaced by the FUND PROT 1992, 1110 UNTS 57; ATS 1995 No. 2.

Protocol [of 1976] to the International Convention on the Establishment of an International Fund for Compensation for Oil Pollution Damage, 1971 (FUND PROT 1976), London, 19 November 1976, entry into force: 22 November 1994, 16 ILM 621; UKTS 1996 No. 28 (Cmnd. 3162); RMC II.7.100.

Protocol of 1992 to amend the International Convention on the Establishment of an International Fund for Compensation for Oil Pollution Damage, 1971 (FUND PROT 1992), London, 27 November 1992, entry into force: 30 May 1996, replaces the 1971 Convention (*see* IMO Doc.: LEG/CONF.11/8 of 27 September 2000); UKTS 87 (1996); Cmnd. 3433; ATS 1996 No. 2; RMC II.7.111.

Protocol of 2000 to the International Convention on the Establishment of an International Fund for Compensation for Oil Pollution Damage, 1971, London, 27 September 2000, entry into force: 27 June 2001, IMO Doc.: LEG/CONF.11/6 and 11/8 of 27 September 2000.

Protocol of 2003 to the International Convention on the Establishment of an International Fund for Compensation for Oil Pollution Damage, London, 16 May 2003, entry into force: 3 March 2005, IMO Doc.: LEG/CONF.14/20; RMC II.7.115.

Convention Relating to Civil Liability in the Field of Maritime Carriage of Nuclear Material, 1971 (NUCLEAR), Brussels, 17 December 1971, entry into force 15 July 1975, 974 UNTS 255; 11 ILM 277; RMC II.5.170.

International Convention for the Unification of Certain Rules Relating to the Limitation of the Liability of Owners of Sea-Going Vessels. Brussels, 25 August 1924, entry into force: 2 June 1931, 120 LNTS 123.

International Convention Relating to the Limitation of the Liability of Owners of Sea-Going Ships of 1957. Brussels, 10 October 1057, entry into force: 31 May 1968, RMC II.2.310.

Convention on Limitation of Liability for Maritime Claims, 1976 (LLMC 1976), London, 19 November 1976, entry into force: 1 December 1986, 1456 UNTS 221; 16 ILM 606; ATS 1991 No. 12; UKTS 13 (1990), Cmnd. 955; RMC II.2.330.

Protocol Amending the Convention on Limitation of Liability for Maritime Claims, London, 2 May 1996, entry into force: 13 May 2004, 35 ILM 1433; IMO Doc.: LEG/CONF.10/8 of 9 May 1996, LLMC.3/Cir.8 of 17 February 2004.

International Convention on Liability and Compensation for Damage in Connection with the Carriage of Hazardous and Noxious Substances by Sea (HNS Convention), London, 3 May 1996, not yet in force, IMO Doc.: LEG/CONF.10/8/2 of 9 May 1996; 35 ILM 1406; RMC II.7.125.

International Convention on Civil Liability for Bunker Oil Pollution Damage, London, 23 March 2001, not yet in force, IMO Doc.: LEG/CONF.12/19 of 27 March 2001; RMC II.7.130.

General

Charter of the United Nations. San Francisco, 26 June 1945, entry into force: 24 October 1945, UKTS 67 (1946); ATS 1945 No.1; TS 993; 3 Bevans 1153.

Convention on the International Maritime Organization, Geneva, 6 March 1948, entry into force: 17 March 1958, 289 UNTS 4; 9 UST 621; ATS 1958 No. 5; UKTS 54 (1958), Cmnd. 4; TIAS 4044; RMC II.1.10.

1964 Amendments, adopted 15 September 1964, entry into force: 6 October 1967, 607 UNTS 276; 18 UST 1299; TIAS 6285; UKTS 92 (1967), Cmnd. 3463.

1965 Amendments, adopted: 28 September 1965, entry into force: 3 November 1968, 649 UNTS 334; TIAS 6490; 19 UST 4855; UKTS 105 (1968), Cmnd. 3839.

1974 Amendments, adopted: 17 October 1974, entry into force: 1 April 1978, 1080 UNTS 374; TIAS 8606; 28 UST 4607, 4609; UKTS 69 (1978), Cmnd. 7262.

1975/1977 Amendments, adopted 14 November 1975, rectified: 9 November 1977, entry into force: 22 May/28 July 1982, 1276 UNTS 468; UKTS 34 (1982), Cmnd. 8632; TIAS 10374, 34 UST 497.

1977 Amendments, adopted: 17 November 1977, entry into force: 10 November 1984, 1380 UNTS 268; ATS 1984 No. 27; TIAS 11094.

1979 Amendments, adopted: 15 November 1979, entry into force: 10 November 1984, 1380 UNTS 288; TIAS 11094; ATS 1984 No. 31; UKTS 26 (1986), Cmnd. 9777.

1991 Amendments, adopted 7 November 1991, not yet in force, IMO Doc.: Res. A.724(17).

1993 Amendments, adopted: 4 November 1993, entry into force: 7 November 2002, IMO Doc.: Res.A.735(18); RMC II.1.90.

International Convention on Tonnage Measurement of Ships, 1969 (with annexes and final act). London, 23 June 1969, entry into force: 18 July 1982, UNTS I-21264, 1291 UNTS 3; TIAS 10490; ATS 1982 No. 15; UKTS 1982 No. 50 (Cmnd. 8716); NZTS 1978 No. 1.

United Nations Convention on the Law of the Sea. Montego Bay, Jamaica, 10 December 1982, entry into force: 16 November 1994, UN Doc.: A/CONF.62/122; 1833 UNTS 3, 397; 21 ILM 1261.

Vienna Convention on the Law of Treaties. Vienna, 23 May, 1969, entry into force: 27 January 1980, UNTS I-18232, 1155 UNTS 331; UN Doc. A/Conf.39/27; 8 ILM 679; 63 AJIL 875.

European Union

Council Directive 94/57/EC of 22 November 1994 on common rules and standards for ship inspection and survey organizations and for the relevant activities of maritime administrations (OJ No. L 319, 12 December 1994, 20), as amended by Directive 2001/105/EC of the European Parliament and of the Council of 19 December 2001, OJ No. L 19 of 22 January 2002, 9, last amended by Directive 2002/84/EC of the European Parliament and of the Council of 5 November 2002 (OJ L 324, 29 November 2002, 53).

Commission of the European Communities, Commission Working Document on the control of recognised organisations by the Commission of 11 October 2006, COM(2006) 588 final.

Commission of the European Communities, Proposal for a Directive on common rules and standards for ship inspection and survey organizations and for the relevant activities of the maritime administration of 23 November 2005, COM(2005) 587 final.

Index

About the International Max Planck Research School for Maritime Affairs at the University of Hamburg

The International Max Planck Research School for Maritime Affairs at the University of Hamburg was established by the Max Planck Society for the Advancement of Science, in cooperation with the Max Planck Institute for Comparative and International Private Law (Hamburg), the Max Planck Institute for Comparative Foreign Public Law and International Law (Heidelberg), the Max Planck Institute for Meteorology (Hamburg) and the University of Hamburg. The School's research is focused on the legal, economic, and geophysical aspects of the use, protection, and organization of the oceans. Its researchers work in the fields of law, economics, and natural sciences. The School provides extensive research capacities as well as its own teaching curriculum. Currently, the School has 15 Directors who determine the general work of the School, act as supervisors for dissertations, elect applicants for the School's PhD-grants, and are the editors of this book series:

Prof. Dr. Dr. h.c. Jürgen Basedow is Director of the Max Planck Institute for Foreign Private Law and Private International Law; *Prof. Dr. Peter Ehlers* is the Director of the German Federal Maritime and Hydrographic Agency; *Prof. Dr. Dr. h.c. Hartmut Graßl* is Director of the Max Planck Institute for Meteorology; *Prof. Dr. Hans-Joachim Koch* is Managing Director of the Seminar of Environmental Law of the Faculty of Law at the University of Hamburg; *Prof. Dr. Rainer Lagoni* is Managing Director of the Institute of Maritime Law and the Law of the Sea at the University of Hamburg; *PD Dr. Gerhard Lammel* is Senior Scientist at the Max Planck Institute for Meteorology; *Prof. Dr. Ulrich Magnus* is Managing Director of the Seminar of Foreign Law and Private International Law at the University of Hamburg; *Prof. Dr. Peter Mankowski* is Director of the Seminar of Foreign and Private International Law at the University of Hamburg; *Prof. Dr. Marian Paschke* is Director of the Institute of Maritime Law and the Law of the Sea at the University of Hamburg; *PD. Dr. Thomas Pohlmann* is Senior Scientist at the Centre for Marine and Climate Research and Member of the Institute of Oceanography at the University of Hamburg; *Dr. Uwe Schneider* is Assistant Professor at the Research Unit Sustainability and Global Change, Centre for Marine and Climate Research, Departments of Geosciences and Economics at the University of Hamburg; *Prof. Dr. Jürgen Sündermann* is Director at the Centre for Marine and Climate Research at the University of Hamburg; *Prof. Dr. Richard Tol* is Director of the Research Unit Sustainability and Global Change at the University of Hamburg; *Prof. Dr. Dr. h.c. Rüdiger Wolfrum* is Director at the Max Planck Institute for Comparative Foreign Public Law and International Law and a judge at the International Tribunal for the Law of the Sea; *Prof. Dr. Wilfried Zahel* is professor at the Centre for Marine and Climate Research, Departments of Geosciences and Economics at the University of Hamburg.

At present, *Prof. Dr. Dr. h.c. Jürgen Basedow* and *Prof. Dr. Ulrich Magnus* serve as speakers of the International Max Planck Research School for Maritime Affairs at the University of Hamburg.

SPRINGER NATURE

GPSR Compliance

The European Union's (EU) General Product Safety Regulation (GPSR) is a set of rules that requires consumer products to be safe and our obligations to ensure this.

If you have any concerns about our products, you can contact us on ProductSafety@springernature.com

In case Publisher is established outside the EU, the EU authorized representative is:

Springer Nature Customer Service Center GmbH
Europaplatz 3
69115 Heidelberg, Germany

The manufacturer's authorised representative in the EU is Springer Nature Customer Service Centre GmbH, Europaplatz 3, 69115 Heidelberg, Germany. If you have any concerns regarding our products, please contact ProductSafety@springernature.com

Printed and bound by CPI Group (UK) Ltd, Croydon, CR0 4YY
01/10/2026
02225951-0017